HMH Florida Science

EARTH SCIENCE

Earth Science

This Write-In Book belongs to

_____

Teacher/Room

_____

Did you know that Florida is called the
Sunshine State because it has an average of
230 days of sunshine each year along with its
subtropical-to-tropical climate? The state
officially adopted this nickname in 1970.

Houghton Mifflin Harcourt

Consulting Authors

Michael A. DiSpezio
Global Educator
North Falmouth, Massachusetts

Marjorie Frank
*Science Writer and Content-Area Reading
    Specialist*
Brooklyn, New York

Michael R. Heithaus, Ph.D.
*Dean, College of Arts, Sciences & Education
Professor, Department of Biological Sciences*
Florida International University
Miami, Florida

Houghton Mifflin Harcourt.

Cover: ©photovideostock/Getty Images

Printed in the U.S.A.

ISBN   978-1-328-78128-4

10   2331   28 27 26 25 24 23 22 21
4500837552   CDEFG

Contents in Brief

This is a fossil of a primate that lived about 47 million years ago.

Contents

Knowledge of dinosaurs is gained by studying fossils.

Unit test date: _____

All galaxies, no matter their size,
contain millions of stars!

Unit test date: _____

When the seasons change, so does some of the surface of Mars.

"Midnight sun" occurs when the sun never completely sets in a 24-hour period.

New technologies make space exploration possible.

Earth's surface changes
because of Earth's layers.

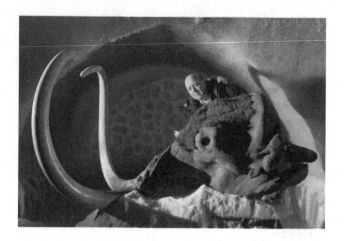

A mammoth's fossils are preserved because they froze.

Sticky tree sap hardens and preserves insect fossils.

I can't wait to learn how this big boulder got here.

Humans impact Earth's land, water, and air.

I wonder how waves form in the ocean.

Unit test date: _____

Strong winds are a sign of severe weather.

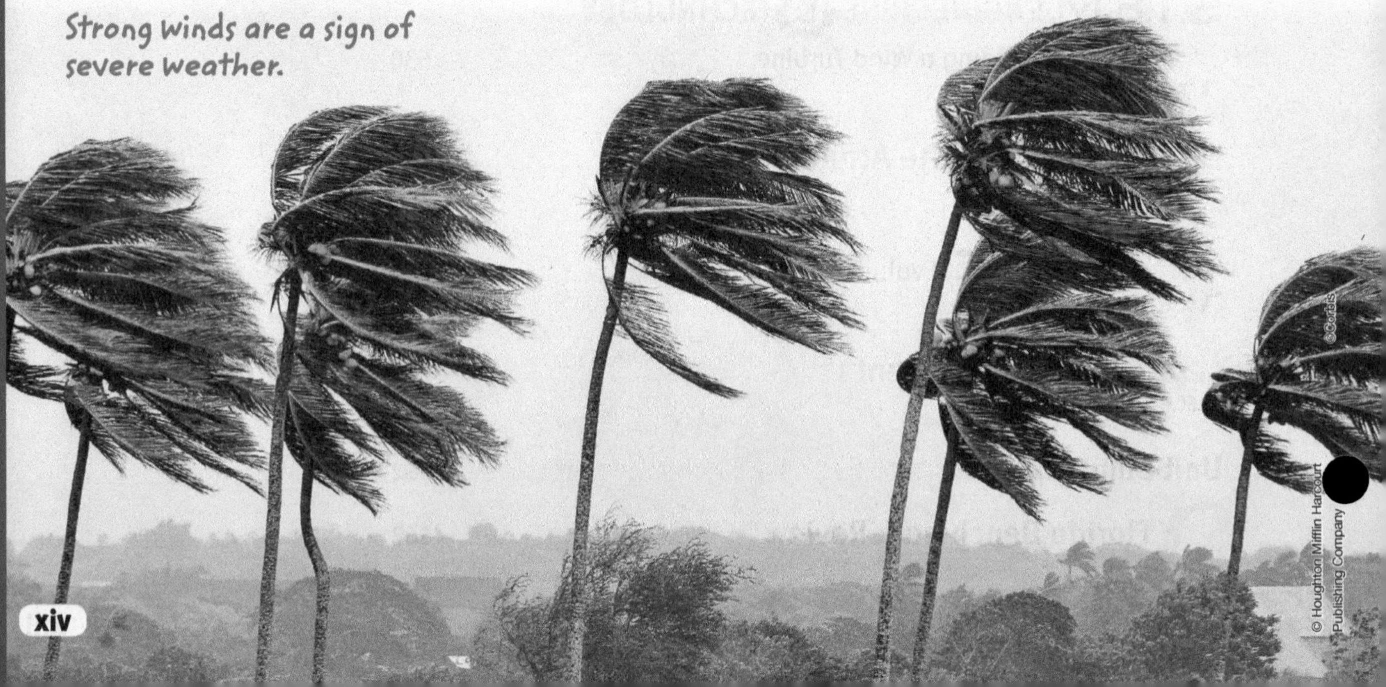

The evaporating water leaves behind a dry, cracked lake bed.

REFERENCES

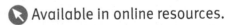

 Available in online resources.

- **Reference Tables**
- **Reading and Study Skills**
- **Science Skills**
- **Math Refresher**

My Assignments:

Nature of Science

Special power drills that can be used in low gravity environments were developed to drill for moon samples. Today, astronauts use these drills for space-station repairs.

The Practice of Science

The Characteristics of Scientific Knowledge

FLORIDA BIG IDEA 3

The Role of Theories, Laws, Hypotheses, and Models

What Do You Think?

Technology helps people perform different tasks, from the everyday to the amazing. How might technology need to be modified for use in space? As you explore this unit, gather evidence to help you state and support a claim.

Nature
of Science

Launching Humanity Into Space

The idea of exploring space was first popularized by science-fiction writers of the late 19th- and early 20th-centuries. It took until the 1940s and 1950s for advances in rocket technology to make the idea of launching humans into space even seem possible. As of today, 12 astronauts have landed on the moon and teams of astronauts have lived on space stations. What is the next step for space exploration?

1926

Robert Goddard was inspired by turn-of-the-century science fiction to develop his theories about rockets that could travel to the moon. In 1926, he launched the world's first liquid-propellant rocket— but the media thought the idea of going to the moon was just too wild.

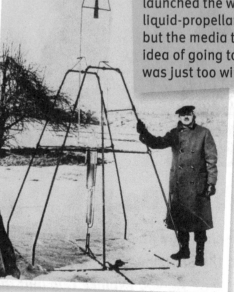

Robert Goddard and his liquid-propellant rocket.

Sputnik 1

Buzz Aldrin

The space shuttle
Columbia

1957

It took several decades to perfect the rocket technology that allowed the Soviet Union to launch the first man-made object into orbit. The Sputnik 1, which weighed only 84 kg, took 96 minutes to orbit Earth.

1981–2010

The new challenge for humans became getting to space as safely and as cost-efficiently as possible. *Columbia* was the first space shuttle NASA developed as a reusable vehicle that could protect astronauts from launch to re-entry.

1969

It only took another 12 years before humans were walking on the moon. Neil Armstrong and Buzz Aldrin became the first humans to set foot on the lunar surface. Back home on Earth, millions of people watched on television.

 Take It Home!

Closer to Home

(1) Think About It

In 2011, the space shuttle program entered retirement. NASA has explored many different options for future launches. Are you familiar with any of the replacement programs? What are they called?

_____

_____

_____

_____

(2) Ask Some Questions

Do some internet research to learn more about the plans NASA has for updating the technology we use for space travel.

- Have new, more stable materials been developed that could be used in construction?

- Have our goals for space exploration changed?

- Are there any new fuels that are more efficient for use in space travel?

- What lessons have we learned from the shuttle program about space travel?

(3) Make A Plan

Identify two vehicles designed to replace the space shuttle and transport astronauts. Design a brochure that describes each option, its features, and its design history. Be sure to include the following information:

- Cost information

- Safety features

Scientific Knowledge

ESSENTIAL QUESTION

What are the types of scientific knowledge?

By the end of this lesson, you should be able to differentiate the methods that scientists use to gain empirical evidence in a variety of scientific fields and explain how this leads to scientific change.

SC.7.N.1.5 Describe the methods used in the pursuit of a scientific explanation as seen in different fields of science such as biology, geology, and physics. **SC.7.N.1.6** Explain that empirical evidence is the cumulative body of observations of a natural phenomenon on which scientific explanations are based. **SC.7.N.1.7** Explain that scientific knowledge is the result of a great deal of debate and confirmation within the science community. **SC.7.N.2.1** Identify an instance from the history of science in which scientific knowledge has changed when new evidence or new interpretations are encountered. **SC.7.N.3.1** Recognize and explain the difference between theories and laws and give several examples of scientific theories and the evidence that supports them.

Under water may seem like an odd place to conduct a science experiment. But scientists often go to faraway places to gather data.

Lesson Labs

Quick Labs
- What's in the Box?
- Pluto on Trial

Exploration Lab
- Mapping the Ocean Floor

Engage Your Brain

1 Predict Check T or F to show whether you think each statement is true or false.

T	F	
☐	☐	All branches of science have scientific theories.
☐	☐	A scientist can use only one method to investigate.
☐	☐	Theories are scientific ideas that have not yet been tested.
☐	☐	Scientific laws describe what happens in the world.

2 Claims • Evidence • Reasoning An aeolipile is a device powered by steam. When heated, water in the bulb produces steam. The bulb rotates as the steam escapes from the nozzles. People were making these devices as long as 2,000 years ago. How do you think they came up with the idea even though they did not have our modern understanding of science? State your claim. Provide evidence to support the claim, and explain your reasoning.

aeolipile

_____
_____
_____
_____

ACTIVE READING

3 Infer The word *empirical* comes from the Greek word *empeirikos*, meaning "experienced." Based on this information, infer how scientists get empirical evidence.

_____
_____
_____
_____

Vocabulary Terms

- empirical evidence
- theory
- law

4 Apply As you learn the definition of each vocabulary term in this lesson, create your own definition or sketch to help you remember the meaning of the term.

...From the **Beginning**

ⓘ Think Outside the Book

5 Define Before you begin reading the lesson, write down what you think science and scientific knowledge are. Reread your definition at the end of the lesson. Has your definition changed?

What is science?

Science is the study of the natural world. Scientists study everything from the deepest parts of the ocean to the objects in outer space. Some scientists study living things. Others study forces such as gravity and magnetism. Name anything you see around you. Chances are, there is a scientist who studies it.

The natural sciences are divided into three areas: biology or life science, geology or Earth science, and physics or physical science. The three areas differ in the subjects they study and the methods they use. Biology is the study of living things. Biologists study everything from the tiniest organisms to human beings. Geology is the study of Earth: what it's made of and the processes that shape it. Physical science is the study of nonliving matter and energy. Chemistry often is included under physical science. A scientist's work sometimes may overlap two or more areas. For example, a biologist often must know chemistry to understand the processes in living things.

Each of the photographs below relates to one of the areas of science in some way. From the captions, can you identify to which area each belongs?

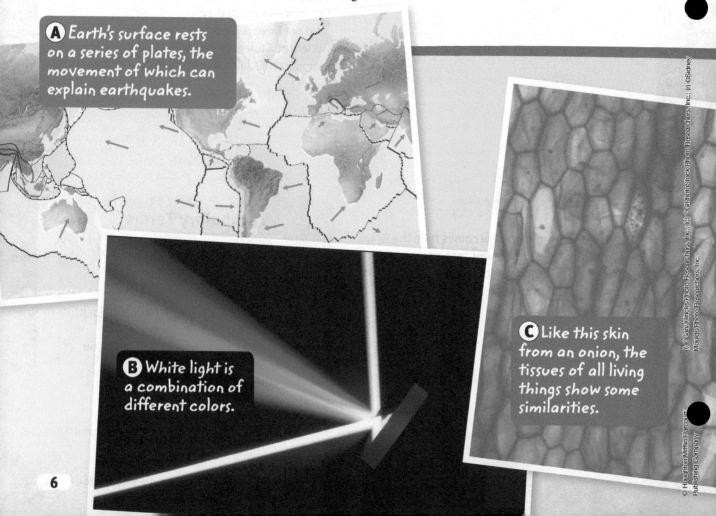

Ⓐ Earth's surface rests on a series of plates, the movement of which can explain earthquakes.

Ⓑ White light is a combination of different colors.

Ⓒ Like this skin from an onion, the tissues of all living things show some similarities.

What does science tell us?

ACTIVE READING

6 Identify Underline what a theory is in science.

You may think that what you read in a science book is accepted by everyone and is unchanging. That is not always the case. The "facts" of science are simply the most widely accepted explanations. Scientific knowledge is and probably always will be changing.

What we learn when we study science are what most scientists agree are the best explanations about how things happen. They are *theories* scientists have about the world. Commonly, we think of a theory as a kind of guess or "hunch." In science, a theory is much more. A scientific theory is an explanation supported by a large amount of evidence. Theories are what most scientists agree to be the best explanations based upon what we now know.

The table below lists three important scientific theories. Each theory relates to one of the areas of science described before. Each also corresponds to a photograph on the previous page. Can you think of what kinds of evidence would support each theory?

Visualize It!

7 Claims • Evidence • Reasoning For each of the three theories listed in the table below, write the letter of the corresponding photograph at the left. On the lines provided, summarize the evidence that supports each theory. Explain your reasoning.

Scientific Theories

	What scientists think	What is some evidence?
Biology	____Cell theory: Living things are made up of cells that perform the basic functions of life.	
Geology	____Plate tectonics: Earth's surface is made up of plates that move.	
Physics	____Wave theory of light: Each color of visible light has a wave of a specific wavelength.	

You Can't Break...

How do scientific theories differ from laws?

ACTIVE READING

8 Identify As you read, underline a real-world example of Boyle's law.

To understand the nature of scientific knowledge, you must understand how scientists use certain words. Often, the meanings are very specialized. *Law* and *theory* are two familiar words that have very special scientific meanings.

○ Laws Describe Principles of Nature

A scientific **law** is a description of a specific relationship under given conditions in the natural world. In short, scientific laws describe the way the world works. They hold anywhere in the universe. You can't escape them.

Boyle's law is one scientific law. According to Boyle's law, at a constant temperature, as the pressure on a gas increases, its volume decreases. To get an appreciation of Boyle's law, think of how it would feel to squeeze a partially deflated beach ball. If you apply pressure by squeezing, the volume, or size, of the ball gets smaller.

You can feel the effects of Boyle's law. A membrane or *eardrum* separates your middle ear from outer ear. Normally, the air spaces on either side are at equal pressure. But sometimes, the pressure on the outer ear can change. For example, the scuba diver in the photo feels an increase in pressure on her eardrum as she descends in the water. By holding her nose and blowing gently, she can force more air into her middle ear. The action momentarily opens the *eustachian tube* connecting the middle ear to the throat. This allows more air from the mouth to rush into the middle ear and equalize the pressure between the two spaces.

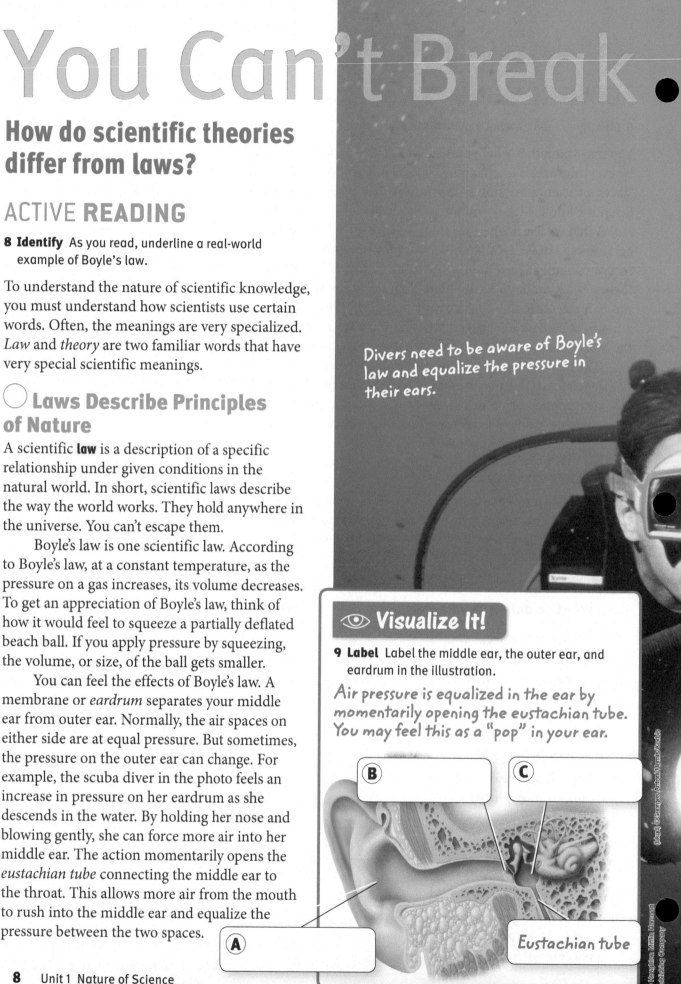

Divers need to be aware of Boyle's law and equalize the pressure in their ears.

◉ Visualize It!

9 Label Label the middle ear, the outer ear, and eardrum in the illustration.

Air pressure is equalized in the ear by momentarily opening the eustachian tube. You may feel this as a "pop" in your ear.

B

C

A

Eustachian tube

(bkgr) ©Georges Antoni/Hemis/Corbis

© Houghton Mifflin Harcourt Publishing Company

Theories Describe How Things Happen

While laws describe what happens, scientific theories attempt to explain how things happen. A scientific **theory** is a well-supported explanation of nature. Theories help us understand the laws we observe.

For example, the kinetic theory of gases can explain Boyle's law. The kinetic theory describes a gas as being composed of quickly-moving particles. The particles of gas constantly bounce off of the walls of the container they occupy. The pressure of the gas increases the more frequently the particles bounce off the sides of the container.

Two factors increase how frequently the particles of a gas will bounce off the walls of their container: temperature and volume. If the temperature of a gas increases, the particles move more quickly. The particles, therefore, come into contact with the container's walls more often. Decreasing volume also increases the encounters because the particles have less distance to travel before hitting the wall. The container walls can be anything: a metal cylinder, a beach ball, or your eardrum. The illustration below will give you some of idea of how this works.

👁 Visualize It!

10 Compare In the table below, circle the signs that show the relationships between the volumes, pressures, and temperatures of the gases in the two cylinders. The first is done for you.

Cylinder 1	Relationship			Cylinder 2
Volume	<	=	(>)	Volume
Pressure	<	=	>	Pressure
Temperature	<	=	>	Temperature

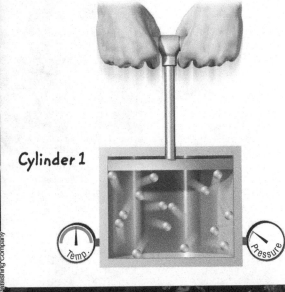

Cylinder 1

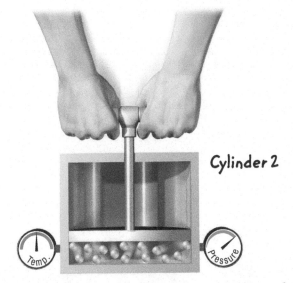

Cylinder 2

What's Your Evidence?

Where do scientists get their evidence?

Scientists are curious. They look at everything going on around them and ask questions. They collect any information that might help them answer these questions.

Scientific knowledge is based on *empirical evidence*. **Empirical evidence** is all the measurements and data scientists gather in support of a scientific explanation. Scientists get empirical evidence in many different places. Generally, scientific work is categorized as field or laboratory work.

ACTIVE READING

11 Identify Underline the definition of empirical evidence.

This scientist is a paleontologist. A paleontologist looks for fossilized bones. Here, he is carefully excavating the remains of a 10,000 year-old rhinoceros.

👁 Visualize It!

12 Gather Evidence What empirical evidence might the scientist in the photograph be trying to gather? Explain your reasoning.

_____

_____

_____

○ In the Field

Generally, gathering empirical evidence outdoors or where conditions cannot be controlled is known as working in the field or *fieldwork*. Fieldwork gives scientists the opportunity to collect data in an original setting. Biologists and geologists do fieldwork.

A biologist might observe how animals behave in their natural environment. They may look at how the animals gather food or interact with other animals. A geologist may be interested in the minerals in rocks found in a certain area. They may be trying to determine how the rocks formed.

○ In the Laboratory

In a laboratory, scientists have the opportunity to collect data in a controlled environment. Unlike in the field, the laboratory allows scientists to control conditions like temperature, lighting, and even what is in the surrounding air. A laboratory is where scientists usually do experiments. In an experiment, scientists try to see what happens under certain conditions. A chemist might be trying to see how two substances react with each other. A physicist might study the energy of a new laser. Even scientists who mainly work in the field, like paleontologists and geologists, may wish to look at a bone or rock in the laboratory.

Laboratories come in many varieties. They can be in the ocean or in the sky. Robotic laboratories even have been sent to Mars!

© Houghton Mifflin Harcourt Publishing Company
(bkgd) ©Reynold Sumayku/Alamy; (inset) ©Pierre-Philippe Marcou/AFP/Getty Images

ACTIVE **READING**

13 Gather Evidence What might a scientist look for to collect evidence about the formation of a volcano? Explain your reasoning.

_____
_____
_____
_____

◉ Visualize It!

14 Claims • Evidence • Reasoning The paleontologists in the photo above have taken a specimen back to the laboratory. Make a claim about what they might be looking for. Provide evidence to support the claim, and explain your reasoning.

_____
_____
_____

The **Debate** Continues

How do scientific ideas change?

Recall that scientific knowledge is agreed-upon knowledge. It is what scientists think are the most-likely explanations for what we see. Over time, these most-likely explanations can change. Sometimes, these changes are very large. More often, they are very small. Why do scientific ideas and explanations change? It's usually because new evidence was found or someone found a better way of explaining the old evidence.

○ By New Evidence

The theory of atoms is a good example of how new evidence can modify an established theory. By the mid-1800s, most scientists agreed matter was made of atoms. However, they were not sure what atoms looked like. At first, they thought atoms probably looked like tiny, solid marbles. They assumed atoms of different substances probably differed by their masses.

Later evidence suggested that atoms most likely contained even smaller parts. Scientists observed that these smaller parts carried electric charges and that most of an atom's mass was concentrated at its center. Scientists still saw atoms as extremely small and still often treated them like they were tiny marbles. They came to realize, however, that to explain how atoms interact in the best way, they needed a more complex picture of them.

Today, scientists are still trying to refine the picture of the atom. Much of what they do involves literally smashing atoms into one another. They examine the patterns made by the crashes. It is almost like an atomic game of marbles.

ACTIVE **READING**

15 Identify Underline an example of a scientific idea that was modified after it was first introduced.

👁 Visualize It!

16 Claims • Evidence • Reasoning How does the early model of the atom differ from the current model? What is similar about the two models? State your claim. Provide evidence to support the claim, and explain your reasoning.

_____

_____

_____

_____

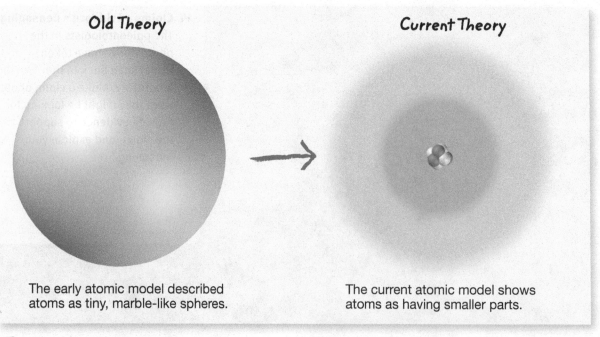

Old Theory

Current Theory

The early atomic model described atoms as tiny, marble-like spheres.

The current atomic model shows atoms as having smaller parts.

By Collaboration and Debate

Most scientists do not work in isolation. They collaborate and share ideas. In a way, all scientists are trying to solve a puzzle. Often, many brains are better than one when solving a puzzle.

Scientists regularly gather at meetings to discuss and debate ideas. This helps them to come to an agreement on their ideas. Many ideas are not accepted at first. It is the nature of science to question every idea. Many times, challenges are even welcomed. This rigorous evaluation ensures that scientific knowledge is solidly supported.

Think Outside the Book

17 Evaluate Describe a time when you had to ask someone's help in solving a problem. Why did you ask for help?

To the left is an example of how scientists study atoms today. The "streaks" show the paths of subatomic particles after two atoms collide. The scientists below study and discuss images like these in a group in hopes to better understand atoms.

Visual Summary

To complete this summary, fill in the blanks with the correct word or phrase. You can use this page to review the main concepts of the lesson.

The facts we may think of as science are simply the most widely accepted explanations.

18 A scientific_____ describes what happens, but a scientific

_____

describes for what reasons it happens.

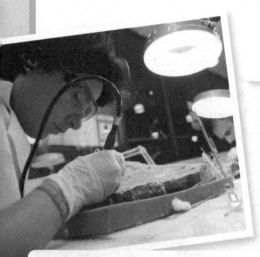

Scientific Knowledge

Empirical evidence is all the measurements and data scientists gather in support of a scientific explanation.

19 Empirical evidence about rocks might be collected by a _____ doing _____

20 Empirical evidence about how substances combine might be collected by a _____ doing work in the _____

Scientific knowledge often changes with new evidence or new interpretations.

21 Scientists often_____ and _____ to help them interpret complex ideas.

22 **Claims • Evidence • Reasoning** Could a scientific theory be thought of as a scientific law that doesn't have as much evidence supporting it? State your claim, and explain your reasoning.

Lesson Review

Vocabulary

Circle the term that best completes each of the following sentences.

1 A scientific *law / theory* is an explanation for how something occurs. It is supported by a great deal of evidence.

2 Scientists look for *empirical evidence / law* either in the field or in the laboratory.

3 A basic principle that applies everywhere and in all situations is best described as a scientific *law / theory*.

Key Concepts

4 List Into what three areas are the natural sciences commonly divided?

_____

_____

5 Distinguish How is the use of the word *theory* in science different from its more common use?

_____

_____

_____

6 Differentiate How would you distinguish a scientific theory from a scientific law?

_____

_____

_____

7 Identify Name two methods scientists use to obtain empirical evidence.

_____

_____

8 Apply What is a difference between research in the field and in the laboratory?

_____

_____

_____

Critical Thinking

Use this picture to answer the following question.

9 Claims • Evidence • Reasoning As the flames heat the gases in the balloon, the volume of the gases increases. At constant pressure, the volume of all gases increases with increasing temperature. Is this statement a scientific theory or law? Provide evidence to support your claim, and explain your reasoning.

_____

_____

10 Claims • Evidence • Reasoning Someone tells you that scientific knowledge cannot be changed or modified. Is this statement true or false? State your claim. Provide evidence to support the claim, and explain your reasoning.

_____

_____

11 Claims • Evidence • Reasoning Each year, the American Chemical Society holds a national meeting and many regional meetings for chemists. Reports of these meetings are then circulated all over the world. Make a claim about why you think this has become standard practice. Provide evidence to support the claim, and explain your reasoning.

_____

_____

SC.7.N.1.5 Describe the methods used in the pursuit of a scientific explanation as seen in different fields of science such as biology, geology, and physics.

Dijanna Figueroa

MARINE BIOLOGIST

Dijanna Figueroa has wanted to be a marine biologist for as long as she can remember. Like many scientists, she now wears a lab coat and safety glasses most days. She spends up to 12 hours a day in the lab. There, she studies the metabolisms of creatures that live in extreme environments. These creatures live more than two kilometers below the ocean's surface, in a habitat that sunlight never reaches. The water pressure is so great that it would crush a human being. Creatures living in these conditions must therefore produce foods in ways that were unknown until only recently. In order to get specimens of these animals for her lab, Dr. Figueroa had to go down to where they live.

Dr. Figueroa's job has taken her onto the big screen, too. She appeared in the IMAX film *Aliens of the Deep*, with other scientists. The film shows footage of expeditions down to the deep-sea ocean vents. These vents may be one of the harshest environments on the planet. The scientists traveled in *Alvin*, a deep-sea submarine.

Dr. Figueroa works to get young people interested in real-life science through fun and exciting hands-on activities. She currently works as the science coordinator for a private school in California.

Dr. Figueroa in Alvin—2,400 m deep!

📖 Language Arts Connection

Think of a science-related job that you would like to know more about. Research the job and write a plan for a documentary film that teaches what you have learned about the job.

JOB BOARD

Museum Educational Interpreter

What You'll Do: Tell students and groups visiting a museum about what they are looking at. You might create educational programs, give tours, and answer questions.

Where You Might Work: Likely places are a science museum or a museum of technology.

Education: Educational interpreters usually need a bachelor's degree in science, and may need extra training in museums or in teaching.

Other Job Requirements: You need to enjoy working with people, be good at public speaking, and be able to answer questions clearly.

Pyrotechnician

What You'll Do: Work with explosives to create explosions and fireworks for special effects. Blow things up in the safest way possible, using a lot of safety measures to keep things from getting out of hand.

Where You Might Work: A company that designs special effects or that creates and performs fireworks shows is a possibility. A pyrotechnician spends time in the workshop and on-site, so you may find yourself on a film set blowing up cars, or on a hillside setting off fireworks.

Education: You need a high-school diploma with additional training in pyrotechnics and safety.

Other Job Requirements: Strong math skills, ability to concentrate, and careful attention to detail are required.

PEOPLE IN SCIENCE NEWS

Jon BOHMER

Cooking with Sunlight

Jon Bohmer isn't the first person to invent an oven that uses sunlight to heat food and water. He's one of many people to use cardboard, foil, and sunlight to build an oven. In some countries, people use firewood for most of their cooking, and must boil all of their water before they drink it. Jon's Kyoto Box oven uses two cardboard boxes painted black on the inside and coated with foil on the outside. It costs only about $5 to make, but it gets hot enough to boil water and cook food.

Scientific Investigations

ESSENTIAL **QUESTION**

How are scientific investigations conducted?

By the end of this lesson, you should be able to summarize the processes and characteristics of different kinds of scientific investigations.

Geologists are able to create artificial earthquakes on this model of a portion of Earth's crust. They can investigate the rock types through which seismic waves travel, all from a computer!

SC.7.N.1.2 Differentiate replication (by others) from repetition (multiple trials). **SC.7.N.1.3** Distinguish between an experiment (which must involve the identification and control of variables) and other forms of scientific investigation and explain that not all scientific knowledge is derived from experimentation. **SC.7.N.1.4** Identify test variables (independent variables) and outcome variables (dependent variables) in an experiment. **SC.7.N.1.5** Describe the methods used in the pursuit of a scientific explanation as seen in different fields of science such as biology, geology, and physics.

Lesson Labs

Quick Labs
- Identifying Minerals
- Soil Structure and Water Flow

Engage Your Brain

1 Predict Check T or F to show whether you think each statement is true or false.

T F

☐ ☐ There is only one correct way to conduct a scientific investigation.

☐ ☐ A hypothesis is a conclusion you draw after you conduct a scientific experiment.

☐ ☐ In a controlled experiment, scientists try to control all but one variable.

☐ ☐ Scientists may come up with different interpretations of the same data.

2 Formulate. Observe the hills shown in the picture. Write some questions you would like to investigate about the sedimentary rock layers.

_____

_____

_____

_____

ACTIVE READING

3 Synthesize You can often define an unknown word if you know the meaning of its word parts. Use the word part and sentence below to make an educated guess about the meaning of the term *independent variable*.

Word part	Meaning
in-	not

Example sentence
In an experiment about how light affects plant growth, the <u>independent variable</u> is the number of hours that a plant is exposed to light.

Independent variable:

_____

_____

Vocabulary Terms

- experiment
- hypothesis
- dependent variable
- observation
- independent variable
- data

4 Identify This list contains the vocabulary terms you'll learn in this lesson. As you read, underline the definition of each term.

Detective Story

What are some types of scientific investigations?

The two basic types of scientific investigations are *experiments* and *observations*. Most scientists use both experiments and observations. Experiments are often based on observations, and they produce additional observations while they are conducted. But observations do not always lead to experiments.

ACTIVE READING

5 Identify As you read these two pages, underline characteristics of the different types of scientific investigations discussed.

Scientific Investigations

Experiments

An **experiment** is an organized procedure to study something under controlled conditions. Scientists often conduct experiments to find out the cause of something they have observed.

In 1928, Alexander Fleming found a fungus growing on a glass plate that was coated with bacteria. He noticed that there were no bacteria around the fungus. He thought that the fungus produced something that killed the bacteria.

Fleming conducted experiments showing that the fungus produced a chemical that could kill bacteria. He named the chemical penicillin after the fungus that produced it. Based on Fleming's work, scientists produced the first antibiotic drugs.

Experiments such as Fleming's are done in a laboratory. Most variables that might affect the outcome of an experiment can be controlled in a laboratory. Experiments can also be done in the field, but fewer conditions can be controlled. However, a field experiment may be needed to show that something found in a laboratory also occurs in nature.

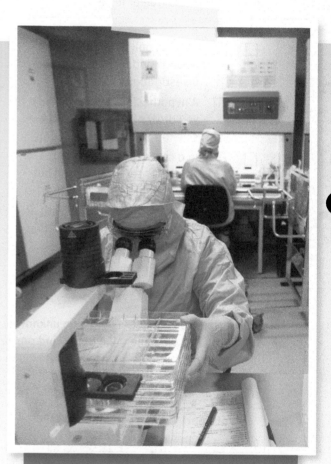

These scientists work in a laboratory called a clean room. A clean room must be free of all possible contaminants.

ACTIVE READING

6 Claims • Evidence • Reasoning Make a claim about why it is harder to control variables in the field than in a laboratory? Provide evidence to support the claim, and explain your reasoning.

_____

_____

Other Types of Investigations

Scientists can make discoveries without conducting experiments. **Observation** is the process of obtaining information by using the senses. The term can also refer to the information obtained by using the senses.

For example, an archaeologist observes a bone at a prehistoric site. The bone is small and does not look like other bones collected there. Based on its size and shape, the scientist wonders if it came from a small animal. She compares the bone to those from various other small animals. After making these observations, she concludes that people kept pets at the site.

Another type of investigation is the creation of models. Models are representations of an object or system. Models are useful for studying things that are very small, large, or complex. For example, computer models of Earth's atmosphere help scientists forecast the weather.

This scientist is observing flies in their natural habitat.

👁 Visualize It!

7 Assess Compare and contrast the kinds of investigations shown in each photo.

Experiment in Clean Room

Observing Flies in Nature

Both

Parts of a Whole

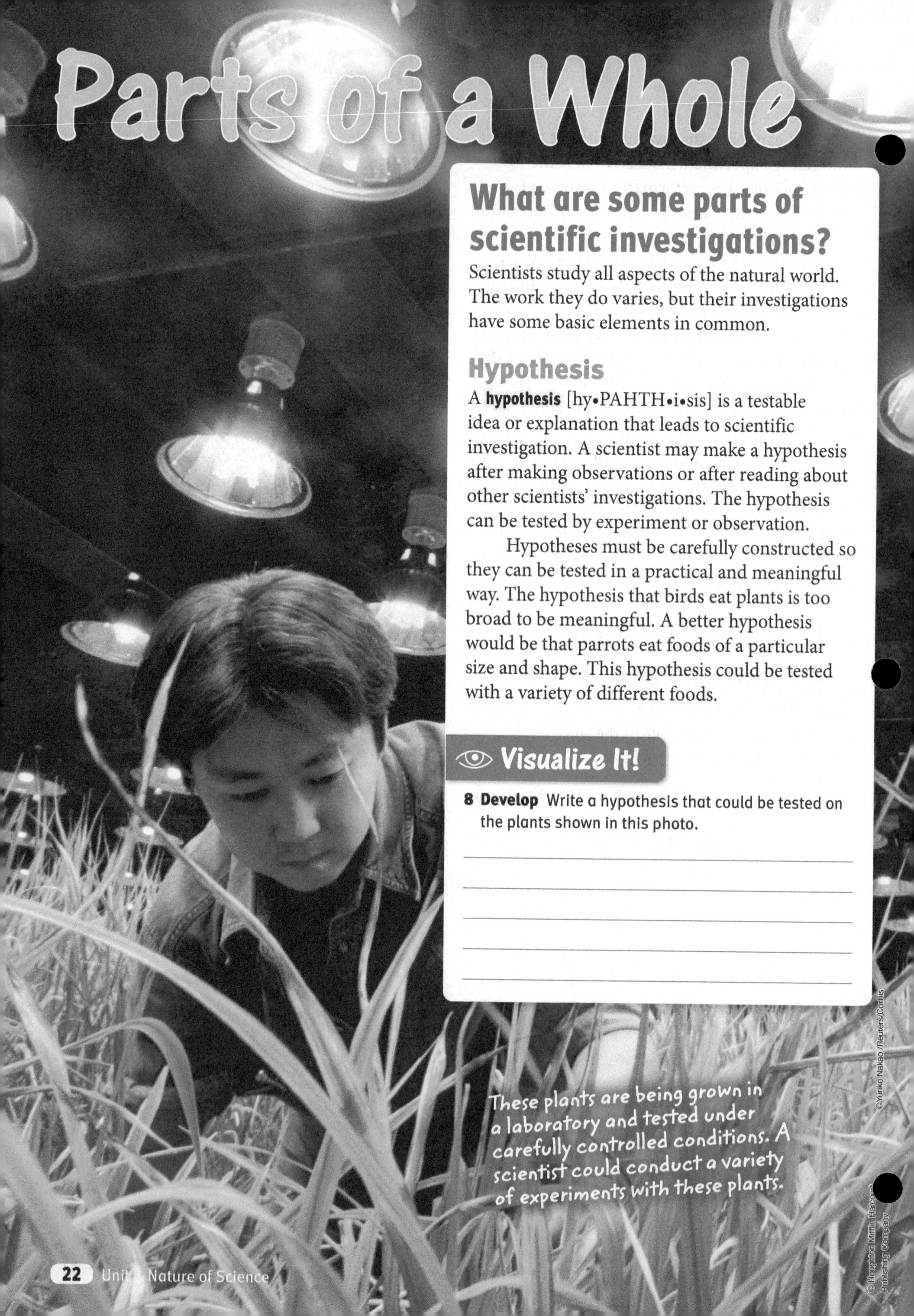

What are some parts of scientific investigations?

Scientists study all aspects of the natural world. The work they do varies, but their investigations have some basic elements in common.

Hypothesis

A **hypothesis** [hy•PAHTH•i•sis] is a testable idea or explanation that leads to scientific investigation. A scientist may make a hypothesis after making observations or after reading about other scientists' investigations. The hypothesis can be tested by experiment or observation.

Hypotheses must be carefully constructed so they can be tested in a practical and meaningful way. The hypothesis that birds eat plants is too broad to be meaningful. A better hypothesis would be that parrots eat foods of a particular size and shape. This hypothesis could be tested with a variety of different foods.

👁 Visualize It!

8 Develop Write a hypothesis that could be tested on the plants shown in this photo.

_____

_____

_____

_____

_____

These plants are being grown in a laboratory and tested under carefully controlled conditions. A scientist could conduct a variety of experiments with these plants.

Elements of Investigations

Independent Variables

Variables are factors that can change in a scientific investigation. An **independent variable**, or test variable, is the factor that is deliberately manipulated in an investigation. The hypothesis determines what the independent variable will be. For example, consider the hypothesis that parrots eat foods of a particular size and shape. The independent variable in an investigation testing that hypothesis is the type of food.

An experiment should have one independent variable. Scientists try to keep all other variables in an experiment constant, or unchanged, so they do not affect the results. However, it may not always be possible to control all the other variables.

Dependent Variables

A **dependent variable**, or outcome variable, is the factor that changes as a result of manipulation of one or more independent variables.

In Fleming's experiments with bacteria, the independent variable was the penicillin fungus. The fungus was either present or absent. The dependent variable was survival of the bacteria. The bacteria either lived or died.

Dependent variables can be measured outside of experiments. Consider the hypothesis that crickets chirp at higher temperatures. The independent variable would be the temperature. The dependent variable would be the cricket chirps. By measuring the dependent variable, you test the hypothesis.

9 Apply Complete the missing parts of the table below, which describes three experiments.

Investigation	Independent Variable	Dependent Variable
How is plant height affected by amount of sunlight it receives?	Hours of sunlight per day	
	Altitude of water	Boiling temperature
How does a person's heart rate change as speed of movement increases?		Heart rate

ACTIVE READING

10 Identify As you read, underline the types of data that scientists record.

Observations and Data

Data are information gathered by observation or experimentation that can be used in calculating or reasoning. Everything a scientist observes must be recorded. The setup and procedures of an experiment also need to be recorded. By carefully recording this information, scientists will not forget important information.

Scientists analyze data to determine the relationship between the independent and dependent variables in an investigation. Then they draw conclusions about whether the data supports the investigation's hypothesis.

Many Methods

What are some scientific methods?

Conducting experiments and other scientific investigations is not like following a cookbook recipe. Scientists do not always use the same steps in every investigation or use steps in the same order. They may even repeat some of the steps. The following graphic shows one path a scientist might follow while conducting an experiment.

👁 Visualize It!

11 Diagram Using a different color, draw arrows showing another path a scientist might follow if the data from an experiment did not support the hypothesis.

Defining a Problem

After making observations or reading scientific reports, a scientist might be curious about some unexplained aspect of a topic. A scientific problem is a specific question that a scientist wants to answer. The problem must be well-defined, or precisely stated, so that it can be investigated.

Planning an Investigation

A scientific investigation must be carefully planned so that it tests a hypothesis in a meaningful way. Scientists need to decide whether an investigation should be done in the field or in a laboratory. They must also determine what equipment and technology are required and how materials for the investigation will be obtained.

Forming a Hypothesis and Making Predictions

When scientists form a hypothesis, they are making an educated guess about a problem. A hypothesis must be tested to see if it is true. Before testing a hypothesis, scientists usually make predictions about what will happen in an investigation.

©Hill Street Studios/Blend Images/Corbis

© Houghton Mifflin Harcourt Publishing Company

Identifying Variables

The independent variable of an experiment is identified in the hypothesis. But scientists need to decide how the independent variable will change. They also must identify other variables that will be controlled. In addition, scientists must determine how they will measure the results of the experiment. The dependent variable often can be measured in more than one way. For example, if the dependent variable is plant growth, a scientist could measure height, weight, or even flower or fruit production.

Collecting and Organizing Data

The data collected in an investigation must be recorded and properly organized so that they can be analyzed. Data such as measurements and numbers are often organized into tables, spreadsheets, or graphs.

Interpreting Data and Analyzing Information

After they finish collecting data, scientists must analyze this information. Their analysis will help them draw conclusions about the results. Scientists may have different interpretations of the same data because they analyze it using different methods.

Drawing and Defending Conclusions

Scientists conclude whether the results of their investigation support the hypothesis. If the hypothesis is not supported, scientists may think about the problem some more and try to come up with a new hypothesis to test. Or they may repeat an experiment to see if any mistakes were made. When they publish the results of their investigation, scientists must be prepared to defend their conclusions if they are challenged by other scientists.

Make it Work

i Think Outside the Book

12 Gather Evidence Choose a plant or animal you would like to study. How would you learn about what it needs to live, grow, and reproduce? Write a paragraph describing the kinds of investigations you would conduct and the type of evidence you would collect to learn more about this organism. Explain your reasoning.

How are scientific methods used?

Scientific methods are used in physical, life, and earth science. The findings of scientific investigations support previous work and add new knowledge.

Different Situations Require Different Methods

After forming a hypothesis, scientists decide how they will test it. Some hypotheses can only be tested through observation. Others must be tested in experiments. However, observation and experiments are often used together to build scientific knowledge.

For example, a biologist wants to study the effects of air pollution on a plant species. He makes observations in the field. He gathers data on the plants and the amount of pollutants in the air. Then he conducts experiments under controlled conditions. He exposes plants to different levels of pollution to test how they are affected. He compares his laboratory data with his field data.

If an investigation does not support a hypothesis, it is still useful. The data can help scientists form a better hypothesis. Scientists often go through many cycles of testing and data analysis before they arrive at a hypothesis that is supported.

This photo shows the large jaw of SuperCroc and the smaller jaw of a modern crocodile.

Scientific Methods Are Used in Earth Science

Earth science includes the study of fossils, which are the remains of organisms that lived long ago. Scientific methods allow scientists to learn about species that died out millions of years ago.

One team of scientists found dinosaur fossils in the Sahara Desert. They found a set of jaws 1.8 meters (6 feet) long. They could tell from the shape of the jaws and teeth that it was not from a dinosaur. They also knew that rivers once flowed through this now extremely dry region. The team hypothesized that the jaws belonged to a giant crocodile that lived in rivers.

To support their hypothesis, the scientists needed more data. They later found skulls, vertebrae, and limb bones. They assembled about half of a complete crocodile skeleton. The scientists measured the fossils and compared them with the bones of modern crocodiles. Their analysis showed that the crocodile grew to a length of 12 meters (40 feet) and weighed as much as 10 tons.

The scientists concluded that the fossils supported their original hypothesis. They published their findings about the crocodile and nicknamed it "SuperCroc."

ACTIVE **READING**

13 Identify As you read, underline a scientific method when it is used and name the method on the lines below.

____

____

____

____

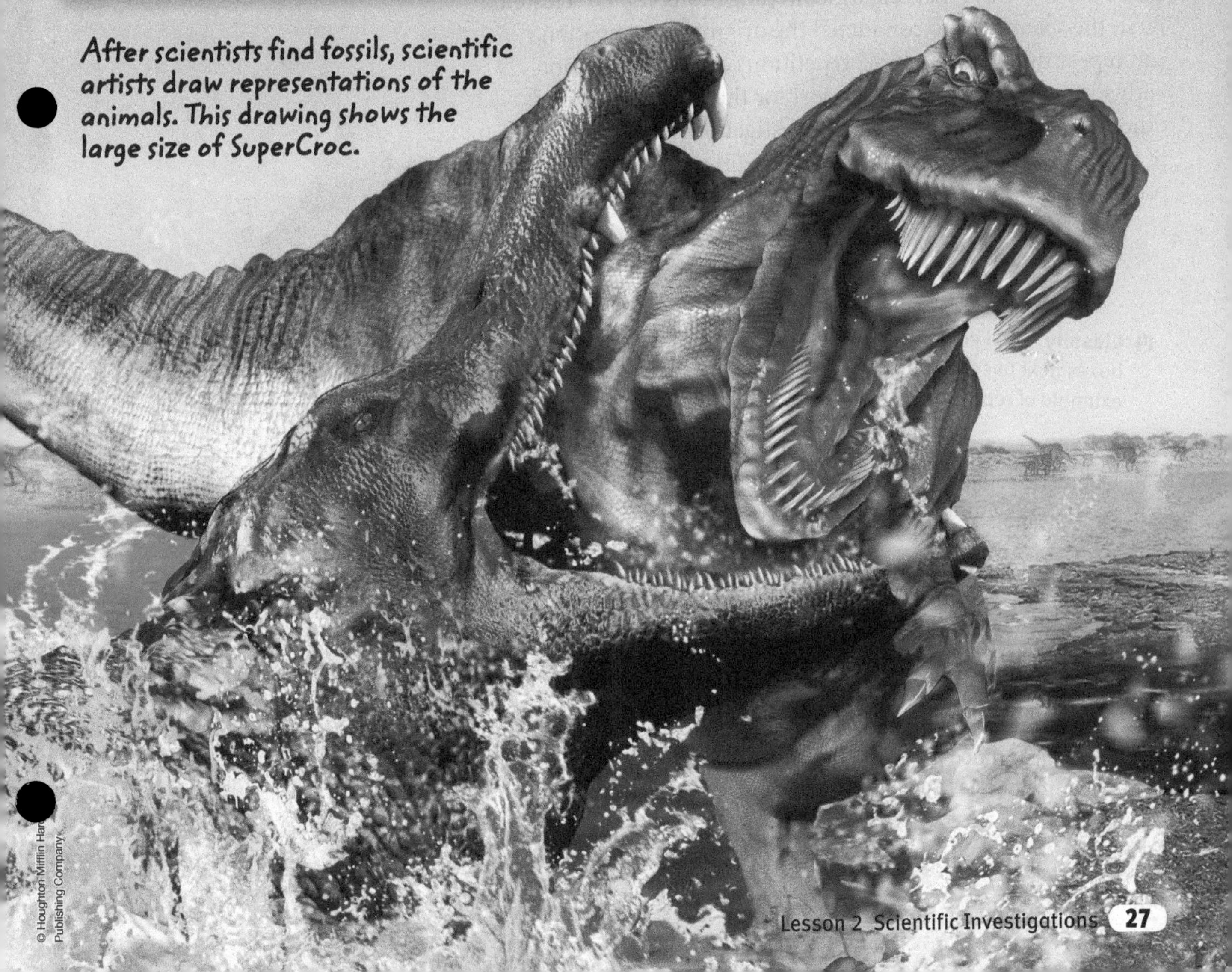

After scientists find fossils, scientific artists draw representations of the animals. This drawing shows the large size of SuperCroc.

Quality Control

What are some characteristics of good scientific investigations?

The standards for scientific investigations are rigorous. Experiments should be verified through repetition and replication. Before a report on an investigation is published in a scientific journal, it should undergo a peer review by scientists not involved in the investigation. Together, these checks help ensure that good scientific practices are followed.

Evaluating Investigations

How is repetition different from replication?

There are two ways that scientific investigations can be retested. First, the scientist who conducted the original investigation can repeat the study. Multiple repetitions of an investigation with similar results provide support for the findings. Second, other scientists can replicate the investigation. Reproduction of the findings by different scientists in different locations also provides support.

14 Classify Read each of the scenarios below. Check one of the boxes next to each statement to classify each scenario as an example of repetition, replication, or both.

Scenario 1: You go to a neighborhood park five times and take notes on the birds you see and hear. You write up your notes.

- ☐ Replication
- ☐ Repetition
- ☐ Both

Scenario 2: You go to the same neighborhood park with a friend. You give your friend a copy of the notes you took when you went to the park on your own. You and your friend both take notes on the birds you see and hear.

- ☐ Replication
- ☐ Repetition
- ☐ Both

Scenario 3: Your friend goes by himself to the same neighborhood park. Your friend takes notes on the birds he sees and hears.

- ☐ Replication
- ☐ Repetition
- ☐ Both

How can you evaluate the quality of scientific information?

The most reliable scientific information is published in peer-reviewed scientific journals. However, these articles are often difficult to understand for people who aren't scientists. Sometimes, reliable summaries of scientific investigations are published in newspapers or magazines or on the Internet.

Many scientists write books for the public. These books are trustworthy if the scientist is writing about his or her field of study. Reliable books and articles may also be written by people who are not scientists but who are knowledgeable about a particular field. The most reliable Internet sources are government or academic webpages. Commercial webpages are often unreliable because they are trying to sell something.

Repetition occurs when an activity is repeated by the same person. When a person bakes a cake multiple times using the same recipe, it should be the same each time. When a scientist repeats her experiment, she should achieve similar results each time.

Replication occurs when an activity is repeated by a different person. When a person bakes a cake using a recipe from someone else, it should be the same as the first person's cake. When a scientist replicates another person's experiment, he should achieve the same results.

Visual Summary

To complete this summary, fill in the blanks with the correct word or phrase. You can use this page to review the main concepts of the lesson.

Scientific Investigations

Types of Scientific Investigations
Scientific investigations may involve observations, experiments, and models.

16 Scientific investigations can be conducted in a _____ or in the _____

17 The _____ of an experiment must be testable.

Scientific Methods
Scientific methods include making observations, planning experiments, collecting data, and drawing conclusions.

18 In an experiment, the variable that a scientist plans to change is the _____ variable.

19 The results of an experiment are the _____ collected.

Characteristics of Good Scientific Investigations
In addition to controlling variables, good scientific investigations should have results that can be reproduced.

20 If your classmate repeats an experiment that you have already conducted, that is an example of _____

21 One way that the quality of scientific information is evaluated is that it is reviewed by _____

22 Claims • Evidence • Reasoning Suppose that you soak ten seeds in water and ten seeds in a mixture of water and vinegar to see how acidity affects the sprouting of seeds. You observe them for two weeks. What are the independent and dependent variables of this experiment? What evidence supports your claim? Explain your reasoning.

Lesson Review

Vocabulary

Circle the term that best completes each of the following sentences.

1 A(n) *hypothesis/observation* is tested in an experiment.

2 In an experiment, the *independent/dependent* variable is the one that scientists manipulate on purpose.

3 The *data/hypothesis* is/are the result(s) obtained from an experiment.

Key Concepts

4 Explain Your Reasoning What is a basic requirement that a scientific hypothesis must have?

_____

_____

5 Claims • Evidence • Reasoning Where are most experiments done? Make a claim about the benefits of this choice. Provide evidence to support the claim, and explain your reasoning.

_____

_____

_____

6 Claims • Evidence • Reasoning Make a claim about the difference between repetition and replication of an investigation? Provide evidence to support your claim, and explain your reasoning.

_____

_____

_____

7 List Write a list of at least five scientific methods.

_____

_____

Critical Thinking

Use this photograph to answer the following questions.

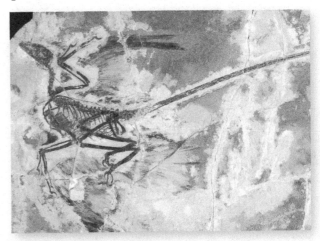

8 Compile Record your observations about the fossil in the photograph. Be sure to include as much detail as you can observe.

_____

_____

_____

9 Produce Write a hypothesis about this fossil that you could test in an investigation.

_____

_____

_____

10 Gather Evidence Describe how you would test your hypothesis. You don't need to identify specific tests or instruments. Rather, describe the kinds of evidence you would want to collect. Explain your reasoning.

_____

_____

_____

LESSON 3

Representing Data

ESSENTIAL **QUESTION**

How do scientists organize, analyze, and present data?

By the end of this lesson, you should be able to use tables, graphs, and models to display and analyze scientific data.

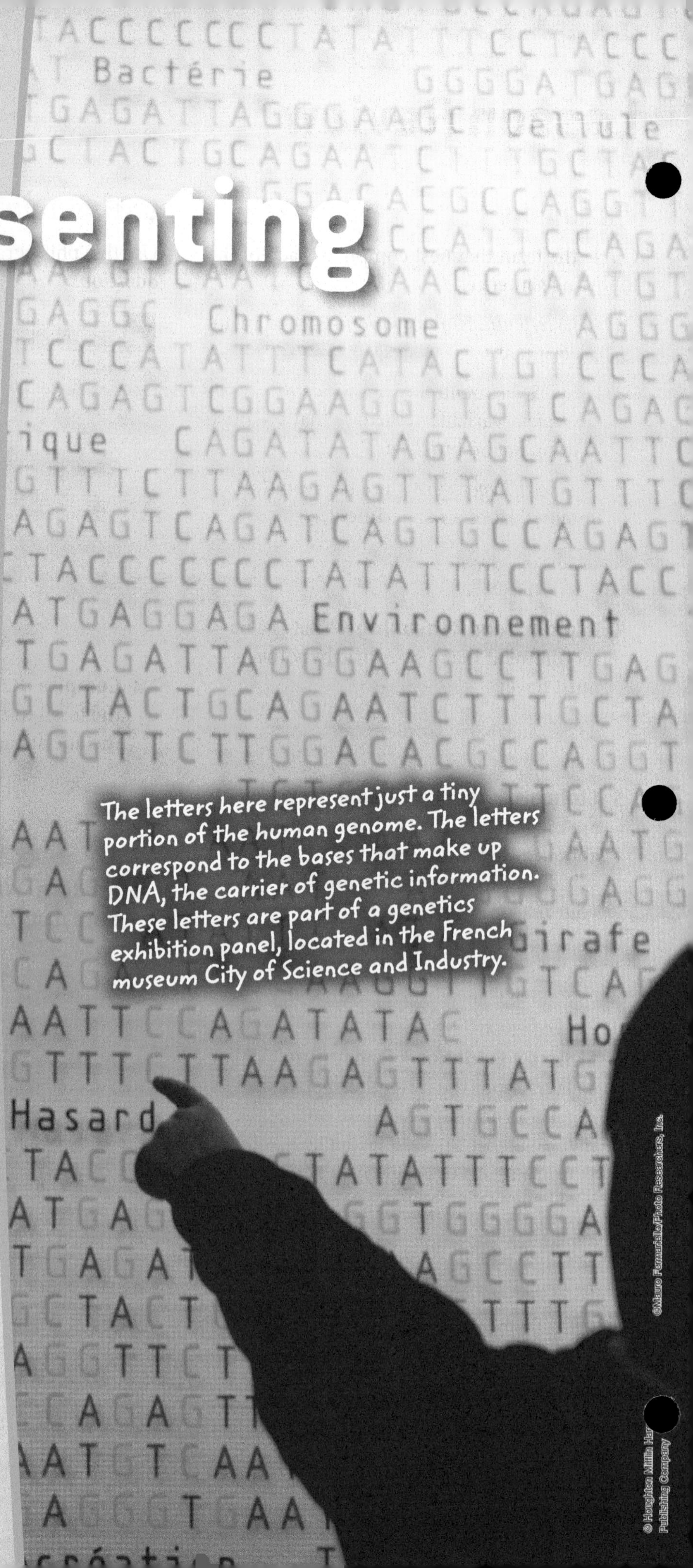

The letters here represent just a tiny portion of the human genome. The letters correspond to the bases that make up DNA, the carrier of genetic information. These letters are part of a genetics exhibition panel, located in the French museum City of Science and Industry.

©Mauro Fermariello/Photo Researchers, Inc.

SC.7.N.1.5 Describe the methods used in the pursuit of a scientific explanation as seen in different fields of science such as biology, geology, and physics. **SC.7.N.3.2** Identify the benefits and limitations of the use of scientific models.

Quick Labs
- Heart Rate and Exercise
- Interpreting Models

Exploration Lab
- Exploring Convection

Engage Your Brain

1 Describe Fill in the blank with the word or phrase that you think correctly completes the following sentences.

Graphs are visual representations of _____.

A map of Florida is an example of a(n) _____.

_____ help show patterns, or trends, in data.

2 Claims • Evidence • Reasoning Identify two things you can understand by looking at this model of our solar system that would be difficult to see if you looked at the sky from Earth. Provide evidence to support your claim, and explain your reasoning.

_____

_____

_____

_____

_____

ACTIVE READING

3 Apply Many words, such as *model,* have multiple meanings. Use context clues to write your own definition for each meaning of the word *model.*

Example sentence
Sports stars are role <u>models</u> for thousands of young people.

model:

_____

_____

Example sentence
They used a computer to <u>model</u> the possible effects of global warming.

model:

_____

_____

Vocabulary Term
- model

4 Apply As you learn the definition of the vocabulary term in this lesson, create your own definition or sketch to help you remember the meaning of the term.

Get Organized!

How do scientists make sense of data?

There are many different kinds of scientific investigations, all of which involve the collection of data. *Data* are the facts, figures, and other evidence scientists gather when they conduct an investigation. The more data a scientist collects, the greater is the need for the data to be organized in some way. Data tables are one easy way to organize a lot of data.

○ Scientists Organize the Data

Scientists design and build tables to hold their data in an orderly way. Typical data include quantities, times, and *frequencies,* or the number of times something happens. Scientists decide where to put each type of data and label the columns and rows accordingly. They include units of measurement, such as feet or seconds, in the column headings.

Scientists use these tables to record observations and measurements during their investigations. Later the data tables become tools of analysis.

Jasmine conducted a survey to determine the types of movies students prefer. She polled 100 students in the seventh grade. Then she organized the data that she collected into the table.

Movie-Type Preferences

Type of movie	Number of students
Action	40
Comedy	30
Drama	15
Horror	5
Other	10
Total	100

👁 Visualize It!

5 Gather Evidence What other kind of evidence could you collect about student preferences?

_____

_____

_____

Scientists Graph and Analyze the Data

In order to analyze data for patterns and trends, it is often helpful to construct a graph. The type of graph you use depends upon the data collected and what you want to show.

A *circle graph* is an ideal way to display data that are parts of a whole. Each section of the circle represents a category of the data. The entire circle represents all of the data. For example, in the movie preference data, the types of movies are the categories.

If you think of a complete circle as 100%, you can express sections of a circle graph as percentages. The table below shows how to find the percentage of students who prefer each type of movie. As shown in the last column, divide the number of students who prefer each movie type by the total number of students. Then multiply by 100 percent to get the percentage.

ACTIVE **READING**

6 Claims • Evidence • Reasoning
Make a claim about the sum of the percentages in a circle graph. Provide evidence to support your claim, and explain your reasoning.

Movie-Type Preferences

Type of movie	Number of students	Percentage of students
Action	40	$\frac{40}{100} \times 100\% = 40\%$
Comedy	30	$\frac{30}{100} \times 100\% = 30\%$
Drama	15	$\frac{15}{100} \times 100\% = 15\%$
Horror	5	$\frac{5}{100} \times 100\% = 5\%$
Other	10	$\frac{10}{100} \times 100\% = 10\%$

👁 Visualize It!

Each section of the circle graph represents the percentage of students who prefer each type of movie. Compare the sizes of the sections to determine how they are related.

7 Claims • Evidence • Reasoning Would you expect the next student Jasmine polled to prefer action movies or horror movies? State your claim. Provide evidence to support the claim, and explain your reasoning.

_____

_____

_____

Movie-Type Preferences

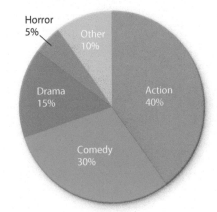

Circle up!

What do graphs show?

Graphs show data in a visual way. Data displayed in a graph are often easier to understand than data displayed in a table. There are many kinds of graphs.

A *circle graph,* or pie chart, is used when showing how each group of data relates to all of the data. A *bar graph* is used to display and compare data in a number of categories. A *line graph* is most often used to show continuous change. Line graphs are useful for showing changes in variables over time.

Do the Math

You Try It

Cara observes the bird feeder in her yard for 3 hours at the same time each day for 3 days. She writes down the types and numbers of birds that visit the feeder. In total, she sees 60 birds. Her data are shown at the right.

Cardinal	ЖІ ЖІ ЖІ
Finch	ЖІ ІІІІ
Mockingbird	ЖІ ЖІ ЖІ ЖІ ІІІІ
Wren	ЖІ ЖІ ІІ

8 Calculate Use the table below to organize the data that Cara collected. In the last column, find the percentage of each bird that Cara saw by dividing the number of each type of bird by the total number of birds and multiplying by 100%.

Type of bird	Number of birds	Percentage of birds

Visualize It!

The circle graph below is divided into equal sections that are 5% of the total circle. Remember that a complete circle is 100%.

9 Graph Make a circle graph using the percentages you calculated for the bird study. Make appropriately sized pie-shaped slices of the graph for each type of bird. Label each section of the graph with the name of the bird type and the total number of birds of that type counted. Then add an appropriate title.

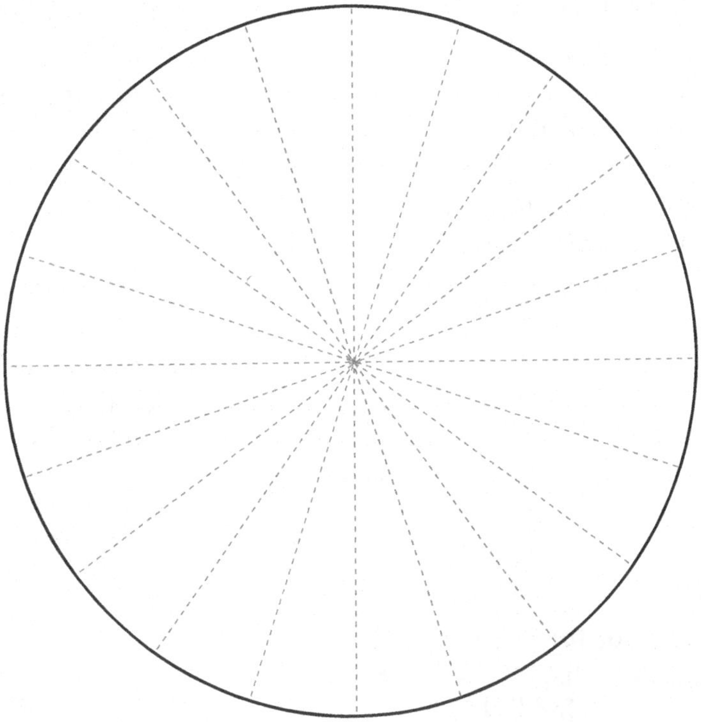

10 Identify Describe something that is easier to see in the circle graph than it is to see in the table.

11 Interpret How does the size of each section of your circle graph relate to the percentage that it represents?

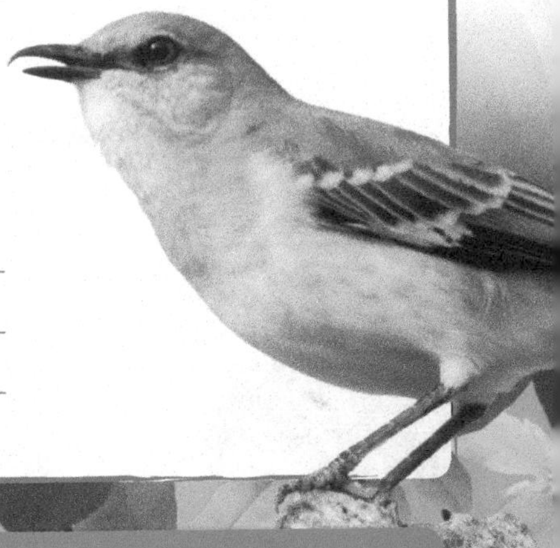

Think Outside the Book

12 Hypothesize Could you have plotted the bird study results in a bar graph? If so, which variable would be shown on the horizontal axis and which would be shown on the vertical axis?

Test Drive the New Model

How do scientists evaluate models?

A scientific **model** can be a visual or mathematical representation of an object or system. Models are useful for showing things that are too small, too large, or too complex to see easily. For example, a globe and an atlas are both visual models of Earth. Scientists who study Earth's atmosphere use mathematical models to try to imitate Earth's climate.

Scientists use models in many ways. They use models to make predictions before an investigation as well as to represent the results after an investigation. Scientists must use models wisely. They must continually look at the models they use to make sure that they are serving their needs. They must be aware of the model's strengths and limitations.

ACTIVE READING

13 Apply As you read, underline examples of scientific models.

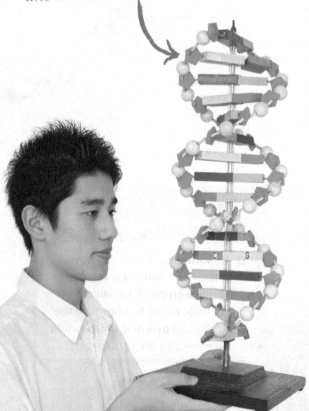

The structure of DNA is a double helix, which is shaped like a twisted ladder.

By How Much They Can Explain

One famous scientific model is that of the DNA (deoxyribonucleic acid) double helix. DNA is the molecule responsible for passing genetic information from one generation to the next. Evidence and data from biology, chemistry, and physics went into developing the DNA model. The model, in a way, is a representsation of that data and evidence.

Models can be created out of a variety of materials. They can be simple or complex. For example, a DNA double helix model can be brightly colored and three-dimensional, similar to the one at the left, or it can be lines on a piece of paper. The important thing is for the model to show what it must in order to be a good representation.

14 Claims • Evidence • Reasoning Explain why it is valuable for some objects to be shown by more than one kind of model. Provide evidence to support your claim.

Visualize It!

15 Compare Both the photo and model below show a plant cell. Identify an advantage and a disadvantage for using the model instead of the photo to study cells.

_____

_____

_____

_____

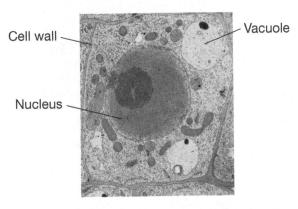

The details of the actual plant cell in this photograph can be fuzzy.

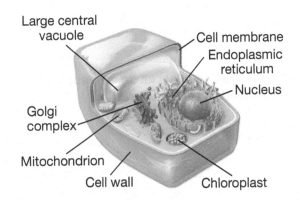

The model of the plant cell shows distinct parts.

By How Well They Can Adapt

When building models, scientists often hope to discover new information. The best models may even explain something that had been puzzling to scientists.

For example, scientists already knew that DNA carries genetic information from one generation to the next. How DNA did this was not obvious. Look at the model at the left. Notice the colors of the horizontal pieces. These pieces represent the way that parts of the molecule attach to one another. The model shows that these attachments follow a certain pattern. The order and pairing of the parts gave scientists a way to speculate about how genetic information is carried.

Scientists had created the model from evidence. Then the model gave scientists more information about how DNA carries genetic information from one generation to the next.

By the Fewest Limitations

Scientists often choose models depending on their limitations. For example, would you want to learn about the parts of a cell using the photo at the top left? The photo is of a plant cell, and many of the cell structures are barely visible. The model of the plant cell at the top right, however, shows the plant cell more clearly. After studying the model for a while, you may even be able to pick out structures in the photo that you did not see before.

Sometimes after building a model scientists find data that do not fit the model they created. So, the model may not take certain data into account. To make sense of the information they gathered, scientists must know the ways in which a model does not act exactly as the real object or system does.

Visual Summary

To complete this summary, check the box that indicates true or false. You can use this page to review the main concepts of the lesson.

Representing Data

A scientific model can be a visual or mathematical representation.

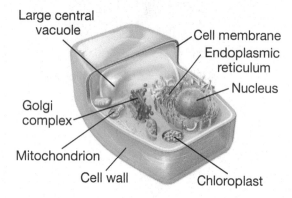

Large central vacuole

Cell membrane

Endoplasmic reticulum

Nucleus

Golgi complex

Mitochondrion

Cell wall

Chloroplast

	T	F
16	☐	☐

Because models are simplified versions of real objects, they often have limitations.

19 Claims • Evidence • Reasoning Sketch a simple model of your yard or a neighborhood park. Include some animals, some plants, and some environmental factors. Make a claim about the limitations of your model. Provide evidence to support the claim, and explain your reasoning.

Different types of graphs can be used to show different types of data.

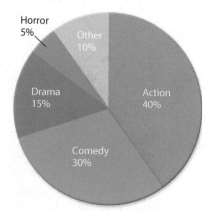

Movie-Type Preferences

Horror 5%
Other 10%
Drama 15%
Action 40%
Comedy 30%

	T	F
17	☐	☐

According to this circle graph, more students preferred horror movies than comedies.

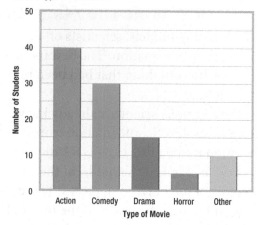

Movie-Type Preferences

	T	F
18	☐	☐

A bar graph is used to compare data in categories.

Lesson Review

Vocabulary

Circle the term that best completes each of the following sentences.

1 A *hypothesis/graph* can be used to represent the results of an investigation.

2 A *model/law* uses familiar things to describe unfamiliar things.

Key Concepts

3 Define What is a model?

_____

_____

_____

4 Explain Your Reasoning Explain why scientists use models.

_____

_____

_____

5 Claims • Evidence • Reasoning Why do scientists use data tables? State your claim. Provide evidence to support the claim, and explain your reasoning.

_____

_____

_____

6 Define What is a circle graph?

_____

_____

_____

7 Explain Your Reasoning Could you use a circle graph to show data about how body mass changes with height? Explain your reasoning.

_____

_____

_____

Critical Thinking

Use this photo to answer the following questions.

8 Compare How similar is this model to a real object?

_____

_____

9 Claims • Evidence • Reasoning How might this model be useful? State your claim. Provide evidence to support the claim, and explain your reasoning.

_____

_____

10 Hypothesize Identify a possible limitation of a model and describe why it might make a model less useful than it could be.

_____

_____

The **Engineering Design Process**

ESSENTIAL QUESTION

What is the engineering design process?

By the end of this lesson, you should be able to explain how the engineering design process is used to develop solutions to meet people's needs.

In 2008, Olympic swimmers competed in a large pool inside the Beijing National Aquatics Center, also known as the Beijing Water Cube. It now houses water rides, a wave pool, and a spa.

SC.7.N.1.1 Define a problem from the seventh grade curriculum, use appropriate reference materials to support scientific understanding, plan and carry out scientific investigation of various types, such as systematic observations or experiments, identify variables, collect and organize data, interpret data in charts, tables, and graphics, analyze information, make predictions, and defend conclusions. **SC.7.N.1.5** Describe the methods used in the pursuit of a scientific explanation as seen in different fields of science such as biology, geology, and physics. **SC.7.N.3.2** Identify the benefits and limitations of the use of scientific models.

Engage Your Brain

1 Predict Check T or F to show whether you think each statement is true or false.

T   F

☐   ☐   The Beijing Water Cube is an example of technology.

☐   ☐   Creativity is not part of the engineering design process.

☐   ☐   Nature can inspire new designs.

2 Observe Both the shape of a structure and the shapes of its individual parts affect the overall strength of a structure. Identify the repeating shapes in each image. List at least two differences between the walls of the Water Cube and the milk bubbles.

_____

_____

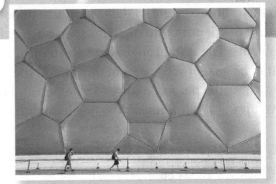

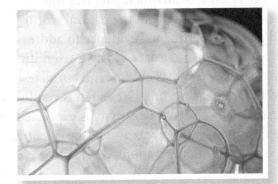

ACTIVE **READING**

3 Synthesize You can often define an unknown word if you know the meanings of its word parts. Use the word parts and sentence below to make an educated guess about the meaning of the word *technology*.

Word part	Meaning
techno	skill
logy	study of

Example sentence
The development of smartphones is viewed as an important advance in computer technology.

technology:

_____

_____

Vocabulary Terms

• **engineering**   • **prototype**
• **technology**

4 Identify This list contains the vocabulary terms you'll learn in this lesson. As you read, underline the vocabulary words whenever they appear in the text.

It's All Relative

How does the goal of science compare to the goal of engineering?

Scientists observe, collect data, and form hypotheses. **Engineering** is the use of scientific and mathematical knowledge to solve practical problems. The goal of engineering is to meet the needs of society while the goal of science is to understand the natural world. Scientists study how the parts of nature work alone and together. Engineers develop ways of improving the quality of life for human beings.

Science Strives to Explain the Natural World

Scientists work in an orderly, logical way. They ask questions about the natural world and gather experimental evidence to address those questions. In order to form a scientific explanation, scientists observe, measure, test, and record data. Scientific research is careful, but it can also be creative. Creativity is expressed in the design of experiments and in the scientific explanations of observations.

Engineering Strives to Meet the Needs of Society

Humans have always needed tools, such as knives and fire, to help them survive. Beginning in the 1700s, people have increasingly used industrial processes. There is a growing need for energy to operate machines and services to support urban populations. Engineers apply scientific discoveries to develop technologies such as electrical power, sanitation systems, and new ways of communicating.

ACTIVE **READING**

5 Claims • Evidence • Reasoning How do engineers contribute to the area where you live? State your claim. Provide evidence to support the claim, and explain your reasoning.

_____

👁 Visualize It!

6 Compare In what ways is the modern lamp a better design than the antique lamp? Explain your reasoning.

_____

_____

_____

_____

A wick carries oil into the globe of this lamp where it burns to produce light.

This light-emitting diode (LED) boat light stays cool. Almost 100% of its energy production is light.

What is the relationship between technology, engineering, math, and science?

Science is the study of the natural world. Engineering applies knowledge to develop technology to solve real-life problems. **Technology** includes the use of tools, materials, or processes to meet human needs. Scientists depend on technology such as digital cameras and instruments to observe and measure when they collect data. With computers, they analyze data to support scientific explanations. Engineers build advances in science into new instruments and processes. Science and engineering support one another to advance our knowledge of the natural world and create technologies to manipulate it. Engineers use science and math to develop new technologies. Scientists use technology in research, and engineers use research results to develop technology.

⊙ Visualize It!

7 Apply Insert the terms *science, technology, engineering,* and *math* into the graphic organizer to see how they are all related.

8 Claims • Evidence • Reasoning How could a biologist studying bird migration use global positioning satellite (GPS) technology? Provide evidence, and explain your reasoning.

_____

_____

_____

9 Support Your Claim Why does the graphic show arrows between technology and both science and engineering? Provide evidence to support your claim.

_____

_____

_____

The Right Tool For the Job

How is technology used in scientific investigations?

Scientists investigate the natural world by making observations and doing experiments. They use tools to measure, collect, and analyze data. Many investigations focus on things that are very big or very small, or located in places that are dangerous or hard to reach. Scientists and engineers design specialized technologies for these investigations. For example, biologists observe bacteria through microscopes. Huge accelerators produce high energy collisions between atoms and other particles. Astronomers probe deep into space using digital cameras with telescopes. Robots transmit data from distant planets and ocean depths. The purpose of all of these tools is to collect samples, take pictures, and acquire data.

Think Outside the Book

11 Apply Imagine a place or situation that would be interesting to explore but is inaccessible to humans. Design, sketch, and label your own explorer. Think about the tasks that the explorer will need to do and the environment in which it will be working.

👁 Visualize It!

10 Identify Label each part with one of the following tasks: generating energy, measuring properties, recording information, communicating data.

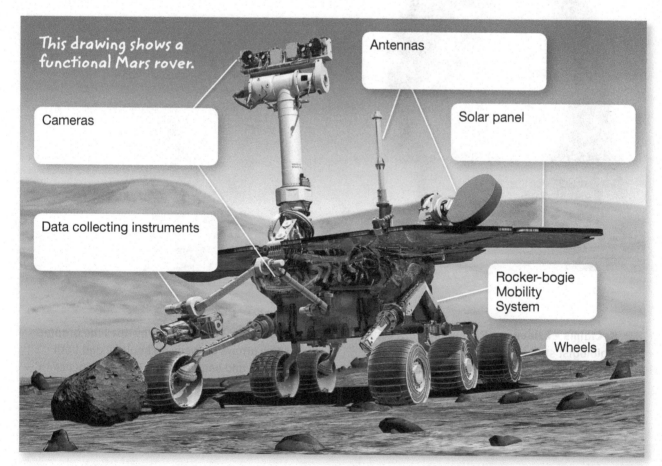

This drawing shows a functional Mars rover.

Antennas

Cameras

Solar panel

Data collecting instruments

Rocker-bogie Mobility System

Wheels

(b) ©NASA/JPL/Cornell University

Students learning about engineering design develop such technical skills as learning to build and test a prototype.

What skills are needed for engineering design?

Look at the world around you. You see computers, cell phones, microwave ovens, and machines for washing dishes and clothes. You see motor vehicles on roads and bridges. You see a world that was designed by engineers.

The goal of engineering design is to meet people's needs. When engineers design solutions to problems, they employ a set of skills that work together.

ACTIVE READING

12 Apply Which type of skills below do you use most often? Give an example.

_____

_____

_____

Research Skills

Engineering design starts with good research skills. Engineers learn all they can about the problem they want to solve, including how similar problems were tackled in the past. Then they must determine whether previous solution attempts were successful and how to adapt them to the current problem. To build on existing approaches, engineers examine new scientific research and apply the results to their design. These adaptations often improve on or replace the previous solutions.

Technical Skills

In solving practical problems, engineers must apply their technical skills in math and science. For example, determining how much weight a bridge can bear requires knowledge of materials and structure and the ability to perform complex calculations. Modern engineering design depends on computer skills in using specialized software for computer-aided design and analysis. Engineering design also requires skill in building **prototypes**, special models built to test a product.

Thinking Skills

Methodical, orderly thinking skills are essential for engineers who must carefully go through every step in the design process. While engineers must pay close attention to every detail in building and testing a prototype, the engineering design process also calls for creativity. Engineers form teams to brainstorm ways of thinking about a problem and proposing solutions. Sometimes they turn a disadvantage into an advantage by finding creative ways to use existing knowledge to solve problems.

Step Right Up

What are the steps of the engineering design process?

When you need to solve a problem, an organized approach leads to the best solution. The steps in the engineering design process provide a logical way of developing a new product or system to solve a real-world problem. People using the process often work in teams. As you will see on the next page, once the need has been identified, the steps of the process often become a cycle.

ACTIVE READING

13 Identify What is the purpose of breaking the engineering design process into specific steps?

_____

1. Identifying a Need

What is the problem? Who has the problem? Why must it be solved? These are the types of questions that identify a problem that needs a technical solution.

2. Conducting Research

By doing research, the design team learns as much as possible about the need that must be met or the problem that must be solved. The research frequently turns up similar problems and the different solutions that have been tried. The design team works more efficiently by learning from the past efforts of others and by identifying new resources and possibilities.

3. Brainstorming and Selecting Solutions

Team members think of possible solution ideas during a brainstorming session. The goal of brainstorming is to come up with as many engineering design solutions as possible. Any idea, even if it does not seem promising, is open for discussion. Then each idea is evaluated: Is the device or product safe? Does it address the problem? What would it cost? Would it be easy to make? The team selects the best solution based on how well it meets the requirements of the need or problem.

4. Building a Prototype

The design team builds a prototype of the device or product they selected as the best technical solution to the need or problem. The team uses the prototype as a working model to test and evaluate how well the product works under real-life conditions. A prototype usually does not work perfectly right away. The team uses the prototype to find out how the solution can be improved and for troubleshooting–finding out why parts of the product or device do not work as expected.

👁 Visualize It!

14 Design In the space provided, sketch a prototype device for rescuing the trapped cat.

5. Testing, Evaluating, and Redesigning a Prototype

The engineering design process calls for testing and changing the prototype until a solution is reached. The team tests the prototype and records the results. After discussing the results, changes are made to improve the prototype design. Testing and redesigning the prototype continues until the prototype addresses the need.

6. Communicating Results

The final step in the engineering design process is communicating the results. It is very important to take good notes and communicate all details about the product or solution. Such details enable others to duplicate the results. Student teams can communicate the results to others in a final report or by posting their results on a display board. Professional engineers often communicate their results through reports in engineering journals.

15 List You want to tell others how you rescued the cat. How will you communicate the results? List two possible ways below.

_____

How does the engineering design process work?

The steps of the engineering design process call for engineers to use both technical skills and creativity. From identifying a need to finding a good solution, engineers are always asking questions. Instead of simply moving from one step to the next, the process goes back and forth between the steps. In the chart below, the rectangles contain steps, and the diamonds contain questions or decision points. Try answering the questions in different ways and see how the path that you follow through the design process depends on the answers to the questions. Keep in mind that the goal is to design a solution to a problem, whether it is rescuing a cat or focusing a beam of charged particles on a tiny target.

ACTIVE READING

16 Claims • Evidence • Reasoning
Make a claim about how asking questions helps the engineering design process. Provide evidence to support the claim, and explain your reasoning.

_____

_____

_____

_____

_____

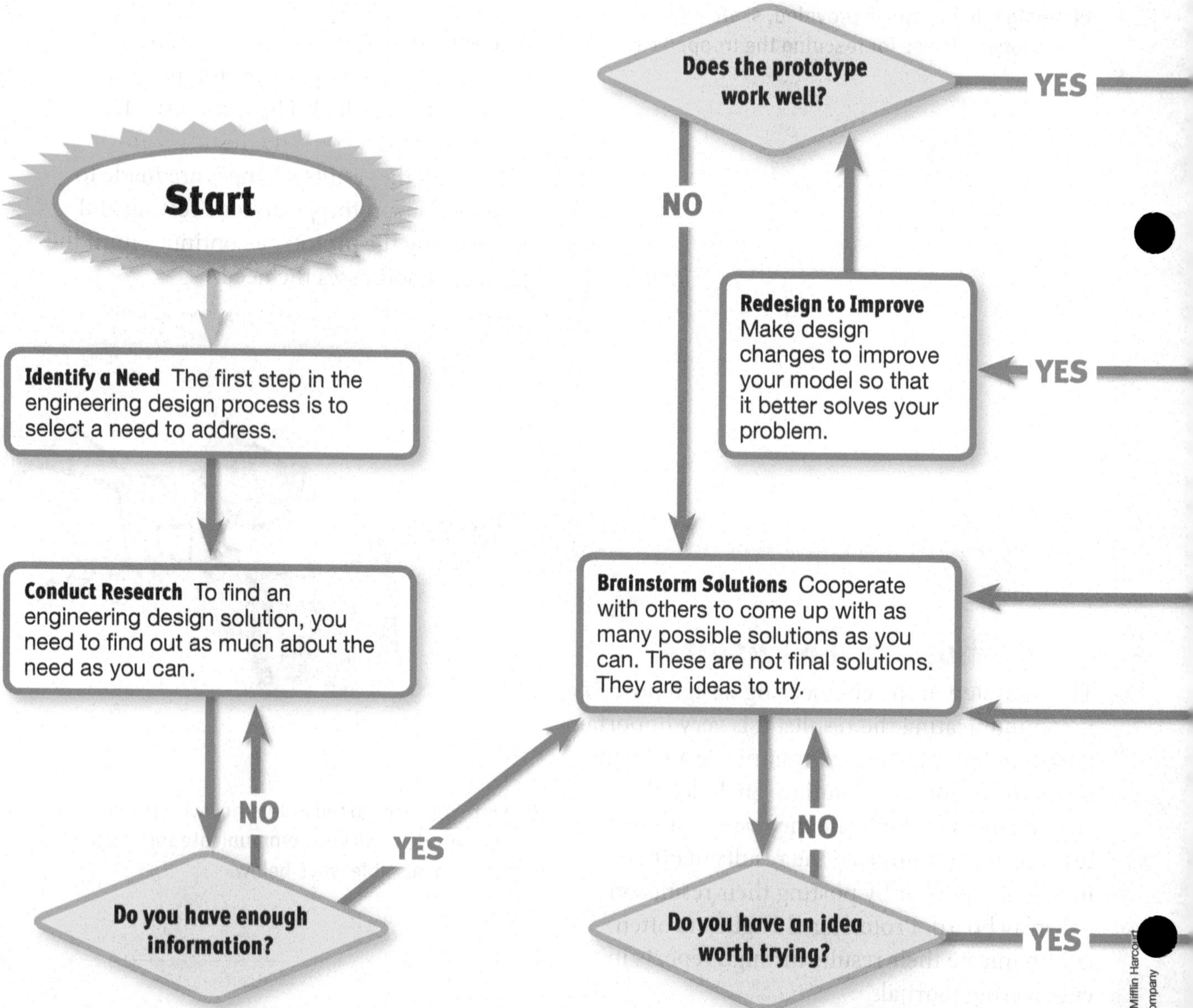

Does the prototype work well? — YES

Start

NO

Identify a Need The first step in the engineering design process is to select a need to address.

Redesign to Improve Make design changes to improve your model so that it better solves your problem. ← YES

Conduct Research To find an engineering design solution, you need to find out as much about the need as you can.

Brainstorm Solutions Cooperate with others to come up with as many possible solutions as you can. These are not final solutions. They are ideas to try.

NO

YES

NO

Do you have enough information?

Do you have an idea worth trying? — YES

This superconducting magnet assembly is one of many magnets designed to focus a beam of charged particles on a target the size of an atom in the Large Hadron Collider. Engineers followed the engineering design process to develop every component of the magnet.

Communicate Your Results When your prototype is finished, you have designed a solution to your problem. Tell others how you did it!

End!

Test and Evaluate Your prototype probably won't be perfect the first time you try it, but it should be on the right track.

Does the prototype show promise?

NO

Build a Prototype Your prototype should be a working model of your solution to the problem.

YES

Can you make a prototype?

NO

Select a Solution Which of your ideas do you want to try? Pick one, and plan how you want to try it.

👁 Visualize It!

17 Apply Oh, no! The test results of your most recent prototype indicate that it doesn't meet the need for which it was designed. List the next four steps in the engineering design process that you might follow.

_____

_____

_____

_____

Visual Summary

To complete this summary, fill in each blank with the correct word or phrase. You can use this page to review the main concepts of this lesson.

The goal of science is to understand the natural world. The goal of engineering is to meet the needs of society.

18 *Engineering applies _____ and math to develop technology.*

The **Engineering Design Process**

The first steps in the process are identifying and doing research about a need.
The next steps involve brainstorming and selecting a solution.

20 *Before selecting the final design, engineers built and tested a _____*

Engineering design starts with good research skills. Engineering design requires a variety of technical skills.

19 *Engineering design calls for both logical and creative _____ skills.*

21 Claims • Evidence • Reasoning As part of an engineering team, you are designing a tool for tracking packages being shipped. Provide some suggestions to be discussed as part of the brainstorming process. Make a claim about your suggested solutions, and support your claim with evidence. Explain your reasoning.

Lesson Review

Vocabulary

Fill in the blank with the term that best completes the following sentences.

1 Engineers solve real-life problems by developing new _____ .

2 Developing new products and systems that meet human needs is the goal of _____ .

3 A working model that engineers use to test a design is called a _____ .

Key Concepts

4 Relate How are scientific discoveries used in engineering design?

_____

_____

5 Summarize List the basic steps in the engineering design process.

_____

_____

6 Claims • Evidence • Reasoning Make a claim about why engineering design calls for good research skills. Provide evidence to support the claim, and explain your reasoning.

_____

_____

7 Claims • Evidence • Reasoning Make a claim about why the engineering design process does not move smoothly from step to step but instead goes back and forth between the steps. Provide evidence to support the claim, and explain your reasoning.

_____

_____

Critical Thinking

8 Infer After an engineering design team communicates its results, how could those results be used?

_____

_____

Use this diagram to answer the following questions.

9 Claims • Evidence • Reasoning Make a claim about the qualities that engineers could test using the prototype of this bicycle. Provide evidence to support your claim, and explain your reasoning.

_____

_____

10 Claims • Evidence • Reasoning Make a claim about one or more changes that could be made to this prototype to reduce wind resistance and increase speed. Provide evidence to support your claim, and explain your reasoning.

_____

_____

Methods of Analysis

© Josh Mitchell/Monsoon/Photolibrary/Corbis

ESSENTIAL **QUESTION**

How can we evaluate technology?

By the end of this lesson you should be able to explain how scientists and engineers determine the costs, benefits, and risks of a new technology.

SC.7.N.1.1 Define a problem from the seventh grade curriculum, use appropriate reference materials to support scientific understanding, plan and carry out scientific investigation of various types, such as systematic observations or experiments, identify variables, collect and organize data, interpret data in charts, tables, and graphics, analyze information, make predictions, and defend conclusions. **SC.7.N.1.5** Describe the methods used in the pursuit of a scientific explanation as seen in different fields of science such as biology, geology, and physics **SC.7.N.2.1** Identify an instance from the history of science in which scientific knowledge has changed when new evidence or new interpretations are encountered. **SC.7.N.3.2** Identify the benefits and limitations of the use of scientific models.

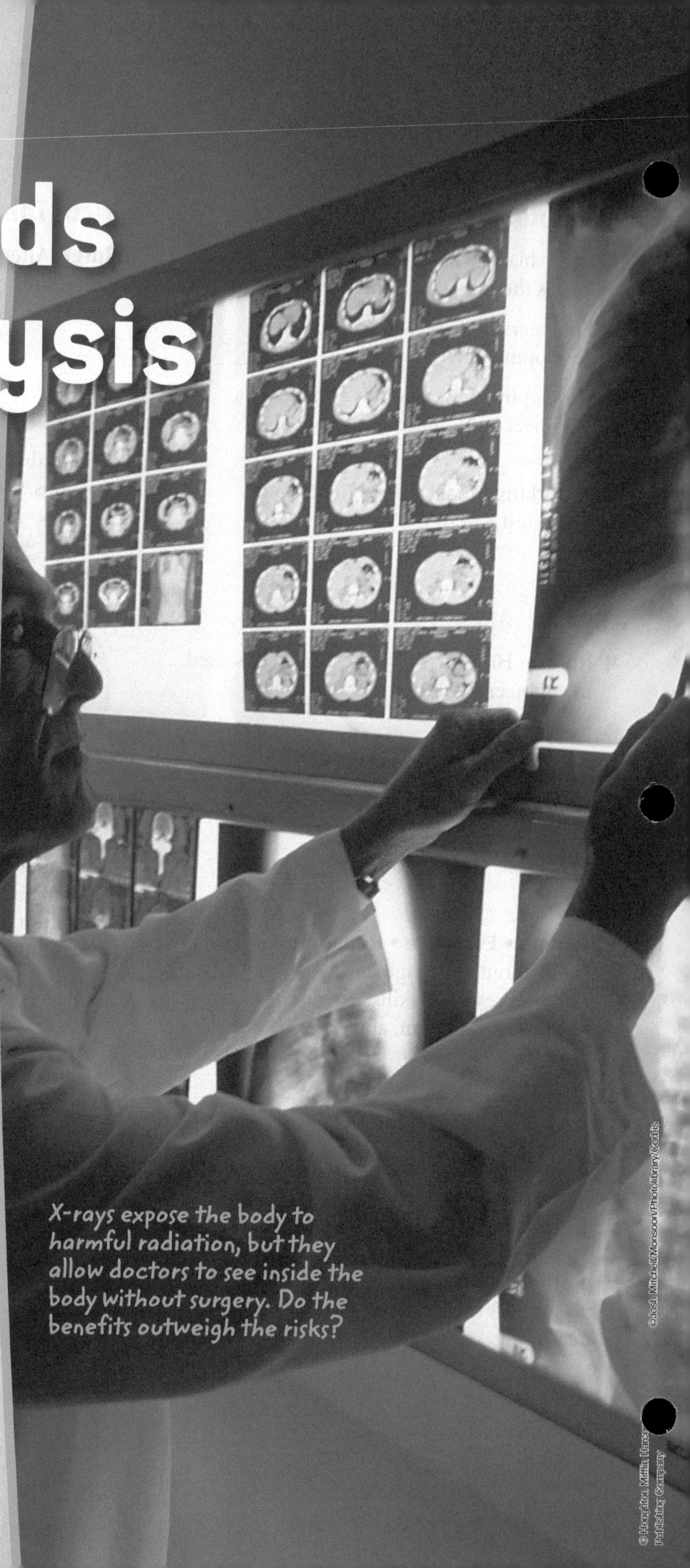

X-rays expose the body to harmful radiation, but they allow doctors to see inside the body without surgery. Do the benefits outweigh the risks?

© Houghton Mifflin Harcourt Publishing Company

Lesson Labs

Quick Labs
- Investigate Mining
- Air Innovation

Engage Your Brain

1 Predict Check T or F to show whether you think each statement is true or false.

T	F	
☐	☐	Sometimes people accept certain risks in exchange for other benefits.
☐	☐	Technology never causes problems.
☐	☐	When comparing technology, you need to examine each feature.
☐	☐	A product only affects the environment when it is thrown away.

2 Identify List advantages and disadvantages of each of the writing utensils shown here.

	Advantages	Disadvantages
A 		
B		

ACTIVE READING

3 Infer The term *life cycle* often describes the stages an organism goes through from birth to death. What do you think *life cycle* means when it is used to talk about a product?

_____

_____

_____

_____

_____

Vocabulary Terms

- trade-off
- risk-benefit analysis
- life cycle analysis
- Pugh chart

4 Apply As you learn the definition of each vocabulary term in this lesson, create your own definition or sketch to help you remember the meaning of the term.

Better or Worse

How can the effects of technology be described?

Technology is the application of science for practical purposes and can include products, processes, and systems. New technology may affect society, the environment, or the economy in several ways. The effects of a new technology can be classified in four ways:

- expected and favorable
- expected and unfavorable
- unexpected and favorable
- unexpected and unfavorable

○ Expected Effects

When people develop technology, they try to predict the effects that it may have. The goal for any new technology is to keep the expected favorable effects greater than any expected unfavorable effects. People make trade-offs when they adopt new technology. A **trade-off** means accepting risks in exchange for benefits or giving up one benefit to gain another. The control of fire is one of the earliest human technologies. Fire improves food and increases the odds of surviving winter. But fire can also destroy homes, crops, and habitats. For thousands of years, people have accepted the risk of fire because the expected benefits outweigh the risk.

○ Unexpected Effects

People cannot always predict the effects of new technology. For example, scientists developed instruments to study how atoms interact with one another. An unexpected favorable result was magnetic resonance imaging (MRI). MRI is a medical technique that looks inside the body without using harmful radiation.

In the mid-twentieth century, nontoxic chemicals made it possible to make better refrigerators for homes. An unexpected unfavorable effect was that these chemicals began destroying the protective ozone layer in the upper atmosphere.

ACTIVE READING

5 Claims • Evidence • Reasoning What is the difference between expected effects and unexpected effects of technology? Provide evidence to support your claim, and explain your reasoning.

Control of fire is one of the earliest technologies to be developed by humans.

Think Outside the Book

6 Claims • Evidence • Reasoning Use the Internet to find out how infectious diseases can spread rapidly from one continent to another. How would you classify the spread of disease as an effect of air travel? State your claim. Provide evidence to support the claim, and explain your reasoning.

Before the invention of freezer technology, many vegetables and fruits could only be eaten during a few months of the year.

	Expected	Unexpected
Favorable	When frozen foods were developed, it was expected that frozen food would last longer than food that was not frozen. As a result, people save money because frozen vegetables do not spoil. Also, people can eat healthy foods even when they are not in season.	Surprisingly, frozen fruits and vegetables turned out to be more nutritious than fresh produce. Produce begins to lose nutrients as soon as it is picked. Food processors usually freeze fruits and vegetables soon after picking so nutrients remain in the product.
Unfavorable	An expected unfavorable effect of selling frozen foods is that local farmers and markets that provide fresh fruits and vegetables lose customers. In addition, frozen foods need more packaging than fresh foods. This adds to the cost of the food and the environmental costs of supplying it. People are willing to make these trade-offs in order to have frozen food.	When frozen foods were first developed, no one could have predicted the variety of frozen foods that would become available. Many frozen foods today contain more fat, sugar, and salt than fresh foods do. Eating too much of these substances can have unfavorable health effects.

7 Analyze Use the comparison table below to analyze the expected and unexpected effects of the development of the World Wide Web.

	Expected	Unexpected
Favorable		
Unfavorable		

Risky Business

How is technology analyzed?

There are many ways to analyze new technology. Three methods that people use are *risk-benefit analysis, life cycle analysis,* and *Pugh charts.*

○ Risk-Benefit Analysis

A **risk-benefit analysis** compares the risks, or unfavorable effects, to the benefits, or favorable effects, of a decision or technology. For example, x-rays are a way for doctors to look inside the body to evaluate broken bones and diagnose disease. However, as x-rays pass through the body, they can damage living cells. Medical x-rays expose patients to very small doses of radiation, so the benefits are considered greater than the risks. At one time, some shoe stores used x-rays to match shoes to customers' feet. This is no longer done because the benefit was very small compared to the risk.

Risks and Benefits of X-rays	
Risks	**Benefits**
damage to cells	quick
increased risk of cancer	painless
	saves lives

Skate parks are popular attractions. But there are definite risks involved for the skaters and the owners of the park.

8 Analyze Fill in the chart below with the risks and benefits of building a new skate park in your community.

Risks and Benefits of a New Skate Park

Life Cycle Analysis

When analyzing technology, it is important to consider the real cost. This is done using a life cycle analysis. A **life cycle analysis** is an evaluation of the materials and energy used for the manufacture, transportation, sale, use, and disposal of a product. This analysis includes everything that the product affects, from obtaining raw materials through disposal. The costs of all of these steps are added together to find the real cost of the product. For example, a life cycle analysis of a glass bottle examines the cost of repairing environmental damage from the mining of raw materials, the cost of fuels consumed to transport materials and finished bottles, and the cost of disposal. A major reason for doing a life cycle analysis is to include environmental effects in the cost. Life cycle analyses are important to manufacturers because the analyses help engineers compare the real costs of different products and find ways to improve production.

Life Cycle of a Television

Resources
A life cycle analysis includes the cost to mine materials for television parts, for manufacturing packaging, and for repairing environmental damage.

Production
The cost of manufacturing is just one part of the overall economic effect of a television.

Consumer Use
Another part of the life cycle analysis is the cost in money and energy when people buy and use the product.

◉ Visualize It!

9 Infer Write a title and a description for the final step in the life cycle of a television.

_____

_____

_____

_____

_____

○ Pugh Chart

A **Pugh chart** is a table used to compare the features of multiple items. Each row of the table shows a different product or solution. Each column of the chart lists one feature. In some Pugh charts, various options are marked as being either present or missing. Other Pugh charts rank each product as being better or worse than a standard for each feature. Another type ranks each product by feature using a numerical scale.

By looking at the table, a person can analyze and compare items. For example, a Pugh chart comparing cell phones would list different phones in the first column on the left. Then each column would be titled based on a characteristic that is important to consumers. These characteristics could include battery life, sound quality, and messaging systems. A quick look at the Pugh chart would tell you which cell phone was the best based on the qualities that you were looking for.

10 Analyze Evaluate the features of different types of containers. Place an X in each box where the quality applies to the container. Then use the chart to answer the following questions.

	Lightweight	Waterproof	Durable	Inexpensive	Transparent	Reusable
Glass jar						
Plastic bag	X					
Cardboard box	X					
Metal box						

11 Infer Suppose that you have a collection of interesting seashells. Use the chart to help you decide which container you would use to display the collection on shelves in your room. Explain your reasoning.

_____

_____

_____

_____

_____

12 Claims • Evidence • Reasoning Why do manufacturers choose cardboard containers for products such as breakfast cereal? State your claim. Provide evidence to support the claim, and explain your reasoning.

_____

_____

_____

_____

_____

WHY IT **MATTERS**

SOCIETY AND TECHNOLOGY

Building Coral Reefs

Recycling large vehicles—ships, jetliners, or railroad cars—is expensive and difficult. Scuba divers exploring wrecked ships found an unexpected solution. Aquatic organisms had moved into the sunken ships and built new coral reefs.

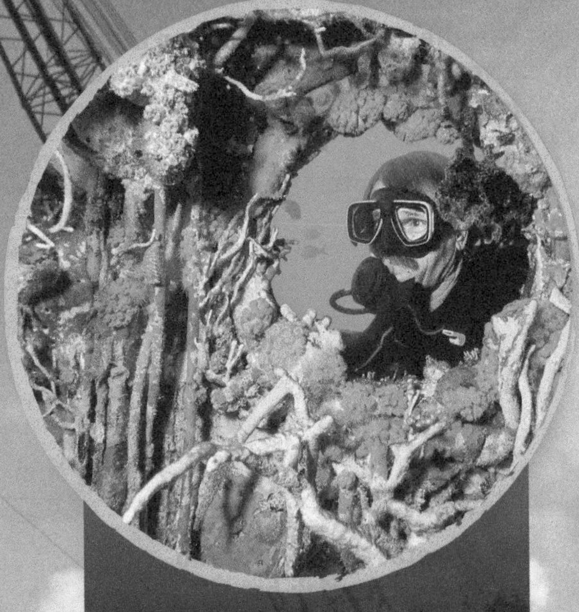

Potential Hazards?

Before sinking, a risk-benefit analysis is done to look for any unfavorable effects such as pollution by leftover fuel.

New Shelters

To the coral organisms, the airplane walls are like an underwater cave. As the new reef grows, many different organisms find their perfect habitat.

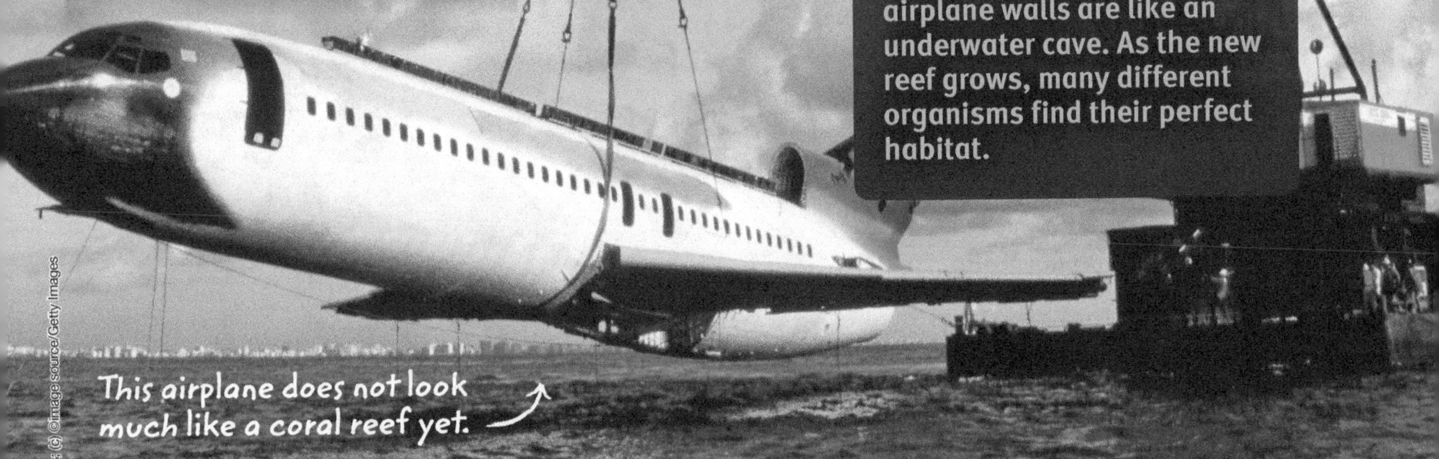

This airplane does not look much like a coral reef yet.

Extend

13 **Identify** How can an artificial reef be considered an unexpected favorable effect of building a plane?

14 **Research** Use the Internet to investigate other positive or negative effects of sinking ships or planes to build artificial reefs. What did you find?

15 **Claims • Evidence • Reasoning** Some people feel that sinking ships and planes on purpose is like dumping our trash in the ocean. In your opinion, do the possible negative effects outweigh the benefits? Provide evidence to support the claim, and explain your reasoning.

Visual Summary

To complete this summary, fill in the blanks with the correct word or phrase. You can use this page to review the main concepts of the lesson.

The effects of technology can be expected favorable, expected unfavorable, unexpected favorable, and unexpected unfavorable.

16 When an effect is predicted and desired, it is an

_____ effect.

Methods of Analysis

Three methods for analyzing technology are risk-benefit analysis, life cycle analysis, and Pugh charts.

17 A _____
examines every aspect of a product from obtaining raw materials through disposal or recycling.

18 A _____
uses a table to compare features of similar products.

19 An analysis that compares the favorable and unfavorable effects of a decision or technology is a

_____

20 **Claims • Evidence • Reasoning** Why do scientists use analysis methods when developing new technology? Provide evidence to support your claim, and explain your reasoning.

Lesson Review

Vocabulary

Fill in the blank with the term that best completes the following sentences.

1 A _____ happens when some benefits are lost to gain other benefits.

2 The evaluation of the materials and energy used for making, selling, using, and disposing of a product is called a _____

_____

3 A _____ is the comparison of the favorable and unfavorable effects of a technology.

Key Concepts

4 Identify What are the four types of effects that can result from technology?

_____

_____

5 Claims • Evidence • Reasoning Which type of analysis would be most useful to someone buying a product at a store? State your claim. Provide evidence to support the claim, and explain your reasoning.

_____

_____

6 Claims • Evidence • Reasoning How is a life cycle analysis used to make decisions about technology? Provide evidence to support your claim, and explain your reasoning.

_____

_____

_____

7 Describe When do the results of a risk-benefit analysis indicate that a technology should be used?

_____

_____

_____

Critical Thinking

Use the Pugh chart below to answer the following questions about digital cameras.

+ = excellent; 0 = good; − = poor

	Zoom	Picture quality	Ease of use	Price
Camera A	−	−	+	0
Camera B	+	−	+	−
Camera C	+	0	0	+

8 Analyze Which camera received the highest overall ratings? Explain your reasoning.

_____

_____

9 Infer If someone chose Camera A based on the ratings in the Pugh chart, which feature was most important to that user?

_____

_____

10 Predict Imagine that a new surgical procedure has been developed to treat spinal cord injury. What are some possible risks and benefits of receiving this procedure?

_____

_____

_____

_____

11 Claims • Evidence • Reasoning How has the development of social networking on the Internet had favorable and unfavorable effects? State your claim. Provide evidence to support the claim, and explain your reasoning.

_____

_____

_____

SC.7.N.1.1 Define a problem from the seventh grade curriculum, use appropriate reference materials to support scientific understanding, plan and carry out scientific investigation of various types, such as systematic observations or experiments, identify variables, collect and organize data, interpret data in charts, tables, and graphics, analyze information, make predictions, and defend conclusions. SC.7.N.3.2 Identify the benefits and limitations of the use of scientific models.

S.T.E.M. ENGINEERING & TECHNOLOGY

Analyzing Technology

Skills
✔ Identify benefits and risks
✔ Evaluate cost of technology
✔ Evaluate environmental impact
Propose improvements
Propose risk reduction
Compare technology
✔ Communicate results

Objectives
Identify the benefits of a specific technology.
Identify the risks of a specific technology.
Conduct a risk-benefit analysis of a specific technology.

Risks and Benefits of Electric Transportation

The growing population in many areas has led to significant transportation problems. People need to move around to get to work, school, or shopping areas. However, without other options, they often end up driving around in cars all by themselves. This contributes to traffic problems, wear and tear on the roads, pollution, and wasted fuel.

Many traffic problems are caused by too many cars on the roads.

1 Observe From a safe place, observe the number of cars driving by your school or driving on a main street in your neighborhood. Record how many cars drive by in a certain amount of time and also how many of those cars contain only the driver.

Cars	Only driver

2 Claims • Evidence • Reasoning What are some of the benefits of people driving around in cars, even though they may often be by themselves? State your claim. Provide evidence to support the claim, and explain your reasoning.

_____

_____

_____

Electric Scooters

Electric scooters are small, open vehicles that use a battery-operated electric motor to propel the rider. Some people say electric scooters are the solution to modern transportation problems. A benefit is something that provides an advantage. Some benefits are that electric scooters take up less space on the road and in parking lots. Electric scooters also do not emit exhaust and can be cheaper to own and operate than cars. A risk is the chance of a dangerous or undesirable outcome.

3 Claims • Evidence • Reasoning Make a claim about some of the problems or risks that could result from the widespread use of electric scooters. Provide evidence to support the claim, and explain your reasoning.

_____

_____

_____

Risk
Even though electric vehicles don't emit exhaust, the power plants that deliver their electricity do have negative environmental effects.

Benefit
Electric scooters take up less room on the road than cars.

🖐 You Try It!

Now it's your turn to evaluate the risks and benefits of students using electric scooters to travel to and from your school.

Analyzing Technology

🖐 You Try It!

Now it's your turn to evaluate the risks and benefits of students using electric scooters to travel to and from your school.

① Identify Risks and Benefits

Suppose all of the students at your school used electric scooters to ride from home to school and back. Think of all the positive and negative aspects of all students riding electric scooters. In the table below, list all of these risks and benefits. List any negative aspects under the "Risks" heading and list any positive aspects under the "Benefits" heading. You may need to add to the table as you complete the rest of this activity.

Risks	Benefits

② Evaluate Cost of Technology

A Imagine that every student in your school rides the school bus. Research the cost per student per year of your school's bus system. To do this, estimate how many miles the students have to ride to and from school and how much gas is needed to travel that distance.

_____

_____

_____

B Research the cost of electric scooters that students might be able to use to get to and from your school. How much would it cost each student to buy a scooter? What other costs do you need to consider?

_____

_____

_____

③ Evaluate Environmental Impact

In what specific ways would the environment be affected by all students riding electric scooters to and from your school? Be sure to think about both positive and negative effects on the environment.

_____

_____

_____

_____

_____

_____

④ Communicate Results

A Based on all the risks and benefits you listed, what conclusion would you make about whether all students should drive electric scooters to and from your school? Explain your reasoning.

_____

_____

_____

_____

_____

_____

B Write a persuasive letter to your local school board attempting to convince members to adopt your conclusion about the use of electric scooters at your school. Be sure to support your argument with evidence from your risk-benefit analysis.

_____

_____

_____

_____

_____

_____

Engineering
and Our World

ESSENTIAL **QUESTION**

How are engineering and society related?

By the end of this lesson, you should be able to explain how engineering, technology, and society affect each other.

Washing machines, dryers, and other appliances are engineered to make our lives easier.

SC.7.N.2.1 Identify an instance from the history of science in which scientific knowledge has changed when new evidence or new interpretations are encountered. **SC.7.N.3.2** Identify the benefits and limitations of the use of scientific models.

(b) ©David Zaitz/Photodisc/Getty Images

Lesson Labs

Quick Labs
- Inventor Trading Cards
- Investigate Energy Efficiency

 Engage Your Brain

1 Describe Write a caption explaining what is going on in this photo.

_____

_____

_____

2 Infer Every kind of technology has advantages and disadvantages. Think of some disadvantages to washing clothes by hand. Think of some advantages. Write your answers below.

_____

_____

_____

_____

ACTIVE **READING**

3 Apply Use context clues to write your own definition for the words *technology* and *design*.

Example sentence
The tools of modern farming <u>technology</u> include chemical fertilizers, diesel-powered tractors, and automatic irrigation systems.

technology:

_____

_____

Example sentence
Landscape engineers <u>design</u> parks so that people have room to relax and play.

design:

_____

_____

Vocabulary

4 Identify As you read, place a question mark next to any words that you don't understand. When you finish reading the lesson, go back and review the text that you marked. If the information is still confusing, consult a classmate or teacher.

Got Tech?

What makes up the designed world?

Your environment is made of a designed world within a natural world. The natural world includes all the parts of the environment that were not made by people. The designed world includes all the parts of the environment that were made by people.

○ Big Structures and Large Machines

Look around you. What do you see? You might see houses, apartments, your school, and roads and bridges and the vehicles on them. These structures are all parts of the designed world. The designed world includes skyscrapers, cars, trains, planes, and other complex technology that require careful engineering. The highways, railroad tracks, and airports needed for transportation have also been engineered.

Other parts of the designed world are not as obvious. For example, within a city park, trees and other plants are used with engineered lights, paths, and bridges. Landscape designers use these natural and human-made things to create natural-looking spaces within cities.

ACTIVE READING

5 Identify What is the designed world?

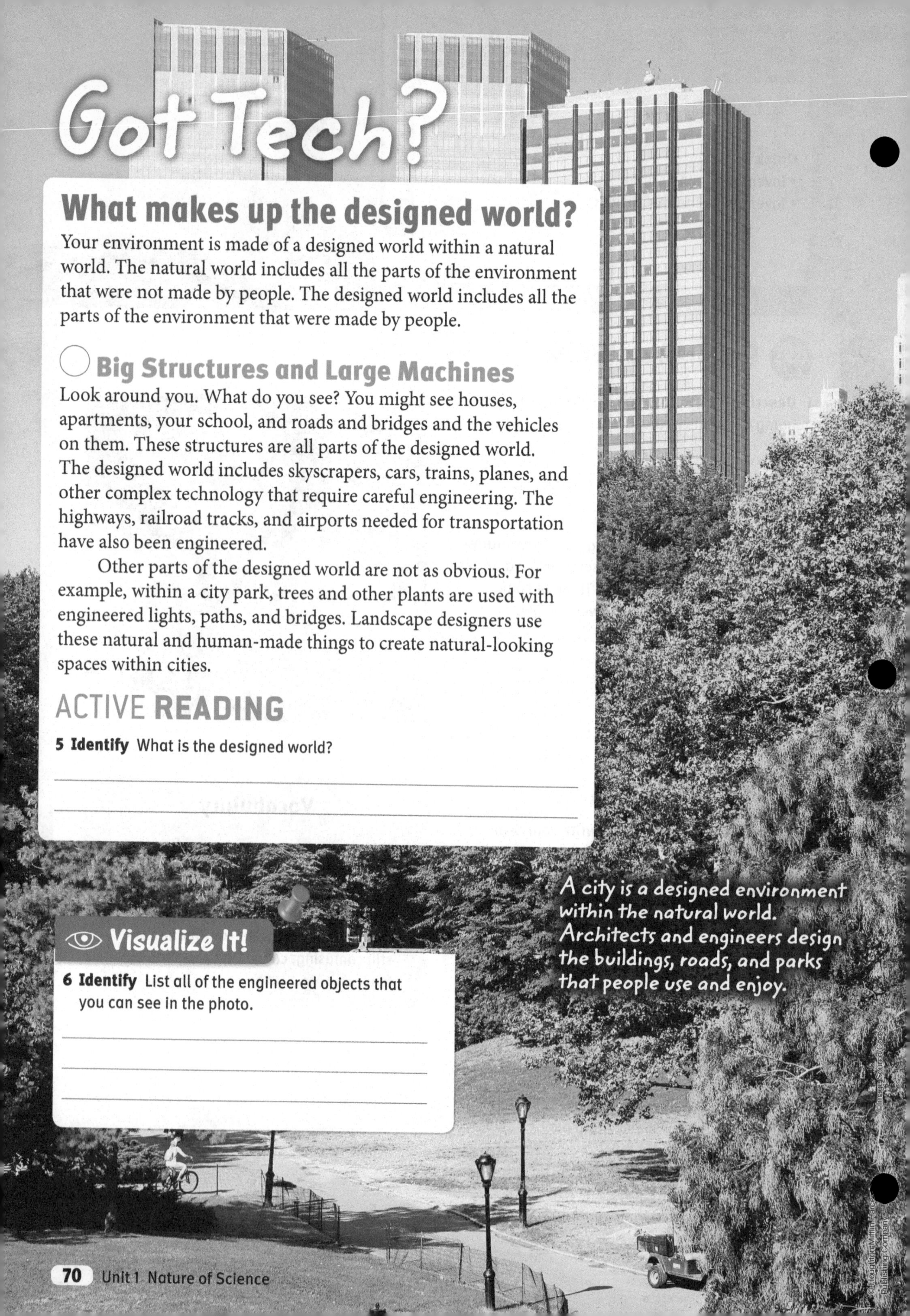

_____

_____

👁 Visualize It!

6 Identify List all of the engineered objects that you can see in the photo.

_____

_____

_____

A city is a designed environment within the natural world. Architects and engineers design the buildings, roads, and parks that people use and enjoy.

○ Products You Use Every Day

The designed world also includes all the products you use every day. Soap, clocks, chairs, and lamps are all engineered to help you live well at home. Books, eyeglasses, and lab equipment are engineered to help you learn at school. Helmets, in-line skates, tennis rackets, and other pieces of sports equipment are designed to help you have fun safely.

Some designed products, such as hand-held games, cell phones, and computers, are complex. Other designed products, such as dinner plates and towels, are fairly simple technology. Some products are a combination of simple and complex. Shoes and waterproof clothing may be made from natural cotton cloth and materials designed by chemical engineers. All of the products you wear and use are part of a designed world.

Personal music players are engineered to store digital music and replay it through earbuds.

Books are a form of technology that people have used for centuries.

Clothing is engineered to be durable, comfortable, and attractive.

Skateboards are engineered to be durable, easy to steer, and fast.

> ### i Think Outside the Book
>
> **7 Apply** Write a script for a podcast ad for a spoon. Imagine that your audience has never seen a spoon before, so describe the spoon's design carefully!

©HMH

Why is technology developed?

The designed world depends on technology. Technology includes all the inventions, processes, and tools that have been developed to meet our needs and wants.

To Meet People's Needs

Basic needs include food, water, clothing, shelter, protection, transportation, and communication. Some simple technology has been meeting people's needs for a long time. For example, people learned how to cook food over fire, use ditches to water crops, weave cloth, and use animals for work and transportation thousands of years ago.

Technology used today still meets these same needs. Modern stoves use electricity or gas to cook food. Modern farms use mechanical irrigation to water crops more efficiently and tractors to pull farm equipment. Clothes are woven using both traditional and new materials. Protective gear is made of modern plastics. Engines power cars, buses, and trains. Modern medical technology helps keep you healthy.

👁 Visualize It!

8 Classify Identify the need that each of the items in the photos addresses.

Needs

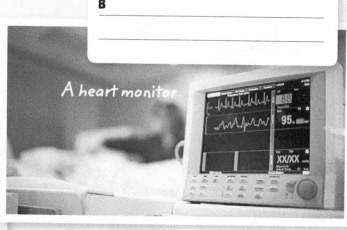
A heart monitor

B
_____
_____

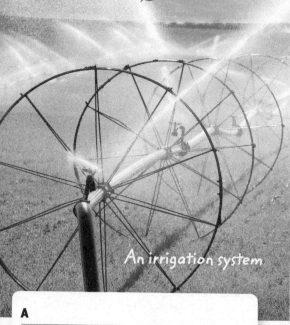
An irrigation system

A
_____
_____

A bicycle helmet

C
_____
_____
_____

Wants

A
_____
_____

Beads

Video game

B
_____
_____

Electronic keyboard

C
_____
_____

👁 Visualize It!

9 Classify Identify the want that each of the items in the photos addresses.

To Meet People's Wants

ACTIVE READING

10 Identify As you read, underline two factors that shape people's wants.

Wants are things that people do not require to survive, but desire anyway. Wants include the desire to be more comfortable, to play, to have beautiful things, or to make music.

Inventors and engineers use technology to develop devices that meet people's wants, such as air conditioners, radios, and telephones. Plastics and other materials are used to meet the desire for play or decoration. The desire for realistic computer games has advanced the field of computer graphics.

People's technological wants often depend on their values and culture. Some cultures embrace all modern technology. Others accept only some technology. For example, some farmers choose to farm using horses instead of tractors. Additionally, wants vary from one culture to another. The definition of beautiful music, art, and fashion differs depending on whom you ask.

11 Claims • Evidence • Reasoning Would you classify a cellular phone as a want or a need? State your claim. Provide evidence to support the claim, and explain your reasoning.

_____
_____
_____
_____
_____

Growing and Changing

Why is technology revised?

Technology is revised as society's needs and wants change. New technology often leads to new needs and wants. These new needs and wants then fuel the development of even newer technology.

Needs and Wants Change

Needs and wants change when society changes. For example, years ago, most people in the United States lived on farms. When new technology made farming more efficient, fewer farmers were needed to grow food. Many people left farms and moved to cities.

The people in cities had new needs. For example, now that they were not growing food, they needed to buy and store food. Refrigerators were developed to keep food fresh. People also had more free time, and new wants. New forms of entertainment, such as movies and recorded music, were developed. All of these wants and needs drove the development of new technology and products.

👁 Visualize It!

Computer technology was developed as society's needs changed. Computers have gotten smaller and more reliable over time. They process data faster and can share data more easily.

In the 1960s and 1970s, computers were large and processed data stored on reels of magnetic tape. Data were shared by moving the reels to another computer.

In the 1980s, engineers worked on making computers smaller. Improved hardware led to the development of personal computers.

Personal computers stored and shared information on floppy disks.

New Technology Generates New Needs

● ACTIVE READING

13 Identify As you read, underline two examples of new technology creating new needs.

When people begin using new technology, they often develop new needs. For example, when people in cities began driving cars, they needed a way of coordinating traffic. So traffic lights were invented. One technology led to another.

Likewise, computers were developed in the 1950s to meet the need to process data. Early computers were very big machines that stored data on giant spools of magnetic tape. Even though they could process large amounts of data, they could not share that data easily. Computer scientists needed a better way to share information. As a result, engineers developed disk storage technology. As computers became smaller and more affordable, more people began using them and more information needed to be shared. Disks improved, and now one DVD can hold more data than an early computer could. Today, computers can transfer data electronically over the Internet. The Internet connects computers directly to each other and makes sharing data and images easy.

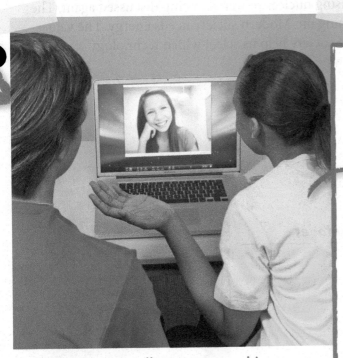

Now, computers all over the world can share data quickly over the Internet. Although the Internet was developed for scientists, people now use it for everyday activities, such as talking to friends.

14 Illustrate How do you think data storage and computer communication will change next? Draw and describe your answer.

How are society and technology related?

Society and technology affect each other. For example, when people choose to buy a technology, manufacturers continue to make and improve it. When people stop buying a technology, manufacturers no longer make it.

Society's technology choices can change in unpredictable ways. For example, in the 1940s, American society had hopes that nuclear technology could supply limitless, clean, and cheap energy. So, in the mid-1950s, engineers planned the first nuclear power plants. However, people discovered that nuclear technology has its disadvantages, too. For example, the plants are costly to build. They need expensive controls to operate safely, and they make dangerous radioactive waste. Accidents at nuclear plants in the 1980s reminded people of the risks of nuclear energy. Companies stopped building nuclear plants and built more plants that burned fossil fuels.

But fossil fuels are limited and becoming more scarce. And a new disadvantage of that technology emerged. Power plants that burn fossil fuels add greenhouse gases to the atmosphere. So the advantages of using nuclear power are being discussed again. The debate is still going on. Modern society needs energy. The values and priorities of society help us select which technology we use.

ACTIVE READING

15 Identify As you read, underline the ways society affects which technology is developed.

16 Identify List some advantages and disadvantages of nuclear energy in the table below.

Advantages	Disadvantages

Society will choose whether nuclear power plants meet our energy needs in the future.

©GFC Collection/Alamy

© Houghton Mifflin Harcourt Publishing Company

WHY IT **MATTERS**

Going Up?

SOCIETY AND TECHNOLOGY

Which technology allows people to climb tall buildings with the push of a button? Elevators! The addition of elevators changed the height of buildings, the skyline of cities, and people's ability to reach the sky.

Need for Skyscrapers

In the middle 1800s, more people started moving to cities. More space was needed for homes and offices. But land in cities was limited and expensive. Building upward was less expensive than spreading out. So architects began designing taller buildings, which meant climbing more stairs to reach the upper floors.

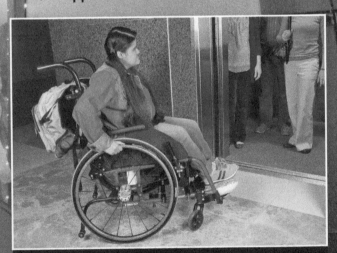

Need for Elevators

Putting elevators in buildings eliminated the need to climb stairs. Elevators make it possible for people who cannot climb stairs to move around easily in any building that has more than one floor.

ⓘ Extend

17 Gather Evidence Why might someone put an elevator in a single-family home? Provide evidence to support your claim.

18 Explain Your Reasoning What might be one disadvantage of elevator technology? Explain your reasoning.

19 Compare Investigate and describe three types of elevator designs: hydraulic, pneumatic, and roped. Describe the advantages and drawbacks of each of the three elevator designs.

© Houghton Mifflin Harcourt Publishing Company

(bg) ©David Grossman/Alamy; (c) ©HMH

Lesson 6 Engineering and Our World **77**

Visual Summary

To complete this summary, fill in the blanks with the correct word or phrase. You can use this page to review the main concepts of the lesson.

Engineering and Our World

The designed world includes large structures and machines and small products. Every product we use is part of the designed world.

20 Large structures in the designed world include _____

As needs and wants change, technologies are revised, too.

22 The need to process, store, and share growing amounts of information led to improved _____

Technologies are developed to meet needs and wants.

21 Clothing, shelter, food, communication, transportation are considered

_____

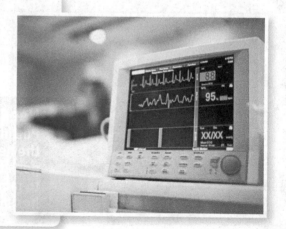

23 Claims • Evidence • Reasoning Make a claim about how society's need to replace coal, oil, and other fossil fuels as energy sources could lead to new technology for automobiles and other motor vehicles. Provide evidence to support the claim, and explain your reasoning.

Lesson Review

Vocabulary

In your own words define the following term.

1 designed world

_____

_____

Key Concepts

2 Identify What makes up the designed world?

_____

_____

3 Apply What drives companies to make batteries that cost less and last longer?

_____

_____

_____

4 Claims • Evidence • Reasoning Why does the designed world change? State your claim. Provide evidence to support the claim, and explain your reasoning.

_____

_____

_____

5 Claims • Evidence • Reasoning Why did computer floppy disks develop? State your claim. Provide evidence to support the claim, and explain your reasoning.

_____

_____

_____

6 Distinguish What is the difference between the designed world and the natural world?

_____

_____

Critical Thinking

Use this table to answer the following question.

Solar Energy	
Advantages	**Disadvantages**
Solar cells use free solar energy.	Solar cells are expensive to make.
Solar cells reduce the need for fossil fuels.	Solar energy cannot supply all of our energy needs right now.
Solar cells do not make pollution.	Solar cells cannot generate electricity at night.

7 Claims • Evidence • Reasoning How would switching to solar power affect a city environmentally and financially? State your claim. Provide evidence to support the claim, and explain your reasoning.

_____

_____

_____

_____

8 Analyze What parts of the designed world were developed to make air travel practical?

_____

_____

9 Claims • Evidence • Reasoning Some farmers in the United States still use horse-drawn equipment. Make a claim about why they might choose to use older technology. Provide evidence to support the claim, and explain your reasoning.

_____

_____

_____

PEOPLE IN SCIENCE

SC.7.N.1.5 Describe the methods used in the pursuit of a scientific explanation as seen in different fields of science such as biology, geology, and physics.

Mitchell W. Pryor

ROBOTICS ENGINEER

Do you think of robots as mostly science fiction? Can you imagine going to college to learn how to build robots? One place where you can do just that is the University of Texas at Austin (UT). Dr. Mitchell Pryor and his colleagues conduct robot research on a regular basis. Dr. Pryor's research group develops and tests new ways to use robots. They are on the cutting edge of robotics.

The group works on robots that operate both with and without human assistance. Today's robots do not look like typical robots from science fiction movies, but they do complete a wide range of tasks. In industrial settings, for example, robots are used to weld, paint, and move and assemble parts. Unlike people, the robots can perform their tasks exactly the same way every time. They also work quickly, do not get injured, can generally work for long periods of time without breaks, and do not require daily pay (although they are not cheap to make or purchase!).

Dr. Pryor, who received his Ph.D. from UT, also teaches graduate and undergraduate courses in mechanical engineering at the university. His ongoing research group gives students an opportunity for some hands-on learning, a dream for many science fiction fans!

This robot cleans areas too hazardous for humans. The robot is controlled by an operator watching a video feed.

📖 Language Arts Connection

Robot speech must be clear, concise, and grammatically correct. Work in a group to generate acceptable robot speech for the information below. Assume that your robot is limited to eight-word statements.

• The lid on the container must be tightened before you can move the container.

• The yellow paint is finished. Red paint will be added next, after drying for 20 minutes.

JOB BOARD

Computer Scientist

What You'll Do: Computer scientists work in a wide range of jobs including Software or Website development, Systems Analyst, Systems Administrator, and Information Technology Specialist.

Where You Might Work: At a computer company, government agency, manufacturing company, software company, large office, or academic institution.

Education: At a minimum a bachelor's degree, but often an advanced degree is needed.

Other Job Requirements: You need research, critical thinking, and problem-solving skills along with knowledge of computer security management and the latest technology.

Materials Scientist

What You'll Do: Study the composition and structure of matter to build new and better products such as shoes, computer chips, vehicles, blue jeans, and baking pans.

Where You Might Work: At a manufacturing plant, environmental consulting firm, or computer company.

Education: A minimum of a bachelor's degree, but typically a master's degree or doctorate in physics or chemistry.

Other Job Requirements: Research skills, verbal and written communication skills, and the ability to solve problems.

PEOPLE IN SCIENCE NEWS

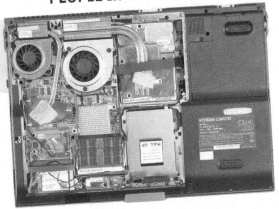

Agnes Riley

A Job for a Problem Solver

A computer is a great time-saving machine—right up until it doesn't work. If your computer isn't working right, you should try some simple steps, such as restarting it. If you are unable to solve the problem yourself, you might need to call an expert. Agnes Riley from Budapest, Hungary, is one such expert. Give her a computer that isn't working correctly, and she will take it apart, find the problem, and fix it.

Agnes learned how to fix computers by trial and error. She worked for a company in Hungary that had old computers, which needed constant repair. By experimenting, she learned to fix them.

In 1999, Agnes moved to New York City and took the exam to become a licensed computer technician. She enjoys the challenge of solving computer problems for people. If you enjoy solving problems, you might want to become a computer technician too!

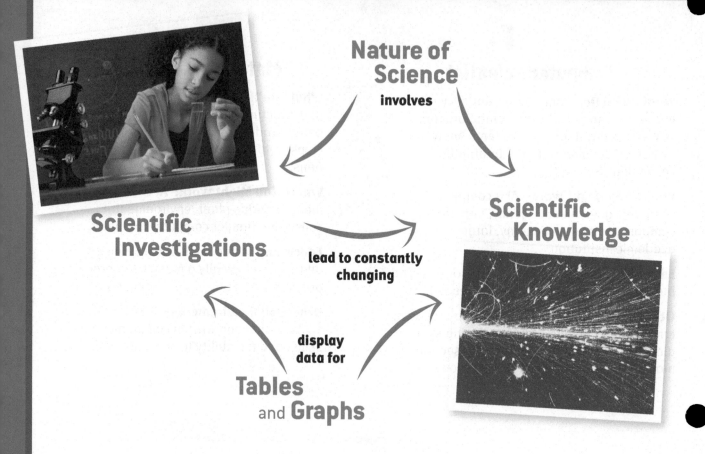

Nature of Science

involves

Scientific Investigations

lead to constantly changing

display data for

Tables and **Graphs**

Scientific Knowledge

1 Interpret According to the Graphic Organizer, there is a relationship between scientific investigations and scientific knowledge. Explain this relationship.

_____

_____

_____

_____

2 Claims • Evidence • Reasoning Why are tables and graphs useful for organizing scientific data? State your claim. Provide evidence to support the claim and explain your reasoning.

_____

_____

_____

_____

3 Claims • Evidence • Reasoning Why is science important for our understanding of the natural world? State your claim. Provide evidence to support the claim and explain your reasoning.

_____

_____

_____

_____

_____

_____

_____

_____

_____

_____

Vocabulary

Name _____

Fill in each blank with the term that best completes the following sentences.

1 Applying science and mathematics to solve real-world problems is called _____.

2 Testing and evaluating a(n) _____ is an important step in the design process.

3 Engineers perform a(n) _____ to compare the possible negative effects of making a decision involving technology with the possible positive effects.

4 To determine how a technology might affect the environment from the time it is made, sold, and used to the time it must be disposed of, engineers make a(n)_____.

5 A(n) _____ must be supported by empirical evidence.

Key Concepts

Identify the choice that best completes the statement or answers the question.

6 Raoul is studying areas of the United States to find the best location for high-rise senior citizen housing.

Major Earthquakes in Northern California					
Year	1906	1911	1979	1980	1984	1989
Magnitude	7.8	6.5	5.7	5.8	6.2	6.9

To help with his decision on the best location, how could Raoul use this table listing the major earthquakes that have occurred in northern California?

A to develop a list of building materials

B to perform a life cycle analysis

C to create a model

D to perform a risk-benefit analysis

7 Jason wants to know how far a shot-putter from the track team can throw a shot. During the experiment, Jason measures test and outcome variables. The drawings below show three trials from the experiment.

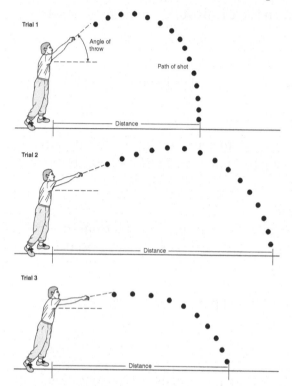

Assuming the shot-putter hurls the shot with the same force each time, what is the test variable?

F force exerted on the shot

G distance traveled by the shot

H angle at which the shot is thrown

I time it takes the shot to hit the ground

8 Which of the following is not a tool used in engineering and technology?

A computer design program

B electron microscope

C suspension bridge

D power drill

Name _____

9 In the early 1900s, geologist Alfred Wegener described a process he called *continental drift.* He proposed that Earth's continents had once been a single landmass that had broken up and the continents had then moved apart. At first, scientists were skeptical, but they accepted Wegener's idea when new discoveries supported it. Which term describes continental drift?

F hypothesis

H law

G theory

I empirical evidence

10 Bryan recorded the mass of a kitten in the table below. What would be the best scale to use for the *mass* variable when making a line graph of the data shown?

Growth of a Kitten

Age (weeks)	Mass (g)
6	2,560
7	2,790
8	2,850
9	2,920
10	3,120

A 0 to 3,500 in units of 10

B 0 to 3,500 in units of 500

C 2,500 to 3,500 in units of 50

D 2,000 to 3,500 in units of 100

11 Which statement best describes technology?

F the tools, machines, materials, and processes that are used for practical purposes

G the application of science and mathematics to solve problems, meeting the needs of society and improving the quality of life

H the study of the natural world

I the exploration of the nature of science

Critical Thinking

Answer the following question in the space provided.

12 Technology used in developing automobiles had some favorable and unfavorable effects.

What is a favorable and unfavorable effect of the automobile shown in the illustration? Use reasoning to explain your answer.

_____

_____

_____

13 The development of refrigeration and frozen-food technology has benefited society in different ways. Identify two ways in which refrigeration has helped people. Support your claims with evidence by identifying two products that developed because of frozen-food technology.

_____

_____

_____

The Universe

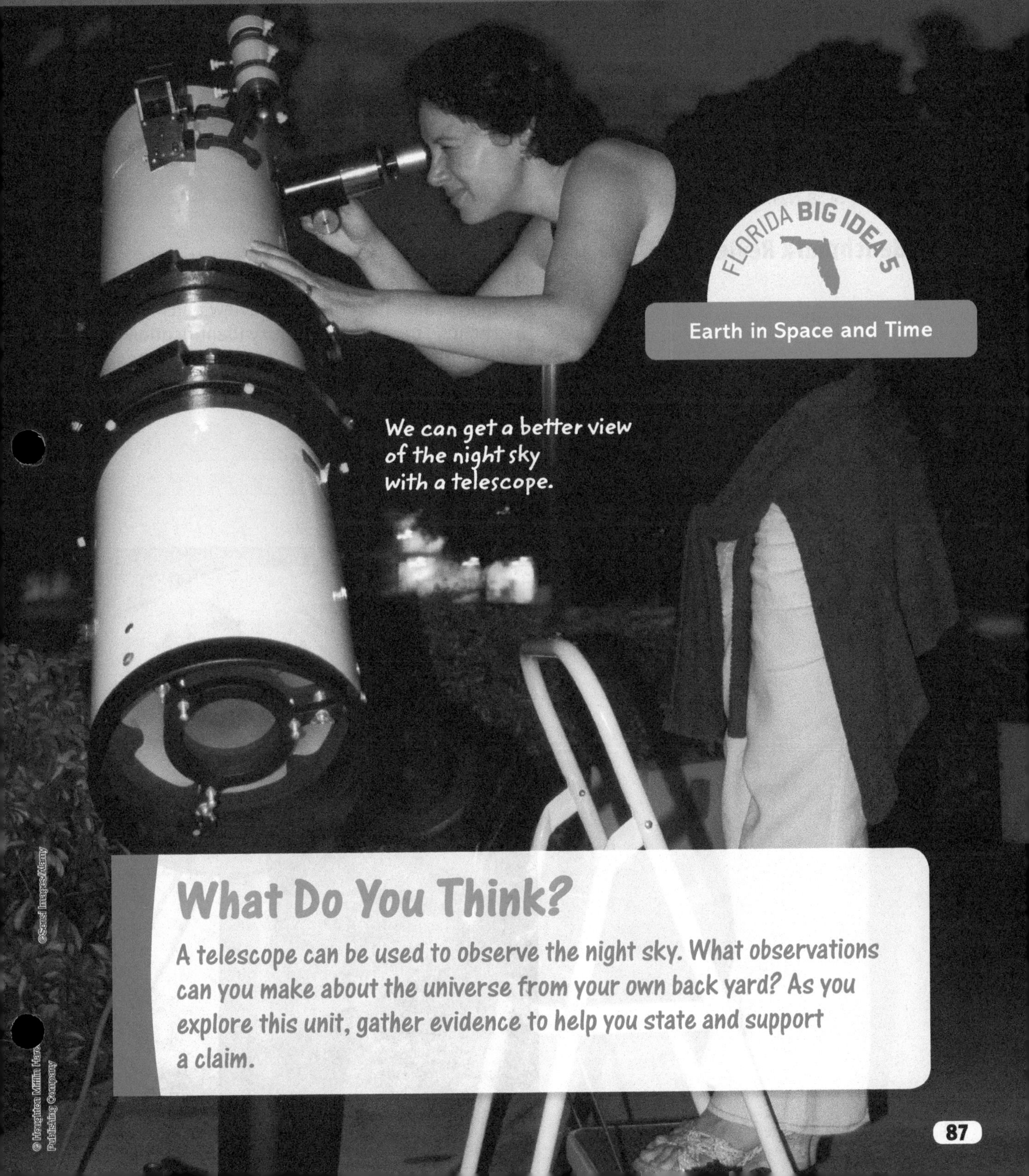

FLORIDA BIG IDEA 5

Earth in Space and Time

We can get a better view
of the night sky
with a telescope.

What Do You Think?

A telescope can be used to observe the night sky. What observations can you make about the universe from your own back yard? As you explore this unit, gather evidence to help you state and support a claim.

The Universe

CITIZEN SCIENCE

Galaxy Zoo

The human eye is far better at identifying characteristics of galaxies than any computer. So Galaxy Zoo has called for everyday citizens to help in a massive identification project. Well over a hundred thousand people have helped identify newly discovered galaxies. Now you can, too.

① Think About It

The scientists using the Sloan Digital Sky Survey telescope can gather far more information than they can review quickly. Humans are better at galaxy identification than computers. Why might this be a difficult task for computers?

_____

_____

_____

Sloan Digital Sky Survey Camera

[Bkgd] AP Images/NASA; (inset) ©Fermilab/Photo Researchers, Inc.

© Houghton Mifflin Harcourt Publishing Company

A galaxy seen edge-on

Spiral galaxy

② Ask a Question

How can people who aren't scientists help aid in galaxy identification?

With a partner, review the instructions on Galaxy Zoo's website and practice identifying galaxies. You will need to pay attention to the Galaxy Zoo classification system. Record your observations about the process.

_____

_____

_____

_____

_____

Things to Consider

Many different people review and classify each image of a galaxy at Galaxy Zoo. This way, scientists are able to control the mistakes that individuals may make.

☐ How can having many different people look at each galaxy help prevent errors?

③ Apply Your Knowledge

A List the characteristics you will be looking for when you examine a galaxy photo.

_____

_____

_____

_____

_____

_____

_____

B Review and classify galaxies on Galaxy Zoo's website.

C Create a classroom guide to the galaxies that you have identified.

⌂ Take It Home!

What has the Citizen Science project known as Galaxy Zoo accomplished so far? Find out how many people have participated and compare that to the number of scientists working on the project.

Structure of the Universe

ESSENTIAL QUESTION

What makes up the universe?

By the end of this lesson, you should be able to describe the structure of the universe, including the scale of distances in the universe.

SC.8.N.1.1 Define a problem from the eighth grade curriculum using appropriate reference materials to support scientific understanding, plan and carry out scientific investigations of various types, such as systematic observations or experiments, identify variables, collect and organize data, interpret data in charts, tables, and graphics, analyze information, make predictions, and defend conclusions. **SC.8.N.1.5** Analyze the methods used to develop a scientific explanation as seen in different fields of science. **SC.8.N.3.1** Select models useful in relating the results of their own investigations. **SC.8.E.5.1** Recognize that there are enormous distances between objects in space and apply our knowledge of light and space travel to understand this distance. **SC.8.E.5.2** Recognize that the universe contains many billions of galaxies and that each galaxy contains many billions of stars. **SC.8.E.5.3** Distinguish the hierarchical relationships between planets and other astronomical bodies relative to solar system, galaxy, and universe, including distance, size, and composition.

This image was taken from the Hubble Space Telescope. It shows just a small number of the galaxies that make up the universe.

✋ Lesson Labs

Quick Labs
- Modeling the Expanding Universe
- Modeling Galaxies

Exploration Lab
- Exploring the Relationship Between Mass and Shape

Engage Your Brain

1 Predict Check T or F to show whether you think each statement is true or false.

T	F	
☐	☐	You live on Earth.
☐	☐	Earth orbits a star called the *moon*.
☐	☐	Earth and the sun have the same composition.
☐	☐	The sun is just one of many stars in the Milky Way galaxy.
☐	☐	Distances in the universe are extremely large.

2 Draw When you look into the night sky, you are seeing only a very small part of the universe. Use the space below to draw what you see in the night sky.

ACTIVE **READING**

3 Synthesize Many English words have their roots in other languages. Use the Latin words below to make an educated guess about the meaning of the word *universe*.

Latin word	Meaning
unus	one
vertere	to turn

Example sentence
Earth is part of the <u>universe</u>.

universe:

_____

_____

_____

Vocabulary Terms

- solar system
- planet
- star
- galaxy
- light-year
- universe

4 Apply This list contains the key terms that you'll learn in this lesson. As you read, circle the definition of each term.

Our place in space

What makes up the universe?

You live on Earth, which is one of eight planets that orbit the sun. As you probably know, the sun is a star. A *star* is a large celestial body that is composed of gas and emits light. Stars are grouped together in structures known as galaxies. A *galaxy* is a large collection of stars, gas, and dust. Based on observations by the Hubble Space Telescope, there are an estimated 100 billion galaxies in the universe. *Universe* is the word that scientists use to describe space and all of the energy and matter in it.

Earth—Our Home Planet

Earth is a special place. Imagine Earth without water. There would be no vast, deep, blue oceans or broad, muddy rivers. If there was no water, there would be no evaporation. Therefore, no clouds would form in Earth's atmosphere, so there would be no rain or snow. Without water, there would be no plants to add oxygen to the atmosphere. And without oxygen, there would be no animal life on Earth.

Earth's atmosphere contains the combination of gases that animals need to breathe. The atmosphere also contains a thin layer of ozone gas. Ozone molecules in this layer absorb radiation from the sun that can be harmful to life. In addition, there are certain gases in the atmosphere that keep temperatures on Earth warm enough for life to exist.

ACTIVE READING

5 Identify As you read the text, underline those characteristics of Earth that make it a special place.

From the moon, you can see Earth's continents, dark-blue oceans, and white clouds swirling in the atmosphere.

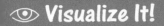
6 Claims • Evidence • Reasoning Make a claim about the relationship between the sizes of the planets and their distances from the sun. Support your claim with evidence, and explain your reasoning.

Neptune
Uranus
Saturn
Jupiter
Earth
Mercury
sun
Mars
Venus

Sizes are roughly to scale.
Distances are not.

The Solar System

ACTIVE **READING**

7 Identify As you read the text, underline the different bodies that make up the solar system.

The **solar system** is the collection of large and small bodies that orbit our central star, the sun. The contents of the solar system are numerous and stretch across a large area of space. For example, the solar system is so big that the distance from the sun to Neptune is 4.5 billion kilometers.

If you crossed the solar system beginning at the sun, you would encounter eight large bodies called *planets*. A **planet** is a spherical body that orbits the sun. Planets are generally larger than the other bodies in the solar system. The four planets that orbit nearest to the sun are the terrestrial planets. They are Mercury, Venus, Earth, and Mars. The terrestrial planets are all rocky, dense, and relatively small. The four planets that orbit farthest from the sun are the gas giant planets. They are Jupiter, Saturn, Uranus, and Neptune. These large planets have thick, gaseous atmospheres; small, rocky cores; and ring systems of ice, rock, and dust.

Orbiting most of the planets are smaller bodies called *moons*. Earth has only one moon, but Jupiter has more than 60. The rest of the solar system is made up of other small bodies. These include dwarf planets, comets, asteroids, and meteoroids. Altogether, there are up to a trillion small bodies in the solar system.

Stars

A **star** is a large celestial body that is composed of gas and emits light. Like the sun, most stars are composed almost entirely of hydrogen and helium. Small percentages of other elements are also found in stars. Energy production takes place in the center, or core, of a star. Energy is produced by the process of nuclear fusion. In this process, stars fuse lighter elements, such as hydrogen, into heavier elements, such as helium. This energy leaves the core and eventually reaches the star's surface. There, energy escapes as visible light, other forms of radiation, heat, and even wind.

Stars vary greatly in size. Small stars, such as white dwarfs, may be about the size of Earth. Giant and supergiant stars may be from 10 to as much as 1,000 times as large as the sun.

ACTIVE **READING**

9 Claims • Evidence • Reasoning Make a claim about how the composition of a star differs from the composition of a planet. Provide evidence to support your claim, and explain your reasoning.

_____

_____

Galaxies

Our solar system is located in the Milky Way galaxy. A **galaxy** (GAL•eck•see) is a large collection of stars, gas, and dust that is held together by gravity. Small galaxies, called *dwarf galaxies,* may contain as few as 100 million stars. Giant galaxies, however, may contain hundreds of billions of stars.

The Milky Way is a spiral galaxy. Spiral galaxies are shaped like pinwheels. They have a central bulge from which two or more spiral arms extend. Stars form in or near the spiral arms. Elliptical galaxies and irregular galaxies are two other kinds of galaxies. Elliptical galaxies look like spheres or ovals, and they do not have spiral arms. Irregular galaxies appear as splotchy, irregularly shaped "blobs." Irregular galaxies are very active areas of star formation.

The Small Magellanic Cloud is an irregular dwarf galaxy that is located near the Milky Way. A few billion stars make up the Small Magellanic Cloud.

This image shows a star formation region within the Small Magellanic Cloud. The blue stars are very young and are still surrounded by the gas and dust from which they formed.

Visualize It!

10 Describe In the boxes below, write in your answers to each of the questions.

You live on Earth. What is Earth's place in the universe?

_____

_____

_____

Not to scale

Earth is part of the solar system. What bodies make up our solar system?

_____

_____

_____

_____

_____

_____

The solar system is located within a spiral arm of the Milky Way galaxy. What is a galaxy?

_____

_____

_____

_____

_____

Lesson 1 Structure of the Universe **95**

How big is

How are distances in the universe measured?

Distances between most objects in the universe are so large that astronomers do not use kilometers to measure distance. Instead, astronomers measure distance using the speed of light. This unit of measure is known as a light-year. A **light-year** is the distance that light travels through space in 1 year. Light travels through space at about 300,000 km/s, or about 9.5 trillion km in 1 year. The closest star to the sun and Earth is Proxima Centauri. It takes light about 4.3 years to travel from Proxima Centauri to us. Therefore, the distance from Proxima Centauri to Earth is around 4.3 light-years. Light from the sun travels to Earth in a little more than 8 minutes. Thus, the distance from the sun to Earth is around 8 light-minutes.

How do distances affect space travel? Our fastest interplanetary spacecraft travel through space at about 58,000 km/h. At this speed, it would take a spacecraft more than 75,000 years to reach Proxima Centauri.

11 Claims • Evidence • Reasoning The Andromeda galaxy is located approximately 2.5 million light-years from Earth. Make a claim about the age of the light that reaches Earth from Andomeda. Provide evidence to support your claim, and explain your reasoning.

_____

_____

©Stocktrek Images/Getty Images

© Houghton Mifflin Harcourt Publishing Company

big?

The Voyager 2 spacecraft was launched in 1977. It explored Jupiter, Saturn, Uranus, and Neptune, and is now close to moving out of the solar system and into interstellar space.

What is the structure of the universe?

The **universe** can be defined as space and all the matter and energy in it. However, this definition does not tell us about the structure of the universe. Astronomers now know that throughout the universe there are areas where galaxies are densely concentrated. These are areas where galaxies are found in what are called *clusters* and *superclusters*. Clusters contain as many as several thousand galaxies. Superclusters can be made up of ten or more clusters of galaxies. There are also areas throughout the universe where very little matter exists. These are huge, spherical areas called *voids*.

Astronomers have begun to think of the universe as having a structure similar to soap bubbles. Clusters and superclusters are located along the thin bubble walls. The interiors of the bubbles are voids. It takes light hundreds of millions of years to cross the largest voids.

i Think Outside the Book

12 Apply In the text, the universe is described as being composed of galaxies and voids. Design and build a model that shows the structure of the universe as you imagine it to be.

ACTIVE **READING**

13 Describe What is the general structure of the universe?

_____

_____

_____

Visual Summary

To complete this summary, fill in the blanks with the correct word or phrase. You can use this page to review the main concepts of the lesson.

Structure
of the **Universe**

Earth is a planet.

14 What is Earth's place in the universe?

_____

Bodies in our solar system orbit the sun.

15 What makes up our solar system?

_____

_____

The sun is a star.

16 What is a star?

_____

The Milky Way is a galaxy.

17 What are galaxies made up of?

_____

18 Claims • Evidence • Reasoning Beginning with Earth, make a claim about the structure of the universe. Summarize evidence to support your claim, and explain your reasoning.

Lesson Review

Vocabulary

Fill in the blank with the term that best completes the following sentences.

1 A _____ is a large collection of stars, gas, and dust that is held together by gravity.

2 Space and all matter and energy in it is called the _____.

3 A _____ consists of a star and all of the bodies in orbit around it.

Key Concepts

In the following table, write the name of the correct structure next to the definition.

Definition	Structure
4 Identify What is a large celestial body that is composed of gas and emits light?	
5 Identify What is a spherical body that orbits the sun?	

6 Claims • Evidence • Reasoning Make a claim that compares the structure of the universe to soap bubbles. Summarize evidence to support your claim, and explain your reasoning.

_____

_____

_____

_____

7 Define Define light-year, and explain how and why light-years are used to measure distances in the universe.

_____

_____

_____

Critical Thinking

Use the table to answer the following questions.

Object	Distance from Earth
sun (nearest star)	8.3 light-minutes
Proxima Centauri (nearest star to sun)	4.2 light-years
center of Milky Way galaxy	28,000 light-years
Andromeda galaxy (nearest large galaxy)	2.5 million light-years

8 Apply Given current spacecraft technology, which of the objects in the table do you think it would be possible for you to travel to in your lifetime? Explain your reasoning.

_____

_____

9 Claims • Evidence • Reasoning A planet in our solar system is located far from the sun. Make a claim about its size and composition. Support your claim with evidence, and explain your reasoning.

_____

_____

_____

_____

_____

10 Claims • Evidence • Reasoning Make a claim about what astronomers mean when they use the term *observable universe*. Provide evidence to support your claim, and explain your reasoning. (Hint: Think of the time it takes for light from very distant objects to reach Earth.)

_____

_____

_____

PEOPLE IN SCIENCE

SC.8.N.1.5 Analyze the methods used to develop a scientific explanation as seen in different fields of science.

Hakeem Oluseyi

ASTROPHYSICIST

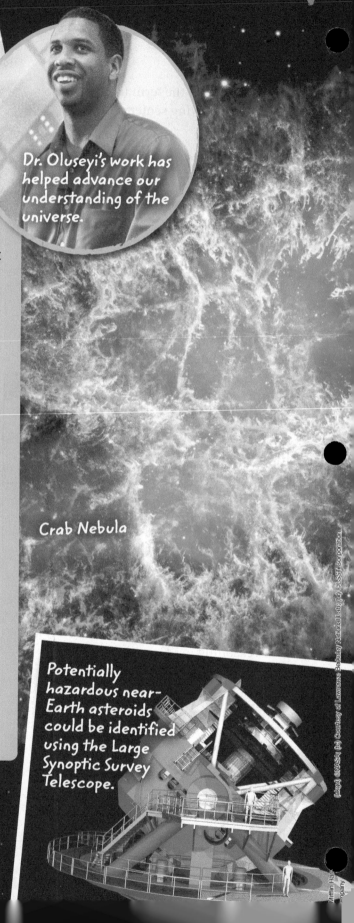

Dr. Oluseyi's work has helped advance our understanding of the universe.

Dr. Hakeem Oluseyi always thought scientists were "supercool." Still, he didn't start right out of high school trying to become a scientist. He spent some time in the Navy before going to college. In college he studied physics and eventually earned a Ph.D. in astrophysics.

Dr. Oluseyi has worked on the manufacture of computer chips, developing ways to both make them smaller and make them operate more quickly. He has also assisted in the development of very sensitive detectors that go on spacecraft. These detectors measure different types of electromagnetic radiation that come from bodies in outer space. Dr. Oluseyi came up with ways to make these detectors more sensitive and stable. This made them better able to work in outer space.

Currently, Dr. Oluseyi is helping to develop the Large Synoptic Survey Telescope (LSST). This telescope will observe the entire sky every night for 10 years. (Other all-sky surveys typically take several years to complete!) Dr. Oluseyi plans to use the data to map out the galactic structure and to search for planets around pulsating stars. Pulsating stars are stars that show changes in brightness due to internal processes happening within the star.

Through work like Dr. Oluseyi's we are gaining a better understanding of the planets and stars. But Dr. Oluseyi would tell you, there is still plenty more he'd like to know.

Crab Nebula

Potentially hazardous near-Earth asteroids could be identified using the Large Synoptic Survey Telescope.

🌐 Social Studies Connection

The Crab Nebula is what remains of an exploding star. Research when the earliest observations of the Crab Nebula were made. Create a timeline of this discovery.

JOB BOARD

Public Education Space Specialist

What You'll Do: You will design, develop, and teach programs on different space topics for an organization. You will also give presentations and tours of space-related workplaces for teachers, students, and the media.

Where You Might Work: Observatories, museums, government buildings, NASA, and the National Science Foundation are places you might work.

Education: Specialists must have a bachelor's degree in astronomy, physical science, science education, or a related field. Experience in public speaking, teaching, and developing educational programs is a plus.

Other Job Requirements: You should be able to present information in a clear and interesting way to people of all ages.

Information Technology (IT) Technician

What You'll Do: Monitor computer systems and help other people use them.

Where You Might Work: Large organizations with mainframe computer systems, like multinational companies, government agencies, hospitals, or colleges.

Education: IT technicians usually have a college certificate in information systems, data processing, electronics technology, mainframe operations, or microcomputer systems.

Other Job Requirements: You need to be able to work on a team and have excellent problem-solving skills.

PEOPLE IN SCIENCE NEWS

Caroline Moore

Seeking Supernovae

Caroline Moore was only 14 years old when she discovered Supernova 2008ha, a new type of supernova, from her backyard observatory. Because the one she discovered is different from other supernovae, her discovery has encouraged scientists to reconsider how stars die. Moore continues to search for supernovae, and is now helping to teach and inspire other young people to take an interest in astronomy.

LESSON 2

Stars

ESSENTIAL **QUESTION**

What are some properties of stars?

By the end of this lesson, you should be able to describe stars and their physical properties.

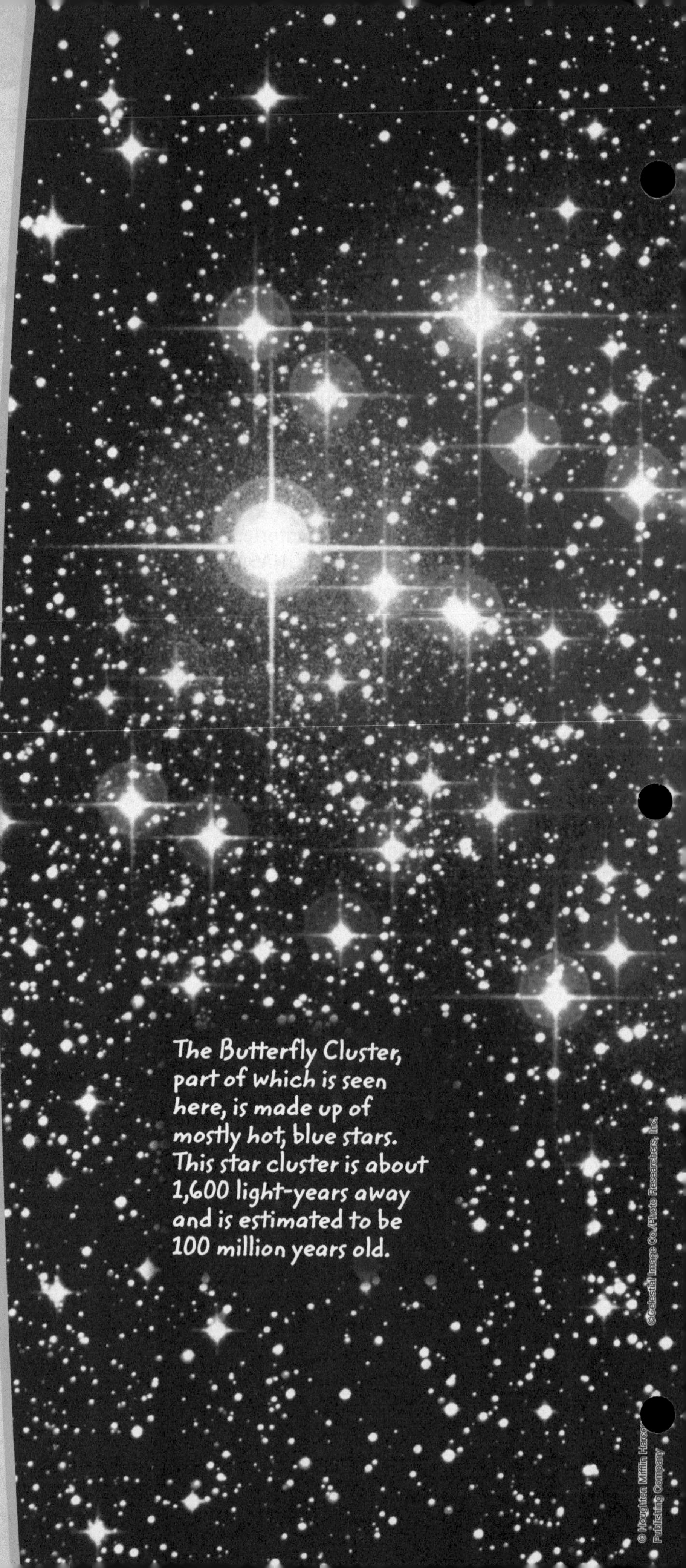

The Butterfly Cluster, part of which is seen here, is made up of mostly hot, blue stars. This star cluster is about 1,600 light-years away and is estimated to be 100 million years old.

SC.8.N.1.6 Understand that scientific investigations involve the collection of relevant empirical evidence, the use of logical reasoning, and the application of imagination in devising hypotheses, predictions, explanations and models to make sense of the collected evidence. **SC.8.N.3.1** Select models useful in relating the results of their own investigations. **SC.8.E.5.5** Describe and classify specific physical properties of stars: apparent magnitude (brightness), temperature (color), size, and luminosity (absolute brightness).

Quick Labs
- Using a Sky Map
- Modeling Star Magnitudes
- Star Graphing

Exploration Labs
- Star Colors and Temperatures

Field Lab
- Investigating Parallax

 Engage Your Brain

1 Predict Check T or F to show whether you think each statement is true or false.

T	F	
☐	☐	The sun is a star.
☐	☐	Stars are made mostly of nitrogen and oxygen.
☐	☐	If two stars have the same apparent magnitude, they are the same distance from Earth.
☐	☐	Red stars have higher surface temperatures than blue stars.
☐	☐	Some stars are about as small as Earth.

2 Describe In the images below, the stars Betelgeuse (left) and Rigel (right) are shown. Both stars are located in the constellation Orion. Describe any differences between these two stars that you see in this pair of images.

_____

_____

_____

Betelgeuse   Rigel

ACTIVE **READING**

3 Synthesize Many English words have their roots in other languages. Use the Latin word below to make an educated guess about the meaning of the word *luminosity*.

Latin word	Meaning
lumen	light

Example sentence
The luminosity of stars is measured relative to the luminosity of the sun.

luminosity:

Vocabulary Terms

- star
- apparent magnitude
- luminosity
- absolute magnitude

4 Apply As you read, place a question mark next to any words that you don't understand. When you finish reading the lesson, go back and review the text that you marked. If the information is still confusing, consult a classmate or a teacher.

Reach for the Stars!

What is a star?

A **star** is a large celestial body that is composed of gas and emits light. The sun is a star. Stars are made mostly of hydrogen and helium. But stars also contain other elements in small amounts. Stars vary in brightness. Although the sun may appear bright from Earth, the sun is not a bright star in comparison to many other stars. The temperatures of stars also vary. These differences in temperature result in differences in color. Stars may range in color from red, which indicates a cool star, to blue, which indicates a very hot star. The sun is a relatively cool yellow star. Stars have different sizes. Stars may be 1/100 as large as the sun or as much as 1,000 times as large as the sun. In addition, two or more stars may be bound together by gravity, which causes those stars to orbit each other. Three or more stars that are bound by gravity are called *multiple stars* or *multiple star systems*.

ACTIVE READING

5 Identify As you read the text, underline any physical properties of stars that are discussed.

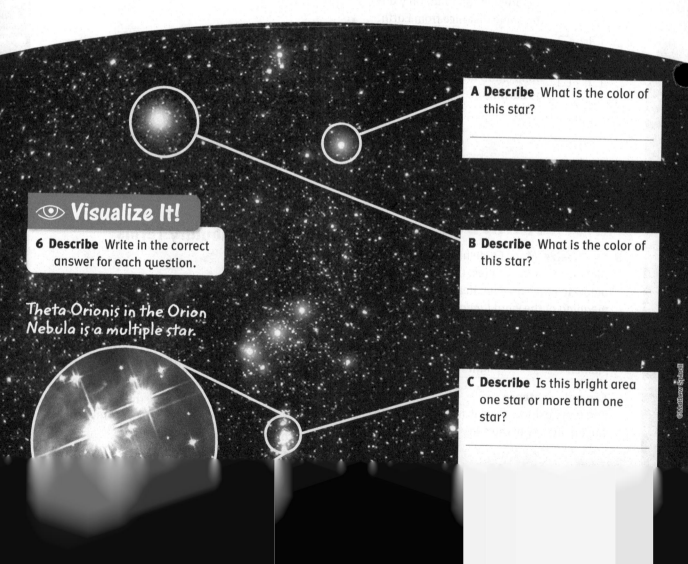

👁 Visualize It!

6 Describe Write in the correct answer for each question.

Theta Orionis in the Orion Nebula is a multiple star.

A Describe What is the color of this star?

_____

B Describe What is the color of this star?

_____

C Describe Is this bright area one star or more than one star?

_____

©Matthew Spinelli

The Sun Is a Star

To see a star, you need look no farther than the sun. The sun, like other stars, is composed mostly of hydrogen and helium. The sun also contains oxygen, carbon, neon, and iron.

At the center of the sun lies the core. In the sun's core, gases are compressed and heated, and temperatures reach 15,000,000 °C. The core is where matter is converted into energy.

The sun's surface, the photosphere, is the layer of the sun's atmosphere that we see from Earth. The photosphere has an average temperature of 5,527 °C. From the core, energy is continuously transferred to the photosphere. There, energy escapes into space as visible light, other forms of radiation, heat, and wind. The sun's atmosphere extends millions of kilometers into space. Temperatures in the sun's middle atmosphere, the chromosphere, are 4,225 °C to 6,000 °C. In the sun's outer atmosphere, or corona, temperatures may reach 2,000,000 °C.

This extreme ultraviolet image of the sun shows areas of different temperature that are found in the sun's atmosphere.

7 Compare Fill in the Venn diagram to compare and contrast the physical properties of the sun with the physical properties of other stars.

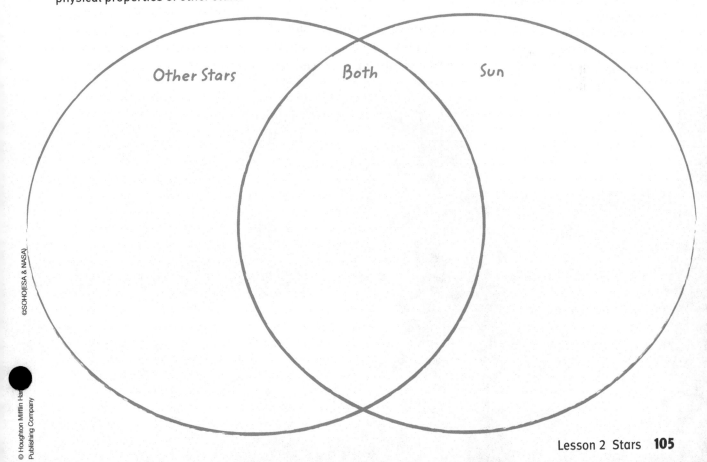

Other Stars   Both   Sun

You're a Shining Star

How is star brightness measured?

When you look at stars in the night sky, you see that stars vary in brightness. Some stars are bright, and other stars are dim. In reality, one star can appear brighter than another star simply because it is located closer to Earth.

By Apparent Magnitude

Apparent magnitude is the measure of a star's brightness as seen from Earth. Some stars are actually more luminous, or brighter, than the sun is. If these stars are located far from Earth, they may not appear bright to us.

Using only their eyes, ancient astronomers described star brightness by magnitude. They called the brightest stars they could see *first magnitude* and the faintest stars they could see *sixth magnitude*. Astronomers using telescopes see many stars that are too dim to see with the naked eye. Rather than replacing the magnitude system, astronomers added to it. Today, the brightest stars have a magnitude of about –2. The faintest stars that we can see with a telescope have a magnitude of +30.

The magnitude scale may seem backward. Faint stars have positive (larger) numbers; bright stars have negative (smaller) numbers. Sirius (SIR•ee•uhz), the brightest star in the night sky, has an apparent magnitude of –1.46. To the naked eye, the sun has an apparent magnitude of –26.8, even though it is not as luminous a star as Sirius is. The sun is simply located closer to Earth.

ACTIVE READING

8 Define As you read the text, underline the definition of *apparent magnitude*.

i 👁 **Visualize It!**

9 Claims • Evidence • Reasoning
How does the light from a flashlight that is shone from two different distances model the apparent magnitude of two stars with the same absolute magnitude? Make a claim, and support it with evidence. Explain your reasoning.

_____

_____

_____

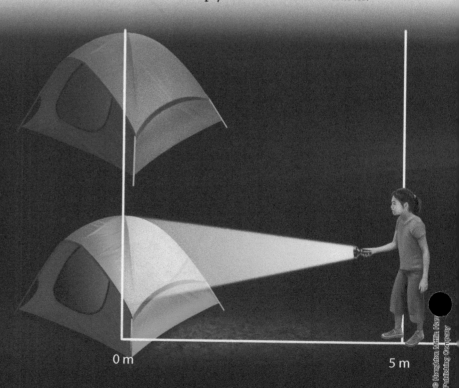

This girl is approaching her tent in the dark. The tent is dimly lit by the flashlight beam when she is 20 m away. The tent is well lit by the flashlight beam when she is 5 m away. The beam appears dimmer at 20 m than at 5 m, but the flashlight is equally bright in both cases.

0 m   5 m

How is star luminosity measured?

When astronomers use the word **luminosity**, they mean the *actual* brightness of a star. To measure a star's luminosity, astronomers use an absolute brightness scale called *absolute magnitude*.

By Absolute Magnitude

Absolute magnitude is a measure of how bright a star would be if the star were located at a standard distance. In other words, absolute magnitude is a measure of the brightness of a star whose distance from Earth is known. Just like apparent magnitude, absolute magnitude uses the magnitude scale.

To understand the difference between apparent magnitude and absolute magnitude, let's use the sun as an example. The apparent magnitude of the sun is –26.8. However, the absolute magnitude of the sun is +4.8, which is typical of many stars. Now compare the sun, which is located 8.3 light-minutes from Earth, to Sirius, which is located 8.6 light-years from Earth. Sirius has an apparent magnitude of –1.46 and an absolute magnitude of +1.4. Therefore, Sirius is much more luminous than the sun is.

Magnitudes of Selected Stars			
Star	Distance from Earth	Apparent Magnitude	Absolute Magnitude
sun	8.3 light-minutes	–26.8	+4.8
Sirius	8.6 light-years	–1.46	+1.4
Betelgeuse	640 light-years	+0.45	–5.6

10 Claims • Evidence • Reasoning
Make a claim about why a star, such as Betelgeuse, which is located far from Earth, has a much greater absolute magnitude than apparent magnitude. Use evidence to support your claim, and explain your reasoning.

_____

_____

_____

_____

_____

_____

_____

_____

10 m   15 m   20 m

Too Hot to Handle

How are the surface temperatures of stars measured?

If you look into the night sky, you may be able to see that stars have different colors. Why do the colors of stars vary? The answer is that differences in the colors of stars are due to differences in their surface temperatures. The same is true of all objects that glow.

By Color

You can see how temperature affects color in heated metal. As shown in the illustrations below, a steel bar glows different colors as it is heated to higher and higher temperatures. If an object's color depends only on temperature, the object is called a *blackbody*. As the temperature of a blackbody rises, it glows brighter and brighter red. As it gets hotter, its color changes to orange, yellow, white, and blue-white. It also glows more brightly.

The table shows the way in which the surface temperatures of stars are related to color. Stars that have the lowest surface temperatures are red. Stars that have the highest surface temperatures are blue.

Color and Surface Temperatures of Stars	
Color	Surface Temperature (°K)
blue	Above 25,000
blue-white	10,000–25,000
white	7,500–10,000
yellow-white	6,000–7,500
yellow	5,000–6,000
yellow-orange	3,500–5,000
red	Below 3,500

A steel bar glows red when heated to about 600 °C.

At about 1,200 °C, the metal glows yellow.

When heated to about 1,500 °C, a steel bar gives off a brilliant white light.

11 Claims • Evidence • Reasoning Make a claim about how the colors of stars that have different surface temperatures are similar to the colors of a steel bar that is heated to different temperatures. Support your claim with evidence, and explain your reasoning.

_____

_____

_____

Think Outside the Book

12 Formulate Come up with a creative way to remember the colors of stars, from coolest to hottest.

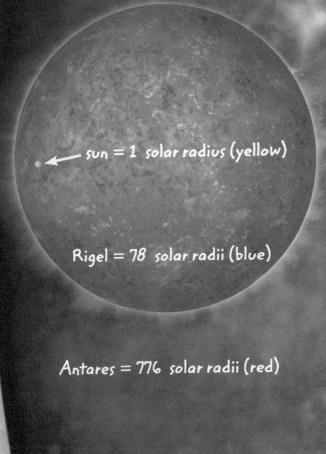

The size of the sun is compared to the blue supergiant star Rigel and the red supergiant star Antares.

← sun = 1 solar radius (yellow)

Rigel = 78 solar radii (blue)

Antares = 776 solar radii (red)

👁 Visualize It!

13 Apply From Earth, the sun appears to be a very large star. In reality, the sun is quite small when compared to stars such as Rigel and Antares. At the scale shown on this page, why would it be impossible to illustrate stars that are smaller than the sun?

_____

_____

_____

_____

_____

How are the sizes of stars measured?

Like the colors of stars, the sizes of stars differ greatly. Stars may be about the same size as Earth or larger than the size of Earth's orbit around the sun. So what do astronomers use to measure star size? It is always easiest to start with an object that is familiar. That is why astronomers use the size of the sun to describe the size of other stars.

Using Solar Radii

Astronomers have indirectly measured the dimensions of the sun. The sun's radius is approximately 695,000 km, or about 109 times the radius of Earth. Astronomers use this measure, the radius of the sun, to measure the size of other stars. Very small stars, which are called _white dwarfs,_ are about the same size as Earth. The size of a white dwarf can be expressed as approximately 0.01 solar radius. Very large stars, which are called _giant stars,_ typically have sizes of between 10 and 100 times the radius of the sun. There are also rare, extremely large stars that have sizes of up to 1,000 solar radii. These stars are called _supergiants._ Supergiants are often red or blue stars.

Visual Summary

To complete this summary, fill in the blanks with the correct word or phrase. You can use this page to review the main concepts of the lesson.

The brightness and luminosity of stars can be measured.

14 _____ is the measure of a star's brightness as seen from Earth.

15 _____ is the measure of how bright a star would be if it were located at a standard distance from Earth.

The color of stars is related to their surface temperature.

17 What is the color and surface temperature of the star in the illustration below?

_____

_____

_____

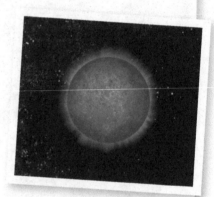

Properties
of Stars

Stars have different sizes.

16 What is the standard unit that astronomers use to measure the size of stars?

_____

_____

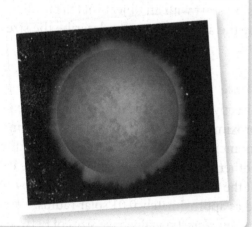

18 What is the color and surface temperature of the star in the illustration below?

_____

_____

19 **Claims • Evidence • Reasoning** Make a claim about how the sun compares to other stars in terms of surface temperature, apparent magnitude, absolute magnitude, and size. Use evidence to support your claim, and explain your reasoning.

Lesson Review

Vocabulary

In your own words, define the following terms.

1 star

_____

_____

2 luminosity

_____

_____

3 apparent magnitude

_____

_____

Key Concepts

4 List What are some of the physical properties of stars?

_____

_____

_____

_____

5 Claims • Evidence • Reasoning Make a claim about why the absolute magnitude of some stars is greater than the apparent magnitude. Support your claim with evidence, and explain your reasoning.

_____

_____

_____

_____

6 Compare How does the size of the sun compare to the sizes of other stars?

_____

_____

_____

7 Apply Mizar is a star system that is composed of two pairs of stars, Mizar A and Mizar B, or four stars in total. What do astronomers call a system that is composed of more than two stars?

_____

_____

Critical Thinking

Use the table to answer the following questions.

Color and Surface Temperature of Stars	
Color	Surface Temperature (K)
blue	Above 25,000
blue-white	10,000–25,000
white	7,500–10,000
yellow-white	6,000–7,500
yellow	5,000–6,000
yellow-orange	3,500–5,000
red	Below 3,500

8 State Your Claim Which stars have the highest surface temperatures, red stars or blue stars?

_____

_____

9 Gather Evidence The sun has a surface temperature of about 5,800 K. What is the color of the sun?

_____

_____

10 Calculate The star *Vega* has a surface temperature of about 17,000 K. How many times hotter is *Vega* than the sun?

_____

The **Universe**

contains

Stars

which are parts of galaxies that, together with voids, make up the

Structure of the **Universe**

1 Interpret The Graphic Organizer above shows the basic organization of the universe. Where would you include the solar system in this diagram? Show your changes above.

2 Claims • Evidence • Reasoning What is Earth's place in the universe? Make a claim and use evidence to support it. Explain your reasoning.

_____

_____

_____

_____

_____

3 Apply Explain why the sun has a greater apparent magnitude than absolute magnitude.

_____

_____

_____

_____

_____

4 Claims • Evidence • Reasoning Make a claim about how the structure of the Milky Way galaxy is similar to the structure of the solar system. Provide evidence to support your claim and explain your reasoning.

_____

_____

_____

_____

_____

©NASA/JPL-Caltech

Vocabulary

Name _____

Fill in each blank with the term that best completes the following sentences.

1 A large celestial body that is composed of gas and that emits light is a(n) _____.

2 A(n) _____ consists of one star or more than one star and all the objects in orbit around the central star.

3 A(n) _____ is a large group of stars, gas, and dust bound together by gravity.

4 The distance that light can travel in one year, also known as a(n) _____, is about 9.5 trillion km.

Key Concepts

Read each question below and circle the best answer.

5 Planets can be classified based on their physical composition. Some planets are small and dense; other planets are large and less dense. Which of the following describes the physical composition of a terrestrial planet?

A icy

B rocky

C liquid

D gaseous

6 Ashni joins the astronomy club. During a trip to an observatory, the members of the astronomy club observe several different stars. Ashni records information about some of the stars in her journal. Of the following four stars, which star should Ashni label as the hottest?

F Wolf, red

G Ceti, yellow

H Cygni B, orange

I Vega, blue-white

7 The sun is much larger than the moon. However, as viewed from Earth, the sun and moon appear to be the same size. Why do the sun and moon appear to be the same size when viewed from Earth?

A The moon is much hotter than the sun is.

B The moon is much denser than the sun is.

C The moon is much brighter than the sun is.

D The moon is much closer to Earth than the sun is.

8 Gloria is at the observatory and is examining a newly discovered star through a powerful telescope. She wants to find out how bright the star actually is. What information will help her calculate the absolute magnitude of the star?

F temperature of the star

G composition of the star

H distance from Earth to the star

I color of the star

9 An astronomer uses a telescope to observe a star. She observes that the color of this star is similar to the color of the sun. Therefore, she infers that the star and the sun have similar sizes and surface temperatures. Using this information, what can the astronomer conclude about the star?

A The star is a white dwarf.

B The star is cooler than a blue star.

C The star is brighter than a red giant star.

D The star is more distant than most other stars in our galaxy.

10 Our solar system contains eight planets. Each planet is classified as either a terrestrial planet or a gas giant planet. Which is a difference between these two types of planets?

F Terrestrial planets are larger than gas giant planets are.

G Gas giant planets are denser than terrestrial planets are.

H Terrestrial planets are located closer to the sun than gas giant planets are.

I Gas giant planets have thinner atmospheres than terrestrial planets have.

Name _____

11 Linda examined the sizes of several different stars. She listed them in order from smallest to largest. Which of the following stars would Linda list first?

A Polaris, 30 solar radii

B Aldebaran, 44.2 solar radii

C Sirius B, 0.008 solar radius

D Barnard's Star, 0.15 solar radius

12 Space exploration has advanced our knowledge of the universe. Which space journey would take the longest?

F a journey from Earth to the sun

G a journey from Earth to the moon

H a journey from Earth to a star in the constellation Centaurus

I a journey from Earth to the farthest planet in our solar system, Neptune

13 The diameter of Saturn is nearly 10 times the diameter of Earth. However, the density of Saturn is much less than the density of Earth. What is the reason for this?

A Earth is farther from the sun than Saturn is.

B Saturn has a ring system around its equator.

C Earth is hotter than Saturn is.

D Saturn is a gaseous planet.

Critical Thinking

Answer the following question in the space provided.

14 Below is a drawing of a galaxy that is similar to the Milky Way Galaxy.

Describe the shape and composition of the Milky Way Galaxy.

_____

_____

_____

15 Study the diagram below.

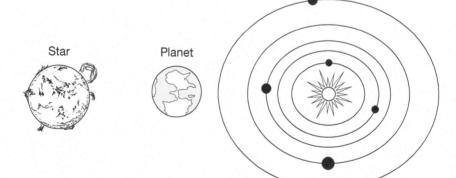

Star   Planet

What are characteristics of planets and stars and what is their relationship within solar systems, galaxies, and the universe?

_____

_____

_____

The Solar System

FLORIDA BIG IDEA 5

Earth in Space and Time

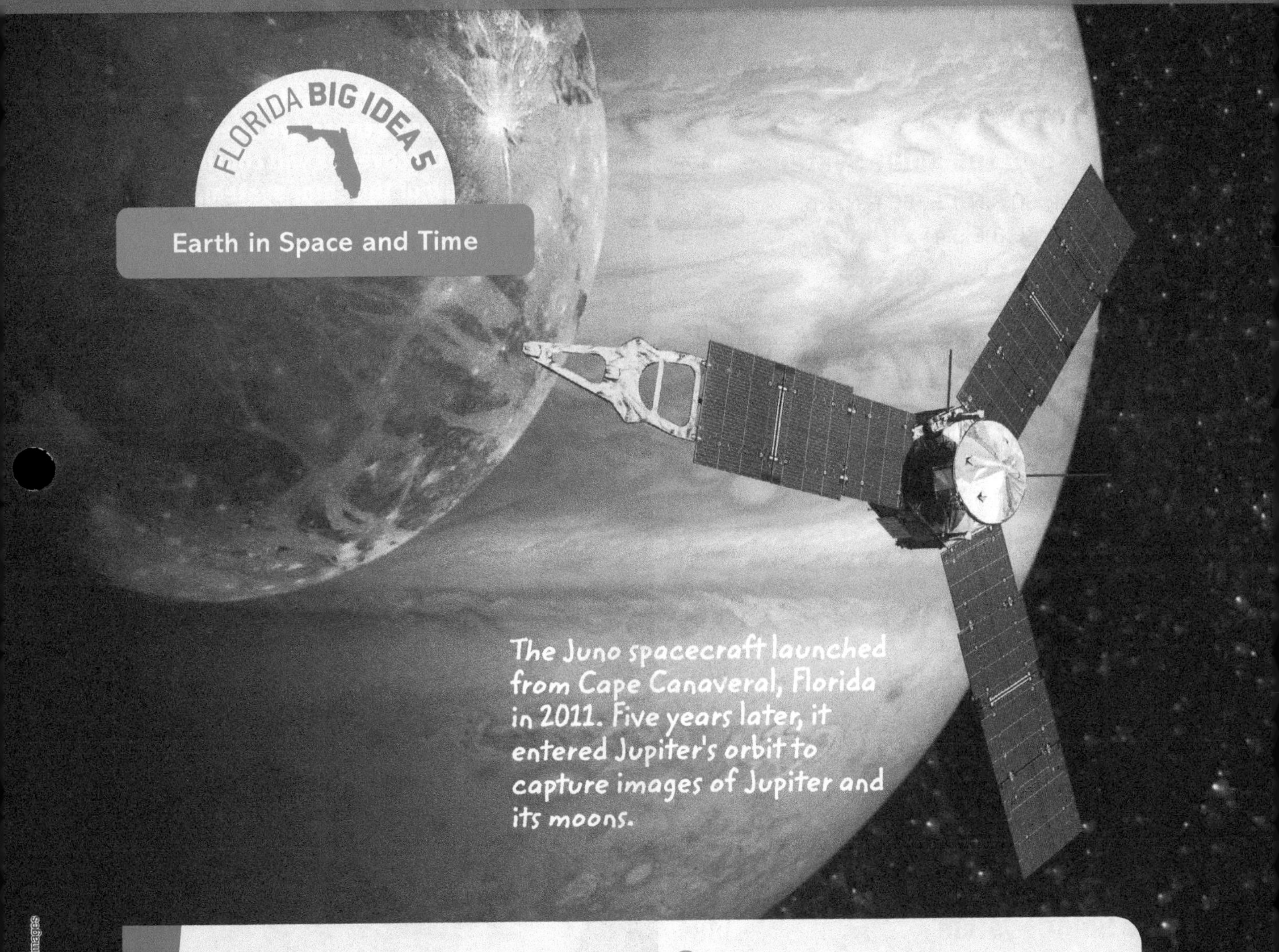

The Juno spacecraft launched from Cape Canaveral, Florida in 2011. Five years later, it entered Jupiter's orbit to capture images of Jupiter and its moons.

What Do You Think?

The Juno spacecraft is one of many spacecrafts that engineers have designed to travel to other planets in our solar system and gather information. How is information about other planets useful for scientists on Earth? As you explore this unit, gather evidence to help you state and support your claim.

The Solar System

CITIZEN **SCIENCE**

Solar System Discoveries

Today's knowledge of the solar system is the result of discoveries that have been made over the centuries. Discoveries will continue to change our view of the solar system.

Moons of Jupiter, 1610

On January 7, 1610, Galileo used a telescope he had improved and discovered the four largest moons of Jupiter. The moons are some of the largest objects in our solar system!

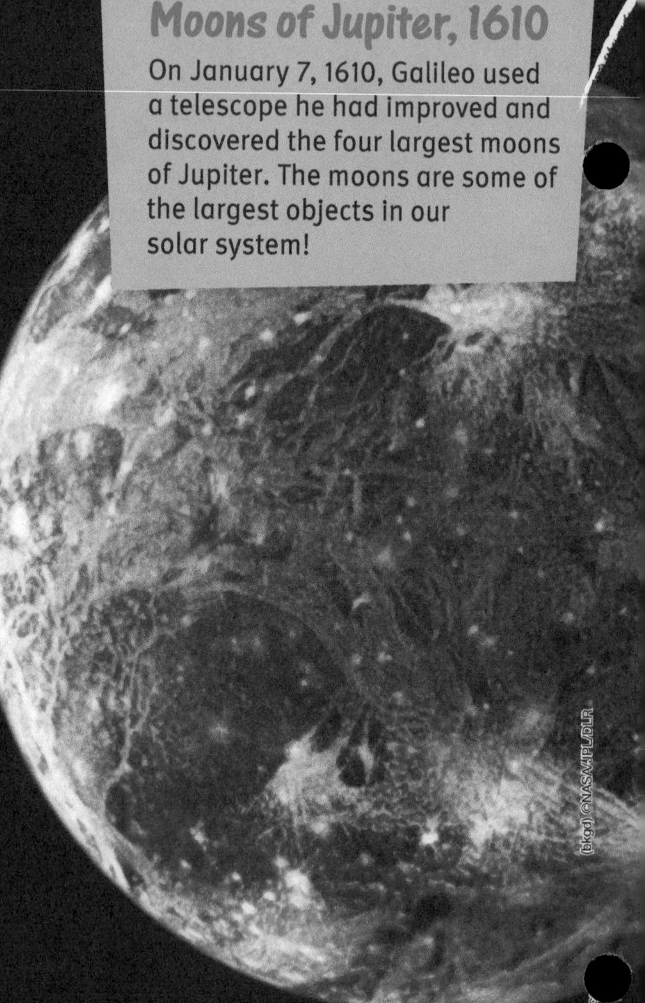

Ganymede is the largest of Jupiter's moons.

(bkg) ©NASA/JPL/DLR

William Herschel

Comet Hyakutake

Comet Hyakutake, 1996

Amateur astronomer Yuji Hyakutake discovered Comet Hyakutake on January 31, 1996, using a pair of powerful binoculars. This comet will approach Earth only once every 100,000 years.

Uranus, 1781

British astronomer Sir William Herschel discovered Uranus on March 13, 1781. It was the first planet discovered with a telescope. Our knowledge of the solar system expanded in ways people had not expected.

Neptune, 1846

Mathematics helped scientists discover the planet Neptune. Astronomers predicted Neptune's existence based on irregularities in Uranus's orbit. On September 23, 1846, Neptune was discovered by telescope almost exactly where it was mathematically predicted to be.

Neptune

 Take It Home!

Future Explorations

① Think About It

What are some recent discoveries that have been made about the solar system?

_____
_____
_____
_____

- Will crewed missions to distant places in the solar system ever be possible? Justify your answer.

_____
_____
_____
_____
_____

② Ask Some Questions

Research efforts like NASA's Stardust spacecraft to learn more about how space is being explored now.

- How is information being transmitted back to Earth?

_____
_____

Make A Plan

Design a poster to explain why humans are exploring the solar system. Be sure to include the following information:

- How we are using technology for exploration
- Why it benefits all of us to learn about the solar system

Historical Models
of the Solar System

ESSENTIAL **QUESTION**

How have people modeled the solar system?

By the end of this lesson, you should be able to compare various historical models of the solar system.

SC.8.N.1.4 Explain how hypotheses are valuable if they lead to further investigations, even if they turn out not to be supported by the data. **SC.8.N.1.5** Analyze the methods used to develop a scientific explanation as seen in different fields of science. **SC.8.N.1.6** Understand that scientific investigations involve the collection of relevant empirical evidence, the use of logical reasoning, and the application of imagination in devising hypotheses, predictions, explanations and models to make sense of the collected evidence. **SC.8.N.3.2** Explain why theories may be modified but are rarely discarded. **SC.8.E.5.8** Compare various historical models of the Solar System, including geocentric and heliocentric.

The Earth-centered model of the solar system was accepted for almost 1,400 years. It was replaced by the sun-centered model of the solar system, which is shown in this 17th-century illustration.

Quick Labs
- The Geocentric Model of the Solar System
- The Heliocentric Model of the Solar System

 Engage Your Brain

1 Predict Check T or F to show whether you think each statement is true or false.

T	F	
☐	☐	The sun and planets circle Earth.
☐	☐	Most early astronomers placed the sun at the center of the solar system.
☐	☐	The planets orbit the sun in ellipses.
☐	☐	The telescope helped to improve our understanding of the solar system.

2 Evaluate What, if anything, is wrong with the model of the solar system shown below?

_____

_____

_____

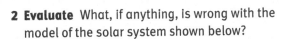

ACTIVE **READING**

3 Synthesis You can often define an unknown word if you know the meaning of its word parts. Use the word parts and sentence below to make an educated guess about the meaning of the word *heliocentric*.

Word part	Meaning
helio-	sun
-centric	centered

Example sentence
The <u>heliocentric</u> model of the solar system was first proposed by Aristarchus.

_____

_____

Vocabulary Terms

- **solar system**
- **heliocentric**
- **geocentric**
- **parallax**

4 Apply As you learn the definition of each vocabulary term in this lesson, create your own definition or sketch to help you remember the meaning of the term.

What is the solar system?

The **solar system** is the sun and all of the bodies that orbit the sun. Our current model of the solar system is the *sun-centered* or *heliocentric* (hee•lee•oh•SEN•trik) model. In the **heliocentric** model, Earth and the other planets orbit the sun. The earliest models for the solar system assumed that the Earth was at the center of the solar system, with the sun, moon, and planets circling it. These models, which used Earth as the center, are called *Earth-centered* or **geocentric** (jee•oh•SEN•trik) models. The heliocentric model was not generally accepted until the work of Copernicus and Kepler in the late 16th to early 17th centuries.

Who proposed some early models of the solar system?

Until Galileo improved on the telescope in 1609, people observed the heavens with the naked eye. To observers, it appeared that the sun, the moon, the planets, and the stars moved around Earth each day. This caused them to conclude that Earth was not moving. If Earth was not moving, then Earth must be the center of the solar system and all other bodies revolved around it.

This geocentric model of the solar system became part of ancient Greek thought beginning in the 6th century BCE. Aristotle was among the first thinkers to propose this model.

ACTIVE READING

5 Identify As you read the text, underline the definitions of geocentric and heliocentric.

Think Outside the Book

6 Research Use different sources to research a geocentric model of the solar system from either ancient Greece, ancient China, or Babylon. Write a short description of the model you choose.

Aristotle (384–322 BCE)

Aristotle

Aristotle (AIR•ih•staht'l) was a Greek philosopher. Aristotle thought Earth was the center of all things. His model placed the moon, sun, planets, and stars on a series of circles that surrounded Earth. He thought that if Earth went around the sun, then the relative positions of the stars would change as Earth moves. This apparent shift in the position of an object when viewed from different locations is known as **parallax** (PAIR•uh•laks). In fact, the stars are so far away that parallax cannot be seen with the naked eye.

of the Solar System?

Aristarchus

Aristarchus (air•i•STAHR•kuhs) was a Greek astronomer and mathematician. Aristarchus is reported to have proposed a heliocentric model of the solar system. His model, however, was not widely accepted at the time. Aristarchus attempted to measure the relative distances to the moon and sun. This was a major contribution to science. Aristarchus's ratio of distances was much too small but was important in the use of observation and geometry to solve a scientific problem.

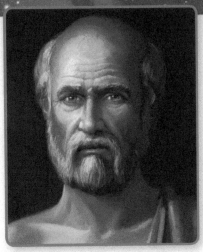

Aristarchus (about 310–230 BCE)

Aristotle thought that if Earth were moving, the positions of the stars should change as Earth moved. In fact, stars are so far away that shifts in their positions can only be observed by telescope.

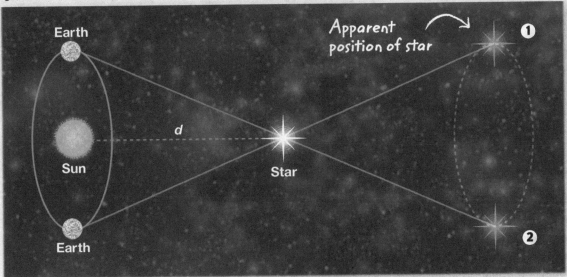

Diagram showing the shift in apparent position of a star at two different times of year seen from a telescope on Earth. A star first seen at point 1 will be seen at point 2 six months later.

👁 Visualize It!

7 Claims • Evidence • Reasoning If a star appears at position 1 during the summer, during which season will it appear at position 2? Summarize evidence from the diagram to support your claim and explain your reasoning.

_____

_____

Ptolemy

Ptolemy (about 100–170 CE)

Ptolemy (TOHL•uh•mee) was an astronomer, geographer, and mathematician who lived in Alexandria, Egypt, which was part of ancient Rome. His book, the *Almagest*, is one of the few books that we have from these early times. It was based on observations of the planets going back as much as 800 years. Ptolemy developed a detailed geocentric model that was used by astronomers for the next 14 centuries. He believed that a celestial body traveled at a constant speed in a perfect circle. In Ptolemy's model, the planets moved on small circles that in turn moved on larger circles. This "wheels-on-wheels" system fit observations better than any model that had come before. It allowed prediction of the motion of planets years into the future.

👁 Visualize It!

8 Claims • Evidence • Reasoning Use the diagram at the right to describe Ptolemy's geocentric model of the solar system.

_____

_____

_____

ℹ Think Outside the Book

9 Claims • Evidence • Reasoning As a class activity, defend Ptolemy's geocentric model of the solar system. Remember that during Ptolemy's time people were limited to what they could see with the naked eye. Clearly state Ptolemy's claim. Summarize the evidence to support the claim and explain your reasoning.

Ptolemaic Model

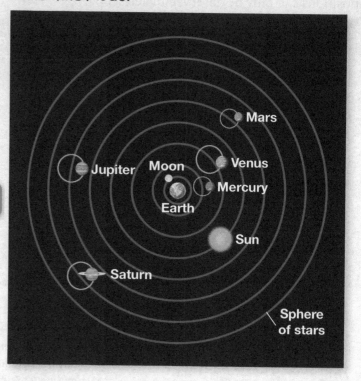

Copernicus

The Polish astronomer Nicolaus Copernicus
(nik•uh•LAY•uhs koh•PER•nuh•kuhs) felt
that Ptolemy's model of the solar system
was too complicated. He was aware of the
heliocentric idea of Aristarchus when he
developed the first detailed heliocentric model
of the solar system. In Copernicus's time,
data was still based on observations with the
naked eye. Because data had changed little
since the time of Ptolemy, Copernicus adopted
Ptolemy's idea that planetary paths should
be perfect circles. Like Ptolemy, he used a
"wheels-on-wheels" system. Copernicus's
model fit observations a little better than the
geocentric model of Ptolemy. The heliocentric
model of Copernicus is generally seen as
the first step in the development of modern
models of the solar system.

Nicolaus Copernicus (1473–1543)

Copernican Model

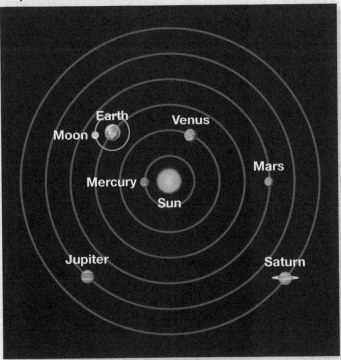

10 Compare How does Copernicus's model
of the solar system differ from Ptolemy's
model of the solar system?

Ptolemaic model	Copernican model

ACTIVE READING

11 Identify Underline text that summarizes Kepler's three laws.

Kepler

Johannes Kepler (yoh•HAH•nuhs KEP•luhr) was a German mathematician and astronomer. After carefully analyzing observations of the planets, he realized that requiring planetary motions to be exactly circular did not fit the observations perfectly. Kepler then tried other types of paths and found that ellipses fit best.

Kepler formulated three principles, which today are known as Kepler's laws. The first law states that planetary orbits are ellipses with the sun at one focus. The second law states that planets move faster in their orbits when closer to the sun. The third law relates the distance of a planet from the sun to the time it takes to go once around its orbit.

Johannes Kepler (1571–1630)

12 Analyze How did Kepler's first law support the idea of a heliocentric solar system? Explain your reasoning.

_____

_____

_____

_____

Kepler's First Law

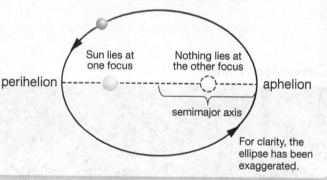

Sun lies at one focus

Nothing lies at the other focus

perihelion

aphelion

semimajor axis

For clarity, the ellipse has been exaggerated.

Galileo

Galileo Galilei (gahl•uh•LAY•oh gahl•uh•LAY) was a scientist who approached questions in the fashion that today we call *scientific method*. Galileo made significant improvements to the newly invented telescope. He then used his more powerful telescope to view celestial objects. Galileo observed the moons Io, Europa, Callisto, and Ganymede orbiting Jupiter. Today, these moons are known as the Galilean satellites. His observations showed that Earth was not the only object that could be orbited. This gave support to the heliocentric model. He also observed that Venus went through phases similar to the phases of Earth's moon. These phases result from changes in the direction that sunlight strikes Venus as Venus orbits the sun.

Galileo Galilei (1564–1642)

SOCIETY AND TECHNOLOGY

Galileo

Galileo Galilei was an Italian mathematician, physicist, and astronomer who lived during the 16th and 17th centuries. Galileo demonstrated that all bodies, regardless of their mass, fall at the same rate. He also argued that moving objects retain their velocity unless an unbalanced force acts upon them. Galileo made improvements to telescope technology. He used his telescopes to observe sunspots, the phases of Venus, Earth's moon, the four Galilean moons of Jupiter, and a supernova.

Galileo's Telescopes
This reconstruction of one of Galileo's telescopes is on exhibit in Florence, Italy. Galileo's first telescopes magnified objects at 3 and then 20 times.

The *Galileo* Spacecraft
The *Galileo* spacecraft was launched from the space shuttle *Atlantis* in 1989. *Galileo* was the first spacecraft to orbit Jupiter. It studied the planet and its moons.

i Extend

13 Identify What were Galileo's most important contributions to astronomy?

14 State Your Claim Galileo invented or improved upon many instruments and technologies, such as the compound microscope, the thermometer, and the geometric compass. Research one of Galileo's technological contributions. Make a claim about how this technology was helpful for society.

15 Create Describe one of Galileo's experiments concerning the motion of bodies by doing one of the following:

- make a poster

- recreate the experiment

- draw a graphic novel of Galileo conducting an experiment

Visual Summary

To complete this summary, fill in the blanks with the correct word or phrase. You can use this page to review the main concepts of the lesson.

Models of the Solar System

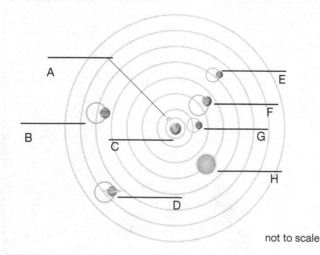

not to scale

Early astronomers proposed a geocentric solar system.

16 Label the solar system bodies as they appear in the geocentric model.

17 Which astronomers are associated with this model of the solar system?

_____

_____

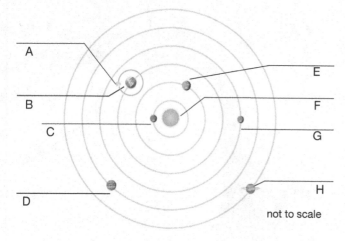

not to scale

The heliocentric solar system is the current model.

18 Label the solar system bodies as they appear in the heliocentric model.

19 Which astronomers are associated with this model of the solar system?

_____

_____

_____

_____

20 Claims • Evidence • Reasoning Make a claim about how the geocentric model of the solar system differs from the heliocentric model of the solar system. Use evidence to support your claim, and explain your reasoning.

Lesson Review

Vocabulary

Fill in the blank with the term that best completes the following sentences.

1 The _____ is the sun and all of the planets and other bodies that travel around it.

2 Until the time of Copernicus, most scientists thought the _____ model of the solar system was correct.

3 An apparent shift in the position of an object when viewed from different locations is called _____ .

Key Concepts

In the following table, write the name of the correct astronomer next to that astronomer's contribution.

Contribution	Astronomer
4 Identify Who first observed the phases of Venus?	
5 Identify Who attempted to measure the relative distances to the moon and the sun?	
6 Identify Who replaced circles with ellipses in a heliocentric model of the universe?	
7 Identify Whose geocentric model of the solar system was accepted for 1,400 years?	
8 Identify Whose heliocentric model is seen as the first step in the development of modern models of the solar system?	

Critical Thinking

Use the illustration to answer the following question.

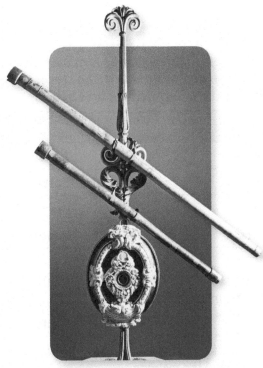

9 Claims • Evidence • Reasoning Explain how the data from Galileo's early telescope provided evidence for the claim that the sun is the center of the solar system.

_____

_____

_____

_____

10 Claims • Evidence • Reasoning Explain why Aristotle proposed a geocentric model of the solar system. Support your claim with evidence based on Aristotle's inability to detect parallax and explain your reasoning.

_____

_____

_____

_____

_____

SC.8.N.1.1 Define a problem from the eighth grade curriculum using appropriate reference materials to support scientific understanding, plan and carry out scientific investigations of various types, such as systematic observations or experiments, identify variables, collect and organize data, interpret data in charts, tables, and graphics, analyze information, make predictions, and defend conclusions.

Mean, Median, Mode, and Range

You can analyze both the measures of central tendency and the variability of data using mean, median, mode, and range.

Tutorial

Orbit eccentricity measures how oval-shaped the elliptical orbit is. The closer a value is to 0, the closer the orbit is to a circle. Examine the eccentricity values below.

Orbit Eccentricities of Planets in the Solar System			
Mercury	0.205	**Jupiter**	0.049
Venus	0.007	**Saturn**	0.057
Earth	0.017	**Uranus**	0.046
Mars	0.094	**Neptune**	0.011

Mean The mean is the sum of all of the values in a data set divided by the total number of values in the data set. The mean is also called the *average*.	$$\frac{0.007 + 0.011 + 0.017 + 0.046 + 0.049 + 0.057 + 0.094 + 0.205}{8}$$ **1** Add up all of the values. **2** Divide the sum by the number of values. **mean = 0.061**
Median The median is the value of the middle item when data are arranged in numerical order. If there is an odd number of values, the median is the middle value. If there is an even number of values, the median is the mean of the two middle values.	0.007 0.011 0.017 0.046 0.049 0.057 0.094 0.205 ⟶ ◄ **1** Order the values. **2** The median is the middle value if there is an odd number of values. If there is an even number of values, calculate the mean of the two middle values. **median = 0.0475**
Mode The mode is the value or values that occur most frequently in a data set. Order the values to find the mode. If all values occur with the same frequency, the data set is said to have no mode.	0.007 0.011 0.017 0.046 0.049 0.057 0.094 0.205 **1** Order the values. **2** Find the value or values that occur most frequently. **mode = none**
Range The range is the difference between the greatest value and the least value of a data set.	0.205 − 0.007 **1** Subtract the least value from the greatest value. **range = 0.198**

You Try It!

The data table below shows the masses and densities of the planets.

Mass and Density of the Planets		
	Mass ($\times 10^{24}$ kg)	**Density (g/cm^3)**
Mercury	0.33	5.43
Venus	4.87	5.24
Earth	5.97	5.52
Mars	0.64	3.34
Jupiter	1,899	1.33
Saturn	568	0.69
Uranus	87	1.27
Neptune	102	1.64

(1)

Using Formulas Find the mean, median, mode, and range for the mass of the planets.

(2)

Using Formulas Find the mean, median, mode, and range for the density of the planets.

(3)

Analyzing Data Find the mean density of the inner planets (Mercury through Mars). Find the mean density of the outer planets (Jupiter through Neptune). Compare these values.

Mean density of the inner planets: ________

Mean density of the outer planets: ________

Comparison:

____

(4)

Claims • Evidence • Reasoning The mean mass of the outer planets is 225 times greater than the mean mass of the inner planets. Use evidence and explain how this data, as well as the data comparing the mean densities of the planets, provide support for the claim that the outer planets are "gas giants."

____

____

Gravity and the Solar System

ESSENTIAL QUESTION

Why is gravity important in the solar system?

By the end of this lesson, you should be able to explain the role that gravity played in the formation of the solar system and in determining the motion of the planets.

Gravity keeps objects, such as these satellites, in orbit around Earth. Gravity also affects the way in which planets move and how they are formed.

SC.8.N.1.4 Explain how hypotheses are valuable...**SC.8.N.1.5** Analyze the methods used to develop a scientific explanation as seen in different fields of science. **SC.8.N.1.6** Understand that scientific investigations involve the collection of relevant empirical evidence, the use of logical reasoning, and the application of imagination in devising hypotheses, predictions, explanations and models to make sense of the collected evidence.
SC.8.N.2.2 Discuss what characterizes science and its methods. **SC.8.E.5.4** Explore the Law of Universal Gravitation...

© NASA/National Geographic/Getty Images

© Houghton Mifflin Harcourt Publishing Company

Lesson Labs

Quick Labs
- Gravity's Effect
- Orbital Ellipses

Exploration Lab
- Weights on Different Celestial Bodies

 Engage Your Brain

1 Predict Check T or F to show whether you think each statement is true or false.

T	F	
☐	☐	Gravity keeps the planets in orbit around the sun.
☐	☐	The planets follow circular paths around the sun.
☐	☐	Sir Isaac Newton was the first scientist to describe how the force of gravity behaved.
☐	☐	The sun formed in the center of the solar system.
☐	☐	The terrestrial planets and the gas giant planets formed from the same material.

2 Draw In the space below, draw what you think the solar system looked like before the planets formed.

ACTIVE **READING**

3 Synthesize You can often define an unknown word if you know the meaning of its word parts. Use the word parts and sentence below to make an educated guess about the meaning of the word *protostellar*.

Word part	Meaning
proto-	first
-stellar	of or having to do with a star or stars

Example sentence
The <u>protostellar</u> disk formed after the collapse of the solar nebula.

protostellar:

_____

_____

Vocabulary Terms

- gravity
- orbit
- aphelion
- perihelion
- centripetal force
- solar nebula
- planetesimal

4 Apply This list contains the key terms you'll learn in this section. As you read, circle the definition of each term.

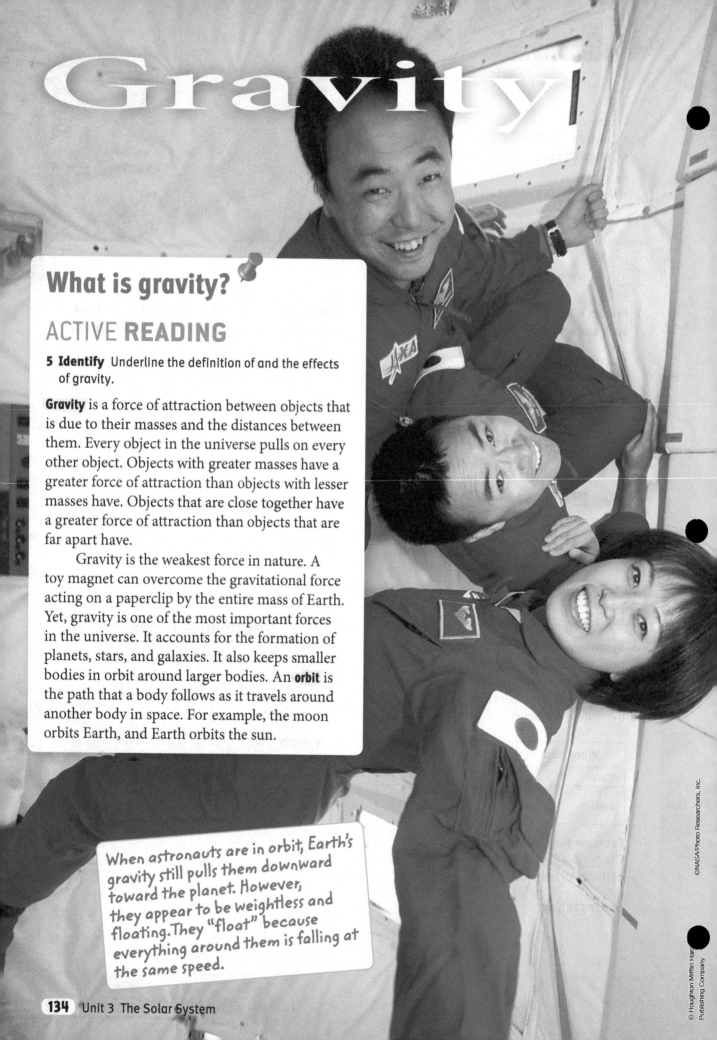

Gravity

What is gravity?

ACTIVE READING

5 Identify Underline the definition of and the effects of gravity.

Gravity is a force of attraction between objects that is due to their masses and the distances between them. Every object in the universe pulls on every other object. Objects with greater masses have a greater force of attraction than objects with lesser masses have. Objects that are close together have a greater force of attraction than objects that are far apart have.

Gravity is the weakest force in nature. A toy magnet can overcome the gravitational force acting on a paperclip by the entire mass of Earth. Yet, gravity is one of the most important forces in the universe. It accounts for the formation of planets, stars, and galaxies. It also keeps smaller bodies in orbit around larger bodies. An **orbit** is the path that a body follows as it travels around another body in space. For example, the moon orbits Earth, and Earth orbits the sun.

When astronauts are in orbit, Earth's gravity still pulls them downward toward the planet. However, they appear to be weightless and floating. They "float" because everything around them is falling at the same speed.

What are Kepler's laws?

The 16th-century Polish astronomer Nicolaus Copernicus (nik•uh•LAY•uhs koh•PER•nuh•kuhs) (1473–1543) changed our view of the solar system. He discovered that the motions of the planets could be best explained if the planets orbited the sun. But, like astronomers who came before him, Copernicus thought the planets followed circular paths around the sun.

Danish astronomer Tycho Brahe (TY•koh BRAH) (1546–1601) built what was at the time the world's largest observatory. Tycho used special instruments to measure the motions of the planets. His measurements were made over a period of 20 years and were very accurate. Using Tycho's data, Johannes Kepler (yoh•HAH•nuhs KEP•luhr) (1571–1630) made discoveries about the motions of the planets. We call these *Kepler's laws of planetary motion.*

Kepler found that objects that orbit the sun follow elliptical orbits. When an object follows an elliptical orbit around the sun, there is one point, called **aphelion** (uh•FEE•lee•uhn), where the object is farthest from the sun. There is also a point, called **perihelion** (perh•uh•HEE•lee•uhn), where the object is closest to the sun. Today, we know that the orbits of the planets are only slightly elliptical. However, the orbits of objects such as Pluto and comets are highly elliptical.

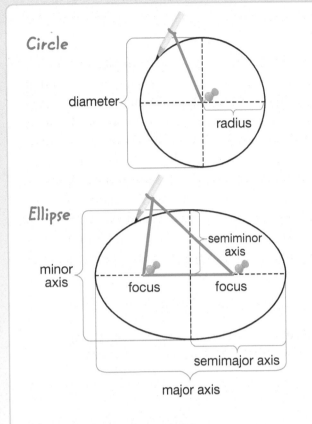

Circle

diameter
radius

Ellipse

semiminor axis
minor axis
focus   focus
semimajor axis
major axis

👁 Visualize It!

6 Support Your Claim How is a circle different from an ellipse? Summarize specific evidence to support your claim.

_____

_____

_____

Kepler's First Law

Kepler's careful plotting of the orbit of Mars kept showing Mars's orbit to be a deformed circle. It took Kepler eight years to realize that this shape was an ellipse. This clue led Kepler to propose elliptical orbits for the planets. Kepler placed the sun at one of the foci of the ellipse. This is Kepler's first law.

ACTIVE READING

7 Contrast What is the difference between Copernicus's and Kepler's description of planetary orbits?

_____

_____

Kepler's First Law

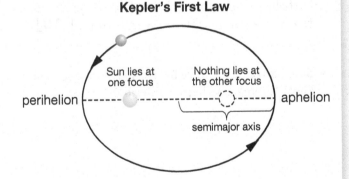

Sun lies at one focus   Nothing lies at the other focus
perihelion   aphelion
semimajor axis

Each planet orbits the sun in an ellipse with the sun at one focus. (For clarity, the ellipse is exaggerated here.)

Kepler's Second Law

Using the shape of an ellipse, Kepler searched for other regularities in Tycho's data. He found that an amazing thing happens when a line is drawn from a planet to the sun's focus on the ellipse. At aphelion, its speed is slower. So, it sweeps out a narrow sector on the ellipse. At perihelion, the planet is moving faster. It sweeps out a thick sector on the ellipse. In the illustration, the areas of both the thin blue sector and the thick blue sector are exactly the same. Kepler found that this relationship is true for all of the planets. This is Kepler's second law.

ACTIVE READING

8 Analyze At which point does a planet move most slowly in its orbit, at aphelion or perihelion?

As a planet moves around its orbit, it sweeps out equal areas in equal times.

Kepler's Second Law

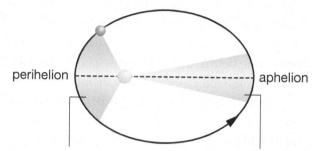

Near perihelion, a planet sweeps out an area that is short but wide.

Near aphelion, in an equal amount of time, a planet sweeps out an area that is long but narrow.

Kepler's Third Law

When Kepler looked at how long it took for the planets to orbit the sun and at the sizes of their orbits, he found another relationship. Kepler calculated the orbital period and the distance from the sun for the planets using Tycho's data. He discovered that the square of the orbital period was proportional to the cube of the planet's average distance from the sun. This law is true for each planet. This principle is Kepler's third law. When the units are years for the period and AU for the distance, the law can be written:

$$(\text{orbital period in years})^2 = (\text{average distance from the sun in astronomical units [AU]})^3$$

The square of the orbital period is proportional to the cube of the planet's average distance from the sun.

Kepler's Third Law

$p^2 \text{ yrs} = a^3 \text{ AU}$

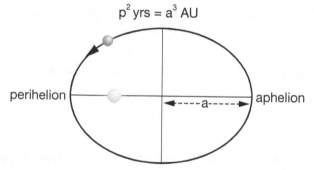

9 Summarize In the table below, summarize each of Kepler's three laws in your own words.

First law	Second law	Third law

What is the law of universal gravitation?

Using Kepler's laws, Sir Isaac Newton (EYE•zuhk NOOT'n) became the first scientist to mathematically describe how the force of gravity behaved. How could Newton do this in the 1600s before the force could be measured in a laboratory? He reasoned that gravity was the same force that accounted for both the fall of an apple from a tree and the movement of the moon around Earth.

In 1687, Newton formulated the *law of universal gravitation*. The law of universal gravitation states that all objects in the universe attract each other through gravitational force. The strength of this force depends on the product of the masses of the objects. Therefore, the gravity between objects increases as the masses of the objects increase. Gravitational force is also inversely proportional to the square of the distance between the objects. Stated another way this means that as the distance between two objects increases, the force of gravity decreases.

Sir Isaac Newton
(1642–1727)

⊞ Do the Math

Newton's law of universal gravitation says that the force of gravity:
- increases as the masses of the objects increase and
- decreases as the distance between the objects increases

In these examples, M = mass, d = distance, and F = the force of gravity exerted by two bodies.

Sample Problems

A. In the example below, when two balls have masses of M and the distance between them is d, then the force of gravity is F. If the mass of each ball is increased to 2M (to the right) and the distance stays the same, then the force of gravity increases to 4F.

B. In this example, we start out again with a distance of d and masses of M, and the force of gravity is F. If the distance is decreased to ½ d, then the force of gravity increases to 4F.

You Try It

Recall that M = mass, d = distance, and F = the force of gravity exerted by two bodies.

10 Claims • Evidence • Reasoning Compare the example below to the sample problems. Make a claim about what the force of gravity would be in the example below. Summarize evidence to support your claim and explain your reasoning.

_____

_____

_____

_____

_____

_____

How does gravity affect planetary motion?

The illustrations on this page will help you understand planetary motion. In the illustration at the right, a girl is swinging a ball around her head. The ball is attached to a string. The girl is exerting a force on the string that causes the ball to move in a circular path. The inward force that causes an object to move in a circular path is called **centripetal** (sehn•TRIP•ih•tuhl) **force**.

In the illustration at center, we see that if the string breaks, the ball will move off in a straight line. This fact indicates that when the string is intact, a force is pulling the ball inward. This force keeps the ball from flying off and moving in a straight line. This force is centripetal force.

In the illustration below, you see that the planets orbit the sun. A force must be preventing the planets from moving out of their orbits and into a straight line. The sun's gravity is the force that keeps the planets moving in orbit around the sun.

As the girl swings the ball, she is exerting a force on the string that causes the ball to move in a circular path.

Centripetal force pulls the ball inward, which causes the ball to move in a curved path.

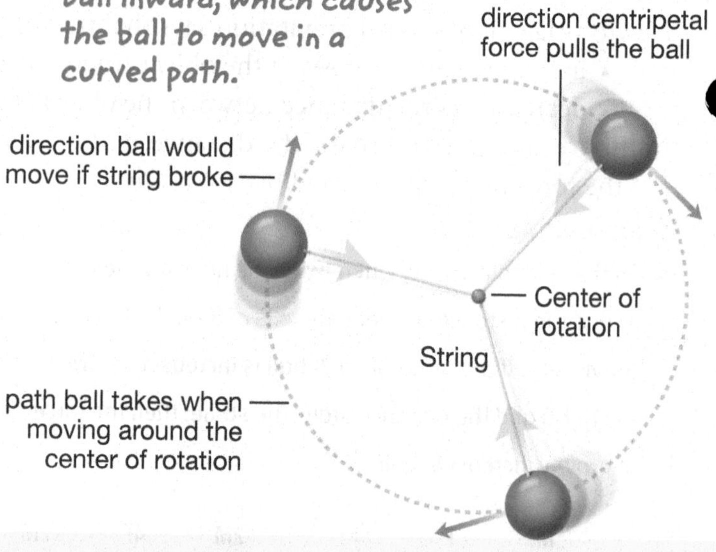

direction centripetal force pulls the ball

direction ball would move if string broke —

— Center of rotation

String

path ball takes when — moving around the center of rotation

Just as the string is pulling the ball inward, gravity is keeping the planets in orbit around the sun.

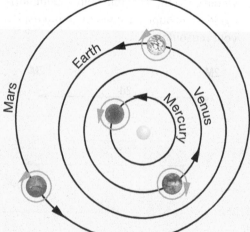

Mars

Earth

Venus

Mercury

11 Explain Your Reasoning In the illustration at the top of the page, what does the hand represent, the ball represent, and the string represent? (Hint: Think of the sun, a planet, and the force of gravity.) Explain your reasoning.

_____

_____

_____

© Houghton Mifflin Harcourt Publishing Company

How did the solar system form?

The formation of the solar system is thought to have begun 4.6 billion years ago when a cloud of dust and gas collapsed. This cloud, from which the solar system formed, is called the **solar nebula** (SOH•ler NEB•yuh•luh). In a nebula, the inward pull of gravity is balanced by the outward push of gas pressure in the cloud. Scientists think that an outside force, perhaps the explosion of a nearby star, caused the solar nebula to compress and then to contract under its own gravity. It was in a single region of the nebula, which was perhaps several light-years across, that the solar system formed. The sun probably formed from a region that had a mass that was slightly greater than today's mass of the sun and planets.

ACTIVE READING

12 Define What is the solar nebula?

_____

_____

A Protostellar Disk Formed from the Collapsed Solar Nebula

As a region of the solar nebula collapsed, gravity pulled most of the mass toward the center of the nebula. As the nebula contracted, it began to rotate. As the rotation grew faster, the nebula flattened out into a disk. This disk, which is called a *protostellar disk* (PROH•toh•stehl•er DISK), is where the central star, our sun, formed.

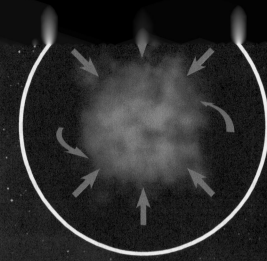

A cloud of dust and gas collapsed 4.6 billion years ago, then began to spin. It may have spun around its axis of rotation once every million years.

As a region of the solar nebula collapsed, it formed a slowly rotating protostellar disk.

The Sun Formed at the Center of the Protostellar Disk

As the protostellar disk continued to contract, most of the matter ended up in the center of the disk. Friction from matter that fell into the disk heated up its center to millions of degrees, eventually reaching its current temperature of 15,000,000 °C. This intense heat in a densely packed space caused the fusion of hydrogen atoms into helium atoms. The process of fusion released large amounts of energy. This release of energy caused outward pressure that again balanced the inward pull of gravity. As the gas and dust stopped collapsing, a star was born. In the case of the solar system, this star was the sun.

ACTIVE READING

13 Identify How did the sun form?

_____
_____
_____
_____
_____

This is an artist's conception of what the protoplanetary disk in which the planets formed might have looked like.

👁 Visualize It!

14 Describe Use the terms *planetesimal* and *protoplanetary disk* to describe the illustration above.

_____
_____
_____
_____
_____
_____

Planetesimals Formed in the Protoplanetary Disk

As the sun was forming, dust grains collided and stuck together. The resulting *dust granules* grew in size and increased in number. Over time, dust granules increased in size until they became roughly meter-sized bodies. Trillions of these bodies occurred in the protostellar disk. Collisions between these bodies formed larger bodies that were kilometers across. These larger bodies, from which planets formed, are called **planetesimals** (plan•ih•TES•ih•muhls). The protostellar disk had become the *protoplanetary disk*. The protoplanetary disk was the disk in which the planets formed.

Dust grains collided and stuck together.

Over time, dust granules grew to become meter-sized bodies.

Planetesimals formed from the collisions of meter-sized bodies.

ⓘ 👁 Visualize It!

15 Claims • Evidence • Reasoning Make a claim about how objects as small as dust grains can become the building blocks of planets. Use evidence to support your claim, and explain your reasoning.

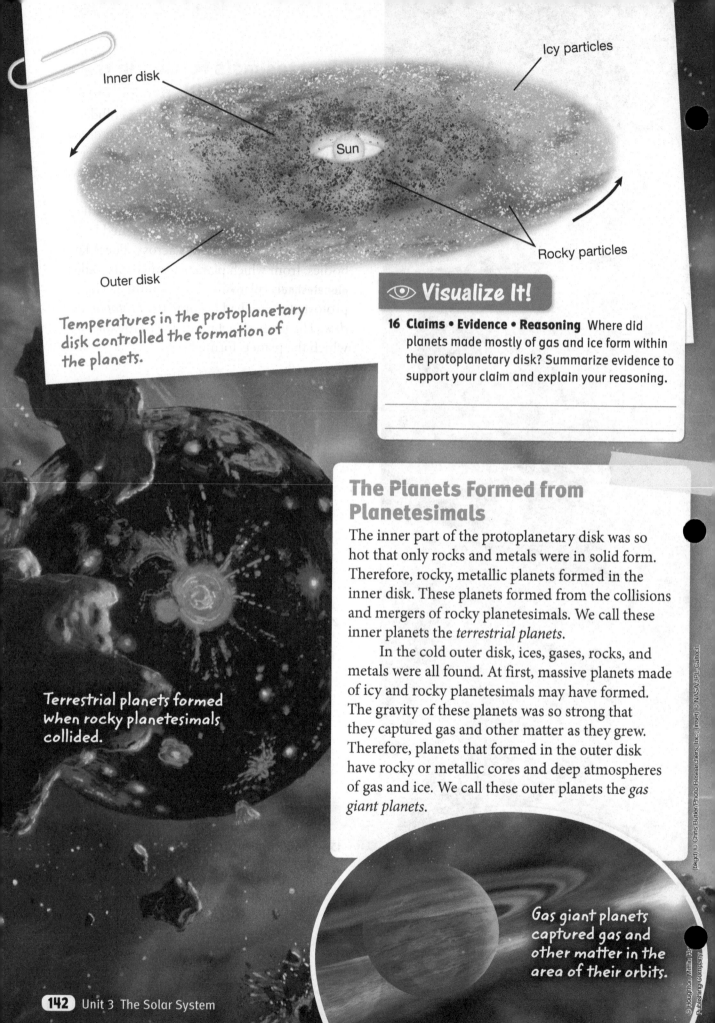

Icy particles

Inner disk

Sun

Rocky particles

Outer disk

Temperatures in the protoplanetary disk controlled the formation of the planets.

Visualize It!

16 Claims • Evidence • Reasoning Where did planets made mostly of gas and ice form within the protoplanetary disk? Summarize evidence to support your claim and explain your reasoning.

_____

_____

Terrestrial planets formed when rocky planetesimals collided.

The Planets Formed from Planetesimals

The inner part of the protoplanetary disk was so hot that only rocks and metals were in solid form. Therefore, rocky, metallic planets formed in the inner disk. These planets formed from the collisions and mergers of rocky planetesimals. We call these inner planets the _terrestrial planets_.

In the cold outer disk, ices, gases, rocks, and metals were all found. At first, massive planets made of icy and rocky planetesimals may have formed. The gravity of these planets was so strong that they captured gas and other matter as they grew. Therefore, planets that formed in the outer disk have rocky or metallic cores and deep atmospheres of gas and ice. We call these outer planets the _gas giant planets_.

Gas giant planets captured gas and other matter in the area of their orbits.

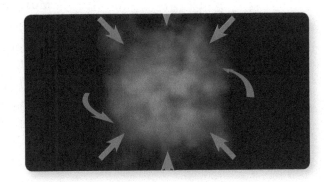

Visualize It!

17 Describe In the spaces on the left, describe Steps 2 and 4 in the formation of the solar system. In the spaces on the right, draw the last two steps in the formation of the solar system.

Steps in the Formation of the Solar System

Step 1 The Solar Nebula Collapses

A cloud of dust and gas collapses. The balance between the inward pull of gravity and the outward push of pressure in the cloud is upset. The collapsing cloud forms a rotating protostellar disk.

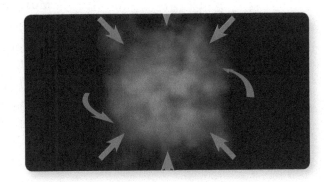

Step 2 The Sun Forms

_____

_____

_____

_____

Step 3 Planetesimals Form

Dust grains stick together and form dust granules. Dust granules slowly increase in size until they become meter-sized objects. These meter-sized objects collide to form kilometer-sized objects called planetesimals.

Step 4 Planets Form

_____

_____

_____

_____

_____

Visual Summary

To complete this summary, fill in the blank with the correct word or phrase. You can use this page to review the main concepts of the lesson.

The **Law** of **Universal Gravitation**

Mass affects the force of gravity.

18 The strength of the force of gravity depends on the product of the _____ of two objects. Therefore, as the masses of two objects increase, the force that the objects exert on one another _____ .

Distance affects the force of gravity.

19 Gravitational force is inversely proportional to the square of the _____ between two objects. Therefore, as the distance between two objects increases, the force of gravity between them _____ .

Gravity affects planetary motion.

20 The sun exerts a _____ , indicated by line B, on a planet so that at point C it is moving around the sun in orbit instead of moving off in a _____ as shown at line A.

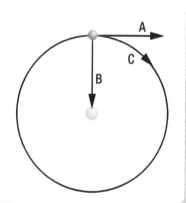

21 Explain Your Reasoning In your own words, explain Newton's law of universal gravitation.

Lesson Review

Vocabulary

Fill in the blank with the term that best completes the following sentences.

1 Small bodies from which the planets formed are called _____

2 The path that a body follows as it travels around another body in space is its _____

3 The _____ is the cloud of gas and dust from which our solar system formed.

Key Concepts

4 Define In your own words, define the word *gravity*.

_____

_____

_____

5 Describe How did the sun form?

_____

_____

_____

_____

_____

_____

6 Describe How did planetesimals form?

_____

_____

_____

_____

_____

_____

_____

Critical Thinking

Use the illustration below to answer the following question.

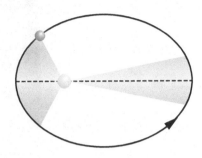

7 Identify What law is illustrated in this diagram?

_____

_____

8 Analyze How does gravity keep the planets in orbit around the sun?

_____

_____

_____

_____

_____

_____

9 Claims • Evidence • Reasoning Explain why the planets are arranged as they are in our solar system. Use the temperature differences in the protoplanetary disk as evidence to support your claim and explain your reasoning.

_____

_____

_____

_____

_____

_____

The Sun

ESSENTIAL QUESTION

What are the properties of the sun?

By the end of this lesson, you should be able to describe the structure and rotation of the sun, energy production and energy transport in the sun, and solar activity on the sun.

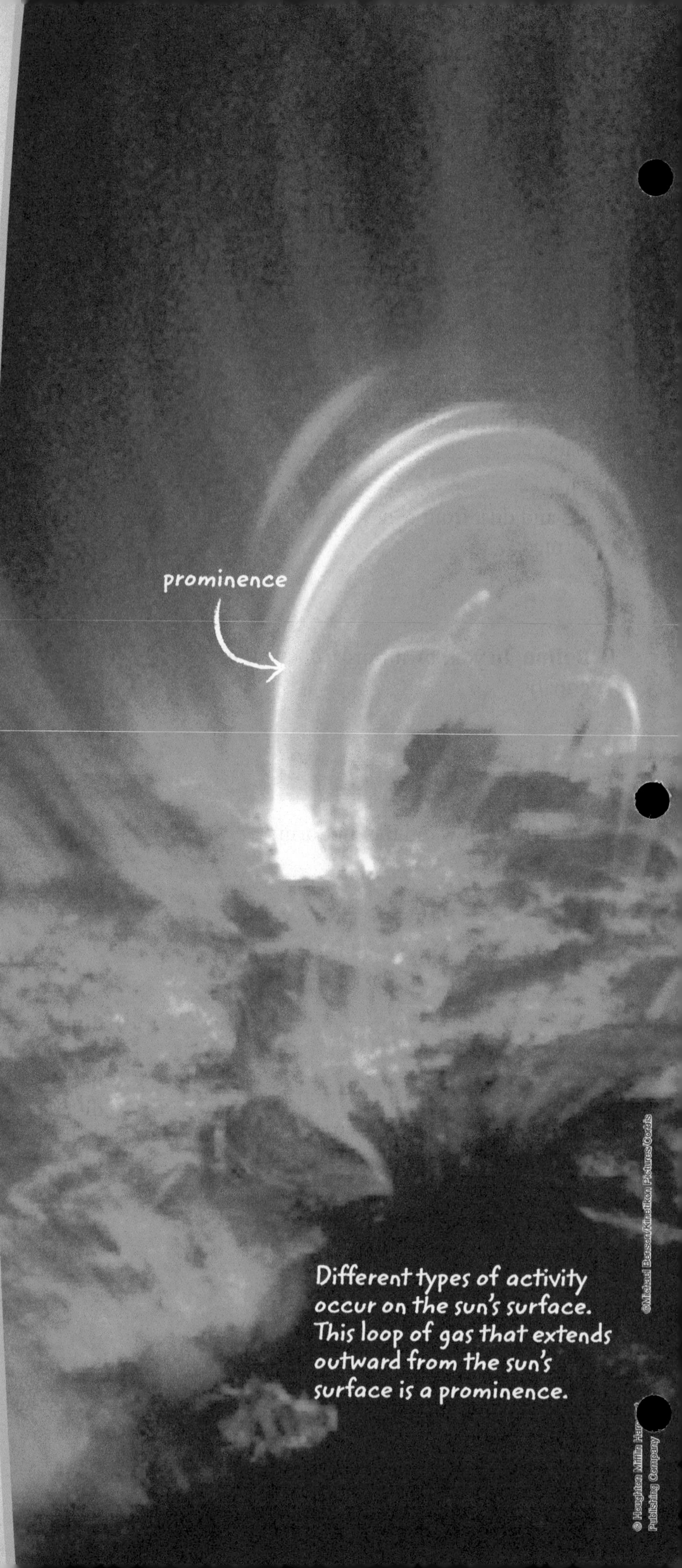

prominence

Different types of activity occur on the sun's surface. This loop of gas that extends outward from the sun's surface is a prominence.

SC.8.E.5.3 Distinguish the hierarchical relationships between planets and other astronomical bodies relative to solar system, galaxy, and universe, including distance, size, and composition.
SC.8.E.5.6 Create models of solar properties including: rotation, structure of the Sun, convection, sunspots, solar flares, and prominences.

Lesson Labs

Quick Labs
- Model Solar Composition
- Model Solar Rotation

Exploration/S.T.E.M. Lab
- Create a Model of the Sun

Engage Your Brain

1 Predict Check T or F to show whether you think each statement is true or false.

T F

☐ ☐ The sun is composed mostly of hydrogen and helium.

☐ ☐ Energy is produced in the sun's core.

☐ ☐ The process by which energy is produced in the sun is known as *nuclear fission*.

☐ ☐ Energy is transferred to the surface of the sun by the processes of radiation and conduction.

☐ ☐ A dark area of the sun's surface that is cooler than the surrounding areas is called a *sunspot*.

2 Explain In your own words, explain the meaning of the word *sunlight*.

_____

_____

_____

_____

_____

_____

_____

_____

_____

ACTIVE READING

3 Synthesize You can often define an unknown word if you know the meaning of its word parts. Use the word parts and sentence below to make an educated guess about the meaning of the word *photosphere*.

Word Part	Meaning
photo-	light
-sphere	ball

Example sentence
Energy is transferred to the sun's <u>photosphere</u> by convection cells.

photosphere:

_____

_____

_____

Vocabulary Terms

- nuclear fusion
- sunspot
- solar flare
- prominence

4 Apply This list contains the key terms you'll learn in this section. As you read, circle the definition of each term.

Here Comes the Sun

What do we know about the sun?

Since early in human history, people have marveled at the sun. Civilizations have referred to the sun by different names. Gods and goddesses who represented the sun were worshipped in different cultures. In addition, early astronomical observatories were established to track the sun's motion across the sky.

By the mid-19th century, astronomers had discovered that the sun was actually a hot ball of gas that is composed mostly of the elements hydrogen and helium. Scientists now know that the sun was born about 4.6 billion years ago. Every second, 4 million tons of solar matter is converted into energy. Of the light emitted from the sun, 41% is visible light, another 9% is ultraviolet light, and 50% is infrared radiation. And, perhaps most important of all, without the sun, there would be no life on Earth.

ACTIVE **READING**

5 Identify As you read the text, underline different discoveries that scientists have made about the sun.

Sun Statistics	
Avg. dist. from Earth	149.6 million km
Diameter	1,390,000 km
Average density	1.41 g/cm³
Period of rotation	25 days (equator); 35 days (poles)
Avg. surface temp.	5,527 °C
Core temp.	15,000,000 °C
Composition	74% hydrogen, 25% helium, 1% other elements

Do the Math

You Try It

6 Calculate The diameter of Earth is 12,756 km. How many times greater is the sun's diameter than the diameter of Earth?

_____

_____

_____

A solar flare, which is shown in this image, is a sudden explosive release of energy in the sun's atmosphere.

What is the structure of the sun?

The composition of the sun and Earth are different. However, the two bodies are similar in structure. Both are spheres. And both have a layered atmosphere and an interior composed of layers.

In the middle of the sun is the core. This is where energy is produced. From the core, energy is transported to the sun's surface through the radiative zone and the convective zone.

The sun's atmosphere has three layers—the photosphere, the chromosphere, and the corona. The sun's surface is the photosphere. Energy escapes the sun from this layer. The chromosphere is the middle layer of the sun's atmosphere. The temperature of the chromosphere rises with distance from the photosphere. The sun's outer atmosphere is the corona. The corona extends millions of kilometers into space.

7 Support Your Claim Why is the structure of the sun different from the structure of Earth? Summarize evidence to support your claim.

_____

_____

_____

_____

_____

_____

Corona The corona is the outer atmosphere of the sun. Temperatures in the corona may reach 2,000,000 °C.

Chromosphere The chromosphere is the middle layer of the sun's atmosphere. Temperatures in the chromosphere increase outward and reach a maximum of about 6,000 °C.

Photosphere The photosphere is the visible surface of the sun. It is the layer from which energy escapes into space. The photosphere has an average temperature of 5,527 °C.

Convective Zone The convective zone is the layer of the sun through which energy travels by convection from the radiative zone to the photosphere.

Radiative Zone The radiative zone is the layer of the sun through which energy is transferred away from the core by radiation.

Core The core is the very dense center of the sun. The core has a temperature of 15,000,000 °C, which is hot enough to cause the nuclear reactions that produce energy in the sun.

Let's Get Together

How does the sun produce energy?

Early in the 20th century, physicist Albert Einstein proposed that matter and energy are interchangeable. Matter can change into energy according to his famous equation $E = mc^2$. E is energy, m is mass, and c is the speed of light. Because c is such a large number, tiny amounts of matter can produce huge amounts of energy. Using Einstein's formula, scientists were able to explain the huge quantities of energy produced by the sun.

By Nuclear Fusion

Scientists know that the sun generates energy through the process of *nuclear fusion*. **Nuclear fusion** is the process by which two or more low-mass atomic nuclei fuse to form another, heavier nucleus. Nuclear fusion takes place in the core of stars. In stars that have core temperatures similar to the sun's, the fusion process that fuels the star starts with the fusion of two hydrogen nuclei. In older stars in which core temperatures are hotter than the sun's, the fusion process involves the fusion of helium into carbon.

Think Outside the Book

8 Claims • Evidence • Reasoning
Einstein's equation $E = mc^2$ is probably the most famous equation in the world. Make a claim about what kinds of technologies rely on the conversion of matter to energy. Summarize evidence to support your claim and explain your reasoning.

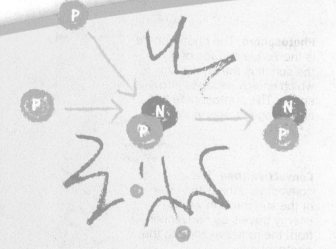

👁 Visualize It!

9 Identify Fill in the circles to label the particles in the diagrams.

P Proton

N Neutron

Three Steps of Nuclear Fusion in the Sun

Step 1: Deuterium Two hydrogen nuclei (protons) collide. One proton emits particles and energy and then becomes a neutron. The proton and neutron combine to produce a heavy form of hydrogen called *deuterium*.

By the Fusion of Hydrogen into Helium

The most common elements in the sun are hydrogen and helium. Under the crushing force of gravity, these gases are compressed and heated in the sun's core, where temperatures reach 15,000,000 °C. In the sun's core, hydrogen nuclei sometimes fuse to form a helium nucleus. This process takes three steps to complete. This three-step process is illustrated below.

Most of the time, when protons are on a collision course with other protons, their positive charges instantly repel them. The protons do not collide. But sometimes one proton will encounter another proton and, at that exact moment, turn into a neutron and eject an electron. This collision forms a nucleus that contains one proton and one neutron. This nucleus is an isotope of hydrogen called *deuterium*. The deuterium nucleus collides with another proton and forms a variety of helium called *helium-3*. Then, two helium-3 nuclei collide and form a helium-4 nucleus that has two protons and two neutrons. The remaining two protons are released back into the sun's core.

The entire chain of fusion reactions requires six hydrogen nuclei and results in one helium nucleus and two hydrogen nuclei. There are approximately 10^{38} collisions between hydrogen nuclei taking place in the sun's core every second, which keeps the sun shining.

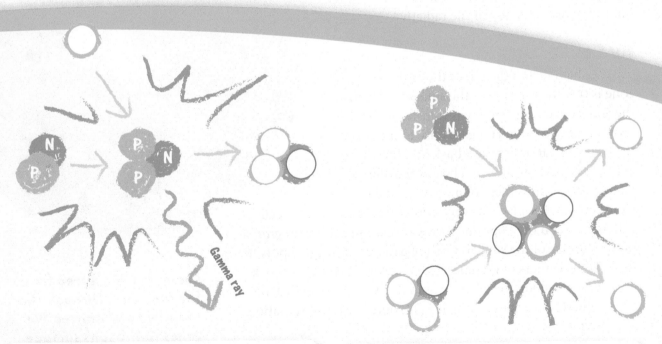

Step 2: Helium-3 Deuterium combines with another hydrogen nucleus to form a variety of helium called *helium-3*. More energy, including gamma rays, is released.

Step 3: Helium-4 Two helium-3 nuclei combine to form helium-4, which releases more energy and a pair of hydrogen nuclei (protons).

Mixing It Up

How is energy transferred to the sun's surface?

Energy is transferred to the surface of the sun by two different processes. Energy that is transferred from the sun's core through the radiative zone is transferred by the process of radiation. Energy that is transferred from the top of the radiative zone through the convective zone to the photosphere is transferred by the process of convection. Energy flow from the sun's core outward to the sun's surface by radiation and convection happens continuously.

By Radiation

When energy leaves the sun's core, it moves into the radiative zone. Energy travels through the radiative zone in the form of electromagnetic waves. The process by which energy is transferred as electromagnetic waves is called *radiation*. The radiative zone is densely packed with particles such as hydrogen, helium, and free electrons. Therefore, electromagnetic waves cannot travel directly through the radiative zone. Instead, they are repeatedly absorbed and re-emitted by particles until they reach the top of the radiative zone.

By Convection

Energy that reaches the top of the radiative zone is then transferred to the sun's surface. In the convective zone, energy is transferred by the movement of matter. Hot gases rise to the surface of the sun, cool, and then sink back into the convective zone. This process, in which heat is transferred by the circulation or movement of matter, is called *convection*. Convection takes place in convection cells. A convection cell is illustrated on the opposite page. Convection cells form *granules* on the surface of the sun. Hot, rising gases cause bright spots to form in the centers of granules. Cold, sinking gases cause dark areas to form along the edges of granules. Once energy reaches the photosphere, it escapes as visible light, other forms of radiation, heat, and wind.

Energy is transferred from the sun's core through the radiative and convective zones to the sun's surface.

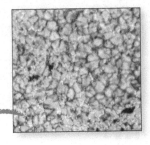

The tops of convection cells form granules on the sun's surface.

11 Compare How is energy transferred from the sun's core to the sun's surface in the radiative zone and in the convective zone?

Radiative zone	Convective zone

Hot, rising gases and colder, sinking gases form convection cells in the convective zone.

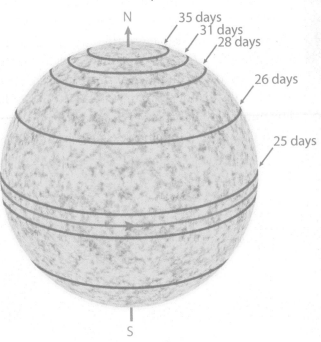

N
35 days
31 days
28 days
26 days
25 days
S

The sun's period of rotation varies with latitude.

How does the sun rotate?

The sun rotates on its axis like other large bodies in the solar system. However, because the sun is a giant ball of gas, it does not rotate in the same way as a solid body like Earth does. Instead, the sun rotates faster at its equator than it does at higher latitudes. This kind of rotation is known as differential rotation. *Differential rotation* is the rotation of a body in which different parts of a body have different periods of rotation. Near the equator, the sun rotates once in about 25 days. However, at the poles, the sun rotates once in about 35 days.

Even stranger is the fact that the sun's interior does not rotate in the same way as the sun's surface does. Scientists think that the sun's core and radiative zone rotate together, at the same speed. Therefore, the sun's radiative zone and core rotate like Earth.

12 Define In your own words, define the term *differential rotation*.

_____

_____

_____

_____

The Ring of Fire

What is solar activity?

Solar activity refers to variations in the appearance or energy output of the sun. Solar activity includes dark areas that occur on the sun's surface known as *sunspots*. Solar activity also includes sudden explosive events on the sun's surface, which are called *solar flares*. Prominences are another form of solar activity. *Prominences* are vast loops of gases that extend into the sun's outer atmosphere.

Sunspots

Dark areas that form on the surface of the sun are called **sunspots**. They are about 1,500 °C cooler than the areas that surround them. Sunspots are places where hot, convecting gases are prevented from reaching the sun's surface.

Sunspots can appear for periods of a few hours or a few months. Some sunspots are only a few hundred kilometers across. Others have widths that are 10 to 15 times the diameter of Earth.

Sunspot activity occurs on average in 11-year cycles. When a cycle begins, the number of sunspots is at a minimum. The number of sunspots then increases until it reaches a maximum. The number then begins to decrease. A new sunspot cycle begins when the sunspot number reaches a minimum again.

Sunspots, solar flares, and prominences are three kinds of solar activity that occur on the sun's surface.

sunspot

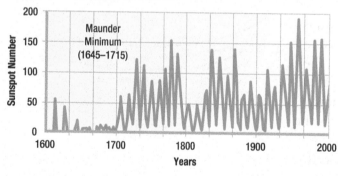

Sunspot Activity from 1600 to 2000

Maunder Minimum (1645–1715)

Sunspot Number

Years

➕➖ Do the Math
✖️➗

You Try It

13 **Support Your Claim** The sunspot range is the difference between the maximum number of sunspots and the minimum number of sunspots for a certain period of time. To find this range, subtract the minimum number of sunspots from the maximum number of sunspots. What is the range of sunspot activity between 1700 and 1800? Summarize evidence from the graph to support your claim.

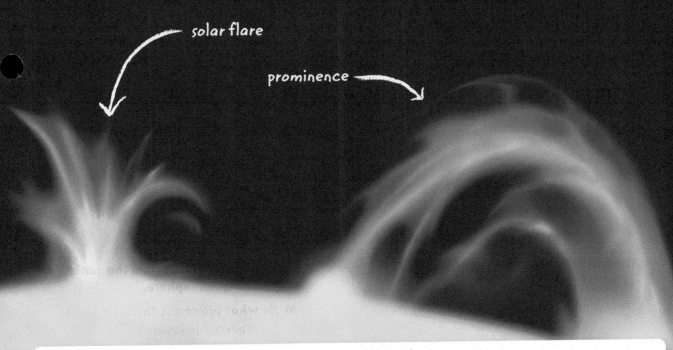

solar flare

prominence

Solar Flares

Solar flares appear as very bright spots on the sun's photosphere. A **solar flare** is an explosive release of energy that can extend outward as far as the sun's outer atmosphere. During a solar flare, enormous numbers of high-energy particles are ejected at near the speed of light. Radiation is released across the entire electromagnetic spectrum, from radio waves to x-rays and gamma rays. Temperatures within solar flares reach millions of degrees Celsius.

Prominences

Huge loops of relatively cool gas that extend outward from the photosphere thousands of kilometers into the outer atmosphere are called **prominences**. Several objects the size of Earth could fit inside a loop of a prominence. The gases in prominences are cooler than the surrounding atmosphere.

Prominences generally last from several hours to a day. However, some prominences can last for as long as several months.

14 Compare Use the Venn diagram below to compare solar flares and prominences.

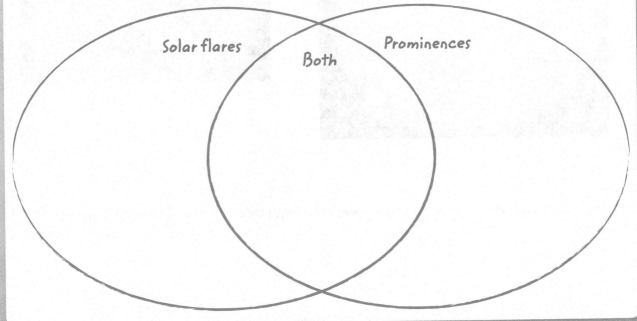

Solar flares   Both   Prominences

Visual Summary

To complete this summary, fill in the blanks with the correct word or phrase. You can use this page to review the main concepts of the lesson.

Properties of the Sun

The sun is composed of layers.

15 Identify the six layers of the sun, beginning with the innermost layer.

_____

_____

_____

_____

_____

_____

Energy is transferred from the sun's core to the photosphere.

16 By what process is the sun's energy transported in layer A?

_____

By what process is the sun's energy transported in layer B?

_____

17 **State Your Claim** Make a claim about the process of energy production by nuclear fusion in the sun.

Lesson Review

Vocabulary

Fill in the blank with the term that best completes the following sentences.

1 The process by which two or more low-mass atomic nuclei fuse to form another, heavier nucleus is called _____.

2 A _____ is a dark area on the surface of the sun that is cooler than the surrounding areas.

3 A _____ is a loop of relatively cool gas that extends above the photosphere.

Key Concepts

In the following table, write the name of the correct layer next to the definition.

Definition	Layer
4 Identify What is the layer of the sun from which energy escapes into space?	
5 Identify What is the layer of the sun in which energy is produced?	
6 Identify What is the layer of the sun through which energy is transferred away from the core by radiation?	

7 Identify What is the composition of the sun?

_____

_____

8 Explain What is the sunspot cycle?

_____

_____

_____

_____

Critical Thinking

Use the illustration to answer the following questions.

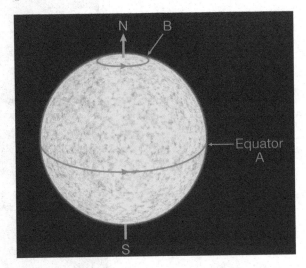

9 Claims • Evidence • Reasoning How many days does it take for the sun to spin once on its axis at location A? How many days does it take for the sun to spin once on its axis at location B? Summarize evidence to support your claims and explain your reasoning.

_____

_____

10 Compare How is the rotation of the sun different from the rotation of Earth?

_____

_____

11 Explain In your own words, explain how energy is transported from the core to the surface of the sun by radiation and by convection.

_____

_____

_____

_____

_____

The **Terrestrial Planets**

Mars

ESSENTIAL **QUESTION**

What is known about the terrestrial planets?

By the end of this lesson, you should be able to describe some of the properties of the terrestrial planets and how the properties of Mercury, Venus, and Mars differ from the properties of Earth.

Earth

Venus

Mercury

The terrestrial planets are the four planets that are closest to the sun. Distances between the planets shown here are not to scale.

sun

SC.8.N.1.5 Analyze the methods used to develop a scientific explanation as seen in different fields of science. SC.8.E.5.3 Distinguish the hierarchical relationships between planets and other astronomical bodies relative to solar system, galaxy, and universe, including distance, size, and composition. SC.8.E.5.7 Compare and contrast the properties of objects in the Solar System including the Sun, planets, and moons to those of Earth, such as gravitational force, distance from the Sun, speed, movement, temperature, and atmospheric conditions.

Lesson Labs

Quick Labs
• Schoolyard Solar System
• How Do the Layers Inside Planets Form?

 Engage Your Brain

1 Define Circle the term that best completes the following sentences.

Venus/Earth/Mars is the largest terrestrial planet.

Mercury/Venus/Mars has clouds that rain sulfuric acid on the planet.

Huge dust storms sweep across the surface of *Mercury/Venus/Mars*.

Venus/Earth/Mars is the most geologically active of the terrestrial planets.

Mercury/Venus/Earth has the thinnest atmosphere of the terrestrial planets.

2 Identify What are properties of Earth that make it a special place in the solar system?

_____

_____

_____

_____

ACTIVE **READING**

3 Synthesize Many English words have their roots in other languages. Use the Latin words below to make an educated guess about the meaning of the word *astronomy*.

Latin word	Meaning
astrón	star
nomos	law

Example sentence
Some students who are interested in the night sky enter college to study <u>astronomy</u>.

astronomy:

_____

_____

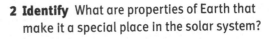 **Vocabulary Terms**

• terrestrial planet
• astronomical unit

4 Apply As you learn the definition of each vocabulary term in this lesson, create your own definition or sketch to help you remember the meaning of the term.

Extreme
to the
Core

What are the terrestrial planets?

The **terrestrial planets** are the four small, dense, rocky planets that orbit closest to the sun. In order by distance from the sun, these planets are Mercury, Venus, Earth, and Mars. The terrestrial planets have similar compositions and consist of an outer crust, a central core, and a mantle that lies between the crust and core.

What is known about Mercury?

Mercury (MUR•kyuh•ree) is the planet about which we know the least. Until NASA's *Mariner 10* spacecraft flew by Mercury in 1974, the planet was seen as a blotchy, dark ball of rock. Today, scientists know that the planet's heavily cratered, moon-like surface is composed largely of volcanic rock and hides a massive iron core.

Mercury orbits only 0.39 AU from the sun. The letters *AU* stand for *astronomical unit*, which is the term astronomers use to measure distances in the solar system. One **astronomical unit** equals the average distance between the sun and Earth, or approximately 150 million km. Therefore, Mercury lies nearly halfway between the sun and Earth.

ACTIVE READING

5 Identify As you read the text, underline important characteristics of the planet Mercury.

Statistics Table for Mercury	
Distance from the sun	0.39 AU
Period of rotation (length of Mercury day)	58 days 15.5 h
Period of revolution (length of Mercury year)	88 days
Tilt of axis	0°
Diameter	4,879 km
Density	5.44 g/cm³
Surface temperature	-184 °C to 427 °C
Surface gravity	38% of Earth's gravity
Number of satellites	0

Although this may look like the moon, it is actually the heavily cratered surface of the planet Mercury.

© J Marshall-Tribaleye Images/Alamy

© Houghton Mifflin Harcourt Publishing Company

Mercury Has the Most Extreme Temperature Range in the Solar System

On Earth, a day lasts 24 h. On Mercury, a day lasts almost 59 Earth days. What does this fact have to do with temperatures on Mercury? It means that temperatures on that part of Mercury's surface that is receiving sunlight can build for more than 29 days. When it is day on Mercury, temperatures can rise to 427 °C, a temperature that is hot enough to melt certain metals. It also means that temperatures on the part of Mercury's surface that is in darkness can fall for more than 29 days. When it is night on Mercury, temperatures can drop to –184 °C. This means that surface temperatures on Mercury can change by as much as 600 °C between day and night. This is the greatest difference between high and low temperatures in the solar system.

Mercury Has a Large Iron Core

Mercury is the smallest planet in the solar system. It has a diameter of only 4,879 km at its equator. Amazingly, Mercury's central core is thought to be around 3,600 km in diameter, which accounts for most of the planet's interior. Scientists originally thought that Mercury had a core of solid iron. However, by observing changes in Mercury's spin as it orbits the sun, astronomers now think that the core is at least partially molten. Why is the core so large? Some scientists think that Mercury may have been struck by another object in the distant past and lost most of the rock that surrounded the core. Other scientists think that long ago the sun vaporized the planet's surface and blasted it away into space.

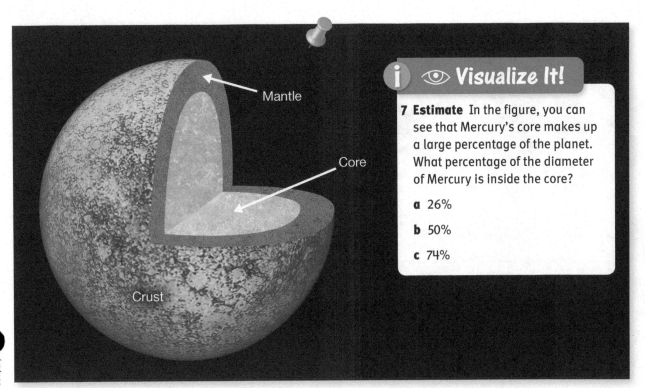

Mantle

Core

Crust

Think Outside the Book

6 Claims • Evidence • Reasoning
You are an astronaut who will be exploring Mercury. Make a claim about what equipment you would take to Mercury to help you survive. Use evidence to support your claim, and explain your reasoning.

ⓘ ◉ Visualize It!

7 Estimate In the figure, you can see that Mercury's core makes up a large percentage of the planet. What percentage of the diameter of Mercury is inside the core?

a 26%

b 50%

c 74%

Harsh Planet

What is known about Venus?

Science-fiction writers once imagined Venus (VEE•nuhs) to be a humid planet with lush, tropical forests. Nothing could be further from the truth. On Venus, sulfuric acid rain falls on a surface that is not much different from the inside of an active volcano.

Venus Is Similar to Earth in Size and Mass

Venus has often been called "Earth's twin." At 12,104 km, the diameter of Venus is 95% the diameter of Earth. Venus's mass is around 80% of Earth's. And the gravity that you would experience on Venus is 89% of the gravity on Earth.

The rotation of Venus is different from the rotation of Earth. Earth has prograde rotation. *Prograde rotation* is the counterclockwise spin of a planet about its axis as seen from above the planet's north pole. Venus, however, has retrograde rotation. *Retrograde rotation* is the clockwise spin of a planet about its axis as seen from above its north pole.

Venus differs from Earth not only in the direction in which it spins on its axis. It takes more time for Venus to rotate once about its axis than it takes for the planet to revolve once around the sun. Venus has the slowest period of rotation in the solar system.

Venus has landforms such as highlands and plains, volcanoes, and impact craters.

Statistics Table for Venus

Distance from the sun	0.72 AU
Period of rotation	243 days (retrograde rotation)
Period of revolution	225 days
Tilt of axis	177.4°
Diameter	12,104 km
Density	5.20 g/cm³
Average surface temperature	465 °C
Surface gravity	89% of Earth's gravity
Number of satellites	0

©NASA/Science Source/Photo Researchers Inc.

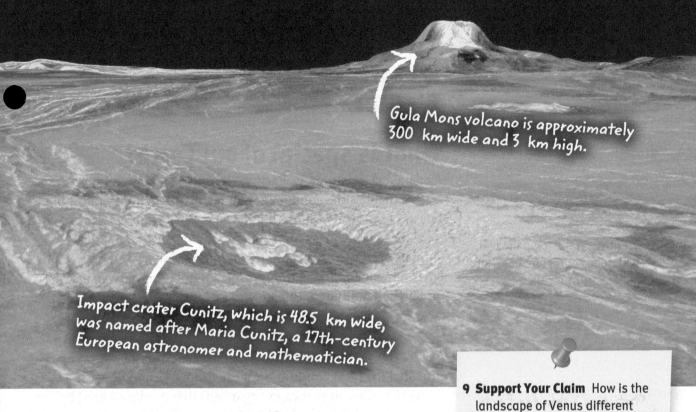

Gula Mons volcano is approximately 300 km wide and 3 km high.

Impact crater Cunitz, which is 48.5 km wide, was named after Maria Cunitz, a 17th-century European astronomer and mathematician.

Venus Has Craters and Volcanoes

In 1990, the powerful radar beams of NASA's *Magellan* spacecraft pierced the dense atmosphere of Venus. This gave us our most detailed look ever at the planet's surface. There are 168 volcanoes on Venus that are larger than 100 km in diameter. Thousands of volcanoes have smaller diameters. Venus's surface is also cratered. These craters are as much as 280 km in diameter. The sizes and locations of the craters on Venus suggest that around 500 million years ago something happened to erase all of the planet's older craters. Scientists are still puzzled about how this occurred. But volcanic activity could have covered the surface of the planet in one huge outpouring of magma.

The Atmosphere of Venus Is Toxic

Venus may have started out like Earth, with oceans and water running across its surface. However, after billions of years of solar heating, Venus has become a harsh world. Surface temperatures on Venus are hotter than those on Mercury. Temperatures average around 465 °C. Over time, carbon dioxide gas has built up in the atmosphere. Sunlight that strikes Venus's surface warms the ground. However, carbon dioxide in the atmosphere traps this energy, which causes temperatures near the surface to remain high.

Sulfuric acid rains down onto Venus's surface, and the pressure of the atmosphere is at least 90 times that of Earth's atmosphere. No human—or machine—could survive for long under these conditions. Venus is a world that is off limits to human explorers and perhaps all but the hardiest robotic probes.

9 Support Your Claim How is the landscape of Venus different from the landscape of Earth? Summarize evidence to support your claim.

_____
_____
_____
_____
_____

ACTIVE READING

10 Identify As you read the text, underline those factors that make Venus an unlikely place for life to exist.

No Place Like Home

What is special about Earth?

As far as scientists know, Earth is the only planet in the solar system that has the combination of factors needed to support life. Life as we know it requires liquid water and an energy source. Earth has both. Earth's atmosphere contains the oxygen that animals need to breathe. Matter is continuously cycled between the environment and living things. And a number of ecosystems exist on Earth that different organisms can inhabit.

ACTIVE READING

11 Identify As you read the text, underline characteristics that make Earth special.

Earth Has Abundant Water and Life

Earth's vast liquid-water oceans and moderate temperatures provided the ideal conditions for life to emerge and flourish. Around 3.5 billion years ago, organisms that produced food by photosynthesis appeared in Earth's oceans. During the process of making food, these organisms produced oxygen. By 560 million years ago, more complex life forms arose that could use oxygen to release energy from food. Today, the total number of species of organisms that inhabit Earth is thought to be anywhere between 5 million and 30 million.

Statistics Table for Earth

Distance from the sun	1.0 AU
Period of rotation	23 h 56 min
Period of revolution	365.3 days
Tilt of axis	23.45°
Diameter	12,756 km
Density	5.52 g/cm³
Temperature	-89 °C to 58 °C
Surface gravity	100% of Earth's gravity
Number of satellites	1

From space, Earth presents an entirely different scene from that of the other terrestrial planets. Clouds in the atmosphere, blue bodies of water, and green landmasses are all clues to the fact that Earth is a special place.

Earth Is Geologically Active

Earth is the only terrestrial planet whose surface is divided into tectonic plates. These plates move around Earth's surface, which causes the continents to change positions over long periods of time. Tectonic plate motion, together with weathering and erosion, has erased most surface features older than 500 million years.

Humans Have Set Foot on the Moon

Between 1969 and 1972, 12 astronauts landed on the moon. They are the only humans to have set foot on another body in the solar system. They encountered a surface gravity that is only about one-sixth that of Earth. Because of the moon's lower gravity, astronauts could not walk normally. If they did, they would fly up in the air and fall over.

Like Mercury, the moon's surface is heavily cratered. It is estimated that about 500,000 craters larger than 1 km dot the moon. There are large dark areas on the moon's surface. These are plains of solidified lava. There are also light-colored areas. These are the lunar highlands.

The moon rotates about its axis in the same time it orbits Earth. Therefore, it keeps the same side facing Earth. During a lunar day, which is a little more than 27 Earth days, the daytime surface temperature can reach 127 °C. The nighttime surface temperature can fall to −173 °C.

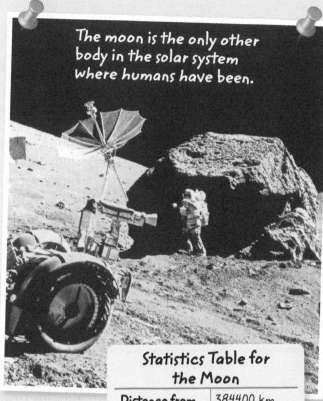

The moon is the only other body in the solar system where humans have been.

Statistics Table for the Moon

Distance from Earth	384,400 km (0.0026 AU)
Period of rotation	27.3 days
Period of revolution	27.3 days
Axial tilt	1.5°
Diameter	3,476 km
Density	3.34 g/cm³
Temperature	−173°C to 127°C
Surface gravity	16.5% of Earth's gravity

👁 Visualize It!

12 Identify In the image, circle any signs of life that you see.

Is It Alive?

What is known about Mars?

A fleet of spacecraft is now in orbit around Mars (MARZ) studying the planet. Space rovers have also investigated the surface of Mars. These remote explorers have discovered a planet with an atmosphere that is 100 times thinner than Earth's and temperatures that are little different from the inside of a freezer. They have seen landforms on Mars that are larger than any found on Earth. And these unmanned voyagers have photographed surface features on Mars that are characteristic of erosion and deposition by water.

Mars Is a Rocky, Red Planet

The surface of Mars is better known than that of any other planet in the solar system except Earth. It is composed largely of dark volcanic rock. Rocks and boulders litter the surface of Mars. Some boulders can be as large as a house. A powdery dust covers Martian rocks and boulders. This dust is the product of the chemical breakdown of rocks rich in iron minerals. This is what gives the Martian soil its orange-red color.

Think Outside the Book

13 Claims • Evidence • Reasoning
Research the surface features of the northern and southern hemispheres of Mars. Decide which hemisphere you would rather explore. With your class, debate the merits of exploring one hemisphere versus the other. Summarize evidence to support your claim and explain your reasoning.

Statistics Table for Mars

Distance from the sun	1.52 AU
Period of rotation	24 h 37 min
Period of revolution	1.88 y
Tilt of axis	25.3°
Diameter	6,792 km
Density	3.93 g/cm³
Temperature	-140°C to 20°C
Surface gravity	37% of Earth's gravity
Number of satellites	2

Mars's northern polar ice cap is composed of carbon dioxide ice and water ice. Its size varies with the seasons.

Mars Has Interesting Surface Features

The surface of Mars varies from hemisphere to hemisphere. The northern hemisphere appears to have been covered by lava flows. The southern hemisphere is heavily cratered.

Large volcanoes are found on Mars. At 27 km high and 600 km across, Olympus Mons (uh•LIM•puhs MAHNZ) is the largest volcano and mountain in the solar system. Mars also has very deep valleys and canyons. The canyon system Valles Marineris (VAL•less mar•uh•NAIR•iss) runs from west to east along the Martian equator. It is about 4,000 km long, 500 km wide, and up to 10 km deep. It is the largest canyon in the solar system.

Mars Has a Thin Atmosphere

Mars has a very thin atmosphere that is thought to have been thicker in the past. Mars may have gradually lost its atmosphere to the solar wind. Or a body or bodies that collided with Mars may have caused much of the atmosphere to have been blown away.

Unlike Earth, Mars's atmosphere is composed mostly of carbon dioxide. During the Martian winter, temperatures at the planet's poles grow cold enough for carbon dioxide to freeze into a thin coating. During the summer, when temperatures grow warmer, this coating vanishes.

Winds on Mars can blow with enough force to pick up dust particles from the planet's surface. When this happens, giant dust storms can form. At times, these storms cover the entire planet.

Olympus Mons is the largest volcano in the solar system.

ACTIVE READING

14 Explain What are two possible reasons why the atmosphere on Mars is so thin?

_____

_____

_____

15 Compare Compare and contrast the physical properties of Mars to the physical properties of Earth.

Hebes Chasma is a 6,000 m–deep depression that is located in the Valles Marineris region.

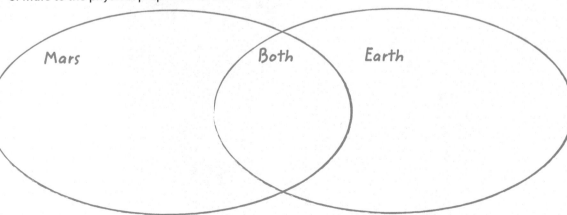

Mars   Both   Earth

Liquid Water Once Flowed on Mars

A number of features on Mars provide evidence that liquid water once flowed on the planet's surface. Many of these features have been struck by asteroids. These asteroid impacts have left behind craters that scientists can use to find the approximate dates of these features. Scientists estimate that many of these features, such as empty river basins, existed on Mars more than 3 billion years ago. Since then, little erosion has taken place that would cause these features to disappear.

In 2000, the *Mars Global Surveyor* took before-and-after images of a valley wall on Mars. Scientists observed the unmistakable trace of a liquid substance that had flowed out of the valley wall and into the valley. Since 2000, many similar features have been seen. The best explanation of these observations is that water is found beneath Mars's surface. At times, this water leaks out onto the Martian surface like spring water on Earth.

👁 Visualize It!

16 Claims • Evidence • Reasoning Make a claim about whether the features in the image at the right indicate that liquid water once flowed on Mars. Summarize evidence to support your claim and explain your reasoning.

_____

_____

_____

_____

This image shows gullies on the wall of a Martian crater. Water that may be stored close to the Martian surface has run downhill into the crater.

Water ice sits on the floor of a crater that is located about 20 degrees below Mars's north pole.

WHY IT **MATTERS**

Roving Mars

NUEVAS FRONTERAS

The Mars Exploration Rovers *Spirit* and *Opportunity* landed safely on Mars in January 2004. These robotic geologists were sent to find out if Mars ever had water. They found landforms shaped by past water activity as well as evidence of past groundwater. The last communication from *Spirit* was received in 2010. *Opportunity* was still exploring Mars in 2015.

Curiosity

Curiosity landed on Mars in 2012 to find out if Mars could have once supported life. It has been exploring ever since then and has found the ingredients needed to support life in some of Mars' rocks.

Testing the Rovers on Earth
Before leaving Earth, the rovers were tested under conditions that were similar to those that they would encounter on the Martian surface.

Collecting Data on Mars
The Mars rover *Spirit* took this picture of itself collecting data from the Martian surface.

i Extend

17 Claims • Evidence • Reasoning What advantages would a robotic explorer have over a manned mission to Mars? Summarize evidence to support your claim and explain your reasoning.

18 Claims • Evidence • Reasoning What kind of evidence would the Mars Exploration Rovers be looking for that would support the claim that water once flowed on Mars? Support your claim with evidence, and explain your reasoning.

Visual Summary

To complete this summary, write the answers to the questions on the lines. You can use this page to review the main concepts of the lesson.

Properties of Terrestrial Planets

Mercury orbits near the sun.

19 Why do temperatures on Mercury vary so much?

_____

_____

_____

Venus is covered with clouds.

20 Why is Venus's surface temperature so high?

_____

_____

_____

Mars is a rocky planet.

22 What makes up the surface of Mars?

_____

_____

_____

Earth has abundant life.

21 What factors support life on Earth?

_____

_____

_____

23 Claims • Evidence • Reasoning How are important properties of Mercury, Venus, and Mars different from important properties of Earth? Summarize evidence to support your claim, and explain your reasoning.

Lesson Review

Vocabulary

Fill in the blanks with the terms that best complete the following sentences.

1 The _____ are the dense planets nearest the sun.

2 An _____ is equal to the distance between the sun and Earth.

Key Concepts

In the following table, write the name of the correct planet next to the property of that planet.

Properties	Planet
3 Identify Which planet has the highest surface temperature in the solar system?	
4 Identify Which planet has very large dust storms?	
5 Identify Which planet is the most heavily cratered of the terrestrial planets?	
6 Identify Which planet has the highest surface gravity of the terrestrial planets?	

7 Explain What is the difference between prograde rotation and retrograde rotation?

_____

_____

_____

8 Describe What characteristics of Venus's atmosphere make the planet so harsh?

_____

_____

_____

_____

Critical Thinking

Use this table to answer the following questions.

Planet	Period of rotation	Period of revolution
Mercury	58 days 15.5 h	88 days
Venus	243 days (retrograde rotation)	225 days
Earth	23 h 56 min	365.3 days
Mars	24 h 37 min	1.88 y

9 Analyze Which planet rotates most slowly about its axis?

_____

10 Analyze Which planet revolves around the sun in less time than it rotates around its axis?

_____

11 Analyze Which planet revolves around the sun in the shortest amount of time?

_____

12 Claims • Evidence • Reasoning Why are the temperatures on each of the other terrestrial planets more extreme than the temperatures on Earth? Summarize evidence to support your claim and explain your reasoning.

_____

_____

_____

_____

_____

_____

_____

_____

_____

PEOPLE IN SCIENCE

SC.8.N.2.2 Discuss what characterizes science and its methods.

A. Wesley Ward

GEOLOGIST

Geologist Dr. Wesley Ward lives in a desert region of the western United States. The living conditions are sometimes harsh, but the region offers some fascinating places to study. For a geologist like Dr. Ward, who tries to understand the geologic processes on another planet, the desert may be the only place to be.

Dr. Ward was a leading scientist on the Mars Pathfinder mission. The surface of Mars is a lot like the western desert. Dr. Ward helped scientists map the surface of Mars and plan for the Pathfinder's landing. Using data from the Pathfinder, Dr. Ward studied how Martian winds have shaped the planet's landscape. This information will help scientists better understand what conditions are like on the surface of Mars. More importantly, the information will guide scientists in choosing future landings sites. Dr. Ward's work may determine whether human beings can safely land on Mars.

You could say that Dr. Ward's scientific career has hit the big-time. He helped in the making of the Discovery Channel's documentary *Planet Storm*. The program features scientists describing weather conditions on other planets. Dr. Ward and the scientists worked with special effects artists to simulate what these conditions might feel like to astronauts.

The Mars Pathfinder rover Sojourner was designed to withstand the fierce Martian dust storms, such as the one shown.

🌐 Social Studies Connection

The Pathfinder is not the first attempt scientists have made to explore the surface of Mars. In fact, scientists in different countries have been exploring Mars for over 50 years. Research other missions to Mars and attempts to send rovers to Mars, and present your research in a timeline. Remember to identify where the mission started, what its goals were, and whether it achieved them.

JOB BOARD

Science Writer

What You'll Do: Research and write articles, press releases, reports, and sometimes books about scientific discoveries and issues for a wide range of readers. Science writers who write for a broad audience must work to find the stories behind the science in order to keep readers interested.

Where You Might Work: For a magazine, a newspaper, or a museum, or independently as a freelance writer specializing in science. Some science writers may work for universities, research foundations, government agencies, or non-profit science and health organizations.

Education: A bachelor's degree in a scientific field, with courses in English or writing.

Other Job Requirements: Strong communications skills. Science writers must not only understand science, but must also be able to interview scientists and to write clear, interesting stories.

Telescope Mechanic

What You'll Do: Keep telescopes at large observatories working, climbing heights of up to 30 meters to make sure the telescope's supports are in good shape, which includes welding new components, cleaning, and sweeping.

Where You Might Work: A large observatory or research institution with large telescopes, possibly in the desert.

Education: A high-school diploma with some experience performing maintenance on delicate equipment.

Other Job Requirements: Strong communications skills to consult with other mechanics and the scientists who use the telescopes. Mechanics must be able to weld and to use tools. Mechanics must also have good vision (or wear glasses to correct their vision), and be able to climb up high and carry heavy equipment.

PEOPLE IN SCIENCE NEWS

Anthony Wesley

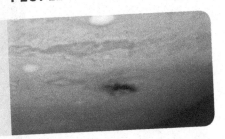

Witnessing Impact

Anthony Wesley was sitting in his backyard in Australia on July 19, 2009, gazing at Jupiter through his custom-built telescope, when he saw a dark spot or "scar" on the planet (shown). Wesley sent his tip to the National Aeronautics and Space Administration (NASA).

NASA has much more powerful telescopes than a citizen scientist usually does. Scientists at NASA confirmed that a comet had crashed into the planet, leaving a scar. Coincidentally, this crash happened almost exactly 15 years after another comet crashed into Jupiter.

The Gas Giant Planets

The gas giant planets are the four planets that orbit farthest from the sun. Distances between the planets shown here are not to scale.

Neptune

Uranus

Saturn

Jupiter

ESSENTIAL QUESTION

What is known about the gas giant planets?

By the end of this lesson, you should be able to describe some of the properties of the gas giant planets and how these properties differ from the physical properties of Earth.

SC.8.E.5.3 Distinguish the hierarchical relationships between planets and other astronomical bodies relative to solar system, galaxy, and universe, including distance, size, and composition.
SC.8.E.5.7 Compare and contrast the properties of objects in the Solar System including the Sun, planets, and moons to those of Earth, such as gravitational force, distance from the Sun, speed, movement, temperature, and atmospheric conditions.

 **Lesson Labs**

Quick Labs
- Modeling Saturn's Rings
- The Winds on Neptune

 Engage Your Brain

1 Predict Circle the term that best completes the following sentences.

Jupiter/Saturn/Uranus is the largest planet in the solar system.

Jupiter/Uranus/Neptune has the strongest winds in the solar system.

Saturn/Uranus/Neptune has the largest ring system of the gas giant planets.

Jupiter/Saturn/Neptune has more moons than any other planet in the solar system.

Jupiter/Uranus/Neptune is tilted on its side as it orbits the Sun.

2 Identify What are the objects that circle Saturn? What do you think they are made of?

_____

_____

_____

ACTIVE **READING**

3 Apply Many scientific words, such as *gas*, also have everyday meanings. Use context clues to write your own definition for each meaning of the word *gas*.

Example sentence
Vehicles, such as cars, trucks, and buses, use gas as a fuel.

gas:

_____

_____

Example sentence
Gas is one of the three common states of matter.

gas:

_____

_____

_____

Vocabulary Terms
- **gas giant**
- **planetary ring**

4 Apply This list contains the key terms you'll learn in this section. As you read, circle the definition of each term.

A Giant Among

Jupiter's high winds circle the planet and cause cloud bands to form. Storms, such as the Great Red Spot shown here, form between the cloud bands.

Callisto

Ganymede

Statistics Table for Jupiter	
Distance from the sun	5.20 AU
Period of rotation	9 h 55 min
Period of revolution	11.86 y
Tilt of axis	3.13°
Diameter	142,984 km
Density	1.33 g/cm³
Mean surface temperature	−145 °C
Surface gravity	253% of Earth's gravity
Number of known satellites	62

(t) ©NASA/Science Source/Photo Researchers, Inc.; (b) ©NASA/JPL/DLR

What is a gas giant planet?

Jupiter, Saturn, Uranus, and Neptune are the gas giant planets. They orbit far from the sun. **Gas giants** have deep, massive gas atmospheres, which are made up mostly of hydrogen and helium. These gases become denser the deeper you travel inside. All of the gas giants are large. Neptune, the smallest gas giant planet, is big enough to hold 60 Earths within its volume. The gas giant planets are cold. Mean surface temperatures range from −145 °C on Jupiter to −220 °C on Neptune.

What is known about Jupiter?

Jupiter (JOO•pih•ter) is the largest planet in the solar system. Its volume can contain more than 900 Earths. Jupiter is also the most massive planet. Its mass is twice that of the other seven planets combined. Jupiter has the highest surface gravity in the solar system at 253% that of Earth. And, although all of the gas giant planets rotate rapidly, Jupiter rotates the fastest of all. Its period of rotation is just under 10 h. Wind speeds on Jupiter are high. They can reach 540 km/h. By contrast, Earth's wind speed record is 372 km/h.

ACTIVE READING

5 Identify As you read the text, underline important physical properties of the planet Jupiter.

© Houghton Mifflin Ha Publishing Company

Giants!

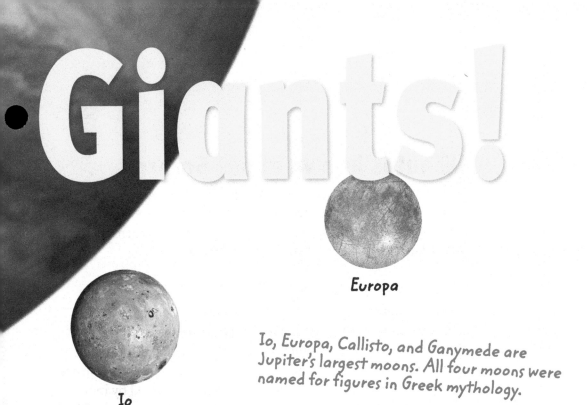

Europa

Io

Io, Europa, Callisto, and Ganymede are Jupiter's largest moons. All four moons were named for figures in Greek mythology.

Huge Storms Travel Across Jupiter's Surface

Jupiter has some of the strangest weather conditions in the solar system. The winds on Jupiter circle the planet. Clouds are stretched into bands that run from east to west. Storms appear as white or red spots between cloud bands. The best known of these storms is the Great Red Spot. The east–west width of this storm is three times the diameter of Earth. Incredibly, this storm has been observed by astronomers on Earth for the past 350 years.

Jupiter Has the Most Moons

More than 60 moons have been discovered orbiting Jupiter. This is the greatest number of moons to orbit any planet. Jupiter's moons Io (EYE•oh), Europa (yu•ROH•puh), Callisto (kuh•LIS•toh), and Ganymede (GAN•uh•meed) are particularly large. In fact, Ganymede is larger than the planet Mercury.

Jupiter's moon Io is the most volcanically active place in the solar system. There are at least 400 active volcanoes on Io's surface. Jupiter's gravity tugs and pulls on Io. This causes the interior of Io to reach the temperature at which it melts. Lava erupts from Io's volcanoes, which throw tremendous geysers of sulfur compounds into space. Over time, the orbit of Io has become a ring of ejected gases that is visible to the Hubble Space Telescope.

Jupiter's moon Europa has an icy surface. Recent evidence suggests that an ocean of liquid water may lie beneath this surface. Because liquid water is essential for life, some scientists are hopeful that future spacecraft may discover life inside Europa.

6 Claims • Evidence • Reasoning
Io, Europa, Callisto, and Ganymede are known as the *Galilean moons*. The astronomer Galileo discovered these moons using one of the first telescopes. Make a claim about why the Galilean moons were the first objects to be discovered with a telescope. Use evidence to support your claim, and explain your reasoning.

_____

_____

_____

Think Outside the Book

7 Model Select one of the following topics about weather on Jupiter to research: belts and zones; jet streams; storms. Present your findings to the rest of the class in the form of a model. Your model may be handcrafted, or may be an art piece, or may be a computer presentation.

King Rings!
of the

What is known about Saturn?

Saturn (SAT•ern) is a near-twin to Jupiter. It is the second-largest gas giant planet and is made mostly of hydrogen and helium. About 800 Earths could fit inside the volume of Saturn. Amazingly, the planet's density is less than that of water.

Saturn Has a Large Ring System

The planetary ring system that circles Saturn's equator is the planet's most spectacular feature. A **planetary ring** is a disk of material that circles a planet and consists of orbiting particles. Saturn's ring system has many individual rings that form complex bands. Between bands are gaps that may be occupied by moons.

Saturn's rings span up to hundreds of kilometers in width, but they are only a few kilometers thick. They consist of trillions of small, icy bodies that are a few millimeters to several hundred meters in size. The rings are mostly pieces left over from the collision of Saturn's moons with comets and asteroids.

ACTIVE READING

8 Identify As you read the text, underline important physical properties about the planet Saturn.

Statistics Table for Saturn

Distance from the sun	9.58 AU
Period of rotation	10 h 39 min
Period of revolution	29.5 y
Tilt of axis	26.73°
Diameter	120,536 km
Density	0.69 g/cm³
Mean surface temperature	−180 °C
Surface gravity	106% of Earth's gravity
Number of known satellites	53

Saturn's rings

Saturn's southern aurora

©NASA/ESA/Space Telescope Science Institute/Science Source/Photo Researchers, Inc

© Houghton Mifflin Harcourt Publishing Company

Saturn's Moon Enceladus Has Water Geysers

In the inner solar system, liquid rock erupts from volcanoes. In some parts of the outer solar system, liquid water erupts from volcanoes. When NASA's *Cassini* spacecraft explored Saturn's moon Enceladus (en•SEL•uh•duhs), it found an icy surface. Scientists believe that Enceladus has a liquid interior beneath this icy surface. Liquid water flows up through cracks in the moon's surface. It either freezes at the surface or forms spectacular water geysers. These geysers are the largest in the solar system.

Saturn's Moon Titan Has a Dense Atmosphere

Titan (TYT'in), the largest moon of Saturn, has an atmosphere that is denser than Earth's. The moon's atmosphere is composed mostly of nitrogen and has traces of compounds such as methane and ethane. Methane clouds form in Titan's atmosphere. From these clouds, methane rain may fall. Unlike Earth, Titan has a crust of ice, which is frozen at a temperature of –180 °C.

In 2005, the *Huygens* (HY•guhnz) Titan probe descended through Titan's atmosphere. It took pictures of a surface with lakes and ponds. The liquid that fills these lakes and ponds is mostly methane.

9 Explain In your own words, write a caption for this illustration of Saturn's moon Enceladus.

_____

_____

_____

Particles that make up Saturn's ring system

Cassini Division in Saturn's ring system

10 Describe Complete this table by writing a description of each structure in Saturn's ring system.

Structure	Description
ring	
gap	
ring particles	

Just Rollin' Along

How is Uranus unique?

ACTIVE READING

11 Identify As you read the text, underline important physical properties of the planet Uranus.

The atmosphere of Uranus (YUR•uh•nuhs) is composed mostly of hydrogen and helium. However, the atmosphere also contains methane. The methane in Uranus's atmosphere absorbs red light, which gives the planet a blue-green color.

Uranus Is a Tilted World

Uranus's axis of rotation is tilted almost 98°. This means that unlike any other planet in the solar system, Uranus is tilted on its side as it orbits the sun. The planet's 27 moons all orbit Uranus's equator, just like the moons of other planets do. The ring system of Uranus also orbits the equator. Scientists are not sure what event caused Uranus's odd axial tilt. But computer models of the four gas giant planets as they were forming may offer an explanation. The huge gravities of Jupiter and Saturn may have caused the orbits of Uranus and Neptune to change. There may also have been many close encounters between Uranus and Neptune that could have tilted the axis of Uranus.

Statistics Table for Uranus

Distance from the sun	19.2 AU
Period of rotation	17 h 24 min (retrograde)
Period of revolution	84 y
Tilt of axis	97.8°
Diameter	51,118 km
Density	1.27 g/cm³
Mean surface temperature	−210 °C
Surface gravity	79% of Earth's gravity
Number of known satellites	27

12 Claims • Evidence • Reasoning Earth has an axial tilt of 23.5°, whereas Uranus has an axial tilt of almost 98°. If Earth had the same axial tilt as Uranus, how would the conditions be different at Earth's North and South Poles? Summarize evidence to support your claim and explain your reasoning.

_____

_____

_____

_____

_____

_____

_____

_____

_____

_____

_____

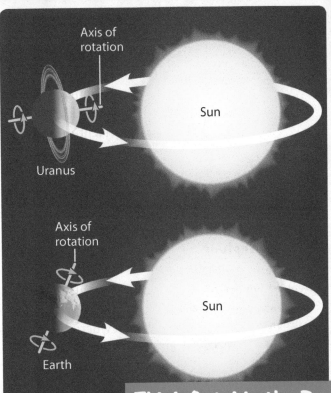

Axis of rotation

Sun

Uranus

Axis of rotation

Sun

Earth

Think Outside the Boo

13 Research Astronomers are discovering planets orbiting stars in other solar systems. Find out what kinds of planets astronomers are discovering in these solar systems.

Seasons on Uranus Last 21 Years

It takes Uranus 84 years to make a single revolution around the sun. For about 21 years of that 84-year period, the north pole faces the sun and the south pole is in darkness. About halfway through that 84-year period, the poles are reversed. The south pole faces the sun and the north pole is in darkness for 21 years. So, what are seasons like on Uranus? Except for a small band near the equator, every place on Uranus has winter periods of constant darkness and summer periods of constant daylight. But, during spring and fall, Uranus has periods of both daytime and nighttime just like on Earth.

Uranus's Moon Miranda Is Active

Miranda (muh•RAN•duh) is Uranus's fifth-largest moon. It is about 470 km in diameter. NASA's _Voyager 2_ spacecraft visited Miranda in 1989. Data from _Voyager 2_ showed that the moon is covered by different types of icy crust. What is the explanation for this patchwork surface? The gravitational forces of Uranus pull on Miranda's interior. This causes material from the moon's interior to rise to its surface. What we see on the surface is evidence of the moon turning itself inside out.

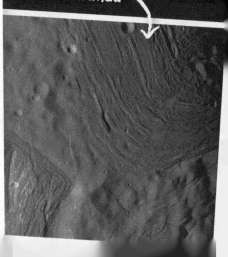

The surface of Uranus's moon Miranda

A Blue, Windy Giant

What is known about Neptune?

Neptune (NEP•toon) is the most distant planet from the sun. It is located 30 times farther from the sun than Earth is. So, sunlight on Neptune is 900 times fainter than sunlight on Earth is. High noon on Neptune may look much like twilight on Earth.

Neptune Is a Blue Ice Giant

Neptune is practically a twin to Uranus. Neptune is almost the same size as Uranus. It also has an atmosphere that is composed of hydrogen and helium, with some methane. The planet's bluish color is caused by the absorption of red light by methane. But because Neptune does not have an atmospheric haze like Uranus does, we can see deeper into the atmosphere. So, Neptune is blue, whereas Uranus is blue-green.

When *Voyager 2* flew by Neptune in 1989, there was a huge, dark area as large as Earth in the planet's atmosphere. This storm, which was located in Neptune's southern hemisphere, was named the *Great Dark Spot*. However, in 1994, the Hubble Space Telescope found no trace of this storm. Meanwhile, other spots that may grow larger with time have been sighted in the atmosphere.

Statistics Table for Neptune

Distance from the sun	30.1 AU
Period of rotation	16 h 7 min
Period of revolution	164.8 y
Tilt of axis	28.5°
Diameter	49,528 km
Density	1.64 g/cm³
Mean surface temperature	−220 °C
Surface Gravity	112% of Earth's gravity
Number of known satellites	13

Great Dark Spot

👁 Visualize It!

14 Claims • Evidence • Reasoning The wind speeds recorded in Neptune's Great Dark Spot reached 2,000 km/h. Make a claim about what kind of destruction might result on Earth in wind speeds if hurricanes approached 2,000 km/h. Provide evidence to support your claim, and explain your reasoning.

_____

_____

Neptune Has the Strongest Winds

Where does the energy come from that powers winds as fast as 2,000 km/h? Neptune has a warm interior that produces more energy than the planet receives from sunlight. Some scientists believe that Neptune's weather is controlled from inside the planet and not from outside the planet, as is Earth's weather.

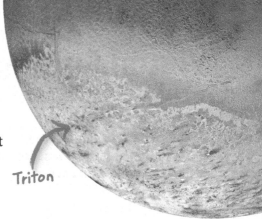

Triton

Neptune's Moon Triton Has a Different Orbit Than Neptune's Other Moons

Triton (TRYT'in) is the largest moon of Neptune. Unlike the other moons of Neptune, Triton orbits Neptune in the opposite direction from the direction in which Neptune orbits the sun. One explanation for this oddity is that, long ago, there were several large moons that orbited Neptune. These moons came so close together that one moon was ejected. The other moon, Triton, remained behind but began traveling in the opposite direction.

Triton's days are numbered. The moon is slowly spiraling inward toward Neptune. When Triton is a certain distance from Neptune, the planet's gravitational pull will begin pulling Triton apart. Triton will then break into pieces.

15 Conclude Complete the cause-and-effect chart by answering the question below.

> Triton spirals inward toward Neptune.

> The gravitational pull of Neptune causes Triton to pull apart.

> Triton breaks into pieces.

What do you think will happen next?

_____
_____
_____
_____
_____

A category 5 hurricane on Earth has sustained wind speeds of 250 km/h. Some effects of the winds of a category 5 hurricane can be seen in this image.

Visual Summary

To complete this summary, write the answers to the questions on the lines. You can use this page to review the main concepts of the lesson.

Properties of Gas Giant Planets

Mercury Venus Earth Mars Jupiter Saturn Uranus Neptune

Terrestrial planets

Gas giant planets

Not to scale

Jupiter has cloud bands.

16 What causes cloud bands to form on Jupiter?

_____

_____

Saturn has a complex ring system.

17 What are Saturn's rings made up of?

_____

_____

Uranus is tilted on its side.

18 What is the tilt of Uranus's axis of rotation?

_____

_____

Neptune is a blue planet.

19 What gives Neptune its bluish color?

_____

_____

20 Claims • Evidence • Reasoning Make a claim about how the properties of the gas giant planets compare with properties of Earth. Support your claim with evidence, and explain your reasoning.

Lesson Review

Vocabulary

Fill in the blank with the term that best completes the following sentences.

1 A large planet that has a deep, massive atmosphere is called a _____.

2 A _____ is a disk of matter that circles a planet and consists of numerous particles in orbit that range in size from a few millimeters to several hundred meters.

Key Concepts

In the following table, write the name of the correct planet next to the property of that planet.

Properties	Planet
3 Identify Which planet has a density that is less than that of water?	
4 Identify Which planet has the strongest winds in the solar system?	
5 Identify Which planet is tilted on its side as it orbits the sun?	
6 Identify Which planet is the largest planet in the solar system?	

7 Compare How does the composition of Earth's atmosphere differ from the composition of the atmospheres of the gas giant planets?

_____

_____

8 Compare How do the periods of rotation and revolution for the gas giant planets differ from those of Earth?

_____

_____

Critical Thinking

Use this diagram to answer the following questions.

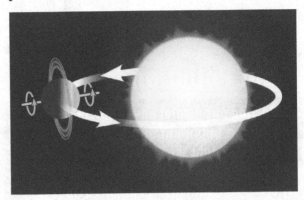

9 Identify Which planet is shown in the diagram? Explain your reasoning.

_____

_____

10 Claims • Evidence • Reasoning Make a claim about how the axial tilt of this planet affects its seasons. Use evidence to support your claim, and explain your reasoning.

_____

_____

_____

11 Claims • Evidence • Reasoning Why do you think the wind speeds on the gas giant planets are so much greater than the wind speeds on Earth? Summarize evidence to support your claim and explain your reasoning.

_____

_____

12 Compare List Earth and the gas giant planets in order from the hottest to the coldest planet. How does the temperature of each planet relate to its distance from the sun?

_____

_____

SC.8.N.4.1 Explain that science is one of the processes that can be used to inform decision making at the community, state, national, and international levels. SC.8.N.4.2 Explain how political, social, and economic concerns can affect science, and vice versa.

Florida Stargazing

Light Pollution

Protecting our natural environment from pollution is important. But we need to protect our night skies from pollution, too. Light pollution is the brightening of our sky by artificial lighting. Streetlights, lights on buildings, and lights on signs are all causes of the problem.

Bright night skies prevent people from viewing the stars. Light pollution also confuses animals that live in the area. Herbivores feed less frequently when it never gets totally dark. Sea turtles attempting to find their way to the ocean may head away from the ocean. And birds are disoriented by lights on communications towers.

Many people are making an effort to turn lights off and bring back the night. Using flashing lights instead of steady-burning ones and turning off porch and landscaping lights help to keep our night skies dark.

Florida's Night Sky

Florida is home to many different astronomical societies all dedicated to observing the night sky. No matter if you live in the Everglades or in the Panhandle, there is an organization that can help you to locate the constellations and other features visible in the night sky. You can also visit one of Florida's many planetariums to view constellation shows, learn about space, and look through a variety of telescopes. You might even be able to join in a star party to view a meteor shower, like the Leonid meteor shower shown here.

Preserving the Dark

The town of Harmony, Florida, has taken steps to combat light pollution and promote astronomy. Every year, Harmony is the site of a Dark Sky Festival attended by amateur and professional astronomers from all over the world.

Harmony is a planned community that is dedicated to preserving the environment, which includes keeping the skies dark. Every light fixture, from streetlights to porch lights, must meet standards of darkness to protect the natural systems around the town. Harmony has done such a good job protecting their night skies that the town was recognized by the International Dark Sky Association.

🏠 Take It Home!

Research your local astronomy organization. Attend or read about a recent gathering and record what people saw as they surveyed the sky. Use their input to determine what you can do to help reduce light pollution and make a pamphlet to share with the class.

🌐 Social Studies Connection

This photograph shows Florida at night. What areas have a lot of light pollution? Where would you expect to have a good view of the night sky? Look around your town and identify sources of light pollution.

Small Bodies in the Solar System

ESSENTIAL QUESTION

What is found in the solar system besides the sun, planets, and moons?

By the end of this lesson, you should be able to compare and contrast the properties of small bodies in the solar system.

Comet Hale-Bopp was discovered in 1995 and was visible from Earth for 18 months. It is a long-period comet that is thought to take about 2,400 years to orbit the sun.

SC.8.N.1.1 Define a problem from the eighth grade curriculum using appropriate reference materials to support scientific understanding, plan and carry out scientific investigations of various types, such as systematic observations or experiments, identify variables, collect and organize data, interpret data in charts, tables, and graphics, analyze information, make predictions, and defend conclusions. **SC.8.E.5.3** Distinguish the hierarchical relationships between planets and other astronomical bodies relative to solar system, galaxy, and universe, including distance, size, and composition. **SC.8.E.5.7** Compare and contrast the properties of objects in the Solar System including the Sun, planets, and moons to those of Earth, such as gravitational force, distance from the Sun, speed, movement, temperature, and atmospheric conditions.

Lesson Labs

Quick Labs
- Orbits of Comets
- Modeling Crater Formation

 ## Engage Your Brain

1 Predict Check T or F to show whether you think each statement is true or false.

T	F	
☐	☐	Pluto is a planet.
☐	☐	The Kuiper Belt is located beyond the orbit of Neptune.
☐	☐	Comets are made of ice, rock, and dust.
☐	☐	All asteroids have the same composition.
☐	☐	Most meteoroids that enter Earth's atmosphere burn up completely.

2 Identify Can you identify the object that is streaking through the sky in the photograph? What do you think makes this object glow?

_____

_____

_____

_____

_____

ACTIVE **READING**

3 Apply Many scientific words, such as *belt*, also have everyday meanings. Use context clues to write your own definition for each meaning of the word *belt*.

Example sentence
I found a <u>belt</u> to go with my new pants.

belt:

_____

_____

Example sentence
Short-term comets originate in the Kuiper <u>Belt</u>.

belt:

_____

_____

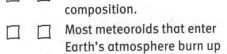
Vocabulary Terms

- dwarf planet
- Kuiper Belt
- Kuiper Belt object
- comet
- Oort cloud
- asteroid
- meteoroid
- meteor
- meteorite

4 Apply As you learn the definition of each vocabulary term in this lesson, create your own definition or sketch to help you remember the meaning of the term.

Where are small bodies in the solar system?

The sun, planets, and moons are not the only objects in the solar system. Scientists estimate that there are up to a trillion small bodies in the solar system. These bodies lack atmospheres and have weak surface gravity. The largest of the small bodies, the dwarf planets, are found in regions known as the *asteroid belt* and the *Kuiper Belt*. The Kuiper (KAHY•per) Belt is located beyond the orbit of Neptune. Kuiper Belt objects, as you might guess, are located in the Kuiper Belt. Comets, too, are found in the Kuiper Belt. However, comets are also located in the Oort cloud. The Oort (OHRT) cloud is a region that surrounds the solar system and extends almost halfway to the nearest star. Two other types of small bodies, asteroids and meteoroids, are located mostly between the orbits of Venus and Neptune.

ACTIVE READING

5 Identify As you read the text, underline the names of different kinds of small bodies that are found in the solar system.

Sizes and distances are not to scale.

Mercury   Venus   Earth   Mars   Ceres   Jupiter

What are dwarf planets?

In 2006, astronomers decided that Pluto would no longer be considered a planet. It became the first member of a new group of solar system bodies called *dwarf planets*. Like planets, a **dwarf planet** is a celestial body that orbits the sun and is round because of its own gravity. However, a dwarf planet does not have the mass to have cleared other bodies out of its orbit around the sun.

Five dwarf planets, made of ice and rock, have been identified. Ceres (SIR•eez), located between the orbits of Mars and Jupiter, is about 950 km in diameter and travels at around 18 km/s. Pluto, Eris (IR•is), Haumea (HOW•may•uh), and Makemake (MAH•kay•MAH•kay) are located beyond the orbit of Neptune. They range in size from about 1,500 km (Haumea) to about 2,400 km (Eris). Their orbital periods around the sun range from 250 to 560 years. All travel at speeds of between 3 km/s and 5 km/s.

ACTIVE READING

6 Describe Describe two properties of dwarf planets.

_____

_____

_____

_____

_____

_____

_____

Saturn

Uranus

Neptune

Pluto   Haumea   Makemake   Eris

👁 Visualize It!

7 Claims • Evidence • Reasoning Make a claim about where in the solar system most of the dwarf planets are located. Use evidence to support your claim, and explain your reasoning.

_____

_____

KBOs

What are Kuiper Belt objects?

The **Kuiper Belt** is a region of the solar system that begins just beyond the orbit of Neptune and contains small bodies made mostly of ice. It extends outward to about twice the orbit of Neptune, a distance of about 55 astronomical units (AU). An AU is a unit of length that is equal to the average distance between Earth and the sun, or about 150,000,000 km. The Kuiper Belt is thought to contain matter that was left over from the formation of the solar system. This matter formed small bodies instead of planets.

A **Kuiper Belt object (KBO)** is any of the minor bodies in the Kuiper Belt outside the orbit of Neptune. Kuiper Belt objects are made of methane ice, ammonia ice, and water ice. They have average orbital speeds of between 1 km/s and 5 km/s. The first Kuiper Belt object was not discovered until 1992. Now, about 1,300 KBOs are known. Scientists estimate that there are at least 70,000 objects in the Kuiper Belt that have diameters larger than 100 km.

Quaoar is a KBO that orbits 43 AU from the sun. It is around 1,260 km in diameter and has one satellite.

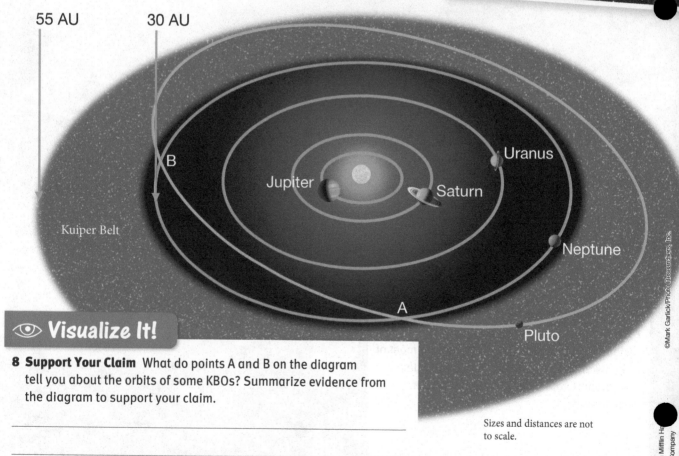

55 AU

30 AU

B

Jupiter

Saturn

Uranus

Neptune

Kuiper Belt

A

Pluto

👁 Visualize It!

8 Support Your Claim What do points A and B on the diagram tell you about the orbits of some KBOs? Summarize evidence from the diagram to support your claim.

_____

_____

Sizes and distances are not to scale.

NEW FRONTIERS

Pluto: From Planet to KBO

From its discovery in 1930 until 2006, Pluto was considered to be the ninth planet in the solar system. However, beginning in 1992, a new group of small bodies called *Kuiper Belt objects*, or simply KBOs, began to be discovered beyond the orbit of Neptune. Not only are some of the KBOs close to Pluto in size, but some have a similar composition of rock and ice. Astronomers recognized that Pluto was, in fact, a large KBO and not the ninth planet. In 2006, Pluto was redefined as a "dwarf planet" by the International Astronomical Union (IAU).

Charon

Pluto

Pluto and Charon

At 2,306 km in diameter, Pluto is the second largest KBO. It is shown in this artist's rendition with Charon (KAIR•uhn), its largest satellite. Many large KBOs have satellites. Some KBOs and their satellites, such as Pluto and Charon, orbit each other.

The Kuiper Belt

The Kuiper Belt is located between 30 AU (the orbit of Neptune) and approximately 55 AU. However, most KBOs have been discovered between 42 and 48 AU, where their orbits are not disturbed by the gravitational attraction of Neptune.

i Extend

9 **Explain** Why is Pluto no longer considered a planet?

10 **Research** Astronomer Clyde Tombaugh discovered Pluto in 1930. Research why Tombaugh was searching beyond Neptune for "Planet X" and how he discovered Pluto.

11 **Claims • Evidence • Reasoning** Research the 2006 IAU decision to redefine Pluto as a "dwarf planet." Combine this research with your research on Pluto. Make a claim about whether Pluto should be considered a "dwarf planet" or return to being called the ninth planet in the solar system. Summarize evidence to support your claim and explain your reasoning in a debate.

What do we know about comets?

ACTIVE READING

12 Identify As you read the text, underline the different parts of a comet and their properties.

A **comet** is a small body of ice, rock, and dust that follows a highly elliptical orbit around the sun. As a comet passes close to the sun, it gives off gas and dust in the form of a coma and a tail.

The speed of a comet will vary depending on how far from or how close to the sun it is. Far from the sun, a comet may travel at speeds as low as 0.32 km/s. Close to the sun, a comet may travel as fast as 445 km/s.

Comets Are Made of a Nucleus and a Tail

All comets have a *nucleus* that is composed of ice and rock. Most comet nuclei are between 1 km and 10 km in diameter. If a comet approaches the sun, solar radiation and heating cause the comet's ice to change to gas. A *coma* is a spherical cloud of gas and dust that comes off of the nucleus. The *ion tail* of a comet is gas that has been ionized, or stripped of electrons, by the sun. The solar wind—electrically charged particles expanding away from the sun—pushes the gas away from the comet's head. So, regardless of the direction a comet is traveling, its ion tail points away from the sun. A second tail made of dust and gas curves backward along the comet's orbit. This *dust tail* can be millions of kilometers long.

👁 Visualize It!

13 Identify Use the write-on lines in the diagram to identify the structures of a comet.

Dust tail

 A

 B

 C

Comets Come from the Kuiper Belt and the Oort Cloud

There are two regions of the solar system where comets come from. The first region is the Kuiper Belt, which is where short-period comets originate. The second region is the Oort cloud, which is where long-period comets originate.

Collisions between objects in the Kuiper Belt produce fragments that become comets. These comets are known as *short-period comets*. Short-period comets take less than 200 years to orbit the sun. Therefore, they return to the inner solar system quite frequently, perhaps every few decades or centuries. Short-period comets also have short life spans. Every time a comet passes the sun, it may lose a layer as much as 1 m thick.

Some comets originate in the Oort cloud. The **Oort cloud** is a spherical region that surrounds the solar system and extends almost halfway to the nearest star. Comets can form in the Oort cloud when two objects collide. Comets can also form when an object in the Oort cloud is disturbed by the gravity of a nearby star and is sent into the inner solar system. Comets that originate in the Oort cloud are called *long-period comets*. Long-period comets may take up to hundreds of thousands of years to orbit the sun.

👁 Visualize It!

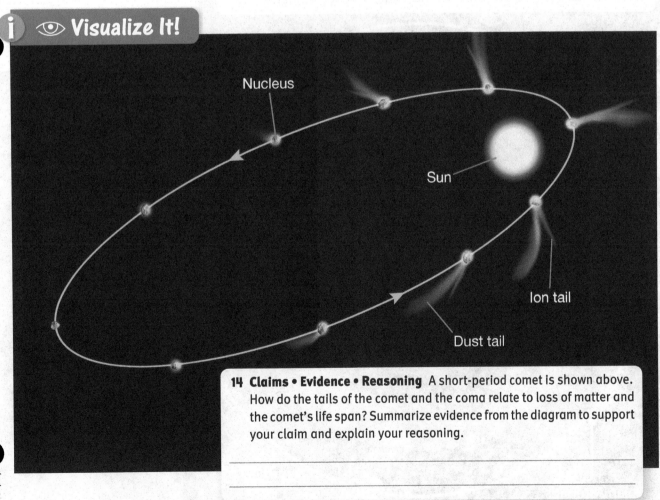

Nucleus

Sun

Ion tail

Dust tail

14 Claims • Evidence • Reasoning A short-period comet is shown above. How do the tails of the comet and the coma relate to loss of matter and the comet's life span? Summarize evidence from the diagram to support your claim and explain your reasoning.

_____

_____

On the rocks

What do we know about asteroids?

ACTIVE READING

15 Identify As you read the text, underline those places in the solar system where asteroids are located.

An **asteroid** is a small, irregularly shaped, rocky object that orbits the sun. Most asteroids are located between the orbits of Mars and Jupiter. This 300 million–km–wide region is known as the *asteroid belt*. The asteroid belt contains hundreds of thousands of asteroids, called *main-belt asteroids*. The largest main-belt asteroid by diameter is Pallas, which has a diameter of 570 km. The smallest asteroid is 4 m in diameter. Groups of asteroids are also located in the orbits of Jupiter and Neptune (called *Trojan asteroids*) and in the Kuiper Belt. Still other asteroids are called *near-Earth asteroids*. Some of these asteroids cross the orbits of Earth and Venus.

Asteroids in the asteroid belt orbit the sun at about 18 km/s and have orbital periods of 3 to 8 years. Although most asteroids rotate around their axis, some tumble end over end through space.

16 Analyze Where is the asteroid belt located?

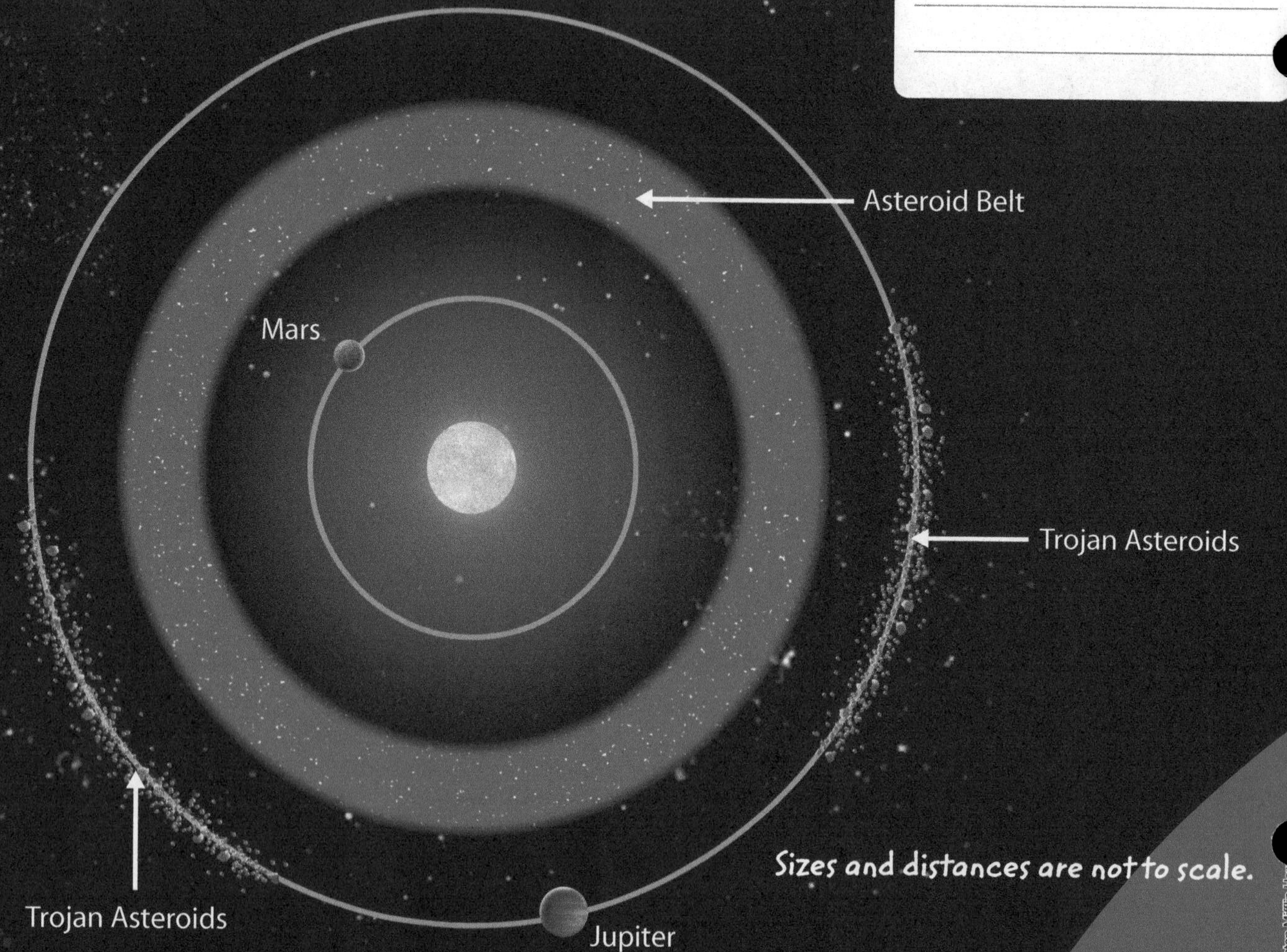

_____

_____

_____

_____

_____

_____

Asteroid Belt

Mars

Trojan Asteroids

Trojan Asteroids

Jupiter

Sizes and distances are not to scale.

Asteroids Have Different Compositions

The composition of asteroids varies. Many asteroids have dark surfaces. Scientists think that these asteroids are rich in carbon. Other asteroids are thought to be rocky and to have a core made of iron and nickel. Still other asteroids may have a rocky core surrounded largely by ice. Small, rocky asteroids have perhaps the strangest composition of all. They appear to be piles of rock loosely held together by gravity. Asteroid Itokawa (ee•TOH•kah•wah), shown below, is a rocky asteroid known as a "rubble-pile" asteroid.

Some asteroids contain economic minerals like those mined on Earth. Economic minerals that are found in asteroids include gold, iron, nickel, manganese, cobalt, and platinum. Scientists are now investigating the potential for mining near-Earth asteroids.

Itokawa is a rubble-pile asteroid. Astronomers think that the 500 m–long asteroid may be composed of two asteroids that are joined.

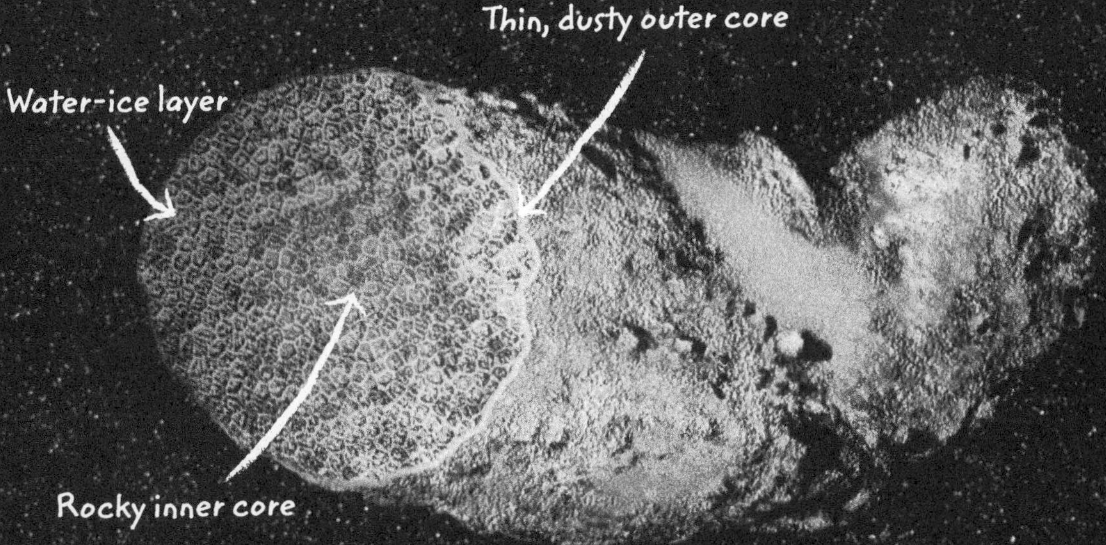

Thin, dusty outer core

Water-ice layer

Rocky inner core

Greetings *from Eros!*

Think Outside the Book

17 Describe Eros is a near-Earth asteroid that tumbles through space. Imagine that you are the first human to explore Eros. Write a postcard that describes what you found on Eros. Then research the asteroid and find out how close your description came to reality.

Burned Out

What do we know about meteoroids, meteors, and meteorites?

A sand grain- to boulder-sized, rocky body that travels through space is a **meteoroid**. Meteoroids that enter Earth's atmosphere travel at about 52 km/s, as measured by radar on Earth. Friction heats these meteoroids to thousands of degrees Celsius, which causes them to glow. The atmosphere around a meteoroid's path also gets hotter and glows because of friction between the meteoroid and air molecules. A bright streak of light that results when a meteoroid burns up in Earth's atmosphere is called a **meteor**. A **meteorite** is a meteoroid that reaches Earth's surface without burning up.

👁 **Visualize It!**

18 Identify Use the write-on lines below to identify the three objects that are shown.

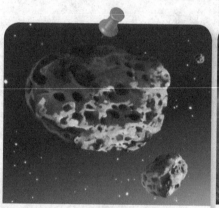

A A small, rocky body that travels through space is a _____

B The glowing trail of a body that is burning up in Earth's atmosphere is a _____

C A body that reaches Earth's surface without burning up is a _____

A meteorite 45 m across produced kilometer-wide Barringer Crater in Arizona about 50,000 years ago.

Meteorites Reach Earth

Meteoroids come from the asteroid belt, Mars, the moon, and comets. Most of the meteoroids that enter Earth's atmosphere do not reach Earth's surface. Many meteoroids explode in the upper atmosphere. These explosions are often recorded by military satellites in orbit around Earth. Other meteoroids skip back into space after briefly crossing the upper atmosphere. However, some large meteoroids that enter Earth's lower atmosphere or strike Earth's surface can be destructive. Scientists estimate that a destructive meteorite impact occurs every 300 to 400 years.

Meteorites Have Different Compositions

Meteorites can be divided into three general groups. The first group of meteorites are the stony meteorites. They are the most common form of meteorite. Stony meteorites are made of silicate minerals, just like rocks on Earth. Some stony meteorites also contain small amounts of organic matter. A much smaller group of meteorites are the iron meteorites. Iron meteorites are composed of iron and nickel. The rarest group of meteorites are stony-iron meteorites. Stony-iron meteorites are composed of both silicate minerals and iron and nickel. All three groups of meteorites can originate from asteroids. However, some stony meteorites come from the moon and Mars.

Visualize It!

19 Describe In the boxes below, describe the composition and origin of each group of meteorite. Also, indicate how common each group of meteorite is.

Stony meteorite

_____
_____
_____
_____
_____

Iron meteorite

_____
_____
_____
_____
_____

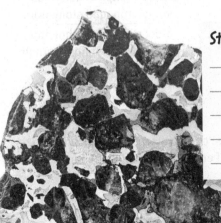

Stony-iron meteorite

_____
_____
_____
_____
_____

Visual Summary

To complete this summary, answer the questions below. You can use this page to review the main concepts of the lesson.

Small Bodies in the Solar System

Small bodies are found throughout the solar system.

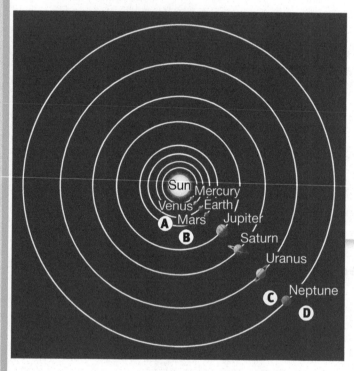

20 Enter the correct letter or letters that indicate a location for each small body in the solar system.

Asteroids	
Dwarf planets	
Kuiper Belt objects	

21 Check true or false to answer the questions below.

T	F	
☐	☐	Comets originate in the asteroid belt and the Kuiper Belt.
☐	☐	Three groups of asteroids are stony, iron, and stony-iron.
☐	☐	Most meteoroids that enter Earth's atmosphere burn up.

22 Gather Evidence Make a table in which you compare and contrast comets and asteroids. Summarize evidence to support the comparison, including the composition of each object, its location in the solar system, and its size.

Lesson Review

Vocabulary

Fill in the blank with the term that best completes the following sentences.

1 The _____ is a spherical region that surrounds the solar system and extends almost halfway to the nearest star.

2 A region of the solar system that extends from the orbit of Neptune to about twice the orbit of Neptune is the _____.

3 Most _____ are located between the orbits of Mars and Jupiter.

4 A meteoroid that reaches Earth's surface without burning up is a _____.

Key Concepts

In the following table, write the name of the correct body next to the property of that body.

Property	Body
5 Identify What is a minor body that orbits outside the orbit of Neptune?	
6 Identify What is a small body that follows a highly elliptical orbit around the sun?	
7 Identify What is the largest of the small bodies that are found in the solar system?	
8 Identify What is the glowing trail that results when a meteoroid burns up in Earth's atmosphere?	

Critical Thinking

Use this table to answer the following questions.

Comet	Orbital Period (years)
Borrelly	6.9
Halley	76
Hale-Bopp	2,400
Hyakutake	100,000

9 Apply Which of the comets in the table are short-period comets?

_____

10 Claims • Evidence • Reasoning Make a claim about which of the comets in the table most likely originated in the Oort cloud. Summarize evidence to support your claim and explain your reasoning.

_____

_____

11 Claims • Evidence • Reasoning Make a claim about why the speeds of comets increase as they near the sun. Provide evidence to support your claim, and explain your reasoning.

_____

_____

12 Claims • Evidence • Reasoning Make a claim about why some asteroids tumble end over end through space while other asteroids rotate around their axis. Support your claim with evidence, and explain your reasoning.

_____

_____

The **Terrestrial Planets**

The **Gas Giant Planets**

Small Bodies in the **Solar System**

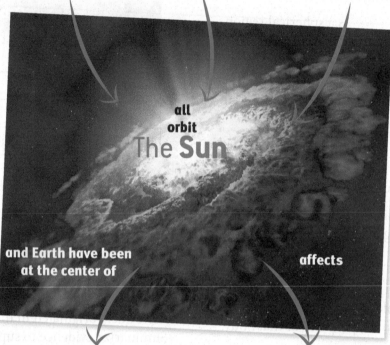

all orbit **The Sun**

and Earth have been at the center of

affects

Historical Models of the **Solar System**

Gravity and the **Solar System**

1 Interpret The Graphic Organizer above shows the sun at the center. Why do you think the sun has been placed at the center?

_____

_____

_____

2 Claims • Evidence • Reasoning You are suddenly transported to another planet. Make a claim about how you would know if that planet were a terrestrial planet or a gas giant planet. Summarize the evidence that would support your claim. Explain your reasoning.

_____

_____

_____

3 Recognize What is the importance of Newton's law of universal gravitation?

_____

_____

_____

_____

4 Apply How is energy transferred to the surface of the sun?

_____

_____

_____

_____

_____

Vocabulary

Fill in each blank with the term that best completes the following sentences.

1 _____ is the process in which energy is released as the nuclei of small atoms combine to form a larger nucleus.

2 The solar system formed from a(n) _____, which is a rotating cloud of gas and dust that formed into the sun and planets.

3 When an object looks as if the position has shifted when it is viewed from different locations, this is referred to as _____.

4 Earth, Venus, Mars, and Mercury are considered _____, which are highly dense planets nearest the sun.

5 A(n) _____ is a small, rocky object that orbits the sun; many of these objects are located in a band between the orbits of Mars and Jupiter.

Key Concepts

Read each question below and circle the best answer.

6 People sometimes talk about seeing shooting stars. What do they actually see?

   A a meteoroid traveling through space

   B a meteoroid that burns up in the atmosphere close enough to see

   C a star that is moving through the galaxy

   D a comet that has come close enough to Earth's atmosphere to be seen

7 Chase is making a model of the solar system. He is labeling the planets as terrestrial planets and gas giants. Which planet should he label as a gas giant?

   F Earth

   G Mars

   H Uranus

   I Venus

8 Weight depends on the force of gravity. The greater the gravitational attraction of a planet, the more an object weighs on that planet. On which planet would you weigh less than you would weigh on Earth?

A Jupiter, which has a surface gravity that is 253% of Earth's

B Neptune, which has a surface gravity that is 112% of Earth's

C Saturn, which has a surface gravity that is 106% of Earth's

D Uranus, which has a surface gravity that is 79% of Earth's

9 The sun is made up of different elements. Which element makes up more than 70 percent of the sun?

F carbon

G helium

H hydrogen

I oxygen

10 Convection cells in the sun's convective zone carry energy from the top of the radiative zone to the photosphere. In convection cells, hot gases rise to the photosphere, cool, and then sink back into the convective zone. What causes the transfer of energy in this process?

A the absorption and re-emission of electromagnetic waves

B the condensation of hot gas into liquid

C the movement of matter

D the process of nuclear fusion

11 Venus has the highest average surface temperature of any planet in the solar system. Which of the following **best** describes why Venus is so hot?

F Venus has a thin atmosphere and solar energy reaches the surface easily.

G The thick atmosphere of Venus reflects most incoming solar energy back into space.

H Carbon dioxide in Venus's atmosphere traps solar energy that reaches Venus's surface.

I Energy from within Venus is transferred to the surface.

Name _____

12 All bodies in the solar system orbit the sun. Of the different bodies that orbit the sun, which body has the fastest orbital speed ?

A a dwarf planet between Mars and Jupiter

B a comet as it nears the sun

C an asteroid

D a Kuiper Belt object

13 The diagrams below illustrate different laws of planetary motion and gravity. Which diagram illustrates Kepler's second law?

F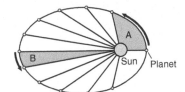

H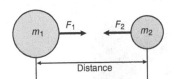

G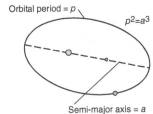

I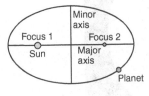

14 Kevin is describing the orbit of Earth. At what point in Earth's orbit is Earth closest to the sun?

A when Earth reaches aphelion

B when Earth reaches its average distance from the sun

C when Earth reaches perihelion

D when Earth reaches its slowest speed

15 Copernicus challenged the way in which people of his time thought about the solar system. How did Copernicus describe the motion of the sun?

F The sun is stationary.

G The sun revolves around Earth.

H The sun moves in an elliptical orbit.

I The sun moves in a straight line through space.

16 An atmosphere acts as insulation to keep a planet's surface warm. Mercury has almost no atmosphere. How does the lack of atmosphere affect temperatures on Mercury?

A Temperatures vary less than they would if Mercury had an atmosphere.

B Temperatures vary more than they would if Mercury had an atmosphere.

C Temperatures would not be affected if Mercury had an atmosphere.

D Temperatures would be affected only when Mercury is closest to the sun.

17 The sun does not rotate in the same way Earth does. The sun has different periods of rotation at different latitudes. The figure below shows the rotation of the sun.

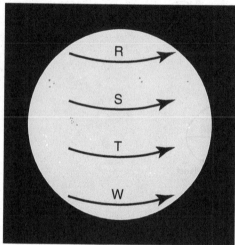

Which arrow indicates the latitude at which the sun rotates the fastest?

F R

G S

H T

I W

18 Aristotle thought that if Earth were moving, he would see the positions of the stars change as Earth moved. However, he could not observe parallax, which is the apparent shift in the position of an object, such as a star, when viewed from different positions. How might Aristotle have interpreted this problem?

A Earth is unmoving.

B The stars are very far away.

C Parallax is undetectable to the naked eye.

D Observers need to change position to view parallax.

© Houghton Mifflin Har Publishing Company

Name _____

19 The sun is made up of six different layers. Three of these layers make up the interior of the sun. The remaining three layers make up the sun's atmosphere. Which is the innermost layer of the sun?

F chromosphere

G convective zone

H core

I corona

20 The Kuiper Belt, pictured below, is generally thought to contain leftover bits from the formation of the solar system.

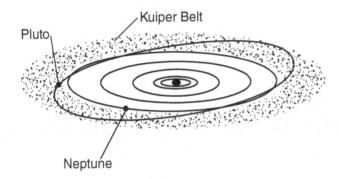

Which of the following describes Kuiper Belt objects?

A often larger than some planets in the solar system

B extremely hot

C minor planet-sized objects that orbit the sun in a flat belt beyond Neptune's orbit

D 100 AU wide

21 Lindsay sees an object fall from a tree to Earth. Which answer **best** describes the example of what Lindsay is observing?

F planetary motion

G nuclear fusion

H centripetal force

I gravitational attraction

Critical Thinking

Answer the following questions in the space provided.

22 A student claims that he could observe a meteoroid, a meteor, and a meteorite on Earth's surface. Do you agree? Summarize evidence to support your claim and explain your reasoning.

_____

_____

_____

_____

_____

_____

23 Name three characteristics of gas giants that make them different from terrestrial planets.

_____

_____

_____

_____

_____

24 Study the diagrams below.

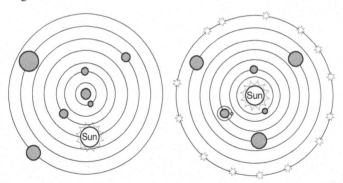

Explain what the two diagrams show. What is significant about them? How were these models developed and by whom? How do the models affect the way we study and think about our solar system?

_____

_____

_____

_____

The Earth-Moon-Sun System

FLORIDA **BIG IDEA 5**

Earth in Space and Time

What Do You Think?

Earth is affected by its sun and moon. The sun provides light and energy. The moon regulates the tides. Why is a regular tide system important? As you explore this unit, gather evidence to help you state and support a claim.

The Earth-Moon-Sun System

CITIZEN **SCIENCE**

Measuring Shadows

Do the lengths of shadows created by the sun change throughout the year? The answer to this question tells us about Earth's rotation and its orbit. Help students with an ongoing research project, called the Sun Shadows Project. The results are presented at the American Geophysical Union's Annual Conference.

① Think About It

Students at James Monroe Middle School in Albuquerque, New Mexico, asked the following questions: The seasons change, but do the length of shadows? How could this be measured?

_____

_____

_____

Scientists in Antarctica measure shadows.

② Ask A Question

What effects do seasons have on the lengths of shadows in your area?

As a class, come up with a prediction. Then, research what students at James Monroe Middle School are doing to gather information.

Things to Consider

Some parts of the world participate in Daylight Savings Time. People move their clocks forward by an hour in the spring, and back by an hour in the fall. In other parts of the world, Daylight Savings Time is not practiced. Daylight Savings Time may affect your measurements, so make sure that your group is taking measurements when shadows are the shortest.

③ Apply Your Knowledge

A List the materials your class will need in order to make and record the measurements to gather the information needed by the students at James Monroe Middle School.

_____

_____

_____

B Decide on a time frame for your class project. Will you participate for an entire season? What factors influence your decision?

_____

_____

_____

_____

C Track the information gathered by your class and draw your own preliminary conclusions.

_____

_____

_____

_____

⌂ Take It Home!

Who else is participating in the Sun Shadows Project? Research the various national and international groups taking part, such as the U.S. Antarctic Program.

Earth's Days, Years, and Seasons

ESSENTIAL **QUESTION**

How are Earth's days, years, and seasons related to the way Earth moves in space?

By the end of this lesson, you should be able to relate Earth's days, years, and seasons to Earth's movement in space.

SC.8.E.5.9 Explain the impact of objects in space on each other including: 1. The Sun on the Earth including seasons and gravitational attraction, 2. The Moon on the Earth, including phases, tides, and eclipses, and the relative position of each body.

In many parts of the world, blooming flowers are one of the first signs that spring has arrived. Spring flowers start blooming with the warmer temperatures of spring, even if there is still snow on the ground.

Quick Labs
• Earth's Rotation and Revolution
• Seasons Model

 Engage Your Brain

1 Predict Check T or F to show whether you think each statement is true or false.

T	F	
☐	☐	A day is about 12 hours long.
☐	☐	A year is about 365 days long.
☐	☐	When it is summer in the Northern Hemisphere, it is summer all around the world.

2 Apply Write your own caption for this photo of leaves in the space below.

_____
_____
_____
_____
_____
_____

ACTIVE **READING**

3 Synthesize The term *rotation* can be tricky to remember because it is used somewhat differently in science than it is in everyday life. In baseball, a pitching *rotation* lists the order of a team's starting pitchers. The order starts over after the last pitcher on the list has played. On the lines below, write down any other examples you can think of that use the term *rotation*.

rotation:

_____
_____
_____

Vocabulary Terms

• rotation	• season
• day	• equinox
• revolution	• solstice
• year	

4 Apply As you learn the definition of each vocabulary term in this lesson, create your own definition or sketch to help you remember the meaning of the term.

Spinning in

What determines the length of a day?

ACTIVE READING

5 Identify As you read, underline the places on Earth's surface at which the ends of Earth's axis would be.

Each planet spins on its axis. Earth's axis (ACK•sis) is an imaginary straight line that runs from the North Pole to the South Pole. The spinning of a body, such as a planet, on its axis is called **rotation**. The time it takes a planet to complete one full rotation on its axis is called a **day**.

The Time It Takes for Earth to Rotate Once

Earth rotates in a counterclockwise motion around its axis when viewed from above the North Pole. This means that as a location on Earth's equator rotates from west to east, the sun appears to rise in the east. The sun then appears to cross the sky and set in the west.

As Earth rotates, only one-half of Earth faces the sun at any given time. People on the half of Earth facing the sun experience daylight. This period of time in daylight is called *daytime*. People on the half of Earth that faces away from the sun experience darkness. This period of time in darkness is called *nighttime*.

Earth's rotation is used to measure time. Earth completes one rotation on its axis in 24 hours, or in one day. Most locations on Earth's surface move through daylight and darkness in that time.

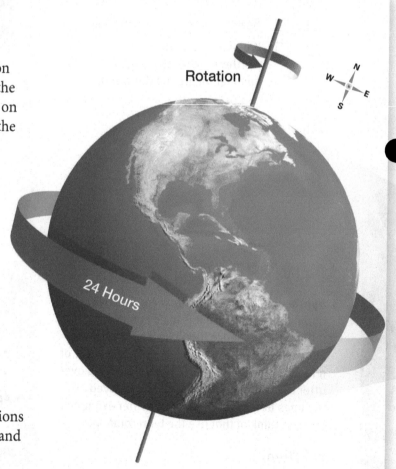

Rotation

24 Hours

Earth's motion is used to measure the length of an Earth day.

Circles

What determines the length of a year?

As Earth rotates on its axis, Earth also revolves around the sun. Although you cannot feel Earth moving, it is traveling around the sun at an average speed of nearly 30 km/s. The motion of a body that travels around another body in space is called **revolution** (reh•vuh•LOO•shun). Earth completes a full revolution around the sun in 365 ¼ days, or about one **year**. We have divided the year into 12 months, each month lasting from 28 to 31 days.

Earth's orbit is not quite a perfect circle. In January, Earth is about 2.5 million kilometers closer to the sun than it is in July. You may be surprised that this distance makes only a tiny difference in temperatures on Earth.

◉ Visualize It!

7 Support Your Claim Imagine that Earth's current position is at point A below. Write the label B to show Earth's position 6 months from now in the same diagram. Explain your reasoning.

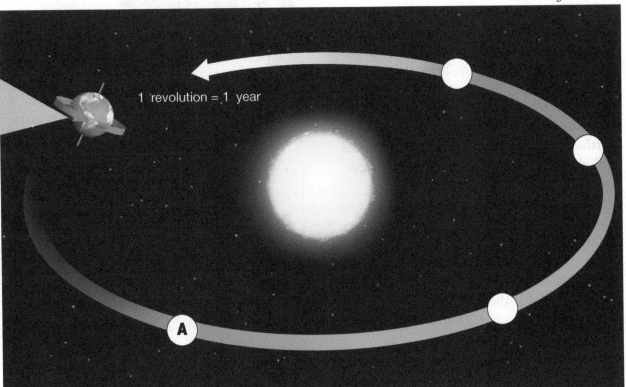

This drawing is not to scale.

1 revolution = 1 year

Tilt-a-Whirl

What conditions are affected by the tilt of Earth's axis?

Earth's axis is tilted at 23.5°. Earth's axis always points toward the North Star as Earth revolves around the sun. Thus, during each revolution, the North Pole may be tilted toward the sun or away from the sun, as seen below. When the North Pole is tilted toward the sun, the Northern Hemisphere (HEHM•ih•sfeer) has longer periods of daylight than does the Southern Hemisphere. When the North Pole is tilted away from the sun, the opposite is true.

The direction of tilt of Earth's axis remains the same throughout Earth's orbit around the sun.

23.5°

23.5°

orbit

This drawing is not to scale.

Temperature

The angle at which the sun's rays strike each part of Earth's surface changes as Earth moves in its orbit. When the North Pole is tilted toward the sun, the sun's rays strike the Northern Hemisphere more directly. Thus, the region receives a higher concentration of solar energy and is warmer. When the North Pole is tilted away from the sun, the sun's rays strike the Northern Hemisphere less directly. When the sunlight is less direct, the solar energy is less concentrated and the region is cooler.

The spherical shape of Earth also affects how the sun warms up an area. Temperatures are high at point A in the diagram. This is because the sun's rays hit Earth's surface at a right angle and are focused in a small area. Toward the poles, the sun's rays hit Earth's surface at a lesser angle. Therefore, the rays are spread out over a larger area and the temperatures are cooler.

👁 Visualize It!

8 Apply Which location on the illustration of Earth below receives more direct rays from the sun?
- ☐ A
- ☐ B
- ☐ They receive equal amounts.

9 Identify Which location is cooler? Explain your reasoning._____

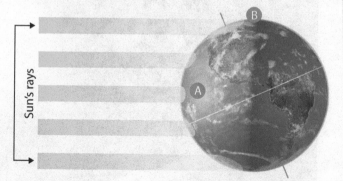

Sun's rays

B

A

Daylight Hours

All locations on Earth experience an *average* of 12 hours of light a day. However, the *actual* number of daylight hours on any given day of the year varies with location. Areas around Earth's equator receive about 12 hours of light a day. Areas on Earth's surface that are tilted toward the sun have more hours of daylight. These areas travel a longer path through the lit part of Earth than areas at the equator. Areas on Earth's surface that are tilted away from the sun have less than 12 hours of light a day. These areas travel a shorter path through the lit part of Earth, as shown below.

This drawing is not to scale.

Sun's Rays

During summer in the Northern Hemisphere, a person has already had many daylight hours by the time a person in the Southern Hemisphere reaches daylight.

About twelve hours later, the person in the Northern Hemisphere is close to daylight again, while the person in the Southern Hemisphere still has many hours of darkness left.

Midnight Sun

When it is summer in the Northern Hemisphere, the time in each day that it is light increases as you move north of the equator. Areas north of the Arctic Circle have 24 hours of daylight, called the "midnight sun," as seen in the photo. At the same time, areas south of the Antarctic Circle receive 24 hours of darkness, or "polar night." When it is winter in the Northern Hemisphere, conditions in the polar areas are reversed.

👁 Visualize It!

10 Claims • Evidence • Reasoning Make a claim about why the area in the photo isn't very warm even though the sun is up all night long. Summarize evidence to support the claim and explain your reasoning.

_____

_____

_____

This composite image shows that the sun never set on this Arctic summer day.

Seasons change...

What causes seasons?

Most locations on Earth experience seasons. Each **season** is characterized by a pattern of temperature and other weather trends. Near the equator, the temperatures are almost the same year-round. Near the poles, there are very large changes in temperatures from winter to summer. We experience seasons due to the changes in the intensity of sunlight and the number of daylight hours as Earth revolves around the sun. So, both the tilt of Earth's axis and Earth's spherical shape play a role in Earth's changing seasons.

As Earth travels around the sun, the area of sunlight in each hemisphere changes. At an **equinox** (EE•kwuh•nahks), sunlight shines equally on the Northern and Southern Hemispheres. Half of each hemisphere is lit, and half is in darkness. As Earth moves along its orbit, the sunlight reaches more of one hemisphere than the other. At a **solstice** (SAHL•stis), the area of sunlight is at a maximum in one hemisphere and at a minimum in the other hemisphere.

- **September Equinox** When Earth is in this position, sunlight shines equally on both poles.
- **December Solstice** About three months later, Earth has traveled a quarter of the way around the sun, but its axis still points in the same direction into space. The North Pole leans away from the sun and is in complete darkness. The South Pole is in complete sunlight.
- **March Equinox** After another quarter of its orbit, Earth reaches another equinox. Half of each hemisphere is lit, and the sunlight is centered on the equator.
- **June Solstice** This position is opposite to the December solstice. Now the North Pole leans toward the sun and is in complete sunlight, and the south pole is in complete darkness.

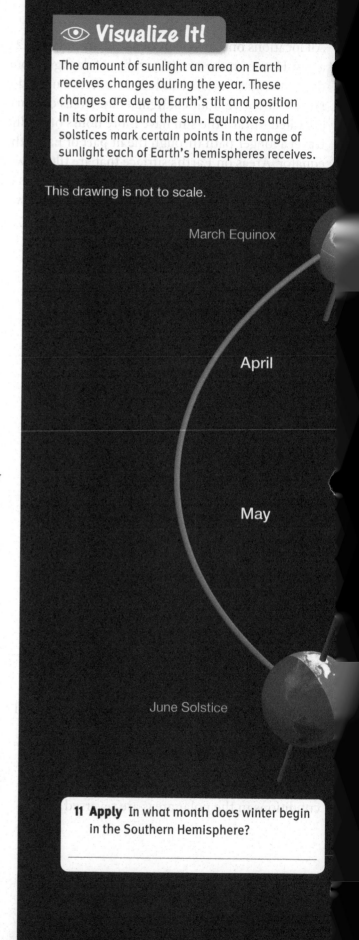

The amount of sunlight an area on Earth receives changes during the year. These changes are due to Earth's tilt and position in its orbit around the sun. Equinoxes and solstices mark certain points in the range of sunlight each of Earth's hemispheres receives.

This drawing is not to scale.

March Equinox

April

May

June Solstice

11 Apply In what month does winter begin in the Southern Hemisphere?

_____

12 Infer During which solstice would the sun be at its highest point in the sky in the Northern Hemisphere? Explain your reasoning.

_____

_____

Solstices

The seasons of summer and winter begin on days called *solstices*. Each year on June 21 or 22, the North Pole's tilt toward the sun is greatest. This day is called the *June solstice*. This solstice marks the beginning of summer in the Northern Hemisphere. By December 21 or 22, the North Pole is tilted to the farthest point away from the sun. This day is the December solstice.

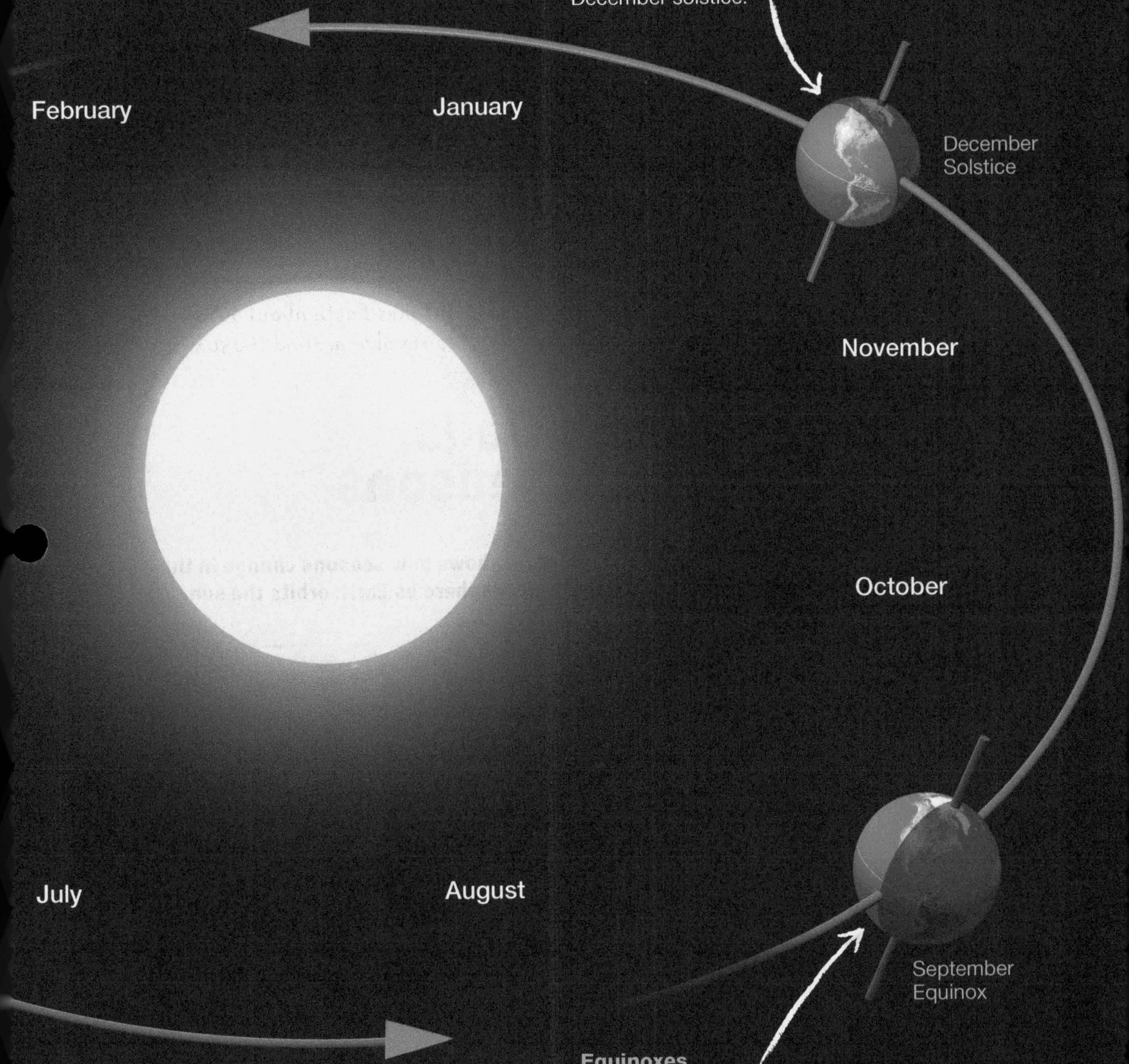

February

January

December Solstice

November

October

July

August

September Equinox

Equinoxes

The seasons fall and spring begin on days called *equinoxes*. The hours of daylight and darkness are approximately equal everywhere on Earth on these days. The *September equinox* occurs on September 22 or 23 of each year. This equinox marks the beginning of fall in the Northern Hemisphere. The March equinox on March 20 or 21 of each year

13 Infer In which parts of the world is an equinox most different from other days of the year?

_____

_____

Visual Summary

To complete this summary, circle the correct word. You can use this page to review the main concepts of the lesson.

The length of a day is determined by Earth's rotation.

14 It takes Earth 24 seconds/hours to make one rotation on its axis.

The length of a year is determined by Earth's revolution around the sun.

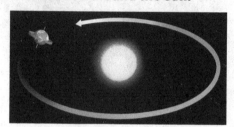

15 It takes Earth about 365 hours/days to revolve around the sun.

Earth's Days, Years, and Seasons

Earth's tilt affects temperatures and daylight hours at different locations on Earth.

Sun's rays

16 Earth's temperatures and hours of daylight stay the most constant at the equator/poles.

This diagram shows how seasons change in the Northern Hemisphere as Earth orbits the sun.

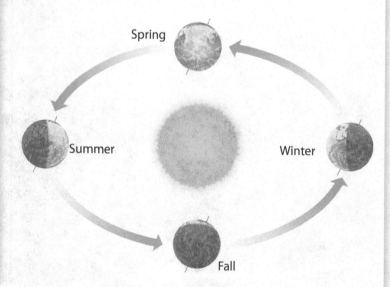

Spring

Summer

Winter

Fall

17 When it is summer in the Northern Hemisphere, it is summer/winter in the Southern Hemisphere.

18 Claims • Evidence • Reasoning Make a claim about how conditions on Earth would change if Earth stopped rotating on its axis. Summarize evidence to support the claim and explain your reasoning.

Lesson Review

Vocabulary

In the space provided below, describe how each set of words are related.

1 revolution, year

_____

_____

2 rotation, day

_____

_____

3 season, equinox, solstice

_____

_____

_____

_____

_____

Key Concepts

4 Identify About how many days are in an Earth year? And how many hours in an Earth day?

_____

5 Describe How does the tilt of Earth's axis affect how the sun's rays strike Earth?

_____

_____

_____

_____

_____

6 Synthesize How does the tilt of Earth's axis affect the number of daylight hours and the temperature of a location on Earth?

_____

_____

_____

_____

Critical Thinking

Use this image to answer the questions below.

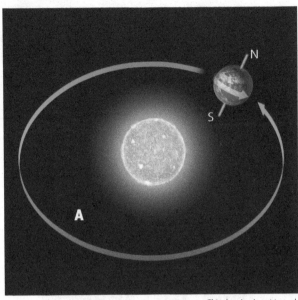

This drawing is not to scale.

7 Identify What season is the Northern Hemisphere experiencing in the image above?

_____

8 Explain How do the tilt of Earth's axis and Earth's movements around the sun cause seasons? Explain your reasoning.

_____

_____

_____

_____

9 Claims • Evidence • Reasoning Make a claim about which season the Northern Hemisphere will experience if Earth moves to point A in the image above. Summarize evidence to support the claim and explain your reasoning.

_____

_____

_____

_____

Moon Phases and Eclipses

ESSENTIAL QUESTION

How do Earth, the moon, and the sun affect each other?

By the end of this lesson, you should be able to describe the effects the sun and the moon have on Earth, including gravitational attraction, moon phases, and eclipses.

Why is part of the moon orange? Because Earth is moving between the moon and the sun, casting a shadow on the moon.

SC.8.E.5.9 Explain the impact of objects in space on each other including: 1. The Sun on the Earth including seasons and gravitational attraction, 2. The Moon on the Earth, including phases, tides, and eclipses, and the relative position of each body.

Lesson Labs

Quick Labs
- Moon Phases
- Lunar Eclipse

Exploration/S.T.E.M. Lab
- What the Moon Orbits

Engage Your Brain

1 Identify Fill in the blanks with the word or phrase you think correctly completes the following sentences.

We can see the moon because it _____ the light from the sun.

The moon's _____ affects the oceans' tides on Earth.

The impact craters on the moon were created by collisions with _____, meteorites, and asteroids.

2 Describe Write your own caption for this photo in the space below.

_____
_____
_____
_____
_____
_____
_____

ACTIVE READING

3 Synthesize You can often define an unknown word if you know the meaning of its word parts. Use the word parts and sentence below to make an educated guess about the meaning of the word *penumbra*.

Word part	Meaning
umbra	shade or shadow
pen-, from the Latin *paene*	almost

Example sentence
An observer in the <u>penumbra</u> experiences only a partial eclipse.

penumbra:

_____
_____

© Houghton Mifflin Har Publishing Company

Vocabulary Terms

- satellite
- gravity
- lunar phases
- eclipse
- umbra
- penumbra

4 Apply As you learn the definition of each vocabulary term in this lesson, create your own definition or sketch to help you remember the meaning of the term.

How are Earth, the moon, and the sun related in space?

Earth not only spins on its axis, but like the seven other planets in our solar system, Earth also orbits the sun. A body that orbits a larger body is called a **satellite** (SAT'l•yt). Six of the planets in our solar system have smaller bodies that orbit around each of them. These natural satellites are also called moons. Our moon is Earth's natural satellite.

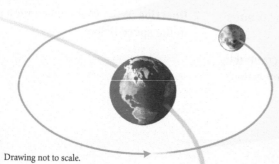

Drawing not to scale.

Earth revolves around the sun as the moon revolves around Earth.

ACTIVE READING

5 Identify As you read, underline the reason that the moon stays in orbit around Earth.

Earth and the Moon Orbit the Sun

All bodies that have mass exert a force that pulls other objects with mass toward themselves. This force is called **gravity.** The mass of Earth is much larger than the mass of the moon, and therefore Earth's gravity exerts a stronger pull on the moon than the moon does on Earth. It is Earth's gravitational pull that keeps the moon in orbit around Earth, forming the Earth-moon system.

The Earth–moon system is itself in orbit around the sun. Even though the sun is relatively far away, the mass of the sun exerts a large gravitational pull on the Earth–moon system. This gravitational pull keeps the Earth–moon system in orbit around the sun.

The Moon Orbits Earth

The pull of Earth's gravity keeps the moon, Earth's natural satellite, in orbit around Earth. Even though the moon is Earth's closest neighbor in space, it is far away compared to the sizes of Earth and the moon themselves.

The distance between Earth and the moon is roughly 383,000 km (238,000 mi)—about a hundred times the distance between New York and Los Angeles. If a jet airliner could travel in space, it would take about 20 days to cover a distance that huge. Astronauts, whose spaceships travel much faster than jets, need about 3 days to reach the moon.

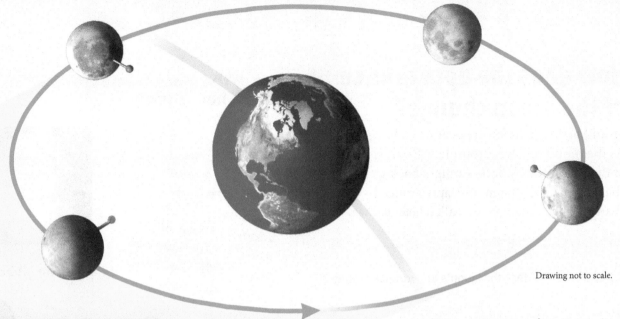

Drawing not to scale.

The moon completes one rotation for every revolution it makes around Earth.

👁 **Visualize It!**

6 Analyze Draw the correct position of the pin when the moon is in the position shown in the top right corner of this figure. Explain your reasoning.

What does the moon look like from Earth?

The moon is only visible from Earth when it reflects the sunlight that reaches the moon. Although the moon is most easily seen at night, you have probably also seen it during daytime on some days. In the daytime, the moon may only be as bright as a thin cloud and can be easily missed. On some days you can see the moon during both the daytime and at night, whereas on other days, you may not see the moon at all.

When you can look at the moon, you may notice darker and lighter areas. Perhaps you have imagined them as features of a face or some other pattern. People around the world have told stories about the animals, people, and objects they have imagined while looking at the light and dark areas of the moon. The dark and light spots do not change over the course of a month because only one side of the moon faces Earth, often called the near side of the moon. This is because the moon rotates once on its own axis each time it orbits Earth. The moon takes 27.3 days or about a month to orbit Earth once.

7 Claims • Evidence • Reasoning Make a claim about how the moon would appear to an observer on Earth if the moon did not rotate. Summarize evidence to support the claim and explain your reasoning.

_____

_____

_____

_____

It's Just a Phase!

How does the appearance of the moon change?

From Earth, the moon's appearance changes. As the moon revolves around Earth, the portion of the moon that reflects sunlight back to Earth changes, causing the moon's appearance to change. These changes are called **lunar phases.**

ACTIVE READING

8 Describe Why does the moon's appearance change?

_____

_____

Lunar Phases Cycle Monthly

The cycle begins with a new moon. At this time, Earth, the moon, and the sun are lined up, such that the near side of the moon is unlit. And so there appears to be no moon in the sky.

As the moon moves along its orbit, you begin to see the sunlight on the near side as a thin crescent shape. The crescent becomes thicker as the moon waxes, or grows. When half of the near side of the moon is in the sunlight, the moon has completed one-quarter of its cycle. This phase is called the *first quarter.*

More of the moon is visible during the second week, or the *gibbous* (GIB•uhs) *phase.* This is when the near side is more than half lit but not fully lit. When the moon is halfway through its cycle, the whole near side of the moon is in sunlight, and we see a full moon.

During the third week, the amount of the moon's near side in the sunlight decreases and it seems to shrink, or wane. When the near side is again only half in sunlight, the moon is three-quarters of the way through its cycle. The phase is called the *third quarter.*

In the fourth week, the area of the near side of the moon in sunlight continues to shrink. The moon is seen as waning crescent shapes. Finally, the near side of the moon is unlit—*new moon.*

Views of the moon from Earth's northern hemisphere

The waxing moon appears to grow each day. This is because the sunlit area that we can see from Earth is getting larger each day.

Waxing gibbous

Full moon

Waning gibbous

Think Outside the Book

9 Apply Look at the night sky and keep a moon journal for a series of nights. What phase is the moon in now?

10 Analyze What shape does the moon appear to be when it is closer to the sun than Earth is?

_____

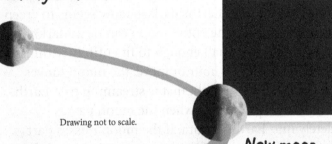

First quarter

Waxing crescent

Drawing not to scale.

New moon

Third quarter

Waning crescent

The waning moon appears to shrink each day. When the moon is waning, the sunlit area is getting smaller. Notice above that even as the phases of the moon change, the total amount of sunlight that the moon gets remains the same. Half the moon is always in sunlight, just as half of Earth is always in sunlight. The moon phases have a period of 29.5 days.

Exploring Eclipses

How do lunar eclipses occur?

An **eclipse** (ih•KLIPS) is an event during which one object in space casts a shadow onto another. On Earth, a lunar eclipse occurs when the moon moves through Earth's shadow. There are two parts of Earth's shadow, as you can see in the diagram below. The **umbra** (UHM•bruh) is the darkest part of a shadow. Around it is a spreading cone of lighter shadow called the **penumbra** (pih•NUHM•bruh). Just before a lunar eclipse, sunlight streaming past Earth produces a full moon. Then the moon moves into Earth's penumbra and becomes slightly less bright. As the moon moves into the umbra, Earth's dark shadow seems to creep across and cover the moon. The entire moon can be in darkness because the moon is small enough to fit entirely within Earth's umbra. After an hour or more, the moon moves slowly back into the sunlight that is streaming past Earth. A total lunar eclipse occurs when the moon passes completely into Earth's umbra. If the moon misses part or all of the umbra, part of the moon stays light and the eclipse is called a partial lunar eclipse.

You may be wondering why you don't see solar and lunar eclipses every month. The reason is that the moon's orbit around Earth is tilted—by about 5°—relative to the orbit of Earth around the sun. This tilt is enough to place the moon out of Earth's shadow for most full moons and Earth out of the moon's shadow for most new moons.

This composite photo shows the partial and total phases of a lunar eclipse over several hours.

Lunar eclipse

👁 Visualize It!

11 Claims • Evidence • Reasoning Make a claim about which type of lunar eclipse would occur if the moon were in the areas being pointed to. Summarize evidence to support the claim and explain your reasoning.

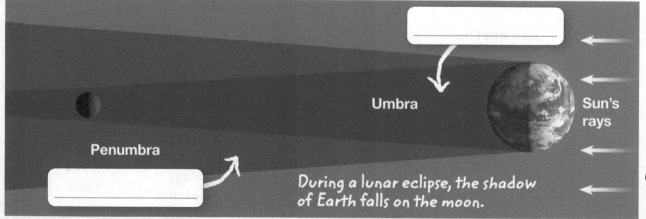

Umbra

Sun's rays

Penumbra

During a lunar eclipse, the shadow of Earth falls on the moon.

Drawing not to scale.

How do solar eclipses occur?

When the moon is directly between the sun and Earth, the shadow of the moon falls on a part of Earth and causes a solar eclipse. During a total solar eclipse, the sun's light is completely blocked by the moon, as seen in this photo. The umbra falls on the area of Earth that lies directly in line with the moon and the sun. Outside the umbra, but within the penumbra, people see a partial solar eclipse. The penumbra falls on the area that immediately surrounds the umbra.

The umbra of the moon is too small to make a large shadow on Earth's surface. The part of the umbra that hits Earth during an eclipse is never more than a few hundred kilometers across, as shown below. So, a total eclipse of the sun covers only a small part of Earth and is seen only by people in particular parts of Earth along a narrow path. A total solar eclipse usually lasts between one to two minutes at any one location. A total eclipse will not be visible in the United States until 2024, even though there is a total eclipse somewhere on Earth about every one to two years.

Solar eclipse

During a solar eclipse, the moon passes between the sun and Earth so that the sun is partially or totally obscured.

ACTIVE READING

12 Claims • Evidence • Reasoning
Make a claim about why it is relatively rare to observe a solar eclipse. Summarize evidence to support the claim and explain your reasoning.

_____

_____

_____

_____

 **Visualize It!**

13 Describe Explain what happens during a solar eclipse.

_____

_____

_____

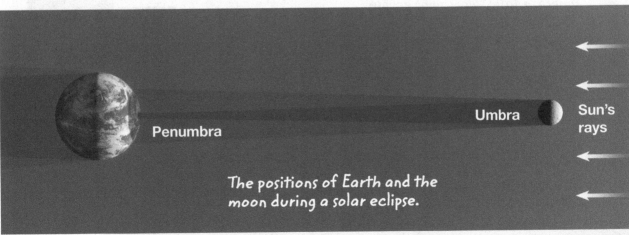

Penumbra

Umbra

Sun's rays

The positions of Earth and the moon during a solar eclipse.

Drawing not to scale.

Visual Summary

To complete this summary, circle the correct word. You can use this page to review the main concepts of the lesson.

Moon Phases and Eclipses

The Earth–moon system orbits the sun.

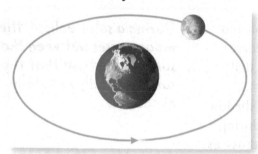

14 The moon takes about one day/month/year to orbit Earth.

Shadows in space cause eclipses.

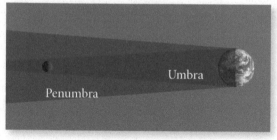

Umbra

Penumbra

15 When the moon is in Earth's umbra, a total solar/lunar eclipse is occurring.

The appearance of the moon depends on the positions of the sun, the moon, and Earth.

16 The fraction of the moon that receives sunlight always/never changes.

17 Claims • Evidence • Reasoning Make a claim about what causes the lunar phases that we see from Earth. Summarize evidence to support the claim and explain your reasoning.

Lesson Review

Vocabulary

In your own words, define the following terms.

1 gravity

_____

_____

2 satellite

_____

_____

3 umbra

_____

_____

Key Concepts

4 Describe What are two phases of a waxing moon, and how do they appear?

_____

_____

_____

_____

5 Identify Explain why the moon can be seen from Earth.

_____

_____

_____

6 Describe What is the relationship between Earth, the sun, and the moon in space?

_____

_____

_____

_____

Critical Thinking

Use the image below to answer the following question.

7 Identify What type of eclipse is shown in the diagram?

_____

8 Describe Where is the moon in its orbit at the time of a solar eclipse?

_____

9 Infer What phase is the moon in when there is a total solar eclipse?

_____

10 Predict Which shape of the moon will you never see during the daytime, after sunrise and before sunset? *Hint:* Consider the directions of the sun and moon from Earth.

_____

11 Claims • Evidence • Reasoning Make a claim on how the ground around you would look if you were an astronaut in the middle of the near side of the moon during a full moon. Summarize evidence about what is in sunlight and what is in darkness to support the claim and explain your reasoning.

_____

_____

_____

_____

_____

SC.8.N.1.6 Understand that scientific investigations involve the collection of relevant empirical evidence, the use of logical reasoning, and the application of imagination in devising hypotheses, predictions, explanations and models to make sense of the collected evidence. **SC.8.N.2.2** Discuss what characterizes science and its methods.

Analyzing Scientific Explanations

Scientists use different methods to develop scientific explanations in different fields of study. Scientists base their explanations on data collected through observation and measurement. After scientists make observations and collect data, they analyze current explanations for what they observed. If a new observation doesn't fit an existing explanation, scientists might work to revise the explanation or to offer a new one.

Tutorial

The text below describes how Ptolemy, a Greek astronomer in the second century C.E., described the universe. Consider the following steps as you analyze scientific explanations.

As Aristotle put forth, Earth is at the center of the universe. All other planets and the Sun revolve around Earth, each on its own sphere. The spheres follow this order outward from Earth: Mercury, Venus, the Moon, the Sun, Mars, Jupiter, Saturn, and the Fixed Stars. Each sphere turns at its own steady pace. Bodies do appear to move backward during their wanderings, but that does not mean the spheres do not keep a steady pace. This is explained by the movement of the bodies along smaller spheres that turn along the edge of the larger spheres. My calculations and models agree with and predict the motions of the spheres. The constant turning of the spheres also moves the bodies closer to Earth and farther from Earth, which explains why the bodies appear brighter or darker at different times. Thus, the heavens remain perfect. This perfection leads to music in the heavens, created by the spheres.

Identify the evidence that supports the explanation. At least two different lines of evidence are needed to be considered valid.

Identify any evidence that does not support the explanation. A single line of evidence can disprove an explanation. Often, new evidence makes scientists reevaluate an explanation. By the 1500s, Ptolemy's model was not making accurate predictions. In 1543, Copernicus, a Polish astronomer, proposed a new explanation of how planets move.

Identify any additional lines of evidence that should be considered. They might point to additional investigations to further examine the explanation. The gravitational force between objects was not known in Ptolemy's time. However, it should be considered when explaining the motion of planets.

Decide whether the original explanation is supported by enough evidence. An alternative explanation might better explain the evidence or might explain a wider range of observations.

If possible, propose an alternative explanation that could fit the evidence. Often, a simpler explanation is better if it fits the evidence. Copernicus explained the apparent backward movement and changing brightness of planets by placing the sun at the center of the solar system with the planets revolving around it.

You Try It!

In 2006, an official definition of a planet was determined. Read and analyze the information below concerning the classification of the largest Main Belt asteroid, Ceres.

The members of the International Astronomical Union (IAU) voted for the official definition of a planet to be a celestial body that

1. orbits the sun,
2. has enough mass so that its gravity helps it to maintain a nearly round shape,
3. has cleared the neighborhood around its orbit.

A group suggests that Ceres be considered a planet under the new definition. As the largest Main Belt asteroid, Ceres orbits the sun along with thousands of smaller asteroids. Images of Ceres clearly show its nearly round shape. These points, says the group's leader, should qualify Ceres as a planet.

1 Making Observations Underline lines of evidence that support the explanation.

2 Evaluating Data Circle any lines of evidence that do not support the proposed explanation. Explain why this evidence does not support the classification.

_____

_____

_____

_____

_____

3 Gather Evidence Identify any additional evidence that should be considered when evaluating the explanation.

_____

_____

_____

4 Communicating Ideas If possible, propose an alternative explanation that could fit the evidence.

_____

_____

_____

_____

_____

_____

🏠 Take It Home!

Pluto was recently reclassified as a dwarf planet. Make a claim about whether or not this was the right decision. Summarize evidence to support the claim. How does this compare to the proposed reclassification of Ceres? List similarities of the two explanations in a chart.

Earth's Tides

ESSENTIAL QUESTION

What causes tides?

By the end of this lesson, you should be able to explain what tides are and what causes them in Earth's oceans and to describe variations in the tides.

You may wonder why this boat is sitting in such shallow water. This photo was taken at low tide, when the ocean water is below average sea level.

SC.8.N.1.1 Define a problem from the eighth grade curriculum using appropriate reference materials to support scientific understanding, plan and carry out scientific investigations of various types, such as systematic observations or experiments, identify variables, collect and organize data, interpret data in charts, tables, and graphics, analyze information, make predictions, and defend conclusions. **SC.8.E.5.9** Explain the impact of objects in space on each other including: 1. The Sun on the Earth including seasons and gravitational attraction, 2. The Moon on the Earth, including phases, tides, and eclipses, and the relative position of each body.

Lesson Labs

Quick Labs
• Tides and Beaches
• Tidal Math

S.T.E.M. Lab
• Using Water to Do Work

 Engage Your Brain

1 Describe Fill in the blank with the word that you think correctly completes the following sentences.

The motion of the _____ around Earth is related to tides.

The daily rotation of _____ is also related to tides.

During a _____ tide, the water level is higher than the average sea level.

During a _____ tide, the water level is lower than the average sea level.

2 Label Draw an arrow to show where you think high tide might be.

Low tide ▶

ACTIVE **READING**

3 Synthesize The word *spring* has different meanings. Use the meanings of the word *spring* and the sentence below to make an educated guess about the meaning of the term *spring tides*.

Meanings of *spring*
the season between winter and summer
a source of water from the ground
jump, or rise up
a coiled piece of metal

Example sentence
During <u>spring tides</u>, the sun, the moon, and Earth are in a straight line, resulting in very high tides.

spring tides:

_____

_____

Vocabulary Terms

• tide   • spring tide
• tidal range   • neap tide

4 Apply As you learn the definition of each vocabulary term in this lesson, create your own definition or sketch to help you remember the meaning of the term.

A **Rising Tide** of Interest

What causes tides?

The photographs below show the ocean at the same location at two different times. **Tides** are daily changes in the level of ocean water. Tides are caused by the difference in the gravitational force of the sun and the moon across Earth. This difference in gravitational force is called the *tidal force*. The tidal force exerted by the moon is stronger than the tidal force exerted by the sun because the moon is much closer to Earth than the sun is. So, the moon is mainly responsible for tides on Earth.

How often tides occur and how tidal levels vary depend on the position of the moon as it revolves around Earth. The gravity of the moon pulls on every particle of Earth. But because liquids move more easily than solids do, the pull on liquids is much more noticeable than the pull on solids is. The moon's gravitational pull on Earth decreases with the moon's distance from Earth. The part of Earth facing the moon is pulled toward the moon with the greatest force. So, water on that side of Earth bulges toward the moon. The solid Earth is pulled more strongly toward the moon than the ocean water on Earth's far side is. So, there is also a bulge of water on the side of Earth farthest from the moon.

ACTIVE READING

5 Identify Underline the sentence that identifies which object is mainly responsible for tides on Earth.

At low tide, the water level is low, and the boats are far below the dock.

At high tide, the water level has risen, and the boats are close to the dock.

What are high tides and low tides?

The bulges that form in Earth's oceans are called high tides. *High tide* is a water level that is higher than the average sea level. Low tides form in the areas between the high tides. *Low tide* is a water level that is lower than the average sea level. At low tide, the water levels are lower because the water is in high-tide areas.

As the moon moves around Earth and Earth rotates, the tidal bulges move around Earth. The tidal bulges follow the motion of the moon. As a result, many places on Earth have two high tides and two low tides each day.

Visualize It!

6 Identify Label the areas where high tides form and the area where the other low tide forms.

Note: Drawing is not to scale.

Moon

A _____

B _____

Earth

Low tide

C _____

This grizzly bear in Alaska is taking advantage of low tide by digging for clams.

7 Claims • Evidence • Reasoning Make a claim about what will happen to the bear when the tide comes in. Summarize evidence to support the claim and explain your reasoning.

_____

_____

Tide Me Over

What are two kinds of tidal ranges?

Tides are due to the *tidal force,* the difference between the force of gravity on one side of Earth and the other side of Earth. Because the moon is so much closer to Earth than the sun is, the moon's tidal force is greater than the sun's tidal force. The moon's effect on tides is twice as strong as the sun's effect. The combined gravitational effects of the sun and the moon on Earth result in different tidal ranges. A **tidal range** is the difference between the levels of ocean water at high tide and low tide. Tidal range depends on the positions of the sun and the moon relative to Earth.

ACTIVE READING

8 Identify As you read, underline the two kinds of tidal range.

Spring Tides: The Largest Tidal Range

Tides that have the largest daily tidal range are **spring tides**. Spring tides happen when the sun, the moon, and Earth form a straight line. So, spring tides happen when the moon is between the sun and Earth and when the moon is on the opposite side of Earth, as shown in the illustrations below. In other words, spring tides happen during the new moon and full moon phases, or every 14 days. During these times, the gravitational effects of the sun and moon add together, causing one pair of very large tidal bulges. Spring tides have nothing to do with the spring season.

Note: Drawings are not to scale.

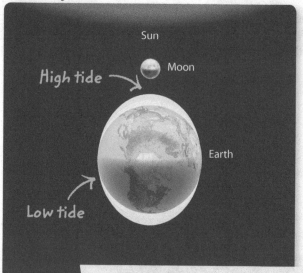
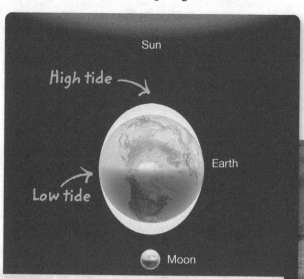

During spring tides, the tidal force of the sun on Earth adds to the tidal force of the moon. The tidal range increases.

9 Claims • Evidence • Reasoning Make a claim about why spring tides happen twice a month. Summarize evidence to support the claim and explain your reasoning.

_____

_____

Neap Tides: The Smallest Tidal Range

Tides that have the smallest daily tidal range are **neap tides**. Neap tides happen when the sun, Earth, and the moon form a 90° angle, as shown in the illustrations below. During a neap tide, the gravitational effects of the sun and the moon on Earth do not add together as they do during spring tides. Neap tides occur halfway between spring tides, during the first quarter and third quarter phases of the moon. At these times, the sun and the moon cause two pairs of smaller tidal bulges.

Note: Drawings are not to scale.

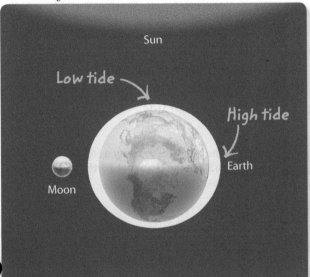
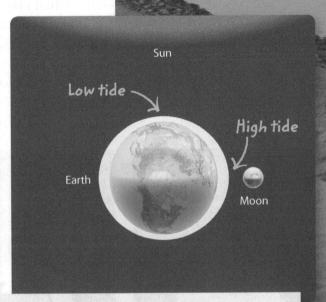

During neap tides, the gravitational effects of the sun and the moon on Earth do not add together. The tidal range decreases.

10 Compare Fill in the Venn diagram to compare and contrast spring tides and neap tides.

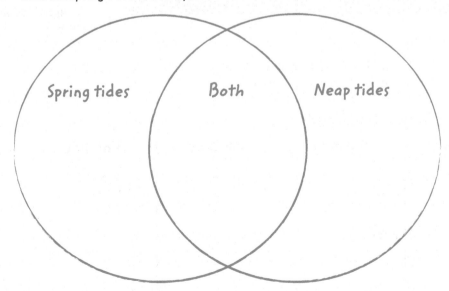

Spring tides   Both   Neap tides

What causes tidal cycles?

The rotation of Earth and the moon's revolution around Earth determine when tides occur. Imagine that Earth rotated at the same speed that the moon revolves around Earth. If this were true, the same side of Earth would always face the moon. And high tide would always be at the same places on Earth. But the moon revolves around Earth much more slowly than Earth rotates. A place on Earth that is facing the moon takes 24 h and 50 min to rotate to face the moon again. So, the cycle of high tides and low tides at that place happens 50 min later each day.

In many places there are two high tides and two low tides each day. Because the tide cycle occurs in 24 h and 50 min intervals, it takes about 6 h and 12.5 min (one-fourth the time of the total cycle) for water in an area to go from high tide to low tide. It takes about 12 h and 25 min (one-half the time of the total cycle) to go from one high tide to the next high tide.

Note: Drawings are not to scale.

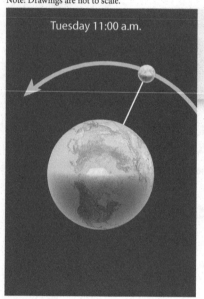
Tuesday 11:00 a.m.

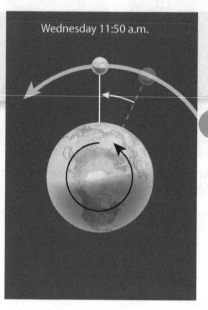
Wednesday 11:50 a.m.

The moon moves only a fraction of its orbit in the time that Earth rotates once.

i Think Outside the Book

11 Claims • Evidence • Reasoning
Make a claim about what Earth's tides would be like if the moon revolved around Earth at the same speed Earth rotates. Draw a diagram to illustrate your claim, then summarize evidence to support the claim and explain your reasoning.

12 Predict In the table, predict the approximate times of high tide and low tide for Clearwater, Florida.

Tide Data for Clearwater, Florida

Date (2009)	High tide	Low tide	High tide	Low tide
August 19	12:14 a.m.		12:39 p.m.	
August 20	1:04 a.m.	7:17 a.m.		
August 21				

WEIRD SCIENCE

Extreme Living Conditions

Some organisms living along ocean coastlines must be able to tolerate extreme living conditions. At high tide, much of the coast is under water. At low tide, much of the coast is dry. Some organisms must also survive the constant crashing of waves against the shore.

Barnacle Business
Barnacles must be able to live in water as well as out of water. They must also tolerate the air temperature, which may differ from the temperature of the water.

Ghostly Crabs
Ghost crabs live near the high tide line on sandy shores. They scurry along the sand to avoid being underwater when the tide comes in. Ghost crabs can also find cover between rocks.

Stunning Starfish
Starfish live in tidal pools, which are areas along the shore where water remains at low tide. Starfish must be able to survive changes in water temperature and salinity.

i Extend

13 Claims • Evidence • Reasoning Make a claim about how living conditions change for two tidal organisms. Summarize evidence to support the claim and explain your reasoning.

14 Research and Record List the names of two organisms that live in the high tide zone or the low tide zone along a coastline of your choice.

15 Describe Imagine a day in the life of an organism you researched in question 14 by doing one of the following:
- make a poster
- write a play
- record an audio story
- make a cartoon

Visual Summary

To complete this summary, fill in the blanks with the correct word. You can use this page to review the main concepts of the lesson.

In many places, two high tides and two low tides occur every day.

16 The type of tide shown here is

_____

The gravitational effects of the moon and the sun cause tides.

17 Tides on Earth are caused mainly by the

_____

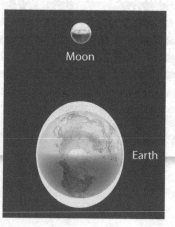

Moon

Earth

Note: Drawings are not to scale.

There are two kinds of tidal ranges: spring tides and neap tides.

Sun

Moon

Earth

Sun

Moon

Earth

18 During a spring tide, the sun, moon, and Earth are in a/an

_____

19 During a neap tide, the sun, moon, and Earth form a/an

_____

20 **Claims • Evidence • Reasoning** Make a claim about how the moon causes tides. Summarize evidence to support the claim and explain your reasoning.

Lesson Review

Vocabulary

Answer the following questions in your own words.

1 Use *tide* and *tidal range* in the same sentence.

_____

_____

2 Write an original definition for *neap tide* and for *spring tide*.

_____

_____

_____

_____

Key Concepts

3 Describe Explain what tides are. Include *high tide* and *low tide* in your answer.

_____

_____

_____

_____

_____

4 Explain State what causes tides on Earth.

_____

_____

_____

5 Identify Write the alignment of the moon, the sun, and Earth that causes a spring tide.

_____

_____

6 Describe Explain why tides happen 50 min later each day.

_____

_____

Critical Thinking

Use this diagram to answer the next question.

Note: Drawing Is not to scale.

Last quarter moon

7 Claims • Evidence • Reasoning Make a claim about the type of tidal range Earth will have when the moon is in this position. Summarize evidence to support the claim and explain your reasoning.

_____

_____

_____

8 Apply How many days pass between the minimum and the maximum of the tidal range in any given area? Explain your reasoning.

_____

_____

_____

9 Claims • Evidence • Reasoning Make a claim about how the tides on Earth would be different if the moon revolved around Earth in 15 days instead of 30 days. Summarize evidence to support the claim and explain your reasoning.

_____

_____

_____

S.T.E.M. ENGINEERING & TECHNOLOGY

Engineering Design Process

Skills
Identify a need
Conduct research
Brainstorm solutions
✓ Select a solution
✓ Design a prototype
✓ Build a prototype
✓ Test and evaluate
✓ Redesign to improve
✓ Communicate results

Objectives
Explain several advantages of tidal energy over conventional energy sources.
Design a technological solution to harnessing changing water levels.
Test and modify a prototype to raise a mass as water levels change.

Harnessing Tidal Energy

Our society uses a lot of electrical energy. If the energy is generated by nuclear power plants or by burning fossil fuels, the waste products tend to harm the environment. However, in many places, these methods of obtaining energy are still used.

Scientists and engineers have been investigating alternative energy sources, such as solar, wind, and tidal energy. Tidal energy is energy from *tides,* the daily, predictable changes in the level of ocean water. The mechanical energy of the moving water can be transformed to other forms of energy that are useful in human activities. Tidal power facilities have less of an impact on nature and have low operating costs. And unlike fossil fuels or the uranium ore used in nuclear power plants, water is not used up in the generation of tidal energy. Generating electrical energy from tides and other alternative energy sources can be less harmful to the environment, but challenges must still be overcome.

Barrage tidal power facility at La Rance, France

1 Compare What are some advantages of generating electrical energy from tides instead of from fossil fuels?

_____

_____

_____

Types of Tidal Power Generators

There are three main types of tidal energy generators. One type is a system that uses a dam with turbines. The dam is called a *barrage*. The barrage allows water in during high tide and releases water during low tide. Barrage tidal power stations can affect marine life behind the barrage. Also, silt settles behind the barrage and must be dredged up and hauled out to sea. This is an older system of generating electrical energy from tides.

The other two types of tidal power generators are *horizontal-axis turbines* and *vertical-axis turbines*. These systems are like huge underwater fans turned by tidal currents instead of by wind. Because water is denser than air, slow-moving water can still produce a lot of power. These facilities have fewer effects on the environment.

2 Claims • Evidence • Reasoning Make a claim about the advantage of using horizontal-axis turbines and vertical-axis turbines instead of barrage tidal power stations. Summarize evidence to support the claim and explain your reasoning.

_____

_____

_____

Four vertical-axis tidal power turbines are seen here. The blades rotate on an axis perpendicular to the ocean floor.

Two horizontal-axis tidal power turbines are seen here. The blades rotate on an axis parallel to the ocean floor.

You Try It!

Now it's your turn to design and build a tidal power device.

Engineering Design Process

 **You Try It!**

Now it's your turn to design and build a tidal power device that will lift two masses. You will lift the masses by harnessing energy from the changing water levels in a sink or tub. Adding water to the sink or tub will simulate a rising tide, and removing water will simulate a falling tide. One mass must be raised when the tide rises, and the other mass must be raised when the tide falls. Both masses must be outside the sink or tub.

① Select a Solution

A How will you use the falling tide to raise a mass?

_____

_____

_____

_____

B How will you use the rising tide to raise a mass?

_____

_____

_____

_____

② Design a Prototype

In the space below, draw and label a prototype of your tidal power device. You may have one idea for harnessing the falling tide and a different idea for harnessing the rising tide.

You Will Need

- ✔ block, wooden or foam
- ✔ bucket
- ✔ dowels, wooden
- ✔ duct tape
- ✔ masses, 50 g or 100 g (2)
- ✔ milk jug, 1 gallon, empty
- ✔ siphon hose
- ✔ string
- ✔ tub, plastic or sink
- ✔ water

③ Build a Prototype

Now build your tidal power device. As you built your device, were there some aspects of your design that could not be assembled as you had predicted? What aspects did you have to revise as you were building the prototype?

_____
_____
_____
_____

④ Test and Evaluate

Place your device in the tub. Add water to the tub to simulate a rising tide. Then drain water from the tub. Observe the motion of the masses as the tide rises and falls, and record your observations.

_____
_____
_____
_____

⑤ Redesign to Improve

Keep making revisions, one at a time, until your tidal power device can lift both masses. Describe the revisions you made.

_____
_____
_____

⑥ Communicate Results

Were you able to raise a mass more easily when the simulated tide was rising or falling? Why do you think that was? Explain your reasoning. Then, compare your results with those of your classmates.

_____
_____
_____
_____
_____

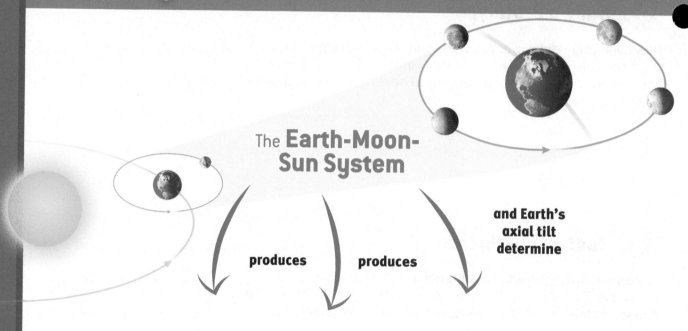

The **Earth-Moon-Sun System**

produces → produces → and Earth's axial tilt determine →

Moon Phases and Eclipses

Earth's Tides

Earth's Days, Years, and Seasons

1 Interpret Review the Graphic Organizer above. What causes the moon's phases and eclipses?

_____

_____

_____

_____

_____

2 Claims • Evidence • Reasoning Make a claim about why the moon has a greater influence on tides on Earth than the sun. Support your claim with evidence and explain your reasoning.

_____

_____

_____

3 Explain How does the tilt of Earth's axis account for differences in the area of sunlight each hemisphere receives during the summer solstice and winter solstice?

_____

_____

_____

_____

_____

_____

_____

4 Recognize Why do we always see the same side of the moon from Earth?

_____

_____

_____

_____

Vocabulary

Name _____

Fill in each blank with the term that best completes the following sentences.

1 A _____ is the periodic rise and fall of the water level in the oceans and other large bodies of water.

2 A _____ is the motion of a body that travels around another body in space.

3 The force of _____ keeps Earth and other planets of the solar system in orbit around the sun and keeps the moon in orbit around Earth.

4 A natural or artificial body that revolves around a celestial body that is greater in mass is called a(n) _____.

5 _____ is the counterclockwise spin of a planet or moon as seen from above a planet's north pole.

Key Concepts

Read each question below and circle the best answer.

6 The moon travels around Earth at a speed of about 1 km/s. Which of the following keeps the moon in orbit around Earth?

A gravity

B magnetism

C ocean tides

D the sun's heat and light

7 Astronomers use cameras on Earth and in orbit to observe the solar system and other objects in space. Suppose that a camera on Earth takes a picture of an astronomical event. The picture shows an object that is large and dark and has a bright area immediately around it. Which event does this picture most likely show?

F total solar eclipse

G total lunar eclipse

H waning gibbous moon

I waxing crescent moon

8 In most places on Earth that are not near the equator, the seasons of summer and winter have very different characteristics. Which of the following is a common characteristic of winter compared to summer?

A noon sun lower in the sky

B higher daytime temperatures

C fewer daily hours of sunlight

D sun rises earlier

9 Luis created a clay model of Earth and the sun. To show how Earth rotates, Luis wants to use a toothpick to represent Earth's axis of rotation.

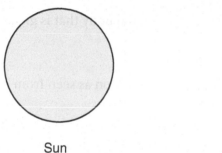

Sun   Earth

Where should Luis place the toothpick?

F horizontally through Earth in the direction Earth is traveling

G vertically through the center of Earth and through each pole

H horizontally through Earth from one side of the equator to the other side

I diagonally across Earth, halfway between the equator and the two poles

10 A specific region on Earth's surface always has its highest temperatures in June and its lowest temperatures in December. Which of these statements explains why the temperatures are LOWEST in December?

A This region is tilted the most toward the sun in December.

B This region is tilted the most away from the sun in December.

C This region is farthest from the sun in December.

D This region is closest to the sun in December.

Name _____

11 Cassie is writing a formula to show the effect of the gravitational pull of the sun and the moon on tidal range. Which formula would Cassie use to show the effect of the sun and the moon on spring tides?

F sun + moon = spring tides

G sun + Earth = spring tides

H sun – moon = spring tides

I Earth – moon = spring tides

12 Sara is recording water levels in the ocean near her home once an hour for one day. She observes the water level slowly rising and falling twice that day. What is Sara observing?

A currents

B gravity

C tides

D waves

13 The table below shows a tide chart from a location in Canada.

Date	High tide time	High tide height (m)	Low tide time	Low tide height (m)
June 4	6:58 a.m.	5.92	12:54 a.m.	1.87
June 5	7:51 a.m.	5.80	1:47 a.m.	1.90
June 6	8:42 a.m.	5.75	2:38 a.m.	1.87
June 7	9:30 a.m.	5.79	3:27 a.m.	1.75
June 8	10:16 a.m.	5.90	4:13 a.m.	1.56
June 9	11:01 a.m.	6.08	4:59 a.m.	1.32
June 10	11:46 a.m.	6.28	5:44 a.m.	1.05
June 11	12:32 p.m.	6.47	6:30 a.m.	0.78

What was the tidal range on June 7?

F 1.75 m

G 4.04 m

H 5.79 m

I 7.54 m

14 Eclipses are predictable solar system events. The answer choices below list relative positions of Earth, the sun, and the moon. Which list represents the position of Earth, the sun, and the moon during a lunar eclipse?

A sun, Earth, moon

B Earth, sun, moon

C sun, moon, Earth

D moon, sun, Earth

Critical Thinking

Answer the following questions in the space provided.

15 If the Earth rotated more slowly about its axis, how would this affect the length of a day on Earth? Use evidence to support your claim and explain your reasoning.

_____

_____

_____

_____

16 Explain what causes tides on Earth and why high and low tides occur.

_____

_____

_____

_____

_____

_____

_____

_____

Space Exploration

FLORIDA BIG IDEA 5

Earth in Space and Time

What Do You Think?

Mars rovers send information about the geology of Mars back to scientists on Earth. How might humans benefit from space exploration? As you explore this unit, you will gather evidence to help you state and support a claim.

UNIT 5

Space Exploration

Exploring Space!

The exploration of space began in 1957 with the launch of Sputnik I. Since 1957, humans have walked on the moon, rovers have investigated the surface of Mars, and spacecraft have flown by the most distant planets in the solar system.

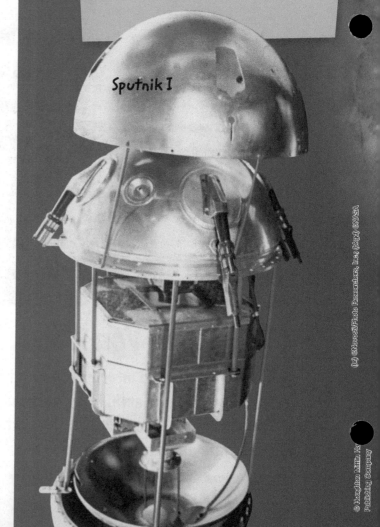

Sputnik I, 1957

On October 4, 1957, the successful launch of the Russian satellite Sputnik I kicked off the race for space.

Sputnik I

(t) ©Novosti/Photo Researchers, Inc; (bg) ©NASA

© Houghton Mifflin Harcourt Publishing Company

Apollo 11

Apollo 11, 1969

Just 12 years later, on July 16, 1969, Neil Armstrong and Buzz Aldrin became the first humans to walk on the moon.

International Space Station, 1998

Assembled in Low-Earth Orbit (LEO), the International Space Station is a long-term research laboratory in space. On clear nights, it can be seen without the use of a telescope.

New Horizons, 2015

On July 14, 2015, NASA's Horizon probe performed the first-ever flyby of the dwarf planet Pluto. The more than 1200 images it sent to Earth have given researchers the first detailed views of Pluto's surface and moons.

International Space Station

Take It Home!

New Ideas

Research the X Prize and the technological innovations and discoveries about space exploration that are coming out of private competition. Choose one prize winner and learn about the project.

A What is the project called?

_____

B Describe the project. How does it build on earlier knowledge? How is it different?

_____
_____
_____

Images from Space

ESSENTIAL QUESTION

What can we learn from space images?

By the end of this lesson, you should be able to describe ways of collecting information from space and analyze how different wavelengths of the electromagnetic spectrum provide different information.

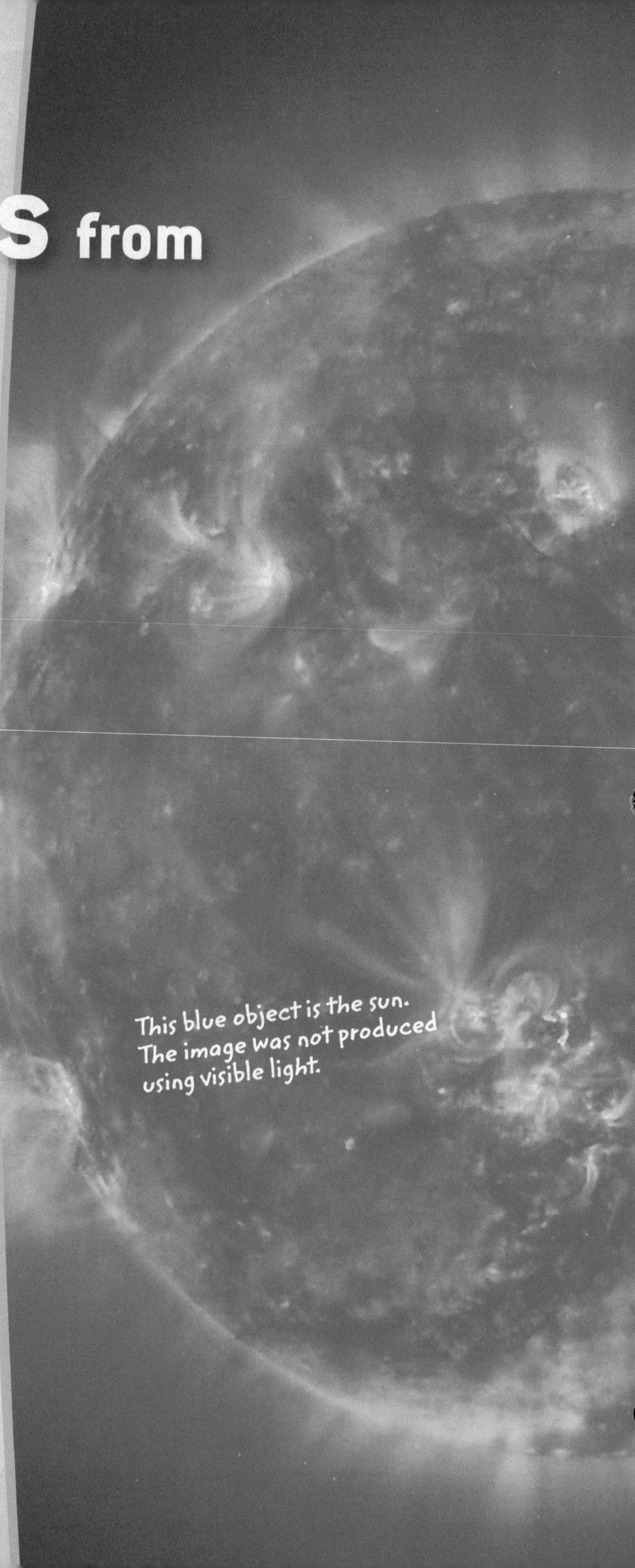

This blue object is the sun. The image was not produced using visible light.

SC.8.N.4.2 Explain how political, social, and economic concerns can affect science, and vice versa.
SC.8.E.5.10 Assess how technology is essential to science for such purposes as access to outer space and other remote locations, sample collection, measurement, data collection and storage, computation, and communication of information.
SC.8.E.5.11 Identify and compare characteristics of the electromagnetic spectrum such as wavelength, frequency, use, and hazards and recognize its application to an understanding of planetary images and satellite photographs.

Lesson Labs

Quick Lab
- A Model of the Expanding Universe
- Using Invisible Light

S.T.E.M./Field Lab
- Making a Telescope

Engage Your Brain

1 Predict Check T or F to show whether you think each statement is true or false.

T	F	
☐	☐	Visible light is a type of electromagnetic radiation.
☐	☐	Artificial satellites can produce images of Earth only.
☐	☐	Earth's atmosphere blocks all ultraviolet radiation from space.
☐	☐	Optical telescopes are used to study objects in the universe.

2 Identify Look at the picture below. Write a caption that explains what the picture shows.

_____

_____

_____

_____

_____

_____

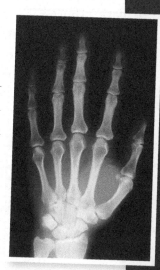

ACTIVE READING

3 Synthesize You can often define an unknown word if you know the meaning of its word parts. Use the word parts and sentence below to make an educated guess about the meaning of the word *microwave*.

Word part	Meaning
micro-	small
-wave	a movement of up or down or back and forth

Example sentence
Microwaves can be used to heat food.

microwave:

_____

_____

Vocabulary Terms
- wavelength
- electromagnetic spectrum
- spectrum

4 Apply As you learn the definition of each vocabulary term in this lesson, create your own definition or sketch to help you remember the meaning of the term.

(bkgd) ©Solar & Heliospheric Observatory consortium (ESA & NASA)/Science Source/Photo Researchers, Inc; (t) ©Photodisc/Getty Images

© Houghton Mifflin Harcourt Publishing Company

What is electromagnetic radiation?

Energy traveling as electromagnetic waves is called *electromagnetic radiation*. Waves can be described by either their wavelength or frequency. **Wavelength** is the distance between two adjacent crests or troughs of a wave. *Frequency* measures the number of waves passing a point per second. Higher-frequency waves have a shorter wavelength. Energy carried by electromagnetic radiation depends on both the wavelength and the amount of radiation at that wavelength. A higher-frequency wave carries higher energy than a lower-frequency wave.

How is electromagnetic radiation classified?

ACTIVE READING

5 Identify As you read, underline the name of each part of the electromagnetic spectrum.

There are many different wavelengths and frequencies of electromagnetic radiation. All these wavelengths and frequencies make up what is called the **electromagnetic spectrum**. A **spectrum** is a continuous range of a single feature, in this case wavelength. The form of electromagnetic radiation with the longest-wavelength and the lowest-frequency is radio waves. Radios and televisions receive radio waves. These receivers then produce sound waves. Sound waves are not electromagnetic radiation. Microwaves have shorter wavelengths and higher frequencies than radio waves. The next shorter wavelength radiation is called infrared. Infrared is sometimes called "heat radiation." Visible light has a shorter wavelength than infrared. You see an object when visible light from the object reaches your eyes. Images produced in visible light are the only images we can see without computer enhancement. Even shorter in wavelength is ultraviolet radiation. The shortest wavelengths belong to x-rays and gamma rays.

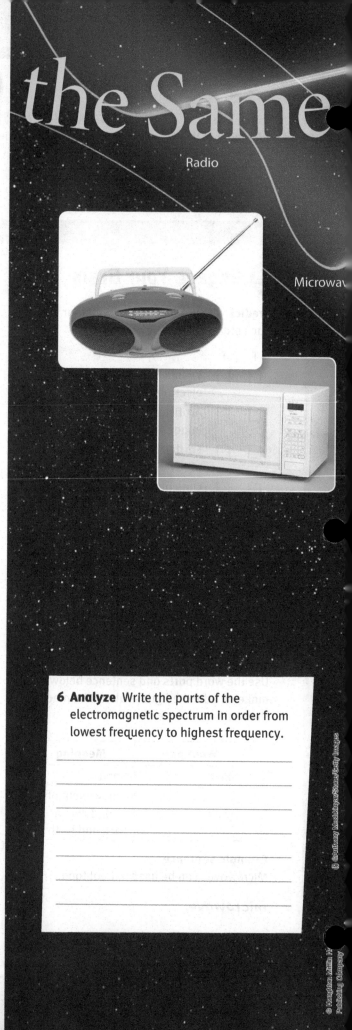

On the Same

Radio

Microwav

6 Analyze Write the parts of the electromagnetic spectrum in order from lowest frequency to highest frequency.

_____

_____

_____

_____

_____

_____

_____

Wavelength?

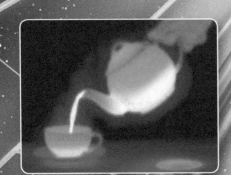

Infrared

Ultraviolet

Visible light

7 Complete Electromagnetic _____ that has a shorter wavelength has a _____ frequency.

X-rays

Gamma rays

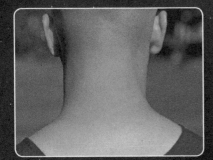

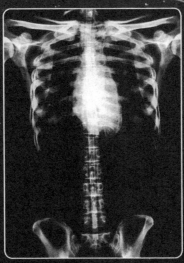

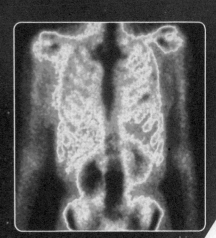

The Better to See You With

What are some characteristics of electromagnetic radiation?

Electromagnetic waves can be generated by devices such as cell phones, microwave ovens, and flashlights. Electromagnetic radiation is also generated by heat. Very cool material radiates, or emits energy, mostly as radio waves. Warmer objects may radiate mainly in the infrared. To emit visible light, an object must be hot. Light bulbs are good examples of hot objects that emit light.

Different portions of the electromagnetic spectrum interact differently with matter. Radio waves pass easily through space and the atmosphere. Using special equipment, infrared radiation allows someone to see room-temperature objects, even at night. Microwaves penetrate a small distance into many materials, where they are absorbed. The energy is released as heat. A microwave oven uses this property to cook food. Ultraviolet rays can cause materials to fluoresce (flu•RES), or glow. This property is used for many purposes, from criminal investigation to document protection. For example, documents can be protected against counterfeiting (KOUN•ter•fit•ing) if they use symbols that are detectable only by special lamps. X-rays pass through flesh easily but less easily through bone. Physicians and other doctors can use x-rays to examine the insides of your body.

In small amounts, electromagnetic radiation can be very useful. Large amounts of any type of radiation can cause problems because of the total amount of energy carried. For example, ultraviolet radiation can cause skin cancer. Gamma rays are especially dangerous to living organisms.

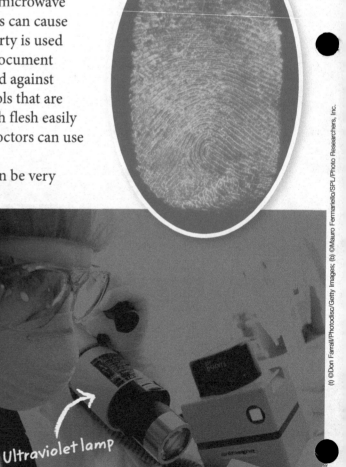

Under an ultraviolet lamp, fingerprints glow.

Ultraviolet lamp

(t) ©Don Farrall/Photodisc/Getty Images; (b) ©Mauro Fermariello/SPL/Photo Researchers, Inc.

© Houghton Mifflin Harcourt Publishing Company

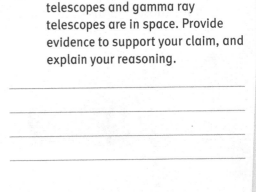

Electromagnetic Radiation and Earth's Surface

Radio Microwave Infrared Visible ↓ Ultraviolet X-ray Gamma rays

What electromagnetic radiation reaches Earth?

If Earth had no atmosphere, energy from the entire electromagnetic spectrum would reach Earth's surface. But not all wavelengths of the electromagnetic spectrum reach Earth's surface, as shown in the illustration above. In the atmosphere, atoms and molecules reflect some of the incoming radiation back into space. Atoms and molecules can also absorb some forms of electromagnetic radiation. For example, water vapor and carbon dioxide molecules absorb much of the infrared and microwave radiation. Most visible light and radio radiation reach Earth's surface.

The higher frequencies of ultraviolet radiation are absorbed by ozone in the atmosphere. Oxygen and nitrogen atoms absorb x-rays and gamma rays. X-rays and gamma rays have high enough energies to damage living tissue and other materials. Fortunately, they are absorbed by molecules in the atmosphere. Therefore, x-rays and gamma rays from space do not reach Earth's surface.

> **ⓘ 10 Claims • Evidence • Reasoning**
> Make a claim about why x-ray telescopes and gamma ray telescopes are in space. Provide evidence to support your claim, and explain your reasoning.
>
> _____
> _____
> _____
> _____

To See or Not to See

How do people detect electromagnetic radiation from objects in space?

Visible light from the sun, moon, planets, and stars can be detected by the human eye or a camera to form an image. Images of objects in space can tell us about their positions and properties. Telescopes are one way to learn about objects in space. They can be placed on mountain tops. Telescopes are also placed in space to collect radiation that does not reach Earth's surface.

All forms of electromagnetic radiation from space can be collected by telescopes. However, special detectors must be used to form images from radiation other than visible light. A radio receiver is used for radio waves. Infrared, x-ray, and gamma-ray detectors are used for those regions of the electromagnetic spectrum.

The Keck Observatory is on top of Mauna Kea, in Hawaii.

With Optical Telescopes
ACTIVE READING

11 Identify As you read, underline two types of optical telescopes.

Optical telescopes collect visible light with a mirror or a lens. A mirror reflects light, and a lens changes the direction of light rays as they pass through the lens. A telescope that uses a mirror to collect light is called a *reflecting telescope*. A telescope that uses a lens to collect light is a called a *refracting telescope*. The larger the lens or mirror, the more light that can be collected. With more light, the observer can view fainter objects. The light collected is then detected by the eye or other detector, such as a camera.

A reflecting telescope uses a mirror to gather and focus light.

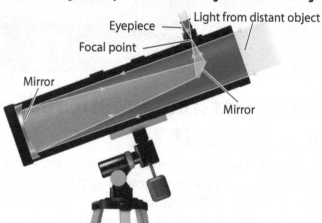

Eyepiece — Light from distant object
Focal point
Mirror
Mirror

A refracting telescope uses a lens to gather and focus light.

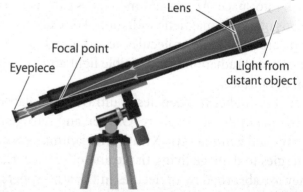

Lens
Focal point
Eyepiece
Light from distant object

With Non-Optical Telescopes
ACTIVE READING

12 Identify As you read, underline one example of electromagnetic radiation that non-optical telescopes detect.

The first telescopes were used to collect visible light. Today, however, astronomers use telescopes to observe in all parts of the electromagnetic spectrum. Most radio telescopes use metal mirrors to reflect radio waves. Radio waves are reflected onto a radio receiver at the focus. A satellite dish is an example of this kind of radio telescope. Radio waves have long wavelengths. Therefore, many radio telescopes are very large.

Telescopes are often used to produce images. First, the electromagnetic radiation that is collected must reach a detector that is sensitive to that wavelength, just like x-rays that pass through your teeth must reach a material sensitive to x-rays. Then the electromagnetic radiation is collected and processed through a computer to produce an image that we can see.

The computer software also adds color, called *false color*. The addition of false color highlights important details. For example, an image might be colored so that areas emitting low energy are dark and areas emitting high energy are bright. The brightness of an object tells the scientists how much energy that object is producing.

👁 Visualize It!

14 Claims • Evidence • Reasoning Compare the mirror in the reflecting telescope with the radio telescope. Make a claim about how the radio telescope is like a reflecting telescope. Summarize evidence to support your claim, and explain your reasoning.

_____

_____

_____

i Think Outside the Book

13 Apply Choose a wavelength from the electromagnetic spectrum other than visible light or x-rays. Imagine that you could look at an image of your hand produced using that wavelength. Then draw a picture of what you think your hand would look like.

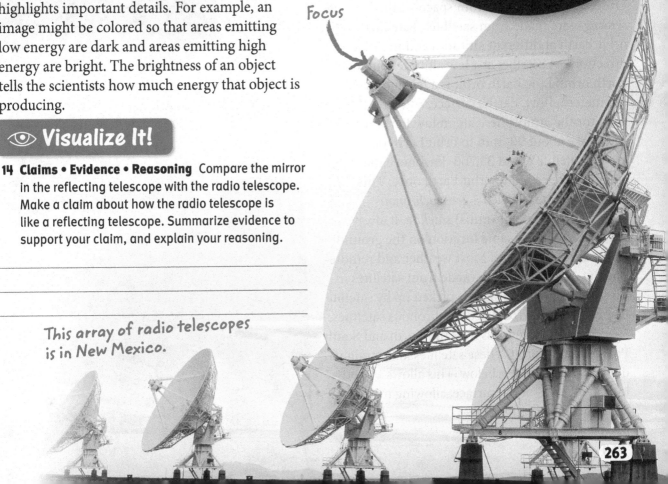

An artist's depiction of the Chandra X-ray Observatory in front of a nebula

Focus

This array of radio telescopes is in New Mexico.

The View from Above

The satellite scans the surface of the Earth.

The satellite transmits the data to a station on the ground.

How can people observe Earth from space?

ACTIVE READING

15 Identify As you read, underline three examples of satellite orbits.

Observations of Earth from space—called *remote sensing*—are made from satellites. Satellites orbit Earth at different altitudes and in different directions. A satellite at a low altitude is in low Earth orbit. Low Earth orbit is a few hundred kilometers above Earth's surface. Satellites that monitor the atmosphere are in low Earth orbits. They take about 90 min to orbit Earth once.

A satellite about 35,700 km above the equator takes 24 h to orbit Earth once. This type of satellite is called a *geosynchronous* (jee•oh•SINGK•kruh•nuhs) *satellite*. It always remains above the same location on the ground as Earth rotates below. Most weather and remote-sensing observations are made from satellites in this orbit. Television signals picked up by satellite dishes also come from geosynchronous satellites.

Some satellites pass over the North and South Poles on every orbit. These satellites look straight down as Earth rotates below. This allows a good look at all areas of the surface, allowing mapping and other observations.

What can you learn about Earth from satellite images?

Images from remote-sensing satellites provide a variety of information. They show evidence of human activity, such as cities. Remote-sensing images of the same place taken on different dates show how things change over time. For example, images of populated areas can show how development has changed over several years, as shown in the two images below of Las Vegas.

The lights seen in images taken at night indicate populated areas and highways. Infrared images can show forests and cleared areas, because trees appear cooler than bare land in infrared images. Images can also show forest fires and can be used to warn people of the danger. Weather satellites provide images of clouds and storms, such as hurricanes. Other images can show features in the atmosphere, such as the aurora and ozone variations.

Think Outside the Book

16 Apply Design your own remote-sensing satellite. Give it a function—what would you like your satellite to monitor? Give your satellite a name.

👁 Visualize It!

17 Claims • Evidence • Reasoning Make a claim about the change in urbanization between 1973 and 2006. Support your claim with evidence from these two images, and explain your reasoning.

_____

_____

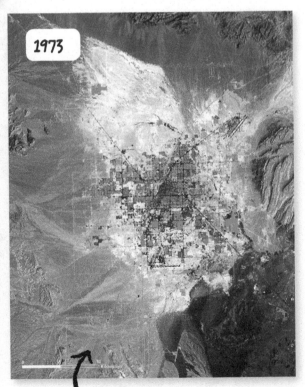

These false-color images of Las Vegas were produced by a satellite called Landsat. The green represents vegetation, and the lines represent city streets.

Seeing Is Believing

What can you learn from space images?

Visible light allows you to see the surfaces of planets and how other objects in space might look. Different types of radiation can be used to produce images to reveal features not visible to the eye. For example, infrared radiation can reveal the temperature of objects. Dust blocks visible light, but some wavelengths of infrared pass through dust, so scientists can see objects normally hidden by dust clouds in space. High-energy objects may be very bright in x-ray or gamma-ray radiation, although difficult to see at longer wavelengths. The four images of the Andromeda galaxy on the right were produced using wavelengths other than visible light, so the colors are all false colors.

👁 Visualize It!

18 Analyze Compare one image of the Andromeda galaxy on the opposite page with the image in visible light on this page.

_____

_____

_____

_____

_____

_____

_____

_____

The Andromeda galaxy in visible light

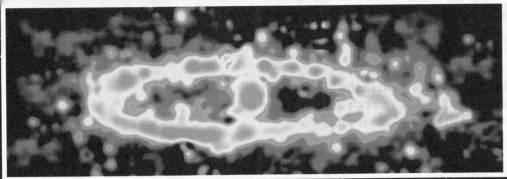

This image of the Andromeda galaxy was produced using radio waves. The reddish-orange color in the center and in the ring represents a source of radio waves. New stars are forming in the ring area.

In this infrared image of the Andromeda galaxy, you can see more detail in the structure of the galaxy. The dark areas within the bright rings are dust. The dust is so thick in some areas that radiation behind the dust is not getting through.

This image of the Andromeda galaxy was produced with a combination of ultraviolet and infrared radiation. The blue areas represent large, young, hot stars. The green areas represent older stars. The bright yellow spot at the very center of the galaxy represents an extremely dense area of old stars.

Visual Summary

To complete this summary, fill in the blanks with the correct word or phrase. You can use this page to review the main concepts of the lesson.

Images from Space

The electromagnetic spectrum is all the wavelengths and frequencies of electromagnetic radiation.

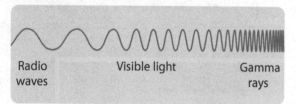

Radio waves   Visible light   Gamma rays

19 *Two parts of the electromagnetic spectrum between visible light and gamma rays are*

_____

_____

Different types of telescopes are used to detect different ranges of electromagnetic radiation.

20 *Optical telescopes detect*

_____

Telescopes are available for every portion of the electromagnetic spectrum. Different types of radiation reveal various features not visible to the eye.

21 *These two images of Saturn are different because they were made using different wavelengths of*

_____

_____

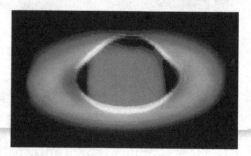

22 Claims • Evidence • Reasoning Make a claim about how images from space of Earth and other objects are useful. Provide evidence to support your claim, and explain your reasoning.

Lesson Review

Vocabulary

Fill in the blank with the term that best completes the following sentences.

1 The distance between two adjacent crests of a wave is called its _____.

2 The _____ is all the wavelengths of electromagnetic radiation.

3 A _____ is a continuous range of a single feature, such as wavelength.

Key Concepts

4 Claims • Evidence • Reasoning State why telescopes that detect non-optical radiation are useful for studying objects in space. Support your claim with evidence and an example, and explain your reasoning.

_____

_____

_____

5 Identify List three examples of telescopes that detect different types of electromagnetic radiation.

_____

_____

_____

6 Explain Describe how wavelength, frequency, and energy are related.

_____

_____

_____

7 Explain Describe one type of electromagnetic radiation that can cause harm to humans.

_____

_____

_____

Critical Thinking

Use this diagram to answer the following questions.

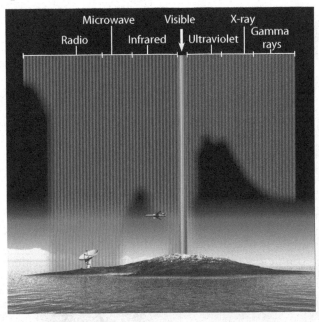

8 Analyze Some infrared radiation reaches Earth, and some does not. Which part does reach Earth—longer wavelength infrared or shorter wavelength infrared?

_____

_____

9 Analyze List two other types of electromagnetic radiation that reach Earth's surface.

_____

_____

10 Claims • Evidence • Reasoning Make a claim about how remote sensing satellites can help people stay safe from massive fires. Summarize evidence to support your claim, and explain your reasoning.

_____

_____

_____

_____

_____

PEOPLE **IN SCIENCE**

SC.8.N.4.1 Explain that science is one of the processes that can be used to inform decision making at the community, state, national, and international levels.

Sandra Faber

ASTRONOMER

What do you do when you send a telescope into space and then find out that it is broken? You call Dr. Sandra Faber, a professor of astronomy at the University of California, Santa Cruz (UCSC). In April 1990, after the *Hubble Space Telescope* went into orbit, scientists found that the images the telescope collected were not turning out as expected. Dr. Faber's team at UCSC was in charge of a device on *Hubble* called the *Wide Field Planetary Camera*. Dr. Faber and her team decided to test the telescope to determine what was wrong.

To perform the test, they centered *Hubble* onto a bright star and took several photos. From those photos, Dr. Faber's team created a model of what was wrong. After reporting the error to NASA and presenting the model they had developed, Dr. Faber and a group of experts began to correct the problem. The group's efforts were a success and put *Hubble* back into operation so that astronomers could continue researching stars and other objects in space.

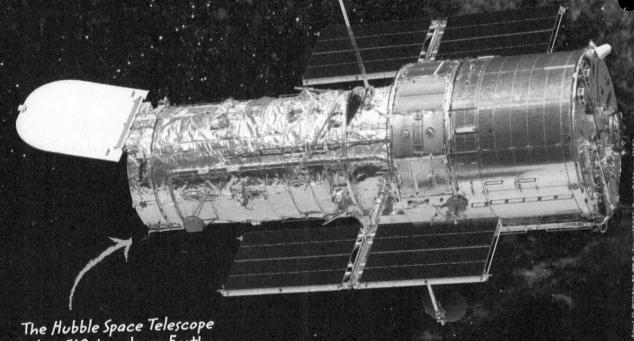

The Hubble Space Telescope orbits 569 km above Earth.

📖 Language Arts Connection

Suppose you are a journalist preparing to interview Dr. Sandra Faber. List four questions you would ask her.

JOB BOARD

Astronautical Engineer

What You'll Do: Work on spacecraft that operate outside of Earth's atmosphere, like satellites or space shuttles. Other tasks include planning space missions, determining orbits of spacecraft, and designing rockets and communications systems.

Where You Might Work: Most likely with space agencies. You may also find jobs with aerospace companies or the military.

Education: All engineers must have a four-year college degree in aerospace or astronautical engineering. Many engineers go on to earn a master's degree and a doctorate. Basic engineering classes include algebra, calculus, physics, and computer programming.

Other Job Requirements: You should be able to work well with a team. You should be very careful and exact in your calculations and measurements.

Robotics Technician

What You'll Do: Help engineers build and operate robots, and work with robotic engineers on robotic tools for spacecraft. Use software to solve problems and to test equipment as part of your daily routine.

Where You Might Work: Government space agencies such as NASA, the auto industry, schools, laboratories, and manufacturing plants.

Education: Most technicians complete a two-year technical certificate. Technicians should have a strong interest in math and science. Professional certification is offered to technicians who have at least four years of work experience.

Other Job Requirements: You may also be asked to read blueprints, use microcomputers, and use oscilloscopes.

Technology for Space Exploration

ESSENTIAL QUESTION

How do people explore space?

By the end of this lesson, you should be able to analyze the ways people explore outer space and assess the role of technology in these efforts.

SC.8.N.1.5 Analyze the methods used to develop a scientific explanation as seen in different fields of science. **SC.8.N.4.1** Explain that science is one of the processes that can be used to inform decision making at the community, state, national, and international levels. **SC.8.N.4.2** Explain how political, social, and economic concerns can affect science, and vice versa. **SC.8.E.5.10** Assess how technology is essential to science for such purposes as access to outer space and other remote locations, sample collection, measurement, data collection and storage, computation, and communication of information.

This artist's depiction shows the rover named Spirit on Mars. Sending robots to other bodies in the solar system is just one way to explore distant objects.

Lesson Labs

Quick Lab
• Splitting White Light

S.T.E.M. Lab
• Build a Rocket

Engage Your Brain

1 Predict Check T or F to show whether you think each statement is true or false.

T   F

☐   ☐   The space shuttle can travel to the moon.

☐   ☐   Satellites in space can help you find directions on Earth.

☐   ☐   Objects farther than the moon are so far away that it can take years to reach them.

☐   ☐   Satellites orbiting Earth can provide a wealth of information on weather and Earth's surface features.

2 Identify Look at the picture below. Write a caption that explains what the picture shows.

ACTIVE **READING**

3 Synthesize You can often define an unknown word if you know the meaning of its word parts. Use the word parts and sentence below to make an educated guess about the meaning of the word *composite*.

Word part	Meaning
com-	together
-posit	put, place

Example sentence
The satellite took all the available data and created a <u>composite</u> image of Earth's surface.

composite:

_____

_____

Vocabulary Terms

• **probe**   • **artificial satellite**

4 Apply As you learn the definition of each vocabulary term in this lesson, create your own definition or sketch to help you remember the meaning of the term.

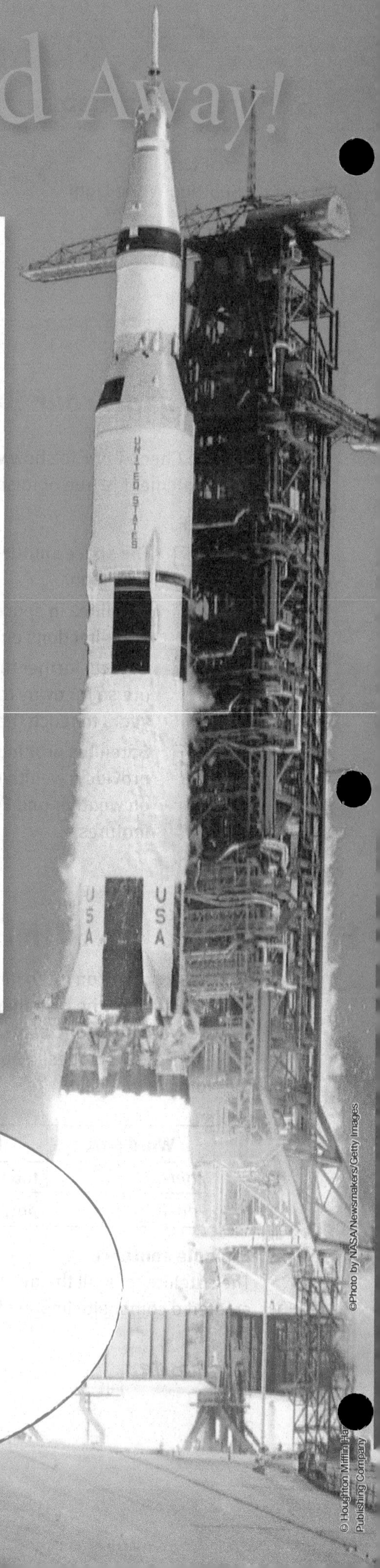

How do people travel to space?

On April 21, 1961, Yuri Gagarin became the first human to orbit Earth. Since then, people have continued to travel to space to learn more about the universe. Large rockets were the first method of transportation into space. The space shuttle, which was first launched in 1981, uses smaller rockets.

With Large Rockets

Humans visited the moon six times between 1969 and 1972, during the *Apollo* program. To travel away from Earth, large rockets were needed to overcome the pull of Earth's gravity. The capsules (KAP•suhls) containing the astronauts detached from the large rockets. The capsules were not reusable.

With Space Shuttles

Columbia, the first space shuttle, was launched on April 12, 1981. Space shuttles were used to travel to and from orbits close to Earth. The space shuttle missions helped build, man, and supply the *International Space Station (ISS)*. NASA, the space agency of the United States, completed 135 shuttle missions before the program ended in 2011. After the space shuttle program ended, astronauts traveled to the ISS in the *Soyuz* Russian spacecraft.

5 Compare Fill in the Venn diagram to compare and contrast two ways of traveling to space.

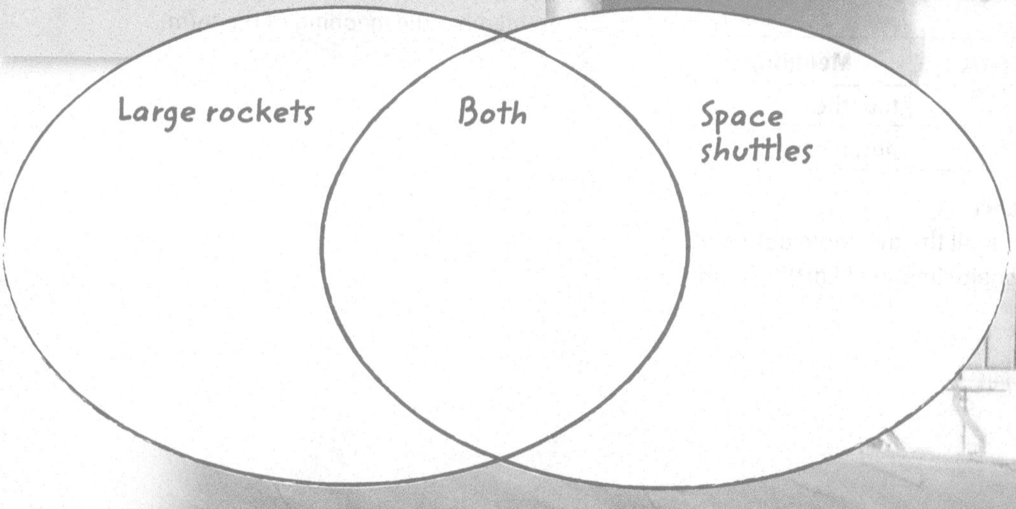

Large rockets   Both   Space shuttles

How do people return from space?

ACTIVE READING

6 Identify As you read, underline three ways that people return to Earth from space.

The space shuttle returned to Earth on a runway, like an airplane runway. When the shuttle landed, a parachute opened to help slow it down. In earlier space missions, the astronauts returned to Earth in a capsule and landed in the ocean. This type of landing was called a "splashdown." The astronauts from the *Apollo* moon missions landed this way. There is another method to return to Earth from space. The capsules containing the crew can parachute to land instead of water. When Russian crew members return to Earth from the *International Space Station*, they use parachutes to land their *Soyuz* capsule on the ground.

The space shuttle lands on a runway.

How are people limited when traveling in space?

People may someday travel to other objects in the solar system, such as Mars. There are many technological challenges to overcome first, such as having enough fuel for a long, return voyage. Other challenges are having enough air, water, and food for the return trip. Another serious challenge is having a spacecraft that is well insulated from the intense cold in space as well as the dangerous radiation from the sun and from deep space.

Astronauts can spend only a short amount of time living on a space shuttle or in a space station. Although the shuttle and the space station have everything necessary for humans to live and work in space, the living space is very limited. Also, in a space environment everything seems weightless (WAYT•lis). Everyday tasks like going to the washroom and sleeping are difficult. The toilet on the space station is a large vacuum toilet with a strong suction, which is not very pleasant. To avoid drifting away when they sleep, crew members strap themselves to their beds.

In space, the astronauts do not use their legs and back the way they do on Earth. So the bones and muscles weaken. To help strengthen their bones and muscles, the astronauts must exercise every day they are in space.

Astronauts must exercise daily.

7 Identify List three limitations of human space travel.

_____

_____

_____

Looking Up

This false-color image of a nebula was taken by the Hubble Space Telescope.

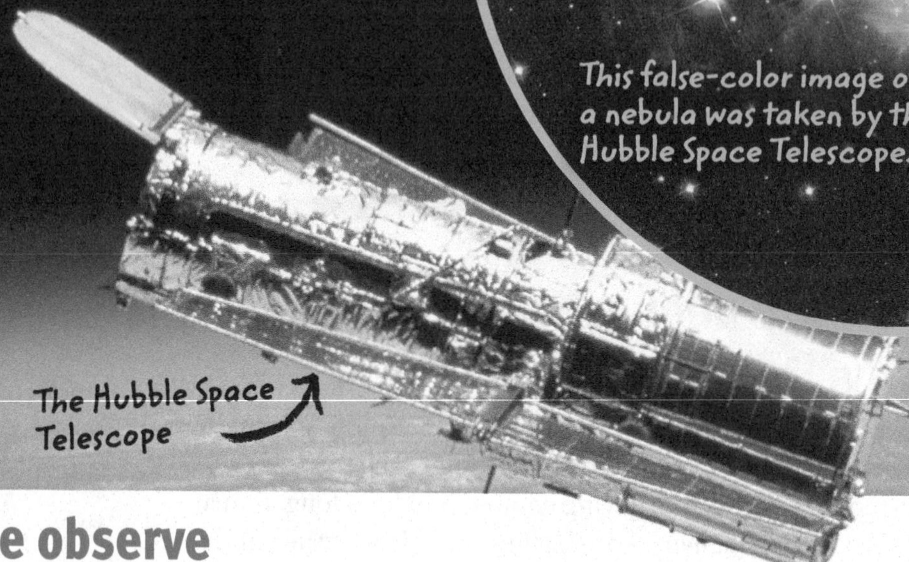

The Hubble Space Telescope

How can people observe distant objects in space?

ACTIVE READING

8 Identify As you read, underline three ways that people can observe distant objects in space.

Most objects in space are just too far away for people to visit. To learn about distant objects, scientists and engineers have developed different ways to gather information about them. Because Earth's atmosphere distorts the light entering it, some telescopes are placed in space above the atmosphere. The computers on the telescopes gather data on an object and send the data to Earth. Scientists and engineers also send spacecraft to fly near or land on distant objects and collect information.

Another way to study distant objects such as planets and comets is to send a probe to gather data and analyze samples. No matter which method is used, all require computer technology.

Using Telescopes in Space

Telescopes in space, such as the Hubble Space Telescope shown above, have produced many exciting images. The Hubble Space Telescope is a reflecting telescope. It was placed in orbit around Earth in 1990, about 600 km above Earth's surface. The Hubble Space Telescope detects light from objects in space, and sends images back to Earth. The telescope also detects radiation other than visible light, such as ultraviolet and infrared radiation.

Other telescopes detect information from different types of electromagnetic radiation. The Compton Gamma-Ray Observatory was sent into orbit in 1991. The Chandra X-Ray Observatory was launched eight years later. The Spitzer Space Telescope was launched in 2003, the Fermi Gamma-Ray Space Telescope in 2008, and the Herschel Space Observatory in 2009. These telescopes were placed in space because Earth's atmosphere blocks most x-rays and gamma rays.

Cassini was launched in 1997 and reached Saturn in 2004. (Artist's impression)

Pieces of the comet particle trapped in aerogel

Using Uncrewed Spacecraft

At the present time, humans cannot travel to other planets. One obstacle to such a trip is that it would take years because the planets are so far away. Another obstacle is the harsh conditions on other planets, such as extreme temperatures. Some planets, such as Saturn, do not even have solid surfaces to land on.

Using uncrewed spacecraft (no humans aboard) is one way to explore such remote places. Uncrewed spacecraft pose no risk to human life and are less expensive than missions involving astronauts. After traveling for seven years and about 3.5 billion km, the spacecraft *Cassini* reached Saturn and returned exciting images.

Using Space Probes

A space **probe** is an uncrewed vehicle that carries scientific instruments to distant objects in space. A probe's instruments can identify gases and measure properties such as temperature. Probes are especially useful for exploring the deep atmospheres of the gas giant planets.

In 2004, NASA's *Stardust* space probe flew close to Comet Wild (VILT) 2. The probe collected samples from the comet. *Stardust* used a silicon-based substance called *aerogel* to collect the comet particles. The image above shows a section of an aerogel block that a comet particle crashed into. The space probe returned the particles to Earth in 2006 for analysis. For the first time, samples from beyond the orbit of the moon were brought back to Earth.

Using Computer Technology

Space exploration cannot happen without computers. Computers and other technologies are used to launch and control spacecraft and instruments, to navigate spacecraft, and to send and receive instructions and information. Computers collect data of many types and send the data to Earth. Once the data are collected, computers are used to analyze the data. For example, computers process data from space telescopes and probes to produce images.

Think Outside the Book

9 Identify Make a poster that compares sending probes into space with sending humans into space.

Looking Down

How are satellites used?

Satellites affect our lives everyday, even if we do not realize it. An **artificial satellite** is any human-made object placed in orbit around a body in space. Some examples are remote-sensing, weather, and communication satellites. Navigation satellites, such as those used in search and rescue operations, are also in Earth orbit. Images taken by satellites can be combined to produce composite images. Military satellites monitor the movement of military equipment on the ground. They can also detect missile launches.

ACTIVE READING

10 Identify As you read, underline five examples of different satellites.

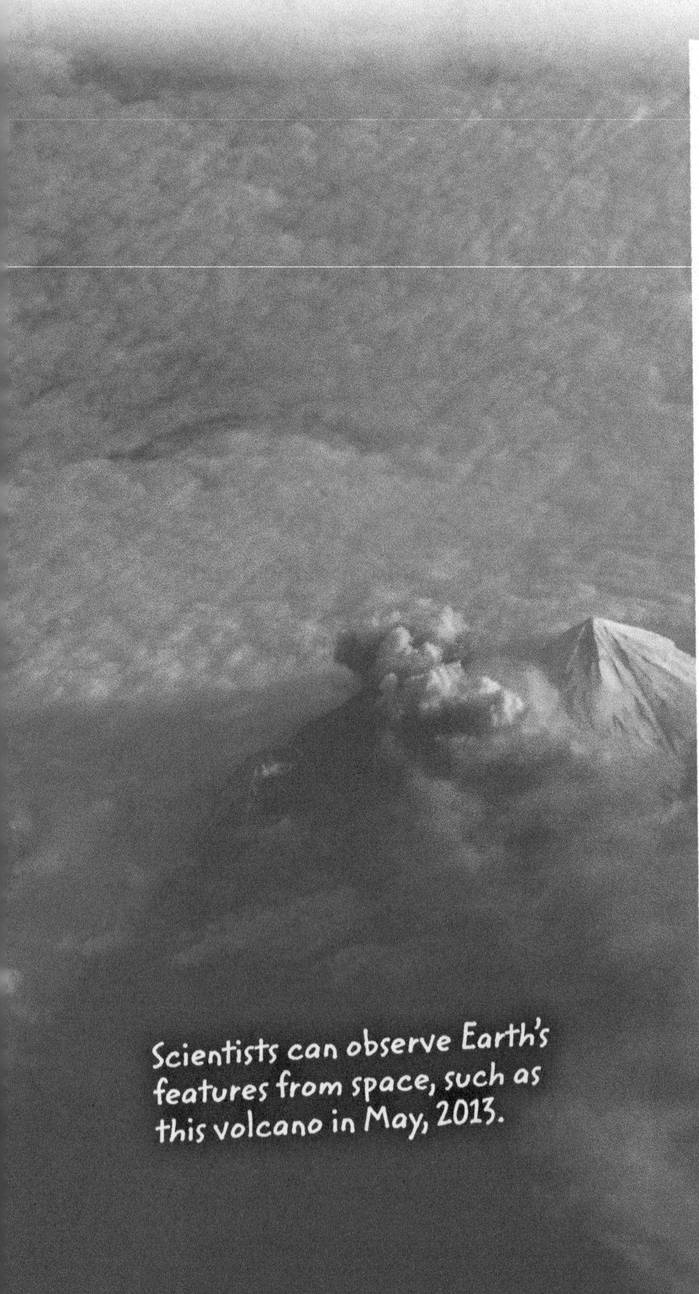

To Study Earth's Surface Features

Scientists can use remote-sensing satellites to study Earth. Remote sensing is a way to collect information about something without physically being there. Remote-sensing satellites are used to map and monitor Earth's resources. For example, remote-sensing satellites identify sources of pollution, monitor crops to watch the spread of disease, and monitor global temperatures as well as ocean and land heights. They also monitor the amount of freshwater ice and sea ice.

The crew onboard the *International Space Station* acted like a remote-sensing satellite when they photographed a volcano during an early stage of eruption, shown here. Photos of volcanoes taken from space are valuable because they show viewpoints that scientists would not have been able to see from Earth.

11 Claims • Evidence • Reasoning Make a claim about two features on Earth's surface, not given as an example here, that might be studied from space. Support your claim with evidence, and explain your reasoning.

_____

_____

_____

Scientists can observe Earth's features from space, such as this volcano in May, 2013.

To Monitor Changes Over Time

Remote-sensing data can also provide valuable information on how Earth's surface is changing over time. For example, for over 30 years, satellites have been observing the Arctic sea ice. Images from the European Space Agency's ENVISAT satellite show that there has been a large decline in Arctic sea ice coverage over the past several years. Satellite images help scientists track the changes in Arctic ice cover so they can understand why the ice coverage is changing.

Images taken by the remote-sensing satellite called Landsat show changes in the Mississippi delta over time. When comparing an image taken in 1984 with an image taken in 2014 (shown on the right), scientists can see how the delta has changed shape. Scientists can also monitor how much land is under water now compared with how much land was under water in 1984.

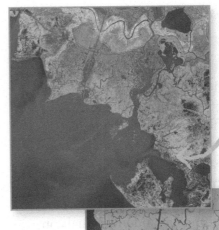

The light blue shows the shape of the delta in 1984.

The light blue here shows the shape of the delta in 2014. The black represents the water in the dark blue Gulf of Mexico.

To Collect Weather Information

It is difficult to imagine life without reliable weather forecasts. Every day, millions of people make decisions based on information provided by weather satellites. Weather satellites provide a big-picture view of Earth's atmosphere. These satellites constantly monitor the atmosphere for the events that lead to severe weather conditions. For example, weather satellites can provide images of hurricanes. Images of a hurricane can help scientists predict the path the hurricane might take. In this way, people living in the hurricane path can be warned to move to a safer place until the hurricane passes.

Weather satellites also monitor changes in cloud formation and heat coming from Earth. In addition, aircraft pilots depend on weather satellites for information to make sure they avoid dangerous weather.

In 2017, Hurricane Irma spanned almost 700 kilometers across as it move through the Caribbean and through the state of Florida.

12 Claims • Evidence • Reasoning Make a claim that tells three ways weather satellite information is useful to people. Use evidence to support your claim, and explain your reasoning.

_____

_____

_____

For Search and Rescue Operations

The U.S. National Oceanic and Atmospheric Administration (NOAA) has many different satellites. NOAA's environmental satellites carry an instrument package called SARSAT. The SARSAT instruments detect distress signals from emergency beacons (BEE•kuhnz). Many ships, airplanes, and individuals on land have emergency beacons. The beacons can be used anywhere in the world, at any time of day. Once the distress signals are received, the satellites relay the signals to a network of rescue coordination centers, as shown in the illustration. In the end, the signals go to the U.S. Mission Control Center in Maryland. The Mission Control Center processes the emergency and puts the search and rescue operation into action.

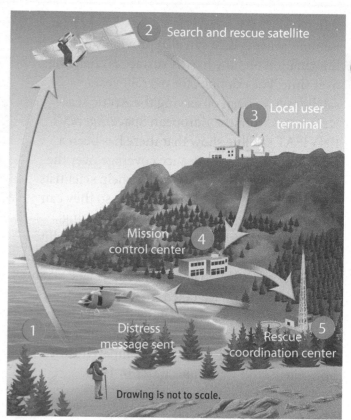

2 Search and rescue satellite

3 Local user terminal

Mission control center 4

1 Distress message sent

5 Rescue coordination center

Drawing is not to scale.

Steps involved in a search and rescue operation

The red areas produce the most light.

To Provide Composite Images

Data from satellites can be combined into one image to get more complete information. The combined image is called a *composite* image. Composite satellite images can give very detailed information about an area's surface features and other features. For example, satellite images can be combined to produce a dramatic image that shows where most of the sources of artifical light are located, as shown here. A composite image that shows aritifical light sources would include images of Earth with no cloud clover.

13 Claims • Evidence • Reasoning Why might it have been necessary to combine two images to produce a picture of this part of Earth's surface? Support your claim by summarizing evidence, and explain your reasoning.

_____

_____

_____

_____

Exploring the Ocean

It may not seem like it, but deep-sea exploration and space exploration have something in common. Both use advanced technologies to observe locations that are difficult or dangerous for humans to explore.

Ocean Submersibles

Both marine scientists and space scientists investigate areas most humans will never visit. Ocean submersibles can be crewed or uncrewed.

Black Smokers
Hydrothermal vents are on the ocean floor where the pressure is too great for humans to withstand.

Tube Worms
In the 1970s, scientists aboard a submersible discovered giant tube worms living near an ocean vent. NASA scientists examine the extreme conditions of Mars and other planets for any signs of life.

(top) ©Ralph White/Corbis; (l) ©B. Murton/Southampton Oceanography Centre/Photo Researchers, Inc.; (r) ©NURP/UNCW and NOAA/FGBNMS

©Houghton Mifflin Harcourt Publishing Company

Extend

14 Support Your Claim Deep sea exploration and space exploration are similar. Support this claim with evidence.

15 Research and Record List some features of an ocean submersible, for example, *Alvin*. How is the submersible's structure similar to that of spacecraft?

16 Recommend Support more funding for deep-sea exploration by doing one of the following:
• write a letter
• design an ad for a science magazine
• write a script for a radio commercial

For Communication

Communications satellites relay data, including Internet service and some television and radio broadcasts. They are also used to relay long-distance telephone calls. One communications satellite can relay thousands of telephone calls or several television programs at once. Communications satellites are in use continuously.

Communications satellites relay the television signals to the consumers.

ACTIVE READING

17 Identify As you read, number the sequence of steps required to get a television signal to your television set.

For Relaying Information to Distant Locations on Earth

How do you send a television signal to someone on the other side of Earth? The problem is that Earth is round, and the signals travel in a straight line. Communications satellites are the answer. A television signal is sent from a point on Earth's surface to a communications satellite. Then, the satellite sends the signal to receivers in other locations, as shown in the diagram. Small satellite dishes on the roofs of houses or outside apartments collect the signals. The signals are then sent to the customer's television set.

18 Claims • Evidence • Reasoning Make a claim about whether satellites are useful for communication. Use evidence to support your claim, and explain your reasoning.

_____

_____

_____

_____

Drawing is not to scale.

19 Apply Write a caption for the image shown here.

For GPS Satellites

Did you know that satellite technology can actually help keep you from getting lost? The Global Positioning System (GPS) is a network of 24 satellites that orbit Earth. GPS satellites continuously send microwave signals. A GPS receiver receives signals from at least four satellites at one time. Once a GPS receiver on Earth picks up the signals, the technology in the receiver can determine the location of the receiver on Earth's surface. Airplane and boat pilots use GPS for navigation. Many cars now have GPS units that show information on a screen on the dashboard.

The satellites shown here are GPS satellites.

Modern GPS units are small enough to hold in your hand, so you can take them with you and know your location anywhere you go!

Visual Summary

To complete this summary, fill in the blanks with the correct word or phrase. You can use this page to review the main concepts of the lesson.

Space Exploration Technology

There are different ways that humans travel to and from space.

20 The space shuttle and vehicles traveling farther than the space shuttle use

_____

Different technologies are used to study distant objects in space.

21 Three different ways that scientists study distant objects in space are

_____

_____

_____

Artificial satellites provide a wealth of information about Earth.

22 Satellites can provide images for remote sensing, communications, navigation, and

_____

The GPS system of satellites helps with navigation.

23 GPS receivers on Earth pick up signals from satellites, which can then be used to determine your

_____

24 **Claims • Evidence • Reasoning** Make a claim about the role of technology in efforts to explore space. Summarize evidence to support your claim, and explain your reasoning.

Lesson Review

Vocabulary

Fill in the blank with the term that best completes the following sentences.

1 A/An _____ is a manufactured object that orbits Earth or another celestial object.

2 A space _____ is an uncrewed vehicle that carries scientific instruments into space to collect scientific data.

Key Concepts

Use this diagram to answer the following question.

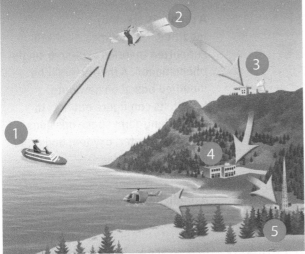

Drawing is not to scale.

3 Analyze Write the steps for each stage in the search and rescue operation.

_____

_____

_____

_____

_____

4 Describe Provide one example of how satellites are useful for communication.

_____

_____

5 Identify List three technologies that humans use to observe objects that are difficult to visit.

_____

_____

_____

6 Provide List three examples of observations of Earth by remote-sensing satellites.

_____

_____

_____

7 Explain Describe one technology used to travel to space and one technology used to return from space.

_____

_____

_____

8 Claims • Evidence • Reasoning Make a claim about how technology assists people with data and sample collection. Use evidence to support your claim, and explain your reasoning.

_____

_____

_____

_____

Critical Thinking

9 Claims • Evidence • Reasoning Make a claim about one limit of human space exploration not mentioned in the text. Use evidence to support your claim, and explain your reasoning.

_____

_____

_____

10 Apply List two instances in your daily life in which you could benefit from using a GPS unit.

_____

_____

SC.8.N.1.3 Use phrases such as "results support" or "fail to support" in science, understanding that science does not offer conclusive 'proof' of a knowledge claim.
SC.8.N.3.2 Explain why theories may be modified but are rarely discarded.

Testing and Modifying Theories

When scientists develop a theory, they use experiments to investigate the theory. The results of experiments can support or disprove theories. If the results of several experiments do not support a theory, it may be modified.

Tutorial

Read below about the Tomatosphere Project to find out more about how theories are tested and modified. This project exposes tomato seeds to simulated Martian conditions to observe later seed germination.

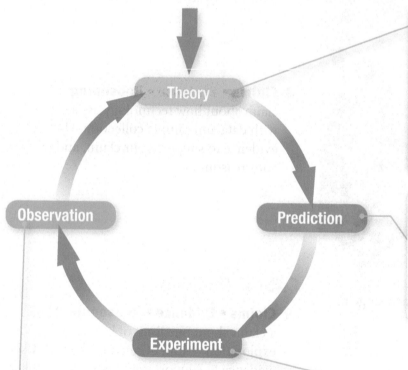

A theory is created/ modified. Sometimes, two well-supported theories explain a single phenomenon. A theory might be modified based on new data. Scientists can figure out how to supply long-term space missions with food, water, oxygen, and other life-support needs.

A prediction is made. Predictions are based on prior knowledge. Scientists might predict that if tomato seeds are exposed to Martian conditions, they will still be able to germinate and grow into healthy, fruit-bearing plants.

Observations are made. Scientists evaluate their observations to see whether or not the results support their hypothesis. If any data disprove the original prediction, scientists may have to modify their theory. The results of the blind studies are gathered and analyzed to see whether exposure to harsh conditions affected the germination of the seeds.

Experiments are done. Setting up the proper scientific procedure to test the prediction is important. In the Tomatosphere Project, a set of exposed seeds, along with a control group of regular seeds, are planted in thousands of classrooms. At least 20 of each type were planted, to ensure a large enough sample size. The type of seeds were not revealed, as part of a blind study.

You Try It!

Two scientists describe theories that try to explain the motion of galaxies. Use the information provided to answer the questions that follow.

Background

Any objects that have mass, such as Earth and you, exert a gravitational force that pulls them toward each other. An unexpected motion of an object in space, such as a galaxy, could be the result of an unseen object pulling on it. Scientists use electromagnetic radiation, such as visible, infrared, and ultraviolet light, to detect and study visible matter. However, dark matter is a hypothetical material that does not give off electromagnetic radiation that we can detect.

Scientist A

There is more dark matter than visible matter in galaxies. There is just too little visible matter to exert the force that would explain how the galaxies move. The additional force exerted by dark matter would explain the motion we see without having to change our understanding of gravitational force.

Scientist B

We must change our understanding of gravitational force. The farther away from the center of a galaxy you go, the stronger (not weaker) the gravitational force becomes. With this change, the amount of visible matter is enough to explain how the galaxies move. Dark matter is not needed.

1 Claims • Evidence • Reasoning Make a claim about how each scientist's theory would be affected if there were proof that dark matter exists. Provide evidence to support your claim, and explain your reasoning.

_____

_____

_____

_____

_____

3 Claims • Evidence • Reasoning Make a claim about what evidence would require both scientists to modify their theories. Support your claim with evidence, and explain your reasoning.

_____

_____

_____

_____

_____

2 Predicting Outcomes If experiments fail to detect dark matter, does Scientist A's theory need to be modified? Explain your reasoning.

_____

_____

_____

_____

Take It Home!

Using the Internet, research a scientific theory that has been reproduced in two different experiments. Write a short report that explains how the observations helped develop the theory. How else could this theory could be investigated?

Space Exploration and Florida

ESSENTIAL QUESTION

How has space exploration affected Florida?

By the end of this lesson, you should be able to summarize the effects of space exploration on the economy and culture of Florida.

The space shuttle Atlantis lifts off from the Kennedy Space Center.

SC.8.N.4.1 Explain that science is one of the processes that can be used to inform decision making at the community, state, national, and international levels. **SC.8.N.4.2** Explain how political, social, and economic concerns can affect science, and vice versa. **SC.8.E.5.12** Summarize the effects of space exploration on the economy and culture of Florida.

Lesson Labs

Quick Labs
- Florida Economics without NASA
- Florida Culture without NASA

Field Lab
- Build a Rocket

 Engage Your Brain

1 Predict Underline the correct word or words to complete each statement.

Florida is *north/south* of the equator.

A rocket or spacecraft is set in motion by a *space elevator/launch* at a space complex.

Launch sites are near an ocean to *capture rocket debris/provide recreation for the astronauts*.

The space exploration industry brings *little/much* revenue to the state of Florida.

A spinoff is a type of *technology/cycling competition*.

2 Identify On the map below, label the state of Florida and the equator.

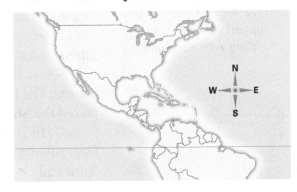

ACTIVE **READING**

3 Synthesize An acronym is a word that is formed from the first letter or letters of each of the successive major parts of a term. For example, the word *laser* is an acronym for **L**ight **A**mplification by **S**timulated **E**mission of **R**adiation. Use the letters in the table below to make an educated guess about the words that make up the acronym *NASA*.

Letter	Word
N	
A	
S	
A	

Vocabulary Terms

- NASA
- spinoff
- launch

4 Apply As you learn the definition of each vocabulary term in this lesson, create your own definition or sketch to help you remember the meaning of the term.

A History of Space

ACTIVE READING

5 Identify As you read, underline the four words that make up the acronym *NASA*.

6 Claims • Evidence • Reasoning Make a claim about how the focus of the missions changed after 1972. Provide evidence to support your claim, and explain your reasoning.

_____

_____

_____

_____

_____

What is NASA's history?

The National Aeronautics and Space Administration, or **NASA**, was formed in 1958. In 1961, President Kennedy announced his goal of sending humans to the moon. So, NASA's earlier programs focused on launches of spacecraft to prepare for flights to the moon. A **launch** is the process of setting a rocket or spacecraft in motion. The first such NASA flight was project *Mercury*, between 1961 and 1963. Project *Gemini*, between 1965 and 1966, was next. The moon flights of the *Apollo* program took place between 1968 and 1972. The first space station, called *Skylab*, operated between 1973 and 1974. Space shuttle flights began in 1981. In 1998, assembly of the *International Space Station* was begun.

NASA also launches Earth satellites and probes to other planets. The highly successful *Mars Pathfinder*, launched in 1996, placed the Mars rover called *Sojourner* on the surface of that planet in 1997. In 2004, NASA sent two more rovers, called *Spirit* and *Opportunity*, to explore the Martian surface for several months. *Spirit* and *Opportunity* remained active for over five years.

1970

1960

1950

1961–1963 The first American astronauts flew in the *Mercury* program. Only one astronaut at a time flew in each *Mercury* spacecraft.

John Glenn

1965–1966 Pairs of astronauts flew in the *Gemini* spacecraft. The word "gemini" means *twins* in Latin.

Tom Stafford (left) and Wally Schirra (right)

1968–1972 The flights to the moon carried three astronauts. The first moon landing was in 1969, with *Apollo 11*. The last moon landing was *Apollo 17* in 1972. A total of 12 astronauts have walked on the moon.

Neil Armstrong (left), Michael Collins (center), Buzz Aldrin (right)

2017

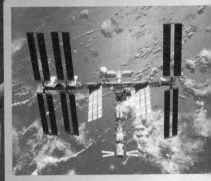

2000

The launch of the space shuttle *Atlantis*

1990

1980

Present Many countries participate in scientific research aboard the *International Space Station*. Rovers *Spirit* and *Opportunity* have spent over a decade providing new information to help prepare for the next mission, manned flight to Mars.

1997 The *Mars Pathfinder* placed a vehicle, called a rover, on Mars. The *Sojourner* rover explored the Martian surface for nearly three months.

1981 Shuttle flights began in 1981. From Earth orbit, the space shuttle launched and retrieved satellites. The space shuttle also went to the *International Space Station*. The space shuttle mission ended in 2011.

1973–1979 Three groups of astronauts, three at a time, were on *Skylab* from 1973 to 1974. In 1979, *Skylab* re-entered Earth's atmosphere.

7 Calculate For approximately how many years has NASA been in existence?

_____

_____

Cape Space

What are the NASA sites in Florida?

ACTIVE READING

8 Identify As you read, underline two NASA sites in Florida.

The first NASA space operations were carried out at the Cape Canaveral Air Force Station, which is on the coast of Florida, east of Orlando, in Brevard County. In 1962, NASA established the Kennedy Space Center on Merritt Island near Cape Canaveral. The space center is the largest launch complex in the United States. NASA conducts scientific research and launches space probes and satellites from Cape Canaveral. The *Apollo* moon missions launched from a launch complex at the Kennedy Space Center. The space shuttles launched from the Kennedy Space Center. Also located at the Kennedy Space Center is the Kennedy Space Center Visitor Complex, which has interesting and educational public activities.

Jacksonville

Orlando

Launch complex at Cape Canaveral

Naples

Kennedy Space Center

Miami

Florida Keys

👁 Visualize It!

9 Identify Are the NASA sites located on the east coast or west coast of Florida?

_____

_____

Why launch from Cape Canaveral?

The first suggestion to launch spacecraft from Florida appeared in Jules Verne's novel *From the Earth to the Moon*, in 1865. His characters select Florida as the launch site because Florida is close to the equator. Almost 100 years later, NASA chose Florida for the same reason. At the equator, Earth's surface rotates toward the east at about 1,670 km/h because of Earth's rotation. The speed becomes smaller as you move toward the poles. A rocket launched from Cape Canaveral starts out with about 1,467 km/h added speed when launched toward the east. A rocket launched from a location near the equator needs less fuel to reach orbit than a rocket launched farther from the equator needs.

Eastward launches over open water also provide a safe place for booster rockets and fuel tanks to fall. In addition, early in NASA's history, Brevard County was a rural citrus-growing region with a low population density. There also were nearby military bases available, so the area already had good roads.

45°N Circumference = 28,337 km
Speed = 1,181 km/h

28.5°N Circumference = 35,218 km
Speed = 1,467 km/h

Earth's rotation

0° Equator Circumference = 40,074 km
Speed = 1,670 km/h

N
W — E
S

At latitudes above and below the equator, Earth's circumference is smaller so the speed of Earth's rotation is slower.

10 Claims • Evidence • Reasoning Make a claim about why NASA chose Cape Canaveral as its launch site. Give four reasons as evidence to support your claim, and explain your reasoning.

_____
_____
_____
_____
_____
_____

An Economy of Space

How does the space program affect Florida's economy?

ACTIVE READING

11 Identify As you read, underline each way the space program benefits Florida's economy.

The state of Florida has invested millions of dollars to support the space industry in the state. The excitement of space travel draws many tourists every year. Many aerospace companies and military industries have located in Florida to support the space program. These industries attract scientists and others to the state. NASA and NASA-related industries and activities brought about $2 billion into Florida's economy in 2008. NASA and the space industry also provide many jobs in Florida.

By Encouraging Tourism

Since the first satellite launches, tourists have flocked to the Cape Canaveral area to see them. Thousands watched as *Apollo 11* launched to the moon. In 2010, the Kennedy Space Center Visitor Complex attracted 1.2 million out-of-state tourists. These visitors may have spent over $71 million at the Kennedy Space Center Visitor Complex. Much more is spent in the surrounding communities and the state itself, when tourists visit the many sites, restaurants, hotels, and local businesses.

Visitors to the Kennedy Space Center Visitor Complex view a large rocket.

By Increasing Revenue

The space exploration industry provides revenue to businesses in Florida. Retail stores and small businesses all over the state benefit from the purchasing power of space industry workers. Employees and tourists visit the restaurants and stay in the local hotels and motels. They also visit the local businesses and shops and buy space-related souvenirs. It has been estimated that $2.83 are generated for Florida's economy for every dollar spent by the space industry.

© Houghton Mifflin Harcourt Publishing Company

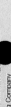

By Encouraging Private Industry

Other activities take place at Cape Canaveral. NASA hired private companies to help build and support the *International Space Station*. NASA and the U.S. Air Force rent launch complexes 36 and 40 to private firms for a growing number of launches each year, in addition to space probe launches. Private firms and the military launch satellites for communication, observing weather, the global positioning system (GPS) of satellites, and other purposes. These satellites are built by NASA and by private firms.

12 Claims • Evidence • Reasoning Make a claim about whether launches by private companies benefit Florida's economy. Use evidence to support your claim, and explain your reasoning.

_____

_____

_____

This rocket is launching a communication satellite.

By Providing Jobs

The space program and aerospace firms employ many researchers, scientists, and engineers. The space industry also employs technicians, managers, and other support staff. In 2011, there were 26,000 jobs related to NASA activities in Florida. The businesses that supply the space industry employ workers in many fields. Science and mathematics teachers are also employed to train the workers of tomorrow and to teach the teachers of tomorrow.

13 Claims • Evidence • Reasoning Make a claim about what would happen to the economy of Florida if the space program were discontinued. Provide evidence to support your claim, and explain your reasoning.

_____

_____

_____

A NASA technician on a forklift removes an engine from the space shuttle *Discovery*.

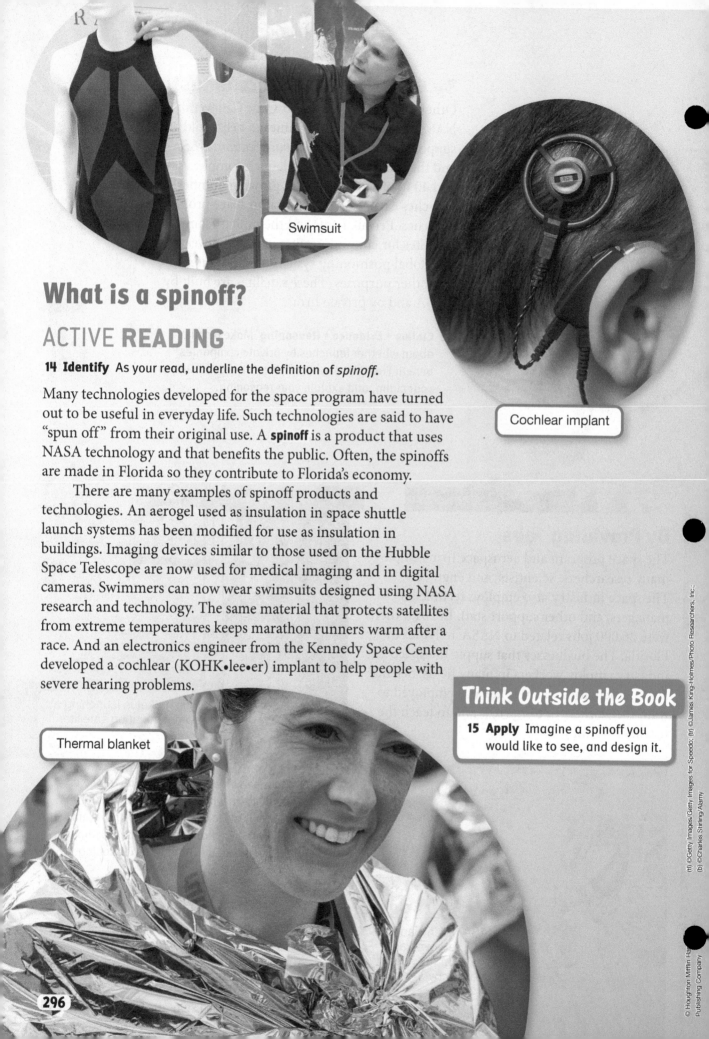

Swimsuit

Cochlear implant

What is a spinoff?

ACTIVE READING

14 Identify As your read, underline the definition of *spinoff*.

Many technologies developed for the space program have turned out to be useful in everyday life. Such technologies are said to have "spun off" from their original use. A **spinoff** is a product that uses NASA technology and that benefits the public. Often, the spinoffs are made in Florida so they contribute to Florida's economy.

There are many examples of spinoff products and technologies. An aerogel used as insulation in space shuttle launch systems has been modified for use as insulation in buildings. Imaging devices similar to those used on the Hubble Space Telescope are now used for medical imaging and in digital cameras. Swimmers can now wear swimsuits designed using NASA research and technology. The same material that protects satellites from extreme temperatures keeps marathon runners warm after a race. And an electronics engineer from the Kennedy Space Center developed a cochlear (KOHK•lee•er) implant to help people with severe hearing problems.

Thermal blanket

Think Outside the Book

15 Apply Imagine a spinoff you would like to see, and design it.

Living Together

The Kennedy Space Center shares its site with the Merritt Island National Wildlife Refuge. The refuge is home to many plants and animals, including several endangered species. The presence of the Kennedy Space Center protects this area from extensive human access. So, endangered species, like the Florida tortoise below, get the protection they need to survive.

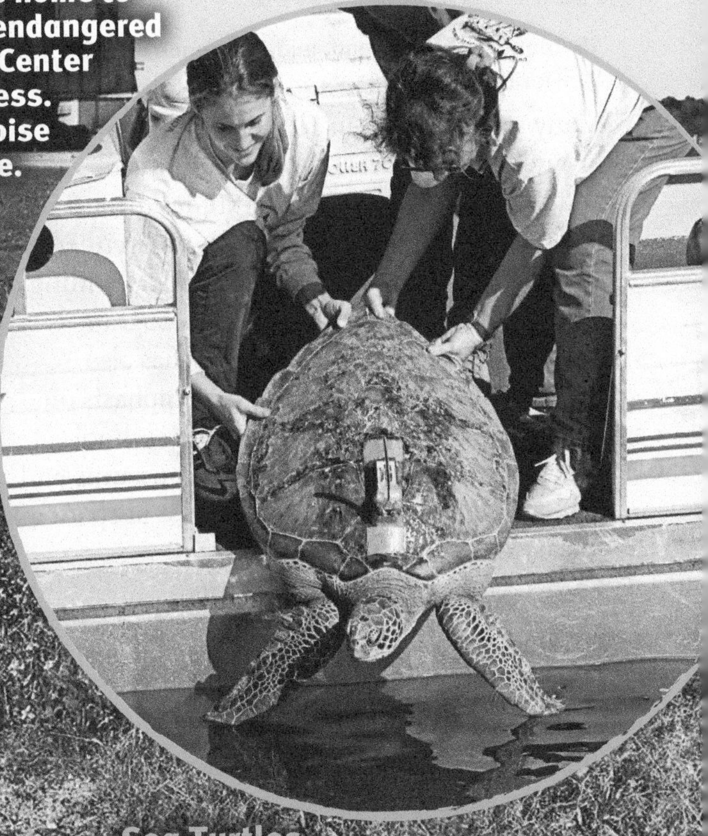

West Indian Manatee

The West Indian manatee is Florida's state marine mammal. An adult manatee may weigh as much as 800 kg. Conservationists estimate that there are about 6,250 West Indian manatees left in the United States.

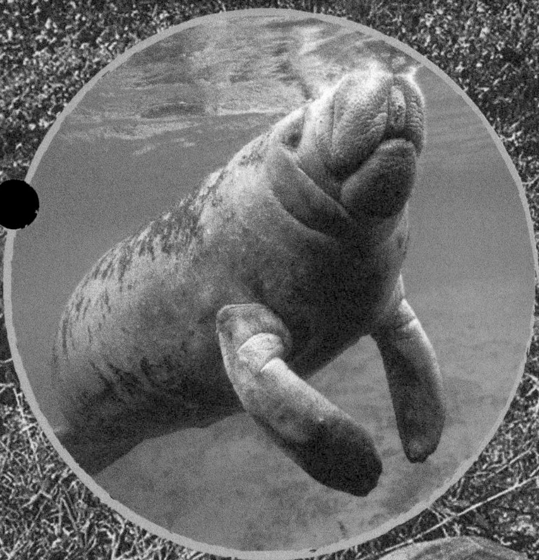

Sea Turtles

The refuge is home to five species of endangered sea turtles. These turtles nest on beaches but usually have to travel far to find food. Scientists tag some sea turtles near the refuge in order to track their travels.

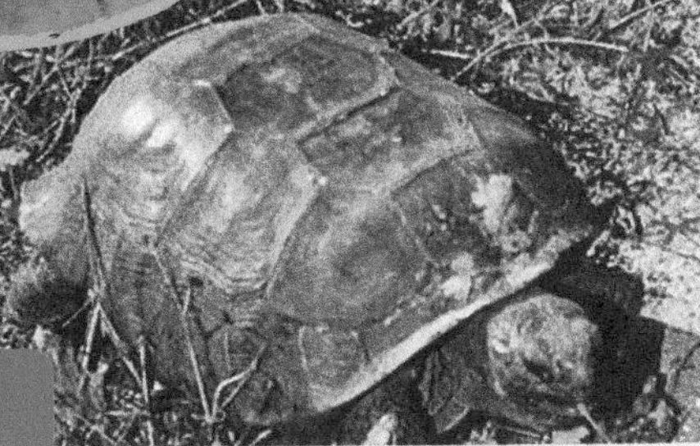

i Extend

16 Identify Name two endangered species that live at the Merritt Island National Wildlife Refuge.

17 Research and Record List five other endangered species at the Merritt Island National Wildlife Refuge.

18 Claims • Evidence • Reasoning Make a claim about the importance of protecting one of the species from question 17. Present evidence to support your claim, and explain your reasoning by doing one of the following:

- make a poster
- write a play
- write a song
- draw a graphic novel

On Solid Ground

How has the space program affected Florida's culture?

ACTIVE READING

19 Identify As you read, underline each way the space program benefits Florida's culture.

Many aspects of life in Florida have been affected by the space program. The effects range from more job opportunities and high-tech industries to attitudes toward science and education. Tourists who visit the Kennedy Space Center come away with a better understanding of Florida's involvement in the space program. The presence of the space industry has also affected education. There is more emphasis on science and mathematics in Florida's schools, colleges, and universities. Florida museums and planetariums also encourage interest in space and space exploration.

Florida Has Become an Important High-Tech Center

Since the beginning of the space age, Florida has been a leader in space exploration, commercial flight, and aviation activities. The needs of the space program have led to the establishment or growth of many high-tech industries. This is especially true in the Orlando area and along the east and west coasts of the state. Some technologies represented are optics, electronics, computers, material science, and satellite communications. These industries, as well as research and development programs, attract new high-tech companies and scientists to Florida.

Workers Have Moved to Florida

Workers have been drawn to Florida by the possibilities represented by the space program. Workers have come from all parts of the United States, as well as from abroad. The presence of aerospace firms has also led to the formation of new companies. New companies offer many new products needed by the space industry. These new companies have also created jobs for workers from Florida and the rest of the country.

The South Florida Science Museum is in West Palm Beach.

Crowds watch the space shuttle *Discovery* lift off from the Kennedy Space Center.

in Florida
More Academic Opportunities Are Available

Some of the best aeronautical and space-related educational programs are in Florida. Both the State University System and private universities offer programs of study in mathematics, science, and engineering. The United States' largest degree programs in aeronautical science and engineering are based in Florida. The Florida Institute of Technology offers a Bachelor of Science in Space Sciences degree. This was the first degree program in Space Science in the United States.

Funded by NASA, the Florida Space Grant Consortium provides scholarships and fellowships for students. The consortium also provides grants to university teachers.

NASA sponsors different competitions for high school and university students. One example is the FIRST Robotics Regional Competition, shown in the photograph at the right.

The effect of the space program on Florida's culture is so extensive that the space shuttle is on Florida's quarter.

Florida high school students compete in a NASA-sponsored robotics competition.

20 Claims • Evidence • Reasoning Make a claim about the effects of the space exploration industry on the culture of Florida. Support your claim by summarizing evidence, and explain your reasoning.

_____
_____
_____
_____

Visual Summary

To complete this summary, fill in the blanks with the correct word. You can use this page to review the main concepts of the lesson.

Florida and Space Exploration

Cape Canaveral, Florida, is the largest launch center in the United States.

21 Cape Canaveral is on the east coast of Florida and includes the following two NASA facilities:

_____

_____

The aerospace and space exploration industries affect Florida's culture.

22 The aerospace and space exploration industries help create interest in

_____

The aerospace and space exploration industries affect Florida's economy.

23 One example of the impact of the aerospace and space exploration industries on Florida's economy is the creation of _____

Spinoffs from the space program have contributed to Florida's economy.

24 A spinoff is a technology that was developed for the space program and now benefits the

_____

25 Claims • Evidence • Reasoning Make a claim about the effects of the space program on the economy and culture of Florida. Summarize evidence to support your claim, and explain your reasoning.

Vocabulary

Fill in the blanks with the term that best completes the following sentences.

1 The national organization in the United States that is responsible for exploring space was formed in _____ and is called _____.

2 When a rocket is _____, the rocket is propelled far above Earth's surface.

3 A _____ is a product that uses NASA technology and benefits the public.

Key Concepts

4 Identify Write the words that make up the acronym NASA.

_____

_____

_____

5 List Write two reasons why Cape Canaveral was chosen as NASA's Florida launch site.

_____

_____

_____

_____

6 Identify State one way the aerospace industry and space program affect Florida's economy.

_____

_____

_____

7 Explain Describe how bringing thousands of workers and their families from all over the country to Florida has affected Florida's culture.

_____

_____

_____

8 Identify List two NASA sites in Florida, and describe what happens at each.

_____

_____

_____

_____

_____

Critical Thinking

Use this map to answer the following questions.

9 Apply Draw an arrow on the map that points to approximately where the Kennedy Space Center is located.

10 Claims • Evidence • Reasoning Galveston, Texas, is located at near the same latitude as Orlando, Florida. Galveston is also near a large body of water, the Gulf of Mexico. Make a claim about why NASA does not launch from Galveston. Summarize evidence to support your claim, and explain your reasoning.

_____

_____

_____

Space Exploration and Florida

depends on

Technology for Space Exploration

which produces

Images from Space

1 Interpret The Graphic Organizer above shows that technology for space exploration produces images from space. Describe one type of technology that is useful in producing images from space.

_____

_____

_____

2 Claims • Evidence • Reasoning Make a claim that tells why Florida was chosen as the center of space exploration in the United States. Summarize evidence to support your claim and explain your reasoning.

_____

_____

_____

_____

_____

3 Describe Having a good understanding of the technology used in space exploration is important for astronauts. Describe how an understanding of this technology could also be important for Floridians who will not travel in space.

_____

_____

_____

_____

_____

_____

_____

_____

_____

Vocabulary

Fill in each blank with the term that best completes the following sentences.

1 A(n) _____ is any human-made object placed in orbit around a body in space, either with or without a crew.

2 _____ is the United States agency that explores space through crewed and uncrewed missions.

3 The _____ refers to all of the frequencies or wavelengths of electromagnetic radiation.

4 _____ provide information about weather, temperature, land use, and changes on Earth over time.

5 A mobile, uncrewed vehicle that is used to explore the surface of another plant is called a(n) _____.

Key Concepts

Read each question below and circle the best answer.

6 Firefighters use air tanks when they go into burning buildings. NASA has created new air tanks that weigh 13 pounds less than typical air tanks. These tanks also have a warning device that tells the firefighters when they are running out of air. Which of these terms best describes these air tanks?

A launch

B aerogel

C spinoff

D divestiture

7 Some planetary images and satellite photographs are made using visible light. Other images are made with radiation from the non-visible portions of the electromagnetic spectrum. Why do scientists study images made with parts of the electromagnetic spectrum other than visible light?

F These images are the only way to observe galaxies beyond our own.

G These images reveal information that visible light does not show.

H These images show important data from optical telescopes.

I These images are the only way to observe space from Earth's surface.

8 Karen is studying types of spacecraft. Which of these spacecraft can people use to travel to and from orbits close to Earth?

A space probe

B space shuttle

C space station

D space telescope

9 Scientists come from all over the world to live and work in Brevard County. These people have a direct impact on Florida's economy, particularly their local economies. The map below shows the concentration of aerospace employment in Florida.

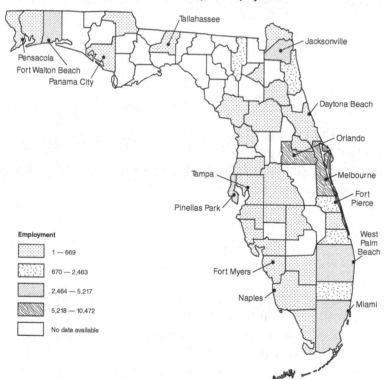

Concentration of Aerospace Employment

Source: Florida Agency for Workforce Innovation, Labor Market Statistics Center, Quarterly Census of Employment and Wages, 2008, Q1, December 2008

Where do most people in Florida who work in aerospace live?

F near Miami

H near Melbourne

G near Tampa

I near Jacksonville

Name _____

10 The Hubble Space Telescope is a telescope that orbits Earth and collects data and images from distant parts of the universe. What type of spacecraft is the Hubble Space Telescope?

   A space station

   B rocket

   C space probe

   D artificial satellite

11 The space industry in Florida has influenced the state in many ways. Many programs exist to get students interested in space and space exploration. Which of these programs in schools likely create the most interest in the space program?

   F art and music

   G math and science

   H literature and language

   I geography and history

12 Suppose that you were in charge of placing a detector aboard a spacecraft that will travel into deep space. Your first step is to analyze the electromagnetic spectrum, which is shown below.

The Electromagnetic Spectrum

Gamma ray	X-ray	Ultraviolet	Visible	Infrared	Microwave	Radio
10^{-13} cm	10^{-9} cm	10^{-6} cm	10^{-4} cm	10^{-2} cm	1 cm	1 km

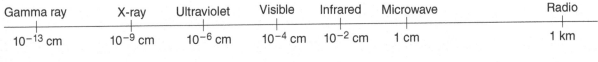

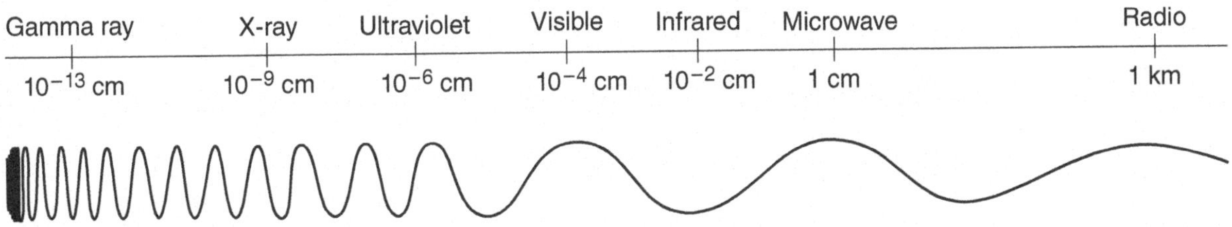

Which type of detector would you place aboard the spacecraft to study wavelengths coming from space that measure 10^{-4} cm?

   A radio telescope

   B optical telescope

   C ultraviolet sensor

   D gamma-ray observatory

13 Refracting telescopes use lenses. Reflecting telescopes use mirrors. However, both types of telescopes have something in common. How are both types of telescopes similar?

F They both magnify tiny nearby objects.

G They both reflect light that enters the telescope.

H They both concentrate electromagnetic radiation.

I They are both classified as non-optical telescopes.

Critical Thinking

Answer the following questions in the space provided.

14 Satellites provide us with various forms of communication.

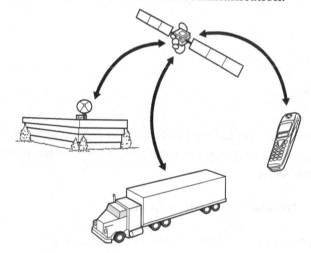

Describe how satellites can aid in communication.

_____

_____

_____

_____

15 Is there a distinction between astronomy and space exploration? Use evidence about how each affects our society to support your claim and explain your reasoning.

_____

_____

_____

_____

Earth's Structures

FLORIDA **BIG IDEA** 6

Earth Structures

This delta may look different than it did 10 years ago.

What Do You Think?

Earth is continuously changing. How did the rock cycle change the delta over time? As you explore this unit, gather evidence to help you state and support a claim.

Earth's Structures

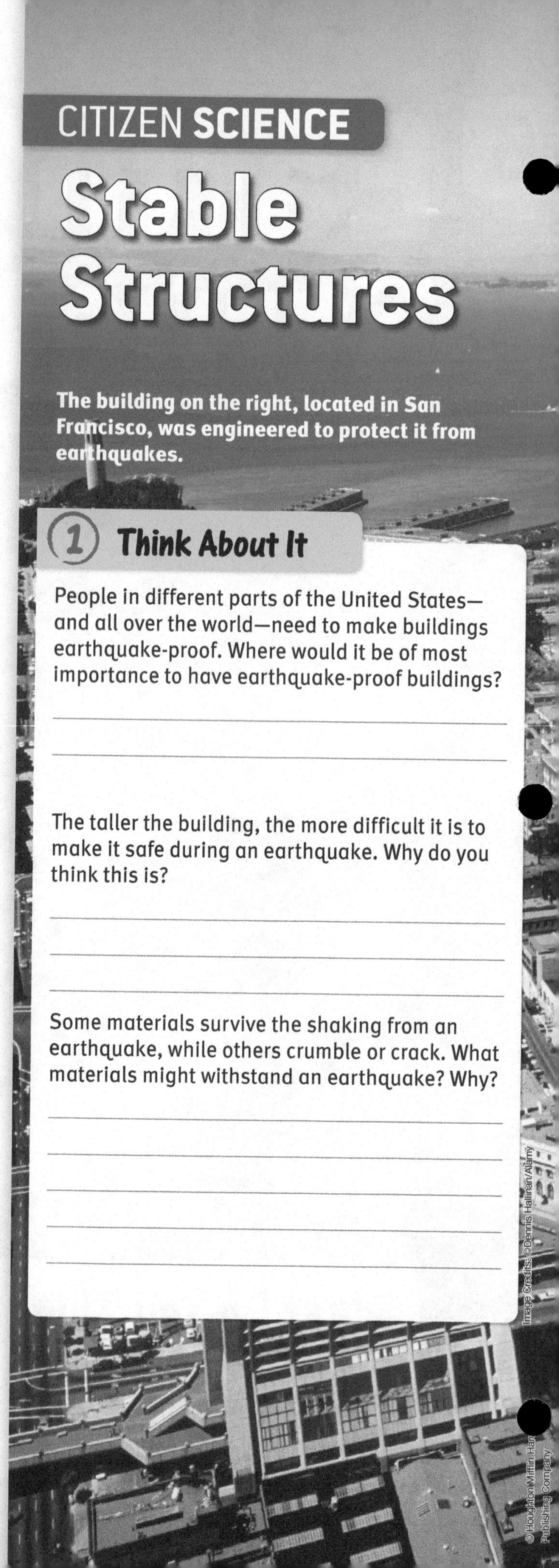

CITIZEN SCIENCE

Stable Structures

The building on the right, located in San Francisco, was engineered to protect it from earthquakes.

① Think About It

People in different parts of the United States—and all over the world—need to make buildings earthquake-proof. Where would it be of most importance to have earthquake-proof buildings?

_____

_____

The taller the building, the more difficult it is to make it safe during an earthquake. Why do you think this is?

_____

_____

_____

Some materials survive the shaking from an earthquake, while others crumble or crack. What materials might withstand an earthquake? Why?

_____

_____

_____

_____

_____

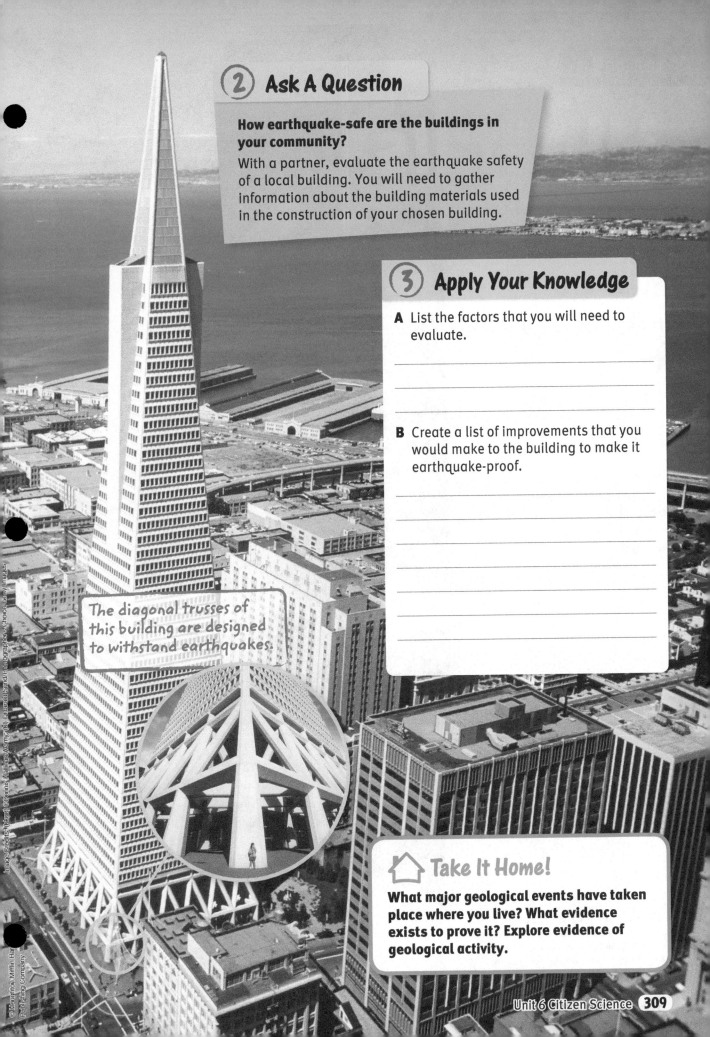

② Ask A Question

How earthquake-safe are the buildings in your community?

With a partner, evaluate the earthquake safety of a local building. You will need to gather information about the building materials used in the construction of your chosen building.

③ Apply Your Knowledge

A List the factors that you will need to evaluate.

_____

_____

_____

B Create a list of improvements that you would make to the building to make it earthquake-proof.

_____

_____

_____

_____

_____

_____

_____

_____

The diagonal trusses of this building are designed to withstand earthquakes.

🏠 Take It Home!

What major geological events have taken place where you live? What evidence exists to prove it? Explore evidence of geological activity.

Minerals

ESSENTIAL QUESTION

What are minerals, how do they form, and how can they be identified?

By the end of this lesson, you should be able to describe the basic structure of minerals and identify different minerals by using their physical properties.

SC.7.E.6.2 Identify the patterns within the rock cycle and relate them to surface events (weathering and erosion) and sub-surface events (plate tectonics and mountain building).

This cave was once full of water. Over millions of years, dissolved minerals in the water slowly formed these gypsum crystals, which are now considered to be the largest mineral crystals in the world!

Lesson Labs

Quick Labs
- Evaporation Rates
- Cooling Rate and Crystal Size
- Scratch Test

Exploration Lab
- Intrinsic Identification of Minerals

Engage Your Brain

1 Identify Which of the materials listed below is a mineral?

Yes	No	
☐	☐	ice
☐	☐	gold
☐	☐	wood
☐	☐	diamond
☐	☐	table salt

2 Explain Describe how you think the minerals in the picture below may have formed.

_____

_____

_____

ACTIVE READING

3 Synthesize Many of this lesson's vocabulary terms are related to each other. Locate the terms in the Glossary and see if you can find connections between them. When you find two terms that are related to each other, write a sentence using both terms in a way that shows the relationship. An example is done for you.

Example Sentence
Each element is made of only one kind of atom.

_____

_____

_____

Vocabulary Terms
- mineral
- element
- atom
- compound
- matter
- crystal
- streak
- luster
- cleavage

4 Apply As you learn the definition of each vocabulary term in this lesson, create your own definition or sketch to help you remember the meaning of the term.

Animal, Vegetable,

What do minerals have in common?

When you hear the word *mineral,* you may think of sparkling gems. But, in fact, most minerals are found in groups that make up rocks. So what is a mineral? A **mineral** is a naturally occurring, usually inorganic solid that has a definite crystalline structure and chemical composition.

○ Definite Chemical Composition

To understand what a definite chemical composition is, you need to know a little about elements. **Elements** are pure substances that cannot be broken down into simpler substances by ordinary chemical means. Each element is made of only one kind of atom. All substances are made up of atoms, so **atoms** can be thought of as the building blocks of matter. Stable particles that are made up of strongly bonded atoms are called *molecules.* And, if a substance is made up of molecules of two or more elements, the substance is called a **compound.**

The chemical composition of a mineral is determined by the element or compound that makes up the mineral. For example, minerals such as gold and silver are composed of only one element. Such a mineral is called a *native element.* The mineral quartz is a compound in which silicon atoms can each bond with up to four oxygen atoms in a repeating pattern.

 5 Claim • Evidence • Reasoning Make a claim about the relationship between elements, atoms, and compounds. Summarize evidence to support the claim and explain your reasoning.

_____

_____

_____

_____

○ Solid

Matter is anything that has volume and mass. *Volume* refers to the amount of space an object takes up. For example, a golf ball has a smaller volume than a baseball does. Matter is generally found in one of three states: solid, liquid, or gas. A mineral is a solid—that is, it has a definite volume and shape. A substance that is a liquid or a gas is not a mineral. However, in some cases its solid form is a mineral. For instance, liquid water is not a mineral, but ice is because it is solid and has all of the other mineral characteristics also.

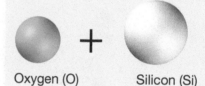

Atoms The mineral quartz is made up of atoms of oxygen and silicon.

Oxygen (O)   Silicon (Si)

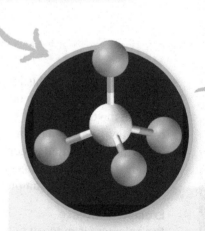

Compound An atom of silicon can typically bond with up to four oxygen atoms to form a molecule. One or more of these molecules form a compound.

or Mineral?

Usually Inorganic

Most substances made by living things are categorized as organic substances, such as kidney stones and wood. However, a few substances made by animals, such as clam shells, are categorized as inorganic. An inorganic substance is usually one that is not made up of living things or the remains of living things. And, although a few organic substances such as kidney stones are categorized as minerals, most minerals are inorganic. And, unlike clam shells, most of the processes that form minerals usually take place in the non-living environment.

Crystalline Structure

Minerals have a crystalline structure because they are composed of crystals. A **crystal** is a solid, geometric form that results from a repeating pattern of atoms or molecules. A crystal's shape is produced by the arrangement of the atoms or molecules within the crystal. This arrangement is determined by the kinds of atoms or molecules that make up the mineral and the conditions under which it forms. All minerals can be placed into crystal classes according to their specific crystal shape. This diagram shows how silica compounds can be arranged in quartz crystals.

Crystal Structure In crystals, molecules are arranged in a regular pattern.

Naturally Occurring

Minerals are formed by many different natural processes that occur on Earth and throughout the universe. On Earth, the mineral halite, which is used for table salt, forms as water evaporates and leaves behind the salt it contained. Some minerals form as molten rock cools. Talc, a mineral that can be used to make baby powder, forms deep in Earth as high temperature and pressure change the rock. Some of the other ways in which minerals form are on the next page.

6 Classify Circle *Y* for "yes" or *N* for "no" to determine whether the two materials below are minerals.

	Cardboard	Topaz
Definite chemical composition?	Y (N)	(Y) N
Solid?	Y N	(Y) N
Inorganic?	Y N	Y N
Naturally occurring?	Y N	Y N
Crystalline structure?	Y (N)	Y N
Mineral?	Y N	Y N

Mineral Crystal Billions of molecules arranged in a crystalline structure form these quartz crystals.

Crystal Clear!

How are minerals formed?

Minerals form within Earth or on Earth's surface by natural processes. Recall that each type of mineral has its own chemical makeup. Therefore, which types of minerals form in an area depends in part on which elements are present there. Temperature and pressure also affect which minerals form.

◯ As Magma and Lava Cool

Many minerals grow from magma. Magma—molten rock inside Earth—contains most of the types of atoms that are found in minerals. As magma cools, the atoms join together to form different minerals. Minerals also form as lava cools. Lava is molten rock that has reached Earth's surface. Quartz is one of the many minerals that crystallize from magma and lava.

◯ By Metamorphism

Temperature and pressure within Earth cause new minerals to form as bonds between atoms break and reform with different atoms. The mineral garnet can form and replace the minerals chlorite and quartz in this way. At high temperatures and pressures, the element carbon in rocks forms the mineral diamond or the mineral graphite, which is used in pencils.

👁 Visualize It!

7 Claims • Evidence • Reasoning Make a claim about the ways in which pluton and pegmatite form in a similar fashion. Summarize evidence to support the claim and explain your reasoning.

_____

_____

Cooling Magma Forms Plutons
As magma rises, it can stop moving and cool slowly. This forms rocks like this granite, which contains minerals like quartz, mica, and feldspar.

Cooling Magma Forms Pegmatites
Magma that cools very slowly can form pegmatites. Some crystals in pegmatites, such as this topaz, can grow quite large.

Metamorphism Minerals like these garnets form when temperature and pressure causes the chemical and crystalline makeup of minerals to change.

From Solutions

Water usually has many substances dissolved in it. As water evaporates, these substances form into solids and come out of solution, or *precipitate*. For example, the mineral gypsum often forms as water evaporates. Minerals can also form from hot water solutions. Hot water can dissolve more materials than cold water. As a body of hot water cools, dissolved substances can form into minerals such as dolomite, as they precipitate out of solution.

8 Summarize Describe three ways minerals form.

A _____

_____

B _____

_____

C _____

_____

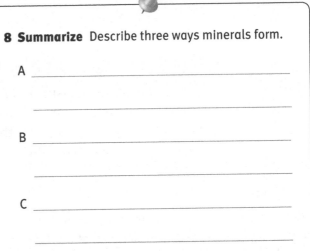

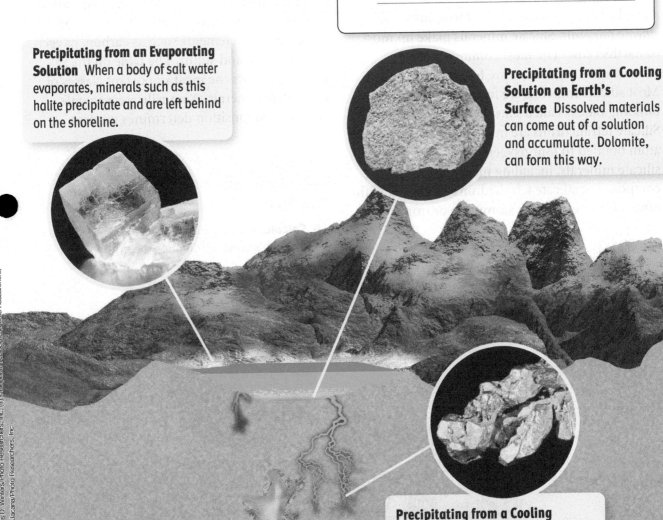

Precipitating from an Evaporating Solution When a body of salt water evaporates, minerals such as this halite precipitate and are left behind on the shoreline.

Precipitating from a Cooling Solution on Earth's Surface Dissolved materials can come out of a solution and accumulate. Dolomite, can form this way.

Precipitating from a Cooling Solution Beneath Earth's Surface Water works its way downward and is heated by magma. It then reacts with minerals to form a solution. Dissolved elements, such as gold, precipitate once the fluid cools to form new mineral deposits.

Think Outside the Book

9 Apply Find out what your state mineral is and how it forms.

Sort It Out

How are minerals classified?

The most common classification of minerals is based on chemical composition. Minerals are divided into two groups based on their composition. These groups are the silicate (SIL'ih•kayt) minerals and the nonsilicate (nawn•SIL'ih•kayt) minerals.

◯ Silicate Minerals

Silicon and oxygen are the two most common elements in Earth's crust. Minerals that contain a combination of these two elements are called *silicate minerals*. Silicate minerals make up most of Earth's crust. The most common silicate minerals in Earth's crust are feldspar and quartz. Most silicate minerals are formed from basic building blocks called *silicate tetrahedrons*. Silicate tetrahedrons are made of one silicon atom bonded to four oxygen atoms. Most silicate minerals, including mica and olivine, are composed of silicate tetrahedrons combined with other elements, such as aluminum or iron.

ACTIVE READING

10 Claims • Evidence • Reasoning Make a claim about why Earth's crust is made up mostly of silicate materials. Summarize evidence to support the claim and explain your reasoning.

_____

_____

The mineral zircon is a silicate mineral. It is composed of the element zirconium and silicate tetrahedrons.

◯ Nonsilicate Minerals

Minerals that do not contain the silicate tetrahedron building block form a group called the *nonsilicate minerals*. Some of these minerals are made up of elements such as carbon, oxygen, fluorine, iron, and sulfur. The table on the next page shows the most important classes of nonsilicate minerals. A nonsilicate mineral's chemical composition determines its class.

＋－×÷ Do the Math

You Try It

11 Calculate Calculate the percent of non-silicates in Earth's crust to complete the graph's key.

Minerals in Earth's Crust

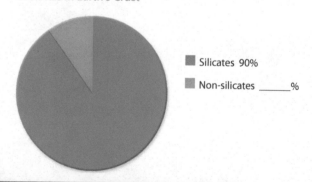

■ Silicates 90%

■ Non-silicates _____ %

Classes of Nonsilicate Minerals

Native elements are minerals that are composed of only one element. Copper (Cu) and silver (Ag) are two examples. Native elements are often used to make electronics.

Silver, Ag

Carbonates are minerals that contain carbon (C) and oxygen (O) in the form of the carbonate ion CO_3^{2-}. We use carbonate minerals in cement, building stones, and fireworks.

Calcite, $CaCO_3$

Halides are compounds that form when elements such as fluorine (F) and chlorine (Cl), combine with elements such as calcium (Ca). Halides are used in the chemical industry and in detergents.

Fluorite, CaF_2

Oxides are compounds that form when an element, such as aluminum (Al) or iron (Fe), combines with oxygen. Oxide minerals are used to make abrasives, aircraft parts, and paint.

Corundum, Al_2O_3

Sulfates are minerals that contain sulfur (S) and oxygen (O) in the form of the sulfate ion SO_4^{2-}. Sulfates are used in cosmetics, toothpaste, cement, and paint.

Barite, $BaSO_4$

Sulfides are minerals that contain one or more elements, such as lead (Pb), or iron (Fe), combined with sulfur (S). Sulfide minerals are used to make batteries and medicines.

Pyrite, FeS_2

👁 Visualize It!

12 Classify Examine the chemical formulas for the two minerals on the right. Classify each mineral as a silicate or a nonsilicate. If it is a nonsilicate, also write its class.

Gypsum, $CaSO_4 \cdot 2H_2O$

Kyanite, Al_2SiO_5

_____

_____

Name That Mineral!

What properties can be used to identify minerals?

If you closed your eyes and tasted different foods, you could probably determine what the foods are by noting properties such as saltiness or sweetness. You can also determine the identity of a mineral by noting different properties. In this section, you will learn about the properties that will help you identify minerals.

○ Color

The same mineral can come in different colors. For example, pure quartz is colorless. However, impurities can make quartz pink, orange, or many other colors. Other factors can also change a mineral's color. Pyrite is normally golden, but it turns black or brown if exposed to air and water. The same mineral can be different colors, and different minerals can be the same color. So, color is helpful but usually not the best way to identify a mineral.

○ Streak

The color of the powdered form of a mineral is its **streak**. A mineral's streak is found by rubbing the mineral against a white tile called a *streak plate*. The mark left is the streak. A mineral's streak is not always the same as the color of the mineral, but all samples of the same mineral have the same streak color. Unlike the surface of a mineral, the streak is not affected by air or water. For this reason, streak is more reliable than color in identifying a mineral.

ACTIVE READING

13 Identify Underline the name of the property on this page that is most reliable for identifying a mineral.

👁 Visualize It!

14 Claims • Evidence • Reasoning Look at these two mineral samples. Make a claim about which property indicates that the two minerals might be the same mineral. Summarize evidence to support the claim and explain your reasoning.

_____

_____

_____

Mineral Lusters

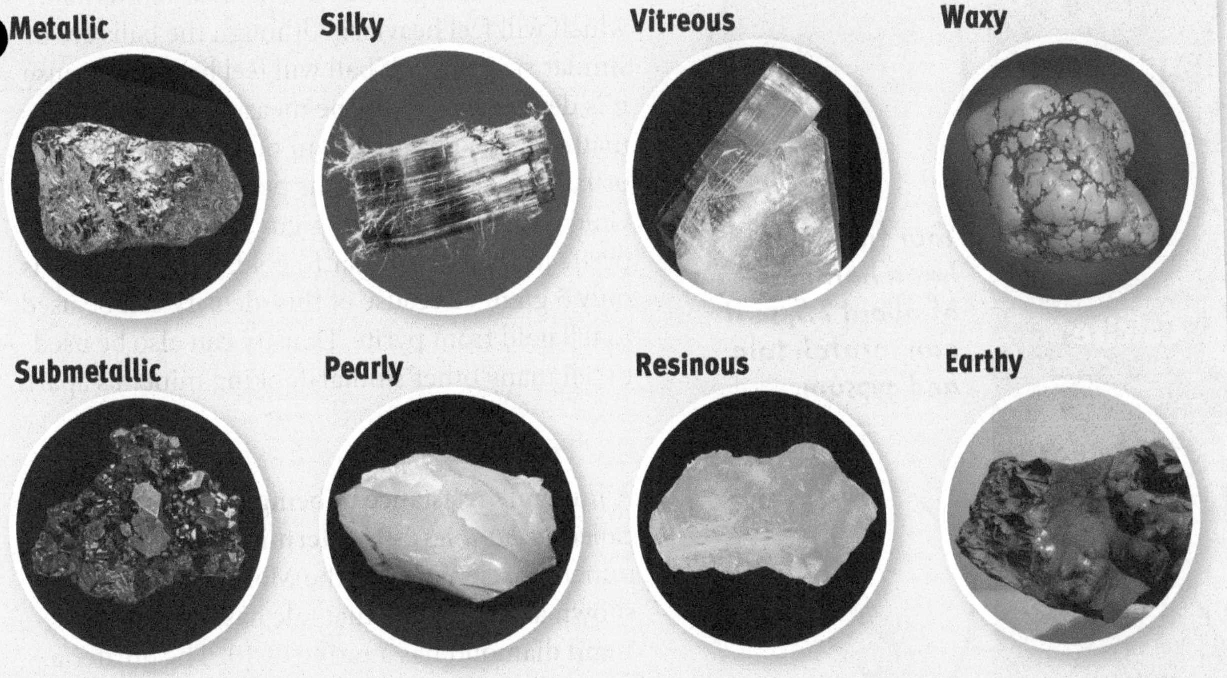

Metallic

Silky

Vitreous

Waxy

Submetallic

Pearly

Resinous

Earthy

Luster

The way a surface reflects light is called **luster**. When you say an object is shiny or dull, you are describing its luster. The two major types of luster are metallic and nonmetallic. Pyrite has a metallic luster. It looks as if it is made of metal. A mineral with a nonmetallic luster can be shiny, but it does not appear to be made of metal. Different types of lusters are shown above.

Cleavage and Fracture

The tendency of a mineral to split along specific planes of weakness to form smooth, flat surfaces is called **cleavage**. When a mineral has cleavage, it breaks along flat surfaces that generally run parallel to planes of weakness in the crystal structure. For example, mica tends to split into parallel sheets. Many minerals, however, do not break along cleavage planes. Instead, they fracture, or break unevenly, into pieces that have curved or irregular surfaces. Scientists describe a fracture according to the appearance of the broken surface. For example, a rough surface has an irregular fracture, and a curved surface has a conchoidal (kahn•KOY•duhl) fracture.

👁 Visualize It!

15 Identify Write the correct description, either *cleavage* or *fracture*, under the two broken mineral crystals shown here.

_____

_____

Mohs Scale

1	Talc
2	Gypsum
3	Calcite
4	Fluorite
5	Apatite
6	Feldspar
7	Quartz
8	Topaz
9	Corundum
10	Diamond

Your fingernail has a hardness of about 2.5, so it can scratch talc and gypsum.

A steel file has a hardness of about 6.5. You can scratch feldspar with it.

Diamond is the hardest mineral. Only a diamond can scratch another diamond.

👁 Visualize It!

16 Determine A mineral can be scratched by calcite but not by a fingernail. What is its approximate hardness?

_____

_____

Density

If you pick up a golf ball and a table-tennis ball, which will feel heavier? Although the balls are of similar size, the golf ball will feel heavier because it is denser. *Density* is the measure of how much matter is in a given amount of space. Density is usually measured in grams per cubic centimeter. Gold has a density of 19 g/cm³. The mineral pyrite looks very similar to gold, but its density is only 5 g/cm³. Because of this, density can be used to tell gold from pyrite. Density can also be used to tell many other similar-looking minerals apart.

Hardness

A mineral's resistance to being scratched is called its *hardness*. To determine the hardness of minerals, scientists use the Mohs hardness scale, shown at left. Notice that talc has a rating of 1 and diamond has a rating of 10. The greater a mineral's resistance to being scratched, the higher its hardness rating. To identify a mineral by using the Mohs scale, try to scratch the surface of a mineral with the edge of one of the 10 reference minerals. If the reference mineral scratches your mineral, the reference mineral is as hard as or harder than your mineral.

Special Properties

All minerals exhibit the properties that were described earlier in this section. However, a few minerals have some additional, special properties that can help identify those minerals. For example, the mineral magnetite is a natural magnet. The mineral calcite is usually white in ordinary light, but in ultraviolet light, it often appears red. Another special property of calcite is shown below.

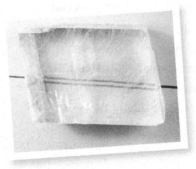

A clear piece of calcite placed over an image will cause a double image.

WHY IT **MATTERS**

Made from Minerals

Many minerals contain useful substances. Rutile and several other minerals contain the metal titanium. Titanium can resist corrosion and is about as strong as steel, but it is 47% lighter than steel. These properties make titanium very valuable.

Devices for Doctors

Surgical procedures like joint replacements require metal implantations. Titanium is used because it can resist body fluid corrosion and its low density and elasticity are similar to human bone.

Marvels for Mechanics

Motorcycle exhaust pipes are often made out of titanium, which dissipates heat better than stainless steel.

An Aid to Architects

Titanium doesn't just serve practical purposes. Architect Frank Gehry used titanium panels to cover the outside of the Guggenheim Museum in Bilbao, Spain. He chose titanium because of its luster.

ℹ Extend

17 Claims • Evidence • Reasoning Make a claim about how the density of titanium-containing minerals would compare to the density of minerals used to make steel. Use evidence to support the claim and explain your reasoning.

18 List Research some other products made from minerals. Make a list summarizing your research.

19 Determine Choose one of the products you researched. How do the properties of the minerals used to make the product contribute to the product's characteristics or usefulness?

Visual Summary

To complete this summary, fill in the blanks with the correct words or phrase. You can use this page to review the main concepts of the lesson.

Minerals make up Earth's crust.

20 A mineral:

- has a definite chemical composition
- is a solid
- is usually inorganic
- is formed in nature
- _____

Minerals are classified by composition.

21 Minerals are classified in two groups as:

Quartz, SiO_2 Calcite, $CaCO_3$
_____   _____

Minerals

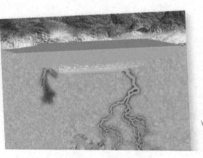

Minerals form by natural processes.

22 Minerals form by:

- metamorphism
- the cooling of magma and lava
- _____

Minerals are identified by their properties.

23 Properties used to identify minerals include:

- color and luster
- _____
- cleavage or fracture
- density and hardness
- special properties

24 Claims • Evidence • Reasoning Make a claim as to whether ice (H_2O) is a silicate or nonsilicate. Summarize evidence to support the claim and explain your reasoning.

Lesson Review

Vocabulary

Fill in the blank with the term that best completes the following sentence.

1 The way light bounces off a mineral's surface is described by the mineral's _____

2 The color of a mineral in powdered form is the mineral's _____

3 Each element is made up of only one kind of _____

Key Concepts

4 Explain How could you determine whether an unknown substance is a mineral?

_____

_____

_____

_____

_____

5 Determine If a substance is a mineral, how could you identify what type of mineral it is?

_____

_____

_____

_____

6 Organize In the space below, draw a graphic organizer showing how minerals can be classified. Be sure to include the six main classes of nonsilicate minerals.

Critical Thinking

Use the diagram below to answer question 7.

Carbon Bonds in Graphite

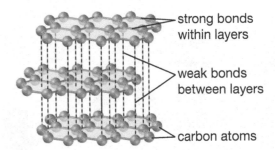

strong bonds within layers

weak bonds between layers

carbon atoms

7 Claims • Evidence • Reasoning The diagram above shows the crystal structure of graphite, a mineral made up of carbon atoms that are bonded together in a regular pattern. Make a claim about whether graphite would more likely display cleavage or fracture. Summarize evidence to support the claim and explain your reasoning.

_____

_____

_____

8 Infer How do you think the hardness and density of a mineral that formed through metamorphism would compare to a mineral that formed through evaporation? Explain your reasoning.

_____

_____

_____

_____

_____

_____

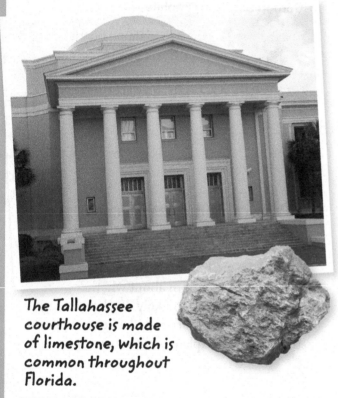
SC.7.E.6.2 Identify the patterns within the rock cycle and relate them to surface events (weathering and erosion) and sub-surface events (plate tectonics and mountain building).

Florida Minerals

The Tallahassee courthouse is made of limestone, which is common throughout Florida.

Calcite in Limestone

Calcite is the primary mineral in limestone. Florida is the second largest producer of limestone in the United States. Most of the limestone mined in Florida is used for road construction. Limestone can also be used to produce cement, glass, and ceramics. Florida's limestone formed over millions of years. Sediment made up of the hard body parts of marine organisms was deposited in thick layers. These layers were later compressed to form limestone.

A key part of the mining process for limestone is following standards to help protect natural resources. The standards include using minimum amounts of water, replanting trees, and making sure an area is not overmined.

Mining

Sandstone, calcite, gypsum, and kaolin are some of the common minerals found in Florida. Kaolin is a clay that is used to make paper, rubber, and china. It is mined mostly in east-central Florida. Kaolin miners drill holes and take samples to locate kaolin deposits. If a deposit is large enough and is of good quality, mining can start. First, the layers of earth above the kaolin are removed—as deep as 30 m. The crude kaolin material is sent to a processing plant where it is dried and separated from other materials. Afterward, the dried kaolin is sent to roller mills, where it is ground into a fine powder. It is then packaged and sent off to manufacturers to make a variety of products. Kaolin can be hazardous. Studies have found that long-term exposure to kaolin may cause miners to develop a respiratory disease called *kaolinosis*.

🌐 Social Studies Connection

Use your school library or the Internet to learn about the state stone of Florida and the minerals it contains. Mark the locations where it can be found on the map shown.

Take It Home

With an adult, find three items in your home that are made from minerals. List the minerals they contain, and research whether these minerals can be found in Florida.

Toothpaste

Phosphate Minerals

Florida's phosphate industry supplies one-fourth of the world's phosphate needs. Mining for phosphate rock, which is rich in phosphate minerals, began in 1883 in Florida. Phosphate is mainly used to make fertilizer, but it is also used in other things, such as vitamins, soft drinks, and even toothpaste!

Like limestone, phosphate rock is formed from sediments of marine organisms deposited on the ocean floor. It is found in a layer of sediment located about 5–15 m below Earth's surface. To get to this layer, miners use a dragline to remove the soil above the layer. The layer is transported to a pit, where it is processed. The phosphate is separated from sediments like sand and clay.

Phosphate mining primarily uses fluoride, radon gas, and sulfur dioxide for processing. These chemicals can be dangerous to the environment and humans. Recent regulations have been put in place to control and reduce the harmful effects of phosphate mining.

This dragline is being used to mine phosphate in Florida.

The **Rock Cycle**

ESSENTIAL **QUESTION**

What is the rock cycle?

By the end of this lesson, you should be able to describe the series of processes and classes of rocks that make up the rock cycle.

SC.7.E.6.2 Identify the patterns within the rock cycle and relate them to surface events (weathering and erosion) and sub-surface events (plate tectonics and mountain building).

It may be hard to believe, but these mountains actually move. Wyoming's Teton Mountains rise by millimeters each year. An active fault is uplifting the mountains. In this lesson, you will learn about uplift and other processes that change rock.

Lesson Labs

Quick Lab
- Crayon Rock Cycle
- Compression

S.T.E.M. Lab
- Modeling Rock Formation

 Engage Your Brain

1 Describe Fill in the blank with the word or phrase that you think correctly completes the following sentences.

Most of Earth is made of _____

Rock is _____ changing.

The three main classes of rock are igneous, metamorphic, and _____

2 Describe Write your own caption for this photo.

_____

_____

_____

ACTIVE **READING**

3 Synthesize Many English words have their roots in other languages. Use the Latin words below to make an educated guess about the meaning of the words *erosion* and *deposition*.

Latin Word	Meaning
erosus	eaten away
depositus	laid down

Vocabulary Terms

- **weathering**
- **erosion**
- **deposition**
- **igneous rock**
- **sedimentary rock**
- **metamorphic rock**
- **rock cycle**
- **uplift**
- **subsidence**
- **rift zone**

4 Apply As you learn the definition of each vocabulary term in this lesson, create your own definition or sketch to help you remember the meaning of the term.

Erosion:

_____

_____

Deposition:

_____

_____

Let's Rock!

What is rock?

The solid parts of Earth are made almost entirely of rock. Scientists define rock as a naturally occurring solid mixture of one or more minerals that may also include organic matter. Most rock is made of minerals, but some rock is made of nonmineral material that is not organic, such as glass. Rock has been an important natural resource as long as humans have existed. Early humans used rocks as hammers to make other tools. For centuries, people have used different types of rock, including granite, marble, sandstone, and slate, to make buildings, such as the pyramids shown below.

It may be hard to believe, but rocks are always changing. People study rocks to learn how areas have changed through time.

5 List How is rock used today?

_____

_____

_____

_____

The ancient Egyptians used a rock called limestone to construct the Great Sphinx and the pyramids at Giza.

These rock formations in Goreme, Turkey, are known as fairy chimneys. They were shaped by erosion.

Think Outside the Book

6 Design Create a travel brochure for Goreme, Turkey.

What processes change rock?

Natural processes make and destroy rock. They change each type of rock into other types of rock and shape the features of our planet. These processes also influence the type of rock that is found in each area of Earth's surface.

ACTIVE READING

7 Identify As you read, underline the processes and factors that can change rock.

◯ Weathering, Erosion, and Deposition

The process by which water, wind, ice, and changes in temperature break down rock is called **weathering**. Weathering breaks down rock into fragments called *sediment*. The process by which sediment is moved from one place to another is called **erosion.** Water, wind, ice, and gravity can erode sediments. These sediments are eventually deposited, or laid down, in bodies of water and other low-lying areas. The process by which sediment comes to rest is called **deposition.**

◯ Temperature and Pressure

Rock that is buried can be squeezed by the weight of the rock or the layers of sediment on top of it. As pressure increases with depth beneath Earth's surface, so does temperature. If the temperature and pressure are high enough, the buried rock can change into metamorphic rock. In some cases, the rock gets hot enough to melt and forms *magma*, or molten rock. If magma reaches Earth's surface, it is called *lava*. The magma or lava eventually cool and solidify to form new rock.

Classified Information!

What are the classes of rocks?

Rocks fall into three major classes based on how they form. **Igneous rock** forms when magma or lava cools and hardens to become solid. It forms beneath or on Earth's surface. **Sedimentary rock** forms when minerals that form from solutions or sediment from older rocks get pressed and cemented together. **Metamorphic rock** forms when pressure, temperature, or chemical processes change existing rock. Each class can be divided further, based on differences in the way rocks form. For example, some igneous rocks form when lava cools on Earth's surface, and others form when magma cools deep beneath the surface. Therefore, igneous rock can be classified based on how and where it forms.

ACTIVE READING

8 Identify As you read the paragraph, underline the three main classes of rocks.

i Think Outside the Book

9 Claims • Evidence • Reasoning Make a claim about the processes that might have shaped the rock formations in the Valley of Fire State Park. Summarize evidence to support the claim and explain your reasoning.

These formations in Valley of Fire State Park in Nevada are made of sandstone, a sedimentary rock.

sandstone

⃝ Sedimentary Rock

Sedimentary rock is composed of minerals formed from solutions or sediments from older rock. Sedimentary rock forms when the weight from above presses down on the layers of minerals or sediment, or when minerals dissolved in water solidify between sediment pieces and cement them together.

Sedimentary rocks are named according to the size and type of the fragments they contain. For example, the rock shown here is made of sand and is called sandstone. Rock made primarily of the mineral calcite (calcium carbonate) is called limestone.

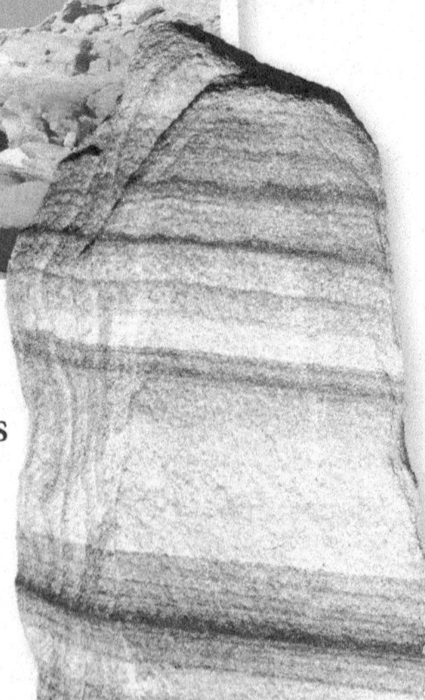

Enchanted Rock in Texas is a large dome made of granite, an intrusive igneous rock.

Igneous Rock

Igneous rock forms from cooling lava and magma. As molten rock cools and becomes solid, the minerals crystallize and grow. The longer the cooling takes, the more time the crystals have to grow. The granite shown here cooled slowly and is made of large crystals. Rock that forms when magma cools beneath Earth's surface is called intrusive igneous rock. Rock that forms when lava cools on Earth's surface is called extrusive igneous rock.

granite

Metamorphic Rock

Metamorphic rock forms when high temperature and pressure change the texture and mineral content of rock. For example, a rock can be buried in Earth's crust, where the temperature and pressure are high. Over millions of years, the solid rock changes, and new crystals are formed. Metamorphic rocks may be changed in four ways: by temperature, by pressure, by temperature and pressure combined, or by fluids or other chemicals. Gneiss, shown here, is a metamorphic rock. It forms at high temperatures deep within Earth's crust.

gneiss

Gneiss is a metamorphic rock that is made up of bands of light and dark minerals.

10 Compare Fill in the chart to compare and contrast sedimentary, igneous, and metamorphic rock.

Classes of Rocks

Sedimentary rock	Igneous rock	Metamorphic rock

What is the rock cycle?

ACTIVE READING

11 Apply As you read, underline the rock types that metamorphic rock can change into.

Rocks may seem very permanent, solid, and unchanging. But over millions of years, any of the three rock types can be changed into another of the three types. For example, igneous rock can change into sedimentary or metamorphic rock, or back into another kind of igneous rock. This series of processes in which rock changes from one type to another is called the **rock cycle**. Rocks may follow different pathways in the cycle. Examples of these pathways are shown here. Factors, including temperature, pressure, weathering, and erosion, may change a rock's identity. Where rock is located on a tectonic plate and whether the rock is at Earth's surface also influence how it forms and changes.

When igneous rock is exposed at Earth's surface, it may break down into sediment. Igneous rock may also change directly into metamorphic rock while still beneath Earth's surface. It may also melt to form magma that becomes another type of igneous rock.

When sediment is pressed together and cemented, the sediment becomes sedimentary rock. With temperature and pressure changes, sedimentary rocks may become metamorphic rocks, or they may melt and become igneous rock. Sedimentary rock may also be broken down at Earth's surface and become sediment that forms another sedimentary rock.

Under certain temperature and pressure conditions, metamorphic rock will melt and form magma. Metamorphic rock can also be altered by heat and pressure to form a different type of metamorphic rock. Metamorphic rock can also be broken down by weathering and erosion to form sediment that forms sedimentary rock.

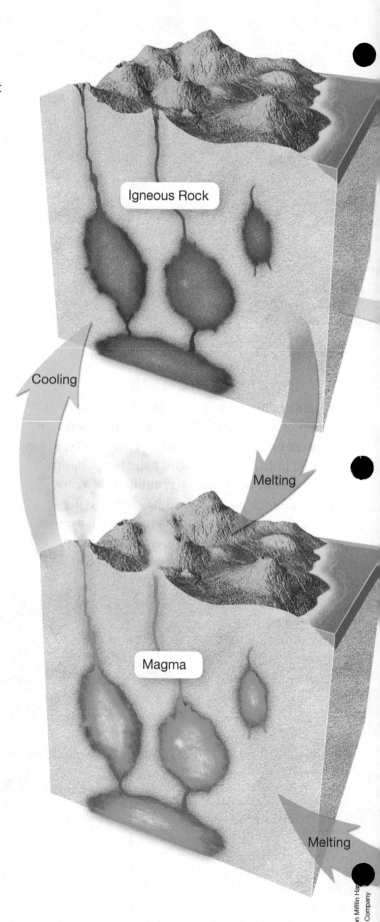

(A) _____

👁 **Visualize It!**

12 Apply Label the missing rock type (B) and processes (A and C) on the diagram of the rock cycle.

(B) _____

Temperature
and
pressure

(C) _____

Weathering,
erosion, and
deposition

Melting

Think Outside the Book

13 Apply Write a series of blog entries from the viewpoint of igneous rock that is changing into sedimentary rock.

Metamorphic Rock

14 Identify List one process that happens above Earth's surface.

_____

List one process that happens below Earth's surface.

_____

How do tectonic plate motions affect the rock cycle?

Tectonic plate motions can move rock around. Rock that was beneath Earth's surface may become exposed to wind and rain. Sediment or rock on Earth's surface may be buried. Rock can also be changed into metamorphic rock by tectonic plate collisions because of increased temperature and pressure.

By Moving Rock Up or Down

There are two types of vertical movements in Earth's crust: uplift and subsidence. **Uplift** is the rising of regions of the crust to higher elevations. Uplift increases the rate of erosion on rock. **Subsidence** is the sinking of regions of the crust to lower elevations. Subsidence leads to the formation of basins where sediment can be deposited.

By Pulling Apart Earth's Surface

A **rift zone** is an area where a set of deep cracks form. Rift zones are common between tectonic plates that are pulling apart. As they pull apart, blocks of crust in the center of the rift zone subside and the pressure on buried rocks is reduced. The reduction in pressure allows rock below Earth's surface to rise up. As the rock rises, it undergoes partial melting and forms magma. Magma can cool below Earth's surface to form igneous rock. If it reaches the surface, magma becomes lava, which can also cool to form igneous rock.

15 Claims • Evidence • Reasoning Make a claim about how uplift differs from subsidence. Summarize evidence to support the claim and explain your reasoning.

_____

_____

_____

_____

⊙ Visualize It!

16 Claims • Evidence • Reasoning Label uplift and subsidence on this diagram. Make a claim about what pathway in the rock cycle might take next if it is subject to uplift. Use evidence to support the claim and explain your reasoning.

_____

_____

_____

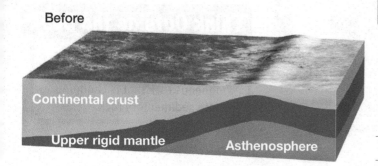

Before

Continental crust

Upper rigid mantle　　Asthenosphere

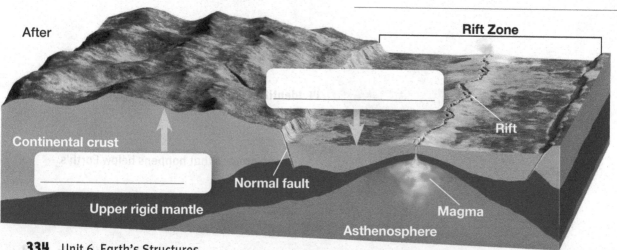

After

Rift Zone

Continental crust

Upper rigid mantle

Normal fault

Rift

Magma

Asthenosphere

WHY IT **MATTERS**

WEIRD SCIENCE

Cliff Dwellings

Can you imagine living on the side of a cliff? Some ancient peoples could! They created dwellings from cliff rock. They also decorated rock with art, as you can see in the pictographs shown below.

Cliff Palace
This dwelling in Colorado is called the Cliff Palace. It was home to the Ancient Puebloans from about 550 to 1300 CE.

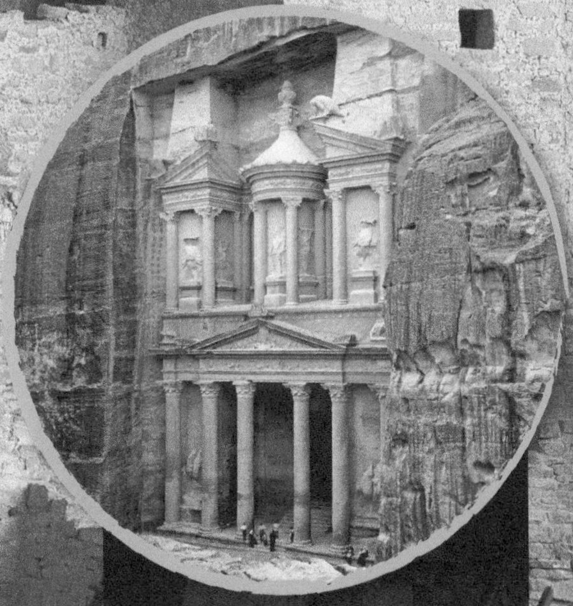

Cliff Art
These pictographs are located at the Gila Cliff Dwellings in New Mexico.

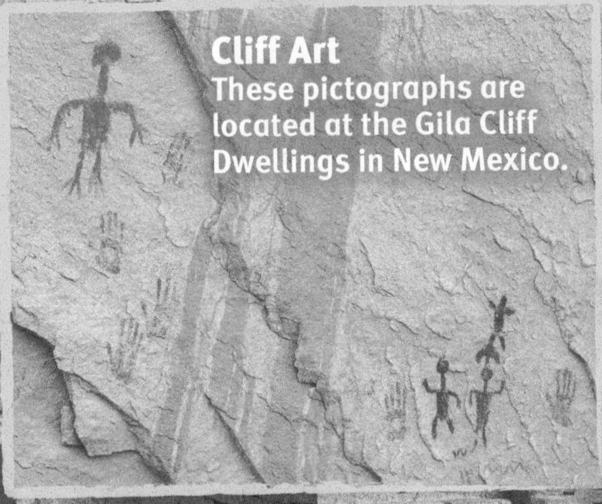

A Palace in Rock
Ancient cliff dwellings are also found outside the United States. These dwellings from about 70 CE are located in Petra, Jordan.

Extend

17 Claims • Evidence • Reasoning Make a claim about how ancient people used rock to create shelter. Summarize evidence to support the claim and explain your reasoning.

18 Research Find out how people lived in one of the cliff dwelling locations. How did living in a rock environment affect their daily lives?

19 Produce Illustrate how the people lived by doing one of the following: write a play, write a song, or create a graphic novel.

Visual Summary

To complete this summary, use what you know about the rock cycle to fill in the blanks below. You can use this page to review the main concepts of the lesson.

Each rock type can change into another of the three types.

20 When sediment is pressed together and cemented, the sediment becomes

_____

21 When lava cools and solidifies,

_____

forms.

22 Metamorphic rock can be altered by temperature and pressure to form a different type of

_____

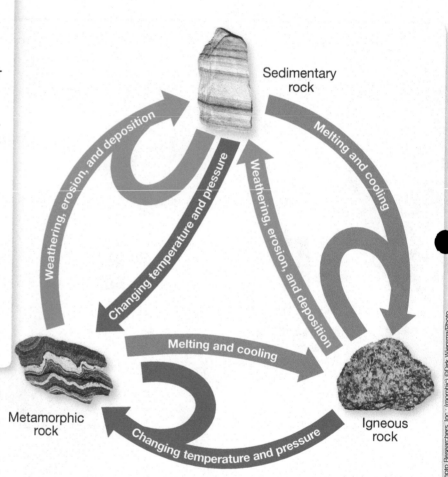

Rock Cycle

Sedimentary rock

Weathering, erosion, and deposition

Melting and cooling

Changing temperature and pressure

Weathering, erosion, and deposition

Melting and cooling

Metamorphic rock

Changing temperature and pressure

Igneous rock

23 Claims • Evidence • Reasoning Make a claim about what factors and processes can affect the pathway that igneous rock takes in the rock cycle. Summarize evidence to support the claim and explain your reasoning.

Lesson Review

Vocabulary

In your own words, define the following terms.

1 Rock cycle

_____

_____

2 Weathering

_____

_____

3 Rift zone

_____

_____

Key Concepts

Use these photos to classify the rock as sedimentary, igneous, or metamorphic.

Example	Type of rock
4 Classify This rock is made up of the mineral calcite, and it formed from the remains of organisms that lived in water.	
5 Classify Through high temperature and pressure, this rock formed from a sedimentary rock.	
6 Classify This rock is made of tiny crystals that formed quickly when molten rock cooled at Earth's surface.	

7 Describe How can sedimentary rock become metamorphic rock?

_____

_____

8 Explain How can subsidence lead to the formation of sedimentary rock?

_____

_____

9 Explain Why are rift zones common places for igneous rock to form?

_____

_____

_____

Critical Thinking

10 Claims • Evidence • Reasoning Make a claim about what would happen to the rock cycle if erosion did not occur. Summarize evidence to support the claim and explain your reasoning.

_____

_____

_____

11 Criticize A classmate states that igneous rock must always become sedimentary rock next, according to the rock cycle. Explain why this statement is not correct.

_____

_____

_____

12 Claims • Evidence • Reasoning Granite is an igneous rock that forms from magma cooled below Earth's surface. Make a claim about why granite would have larger crystals than igneous rocks formed from lava cooled above Earth's surface. Support your claim with evidence and explain your reasoning.

_____

_____

_____

SC.7.N.1.1 Define a problem from the seventh grade curriculum, use appropriate reference materials to support scientific understanding, plan and carry out scientific investigation of various types, such as systematic observations or experiments, identify variables, collect and organize data, interpret data in charts, tables, and graphics, analyze information, make predictions, and defend conclusions.

S.T.E.M. ENGINEERING & TECHNOLOGY

Analyzing Technology

Skills
Identify risks
Identify benefits
✔ Evaluate cost of technology
✔ Evaluate environmental impact
✔ Propose improvements
Propose risk reduction
✔ Compare technology
✔ Communicate results

Objectives
Analyze the life cycle of an aluminum can.
Analyze the life cycle of a glass bottle.
Evaluate the cost of recycling versus disposal of technology.
Analyze the environmental impact of technology.

Analyzing the Life Cycles of Aluminum and Glass

A life cycle analysis is a way to evaluate the real cost of a product. The analysis considers how much money an item costs to make. It also examines how making the product affects the economy and the environment through the life of the product. Engineers, scientists, and technologists use this information to improve processes and to compare products.

Costs of Production

Have you ever wondered where an aluminum soda can comes from? Have you wondered where the can goes when you are done with it? If so, you have started a life cycle analysis by asking the right questions. Aluminum is a metal found in a type of rock called *bauxite*. To get aluminum, first bauxite must be mined. The mined ore is then shipped to a processing plant. There, the bauxite is melted to get aluminum in a process called *smelting*. After smelting, the aluminum is processed. It may be shaped into bicycle parts or rolled into sheets to make cans. Every step in the production involves both financial costs and environmental costs that must be considered in a life cycle analysis.

Many bicycles are made of aluminum because it is lightweight and strong.

©Nordicimages/Alamy

© Houghton Mifflin Harcourt Publishing Company

Costs of Disposal

After an aluminum can is used it can travel either to a landfill or to a recycling plant. The process of recycling an aluminum can does require the use of some energy. However, the financial and environmental costs of disposing of a can and mining ore are much greater than the cost of recycling a can. Additionally, smelting bauxite produces harmful wastes. A life cycle analysis of an aluminum can must include the cost and environmental effects of mining, smelting, and disposing of the aluminum can.

1 Claims • Evidence • Reasoning Make a claim about which steps are no longer part of a can's life cycle after the can is recycled. Summarize evidence to support the claim and explain your reasoning.

_____

_____

_____

_____

Bauxite mining

Most bauxite mining occurs far away from where aluminum is used. Large ships or trains transport the ore before it is made into aluminum products.

Aluminum is one of the easiest materials to recycle. Producing a ton of aluminum by shredding and remelting uses about 5% of the energy needed to process enough bauxite to make a ton of aluminum.

Remelting

Shredding

Smelting

Fabrication

Recycling

Life Cycle of an Aluminum Can

Manufacturing

Consumer use

2 Evaluate In the life cycle shown here, which two steps could include an arrow to indicate disposal?

_____

_____

👋 You Try It!

Now it's your turn to analyze the life cycle of a product.

🖐 You Try It!

Now, apply what you have learned about the life cycle of aluminum to analyze the life cycle of a glass bottle. Glass is made by melting silica from sand or from mineral deposits mined from the Earth. A kiln heats the silica until it melts to form a red-hot gob. Then, the glass is shaped and cooled to form useful items.

① Evaluate Cost of Technology

As a group, discuss the steps that would be involved in making a glass bottle. List the steps in the space below. Start with mining and end at a landfill. Include as many steps in the process as you can think of. Beside each step, tell whether there would be financial costs, environmental costs, or both.

Life Cycle of a Glass Bottle

② Evaluate Environmental Impact

Use the table below to indicate which of the steps listed above would have environmental costs, and what type of cost would be involved. A step can appear in more than one column.

Cause pollution	Consume energy	Damage habitat

(3) Propose Improvements

In your group, discuss how you might improve the life cycle of a glass bottle and reduce the impact on the environment. Draw a life cycle that includes your suggestions for improvement.

(4) Compare Technology

Claims • Evidence • Reasoning How does your improved process decrease the environmental effects of making and using glass bottles? Provide evidence to support your claim and explain your reasoning.

_____

_____

_____

_____

(5) Communicate Results

Imagine that you are an accountant for a company that produces glass bottles. In the space below, write an argument for using recycled glass that is based on financial savings for your company.

_____

_____

_____

_____

Earth's Layers

ESSENTIAL QUESTION

What are Earth's layers?

By the end of this lesson, you should be able to identify Earth's compositional and physical layers and describe their properties.

If you could dig below this canyon, you would discover that Earth is made up of different layers below its surface.

SC.7.E.6.1 Describe the layers of the solid Earth, including the lithosphere, the hot convecting mantle, and the dense metallic liquid and solid cores.
SC.7.E.6.7 Recognize that heat flow and movement of material within Earth causes earthquakes and volcanic eruptions, and creates mountains and ocean basins.

Lesson Labs

Quick Labs
- Tectonic Ice Cubes
- Layers of Earth

S.T.E.M. Lab
- Models of Earth

 Engage Your Brain

1 Predict Check T or F to show whether you think each statement is true or false.

T	F	
☐	☐	The outermost layer of solid Earth is sometimes called the crust.
☐	☐	The crust is the densest layer.
☐	☐	The mantle is the layer between the crust and the core.
☐	☐	Earth's core is divided into five parts.

2 Describe If you were asked to describe this apple, how many layers would you say it has? How would you describe the layers?

_____

_____

_____

_____

_____

ACTIVE **READING**

3 Synthesize You can often define an unknown word if you know the meaning of its word parts. Use the word parts and sentence below to make an educated guess about the meaning of the word *mesosphere*.

Word part	Meaning
meso-	middle
-sphere	ball

Example sentence
The <u>mesosphere</u> is more than 2,000 km thick.

Mesosphere:

_____

_____

Vocabulary Terms

- crust
- mantle
- convection
- core
- lithosphere
- asthenosphere
- mesosphere

4 Apply As you learn the definition of each vocabulary term in this lesson, create your own definition or sketch to help you remember the meaning of the term.

Peeling the Layers

What is inside Earth?

If you tried to dig to the center of Earth, what do you think you would find? Would Earth be solid or hollow? Would it be made of the same material throughout? Actually, Earth is made of several layers. The materials that make up each layer have characteristic properties that vary from layer to layer. Scientists think about Earth's layers in two ways—in terms of their chemical composition and in terms of their physical properties.

i Think Outside the Book

5 Claims • Evidence • Reasoning
Make a claim about why scientists might have two ways for thinking about Earth's layers. Summarize evidence to support the claim and explain your reasoning.

What are Earth's compositional layers?

Earth can be divided into three layers based on chemical composition. These layers are called the *crust*, the *mantle*, and the *core*. Each compositional layer is made up of a different mixture of chemicals.

Earth is divided into three layers based on the chemical composition of each layer.

mantle

core

crust

continental crust

oceanic crust

mantle

Continental crust is thicker than oceanic crust.

Crust

The outermost solid layer of Earth is the **crust.** There are two types of crust—continental and oceanic. Both types are made mainly of the elements oxygen, silicon, and aluminum. However, the denser oceanic crust has almost twice as much iron, calcium, and magnesium. These elements form minerals that are denser than those in the continental crust.

ACTIVE READING

6 Identify List the compositional layers in order of most dense to least dense.

_____

_____

_____

Mantle

The **mantle** is located between the core and the crust. It is a region of hot, slow-flowing, solid rock. When convection takes place in the mantle, cooler rock sinks and warmer rock rises. **Convection** is the movement of matter that results from differences in density caused by variations in temperature. Scientists can learn about the mantle by observing mantle rock that has risen to Earth's surface. The mantle is denser than the crust. It contains more magnesium and less aluminum and silicon than the crust does.

Core

The **core** extends from below the mantle to the center of Earth. Scientists think that the core is made mostly of iron and some nickel. Scientists also think that it contains much less oxygen, silicon, aluminum, and magnesium than the mantle does. The core is the densest layer. It makes up about one-third of Earth's mass.

ACTIVE READING

7 Identify What element makes up most of Earth's core?

_____

What are Earth's physical layers?

Earth can also be divided into layers based on physical properties. The properties considered include whether the layer is solid or liquid, and how the layer moves or transmits waves. The five physical layers are the *lithosphere, asthenosphere, mesosphere, outer core,* and *inner core.*

ACTIVE READING

8 Label Write the names of the compositional layers shown below in the spaces provided.

Lithosphere

The outermost, rigid layer of Earth is the **lithosphere.** The lithosphere is made of two parts—the crust and the rigid, upper part of the mantle. The lithosphere is divided into pieces called *tectonic plates.*

Asthenosphere

The **asthenosphere** is a layer of weak or soft mantle that is made of rock that flows slowly. Tectonic plates move on top of this layer.

Mesosphere

The strong, lower part of the mantle is called the **mesosphere.** Rock in the mesosphere flows more slowly than rock in the asthenosphere does.

Outer Core

The outer core is the liquid layer of Earth's core. It lies beneath the mantle and surrounds the inner core.

Inner Core

The inner core is the solid, dense center of our planet that extends from the bottom of the outer core to the center of Earth, which is about 6,380 km beneath the surface.

Visualize It!

9 Claims • Evidence • Reasoning
Make a claim about which of Earth's compositional layers make up the lithosphere. Summarize evidence to support the claim and explain your reasoning.

A

B

C

Sample Problem

Here's an example of how to find the percentage thickness of the core that is the outer core.

Physical	Compositional
Continental lithosphere (150 km)	Continental crust (50 km)
Asthenosphere (250 km)	Mantle (2,900 km)
Mesosphere (2,550 km)	
Outer core (2,200 km)	Core (3,430 km)
Inner core (1,230 km)	

Identify

A. What do you know?

core = 3,430 km   outer core = 2,200 km

B. What do you want to find out?

Percentage of core that is outer core

Plan

C. Write the formula:

Percentage (%) of core that is outer core =

$$\left(\frac{\text{thickness of outer core}}{\text{thickness of core}} \right) \times 100\%$$

D. Substitute into the formula:

$$\% = \frac{(2,200)}{(3,430)} \times 100\%$$

Solve

E. Calculate and simplify:

$$\% = 0.6414 \times 100\% = 64.14\%$$

Answer: 64.14%

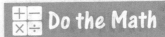

You Try It

10 Calculate What percentage thickness of the continental lithosphere is continental crust?

Identify

A. What do you know?

B. What do you want to find out?

Plan

C. Write the formula:

D. Substitute into the formula:

Solve

E. Calculate and simplify:

Answer:

Visual Summary

To complete this summary, fill in the blanks with the correct word or phrase. You can use this page to review the main concepts of the lesson.

Earth is divided into three compositional layers.

11 The outermost compositional layer of the Earth is the _____ .

12 The _____ is denser than the crust and contains more magnesium.

Earth is divided into five physical layers.

13 The _____ is divided into pieces called tectonic plates.

14 The _____ core is the liquid layer of Earth's core.

Earth's Layers

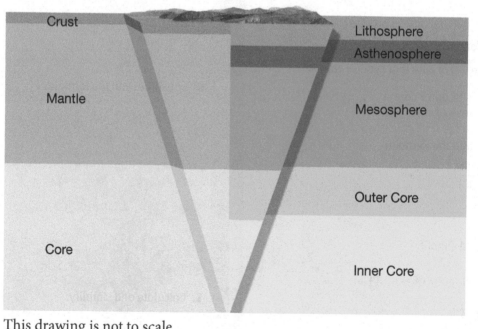

Crust
Mantle
Core

Lithosphere
Asthenosphere
Mesosphere
Outer Core
Inner Core

This drawing is not to scale

15 **Claims • Evidence • Reasoning** Make a claim about which physical layers correspond to which compositional layers. Give evidence to support the claim and explain your reasoning.

Lesson Review

Vocabulary

Fill in the blank with the term that best completes the following sentence.

1 The _____ is a region of hot, slow-flowing, solid rock between the core and the crust.

2 The _____ is the densest compositional layer and makes up one-third of Earth's mass.

3 The _____ is the outermost, rigid physical layer of Earth.

Key Concepts

Use this diagram to answer the following questions.

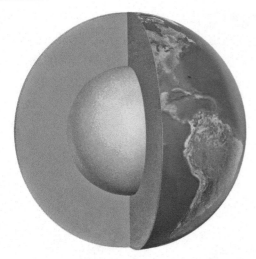

4 Identify Which model of Earth's interior does this image show?

_____

5 Identify Which of these layers is made mostly of iron and nickel?

_____

6 Compare Explain the differences between the inner core and the outer core.

_____

Critical Thinking

7 Compare Explain the difference between the lithosphere and the crust.

_____

_____

_____

_____

8 Claims • Evidence • Reasoning Scientists find dense rock on Earth's surface that is made of magnesium and smaller amounts of aluminum and silicon. Make a claim about which layer of Earth this rock might help scientists study. Summarize evidence to support the claim and explain your reasoning.

_____

_____

_____

_____

_____

_____

_____

9 Apply In a model of Earth's layers that is determined by physical properties, how might the atmosphere be classified? Would it be part of the lithosphere, or a separate layer? Explain your answer.

_____

_____

_____

_____

_____

_____

Plate Tectonics

ESSENTIAL QUESTION

What is plate tectonics?

By the end of this lesson, you should be able to explain the theory of plate tectonics, to describe how tectonic plates move, and to identify geologic events that occur because of tectonic plate movement.

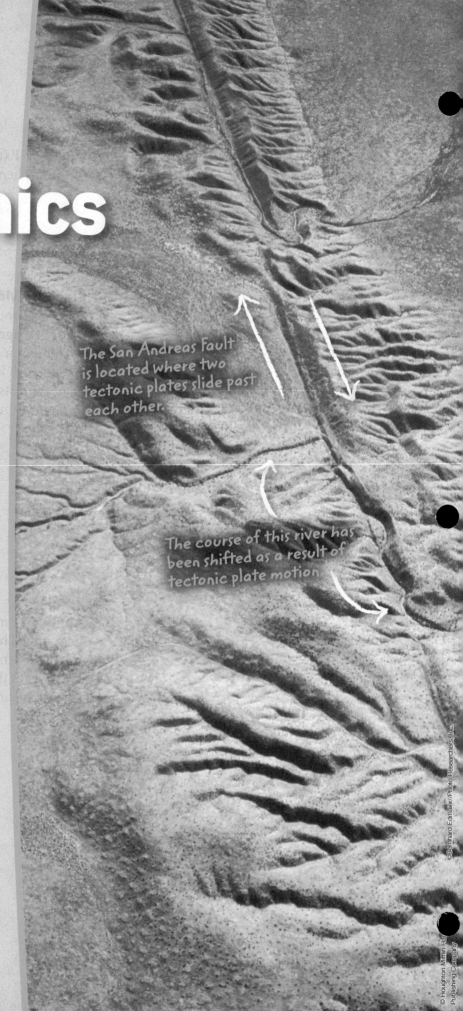

The San Andreas Fault is located where two tectonic plates slide past each other.

The course of this river has been shifted as a result of tectonic plate motion

SC.7.E.6.1 Describe the layers of the solid Earth, including the lithosphere, the hot convecting mantle, and the dense metallic liquid and solid cores. **SC.7.E.6.2** Identify the patterns within the rock cycle and relate them to surface events (weathering and erosion) and sub-surface events (plate tectonics and mountain building). **SC.7.E.6.5** Explore the scientific theory of plate tectonics by describing how the movement of Earth's crustal plates causes both slow and rapid changes in Earth's surface, including volcanic eruptions, earthquakes, and mountain building. **SC.7.E.6.7** Recognize that heat flow and movement of material within Earth causes earthquakes and volcanic eruptions, and creates mountains and ocean basins.

Lesson Labs

Quick Labs
• Reconstructing Land Masses
• What Happens When Objects Collide?
• Mantle Convection

Exploration Lab
• Seafloor Spreading

 Engage Your Brain

1 Identify Check T or F to show whether you think each statement is true or false.

T F

☐ ☐ Earth's surface is all one piece.

☐ ☐ Scientists think the continents once formed a single landmass.

☐ ☐ The sea floor is smooth and level.

☐ ☐ All tectonic plates are the same.

2 Predict Imagine that ice cubes are floating in a large bowl of punch. If there are enough cubes, they will cover the surface of the punch and bump into one another. Parts of the cubes will be below the surface of the punch and will displace the punch. Will some cubes displace more punch than others? Explain your answer.

_____

_____

_____

_____

_____

_____

ACTIVE **READING**

3 Apply Many scientific words, such as *divergent* and *convergent*, also have everyday meanings or are related to words with everyday meanings. Use context clues to write your own definition for each underlined word.

Example sentence
They argued about the issue because their opinions about it were <u>divergent</u>.

divergent:

_____

_____

Example sentence
The two rivers <u>converged</u> near the town.

convergent:

_____

_____

Vocabulary Terms
• Pangaea
• sea-floor spreading
• plate tectonics
• tectonic plates
• convergent boundary
• divergent boundary
• transform boundary
• convection

4 Identify This list contains key terms you'll learn in this lesson. As you read, underline the definition of each term.

Puzzling Evidence

What evidence suggests that continents move?

Have you ever looked at a map and noticed that the continents look like they could fit together like puzzle pieces? In the late 1800s, Alfred Wegener proposed his hypothesis of continental drift. He proposed that the continents once formed a single landmass, broke up, and drifted. This idea is supported by several lines of evidence. For example, fossils of the same species are found on continents on different sides of the Atlantic Ocean. These species could not have crossed the ocean. The hypothesis is also supported by the locations of mountain ranges and rock formations and by evidence of the same ancient climatic conditions on several continents.

Geologic evidence supports the hypothesis of continental drift.

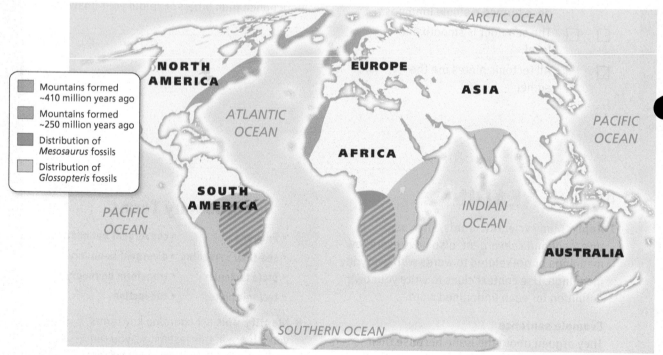

Key:
- Mountains formed ~410 million years ago
- Mountains formed ~250 million years ago
- Distribution of *Mesosaurus* fossils
- Distribution of *Glossopteris* fossils

Visualize It!

5 Summarize Using the map and its key, complete the table to describe evidence that indicates each continent pair was once joined.

	Fossil evidence	Mountain evidence
South America and Africa		
North America and Europe		

What is Pangaea?

ACTIVE READING

6 Identify As you read, underline the description of how North America formed from Pangaea.

Using evidence from many scientific fields, scientists can construct a picture of continental change throughout time. Scientists think that about 245 million years ago, the continents were joined in a single large landmass they call **Pangaea** (pan•JEE•uh). As the continents collided to form Pangaea, mountains formed. A single, large ocean called Panthalassa surrounded Pangaea.

About 200 million years ago, a large rift formed and Pangaea began to break into two continents—*Laurasia* and *Gondwana*. Then, Laurasia began to drift northward and rotate slowly, and a new rift formed. This rift separated Laurasia into the continents of North America and Eurasia. The rift eventually formed the North Atlantic Ocean. At the same time, Gondwana also broke into two continents. One continent contained land that is now the continents of South America and Africa. The other continent contained land that is now Antarctica, Australia, and India.

About 150 million years ago, a rift between Africa and South America opened to form the South Atlantic Ocean. India, Australia, and Antarctica also began to separate from each other. As India broke away from Australia and Antarctica, it started moving northward, toward Eurasia.

As India and the continents moved into their present positions, new oceans formed while others disappeared. In some cases, continents collided with other continents. About 50 million years ago, India collided with Eurasia, and the Himalaya Mountains began to form. Mountain ranges form as a result of these collisions, because a collision welds new crust onto the continents and uplifts some of the land.

The Breakup of Pangaea

245 million years ago

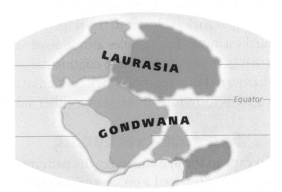

200 million years ago

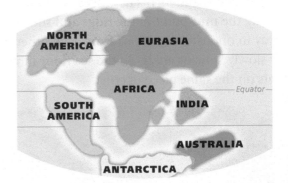

65 million years ago

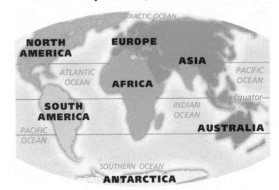

3 million years ago

What discoveries support the idea of continental drift?

Wegener's ideas of continental drift were pushed aside for many years because scientists could not determine how continents moved. Then, in the mid-1900s, scientists began mapping the sea floor. They expected the floor to be smooth and level. Instead, they found huge under-water mountain ranges called *mid-ocean ridges*. The discovery of mid-ocean ridges eventually led to the theory of plate tectonics, which built on some of Wegener's ideas.

○ Age and Magnetic Properties of the Sea Floor

Scientists learned that the mid-ocean ridges form along cracks in the crust. Rock samples from the sea floor revealed that the youngest rock is closest to the ridge, while the oldest rock is farthest away. The samples also showed that even the oldest ocean crust is young compared to continental crust. Scientists also discovered that sea-floor rock contains magnetic patterns. These patterns form mirror images on either side of a mid-ocean ridge.

○ Sea-Floor Spreading

To explain the age and magnetic patterns of sea-floor rocks, scientists proposed a process called **sea-floor spreading**. In this process, molten rock from inside Earth rises through the cracks in the ridges, cools, and forms new oceanic crust. The old crust breaks along the mid-point of the ridge and the two pieces of crust move away in opposite directions from each other. In this way, the sea floor slowly spreads apart. As the sea floor moves, so do the continents on the same piece of crust.

7 Claims • Evidence • Reasoning
Make a claim about why many scientists would not accept the hypothesis of continental drift. Give evidence to support the claim and explain your reasoning.

_____

_____

_____

This map shows where mid-ocean ridges are located.

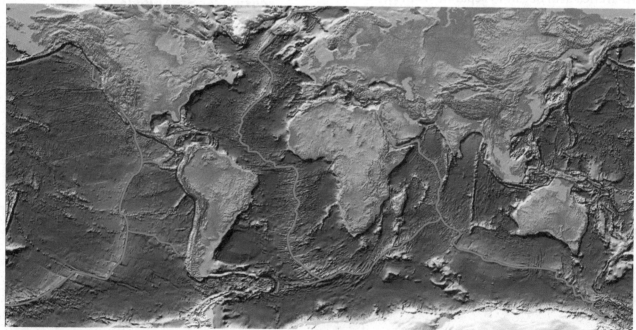

Ocean Trenches

If the sea floor has been spreading for millions of years, why is Earth not getting larger? Scientists discovered the answer when they found huge trenches, like deep canyons, in the sea floor. At these sites, dense oceanic crust is sinking into the asthenosphere as shown in the diagram below. Older crust is being destroyed at the same rate new crust is forming. Thus, Earth remains the same size.

With this new information about the sea floor, sea-floor spreading, and ocean trenches, scientists could begin to understand how continents were able to move.

ACTIVE READING

8 Claims • Evidence • Reasoning Make a claim about why Earth isn't getting larger if the sea floor is spreading. Summarize evidence to support the claim and explain your reasoning.

_____

_____

_____

👁 Visualize It!

9 Provide Label the youngest rock and the oldest rock on this diagram of sea-floor spreading.

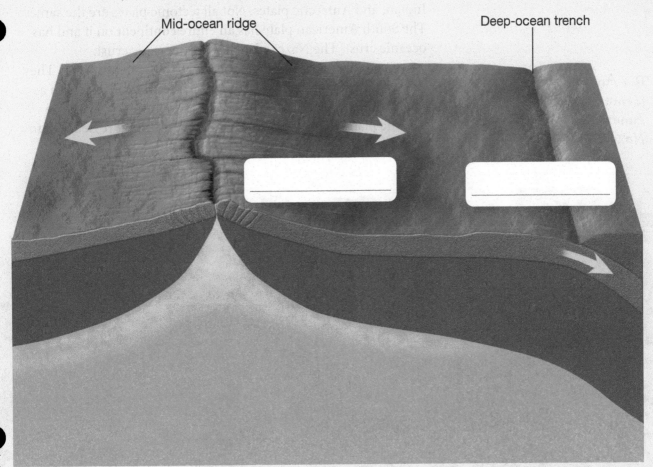

Sea-floor spreading takes place at mid-ocean ridges.

Mid-ocean ridge

Deep-ocean trench

A Giant Jigsaw

Think Outside the Book

10 Apply Imagine that the theory of plate tectonics has just been proposed. Design a magazine ad for the theory.

ACTIVE READING

11 Identify As you read, underline the definition of *tectonic plates*.

The Andes Mountains formed where the South American plate and Nazca plate meet.

What is the theory of plate tectonics?

As scientists' understanding of continental drift, mid-ocean ridges, and sea-floor spreading grew, scientists formed a theory to explain these processes and features. **Plate tectonics** describes large-scale movements of Earth's lithosphere, which is made up of the crust and the rigid, upper part of the mantle. Plate tectonics explains how and why features in Earth's crust form and continents move.

What is a tectonic plate?

The lithosphere is divided into pieces called **tectonic plates.** These plates move around on top of the asthenosphere. The plates are moving in different directions and at different speeds. Each tectonic plate fits together with the plates that surround it. The continents are located on tectonic plates and move around with them. The major tectonic plates include the Pacific, North American, Nazca, South American, African, Australian, Eurasian, Indian, and Antarctic plates. Not all tectonic plates are the same. The South American plate has an entire continent on it and has oceanic crust. The Nazca plate has only oceanic crust.

Tectonic plates cover the surface of the asthenosphere. They vary in size, shape, and thickness. Thick tectonic plates, such as those with continents, displace more asthenosphere than thin oceanic plates do. But, oceanic plates are much more dense than continental plates are.

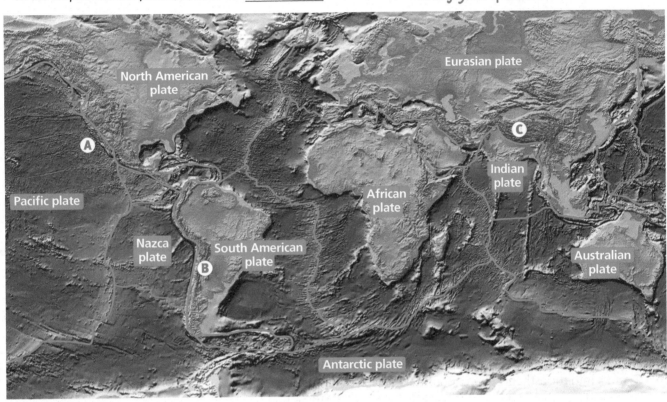

Visualize It!

12 Locate Which letter marks where the Andes Mountains are located on the map of tectonic plates, A, B, or C? _____

The tectonic plates fit together like the pieces of a jigsaw puzzle.

North American plate

Eurasian plate

Pacific plate

C

Indian plate

African plate

Nazca plate

South American plate

B

A

Australian plate

Antarctic plate

The thickest part of the South American plate is the continental crust. The thinnest part of this plate is in the Atlantic Ocean.

Andes mountain range

South American Tectonic plate

Continental crust

Rigid Mantle

Oceanic crust

(bkgd) ©Emil von Maltiz/Gallo Images/Getty Images

©Houghton Mifflin Harcourt Publishing Company

Boundaries

What are the three types of plate boundaries?

The most dramatic changes in Earth's crust occur along plate boundaries. Plate boundaries may be on the ocean floor, around the edges of continents, or even within continents. There are three types of plate boundaries: divergent boundaries, convergent boundaries, and transform boundaries. Each type of plate boundary is associated with characteristic landforms.

ACTIVE READING

13 Identify As you read, underline the locations where plate boundaries may be found.

Convergent Boundaries

Convergent boundaries form where two plates collide. Three types of collisions can happen at convergent boundaries. When two tectonic plates of continental lithosphere collide, they buckle and thicken, which pushes some of the continental crust upward. When a plate of oceanic lithosphere collides with a plate of continental lithosphere, the denser oceanic lithosphere sinks into the asthenosphere. Boundaries where one plate sinks beneath another plate are called subduction zones. When two tectonic plates of oceanic lithosphere collide, one of the plates subducts, or sinks, under the other plate.

 14 Claims • Evidence • Reasoning Make a claim about why the denser plate subducts in a collision. Support the claim with evidence and explain your reasoning.

_____

_____

_____

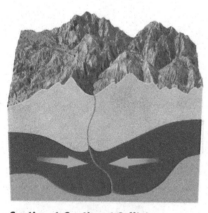

Continent-Continent Collisions
When two plates of continental lithosphere collide, they buckle and thicken. This causes mountains to form.

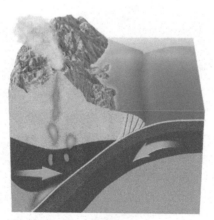

Continent-Ocean Collisions
When a plate of oceanic lithosphere collides with a plate of continental lithosphere, the oceanic lithosphere subducts because it is denser.

Ocean-Ocean Collisions
When two plates of oceanic lithosphere collide, the older, denser plate subducts under the other plate.

Divergent Boundaries

At a **divergent boundary**, two plates move away from each other. This separation allows the asthenosphere to rise toward the surface and partially melt. This melting creates magma, which erupts as lava. The lava cools and hardens to form new rock on the ocean floor.

As the crust and the upper part of the asthenosphere cool and become rigid, they form new lithosphere. This lithosphere is thin, warm, and light. This warm, light rock sits higher than the surrounding sea floor because it is less dense. It forms mid-ocean ridges. Most divergent boundaries are located on the ocean floor. However, rift valleys may also form where continents are separated by plate movement.

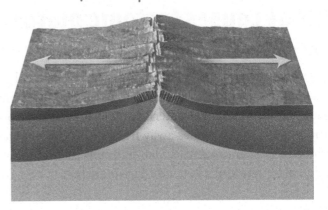

At divergent boundaries, plates separate.

Transform Boundaries

A boundary at which two plates move past each other horizontally is called a **transform boundary**. However, the plate edges do not slide along smoothly. Instead, they scrape against each other in a series of sudden slippages of crustal rock that are felt as earthquakes. Unlike other types of boundaries, transform boundaries generally do not produce magma. The San Andreas Fault in California is a major transform boundary between the North American plate and the Pacific plate. Transform motion also occurs at divergent boundaries. Short segments of mid-ocean ridges are connected by transform faults called fracture zones.

ACTIVE READING

15 Claims • Evidence • Reasoning How are transform boundaries different from convergent and divergent boundaries? Provide evidence to support the claim and explain your reasoning.

_____

_____

_____

At transform boundaries, plates slide past each other horizontally.

Hot Plates

What causes tectonic plates to move?

Scientists have proposed three mechanisms to explain how tectonic plates move over Earth's surface. Mantle convection drags plates along as mantle material moves beneath tectonic plates. Ridge push moves plates away from mid-ocean ridges as rock cools and becomes more dense. Slab pull tugs plates along as the dense edge of a plate sinks beneath Earth's surface.

ACTIVE READING

16 Identify As you read, underline three mechanisms scientists have proposed to explain plate motion.

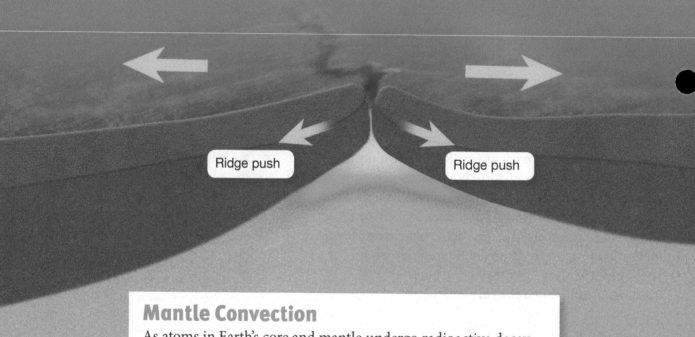

Ridge push   Ridge push

Mantle Convection

As atoms in Earth's core and mantle undergo radioactive decay, energy is released as heat. Some parts of the mantle become hotter than others parts. The hot parts rise as the sinking of cooler, denser material pushes the heated material up. This kind of movement of material due to differences in density is called **convection**. It was thought that as the mantle convects, or moves, it would drag the overlying tectonic plates along with it. However, this hypothesis has been criticized by many scientists because it does not explain the huge amount of force that would be needed to move plates.

Ridge Push

Newly formed rock at a mid-ocean ridge is warm and less dense than older, adjacent rock. Because of its lower density, the new rock rests at a higher elevation than the older rock. The older rock slopes downward away from the ridge. As the newer, warmer rock cools, it also becomes more dense. These cooling and increasingly dense rocks respond to gravity by moving down the slope of the asthenosphere, away from the ridge. This force, called ridge push, pushes the rest of the plate away from the mid-ocean ridge.

Slab Pull

At subduction zones, a denser tectonic plate sinks, or subducts, beneath another, less dense plate. The leading edge of the subducting plate is colder and denser than the mantle. As it sinks, the leading edge of the plate pulls the rest of the plate with it. This process is called slab pull. In general, subducting plates move faster than other plates do. This evidence leads many scientists to think that slab pull may be the most important mechanism driving tectonic plate motion.

Slab pull

17 Compare Complete the chart with brief descriptions to compare and contrast mantle convection, ridge push, and slab pull.

Mechanisms

Mantle convection	Ridge push	Slab pull

Visual Summary

To complete this summary, fill in the blanks to complete the label or caption. You can use this page to review the main concepts of the lesson.

Plate Tectonics

The continents were joined in a single landmass.

18 Scientists call the landmass _____

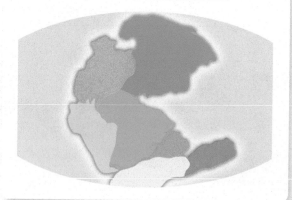

Tectonic plates differ in size and composition.

19 The United States lies on the

_____ plate.

There are three types of plate boundaries: convergent, divergent, and transform.

20 This image shows a

_____

boundary.

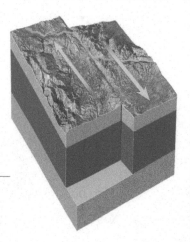

Three mechanisms may drive plate motion. These are mantle convection, slab pull, and ridge push.

21 The mechanism that scientists think is most important is _____

22 **Synthesize** How does the flow of energy as heat in Earth's interior contribute to the movement of tectonic plates? Make a claim about what would happen if Earth were not a convecting system. Use evidence to support your claim, and explain your reasoning.

Lesson Review

Vocabulary

Fill in the blanks with the term that best completes the following sentences.

1 The lithosphere is divided into pieces called

_____

2 The theory that describes large-scale movements of Earth's lithosphere is called

_____

3 The movement of material due to differences in density that are caused by differences in temperature is called _____

_____

Key Concepts

Use this diagram to answer the following questions.

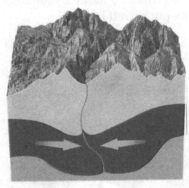

4 Identify What type of plate boundary is shown?

_____

5 Identify Which types of lithosphere are colliding at this boundary?

_____

_____

_____

6 Identify What landforms are likely to form at this boundary?

_____

7 Describe How is continental lithosphere different from oceanic lithosphere?

_____

_____

_____

8 Compare How are convergent boundaries different from divergent boundaries?

_____

_____

_____

Critical Thinking

9 Claims • Evidence • Reasoning Make a claim about why cool rock material sinks when convection takes place in the mantle. Summarize evidence to support the claim and explain your reasoning.

_____

_____

_____

_____

_____

_____

10 Defend A friend says that Earth's continents are too large and massive to move. Explain to your friend why continents move. Defend your claim with evidence.

_____

_____

_____

_____

_____

_____

PEOPLE IN SCIENCE

SC.7.N.1.5 Describe the methods used in the pursuit of a scientific explanation as seen in different fields of science such as biology, geology, and physics.

Estella Atekwana

GEOPHYSICIST

Dr. Estella Atekwana studies changes on Earth's surface. Some of the changes may tell us how life on Earth developed. Others may help us to detect whether life exists somewhere else in the universe.

Some of Dr. Atekwana's work takes her to Botswana and Zambia in Africa. There she is studying the formation of a new rift valley. Rift valleys are places where continents break apart. (For example, long ago a rift valley formed, and Africa broke apart from South America.) Studying this rift valley, Dr. Atekwana hopes to learn more about how new landmasses form. Further, the ground reveals the remains of plants and animals that once lived there. These remains can tell us more about the climate that existed there millions of years ago.

Currently, Dr. Atekwana is doing brand new research in a new field of geology known as biogeophysics. She is looking at the effects that microorganisms have on rocks. She is using new technologies to study how rock changes after microorganisms have mixed with it. This research may one day help scientists detect evidence of life on other planets. Looking for the same geophysical changes in the rocks on Mars might be a way of detecting whether life ever existed on that planet. If the rocks show the same changes as the rocks on Earth, it could be because microorganisms once lived in them.

Dr. Atekwana's research included this visit to Victoria Falls on the Zambezi River in Africa.

Social Studies Connection

Dr. Atekwana studies rift valleys—areas where the tectonic plates are pulling apart. Research to find out where else in the world scientists have located rift valleys.

JOB BOARD

Surveying and Mapping Technicians

What You'll Do: Help surveyors take measurements of outdoor areas. Technicians hold measuring tapes and adjust instruments, take notes, and make sketches.

Where You Might Work: Outdoors and indoors entering measurements into a computer.

Education: Some post-secondary education to obtain a license.

Other Job Requirements: Technicians must be able to visualize objects, distances, sizes, and shapes. They must be able to work with great care, precision, and accuracy because mistakes can be expensive. They must also be in good physical condition.

Petroleum Technician

What You'll Do: Measure and record the conditions in oil or gas wells to find out whether samples contain oil and other minerals.

Where You Might Work: Outdoors, sometimes in remote locations and sometimes in your own town or city.

Education: An associate's degree or a certificate in applied science or science-related technology.

Other Job Requirements: You need to be able to take accurate measurements and keep track of many details.

Geologist

What You'll Do: Study the history of Earth's crust. Geologists work in many different businesses. You may explore for minerals, oil, or gas. You may find and test ground water supplies. You may work with engineers to make sure ground is safe to build on.

Where You Might Work: In the field, where you collect samples, and in the office, where you analyze them. Geologists work in mines, on oil rigs, on the slopes of volcanoes, in quarries, and in paleontological digs.

Education: A four-year bachelor's degree in science.

Other Job Requirements: Geologists who work in the field must be in good physical condition. Most geologists do field training. Geologists need strong math skills, analytical skills, and computer skills. They also need to be able to work well with other members of a team.

Mountain Building

ESSENTIAL QUESTION

How do mountains form?

By the end of this lesson, you should be able to describe how the movement of Earth's tectonic plates causes mountain building.

SC.7.N.1.1 Define a problem from the seventh grade curriculum, use appropriate reference materials to support scientific understanding, plan and carry out scientific investigation of various types, such as systematic observations or experiments, identify variables, collect and organize data, interpret data in charts, tables, and graphics, analyze information, make predictions, and defend conclusions. **SC.7.E.6.5** Explore the scientific theory of plate tectonics by describing how the movement of Earth's crustal plates causes both slow and rapid changes in Earth's surface, including volcanic eruptions, earthquakes, and mountain building. **SC.7.E.6.7** Recognize that heat flow and movement of material within Earth causes earthquakes and volcanic eruptions, and creates mountains and ocean basins.

The highest peak in the Alps mountain range is Mont Blanc at just over 4,800 m tall.

Lesson Labs

Quick Labs
- Modeling Geologic Processes
- Modeling Strike-Slip Faults

 Engage Your Brain

1 Predict Check T or F to show whether you think each statement is true or false.

T   F

☐ ☐ Mountains can originate from a level surface that is folded upward.

☐ ☐ Rocks can be pulled apart by the movement of tectonic plates.

☐ ☐ All mountains are created by volcanoes.

☐ ☐ A mountain range can form only at the edge of a tectonic plate.

Rocky Mountains

Appalachian Mountains

2 Hypothesize The Appalachian Mountains were once taller than the Rocky Mountains. What do you think happened to the mountains? Explain your reasoning.

_____

_____

ACTIVE **READING**

3 Compare The terms *compression* and *tension* have opposite meanings. Compare the two sentences below, then write your own definition for *compression* and *tension*.

Vocabulary	Sentence
compression	The stack of books on Jon's desk caused the bottom book to be flattened by <u>compression</u>.
tension	Keisha pulled the piece of string so hard, the <u>tension</u> caused the string to break.

compression:

_____

_____

tension:

_____

_____

Vocabulary Terms

- deformation
- folding
- fault
- shear stress
- tension
- compression

4 Apply As you learn the definition of each vocabulary term in this lesson, create your own definition or sketch to help you remember the meaning of the term.

Stressed Out

How can tectonic plate motion cause deformation?

The movement of tectonic plates places stress on rocks. A tectonic plate is a block of lithosphere that consists of crust and the rigid outermost part of the mantle. *Stress* is the amount of force per unit area that is placed on an object. Rocks can bend or break under stress. In addition, low temperatures make materials more brittle, or easily broken. High temperatures can allow rock to bend.

When a rock is placed under stress, it deforms, or changes shape. **Deformation** (dee•fohr•MAY•shuhn) is the process by which rocks change shape when under stress. Rock can bend if it is placed under high temperature and pressure for long periods of time. If the stress becomes too great, or is applied quickly, rock can break. When rocks bend, folds form. When rocks break, faults form.

ACTIVE READING

5 Identify As you read, list some objects near you that can bend or break from deformation.

_____

_____

_____

_____

_____

By applying stress, the boy is causing the spaghetti to deform. Similarly, stress over a long period of time can cause rock to bend.

Like the spaghetti, stress over a short period of time or great amounts of stress can cause rock to break.

👁 Visualize It!

6 Claims • Evidence • Reasoning Make a claim about how the same material might bend in one situation but break in another. Provide evidence to support the claim and explain your reasoning.

_____

_____

_____

_____

What are two kinds of folds?

Folded rock layers appear bent or buckled. **Folding** occurs when rock layers bend under stress. The bends are called *folds*. Scientists assume that all rock layers start out as horizontal layers deposited on top of each other over time. Sometimes, different layers of rocks can still be seen even after the rocks have been folded. When scientists see a fold, they know that deformation has happened. Two common types of folds are synclines and anticlines.

Think Outside the Book

7 Model Stack several sheets of paper together. Apply stress to the sides of the paper to create a model of a syncline and an anticline. Share your model with your teacher.

◯ Synclines and Anticlines

Folds are classified based on the age of the rock layers. In a *syncline* (SIN•klyn), the youngest layers of rock are found at the core of a fold. The oldest layers are found on the outside of the fold. Synclines usually look like rock layers that are arched upward, like a bowl. In an *anticline* (AN•tih•klyn), the oldest layers of rock are found at the core of the fold. The youngest layers are found on the outside of the fold. Anticlines often look like rock layers that are arched downwards and high in the middle. Often, both types of folds will be visible in the same rock layers, as shown below.

The hinge is the middle point of the bend in a syncline or anticline.

👁 Visualize It!

8 Claims • Evidence • Reasoning Make a claim about which rock layers are youngest and oldest. Summarize evidence to support the claim and explain your reasoning.

_____

_____

_____

_____

_____

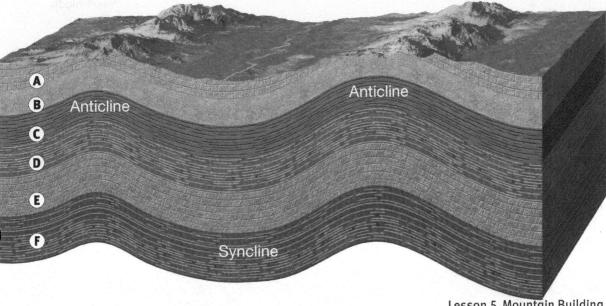

A
B Anticline
C
D
E
F

Anticline

Syncline

Faulted

What are the three kinds of faults?

Rock can be under so much stress that it cannot bend and may break. The crack that forms when large blocks of rock break and move past each other is called a **fault**. The blocks of rock on either side of the fault are called *fault blocks*. The sudden movement of fault blocks can cause earthquakes.

Any time there is a fault in Earth's crust, rocks tend to move in predictable ways. Earth has three main kinds of faults: strike-slip faults, normal faults, and reverse faults. Scientists classify faults based on the way fault blocks move relative to each other. The location where two fault blocks meet is called the *fault plane*. A fault plane can be oriented horizontally, vertically, or at any angle in between. For any fault except a perfectly vertical fault, the block above the fault plane is called the *hanging wall*. The block below the fault plane is the *footwall*.

The movement of faults can create mountains and other types of landforms. At any tectonic plate boundary, the amount of stress on rock is complex. Therefore, any of the three types of faults can occur at almost all plate boundaries.

ACTIVE READING

9 Identify As you read, underline the direction of movement of the fault blocks in each type of fault.

Strike-Slip Faults

In a strike-slip fault, the fault blocks move past each other horizontally. Strike-slip faults form when rock is under shear stress. **Shear stress** is stress that pushes rocks in parallel but opposite directions as seen in the image. As rocks are deformed deep in Earth's crust, energy builds. The release of this energy can cause earthquakes as the rocks slide past each other. Strike-slip faults are common along transform boundaries, where tectonic plates move past each other. The San Andreas fault system in California is an example of a strike-slip fault.

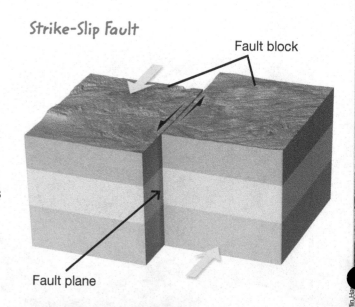

Strike-Slip Fault

Fault block

Fault plane

Normal Faults

In the normal fault shown on the right, the hanging wall moves down relative to the footwall. The faults are called normal because the blocks move in a way that you would *normally* expect as a result of gravity. Normal faults form when the rock is under tension. **Tension** (TEN•shun) is stress that stretches or pulls rock apart. Therefore, normal faults are common along divergent boundaries. Earth's crust can also stretch in the middle of a tectonic plate. The Basin and Range area of the southwestern United States is an example of a location with many normal fault structures.

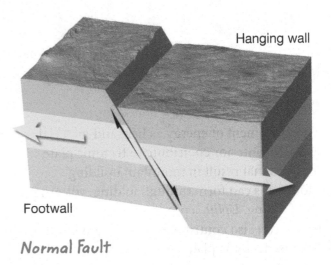

Hanging wall

Footwall

Normal Fault

Reverse Faults

In the reverse fault shown on the right, the hanging wall moves up relative to the footwall. The faults are called reverse because the hanging blocks move up, which is the reverse of what you would expect as a result of gravity. Reverse faults form when rocks undergo compression. **Compression** (kuhm•PRESH•uhn) is stress that squeezes or pushes rock together. Reverse faults are common along convergent boundaries, where two plates collide. The San Gabriel Mountains in the United States are caused by reverse faults.

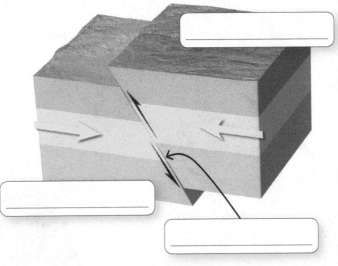

Reverse Fault

👁 Visualize It!

10 Identify Label the fault plane, hanging wall, and footwall on the reverse fault to the right.

ⓘ Think Outside the Book

11 Compile Create a memory matching game of the types of faults. Create as many cards as you can with different photos, drawings, or written details about the types of faults. Use the cards to quiz yourself and your classmates.

Moving On Up

What are the three kinds of mountains?

The movement of energy as heat and material in Earth's interior contribute to tectonic plate motions that result in mountain building. Mountains can form through folding, volcanism, and faulting. *Uplift*, a process that can cause land to rise can also contribute to mountain building. Because tectonic plates are always in motion, some mountains are constantly being uplifted.

ACTIVE READING

12 Identify As you read, underline examples of folded, volcanic, and fault-block mountains.

Folded Mountains

Folded mountains form when rock layers are squeezed together and pushed upward. They usually form at convergent boundaries, where plates collide. For example, the Appalachian Mountains (ap•uh•LAY•chun) formed from folding and faulting when the North American plate collided with the Eurasian and African plates millions of years ago.

In Europe, the Pyrenees (PIR•uh•neez) are another range of folded mountains, as shown below. They are folded over an older, pre-existing mountain range. Today, the highest peaks are over 3,000 m tall.

The Pyrenees Mountains are folded mountains that separate France from Spain.

Visualize It!

13 Claims • Evidence • Reasoning What evidence do you see that the Pyrenees Mountains are folded mountains? Summarize evidence to support the claim and explain your reasoning.

_____

_____

_____

Volcanic Mountains

Volcanic mountains form when melted rock erupts onto Earth's surface. Many major volcanic mountains are located at convergent boundaries. Volcanic mountains can form on land or on the ocean floor. Volcanoes on the ocean floor can grow so tall that they rise above the surface of the ocean, forming islands. Most of Earth's active volcanoes are concentrated around the edge of the Pacific Ocean. This area is known as the Ring of Fire. Many volcanoes, including Mt. Griggs in the image to the right, are located on the Northern rim of the Pacific plate in Alaska.

Mt. Griggs volcano on the Alaskan Peninsula is 2,317 m high.

Fault-Block Mountains

Fault-block mountains form when tension makes the lithosphere break into many normal faults. Along the faults, pieces of the lithosphere drop down compared with other pieces. The pieces left standing form fault-block mountains. The Teton Mountains (TEE•tuhn) and the Sierra Nevadas are fault-block mountains.

The Teton Mountains in Wyoming are fault-block mountains.

14 Identify Draw a simple version of each type of mountain below.

Folded	Volcanic	Faulted

Visual Summary

To complete this summary, fill in the blanks with the correct word or phrase. You can use this page to review the main concepts of the lesson.

Mountain Building

Rocks can bend or break under stress.

15 The process by which rocks change shape under stress is called _____

Folds occur when rock layers bend.

16 A rock structure with the oldest rocks at the core of the fold is called a/an _____

Faults occur when rock layers break.

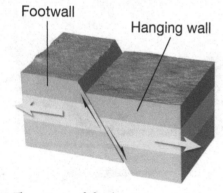

Footwall

Hanging wall

17 The type of fault pictured is a _____ fault.

Mountains form through folding, volcanism, and faulting.

18 The type of mountains pictured are _____ mountains.

19 **Claims • Evidence • Reasoning** The middle of tectonic plates tend to have fewer mountains than locations near tectonic plate boundaries. Make a claim about what might be one possible explanation for this. Summarize evidence to support the claim and explain your reasoning.

Lesson Review

Vocabulary

Fill in the blank with the term that best completes the following sentences.

1 A normal fault is a result of a type of stress known as _____

2 A strike-slip fault is a result of _____ stress.

3 A reverse fault is caused by a type of stress known as _____

Key Concepts

Fill in the table below by identifying the type of mountain described in the example question.

Example	Type of Mountain
4 Identify The Basin and Range province is characterized by many normal faults.	
5 Identify The Cascade Range in the United States has many eruptive mountains.	
6 Identify The Pyrenees Mountains have many syncline and anticline structures.	

7 Describe How does the movement of tectonic plates cause deformation in rock?

_____

_____

_____

8 Compare How do folded, volcanic, and fault-block mountains differ?

_____

_____

_____

Critical Thinking

Use the diagram below to answer the following questions.

9 Correlate What type of stress caused the fault shown in the image?

_____

10 Claims • Evidence • Reasoning Make a claim about along which type of tectonic plate boundary this fault would be common. Provide evidence to support the claim and explain your reasoning.

_____

_____

11 Claims • Evidence • Reasoning Make a claim about whether a rock can undergo compression, tension, and shear stress all at once. Summarize evidence to support the claim and explain your reasoning.

_____

_____

_____

12 Conclude Imagine you are walking along a roadway and see a syncline. What can you conclude about the formation of that fold?

_____

_____

_____

Earthquakes

ESSENTIAL QUESTION

Why do earthquakes happen?

By the end of this lesson, you should be able to describe the causes of earthquakes and to identify where earthquakes happen.

SC.7.N.1.1 Define a problem from the seventh grade curriculum, use appropriate reference materials to support scientific understanding, plan and carry out scientific investigation of various types, such as systematic observations or experiments, identify variables, collect and organize data, interpret data in charts, tables, and graphics, analyze information, make predictions, and defend conclusions. **SC.7.E.6.5** Explore the scientific theory of plate tectonics by describing how the movement of Earth's crustal plates causes both slow and rapid changes in Earth's surface, including volcanic eruptions, earthquakes, and mountain building. **SC.7.E.6.7** Recognize that heat flow and movement of material within Earth causes earthquakes and volcanic eruptions, and creates mountains and ocean basins.

The 1995 Kobe earthquake in Japan destroyed more than 200,000 buildings and structures including this railroad track.

©Pacific Press Service/Alamy

© Houghton Mifflin Harcourt Publishing Company

Lesson Labs

Quick Labs
- Elastic Rebound
- Earthquake Vibrations
- Earthquakes and Buildings

S.T.E.M. Lab
- Use a Seismograph to Determine the Amount of Energy in an Earthquake

 ## Engage Your Brain

1 Predict Fill in any words or numbers that you think best complete each of the statements below.

Each year there are approximately _____ earthquakes detected around the world.

In the United States, the state with the most earthquakes on average is _____

Every year, earthquakes cause _____ of dollars in damages in the United States.

Most earthquakes only last for several _____ of time.

2 Analyze Using the image, list in column 1 some of the hazards that can occur after an earthquake. In column 2, explain why you think these items or situations would be hazardous.

_____

_____

Hazards	Why?

ACTIVE READING

3 Synthesize You can often define an unknown word if you know the meaning of its word parts. Use the word parts and sentence below to make an educated guess about the meaning of the word *epicenter*.

Word part	Meaning
epi-	on, upon, or over
-center	the middle

Example sentence
The <u>epicenter</u> of the earthquake was only 3 km from our school.

epicenter:

_____

_____

Vocabulary Terms

- earthquake
- focus
- epicenter
- tectonic plate boundary
- fault
- deformation
- elastic rebound

4 Apply As you learn the definition of each vocabulary term in this lesson, create your own definition or sketch to help you remember the meaning of the term.

Let's Focus

What is an earthquake?

Earthquakes can cause extreme damage and loss of life. **Earthquakes** are ground movements that occur when blocks of rock in Earth move suddenly and release energy. The energy is released as seismic waves which cause the ground to shake and tremble.

Earthquake waves can be tracked to a point below Earth's surface known as the focus. The **focus** is a place within Earth along a fault at which the first motion of an earthquake occurs. Motion along a fault causes stress. When the stress on the rock is too great, the rock will rupture and cause an earthquake. The earthquake releases the stress. Directly above the focus on Earth's surface is the **epicenter** (EP•i•sen•ter). Seismic waves flow outward from the focus in all directions.

ACTIVE READING

5 Identify As you read, underline the definitions of *focus* and *epicenter*.

👁 Visualize It!

6 Identify Label the epicenter, focus, and fault on the diagram.

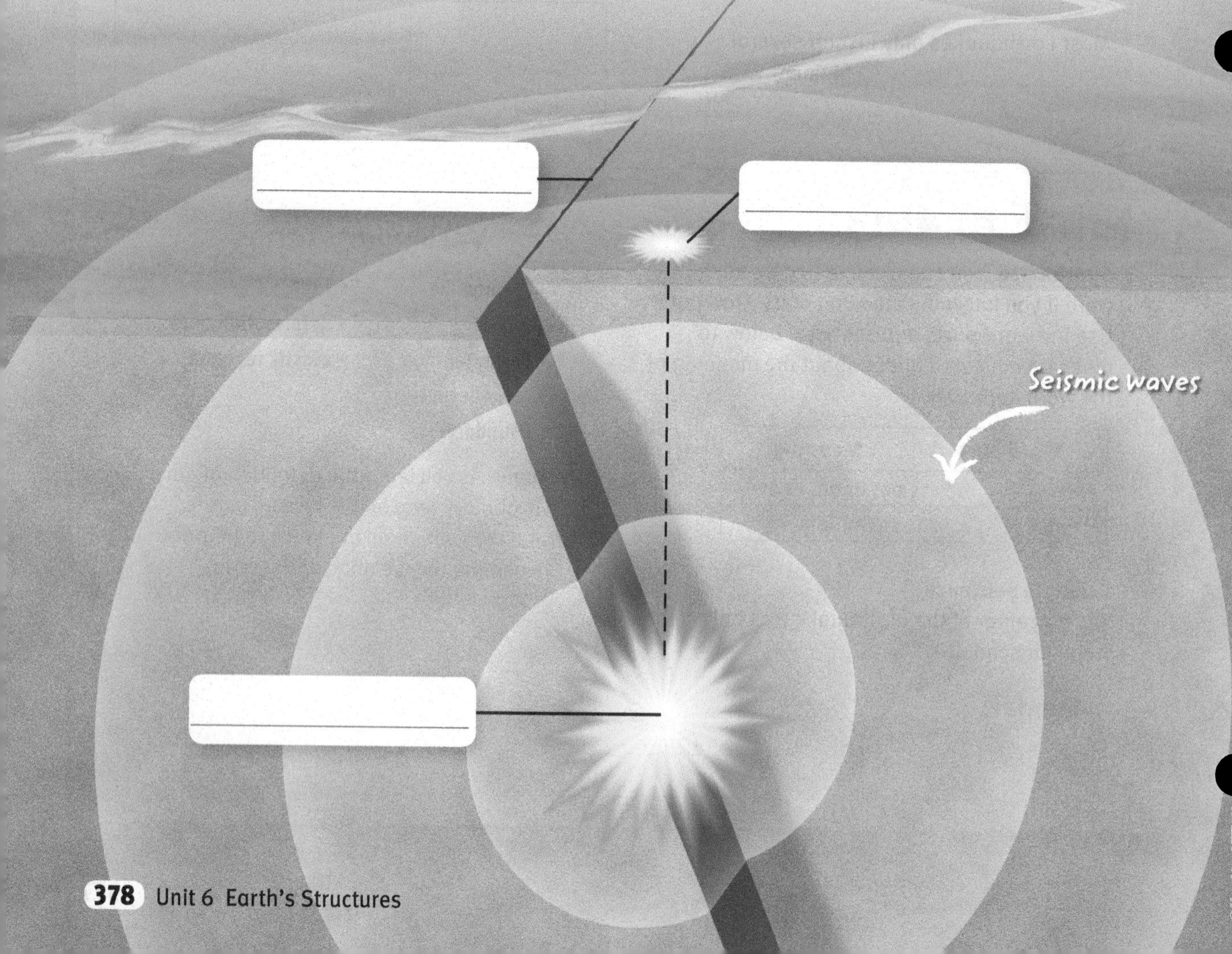

Seismic waves

© Houghton Mifflin Harcourt Publishing Company

What causes earthquakes?

Most earthquakes occur near the boundaries of tectonic plates. A **tectonic plate boundary** is where two or more tectonic plates meet. As tectonic plates move, pressure builds up near the edges of the plates. These movements break Earth's crust into a series of faults. A **fault** is a break in Earth's crust along which blocks of rock move. The release of energy that accompanies the movement of the rock along a fault causes an earthquake.

◯ Elastic Rebound

When rock is put under tremendous pressure, stress may deform, or change the shape of, the rock. **Deformation** (dee•for•MAY•shun) is the process by which rock becomes deformed and changes shape due to stress. As stress increases, the amount of energy that is stored in the rock increases, as seen in image B to the right.

Stress can change the shape of rock along a fault. Once the stress is released, rock may return to its original shape. When rock returns to nearly the same shape after the stress is removed, the process is known as *elastic deformation*. Imagine an elastic band that is pulled tight under stress. Once stress on the elastic band is removed, there is a *snap!* The elastic band returns to its original shape. A similar process occurs during earthquakes.

Similar to an elastic band, rock along tectonic plate boundaries can suddenly return to nearly its original shape when the stress is removed. The sudden *snap* is an earthquake. The return of rock to its original shape after elastic deformation is called **elastic rebound**. Earthquakes accompany the release of energy during elastic rebound. When the rock breaks and rebounds, it releases energy as seismic waves. The seismic wave energy radiates from the focus of the earthquake in all directions. This energy causes the ground to shake for a short time. Most earthquakes last for just a few seconds.

◉ Visualize It!

7 Claims • Evidence • Reasoning Make a claim about whether an earthquake occurred between images A and B or between images B and C. Summarize evidence to support the claim and explain your reasoning.

_____

Along a fault, rocks are pushed or pulled in different directions and at different speeds.

As stress increases and energy builds within the rock, the rock deforms but remains locked in place.

Too much stress causes the rock to break and rebound to its original shape, releasing energy.

Unstable Ground

Where do earthquakes happen?

Each year, approximately 500,000 earthquakes are detected worldwide. The map below shows some of these earthquakes. Movement of material and energy in the form of heat in Earth's interior contribute to plate motions that result in earthquakes.

Most earthquakes happen at or near tectonic plate boundaries. Tectonic plate boundaries are areas where Earth's crust experiences a lot of stress. This stress occurs because the tectonic plates are colliding, separating, or grinding past each other horizontally. There are three main types of tectonic plate boundaries: divergent, convergent, and transform. The movement and interactions of the plates causes the crust to break into different types of faults. Earthquakes happen along these faults.

Plate Tectonic Boundaries and Earthquake Locations Worldwide

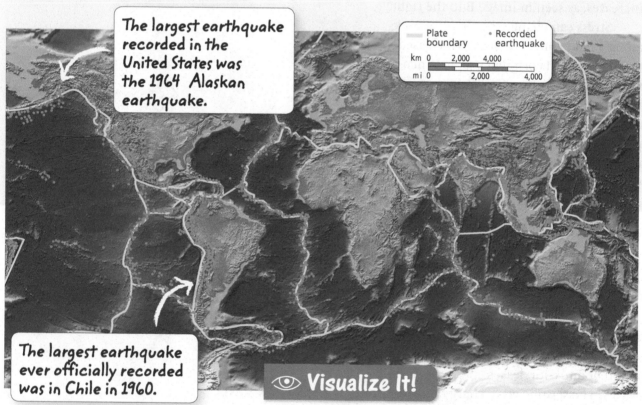

The largest earthquake recorded in the United States was the 1964 Alaskan earthquake.

The largest earthquake ever officially recorded was in Chile in 1960.

Plate boundary	• Recorded earthquake
km 0 2,000 4,000	
mi 0 2,000 4,000	

👁 Visualize It!

9 Claims • Evidence • Reasoning Make a claim about where most of Earth's earthquakes are located. Summarize evidence to support the claim and explain your reasoning.

_____

_____

10 Correlate In the caption for each diagram, write in the type of fault that is common at each of the types of tectonic plate boundaries.

At Divergent Boundaries

At a divergent boundary, plates pull apart, causing the crust to stretch. Stress that stretches rock and makes rock thinner is called *tension*. Normal faults commonly result when tension pulls rock apart.

Most of the crust at divergent boundaries is thin, so the earthquakes tend to be shallow. Most earthquakes at divergent boundaries are no more than 20 km deep. A mid-ocean ridge is an example of a divergent boundary where earthquakes occur.

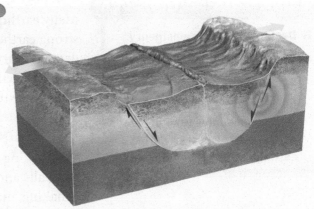

At divergent boundaries, earthquakes are common along _____ faults.

At Convergent Boundaries

Convergent plate boundaries occur when plates collide, causing rock to be squeezed. Stress that shortens or squeezes an object is known as *compression*. Compression causes the formation of reverse faults. Rocks are thrust over one another at reverse faults.

When two plates come together, both plates may crumple up to form mountains. Or one plate can subduct, or sink, underneath the other plate and into the mantle. The earthquakes that happen at convergent boundaries can be very strong. Subduction zone earthquakes occur at depths of up to 700 km.

At convergent boundaries, earthquakes are common along _____ faults.

At Transform Boundaries

A transform boundary is a place where two tectonic plates slide past each other horizontally. Stress that distorts a body by pushing different parts of the body in opposite directions is called *shear stress*. As the plates move, rocks on both sides of the fault are sheared, or broken, as they grind past one another in opposite directions.

Strike–slip faults are common at transform boundaries. Most earthquakes along the faults at transform boundaries are relatively shallow. The earthquakes are generally within the upper 50 km of the crust.

At transform boundaries, earthquakes are common along _____ faults.

Although most of this building is left standing, the entire area is a hazard to citizens in the town.

What are some effects of earthquakes?

Many earthquakes do not cause major damage. However, some strong earthquakes can cause billions of dollars in property damage. Earthquakes may even cause human injuries and loss of life. In general, areas closest to the epicenter of an earthquake experience the greatest damage.

Danger to People and Structures

The shaking of an earthquake can cause structures to move vertically and horizontally. When structures cannot withstand the shaking, major destruction can occur. Following the release of seismic waves, buildings can shake so violently that a total or partial collapse can happen, as shown below.

Much of the injury and loss of life that happen during and after earthquakes is caused by structures that collapse. In addition, fires, gas leaks, floods, and polluted water supplies can cause secondary damages following an earthquake. The debris left after an earthquake can take weeks or months to clean up. Bridges, roadways, homes, and entire cities can become disaster zones.

Tsunamis

An earthquake under the ocean can cause a vertical movement of the sea floor that displaces an enormous amount of water. This displacement may cause a tsunami to form. A *tsunami* (sue•NAH•mee) is a series of extremely long waves that can travel across the ocean at speeds of up to 800 km/h. Tsunami waves travel outward in all directions from the point where the earthquake occurred. As the waves approach a shoreline, the size of the waves increases. The waves can be taller than 30 m. Tsunami waves can cause major destruction and take many lives as they smash and wash away anything in their path. Many people may drown during a tsunami. Floods, polluted water supplies, and large amount of debris are common in the aftermath.

12 Identify List some of the hazards associated with earthquakes on land and underwater.

On Land	Underwater

Killer Quake

Imagine losing half the people in your city. On December 26, 2004, a massive tsunami destroyed approximately one-third of the buildings in Banda Aceh, Indonesia, and wiped out half the population.

How Tsunamis Form

In the ocean, tsunami waves are fast but not very tall. As the waves approach a coast, they slow down and get much taller.

Before

Before the Earthquake

The Banda Aceh tsunami resulted from a very strong earthquake in the ocean. Banda Aceh was very close to the epicenter.

Major Damages

The destruction to parts of Asia were so massive that geographers had to redraw the maps of some of the countries.

After

i Extend

13 Identify In what ocean did the earthquake occur?

14 Research Investigate one other destructive tsunami and find out where the earthquake that caused it originated.

15 Claims • Evidence • Reasoning Many of the people affected by the tsunami were poor. Make a claim about why earthquakes might be more damaging in poor areas of the world. Support the claim with evidence, and explain your reasoning.

Visual Summary

To complete this summary, fill in the correct word. You can use this page to review the main concepts of the lesson.

Earthquakes

Earthquakes occur along faults.

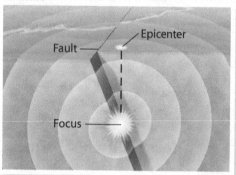

16 The epicenter of an earthquake is directly above the _____

Rocks break and snap back to their original shape in an earthquake.

17 Earthquakes happen when rocks bend and snap back in a process called _____

Earthquakes usually happen along plate boundaries.

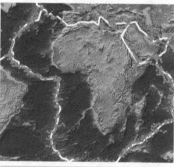

18 The three types of plate boundaries are

_____

_____

_____

Earthquakes can cause a lot of damage.

19 An example of the dangers of earthquakes is _____

20 Claims • Evidence • Reasoning Make a claim about whether or not earthquakes can be prevented. Summarize evidence to support the claim and explain your reasoning.

Lesson Review

Vocabulary

In your own words, define the following terms.

1 Elastic rebound

_____

_____

_____

2 Focus

_____

_____

_____

3 Fault

_____

_____

_____

Key Concepts

Example	Type of Boundary
4 Identify Most of the earthquakes in Japan are a result of one plate sinking under another.	
5 Identify The African Rift Valley is a location where plates are moving apart.	
6 Identify The San Andreas fault is a location where tectonic plates move horizontally past each other.	

7 Explain What causes an earthquake?

_____

_____

_____

Critical Thinking

Use the image to answer the following questions.

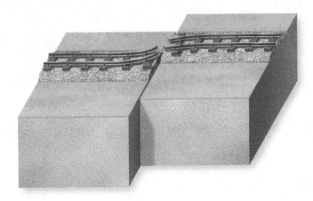

8 Claims • Evidence • Reasoning Make a claim about how the image above demonstrates that a deformation has taken place. Summarize evidence to support the claim and explain your reasoning.

_____

_____

_____

_____

9 Apply How do Earth's surface and the structures on the surface change as a result of an earthquake?

_____

_____

_____

_____

10 Claims • Evidence • Reasoning Make a claim about why there is often only a short amount of time to evacuate an area before an earthquake. Use evidence to support the claim and explain your reasoning.

_____

_____

_____

S.T.E.M. ENGINEERING & TECHNOLOGY

Engineering Design Process

Skills
Identify a need
Conduct research
✔ Brainstorm solutions
✔ Select a solution
Design a prototype
✔ Build a prototype
✔ Test and evaluate
✔ Redesign to improve
✔ Communicate results

Objectives
Explain how scientists measure the energy of earthquakes.
Design a model seismometer to measure motion.
Test and modify a prototype to achieve a desired result.

Building a Seismometer

An earthquake occurs when rocks beneath the ground move suddenly. The energy of this movement travels through Earth in waves. Sometimes the shaking is detected hundreds or thousands of miles away from the origin of the earthquake. Scientists can learn about earthquakes by measuring the earthquake waves.

Measuring Motion

A seismometer is a device for measuring the motion of the ground beneath it. To develop seismometers, scientists had to solve a problem: How do you keep one part of the device from moving when the ground moves? The solution can be seen in the design shown here. A spring separates a heavy weight from the frame of the seismometer. Attached to the weight is a pen. The tip of the pen touches the surface of a circular drum that is covered in paper and slowly turning. When the ground moves, the frame and the rotating drum move along with it. The spring absorbs the ground's movement, so the weight and pen do not move. The pen is always touching the paper on the rotating drum. When the ground is not moving, the pen draws a straight line. When the ground moves, the pen draws this movement.

Waves move the instrument, but the spring and weight keep the pen still.

1 Claims • Evidence • Reasoning This instrument measures the up-and-down motion of earthquake waves. Make a claim about how to change the instrument to measure the side-to-side motion of an earthquake. Support the claim with evidence and explain your reasoning.

_____

_____

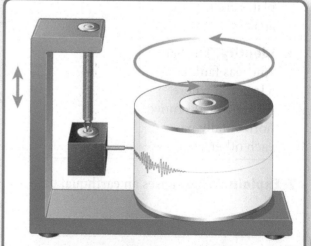

2 Infer In the oval below, write *moves* or *still* to indicate whether the labeled part moves during an earthquake or remains still.

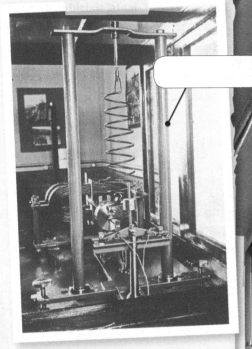

The spring in this older type of seismometer absorbs energy. Modern seismometers use electronic components instead of giant springs.

Drawing the Waves

The drawing produced by a seismometer is called a *seismogram*. A seismogram shows two kinds of earthquake waves: P waves and S waves. P waves move though Earth's crust faster than S waves do. Seismologists measure the time between the arrival of P waves and the arrival of S waves to calculate how far away the earthquake occurred.

Seismogram

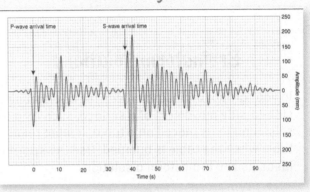

3 Claims • Evidence • Reasoning Make a claim about how geologists might use seismograms to find the exact location of an earthquake. Support the claim with evidence, and explain your reasoning.

_____

_____

_____

_____

🖐 **You Try It!** →

Now it's your turn to design and build a seismometer.

(cd) ©Eye Ubiquitous/Alamy Images; (t) ©Bettmann/Corbis

🖐 You Try It!

Now you will build a seismometer that can detect motion. You will use your seismometer to record the motion of a table. To do this, you will need to determine which parts of your seismometer will move and which parts will remain still. After you design and build the prototype, slowly shake the table back and forth. You may need to redesign and try again.

You Will Need

✓ large square wooden frame
✓ metal weights
✓ string
✓ fine point felt tip pen
✓ long strips or roll of paper
✓ tape
✓ various hooks and hardware

1 Brainstorm Solutions

In your group, brainstorm ideas for a seismometer that will measure side-to-side movement of a surface, such as a table. When the seismometer is placed on a table, it must record the motion of the table when the table is bumped. Use the space below to record ideas as you brainstorm a solution.

2 Select a Solution

Draw a prototype of your group's seismometer idea in the space below. Be sure to include all the parts you will need and show how they will be connected.

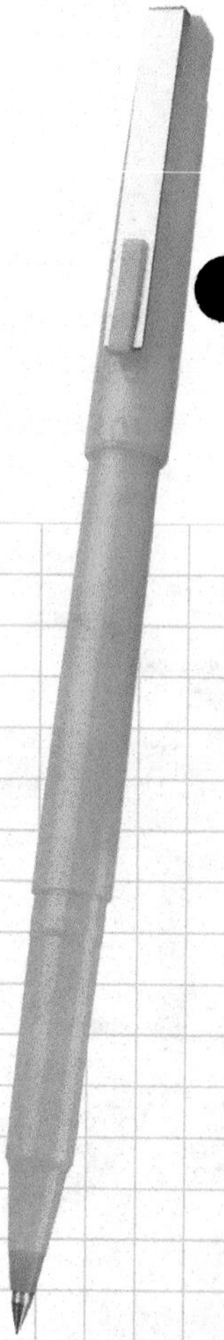

S.T.E.M. ENGINEERING & TECHNOLOGY

③ Build a Prototype

In your group, build the seismometer. As the group builds it, are there some aspects of the design that cannot be assembled as predicted? What did the group have to revise in the prototype?

_____
_____
_____
_____

④ Test and Evaluate

Bump or shake the table under the seismometer. Did the prototype record any motion on the paper strip? If not, what can you revise?

_____
_____
_____

⑤ Redesign to Improve

Choose one aspect to revise, and then test again. Keep making revisions, one at a time, until your seismometer records the motion of the table. How many revisions did the group make?

_____
_____

⑥ Communicate Results

Claims • Evidence • Reasoning Report your observations about the prototype seismometer. Include changes that improved its performance or decreased its performance. Make a claim about ways you could have built a more accurate seismometer, including what additional materials you would need and what they would be used for. Provide evidence to support the claim and explain your reasoning.

_____
_____
_____

Volcanoes

ESSENTIAL QUESTION

How do volcanoes change Earth's surface?

By the end of this lesson, you should be able to describe what the various kinds of volcanoes and eruptions are, where they occur, how they form, and how they change Earth's surface.

SC.7.E.6.5 Explore the scientific theory of plate tectonics by describing how the movement of Earth's crustal plates causes both slow and rapid changes in Earth's surface, including volcanic eruptions, earthquakes, and mountain building.
SC.7.E.6.7 Recognize that heat flow and movement of material within Earth causes earthquakes and volcanic eruptions, and creates mountains and ocean basins.

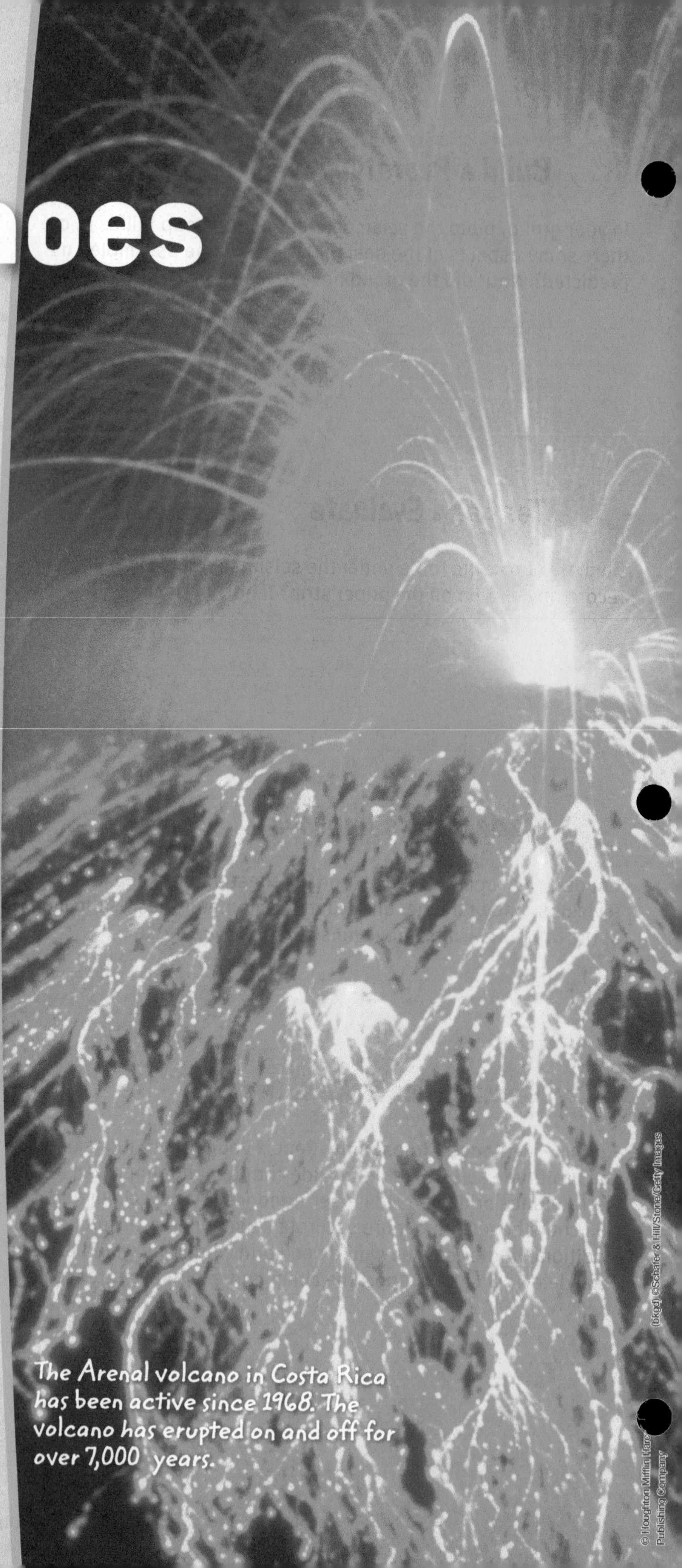

The Arenal volcano in Costa Rica has been active since 1968. The volcano has erupted on and off for over 7,000 years.

© Houghton Mifflin Harcourt Publishing Company

(bkgd) ©Schafer & Hill/Stone/Getty Images

Lesson Labs

Quick Lab
- Modeling an Explosive Eruption
- Volcano Mapping

Engage Your Brain

1 Predict Check T or F to show whether you think each statement is true or false.

T	F	
☐	☐	Volcanoes create new landforms such as mountains.
☐	☐	Tectonic plate boundaries are the only locations where volcanoes form.
☐	☐	Volcanic eruptions are often accompanied by earthquakes.
☐	☐	Volcanoes form new rocks and minerals.

2 Hypothesize You are a news reporter assigned to cover a story about the roadway in the image below. Describe what you think happened in this photo.

_____

_____

_____

_____

ACTIVE READING

3 Synthesize You can often define an unknown word if you know the meaning of its word parts. Use the word parts and sentence below to make an educated guess about the meaning of the word *pyroclastic*.

Word part	Meaning
pyro-	heat or fire
-clastic	pieces

Example sentence
<u>Pyroclastic</u> material was ejected into the atmosphere with explosive force during the eruption of the volcano.

pyroclastic: _____

_____

Vocabulary Terms

- volcano
- magma
- lava
- vent
- tectonic plate
- hot spot

4 Apply As you learn the definition of each vocabulary term in this lesson, create your own definition or sketch to help you remember the meaning of the term.

Magma MAGIC

What is a volcano?

What do volcanoes look like? Most people think of a steep mountain with smoke coming out of the top. In fact, a **volcano** is any place where gas, ash, or melted rock come out of the ground. A volcano can be a tall mountain, as shown below, or a small crack in the ground. Volcanoes occur on land and underwater. There are even volcanoes on other planets. Not all volcanoes actively erupt. Many are *dormant,* meaning an eruption has not occurred in a long period of time.

Volcanoes form as rock below the surface of Earth melts. The melted rock, or **magma**, is less dense than solid rock, so it rises toward the surface. **Lava** is magma that has reached Earth's surface. Lava and clouds of ash can erupt from a **vent**, or opening of a volcano.

👁 Visualize It!

5 Identify Label the parts of the volcano. Include the following terms: *magma, lava, vent, ash cloud.*

Lava can reach temperatures of more than 1,200 °C.

What are the kinds of volcanic landforms?

The location of a volcano and the composition of magma determine the type of volcanic landforms created. Shield volcanoes, cinder cones, composite volcanoes, lava plateaus, craters, and calderas are all types of volcanic landforms.

Volcanic Mountains

Materials ejected from a volcano may build up around a vent to create volcanic mountains. *Viscosity* (vyz•SKAHZ•ih•tee) is the resistance of a liquid material, such as lava, to flow. The viscosity of lava determines the explosiveness of an eruption and the shape of the resulting volcanic mountain. Low-viscosity lava flows easily, forms low slopes, and erupts without large explosions. High-viscosity lava does not flow easily, forms steep slopes, and can erupt explosively. *Pyroclastic materials* (py•roh•KLAHZ•tyk), or hot ash and bits of rock, may also be ejected into the atmosphere.

ACTIVE READING

7 Identify As you read, underline the main features of each type of volcanic mountain.

- **Shield Volcanoes** Volcanoes with a broad base and gently sloping sides are *shield volcanoes*. Shield volcanoes cover a wide area and generally form from mild eruptions. Layers of lava flow out from the vent, harden, and slowly build up to form the cone. The Hawaiian Islands are shield volcanoes.

- **Cinder Cones** Sometimes, ash and pieces of lava harden in the air and can fall to the ground around a small vent. The hardened pieces of lava are called cinders. The cinders and ash build up around the vent and form a steep volcano called a *cinder cone*. A cinder cone can also form at a side vent on other volcanic mountains, such as on shield or composite volcanoes.

- **Composite Volcanoes** Alternating layers of hardened lava flows and pyroclastic material create *composite volcanoes* (kuhm•PAHZ•iht). During a mild eruption, lava flows cover the sides of the cone. During an explosive eruption, pyroclastic material is deposited around the vent. Composite volcanoes commonly develop into large and steep volcanic mountains.

Layers of lava
Magma

Pyroclastic material
Ash and cinders
Conduit

Pyroclastic material
Lava and ash layers

Fissures and Lava Plateaus

Fissure eruptions (FIH•shohr ee•RUHP•shuhnz) happen when lava flows from giant cracks, or *fissures*, in Earth's surface. The fissures are found on land and on the ocean floor. A fissure eruption has no central opening. Lava flows out of the entire length of the fissure, which can be many kilometers long. As a result, a thick and mostly flattened layer of cooled lava, called a *lava plateau* (plah•TOH), can form. One example of a lava plateau is the Columbia Plateau Province in Washington, Oregon, and Idaho, as shown to the right.

The Palouse Falls in Washington plunge deep into exposed layers of the Columbia lava plateau.

Craters and Calderas

A *volcanic crater* is an opening or depression at the top of a volcano caused by eruptions. Inside the volcano, molten rock can form an expanded area of magma called a *magma chamber*, as shown to the right. When the magma chamber below a volcano empties, the roof of the magma chamber may collapse and leave an even larger, basin-shaped depression called a *caldera* (kahl•DAHR•uh). Calderas can form from the sudden drain of a magma chamber during an explosive eruption or from a slowly emptied magma chamber. More than 7,000 years ago, the cone of Mount Mazama in Oregon collapsed to form a caldera. The caldera later filled with water and is now called Crater Lake.

A caldera can be more than 100 km in diameter.

👁 Visualize It!

8 Claims • Evidence • Reasoning Make a claim about how the appearance of land surfaces change before and after a caldera forms. Summarize evidence to support the claim and explain your reasoning.

Before

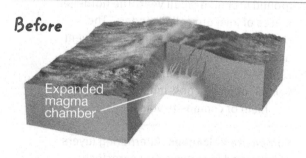

Expanded magma chamber

After

Collapsed magma chamber

ERUPTION!

Where do volcanoes form?

Volcanoes can form at plate boundaries or within the middle of a plate. Recall that **tectonic plates** are giant sections of lithosphere on Earth's surface. Volcanoes can form at *divergent plate boundaries* where two plates are moving away from each other. Most fissure eruptions occur at divergent boundaries. Shield volcanoes, fissure eruptions, and cinder cones can also occur away from plate boundaries within a plate at *hot spots*. The type of lava normally associated with these volcanoes has a relatively low viscosity, few trapped gases, and is usually not explosive.

Composite volcanoes are most common along *convergent plate boundaries* where oceanic plates subduct. In order for the rock to melt, it must be hot and the pressure on it must drop, or water and other fluids must be added to it. Extra fluids from ocean water form magma of higher viscosity with more trapped gases. Thus, composite volcanoes produce the most violent eruptions. The *Ring of Fire* is a name used to describe the numerous explosive volcanoes that form on convergent plate boundaries surrounding the Pacific Ocean.

ACTIVE READING

9 Identify As you read, underline three locations where volcanoes can form.

Plate Tectonic Boundaries and Volcano Locations Worldwide

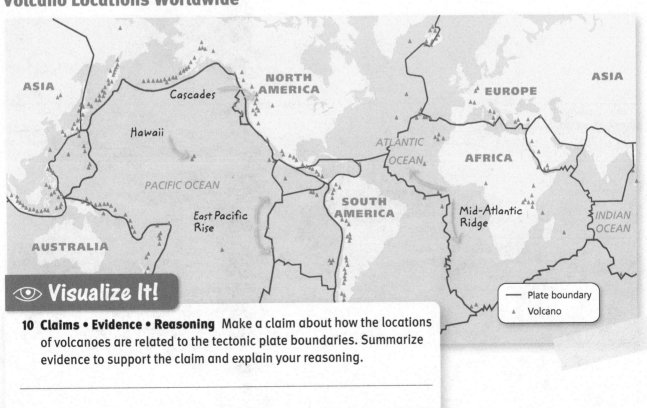

Visualize It!

10 Claims • Evidence • Reasoning Make a claim about how the locations of volcanoes are related to the tectonic plate boundaries. Summarize evidence to support the claim and explain your reasoning.

_____

_____

At Divergent Boundaries

At divergent boundaries, plates move away from each other. The lithosphere stretches and gets thinner, so the pressure on the mantle rock below decreases. As a result, the asthenosphere bulges upward and magma forms. This magma rises through fissures in the lithosphere, out onto the land or the ocean floor.

Most divergent boundaries are on the ocean floor. When eruptions occur in these areas, undersea volcanoes develop. These volcanoes and other processes lead to the formation of a long, underwater mountain range known as a *mid-ocean ridge*. Two examples of mid-ocean ridges are the East Pacific Rise in the Pacific Ocean and the Mid-Atlantic Ridge in the Atlantic Ocean. The youngest rocks in the ocean are located at mid-ocean ridges.

Shield volcanoes and cinder cones are common in Iceland, where the Mid-Atlantic Ridge runs through the country. As the plates move away from each other, new crust forms. When a divergent boundary is located in the middle of a continent, the crust stretches until a rift valley is formed, as shown below.

ACTIVE READING

11 Claims • Evidence • Reasoning Make a claim about what types of volcanic landforms occur at divergent plate boundaries. Support your claim with evidence. Explain your reasoning.

_____

_____

_____

Divergent plate boundaries create fissure eruptions and shield volcanoes.

Fissure

The Great Rift Valley in Africa is a location where the crust is stretching and separating.

Tectonic plates move away from each other at divergent boundaries.

At Convergent Boundaries

At convergent boundaries, two plates move toward each other. In most cases, one plate sinks beneath the other plate. As the sinking plate dives into the mantle, fluids in the sinking plate become super heated and escape. These escaping fluids cause the rock above the sinking plate to melt and form magma. This magma rises to the surface and erupts to form volcanoes.

The magma that forms at convergent boundaries has a high concentration of fluids. As the magma rises, decreasing pressure causes the fluid trapped in the magma to form gas bubbles. But, because the magma has a high viscosity, these bubbles cannot escape easily. As the bubbles expand, the magma rises faster. Eventually, the magma can erupt explosively, forming calderas or composite volcanoes. Gas, ash, and large chunks of rock can be blown out of the volcanoes. The Cascade Range is a chain of active composite volcanoes in the northwestern United States, as shown to the right. In 1980, Mt. St. Helens erupted so violently that the entire top of the mountain was blown away.

Tectonic plates move toward each other at convergent boundaries.

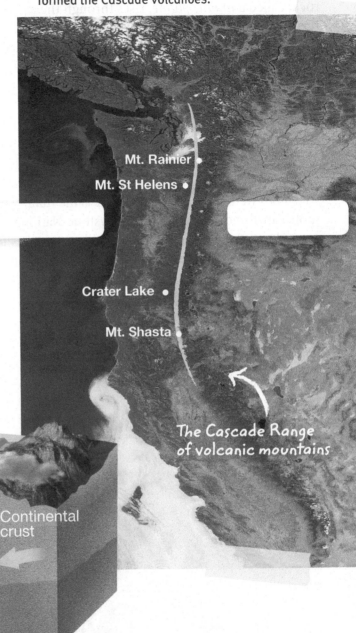

👁 **Visualize It!**

12 Identify Draw two arrows in the white boxes to indicate the direction of motion of the plates that formed the Cascade volcanoes.

Mt. Rainier

Mt. St Helens

Crater Lake

Mt. Shasta

The Cascade Range of volcanic mountains

Oceanic crust

Continental crust

13 Summarize List the characteristics of divergent-boundary volcanoes and convergent-boundary volcanoes below.

Volcanoes at divergent boundaries	Volcanoes at convergent boundaries

At Hot Spots

Volcanoes can form within a plate, away from the plate boundaries. A **hot spot** is a location where a column of extremely hot mantle rock, called a *mantle plume*, rises through the asthenosphere. As the hot rock reaches the base of the lithosphere, it melts partially to form magma that can rise to the surface and form a volcano. Eruptions at a hot spot commonly form shield volcanoes. As tectonic plates move over a mantle plume, chains of volcanic mountains can form, as shown below.

The youngest Hawaiian island, the Big Island, is home to Kilauea (kih•loh•AY•uh). The Kilauea volcano is an active shield volcano located over a mantle plume. To the north and west of Kilauea is a chain of progressively-older shield volcanoes. These volcanoes were once located over the same mantle plume. Hot spots can also occur on land. Yellowstone National Park, for example, contains a huge volcanic caldera that was formed by the same mantle plume that created the Columbia Plateau.

👁 Visualize It!

14 Claims • Evidence • Reasoning Make a claim about which location, A, B, or C, is the oldest volcano. Give evidence to support the claim and explain your reasoning.

_____

_____

_____

Hot spots form over mantle plumes within a tectonic plate.

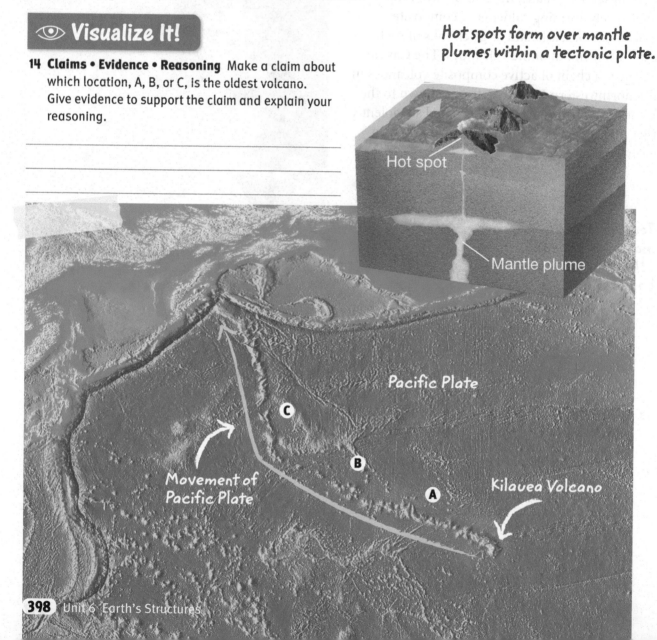

Hot spot

Mantle plume

Pacific Plate

C

B

A

Movement of Pacific Plate

Kilauea Volcano

Living Near a Volcano

Volcanoes occur around the world. Many people live near volcanoes because the soils around a volcano can be very rich with essential minerals. These minerals make the soils fertile for growing a variety of crops. Living near a volcano also has its hazards. Sudden and unexpected eruptions can cause people to lose their homes and their lives.

Not All Bad
Volcanic rocks are used in jewelry, in making concrete, and in water filtration systems. Even cat litter and facial scrubs can contain volcanic rock.

Destruction
Earthquakes, fires, ash, and lava flows during an eruption can destroy entire cities.

Ash in the Air
Volcanic ash can cause breathing problems, bury crops, and damage engines. The weight of falling ash can cause buildings to collapse.

ℹ Extend

15 Claims • Evidence • Reasoning Make a claim about whether all characteristics of volcanoes are dangerous. Summarize evidence to support the claim and explain your reasoning.

16 Apply Research the eruption of a specific volcano of your choice. Describe how the volcano affected the environment and the people near the volcano.

17 Design Create a poster that outlines a school safety plan for events that can occur before, during, and after a volcanic eruption.

Visual Summary

To complete this summary, check the box that indicates true or false. You can use this page to review the main concepts of the lesson.

Lava and magma are different.

T   F
18 ☐   ☐   Lava is inside Earth's crust and may contain trapped gases.

The three types of volcanic mountains are shield volcanoes, cinder cones, and composite volcanoes.

T   F
19 ☐   ☐   The type of volcano shown is a shield volcano.

Volcanoes

Volcanoes can form at tectonic plate boundaries.

T   F
20 ☐   ☐   At divergent plate boundaries, plates move toward each other.

Volcanoes can form at hot spots.

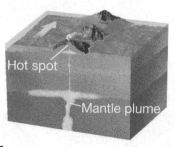

T   F
21 ☐   ☐   Hot spots are restricted to tectonic plate boundaries.

22 Claims • Evidence • Reasoning Make a claim about how volcanoes contribute to the formation of new landforms. Summarize evidence to support the claim and explain your reasoning.

Lesson Review

Vocabulary

Write 1 or 2 sentences that describe the differences between the two terms.

1 magma   lava

_____

_____

2 volcano   vent

_____

_____

3 tectonic plate   hot spot

_____

_____

Key Concepts

Use the image to answer the following question.

4 Identify How did the composite volcano in the image get its layered interior?

_____

5 Analyze Is pyroclastic material likely to form from low-viscosity lava or high-viscosity lava? Explain your answer.

_____

_____

Describe the location and characteristics of the types of volcanic landforms in the table below.

Volcanic landform	Description
6 Hot-spot volcanoes	
7 Cinder cones	
8 Calderas	

Critical Thinking

9 Claims • Evidence • Reasoning In Iceland, the Mid-Atlantic Ridge runs through the center of the country. Make a claim about the appearance of Iceland many thousands of years from now. Summarize evidence to support the claim and explain your reasoning.

_____

_____

10 Analyze Why do you think the location surrounding the Pacific Ocean is known as the Ring of Fire?

_____

_____

_____

Earth's
Layers

influence

Plate
Tectonics

affects

Mountain
Building

explains

Volcanoes

explains

Earthquakes

affects

Minerals and
the Rock Cycle

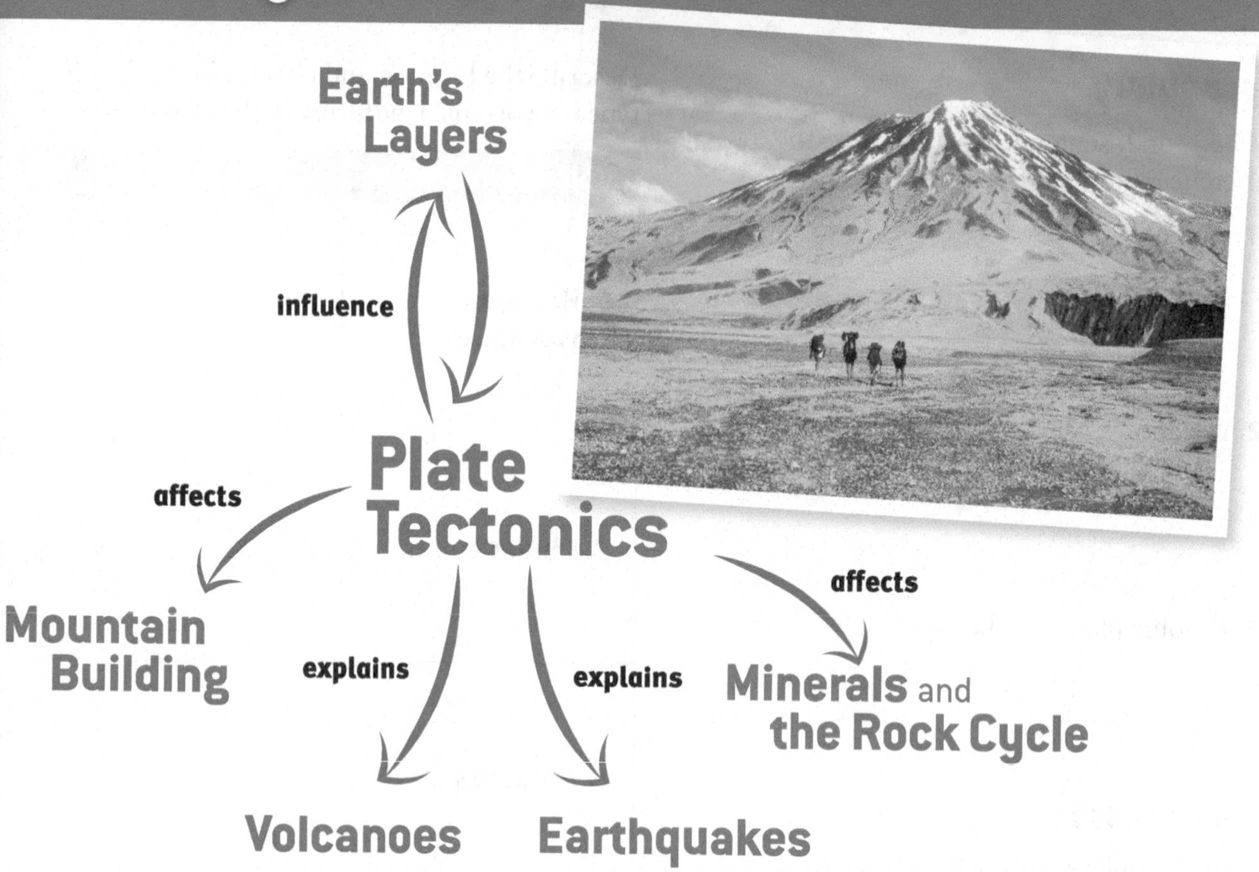

1 Claims • Evidence • Reasoning The Graphic Organizer above shows how Earth's surface changes because of Earth's layers. Make a claim about changes on a planet that has the same composition from core to surface. Use evidence to support the claim and explain your reasoning.

_____
_____
_____
_____
_____
_____
_____

2 Relate How are Earth's crust and mantle involved in the formation of new rock?

_____
_____
_____
_____

3 Apply Explain how a volcanologist can piece together the history of a volcano by studying the rock that makes up the volcano.

_____
_____
_____
_____
_____

Vocabulary

Name _____

Fill in each blank with the term that best completes the following sentences.

1 The hot, convecting _____ is the layer of rock between the Earth's crust and core.

2 _____ is the theory that explains how large pieces of Earth's outermost layer move and change shape.

3 _____is the bending of rock layers due to stress.

4 A(n) _____ is a vent or fissure in the Earth's surface through which magma and gases are expelled.

5 A(n) _____ is a movement or trembling of the ground that is caused by a sudden release of energy when rocks move along a fault.

Key Concepts

Identify the choice that best completes the statement or answers the question.

6 One way of measuring the amount of energy released by an earthquake is the Richter scale. Each increase of one unit on the Richter scale shows a 10-fold increase in the strength of the earthquake. What determines how strong an earthquake will be?

   A distance from the epicenter of the earthquake

   B amount of stress released by the elastic rebound of rock

   C the temperature of the rock just before the earthquake begins

   D the density of population and buildings near the epicenter of the earthquake

7 Earth's core is composed of two separate layers: the inner core and the outer core. What is one difference between these two layers?

   F One is iron, and one is zinc.

   G One is liquid, and one is gas.

   H One is solid, and one is liquid.

   I One is iron, and one is nickel.

8 Scientists study different parts of earthquakes and how they are related. This illustration shows a cross section of the lithosphere when an earthquake is taking place.

Cross Section of Lithosphere during an Earthquake

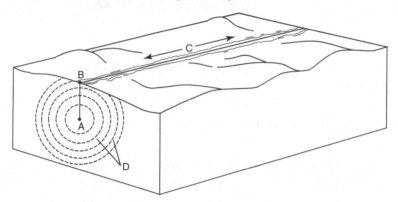

Where is the epicenter of this earthquake located?

A point A

B point B

C along the line labeled C

D along the line between points A and B

9 Convection currents in the mantle contribute to tectonic plate movement. What is a convection current?

F the transfer of energy through materials in direct contact

G the transfer of energy due to the movement of matter

H the transfer of energy as electromagnetic waves

I the transfer of energy from a region of lower temperature to a region of higher temperature

10 Granite forms when liquid magma slowly cools within Earth's crust. If the granite is exposed to intense heat and pressure, it can change to gneiss. Which type of change takes place when granite turns into gneiss?

A Sedimentary rock changes into igneous rock.

B Igneous rock changes into metamorphic rock.

C Metamorphic rock changes into igneous rock.

D Sedimentary rock changes into metamorphic rock.

Name _____

11 Imagine you could travel in a straight line through Earth from a point on one side and come out on the other side. What compositional layer would you travel through in the exact center of Earth?

F core

H lithosphere

G crust

I mesosphere

12 Earth can be divided into three layers: the core, the mantle, and the crust. How are these three layers identified?

A by their plate tectonics

B by their structural features

C by their physical properties

D by their chemical composition

13 The forces of volcanic eruptions vary. Some eruptions explode violently, and others are slow and quiet. Which type of eruption is happening when pyroclastic materials are released?

F a quiet eruption

G a violent eruption

H a moderate eruption

I quiet eruptions alternating with moderate eruptions

14 Unlike Florida, a transform boundary passes through California. What happens at a transform boundary that can cause an earthquake?

A Two plates collide.

B Two plates move in the same direction.

C Two plates move away from each other.

D Two plates slide or glide past each other.

15 Sometimes tectonic plates move toward each other and squeeze large blocks of rocks together, creating folded mountains. Which of the following terms describes a kind of fold in which the youngest rock layers are in the center of the fold?

F syncline

H symmetrical fold

G anticline

I asymmetrical fold

16 Quartz, feldspar, and mica are silicate minerals. Silicate minerals contain atoms of silicon and oxygen and often other elements bonded together. What must be **true** of silicate minerals?

A They are pure elements.

B They are made up of compounds.

C They melt at very low temperatures.

D They are made up of only one kind of atom.

17 The following steps are part of a laboratory exercise that Florida sixth-grade students are doing in their science class.

Step	Procedure
1	Get an ice cube that has been darkly colored with food coloring.
2	Use tongs to place the ice cube in a beaker containing warm water. Be sure to lower the ice cube slowly to keep the water as still as possible.
3	Observe the ice cube and water mixture for at least 5 min.

What are these students modeling?

F plate boundary

G continental drift

H movement of tectonic plates

I convection currents in the mantle

18 Mr. Garcia told his seventh-grade class that as a tectonic plate moves farther from a mid-ocean ridge, it cools and becomes denser. This can cause the plate to sink below another, less dense tectonic plate. The weight of the sinking plate then drags the rest of the plate downward. What is Mr. Garcia describing?

A slab pull

B ridge push

C continental drift

D convection current

Name _____

19 The figure below shows mountains that were formed when large blocks of rock were squeezed together as two tectonic plates collided.

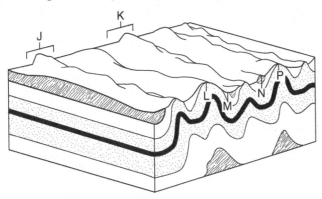

What does the letter K represent?

F syncline

G anticline

H reverse fault

I normal fault

20 Ruben made the chart below to describe the classes of nonsilicate minerals.

Class	Description	Example
Carbonates	contain carbon and oxygen compounds	calcite
Halides	contain ions of chlorine, fluorine, iodine, and bromine	halite
Native elements	contain only one type of atom	gold
Oxides	contain oxygen compounds	hematite
Sulfides	contain sulfur compounds	pyrite

There are actually six classes of nonsilicate minerals. Which class is missing from Ruben's chart?

A feldspars

B micas

C silicates

D sulfates

21 Declan observed a rock that he found at the beach. The rock felt hard, it was yellow, and it appeared to be made of layers. Declan concluded that the rock was sedimentary. Which observation **best** supports this conclusion?

F the yellow color

G the layers within the rock

H the hardness of the rock

I the location where the rock was found

22 Mount Everest formed when two tectonic plates collided. Which process then took place to create Mount Everest?

A erosion

C uplift

B subsidence

D weathering

Critical Thinking

Answer the following questions in the space provided.

23 Explain how a convergent boundary is different from a transform boundary.

_____

_____

Then name one thing that commonly occurs along both convergent boundaries and transform boundaries.

_____

_____

24 The diagram below shows the five physical layers of Earth.

Identify the physical layers A, B, and C. Is the relationship between these layers important to understanding plate tectonics? Use evidence to support your claim and explain your reasoning.

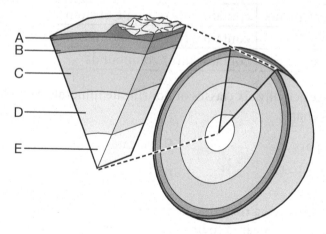

_____

_____

_____

_____

_____

Earth's History

FLORIDA **BIG IDEA** 6

Earth Structures

Florida's unique topography answers questions about Florida's past.

What Do You Think?

Earth's landscape is constantly changing. But Earth's history has not been erased. Look closely at the prominent features of this saber-toothed cat skull. What might the environment have been like when this animal was alive? As you explore this unit, gather evidence to state and support your claim.

Earth's History

CITIZEN SCIENCE

Preserving the Past

Fossils are found throughout Florida. These fossils contain information about the organisms that lived both on land and in the ocean. How would you research Florida's fossil history?

① Think About It

Where can people find fossils?

_____

_____

What are the most common types of fossils found in Florida?

_____

_____

Many important fossil discoveries have been made in Florida. Use the internet to research a fossil discovery site in Florida. Take notes on your findings on a separate sheet of paper.

Scientists use grids to record where things are found.

Ammonite fossils
in limestone

② Ask A Question

Is your area home to fossils?

As a class, evaluate the area in which you live and determine the likelihood of fossils being present. Consider natural changes like weather or earthquakes that might ruin fossil sites, as well as human factors like construction.

What to consider

☐ What kind of rock is common in your area?

☐ Are there any undeveloped areas that will have undisturbed rock?

③ Apply Your Knowledge

A List the kinds of rock in which fossils are found in Florida.

_____

_____

_____

_____

_____

B Use a geologic map to determine where rock that contains fossils can be found close to where you live. Determine how long it will take to travel to one of these sites.

C If you can, plan a trip to a site where you can find fossils. Describe how you will search for fossils.

_____

_____

_____

_____

_____

_____

🏠 Take It Home!

What was your local community like long ago? Research to find out what the most common fossils from your area are. How were the fossils formed?

Geologic Change over Time

ESSENTIAL QUESTION

How do we learn about Earth's history?

By the end of this lesson, you should be able to explain how Earth materials, such as rock, fossils, and ice, show that Earth has changed over time.

Scientists learn about Earth's history by studying materials such as these rhinoceros fossils in Nebraska.

SC.7.N.1.1 Define a problem from the seventh grade curriculum, use appropriate reference materials to support scientific understanding, plan and carry out scientific investigation of various types, such as systematic observations or experiments, identify variables, collect and organize data, interpret data in charts, tables, and graphics, analyze information, make predictions, and defend conclusions. **SC.7.N.1.5** Describe the methods used in the pursuit of a scientific explanation as seen in different fields of science such as biology, geology, and physics. **SC.7.E.6.4** Explain and give examples of how physical evidence supports scientific theories that Earth has evolved over geologic time due to natural processes.

Quick Labs
• Fossil Flipbook
• Connecting Fossils to Climates
• Timeline of Earth's History

S.T.E.M. Lab
• Exploring Landforms

 Engage Your Brain

1 Predict Check T or F to show whether you think each statement is true or false.

T   F

☐   ☐   Once rock forms, it never changes.

☐   ☐   Fossils can tell us which animals lived at a certain time.

☐   ☐   The climate is exactly the same all over the world.

☐   ☐   A volcano erupting is an example of a geologic process.

2 Explain What can you infer about the environment in which this fossil probably formed?

_____

_____

_____

ACTIVE **READING**

3 Synthesize You can often define an unknown word if you know the meaning of its word parts. Use the word parts and sentence below to make an educated guess about the meaning of the word *uniformitarianism*.

Word part	Meaning
uniform-	*the same in all cases and at all times*
-ism	*a system of beliefs or actions*

Example sentence
The idea that erosion has occurred the same way throughout Earth's history is an example of <u>uniformitarianism</u>.

uniformitarianism:

_____

_____

Vocabulary Terms

• uniformitarianism   • climate
• fossil   • ice core
• trace fossil

4 Identify This list contains vocabulary terms you'll learn in this lesson. As you read, circle the definition of each term.

This inactive volcano last erupted over 4,000 years ago.

What is the principle of uniformitarianism?

The principle of **uniformitarianism** (yoo•nu h•fohr•mi•TAIR•ee•uh•niz•uhm) states that geologic processes that happened in the past can be explained by current geologic processes. Processes such as volcanism and erosion that go on today happened in a similar way in the past. Because geologic processes tend to happen at a slow rate, this means that Earth must be very old. In fact, scientists have shown that Earth is about 4.6 billion years old.

Most geologic change is slow and gradual, but sudden changes have also affected Earth's history. An asteroid hitting Earth may have led to the extinction of the dinosaurs. However, scientists see these as a normal part of geologic change.

ACTIVE **READING**

5 Describe In your own words, describe the principle of uniformitarianism.

_____

_____

_____

_____

◉ **Visualize It!**

6 Identify How do these photos show the principle of uniformitarianism?

_____

_____

_____

This is an active volcano.

Done That

How do organisms become preserved as fossils?

Fossils are the trace or remains of an organism that lived long ago, most commonly preserved in sedimentary rock. Fossils may be skeletons or body parts, shells, burrows, or ancient coral reefs. Fossils form in many different ways.

👁 Visualize It!

Trapped in Amber

Imagine that an insect is caught in soft, sticky tree sap. Suppose that the insect is covered by more sap, which hardens with the body of the insect inside. Amber is formed when hardened tree sap is buried and preserved in sediment. Some of the best insect fossils, such as the one shown below, are found in amber. Fossil spiders, frogs, and lizards have also been found in amber.

Trapped in Asphalt

There are places where asphalt wells up at Earth's surface in thick, sticky pools. One such place is La Brea Tar Pits in California. These asphalt pools have trapped and preserved many fossils over the past 40,000 years, such as the one shown below. Fossils such as these show a lot about what life was like in Southern California in the past.

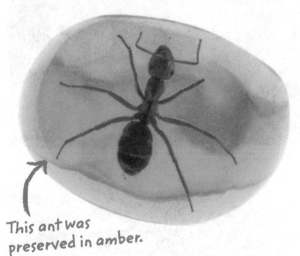

This ant was preserved in amber.

This water beetle was preserved in asphalt.

7 Analyze What features of the ant can you still see in this fossil?

_____

_____

_____

8 Claims • Evidence • Reasoning Make a claim about how this organism became a fossil. Support your claim with evidence, and explain your reasoning.

_____

_____

_____

Buried in Rock

When an organism dies, it often starts to decay or is eaten by other organisms. Sometimes, however, organisms are quickly buried by sediment when they die. The sediment slows down decay and can protect parts of the body from damage. Hard parts of organisms, such as shells and bones, do not break down as easily as soft parts do. So, when sediments become rock, the hard parts of animals are preserved and become part of the rock as the sediments harden.

Ammonites once lived in shells in ancient seas.

👁 Visualize It!

9 Gather Evidence What part of the organism was preserved as a fossil in this rock? Support your claim with evidence.

_____

_____

Become Frozen

In very cold places on Earth, the soil can be frozen all the time. An animal that dies there may also be frozen. It is frozen with skin and flesh, as well as bones. Because cold temperatures slow down decay, many types of frozen fossils are preserved from the last ice age.

This frozen mammoth was discovered in Siberia.

👁 Visualize It!

10 Compare What information can this fossil give that fossils preserved in rock cannot?

_____

_____

Become Petrified

Petrification (pet•ruh•fi•KAY•shuhn) happens when an organism's tissues are replaced by minerals. In some petrified wood, minerals have replaced all of the wood. A sample of petrified wood is shown at the right. This wood is in the Petrified Forest National Park in Arizona.

A similar thing happens when the pore space in an organism's hard tissue, such as bone, is filled up with minerals.

This petrified wood is in Arizona.

What are trace fossils?

ACTIVE READING

11 Identify As you read, underline examples of trace fossils.

Fossils of organisms can tell us a lot about the bodies of life forms. Another type of fossil may also give evidence about how some animals behaved. A **trace fossil** is a fossilized structure that formed in sedimentary rock by animal activity on or in soft sediment.

Tracks, like the ones across this page, are one type of trace fossil. They are footprints made by animals in soft sediment that later became hard rock. Tracks show a lot about the animal that made them, such as how it lived, how big it was, and how fast it moved. For example, scientists have found paths of tracks showing that a group of dinosaurs moved in the same direction. This has led scientists to hypothesize that some dinosaurs moved in herds.

Burrows are another kind of trace fossil. Burrows are pathways or shelters made by animals, such as clams on the sea floor or rodents on land, that dig in sediment. Some scientists also classify animal dung, called coprolite (KAHP•ruh•lyt), as a trace fossil. Some coprolites are shown at the right.

These tracks were made by dinosaurs that once lived in Utah.

⊙ Visualize It!

12 Illustrate Draw two sets of tracks that represent what you might leave for future scientists to study. Draw one set of you walking and another set of you running.

Walking

_____

Running

Time Is on Our Side

Visualize It!

13 Claims • Evidence • Reasoning
Based on these fossils of tropical plants from Antarctica, make a claim about what the climate was once like. Support your claim with evidence, and explain your reasoning.

_____

_____

_____

A piece of
Antarctica's past

Antarctica today

What can fossils tell us?

All of the fossils that have been discovered on Earth are called the _fossil record_. The fossil record shows part of the history of life on Earth. It is only part of the history because some things are still unknown. Not all the organisms that ever lived have left behind fossils. Also, there are many fossils that have not been discovered yet. Even so, fossils that are available do provide important information about Earth's history.

Fossils can tell scientists about environmental changes over time. The types of fossils preserved in sedimentary rock show what the environment was like when the organisms were alive. For example, fish fossils indicate that an aquatic environment was present. Palm fronds mean a tropical environment was present. Scientists have found fossils of trees and dinosaurs in Antarctica, so the climate there must have been warm in the past.

Fossils can also tell scientists how life forms have changed over time. Major changes in Earth's environmental conditions and surface can influence an organism's survival and the types of adaptations that a species must have to survive. To learn about how life on Earth has changed, scientists study relationships between different fossils and between fossils and living organisms.

ACTIVE READING

14 Identify As you read, underline two types of changes on Earth that fossils can give information about.

How does sedimentary rock show Earth's history?

Rock and mineral fragments move from one place to another during erosion. Eventually, this sediment is deposited in layers. As new layers of sediment are deposited, they cover older layers. Older layers become compacted. Dissolved minerals, such as calcite and quartz, separate from water that passes through the sediment. This forms a natural cement that holds the rock and mineral fragments together in sedimentary rock.

Scientists use different characteristics to classify sedimentary rock. These provide evidence of the environment that the sedimentary rock formed in.

Composition

The composition of sedimentary rock shows the source of the sediment that makes up the rock. Some sedimentary rock forms when rock or mineral fragments are cemented together. Sandstone, shown below, forms when sand grains are deposited and buried, then cemented together. Other sedimentary rock forms from the remains of once-living plants and animals. Most limestone forms from the remains of animals that lived in the ocean. Another sedimentary rock, called coal, forms underground from partially decomposed plant material that is buried beneath sediment.

Texture and Features

The texture of sedimentary rock shows the environment in which the sediment was carried and deposited. Sedimentary rock is arranged in layers. Layers can differ from one another, depending on the kind, size, and color of their sediment. Features on sedimentary rock called *ripple marks* record the motion of wind or water waves over sediment. An example of sedimentary rock with ripple marks is shown below. Other features, called *mud cracks*, form when fine-grained sediments at the bottom of a shallow body of water are exposed to the air and dry out. Mud cracks show that an ancient lake, stream, or ocean shoreline was once a part of an area.

ACTIVE READING

15 Describe What processes can cause rock to break apart into sediment?

_____

_____

_____

Sandstone

👁 Visualize It!

16 Identify Which arrow shows the direction that water was moving to make these ripple marks?

_____

A   B   C

These are ripple marks in sandstone.

What do Earth's surface features tell us?

Earth's surface is always changing. Continents change position continuously as tectonic plates move across Earth's surface.

◯ Continents Move

The continents have been moving throughout Earth's history. For example, at one time the continents formed a single landmass called *Pangaea* (pan•JEE•uh). Pangaea broke apart about 200 million years ago. Since then, the continents have been slowly moving to their present locations, and continue to move today.

Evidence of Pangaea can be seen by the way rock types, mountains, and fossils are now distributed on Earth's surface. For example, mountain-building events from tectonic plate movements produced different mountain belts on Earth. As the map below shows, rock from one of these mountain belts is now on opposite sides of the Atlantic Ocean. Scientists think this mountain belt separated as continents have moved to their current locations.

Today's continents were once part of a landmass called Pangaea.

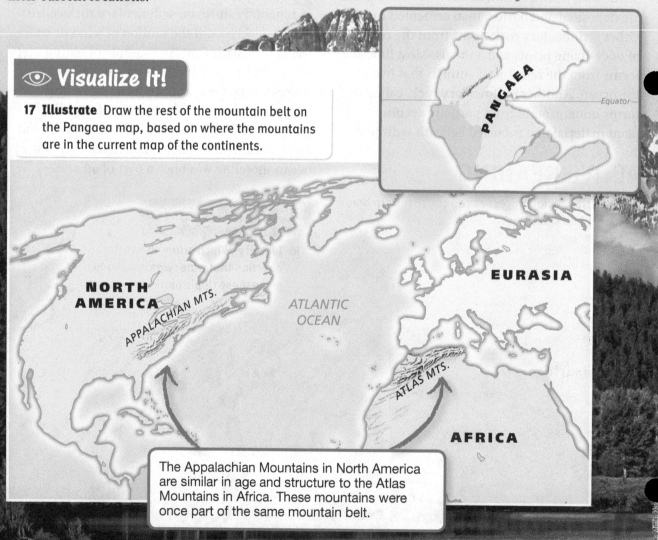

👁 Visualize It!

17 Illustrate Draw the rest of the mountain belt on the Pangaea map, based on where the mountains are in the current map of the continents.

The Appalachian Mountains in North America are similar in age and structure to the Atlas Mountains in Africa. These mountains were once part of the same mountain belt.

Landforms Change over Time

The movement of tectonic plates across Earth has resulted in extraordinary events. When continental plates collide, mountain ranges such as the ones shown below can form. As they pull apart, magma can be released in volcanic eruptions. When they grind past one another, breaks in Earth's surface form, where earthquakes can occur. Collisions between oceanic and continental plates can also cause volcanoes and the formation of mountains.

In addition to forces that build up Earth's surface features, there are forces that break them down as well. Weathering and erosion always act on Earth's surface, changing it with time. For example, high, jagged mountains can become lower and more rounded over time. So, the height and shape of mountains can tell scientists about the geologic history of mountains.

Think Outside the Book

19 **Support** Find out about how the continents continue to move today. Draw a map that shows the relative motion along some of the tectonic plate boundaries.

👁 Visualize It!

18 **Analyze** Label the older and younger mountains below. Explain your reasoning about how you decided which was older and which was younger.

_____

_____

_____

Rocky Mountains

Appalachian Mountains

Back to the Future

What other materials tell us about Earth's climate history?

The **climate** of an area describes the weather conditions in the area over a long period of time. Climate is mostly determined by temperature and precipitation. In addition to using fossils, scientists also analyze other materials to study how Earth's climate and environmental conditions have changed over time.

ACTIVE READING

20 Identify As you read the next two pages, underline the evidence that scientists use to learn about Earth's climate history.

Trees

When most trees grow, a new layer of wood is added to the trunk every year. This forms rings around the circumference (suhr•KUHM•fuhr•uhns) of the tree, as shown at the right. These rings tell the age of the tree. Some trees are over 2,000 years old. Scientists can use tree rings to find out about the climate during the life of the tree. If a tree ring is thick, it means the tree grew well—there was plenty of rain and favorable temperatures existed at that time. Thin tree rings mean the growing conditions were poor.

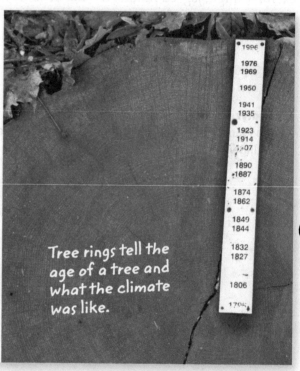

Tree rings tell the age of a tree and what the climate was like.

👁 Visualize It!

21 Claims • Evidence • Reasoning What is the time frame for which this tree can give information about Earth's climate? Use evidence to support your claim, and explain your reasoning.

Sea-Floor Sediments

Evidence about past climates can also be found deep beneath the ocean floor. Scientists remove and study long cylinders of sediment from the ocean floor, such as the one shown at the right. Preserved in these sediments are fossil remains of microscopic organisms that have died and settled on the ocean floor. These remains build up in layers, over time. If certain organisms are present, it can mean that the climate was particularly cold or warm at a certain time. The chemical composition of sediments, especially of the shells of certain microorganisms, can also be important. It shows what the composition was of the ocean water and atmosphere when the organisms were alive.

These scientists are studying sediment from the Ross Sea in Antarctica.

Ice

Icecaps are found in places such as Iceland and islands in the Arctic. The icecaps formed as older snow was squeezed into ice by new snow falling on top of it. Scientists can drill down into icecaps to collect a long cylinder of ice, called an **ice core**.

Ice cores, such as the ones shown in these photographs, give a history of Earth's climate over time. Some ice cores have regular layers, called bands, which form each year. Band size shows how much precipitation fell during a given time. The composition of water and concentration of gases in the ice core show the conditions of the atmosphere at the time that the ice formed.

Scientists study ice cores to find out about amounts of precipitation in the past.

22 State Your Claim Fill in the table by reading the evidence and making a claim about what it could mean.

Evidence	What it could mean
A. A scientist finds a fossil of a shark tooth in a layer of rock that is high in the mountains.	
B. Rocks from mountains on two different continents were found to have formed at the same time and to have the same composition.	
C. Upon studying an ice core, scientists find that a particular band is very wide.	

Visual Summary

To complete this summary, check the box that indicates true or false. You can use this page to review the main concepts of the lesson.

Fossils give information about changes in Earth's environments and life forms.

23 Trace fossils give information about animal activity and movement.

☐ True
☐ False

Sedimentary rocks provide information about Earth's geologic history.

24 These are ripple marks in sedimentary rock.

☐ True
☐ False

Studying Earth's History

Earth's surface features reflect its geologic history.

25 Tall, jagged mountains are older than rounded, smaller mountains.

☐ True
☐ False

Besides fossils, other materials give information about Earth's climate history.

26 Scientists study the width of tree rings to learn about past climate conditions.

☐ True
☐ False

27 **Claims • Evidence • Reasoning** At one point in history, Florida was completely submerged in water. Use evidence to support a claim about which material (wood, sea-floor sediments, ice) would be the most useful in studying Florida's fossil record. Explain your reasoning.

Lesson Review

Vocabulary

In your own words, define the following terms.

1 uniformitarianism _____

_____

_____

2 trace fossil _____

_____

_____

Key Concepts

3 Identify How old is Earth?

_____

4 Explain How can sedimentary rock show Earth's history?

_____

_____

_____

5 List Name three examples of trace fossils.

_____

_____

6 Explain Name five ways that organisms can be preserved as fossils, and explain what fossils can show about Earth's history.

_____

_____

_____

7 Describe How do Earth's surface features indicate changes over time?

_____

_____

_____

_____

8 Describe What are two ways that scientists can study Earth's climate history?

_____

_____

_____

_____

Critical Thinking

9 Claims • Evidence • Reasoning Make a claim about whether or not a piece of pottery is an example of a fossil? Summarize evidence to support your claim and explain your reasoning.

_____

_____

_____

Use this photo to answer the following questions.

10 Synthesize How does the erosion of these mountains support the principle of uniformitarianism? Explain your reasoning.

_____

_____

_____

11 Infer The type and age of rocks found in this mountain range are also found on another continent. What might this mean?

_____

_____

_____

Relative Dating

ESSENTIAL QUESTION

How are the relative ages of rock measured?

By the end of this lesson, you should be able to summarize how scientists measure the relative ages of rock layers and identify gaps in the rock record.

Studying these rock layers can tell scientists a great deal about the order in which the different layers formed.

SC.7.N.1.5 Describe the methods used in the pursuit of a scientific explanation as seen in different fields of science such as biology, geology, and physics. **SC.7.E.6.3** Identify current methods for measuring the age of Earth and its parts, including the law of superposition and radioactive dating.

Lesson Labs

Quick Labs
- Layers of Sedimentary Rock
- Ordering Rock Layers

Exploration Lab
- Earth's History

Engage Your Brain

1 Describe Fill in each blank with the word or phrase that you think completes the following sentences.

An example of something young is

_____

An example of something old is

_____

An example of something that is horizontal is

_____

An example of something older than you is

_____

The Liberty Bell

2 Explain Which came first, the bell or the crack in the bell? Explain your reasoning.

_____

_____

_____

_____

ACTIVE READING

3 Synthesize You can often define an unknown word if you know the meaning of its word parts. Use the word parts below to make an educated guess about the meaning of the word *superposition*, when used to describe layers of rock.

Word part	Meaning
super-	above
-position	specific place

superposition:

_____

_____

Vocabulary Terms

- relative dating
- superposition
- unconformity
- fossil
- geologic column

4 Apply As you learn the definition of each vocabulary term in this lesson, make your own definition or sketch to help you remember the meaning of the term.

Who's First?

What is relative dating?

Imagine that you are a detective at a crime scene. You must figure out the order of events that took place before you arrived. Scientists have the same goal when studying Earth. They try to find out the order in which events happened during Earth's history. Instead of using fingerprints and witnesses, scientists use rocks and fossils. Determining whether an object or event is older or younger than other objects or events is called **relative dating**.

The telephones shown below show how technologies have changed over time. Layers of rock also show how certain things took place in the past. Using different pieces of information, scientists can find the order in which rock layers formed. Once they know the order, a relative age can be determined for each rock layer. Keep in mind, however, that this does not give scientists a rock's age in years. It only allows scientists to find out what rock layer is older or younger than another rock layer.

Think Outside the Book

5 Model In groups of 6–10 people, form a line. Place the oldest person in the front of the line and the youngest person at the end of the line. What is your relative age compared to the person in front of you? Compared to the person behind you?

Visualize It!

6 Explain Use the numbers 1, 2, and 3 to rate these telephones from oldest (1) to youngest (3). Explain your reasoning. Does this tell you the years that the telephones were made?

_____

_____

_____

How these telephones look is a clue to their relative ages.

How are undisturbed rock layers dated?

To find the relative ages of rocks, scientists study the layers in sedimentary rocks. Sedimentary rocks form when new sediments are deposited on top of older rock. As more sediment is added, it is compressed and hardens into rock layers.

Scientists know that gravity causes sediment to be deposited in layers that are horizontal (hohr•ih•ZAHN•tuhl). Over time, different layers of sediment pile up on Earth's surface. Younger layers pile on top of older ones. If left undisturbed, the sediment will remain in horizontal layers. Scientists use the order of these layers to date the rock of each layer.

ACTIVE READING

7 Explain Why does gravity cause layers of sediment to be horizontal? Explain your reasoning.

_____

_____

_____

Using Superposition

Suppose that you have a brother who takes pictures of your family and piles them in a box. Over time, he adds new pictures to the top of the pile. Where are the oldest pictures—the ones taken when you were a baby? Where are the most recent pictures—the ones taken last week? The oldest pictures will be at the bottom of the pile. The youngest pictures will be at the top of the pile. Layers of rock are like the photographs shown below. As you go from top to bottom, the layers get older.

This approach is used to determine the relative age of sedimentary rock layers. The law of **superposition** (soo•per•puh•ZISH•uhn) is the principle that states that younger rocks lie above older rocks if the layers have not been disturbed.

Rock layers are like photographs that have been put in a pile over time.

👁 Visualize It!

8 Claims • Evidence • Reasoning Make a claim about the relative ages of these rock layers. Support your claim with evidence. Explain your reasoning.

_____

_____

_____

How Disturbing!

How are sedimentary rock layers disturbed?

If rock layers are not horizontal, then something disturbed them after they formed. Forces in Earth can disturb rock layers so much that older layers end up on top of younger layers. Some of the ways that rock layers can be disturbed are shown below and on the next page.

By Tilting and Folding

Tilting happens when Earth's forces move rock layers up or down unevenly. The layers become slanted. *Folding* is the bending of rocks that can happen when rock layers are squeezed together. The bending is from stress on the rock. Folding can cause rock layers to be turned over by so much that older layers end up on top of younger layers.

By Faults and Intrusions

Scientists often find features that cut across existing layers of rock. A *fault* is a break or crack in Earth's crust where rocks can move. An *intrusion* (in•TROO•zhuhn) is igneous rock that forms when magma is injected into rock and then cools and becomes hard.

Folding, tilting, faults, and intrusions can make finding out the relative ages of rock layers difficult. This can be even more complicated when a layer of rock is missing. Scientists call this missing layer of rock an *unconformity*.

👁 **Visualize It!**

9 Describe Write a caption for this group of images.

_____

_____

_____

Tilting

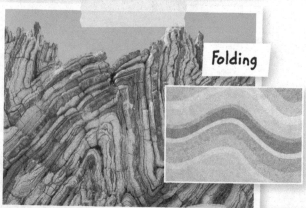
Folding

Faults

Intrusions

By Unconformities

A missing layer of rock forms a gap in Earth's geologic history, also called the geologic record. An **unconformity** (uhn•kuhn•FAWR•mih•tee) is a break in the geologic record that is made when rock layers are eroded or when sediment is not deposited for a long period of time. When scientists find an unconformity, they must question if the "missing layer" was simply never present or if it was removed. Two examples of unconformities are shown below.

ACTIVE READING

10 Claims • Evidence • Reasoning Make a claim about two ways that a rock layer can cause a gap in the geologic record. Support your claim with evidence, and explain your reasoning.

_____

_____

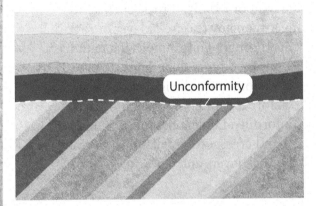

An unconformity can happen between horizontal layers and layers that are tilted or folded. The older layers were tilted or folded and then eroded before horizontal layers formed above them.

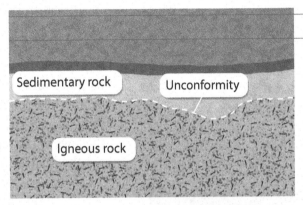

An unconformity can also happen when igneous or metamorphic rocks are exposed at Earth's surface and become eroded. Later, deposited sediment causes the eroded surface to become buried under sedimentary rock.

11 Illustrate Choose two of the following: tilting, folding, fault, intrusion, and an unconformity. Draw and label each one.

I'm Cutting In!

How are rock layers ordered?

Often, the order of rock layers is affected by more than one thing. Finding out what happened to form a group of rock layers is like piecing together a jigsaw puzzle. The law of superposition helps scientists to do this.

The idea that layers of rock have to be in place before anything can disturb them is also used. The law of crosscutting relationships states that a fault or a body of rock, such as an intrusion, must be younger than any feature or layer of rock that the fault or rock body cuts through. For example, if a fault has broken a rock layer, the fault is younger than the rock layer. If a fault has broken through igneous rock, the igneous rock must have been in place, and cool, before it could have been broken. The same is true for an unconformity. Look at the image below and use the laws of superposition and crosscutting relationships to figure out the relative ages of the rock layers and features.

ACTIVE READING

12 Identify As you read, underline the law of crosscutting relationships.

👁 Visualize It!

13 Claims • Evidence • Reasoning Make a claim about the order in which features A through J formed. Support your claim with evidence from the illustration. Fill in the lines according to the relative ages of the layers or features. Explain your reasoning.

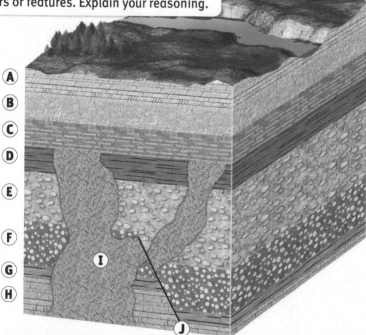

Youngest
_____
_____
_____
_____
_____
_____
_____
_____
_____
Oldest

Dating Mars

NASA's Mars Odyssey orbiter and the Hubble Space Telescope have produced a large collection of images of the surface of Mars. These are studied to find the relative ages of features on Mars, using the laws of superposition and crosscutting relationships. Here are two examples of crosscutting relationships.

The Crater Came First
A crater can be cut by another feature, such as a fracture.

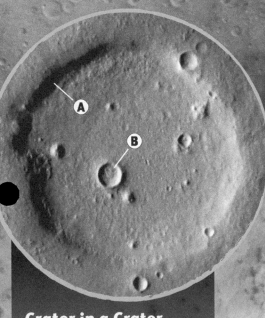

Crater in a Crater
A crater (A) can be cut by another crater (B) that formed from a later impact.

Hellas Crater
The many craters on Mars are studied to determine relative ages of features. This is Hellas Impact Basin, which is almost 2100 km wide.

i Extend

14 Claims • Evidence • Reasoning Make a claim about the relative ages of crater A and crater B. Provide evidence to support your claim, and explain your reasoning.

15 Apply How can scientists use erosion as a way to determine the relative ages of craters on Mars? Describe how erosion could change the appearance of a crater over time.

16 Research Find out how scientists have used relative dating to study the geologic history of other planets, such as Venus. Present what you found out by drawing a graphic novel or making a poster.

How are fossils used to determine relative ages of rocks?

Fossils are the traces or remains of an organism that lived long ago, most commonly preserved in sedimentary rock. Fossil forms of plants and animals show change over time, as they evolve. Scientists can classify fossilized (FAHS•uh•lyzd) organisms based on these changes. Then they can use that classification of fossils to find the relative ages of the rocks in which the fossils are found. Rock that contains fossils of organisms similar to those that live today is most likely younger than rock that contains fossils of ancient organisms. For example, fossilized remains of a 47 million-year-old primate are shown below. Rock that contains these fossils is younger than rock that contains the fossils of a dinosaur that lived over 200 million years ago.

17 Claims • Evidence • Reasoning Make a claim about whether fossils of species that did not change noticeably over time would be useful in determining the relative ages of rocks. Summarize your evidence to support your claim, and explain your reasoning.

_____

_____

_____

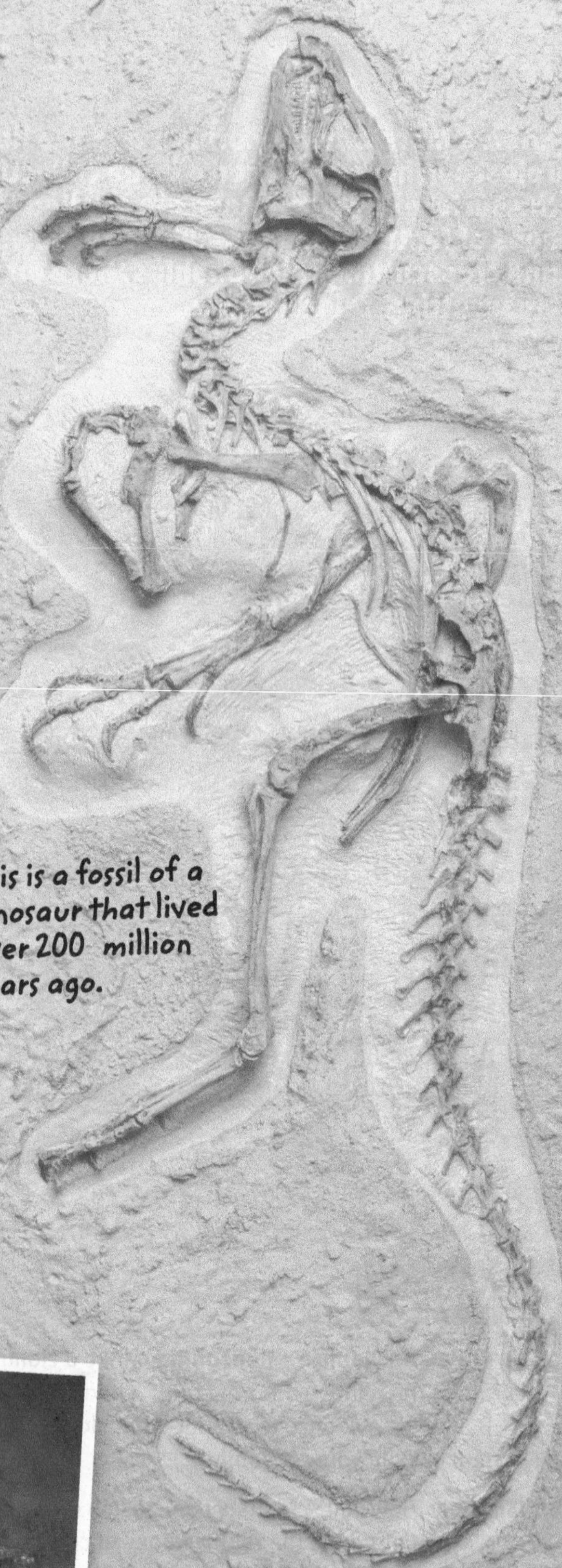

This is a fossil of a dinosaur that lived over 200 million years ago.

This is a fossil of a primate that lived about 47 million years ago.

(bkgd) ©Andy Crawford/Dorling Kindersley/Getty Images; (inset) ©Mario Tama/Getty Images

© Houghton Mifflin Harcourt Publishing Company

How are geologic columns used to compare relative ages of rocks?

Relative dating can also be done by comparing the relative ages of rock layers in different areas. The comparison is done using a geologic column. A **geologic column** is an ordered arrangement of rock layers that is based on the relative ages of the rocks, with the oldest rocks at the bottom of the column. It is made by piecing together different rock sequences from different areas. A geologic column represents an ideal image of a rock layer sequence that doesn't actually exist in any one place on Earth.

The rock sequences shown below represent rock layers from different outcrops at different locations. Each has certain rock layers that are common to layers in the geologic column, shown in the middle. Scientists can compare a rock layer with a similar layer in a geologic column that has the same fossils or that has the same relative position. If the two layers match, then they probably formed around the same time.

👁 Visualize It!

19 Identify Draw lines from the top and bottom of each outcrop to their matching positions in the geologic column.

Outcrop 1

Geologic Column

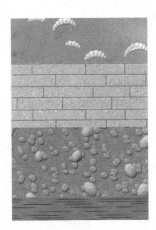

Outcrop 2

Rock layers from different outcrops can be compared to a geologic column.

Visual Summary

To complete this summary, circle the correct words. You can use this page to review the main concepts of the lesson.

If undisturbed, sedimentary rock exists as horizontal layers.

20 For undisturbed rock layers, younger rocks are above/below older rocks.

Forces in Earth can cause horizontal layers of rock to be disturbed.

21 This photo shows folding/tilting.

Relative Dating

Fossils can be used to determine the relative ages of rock layers.

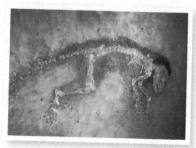

22 In undisturbed rock layers, fossils of a more recent organism will be in rock that is above/below rock containing fossils of older organisms.

Rock layers from different areas can be compared to a geologic column.

23 In geologic columns, the oldest rock layers are at the bottom/top.

24 Claims • Evidence • Reasoning Make a claim as to how the law of superposition relates to a stack of magazines that you have been saving over the past few years. Use evidence to support your claim and explain your reasoning.

Lesson Review

Vocabulary

In your own words, define the following terms.

1 relative dating

_____

_____

2 unconformity

_____

_____

Key Concepts

3 Describe How are sedimentary rock layers deposited?

_____

_____

4 List Name five ways that the order of rock layers can be disturbed.

_____

_____

_____

5 Explain How are the laws of superposition and crosscutting relationships used to determine the relative ages of rocks?

_____

_____

_____

_____

_____

6 Explain How can fossils be used to determine the relative ages of rock layers?

_____

_____

_____

_____

7 Describe How is the geologic column used in relative dating?

_____

_____

_____

Critical Thinking

8 Claims • Evidence • Reasoning Make a claim about which types of rocks the law of crosscutting relationships involves. Summarize evidence to support your claim and explain your reasoning.

_____

_____

_____

Use this image to answer the following questions.

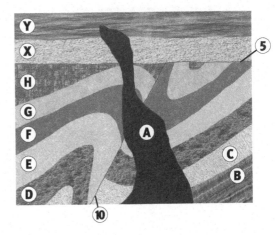

9 Analyze Is intrusion A younger or older than layer X? Explain your reasoning.

_____

_____

10 Analyze What feature is marked by 5?

_____

11 Analyze Other than intrusion and faulting, what happened in layers B, C, D, E, F, G, and H? Support your claim with evidence.

_____

_____

SC.7.N.1.1 Define a problem from the seventh grade curriculum, use appropriate reference materials to support scientific understanding, plan and carry out scientific investigation of various types, such as systematic observations or experiments, identify variables, collect and organize data, interpret data in charts, tables, and graphics, analyze information, make predictions, and defend conclusions.

Forming a Hypothesis

When conducting an investigation to test a hypothesis, a scientist must not let personal bias affect the results of the investigation. A scientist must be open to the fact that the results of an investigation may not completely support the hypothesis. They may even contradict it! Revising or forming a new hypothesis may lead a scientist to make a breakthrough that could be the basis of a new discovery.

Tutorial

The following procedure explains the steps that you will use to develop and evaluate a hypothesis.

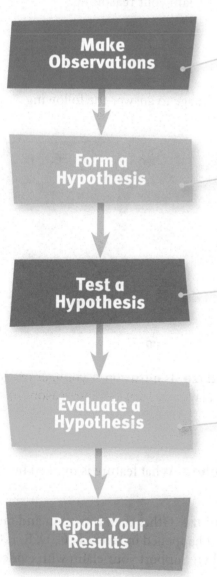

1 Making Observations Scientific investigations commonly begin with observations. Your observations may lead to a question. For example, you may wonder how, why, or when something happens.

2 Forming a Hypothesis To answer your question, you can start by forming a hypothesis. A hypothesis is a clear statement of what you expect will be the answer to your question. Start to form a hypothesis by stating the probable answer to your question based on your observations.

3 Testing a Hypothesis A useful hypothesis must be testable. To determine whether your hypothesis is testable, identify experiments that you can perform or observations that you can make to find out whether the hypothesis is supported or not.

4 Evaluating a Hypothesis After analyzing your data, you can determine if your results support your hypothesis. If your data support your hypothesis, you may want to repeat your observations or experiments to verify your results. If your data do not support your hypothesis, you may have to check your procedure for errors. You may even have to reject your hypothesis and form a new one.

You Try It!

The table provides observations about the latest eruptions of several volcanoes in Hawai'i.

Latest Eruption of Volcanoes in Hawai'i	
Volcano	**Year**
East Maui (Haleakala)	1460
Hualalai	1801
Mauna Loa	1984
Kilauea	still active

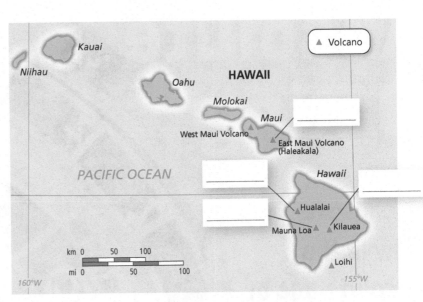

1 Making Observations On the map, label the volcanoes with the years shown. What do you observe about the dates and the locations of the volcanoes?

_____
_____
_____
_____
_____
_____
_____

2 Forming a Hypothesis Use the observations above to form a hypothesis about the history of the area. Focus on the relationship between the activity of the volcanoes and the location of the volcanoes. Your hypothesis should be supported by all of your data. Summarize your completed hypothesis in a single paragraph.

_____
_____
_____
_____
_____

3 Claims • Evidence • Reasoning Loihi is currently active, but West Maui has not erupted in recent history. Make a claim about whether these new observations support your hypothesis or disprove it. Support your claim with evidence, and explain your reasoning.

_____
_____
_____
_____

4 Revising a Hypothesis Share your hypothesis with your classmates. Rewrite your hypothesis so that it includes the changes suggested by your classmates.

_____
_____

 Take It Home!

While you already know the word *hypothesis*, you might not know the word *hypothetical*. Use the dictionary to look up the meaning of the suffix *-ical*. Combine the meanings of these two word parts, and write an original definition of *hypothetical* in your notebook.

Absolute Dating

ESSENTIAL QUESTION

How is the absolute age of rock measured?

By the end of this lesson, you should be able to summarize how scientists measure the absolute age of rock layers, including by radiometric dating.

A clock is one way of measuring absolute time.

[kr] ©James Strachan/Stone/Getty Images

SC.7.N.1.5 Describe the methods used in the pursuit of a scientific explanation as seen in different fields of science such as biology, geology, and physics. SC.7.E.6.3 Identify current methods for measuring the age of Earth and its parts, including the law of superposition and radioactive dating.

© Houghton Mifflin Har
Publishing Company

Engage Your Brain

1 **Predict** Check T or F to show whether you think each statement is true or false.

T   F

☐ ☐ All rocks are made of matter and all matter is made of atoms.

☐ ☐ We use calendars to measure the absolute age of people.

☐ ☐ Someone tells you that he is older than you are. This tells you his absolute age.

☐ ☐ If you cut a clay ball in two and then cut one of the halves in two, you will end up with four pieces of clay.

2 **Explain** What is the age of this person? Explain your reasoning.

_____
_____
_____
_____
_____
_____

ACTIVE **READING**

3 **Synthesize** You can often define an unknown word if you know the meaning of its word parts. Use the word parts and sentence below to make an educated guess about the meaning of the phrase *radiometric dating*.

Word part	Meaning
radio-	relating to radiation
-metric	relating to measurement

Example sentence
By using <u>radiometric dating</u>, the scientist found that the rock was 25 million years old.

radiometric dating:

_____
_____

Vocabulary Terms

• **absolute dating**   • **half-life**
• **radioactive decay** • **radiometric dating**

4 **Apply** As you learn the definition of each vocabulary term in this lesson, create your own definition or sketch to help you remember the meaning of the term.

It's About

How can the absolute age of rock be determined?

Determining the actual age of an event or object in years is called **absolute dating**. Scientists use many different ways to find the absolute age of rock and other materials. One way is by using radioactive isotopes (ray•dee•oh•AK•tiv EYE•suh•tohpz).

Using Radioactive Isotopes

Atoms of the same element that have a different number of neutrons are called isotopes. Many isotopes are stable, meaning that they stay in their original form. But some isotopes are unstable and break down to form different isotopes. The unstable isotopes are called *radioactive*. The breakdown of a radioactive isotope into a stable isotope of the same element or of another element is called **radioactive decay**. As shown on the right, radioactive decay for many isotopes happens when a neutron is converted to a proton, with the release of an electron. A radioactive isotope is called a *parent isotope*. The stable isotope formed by its breakdown is called the *daughter isotope*.

Each radioactive isotope decays at a specific, constant rate. **Half-life** is the time needed for half of a sample of a radioactive substance to undergo radioactive decay to form daughter isotopes. Half-life is always given in units of time.

ACTIVE READING

5 Claims • Evidence • Reasoning Make a claim about how much of a radioactive parent isotope remains after one half-life has passed. Use evidence to support your claim, and explain your reasoning.

_____

_____

6 Identify Label the parent isotope and the daughter isotope.

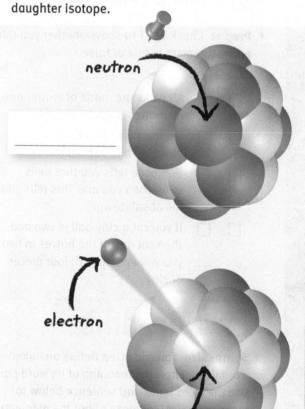

neutron

_____

electron

proton

_____

Time!

By Radiometric Dating

Some radioactive isotopes in mineral crystals can act as clocks. These mineral crystals record the ages of the rocks in which the minerals formed. Scientists study the amounts of parent and daughter isotopes to date samples. If you know how fast a radioactive isotope decays, you can figure out the sample's absolute age. Finding the absolute age of a sample by determining the relative percentages of a radioactive parent isotope and a stable daughter isotope is called **radiometric dating** (ray•dee•oh•MET•rik DAYT•ing). The figure on the right shows how the relative percentages of a parent isotope and a daughter isotope change with the passing of each half-life. The following is an example of how radiometric dating can be used:

- You want to determine the age of a sample that contains a radioactive isotope that has a half-life of 10 million years.
- You analyze the sample and find equal amounts of parent and daughter isotopes.
- Because 50%, or ½, of the parent isotope has decayed, you know that 1 half-life has passed.
- So, the sample is 10 million years old.

What is the best rock for radiometric dating?

Igneous rock is often the best type of rock sample to use for radiometric dating. When igneous rock forms, elements are separated into different minerals in the rock. When they form, minerals in igneous rocks often contain only a parent isotope and none of the daughter isotope. This makes the isotope percentages easier to interpret and helps dating to be more accurate.

Visualize It!

7 Calculate Fill in the number of parent isotopes and daughter isotopes in the spaces beside the images below.

0 years
Parent isotope = 16
Daughter isotope = 0
100% of the sample is parent isotope.

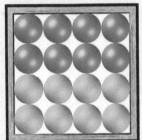

After 1 half-life
Parent isotope = 8
Daughter isotope = 8
50%, or $\frac{1}{2}$, of the sample is parent isotope.

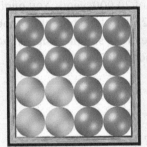

After 2 half-lives
Parent isotope = 4
Daughter isotope = ____
25%, or $\frac{1}{4}$, of the sample is parent isotope.

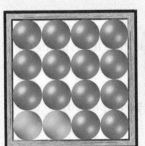

After 3 half-lives
Parent isotope = ____
Daughter isotope = ____
12.5%, or $\frac{1}{8}$, of the sample is parent isotope.

Sample Problem

A crystal contains a radioactive isotope that has a half-life of 10,000 years. One-fourth (25%) of the parent isotope remains in a sample. How old is the sample?

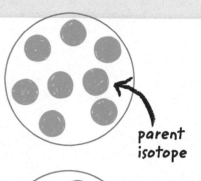

parent isotope

Identify

A. What do you know? Half-life = 10,000 years, parent isotope = 25%

B. What do you want to find out? How old the sample is. So, you need to know how many half-lives have gone by since the crystal formed.

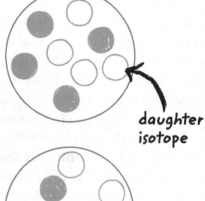

daughter isotope

Plan

C. Draw the parent-to-daughter isotope ratios for each half-life.

Solve

D. The third drawing on the right shows a sample that contains 25% parent isotope. This amount is present after 2 half-lives have passed.

E. Find the age of the sample. Because the half-life of the radioactive isotope is 10,000 years and 2 half-lives have passed, the age of the sample is: $2 \times 10,000$ years $= 20,000$ years

You Try It

8 Claims • Evidence • Reasoning A crystal contains a radioactive isotope that has a half-life of 20,000 years. You analyze a sample and find that one-eighth (12.5%) of the parent isotope remains. Make a claim about the age of the sample. Support your claim with mathematical evidence, and explain your reasoning.

Identify

A. What do you know? _____

B. What do you want to find out? _____

Plan

C. Draw the parent-to-daughter isotope ratios on the right.

Solve

D. Figure out how many half-lives have passed: _____

E. Find the age of the sample: _____

Answer: _____

Time for a Change

What are some radiometric dating methods?

Scientists use many different isotopes for radiometric dating. The half-life of an isotope is very important in determining the time range that it is useful for dating. If the half-life is too short compared with the age of the sample, there will be too little parent isotope left to measure. If the half-life is too long, there will not be enough daughter isotope to measure. Also, different methods may only be useful for certain types of materials.

Radiocarbon Dating

The ages of wood, bones, shells, and other organic remains can be found by radiocarbon dating. The radioactive isotope carbon-14 combines with oxygen to form radioactive carbon dioxide, CO_2. Most CO_2 in the atmosphere contains nonradioactive carbon-12, but radioactive carbon-14 is also present.

Plants absorb CO_2 from the atmosphere, which they use to build their bodies through photosynthesis. As long as a plant is alive, the plant takes in carbon dioxide with the same carbon-14 to carbon-12 ratio. Similarly, animals convert the carbon from the food they eat into bone and other tissues. So, animals inherit the carbon isotope ratio of their food sources.

Once a plant or animal dies, carbon is no longer taken in. The ratio of carbon-14 to carbon-12 decreases in the dead organism because carbon-14 undergoes radioactive decay to nitrogen-14. The half-life of carbon-14 is only 5,730 years. Also, radiocarbon dating can only be used to date organic matter. So this method is used to date things that lived in the last 45,000 years.

Materials such as these woolly mammoth teeth can be radiocarbon dated.

©Kevin Schafer/Corbis

© Houghton Mifflin Harcourt Publishing Company

Radiometric dating has been done on Mammoth Mountain's volcanic rock.

ACTIVE READING

11 Identify As you read this page, underline the time frame for which each method is most useful.

Potassium-Argon Dating

The element potassium (puh•TAS•ee•uhm) occurs in two stable isotopes, potassium-41 and potassium-39, and one radioactive isotope that occurs naturally, potassium-40. Potassium-40 decays to argon and calcium. It has a half-life of 1.25 billion years. Scientists measure argon as the daughter isotope. Potassium-argon dating is often used to date igneous volcanic rocks. This method is used to date rocks that are between about 100,000 years and a few billion years old.

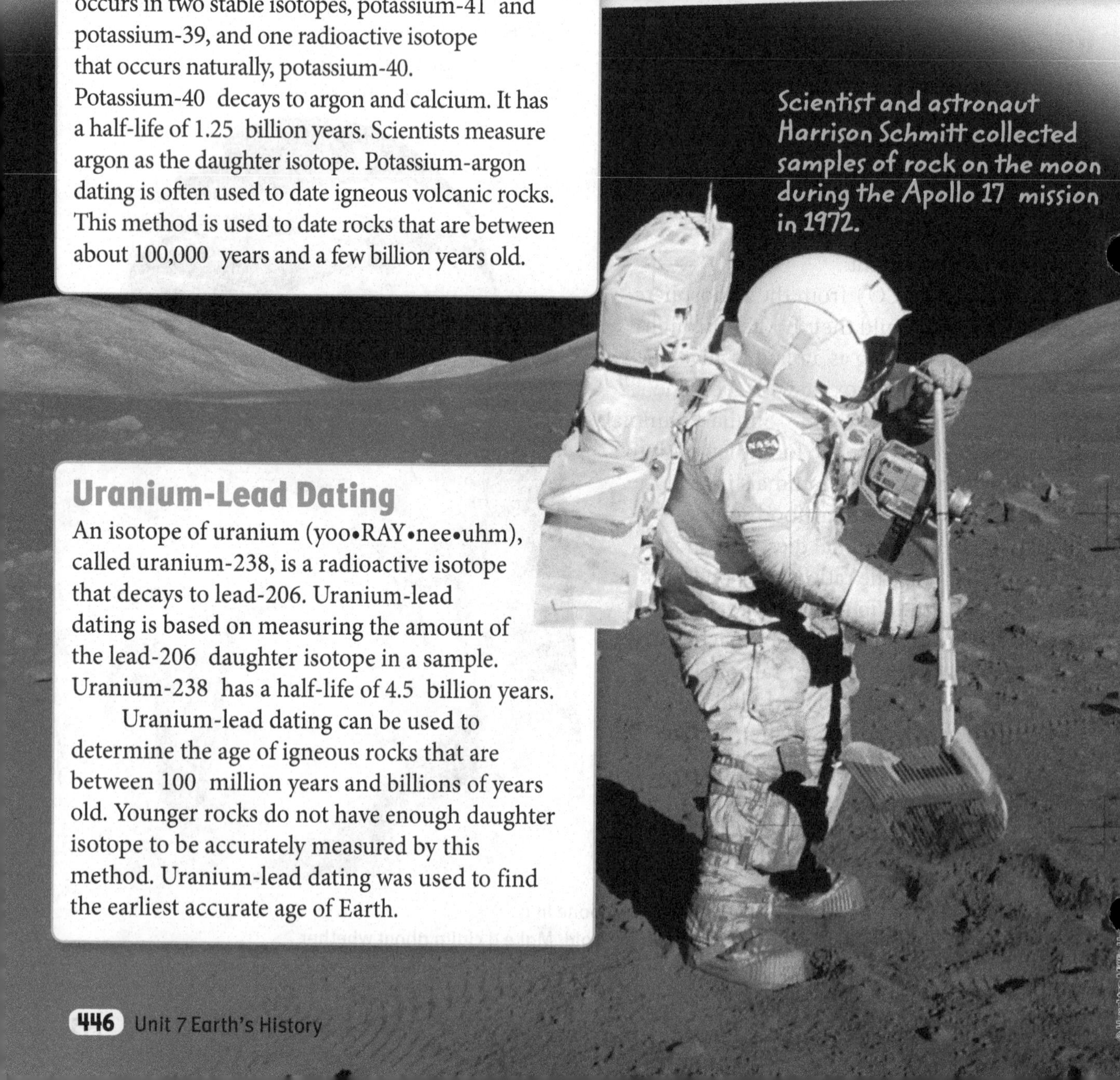

Scientist and astronaut Harrison Schmitt collected samples of rock on the moon during the Apollo 17 mission in 1972.

Uranium-Lead Dating

An isotope of uranium (yoo•RAY•nee•uhm), called uranium-238, is a radioactive isotope that decays to lead-206. Uranium-lead dating is based on measuring the amount of the lead-206 daughter isotope in a sample. Uranium-238 has a half-life of 4.5 billion years.

Uranium-lead dating can be used to determine the age of igneous rocks that are between 100 million years and billions of years old. Younger rocks do not have enough daughter isotope to be accurately measured by this method. Uranium-lead dating was used to find the earliest accurate age of Earth.

Time Will Tell

How is radiometric dating used to determine the age of Earth?

Radiometric dating can be used to find the age of Earth, though not by dating Earth rocks. The first rocks that formed on Earth have long ago been eroded or melted, or buried under younger rocks. So, there are no Earth rocks which can be directly studied that are as old as our planet. But other bodies in space do have rock that is as old as our solar system.

Meteorites (MEE•tee•uh•rytz) are small, rocky bodies that have traveled through space and fallen to Earth's surface. Scientists have found meteorites on Earth, such as the one shown below. Rocks from the moon have also been collected. Radiometric dating has been done on these rocks from other parts of our solar system. The absolute ages of these samples show that our solar system, including Earth, is about 4.6 billion years old.

ACTIVE READING

12 **Identify** As you read, underline the reason why scientists cannot use rocks from Earth to measure the age of Earth.

i Think Outside the Book

13 **Model** Develop a way to help people understand how large the number 4.6 billion is.

This 4.5 billion-year-old rock is part of a meteorite that landed in Antarctica. It is thought to be from Mars.

Showing Your **Age**

How can fossils help to determine the age of sedimentary rock?

Sedimentary rock layers and the fossils within these layers cannot be dated directly. But igneous rock layers on either side of a fossil layer can be dated radiometrically. Once the older and younger rock layers are dated, scientists can assign an absolute age range to the sedimentary rock layer that the fossils are found in.

ACTIVE **READING**

14 Identify As you read, underline the requirements for a fossil to be an index fossil.

Using Index Fossils

Scientists have found that particular types of fossils appear only in certain layers of rock. By dating igneous rock layers above and below these fossil layers, scientists can determine the time span in which the organisms lived. *Index fossils,* such as the ones shown below, are fossils that are used to estimate the absolute age of the rock layers in which they are found. Once the absolute age of an index fossil is known, it can be used to determine the age of rock layers that contain the same index fossil anywhere on Earth.

To be an index fossil, the organism from which the fossil formed must have lived during a relatively short geologic time span. The fossils of the organism must be relatively common and must be found over a large area. Index fossils must also have features that make them different from other fossils.

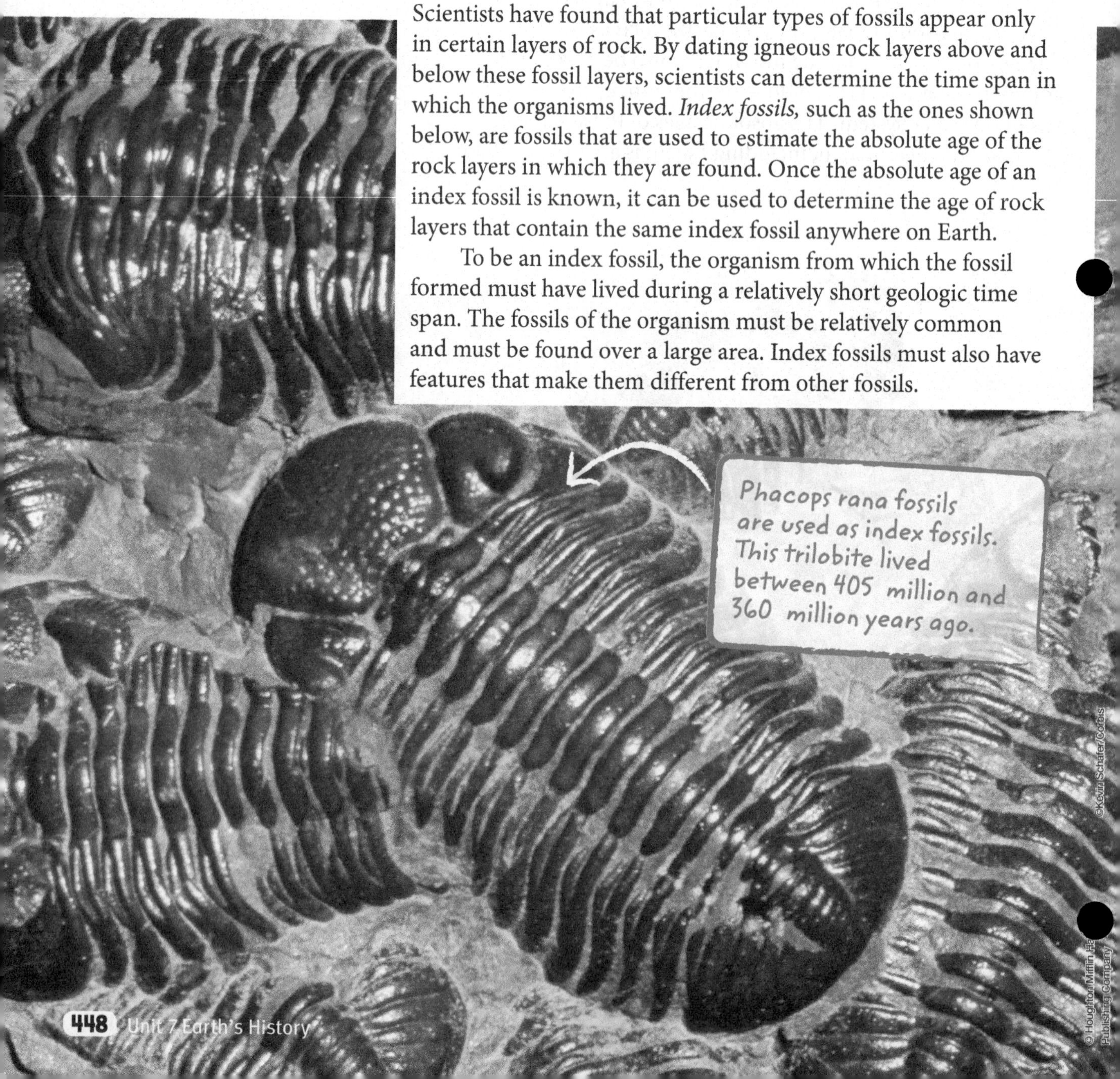

Phacops rana fossils are used as index fossils. This trilobite lived between 405 million and 360 million years ago.

How are index fossils used?

Index fossils act as markers for the time that the organisms lived on Earth. Organisms that formed index fossils lived during short periods of geologic time. So, the rock layer that an index fossil is found in can be dated accurately. For example, ammonites were marine mollusks, similar to a modern squid. They lived in coiled shells in ancient seas. The ammonite *Tropites* (troh•PY•teez) lived between 230 million and 208 million years ago. So, whenever scientists find a fossil of *Tropites*, they know that the rock layer the fossil was found in formed between 230 million and 208 million years ago. As shown below, this can also tell scientists something about the ages of surrounding rock layers.

Trilobite (TRY•luh•byt) fossils are another example of a good index fossil. The closest living relatives of trilobites are the horseshoe crab, spiders, and scorpions. *Phacops rana* is a trilobite that lived between 405 million and 360 million years ago. The *Phacops rana* fossil, shown on the previous page, is the state fossil of Pennsylvania.

Index fossils can also be used to date rock layers in separate areas. The appearance of the same index fossil in rock of different areas shows that the rock layers formed at about the same time.

ACTIVE **READING**

15 **Identify** As you read, underline examples of organisms whose fossils are index fossils. Include the time frame for which they are used to date rock.

👁 Visualize It!

16 **Explain Your Reasoning** *Tropites* fossils are found in the middle rock layer shown below. Place each of the following ages beside the correct rock layer: 215 million/500 million/100 million. Explain your reasoning.

Fossils of a genus of ammonites called Tropites are good index fossils.

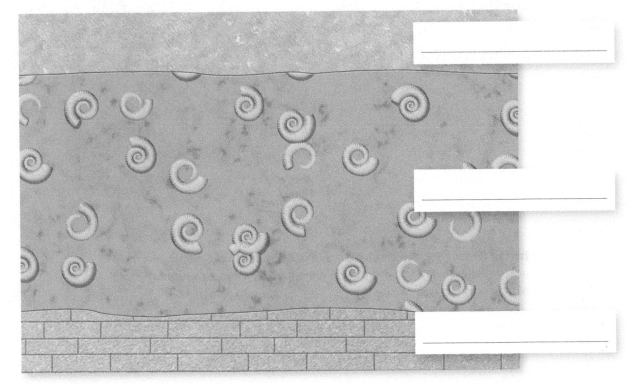

Visual Summary

To complete this summary, fill in the blanks with the correct word or phrase. You can use this page to review the main concepts of the lesson.

Radiometric dating can be used to find the absolute ages of materials such as igneous rocks. This method uses the radioactive decay of an isotope.

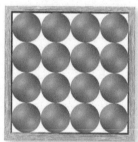  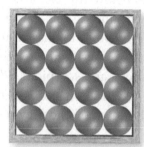

17 During radioactive decay, the amount of _____ isotope

decreases by one-half after every _____

Absolute Dating

Index fossils can be used to estimate the absolute ages of some sedimentary rocks.

18 Four things that index fossils should be:

A _____

B _____

C _____

D _____

19 Claims • Evidence • Reasoning Make a claim about how the use of radioactive decay in absolute dating is similar to how you use a clock. Summarize evidence to support your claim and explain your reasoning.

Lesson Review

Vocabulary

Fill in each blank with the term that best completes the following sentences.

1 The breakdown of a radioactive isotope into a stable isotope is called _____

_____

2 The _____ is the time needed for half of a sample of a radioactive isotope to break down to form daughter isotopes.

3 _____ is a method used to determine the absolute age of a sample by measuring the relative amounts of parent isotope and daughter isotope.

Key Concepts

4 Summarize How are radioactive isotopes used to determine the absolute age of igneous rock? Name two radiometric methods that are used.

_____

_____

5 Describe What happens to an isotope during radioactive decay?

_____

6 Claims • Evidence • Reasoning Make a claim about why igneous rocks are the best type of rock sample for radiometric dating. Support you claim with evidence, and explain your reasoning.

_____

7 Describe How old is Earth and how did scientists find this out?

_____

8 Explain What are index fossils and how are they used to determine the absolute age of sedimentary rock?

_____

_____

Critical Thinking

9 Claims • Evidence • Reasoning An igneous rock sample is about 250,000 years old. Make a claim about whether you would use uranium-lead radiometric dating to find its age. Summarize evidence to support your claim and explain your reasoning.

_____

_____

10 Calculate A sample of wood contains 12.5% of its original carbon-14. What is the estimated age of this sample? Show your work.

_____

_____

Use this graph to answer the following questions.

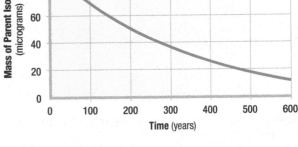

Radioactive Decay

11 Analyze What is the half-life of the radioactive isotope? Explain your reasoning.

_____

12 Analyze What mass of radioactive isotope will be left after three half-lives? Explain your reasoning.

_____

Earth's History

can be studied using

shows

Relative Dating

Absolute Dating

Geologic Change over Time

1 Claims • Evidence • Reasoning As shown in the Graphic Organizer above, both relative and absolute dating are used to study Earth's history. Make a claim about how both techniques could be used together to date igneous and sedimentary rock that are found together. Summarize your evidence to support your claim and explain your reasoning.

_____

_____

_____

_____

_____

_____

_____

2 Apply How can scientists determine the age of Earth?

_____

_____

_____

_____

_____

_____

3 Relate What does sedimentary rock tell us about past environments on Earth?

_____

_____

_____

_____

_____

_____

_____

_____

_____

_____

Vocabulary

Fill in each blank with the term that best completes the following sentences.

1 A _____ is the remains of a once-living organism found in layers of rock, ice, or amber.

2 The time required for half the quantity of a radioactive material to decay is its _____.

3 _____ is the theory stating that Earth's lithosphere is made up of large plates that are in constant motion.

4 _____ is the process in which a radioactive isotope tends to break down into a stable isotope.

5 _____ is the scientific study of the origin, physical history, and structure of Earth and the processes that shape it.

Key Concepts

Identify the choice that best completes the statement or answers the question.

6 A trace fossil includes no physical remains of the organism's body but only a mark or structure that the organism left behind. Which of these choices is not an example of a trace fossil?

A footprint in sediment

B coprolite in sediment

C burrow in the sea floor

D insect in amber

7 Weather is not the same as climate. What is the main difference between these two concepts?

F The main difference is how both are measured.

G Only weather includes information about the temperature.

H Only climate includes information about the precipitation.

I The main difference is the length of time over which both are measured.

8 Ava visited the Grand Canyon. She was very impressed by the rock formations and decided to sketch them. This figure shows what she drew.

What type of rock did Ava see?

A fossilized

C metamorphic

B igneous

D sedimentary

9 A team of scientists is searching for specimens to understand how Earth's climate has changed in the past. The black boxes in the figure below show where this team has drilled to obtain such specimens.

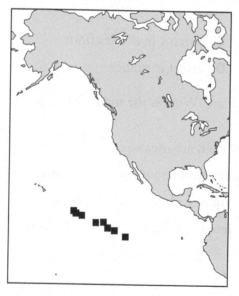

What were these scientists drilling for?

F ice cores

H sea-floor sediments

G surface landforms

I fossils preserved in amber

Name _____

10 Tiny fossils provide evidence that life on Earth began at least 3.5 billion years ago. According to this fossil evidence, about how old was Earth when life first appeared on the planet?

A 4.6 billion years

B 3.5 billion years

C 2.3 billion years

D 1.1 billion years

11 A team of geologists compared the rock layers found in Florida to those found in northwest Africa. They placed all of the rock layers from the two regions in order from youngest to oldest. What did the team make?

F a geologic record

G a fossil reference

H a geologic column

I a topographic map

12 Jacob has one older brother and one younger sister. He wants to explain relative dating to them using their ages as an example. Which of these statements describes their ages using relative dating?

A Their ages are 14, 12, and 9.

B They are all about the same age.

C The boys have different ages than the girl.

D Jacob is younger than his brother but older than his sister.

13 Basalt is a gray or black igneous rock. Pilar uses an absolute dating method to study a sample of basalt. What will the method help her learn about the basalt sample?

F the age of the sample

G the composition of the sample

H the physical structure of the sample

I the geographic distribution of the sample

14 Scientists have determined an approximate age for Earth. To do this, they tested samples of meteorites, rocks from the moon, and rocks from other parts of the solar system. Which method could be used to determine the age of these samples?

A radiocarbon dating

B index fossil dating

C sedimentary rock dating

D uranium-lead dating

15 Which type of evidence acts as a record of changes in species over time and indicates major changes in Earth's surface and climate?

 F fossil record

 G movement of continents

 H ripple marks and mud cracks

 I composition of ice core samples

Critical Thinking

Answer the following questions in the space provided.

16 Scientists study how radioactive isotopes in rocks, such as carbon-14, decay to tell the age of the rock.

Carbon-14 Nitrogen-14 + Particles + Energy

Does knowing the half-life of Carbon 14 help scientists determine the absolute or relative age of a rock? State your claim. Use evidence to support your claim and explain your reasoning.

_____

_____

_____

_____

_____

17 Explain how fossils and other materials can tell us about the conditions of an area at the times it existed. Then explain how you could find the ages of these fossils and other materials.

_____

_____

_____

_____

_____

Weathering, Erosion, Deposition, and Landforms

FLORIDA **BIG IDEA 6**

Earth Structures

Some caves in Florida are under water.

What Do You Think?

Florida has many caves underground. If a cave is close to Earth's surface and its roof is weak, the roof may fall in, forming a sinkhole. As you explore this unit, gather evidence to help you state and support a claim about how these caves might have formed.

Weathering, Erosion, Deposition, and Landforms

CITIZEN SCIENCE

Save a Beach

Like many other features on land, beaches can also change over time. But what could be powerful enough to wash away a beach? Waves and currents.

① Define the Problem

People love to visit the beach. Many businesses along the beach survive because of the tourists that visit the area. But in many places, the beach is being washed away by ocean waves and currents.

Beaches draw lots of tourists.

② Think About It

When waves from the ocean hit the beach at an angle, the waves will often pull some of the sand back into the ocean with them. These sands may then be carried away by the current. In this way, a beach can be washed away. What could you do to prevent a sandy beach from washing away? Looking at the photo below, design a way to prevent the beach from washing away. Then conduct an experiment to test your design.

Check off the questions below as you use them to design your experiment.

☐ How will you create waves?

☐ At what angle should the waves hit the beach?

☐ Will people still be able to use the beach if your method were used?

Waves carry the sands back into the ocean with them.

③ Make a Plan

A Make a list of the materials you will need for your experiment in the space below.

_____

_____

_____

B Draw a sketch of the set up in the space below.

C Conduct your experiment. Briefly state your findings.

_____

_____

_____

Take It Home!

Find an area that may be eroding in your neighborhood, such as the banks of a pond or road. Study the area. Then, prepare a short presentation for your class on how to prevent erosion in this area.

© Houghton Mifflin Harcourt Publishing Company

© Franz Marc Frei/PhotoLibrary

Weathering

ESSENTIAL QUESTION

How does weathering change Earth's surface?

By the end of this lesson, you should be able to analyze the effects of physical and chemical weathering on Earth's surface, including examples of each kind of weathering.

SC.6.E.6.1 Describe and give examples of ways in which Earth's surface is built up and torn down by physical and chemical weathering, erosion, and deposition.

Wave Rock in Australia may look like an ocean wave, but it was actually formed when the rock in the middle of this formation weathered faster than the rock at the top.

©Douglas Pearson/Corbis

Lesson Labs

Quick Labs
• Mechanical Weathering
• Weathering Chalk

Engage Your Brain

1 Predict Check T or F to show whether you think each statement is true or false.

T	F	
☐	☐	Rocks can change shape and composition over time.
☐	☐	Rocks cannot be weathered by wind and chemicals in the air.
☐	☐	A rusty car is an example of weathering.
☐	☐	Plants and animals can cause weathering of rocks.

2 Describe Your class has taken a field trip to a local stream. You notice that the rocks in the water are rounded and smooth. Write a brief description of how you think the rocks changed over time.

_____

_____

_____

_____

_____

_____

_____

_____

ACTIVE READING

3 Synthesize You can often find clues to the meaning of a word by examining the use of that word in a sentence. Read the following sentences and write your own definition for the word *abrasion*.

Example sentences
Bobby fell on the sidewalk and scraped his knee. The <u>abrasion</u> on his knee was painful because of the loss of several layers of skin.

abrasion:

_____

_____

_____

_____

Vocabulary Terms

• weathering
• physical weathering
• abrasion
• chemical weathering
• oxidation
• acid precipitation

4 Apply As you learn the definition of each vocabulary term in this lesson, create your own definition or sketch to help you remember the meaning of the term.

Break It Down

What is weathering?

Did you know that sand on a beach may have once been a part of a large boulder? Over millions of years, a boulder can break down into many smaller pieces. The breakdown of rock material by physical and chemical processes is called **weathering**. Two kinds of weathering are *physical weathering* and *chemical weathering*.

What causes physical weathering?

Rocks can get smaller and smaller without a change in the composition of the rock. This is an example of a physical change. The process by which rock is broken down into smaller pieces by physical changes is **physical weathering**. Temperature changes, pressure changes, plant and animal actions, water, wind, and gravity are all agents of physical weathering.

As materials break apart, they can become even more exposed to physical changes. For instance, a large boulder can be broken apart by ice and water over time. Eventually, the boulder can split in two. Now there are two rocks exposed to the agents of physical weathering. In other words, the amount of surface area exposed to the agents of physical weathering increases. The large boulder can become thousands of tiny rocks over time as each new rock increases the amount of surface area able to be weathered.

ACTIVE **READING**

5 Identify As you read, place the names of some common agents of physical weathering in the graphic organizer below.

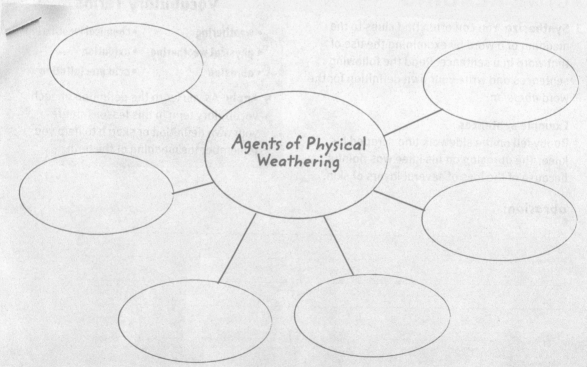

Agents of Physical Weathering

6 Describe Write a caption for each of the images to describe the process of ice wedging

Ice Wedging

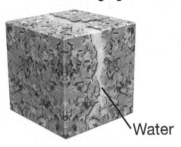

Water

_____

_____

Ice

_____

_____

Water

_____

_____

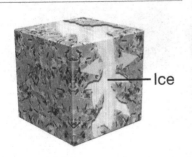

Ice

_____

_____

Temperature Change

Changes in temperatures can cause a rock to break apart. A rise in temperature will cause a rock to expand. A decrease in temperature will cause a rock to contract. Repeated temperature changes can weaken the structure of a rock, causing the rock to crumble. Even changes in temperature between day and night can cause rocks to expand and contract. In desert regions differences in day and night temperatures can be significant. Rocks can weaken and crumble from the stress caused by these temperature changes.

Ice wedging, sometimes known as _frost wedging_, can also cause rocks to physically break apart, as shown in the image below. Ice wedging causes cracks in rocks to expand as water seeps in and freezes. When water collects in cracks in rock and the temperature drops, the water may freeze. Water expands as it freezes to become ice. As the ice expands, the crack will widen. As more water enters the crack, it can expand to an even larger size. Eventually, a small crack in a rock can cause even the largest of rocks to split apart.

7 Claims • Evidence • Reasoning Make a claim about where on Earth physical weathering from temperature changes would be the least and most common. Provide evidence to support your claim and explain your reasoning.

_____

_____

These cracks, which were caused by ice wedging, will continue to expand over time.

Enchanted Rock was once buried deep inside Earth.

Pressure Change

Physical weathering can be caused by pressure changes. Rocks formed under pressure deep within Earth can become exposed at the surface. As overlying materials are removed above the rock, the pressure decreases. As a result, the rock expands, causing the outermost layers of rock to separate from the underlying layers, as shown to the left. *Exfoliation* (ex•foh•lee•AY•shun) is the process by which the outer layers of rock slowly peel away due to pressure changes. Enchanted Rock in Texas is a 130 m–high dome of granite that is slowly losing the outermost layers of rock due to exfoliation and other processes.

Animal Action

Animals can cause physical weathering. Many animals dig burrows into the ground, allowing more rock to be exposed. Common burrowing animals include ground squirrels, prairie dogs, ants, and earthworms. These animals move soils and allow new rocks, soils, and other materials to be exposed at the surface, as shown below. Materials can undergo weathering below the surface, but are more likely to be weathered once exposed at the surface.

👁 Visualize It!

8 Describe Write a caption for each animal describing how it might cause physical weathering.

Prairie dog

A _____
_____
_____

Some pocket gophers can dig burrows up to 240 m in length.

C _____
_____

Earthworm

B _____
_____
_____

Wind, Water, and Gravity

Rock can be broken down by the action of other rocks over time. **Abrasion** (uh•BRAY•zhuhn) is the breaking down and wearing away of rock material by the mechanical action of other rock. Three agents of physical weathering that can cause abrasion are moving water, wind, and gravity. Also, rocks suspended in the ice of a glacier can cause abrasion of other rocks on Earth's surface.

In moving water, rock can become rounded and smooth. Abrasion occurs as rocks are tumbled in water, hitting other rocks. Wind abrasion occurs when wind lifts and carries small particles in the air. The small particles can blast away at surfaces and slowly wear them away. During a landslide, large rocks can fall from higher up a slope and break more rocks below, causing abrasion.

ACTIVE **READING**

9 Identify As you read, underline the agents of weathering that cause abrasion.

Rocks are tumbled in water, causing abrasion.

Wind-blown sand can blast small particles away.

Rocks can be broken down in a landslide.

Plant Growth

You have probably noticed that just one crack in a sidewalk can be the opening for a tiny bit of grass to grow. Over time, a neglected sidewalk can become crumbly from a combination of several agents of physical weathering, including plant growth. Why?

Roots of plants do not start out large. Roots start as tiny strands of plant matter that can grow inside small cracks in rocks. As the plant gets bigger, so do the roots. The larger a root grows, the more pressure it puts on rock. More pressure causes the rock to expand, as seen to the right. Eventually, the rock can break apart.

Think Outside the Book

10 Summarize Imagine you are a rock. Write a short biography of your life as a rock, describing the changes you have gone through over time.

This tree started as a tiny seedling and eventually grew to split the rock in half.

Reaction

What causes chemical weathering?

Chemical weathering changes both the composition and appearance of rocks. **Chemical weathering** is the breakdown of rocks by chemical reactions. Agents of chemical weathering include oxygen in the air and acids.

Reactions with Oxygen

Oxygen in the air or in water can cause chemical weathering. Oxygen reacts with the compounds that make up rock, causing chemical reactions. The process by which other chemicals combine with oxygen is called **oxidation** (ahk•si•DAY•shun).

Rock surfaces sometimes change color. A color change can mean that a chemical reaction has taken place. Rocks containing iron can easily undergo chemical weathering. Iron in rocks and soils combines quickly with oxygen that is dissolved in water. The result is a rock that turns reddish orange. This is rust! The red color of much of the soil in the southeastern United States and of rock formations in the southwestern United States is due to the presence of rust, as seen in the image below.

Reactions with Acid Precipitation

Acids break down most minerals faster than water alone. Increased amounts of acid from various sources can cause chemical weathering of rock. Acids in the atmosphere are created when chemicals combine with water in the air. Rain is normally slightly acidic. When fossil fuels are burned, other chemicals combine with water in the atmosphere to produce even stronger acids. When these stronger acids fall to Earth, they are called **acid precipitation** (AS•id prih•sip•ih•TAY•shun). Acid precipitation is recognized as a problem all around the world and causes rocks to break down and change composition.

These rocks in Arizona are red because of oxidation.

Reactions with Acids in Groundwater

Water in the ground, or groundwater, can cause chemical weathering. As groundwater moves through spaces or cracks in rock, acids in the water can cause rocks to dissolve. A small crack in a rock can result in the formation of extensive cave systems that are carved out over time under Earth's surface, as shown to the right. The dissolved rock material is carried in water until it is later deposited. Stalactites (stuh•LAHK•tyt) and stalagmites (stuh•LAHG•myt) are common features in cave systems as dissolved chemicals are deposited by dripping water underground.

Reactions with Acids in Living Things

Acids are produced naturally by certain living organisms. For instance, lichens (LY•kuhns) and mosses often grow on rocks and trees. As they grow on rocks, they produce weak acids that can weather the rock's surface. As the acids move through tiny spaces in the rocks, chemical reactions can occur. The acids will eventually break down the rocks. As the acids seep deeper into the rocks, cracks can form. The rock can eventually break apart when the cracks get too large.

Stalactites

Stalagmites

The dissolved rock from acidic groundwater can later be deposited in different locations.

This gear is rusted, which indicates that a chemical reaction has taken place.

© Houghton Mifflin Harcourt Publishing Company

Think Outside the Book

13 **Claims • Evidence • Reasoning**
Think of an item made by humans that could be broken down by the agents of physical and chemical weathering. Make a claim about all of the ways the item could change over time. Provide evidence and explain your reasoning.

Visual Summary

To complete this summary, fill in the blanks with the correct word or phrase. You can use this page to review the main concepts of the lesson.

Weathering

Physical weathering breaks rock into smaller pieces by physical means.

Chemical weathering breaks down rock by chemical reactions.

14 Label the images with the type of physical weathering shown.

A _____

B _____

C _____

15 Label the images with the type of chemical weathering shown.

A _____

B _____

16 Claims • Evidence • Reasoning Make a claim about why some rocks are more easily weathered than other rocks. Support your claim with evidence and explain your reasoning.

Lesson Review

Vocabulary

Fill in the blank with the term that best completes the following sentences.

1 Acid precipitation is an agent of _____ weathering.

2 The gradual wearing away or breaking down of rocks by abrasion is a type of _____ weathering.

3 The process of _____ causes rocks to change composition when reacting with oxygen.

4 The mechanical breakdown of rocks by the action of other rocks and sand particles is called_____

Key Concepts

5 Compare What are some similarities and differences between physical and chemical weathering?

_____

_____

6 List Provide examples of agents of physical weathering and chemical weathering in the chart below.

Physical Weathering	Chemical Weathering

7 Compare What are some similarities between ice wedging and plant root growth in a rock?

_____

_____

Critical Thinking

Use the graph to answer the following questions.

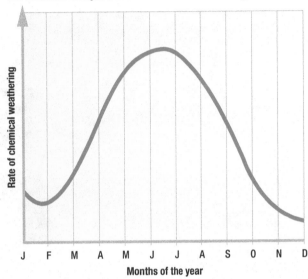

The Effect of Temperature on Rates of Weathering

8 Analyze Which two months had the highest rates of chemical weathering?

_____

_____

9 Apply Why do you think those two months had the highest rates of chemical weathering?

_____

_____

_____

10 Claims • Evidence • Reasoning Make a claim about which processes may cause increased abrasion along a coastal region. Summarize evidence to support the claim and explain your reasoning.

_____

_____

_____

Erosion and Deposition by Water

ESSENTIAL QUESTION

How does water change Earth's surface?

By the end of this lesson, you should be able to relate the processes of erosion and deposition by water to the landforms that result from these processes.

SC.6.E.6.1 Describe and give examples of ways in which Earth's surface is built up and torn down by physical and chemical weathering, erosion, and deposition. **SC.6.E.6.2** Recognize that there are a variety of different landforms on Earth's surface such as coastlines, dunes, rivers, mountains, glaciers, deltas, and lakes and relate these landforms as they apply to Florida.

Rivers aren't only found on Earth's surface. They also flow underground! Underground rivers can carve out caves full of channels, waterfalls, and even lakes.

©Robbie Shone/Aurora/Getty Images

©Houghton Mifflin Harcourt Publishing Company

Lesson Labs

Quick Lab
- Wave Action on the Shoreline
- Moving Sediment

Exploration Labs
- Exploring Stream Erosion and Deposition
- Beach Erosion

Engage Your Brain

1 Predict Check T or F to show whether you think each statement is true or false.

T   F

☐ ☐ Water is able to move rocks as big as boulders.

☐ ☐ Rivers can help to break down mountains.

☐ ☐ Water cannot change rock underneath Earth's surface.

☐ ☐ Waves and currents help to form beaches.

2 Explain Write a caption that explains how you think this canyon formed.

_____

_____

_____

ACTIVE READING

3 Synthesize Several of the vocabulary terms in this lesson are compound words, or two separate words combined to form a new word that has a new meaning. Use the meanings of the two separate words to make an educated guess about the meaning of the compound terms shown below.

flood + plain = floodplain

_____

_____

ground + water = groundwater

_____

_____

shore + line = shoreline

_____

sand + bar = sandbar

_____

_____

Vocabulary Terms

- erosion
- deposition
- floodplain
- delta
- alluvial fan
- groundwater
- shoreline
- beach
- sandbar
- barrier island

4 Apply As you learn the definition of each vocabulary term in this lesson, create your own definition or sketch to help you remember the meaning of the term.

Go with the Flow

How does flowing water change Earth's surface?

If your job was to carry millions of tons of rock and soil across the United States, how would you do it? You might use a bulldozer or a dump truck, but your job would still take a long time. Did you know that rivers and other bodies of flowing water do this job every day? Flowing water, as well as wind and ice, can move large amounts of material, such as soil and rock. Gravity also has a role to play. Gravity causes water to flow and rocks to fall downhill.

By Erosion

Acting as liquid conveyor belts, rivers and streams erode soil, rock, and sediment. *Sediment* is tiny grains of broken-down rock. **Erosion** is the process by which sediment and other materials are moved from one place to another. Eroded materials in streams may come from the stream's own bed and banks or from materials carried to the stream by rainwater runoff. Over time, erosion causes streams to widen and deepen.

By Deposition

After streams erode rock and soil, they eventually drop, or deposit, their load downstream. **Deposition** is the process by which eroded material is dropped. Deposition occurs when gravity's downward pull on sediment is greater than the push of flowing water or wind. This usually happens when the water or wind slows down. A stream deposits materials along its bed, banks, and mouth, which can form different landforms.

5 Compare Fill in the Venn diagram to compare and contrast erosion and deposition.

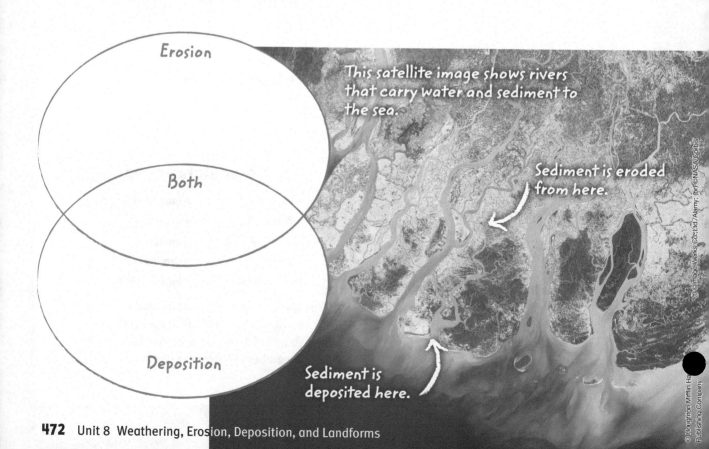

Erosion

Both

Deposition

This satellite image shows rivers that carry water and sediment to the sea.

Sediment is eroded from here.

Sediment is deposited here.

What factors relate to a stream's ability to erode material?

Some streams are able to erode large rocks, while others can erode only very fine sediment. Some streams move many tons of material each day, while others move very little sediment. So what determines how much material a stream can erode? A stream's gradient, discharge, and load are the three main factors that control what sediment a stream can carry.

Gradient

Gradient is the measure of the change in elevation over a certain distance. You can think of gradient as the steepness of a slope. The water in a stream that has a high gradient—or steep slope—moves very rapidly because of the downward pull of gravity. This rapid water flow gives the stream a lot of energy to erode rock and soil. A river or stream that has a low gradient has less energy for erosion, or erosive energy.

Load

Materials carried by a stream are called the stream's *load*. The size of the particles in a stream's load is affected by the stream's speed. Fast-moving streams can carry large particles. The large particles bounce and scrape along the bottom and sides of the streambed. Thus, a stream that has a load of large particles has a high erosion rate. Slow-moving streams carry smaller particles and have less erosive energy.

Discharge

The amount of water that a stream carries in a given amount of time is called *discharge*. The discharge of a stream increases when a major storm occurs or when warm weather rapidly melts snow. As the stream's discharge increases, its erosive energy, speed, and load increase.

ACTIVE READING

6 Explain Why do some streams and rivers cause more erosion and deposition than others?

_____

_____

_____

 **Do the Math**

River Gradient Plot

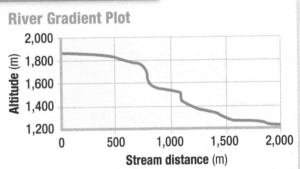

A river gradient plot shows how quickly the elevation of a river falls along its course. The slope of the line is the river's gradient. The line has a steep slope at points along the river where the gradient is steep. The line has a nearly level slope where the river gradient is shallow.

Identify

7 Along this river, at which two approximate altitude ranges are the gradients the steepest?

_____

_____

_____

8 Support Your Claim At which altitude ranges would you expect the highest streambed erosion rate? Provide evidence from the graph.

_____

_____

_____

9 Support Your Claim At which altitude ranges would you expect the slowest streambed erosion rate? Provide evidence from the graph.

_____

_____

_____

Run of a River

10 Apply Discuss with your classmates some landforms near your town that were likely made by flowing water.

What landforms can streams create?

A stream forms as water erodes soil and rock to make a channel. A *channel* is the path that a stream follows. As the stream continues to erode rock and soil, the channel gets wider and deeper. Over time, canyons and valleys can form.

Canyons and Valleys by Erosion

The processes that changed Earth's surface in the past continue to be at work today. For example, erosion and deposition have taken place throughout Earth's history. Six million years ago, Earth's surface in the area now known as the Grand Canyon was flat. The Colorado River cut down into the rock and formed the Grand Canyon over millions of years. Landforms, such as canyons and valleys, are created by the flow of water through streams and rivers. As the water moves, it erodes rock and sediment from the streambed. The flowing water can cut through rock, forming steep canyons and valleys.

👁 Visualize It!

11 Apply On the lines below, label where erosion and deposition are occurring.

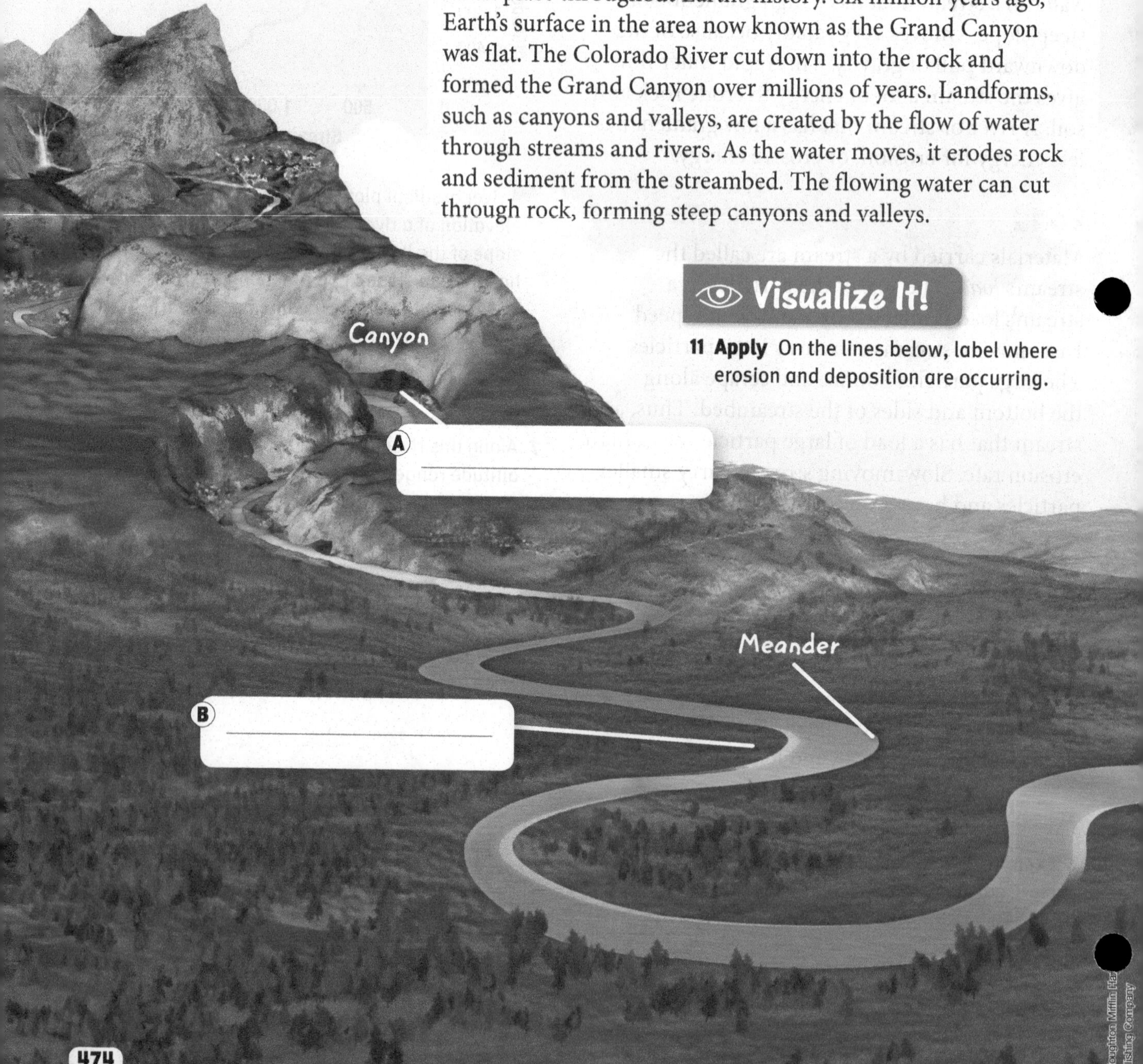

Canyon

A _____

B _____

Meander

Floodplains by Deposition

When a stream floods, a layer of sediment is deposited over the flooded land. Many layers of deposited sediment can form a flat area called a **floodplain**. Sediment often contains nutrients needed for plant growth. Because of this, floodplains are often very fertile.

As a stream flows through an area, its channel may run straight in some parts and curve in other parts. Curves and bends that form a twisting, looping pattern in a stream channel are called *meanders*. The moving water erodes the outside banks and deposits sediment along the inside banks. Over many years, meanders shift position. During a flood, a stream may cut a new channel that bypasses a meander. The cut-off meander forms a crescent-shaped lake, which is called an *oxbow lake*.

Deltas and Alluvial Fans by Deposition

When a stream empties into a body of water, such as a lake or an ocean, its current slows and it deposits its load. Streams often deposit their loads in a fan-shaped pattern called a **delta**. Over time, sediment builds up in a delta, forming new land. Sometimes the new land can extend far into the lake or ocean. A similar process occurs when a stream flows onto a flat land surface from mountains or hills. On land, the sediment forms an alluvial fan. An **alluvial fan** is a fan-shaped deposit that forms on dry land.

ACTIVE READING

12 Identify As you read, underline the definitions of *delta* and *alluvial fan*.

13 Compare Compare and contrast alluvial fans and deltas.

_____
_____
_____
_____
_____

Alluvial fan

Floodplain

C _____

Oxbow lake

Delta

More Waterworks

What landforms are made by groundwater erosion?

As you have learned, rivers cause erosion when water picks up and moves rock and soil. The movement of water underground can also cause erosion. **Groundwater** is the water located within the rocks below Earth's surface. Slightly acidic groundwater can cause erosion by dissolving rock. When underground erosion happens, caves can form. Most of the world's caves formed over thousands of years as groundwater dissolved limestone underground. Although caves are formed by erosion, they also show signs of deposition. Water that drips from cracks in a cave's ceiling leaves behind icicle-shaped deposits known as *stalactites* and *stalagmites*. When the groundwater level is lower than the level of a cave, the cave roof may no longer be supported by the water underneath. If the roof of a cave collapses, it may leave a circular depression called a *sinkhole*.

Stalactites are caused by deposition.

ACTIVE READING

14 Explain How does groundwater cause caves to form?

_____

_____

Groundwater can erode rock, causing caves to form.

<👁 Visualize It!>

15 Claims • Evidence • Reasoning Make a claim about what may have happened underground to cause this sinkhole to form. Summarize evidence to support the claim and explain your reasoning.

_____

_____

_____

_____

What forces shape a shoreline?

A **shoreline** is the place where land and a body of water meet. Ocean water along a shoreline moves differently than river water moves. Ocean waves crashing against the shoreline have a great deal of energy. Strong waves may erode material. Gentle waves may deposit materials. In addition to waves, ocean water has *currents*, or streamlike movements of water. Like waves, currents can also erode and deposit materials.

Waves

Waves play a major part in building up and breaking down a shoreline. Waves slow down as they approach a shoreline. The first parts of the shoreline that waves meet are the *headlands*, or pieces of land that project into the water. The slowing waves bend toward the headlands, which concentrates the waves' energy. A huge amount of energy is released when waves crash into headlands, causing the land to erode. The waves striking the areas between headlands have less energy. Therefore, these waves are more likely to deposit materials rather than erode materials.

Currents

When water travels almost parallel to the shoreline very near shore, the current is called a *longshore current*. Longshore currents are caused by waves hitting the shore at an angle. Waves that break at angles move sediment along the coast. The waves push the sand in the same angled direction in which they break. But the return water flow moves sand directly away from the beach. The end result is a zigzag movement of the sand. As sand moves down a beach, the upcurrent end of the beach is eroded away while the downcurrent end of the beach is built up.

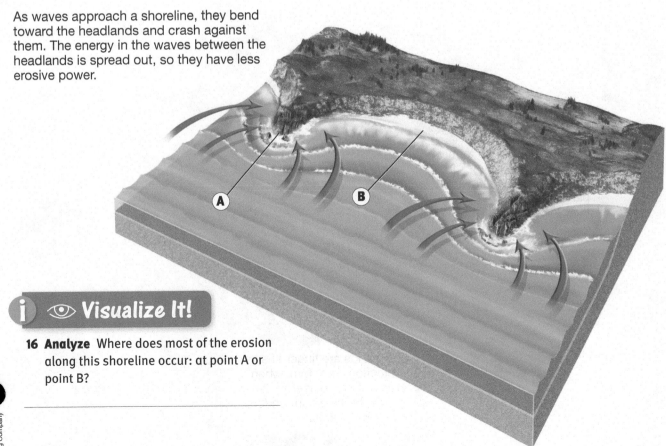

As waves approach a shoreline, they bend toward the headlands and crash against them. The energy in the waves between the headlands is spread out, so they have less erosive power.

ⓘ 👁 Visualize It!

16 Analyze Where does most of the erosion along this shoreline occur: at point A or point B?

_____

Surf Versus Turf

What coastal landforms are made by erosion?

Wave erosion produces a variety of features along a shoreline. The rate at which rock erodes depends on the hardness of the rock and the energy of the waves. Gentle waves cause very little erosion. Strong waves from heavy storms can increase the rate of erosion. During storms, huge blocks of rock can be broken off and eroded away. In fact, a severe storm can noticeably change the appearance of a shoreline in a single day.

In addition to wave energy, the hardness of the rock making up the coastline affects how quickly the coastline is eroded. Very hard rock can slow the rate of erosion because it takes a great deal of wave energy to break up hard rock. Soft rock erodes more rapidly. Many shoreline features are caused by differences in rock hardness. Over time, a large area of softer rock can be eroded by strong waves. As a result, part of the shoreline is carved out and forms a bay.

ACTIVE READING

17 Claims • Evidence • Reasoning
Make a claim about the factors that determine how fast the shoreline erodes. Summarize evidence to support the claim and explain your reasoning.

Sea caves form when waves cut large holes into fractured or weak rock along the base of sea cliffs.

Wave-cut platforms form when a sea cliff is worn back from shore, producing a nearly level platform beneath the water at the base of the cliff.

Headlands are finger-shaped projections that form when cliffs of hard rock erode more slowly than the surrounding softer rock does.

© Houghton Mifflin Harcourt Publishing Company

Sea Cliffs and Wave-cut Platforms

A *sea cliff* forms when waves erode and undercut rock to make steep slopes. Waves strike the cliff's base, wearing away the rock. This process makes the cliff steeper. As a sea cliff erodes above the waterline, a bench of rock usually remains beneath the water at the cliff's base. This bench is called a *wave-cut platform*. Wave-cut platforms are almost flat because the rocks eroded from the cliff often scrape away at the platform.

Sea Caves, Arches, and Stacks

Sea cliffs seldom erode evenly. Often, headlands form as some parts of a cliff are cut back faster than other parts. As the rock making up sea cliffs and headlands erodes, it breaks and cracks. Waves can cut deeply into the cracks and form large holes. As the holes continue to erode, they become *sea caves*. A sea cave may erode even further and eventually become a *sea arch*. When the top of a sea arch collapses, its sides become *sea stacks*.

18 Summarize Complete the chart by filling in descriptions of each coastal landform.

Coastal Landform	Description
Headland	
Sea cave	
Sea arch	
Sea stack	
Wave-cut platform	

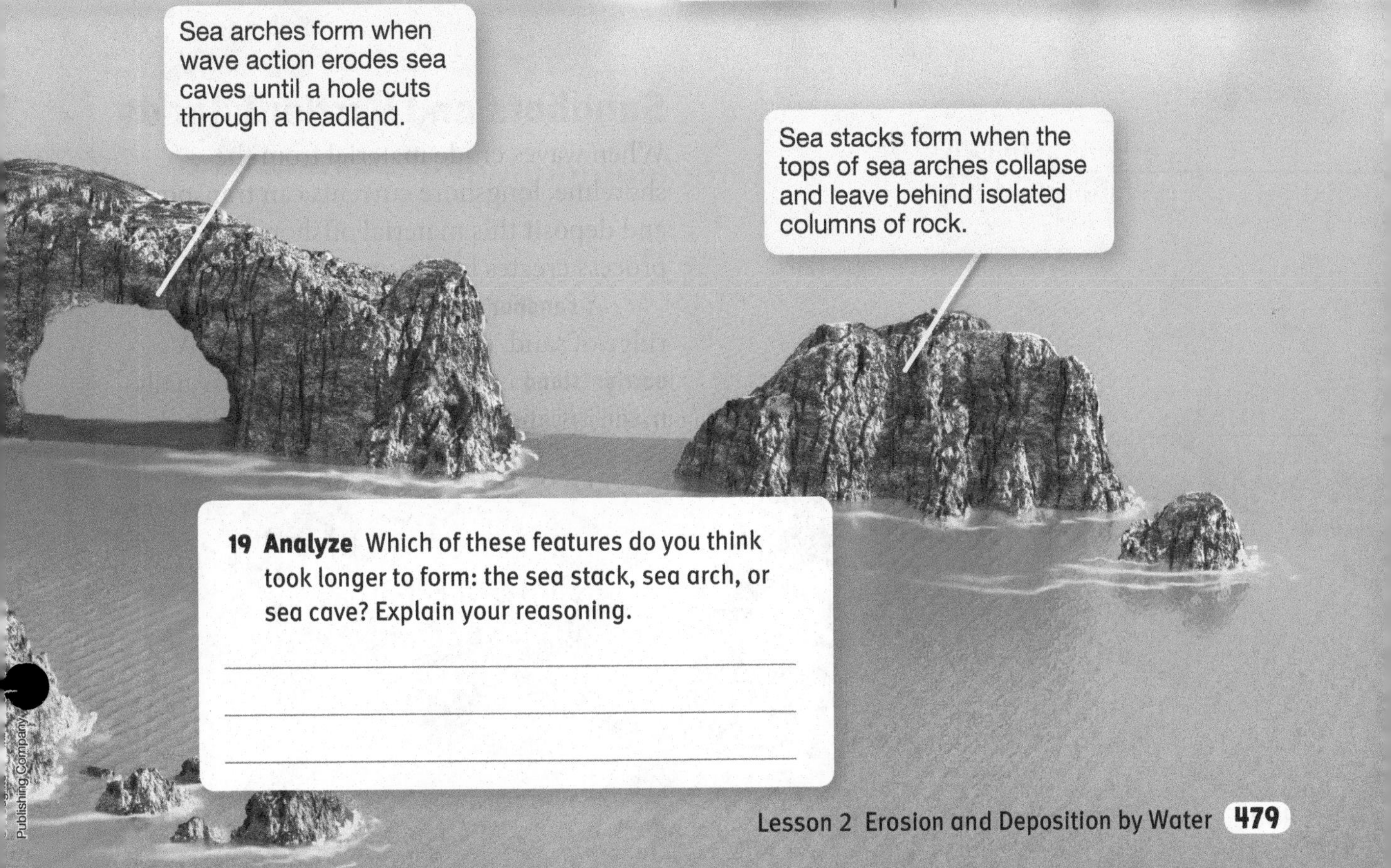

Sea arches form when wave action erodes sea caves until a hole cuts through a headland.

Sea stacks form when the tops of sea arches collapse and leave behind isolated columns of rock.

19 Analyze Which of these features do you think took longer to form: the sea stack, sea arch, or sea cave? Explain your reasoning.

Shifting Sands

What coastal landforms are made by deposition?

Waves and currents carry a variety of materials, including sand, rock, dead coral, and shells. Often, these materials are deposited on a shoreline, where they form a beach. A **beach** is an area of shoreline that is made up of material deposited by waves and currents. A great deal of beach material is also deposited by rivers and then is moved down the shoreline by currents.

Beaches

You may think of beaches as sandy places. However, not all beaches are made of sand. The size and shape of beach material depend on how far the material has traveled from its source. Size and shape also depend on the type of material and how it is eroded. For example, in areas with stormy seas, beaches may be made of pebbles and boulders deposited by powerful waves. These waves erode smaller particles such as sand.

◉ Visualize It!

20 Infer Would it take more wave energy to deposit sand or the rocks shown on this beach? Explain your reasoning.

_____

_____

_____

Barrier islands lie nearly parallel to the shore.

Barrier islands are ridges of sand.

Sandbars and Barrier Islands

When waves erode material from the shoreline, longshore currents can transport and deposit this material offshore. This process creates landforms in open water.

A **sandbar** is an underwater or exposed ridge of sand, gravel, or shell material. A **barrier island** is a long, narrow island, usually made of sand, that forms parallel to the shoreline a short distance offshore.

Living on the Edge

Barrier islands are dynamic landforms that are constantly changing shape. What's here today may be gone tomorrow!

Barrier islands

Landform in Limbo

Barrier islands are found all over the world, including the United States. They can be eroded away by tides and large storms. The barrier island at the left was eroded by a hurricane. Because of erosion, the shape of a barrier island is always changing.

Building on Barriers

Barrier islands are popular spots to build vacation homes and hotels. Residents of barrier islands often use anti-erosion strategies to protect their property from erosion by tides and storms. Short-term solutions include using sand bags, like those shown on the right, to slow down erosion.

ⓘ Extend

21 Claims | Evidence | Reasoning: Make a claim about how a barrier island could form in a step-by-step description. Summarize evidence to support the claim and explain your reasoning.

22 Identify Research different technologies and strategies people can use to slow the erosion of a barrier island.

23 Model Choose one of the anti-erosion methods identified in your research and design an experiment to test how well the technology or strategy slows down the process of erosion.

Visual Summary

To complete this summary, fill in the blanks. You can use this page to review the main concepts of the lesson.

Erosion and Deposition by Water

Streams alter the shape of Earth's surface.

24 Caused by erosion: canyons, valleys

Caused by deposition: floodplains, deltas, _____

Groundwater erodes and deposits materials.

25 Caused by erosion: caves, _____

Caused by deposition: stalactites, stalagmites

Waves and currents change the shape of the shoreline.

26 Caused by erosion: bays, inlets, headlands, wave-cut platforms, sea cliffs, sea caves, sea stacks, _____

Caused by deposition: beaches, sandbars, barrier islands

27 **Claims • Evidence • Reasoning** Make a claim about how erosion and deposition work together to form a delta. Summarize evidence to support the claim and explain your reasoning.

Lesson Review

Vocabulary

Circle the term that best completes the following sentences.

1 *Erosion/Deposition* occurs when materials drop out of wind or water.

2 When a river flows into an ocean, it slows down and deposits materials in its *alluvial fan/delta*.

3 When a river periodically floods and deposits its sediments, a flat area known as a *floodplain/shoreline* forms over time.

Key Concepts

Complete the table below.

Landform	How It Forms
Canyon	**4 Explain**
Sinkhole	**5 Explain**
Sea cave	**6 Explain**

7 **Claims • Evidence • Reasoning** Make a claim about how gravity relates to a stream's ability to erode and deposit materials. Summarize evidence to support the claim and explain your reasoning.

_____

8 **Identify** What are the two main factors that affect how quickly a coastline erodes?

_____

9 **Describe** How does a longshore current change a beach?

_____

Critical Thinking

Use this graph, which shows erosion and deposition on a beach, to answer questions 10–11.

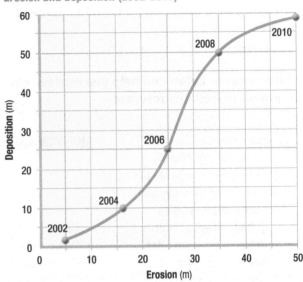

Erosion and Deposition (2002-2010)

10 **Analyze** In 2004, was there more erosion or deposition taking place?

_____

11 **Claims • Evidence • Reasoning** Make a claim about how waves and currents are affecting this beach over time. Summarize evidence to support the claim and explain your reasoning.

_____
_____
_____
_____

12 **Hypothesize** Many communities pump groundwater to irrigate crops and supply homes with water. How do you think overpumping groundwater is related to the formation of sinkholes?

_____
_____
_____

THINK **SCIENCE**

SC.6.N.1.1 Define a problem from the sixth grade curriculum, use appropriate reference materials to support scientific understanding, plan and carry out scientific investigation of various types, such as systematic observations or experiments, identify variables, collect and organize data, interpret data in charts, tables, and graphics, analyze information, make predictions, and defend conclusions.

Searching the Internet

The Internet can be a great tool for finding scientific information and reference material. But, because the Internet contains so much information, finding useful information on it may be difficult. Or, you may find information that is unreliable or not suitable.

Tutorial

The procedure below can help you retrieve useful, reliable information from the Internet.

Choose a search engine There are many search engines available for finding information. Evaluate different search engines using the following criteria:

- number of relevant sites listed in search results;
- how easy the search engine is to use;
- how fast the search is; and
- how easy the documents on the site are to access, and what type of documents they are.

Choose and enter keywords Identify specific keywords for the topic of interest. You can make lists or draw concept maps to help you think of keywords or key phrases. Enter your keyword(s) into the search engine. You can enter one keyword at a time, or you can enter multiple keywords. You can put the word and or + between two keywords to find both words on the site. Use the word or between two keywords to find at least one of the keywords on the site. Use quotations ("like this") around keywords to find exact matches.

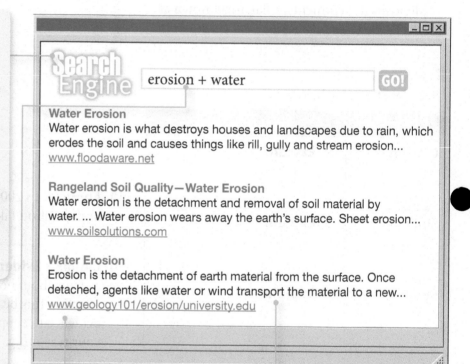

Look at the URL Examine the address in the search results list. Ask yourself if a reliable organization is behind the webpage such as government agencies (.gov or .mil), educational institutions (.edu), and non-profit organizations (.org). Avoid personal sites and biased sources, which may tell only one side of a story. These types of sources may lead to inaccurate information or a false impression.

Look at the content of the webpage Decide whether the webpage contains useful information. Read the page's title and headings. Read the first sentences of several paragraphs. Look at tables and diagrams. Ask yourself: How current is the webpage?; Are the sources documented?; and Are there links to more information? Decide whether the webpage contains the kind of information that you need.

You Try It!

Weathering is the physical and chemical alteration of rock.

Weathering processes have led to the formations you see here in Bryce Canyon. Study the photo and then do some research on the Internet to find out more about weathering processes.

Morning light on Thor's Hammer in Bryce Canyon National Park in Utah

1 Choosing Keywords Think about what you want to learn about mechanical weathering. You may want to focus on one topic, such as frost wedging, exfoliation, or thermal expansion. Choose relevant keyword(s) or phrases for the topic that you are researching.

_____

_____

_____

_____

_____

_____

2 Searching the Internet Enter the keywords in a search engine. Which keywords or phrases prompted the most relevant and reliable sites?

_____

_____

_____

_____

_____

_____

3 State Your Claim Use the table below to make claims about how useful the websites are and the quality of the information. Also make claims about each site's relevance and suitability.

Webpage	Comments

Erosion and Deposition by Wind, Ice, and Gravity

ESSENTIAL **QUESTION**

How do wind, ice, and gravity change Earth's surface?

By the end of this lesson, you should be able to describe erosion and deposition by wind, ice, and gravity as well as identify the landforms that result from these processes.

In this desert, wind has sculpted hills of sand, spreading them out like fingers.

SC.6.N.3.4 Identify the role of models in the context of the sixth grade science benchmarks. **SC.6.E.6.1** Describe and give examples of ways in which Earth's surface is built up and torn down by physical and chemical weathering, erosion, and deposition. **SC.6.E.6.2** Recognize that there are a variety of different landforms on Earth's surface such as coastlines, dunes, rivers, mountains, glaciers, deltas, and lakes and relate these landforms as they apply to Florida.

Lesson Labs

Quick Labs
- Modeling a Glacier
- Modeling a Landslide

Virtual Lab
- Erosion and Deposition of Sand Dunes

Engage Your Brain

1 Predict How do you think wind can erode materials?

_____

_____

_____

_____

2 Infer The dark bands you see in the photo on the right are dirt and rocks frozen in the ice. What do you think will happen to the dirt and rocks when the ice melts?

_____

_____

_____

_____

ACTIVE **READING**

3 Define In this lesson, you will be learning about how different agents of erosion can abrade rock. Use a dictionary to look up the meaning of the word _abrade_. Record the definition.

_____

_____

Now use the word _abrade_ in your own sentence:

_____

_____

As you read this lesson, circle the word _abrade_ whenever you come across it. Compare any sentences that include this word with the sentence you wrote for question 3.

Vocabulary Terms

- dune
- loess
- glacier
- glacial drift
- creep
- rockfall
- landslide
- mudflow

4 Apply As you learn the definition of each vocabulary term in this lesson, create your own definition or sketch to help you remember the meaning of the term.

Gone with the.

How can wind shape Earth?

Have you ever been outside and had a gust of wind blow a stack of papers all over the place? If so, you have seen how wind erosion works. In the same way that wind moved your papers, wind moves soil, sand, and rock particles. When wind moves soil, sand, and rock particles, it acts as an agent of erosion.

Abraded Rock

When wind blows sand and other particles against a surface, it can wear down the surface over time. The grinding and wearing down of rock surfaces by other rock or by sand particles is called *abrasion*. Abrasion happens in areas where there are strong winds, loose sand, and soft rocks. The blowing of millions of grains of sand causes a sandblasting effect. The sandblasting effect slowly erodes the rock by stripping away its surface. Over time, the rock can become smooth and polished.

Desert Pavement

The removal of fine sediment by wind is called *deflation*. This process is shown in the diagram below. During deflation, wind removes the top layer of fine sediment or soil. Deflation leaves behind rock fragments that are too heavy to be lifted by the wind. After a while, these rocks may be the only materials left on the surface. The resulting landscape is known as desert pavement. As you can see in the photo below, desert pavement is a surface made up mostly of pebbles and small, broken rocks.

Wind Direction

Desert Pavement

Visualize It!

5 Claims • Evidence • Reasoning Make a claim about how the desert pavement in this photo most likely formed. Summarize evidence to support the claim and explain your reasoning.

_____

_____

_____

Wind

Dunes

Wind carries sediment in much the same way that rivers do. Just as rivers deposit their loads, winds eventually drop the materials that they are carrying. For example, when wind hits an obstacle, it slows and drops materials on top of the obstacle. As the material builds up, the obstacle gets larger. This obstacle causes the wind to slow more and deposit more material, which forms a mound. Eventually, the original obstacle is buried. Mounds of wind-deposited sand are called **dunes**. Dunes are common in deserts and along the shores of lakes and oceans.

Generally, dunes move in the same direction the wind is blowing. Usually, a dune's gently sloped side faces the wind. Wind constantly moves material up this side of the dune. As sand moves over the crest of the dune, the sand slides down the slip face and makes a steep slope.

Loess

Wind can carry extremely fine material long distances. Thick deposits of this windblown, fine-grained sediment are known as **loess** (LOH•uhs). Loess can feel like the talcum powder a person may use after a shower. Because wind carries fine-grained material much higher and farther than it carries sand, loess deposits are sometimes found far away from their source. Loess deposits can build up over thousands and even millions of years. Loess is a valuable resource because it forms good soil for growing crops.

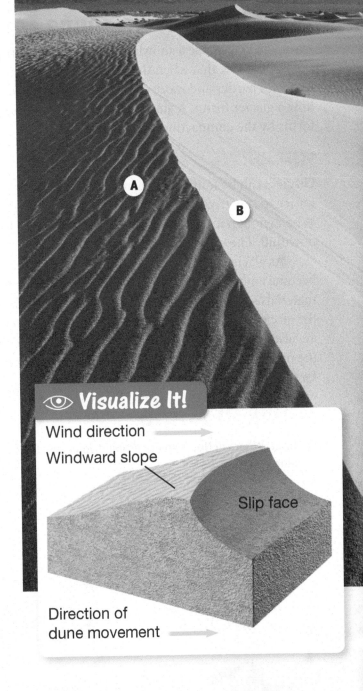

◉ Visualize It!

Wind direction →

Windward slope

Slip face

Direction of dune movement →

Active Reading

6 Claims • Evidence • Reasoning Make a claim about how loess can be carried farther than sand. Summarize evidence to support the claim and explain your reasoning.

_____

_____

_____

7 Determine Look at the photo above the illustration. Which direction does the wind blow across the photographed dune: from left to right or right to left?

_____

8 Identify Which side of the dune in the photograph is the slip face: A or B?

Groovy Glacier

What kinds of ice shape Earth?

Have you ever made a snowball from a scoop of fluffy snow? If so, you know that when the snow is pressed against itself, it becomes harder and more compact. The same idea explains how a glacier forms. A **glacier** is a large mass of moving ice that forms by the compacting of snow by natural forces.

Flowing Ice

Glaciers can be found anywhere on land where it is cold enough for ice to stay frozen year round. Gravity causes glaciers to move. When enough ice builds up on a slope, the ice begins to move downhill. The steeper the slope is, the faster the glacier moves.

As glaciers move, they pick up materials. These materials become embedded in the ice. As the glacier moves forward, the materials scratch and abrade the rock and soil underneath the glacier. This abrasion causes more erosion. Glaciers are also agents of deposition. As a glacier melts, it drops the materials that it carried. **Glacial drift** is the general term for all of the materials carried and deposited by a glacier.

ACTIVE READING

10 Infer Where in North America would you expect to find glaciers?

_____

_____

Think Outside the Book

9 Apply Find out whether glaciers have ever covered your state. If so, what landforms did they leave behind?

As a glacier flowed over this rock, it scratched out these grooves.

This glacier is moving down the valley like a river of ice.

Alpine Glaciers

An alpine glacier is a glacier that forms in a mountainous area. Alpine glaciers flow down the sides of mountains and create rugged landscapes. Glaciers may form in valleys originally created by stream erosion. The flow of water in a stream forms a V-shaped valley. As a glacier slowly flows through a V-shaped valley, it scrapes away the valley floor and walls. The glacier widens and straightens the valley into a broad U-shape. An alpine glacier can also carve out bowl-shaped depressions, called *cirques* (surks), at the head of a valley. A sharp ridge called an *arête* (uh•RAYT) forms between two cirques that are next to each other. When three or more arêtes join, they form a sharp peak called a *horn*.

11 Summarize Use the illustration below to write a description for each of the following landforms.

Landforms made by alpine glaciers	Description
Arête	
Cirque	
Horn	
U-shaped valley	

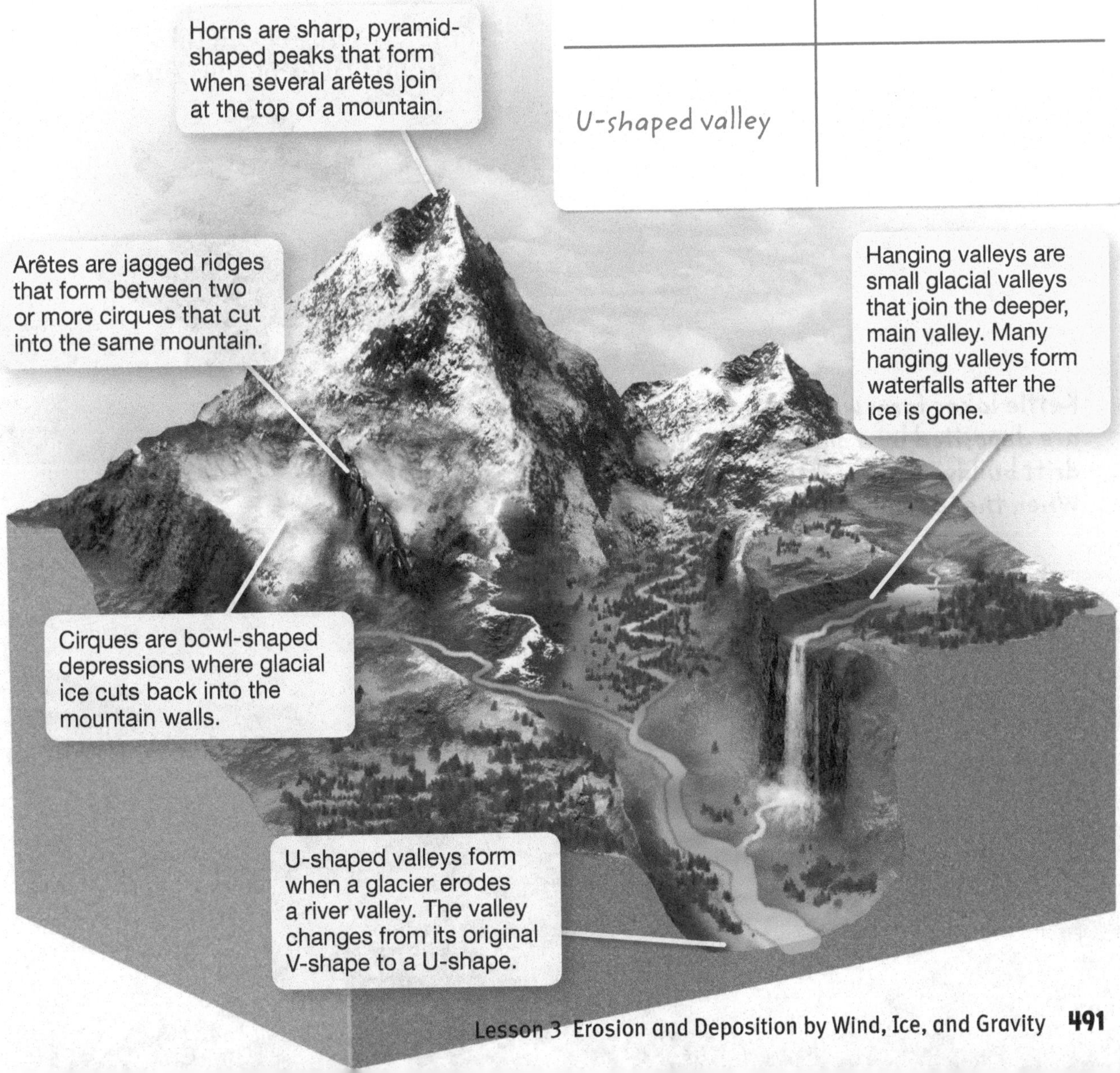

Horns are sharp, pyramid-shaped peaks that form when several arêtes join at the top of a mountain.

Arêtes are jagged ridges that form between two or more cirques that cut into the same mountain.

Hanging valleys are small glacial valleys that join the deeper, main valley. Many hanging valleys form waterfalls after the ice is gone.

Cirques are bowl-shaped depressions where glacial ice cuts back into the mountain walls.

U-shaped valleys form when a glacier erodes a river valley. The valley changes from its original V-shape to a U-shape.

Continental Glaciers

Continental glaciers are thick sheets of ice that may spread over large areas, including across entire continents. These glaciers are huge, continuous masses of ice. Continental glaciers create very different landforms than alpine glaciers do. Alpine glaciers form sharp and rugged features, whereas continental glaciers flatten and smooth the landscape. Continental glaciers erode and remove features that existed before the ice appeared. These glaciers smooth and round exposed rock surfaces in a way similar to the way that bulldozers can flatten landscapes.

Erosion and deposition by continental glaciers result in specific, recognizable landforms. Some of the landforms are shown below. Similar landforms can be found in the northern United States, which was once covered by continental glaciers.

Visualize It!

12 Compare What does the formation of erratics and kettle lakes have in common?

Erratics are large boulders that were transported and deposited by glaciers.

Kettle lakes form when chunks of ice are deposited by a glacier and glacial drift builds up around the ice blocks. When the ice melts, a lake forms.

Melting the Ice

A CHANGING WORLD

What would you do if an Ice Age glacial dam broke and let loose millions of gallons of water? Get out of the way and get ready for some erosion!

A Crack in the Ice

During the last Ice Age, a huge ice dam held back Glacial Lake Missoula, a 320-km-long body of water. Then one day, the dam burst. Water roared out, emptying the lake in less than 48 hours!

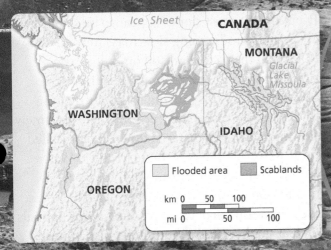

Ice Sheet
CANADA
MONTANA
Glacial Lake Missoula
WASHINGTON
IDAHO

Flooded area   Scablands

km 0   50   100
mi 0   50   100

OREGON

Giant ripple marks from the Missoula floods

Large-Scale Landforms

The erosion caused by the roaring water carved out a landscape of huge waterfalls, deep canyons, and three-story-high ripple marks. Many of these features are in an area called the Scablands.

History Repeats Itself

Lake Missoula eventually reformed behind another ice dam. The breaking of the dam and the floods repeated about 40 more times, ripping away topsoil and exposing and cracking the bedrock.

i Extend

13 Relate Where have you seen ripple marks before and how do they compare to the ripple marks shown in the photo on this page?

14 Claims • Evidence • Reasoning Make a claim about how the three-story-high ripple marks shown here were formed. Summarize evidence to support the claim and explain your reasoning.

15 Model Use sand, pebbles, and other materials to model how a severe flood can alter the landscape. Photograph or illustrate the results of your investigation. Present your results in the form of an animation, slide show, or illustrated report.

Slippery Slope

The shape of this tree trunk indicates that creep has occurred along the slope.

How can gravity shape Earth?

Although you can't see it, the force of gravity, like water, wind, and ice, is an agent of erosion and deposition. Gravity not only influences the movement of water and ice, but it also causes rocks and soil to move downslope. This shifting of materials is called *mass movement*. Mass movement plays a major role in shaping Earth's surface.

Slow Mass Movement

Even though most slopes appear to be stable, they are actually undergoing slow mass movement. In fact, all the rocks and soil on a slope travel slowly downhill. The ground beneath the tree shown on the left is moving so slowly that the tree trunk curved as the tree grew. The extremely slow movement of material downslope is called **creep**. Many factors contribute to creep. Water loosens soil and allows the soil to move freely. In addition, plant roots act as wedges that force rocks and soil particles apart. Burrowing animals, such as gophers and groundhogs, also loosen rock and soil particles, making it easier for the particles to be pulled downward.

◉ Visualize It!

16 Claims • Evidence • Reasoning Make a claim about what is causing the tree to change so that it continues to grow upright. Summarize evidence to support the claim and explain your reasoning.

_____

_____

_____

Rapid Mass Movement

The most destructive mass movements happen suddenly and rapidly. Rapid mass movement can be very dangerous and can destroy everything in its path. Rapid mass movement tends to happen on steep slopes because materials are more likely to fall down a steep slope than a shallow slope.

While traveling along a mountain road, you may have noticed signs along the road that warn of falling rocks. A **rockfall** happens when loose rocks fall down a steep slope. Steep slopes are common in mountainous areas. Gravity causes loosened and exposed rocks to fall down steep slopes. The rocks in a rockfall can range in size from small fragments to large boulders.

Another kind of rapid mass movement is a landslide. A **landslide** is the sudden and rapid movement of a large amount of material downslope. As you can see in the photo on the right, landslides can carry away plants. They can also carry away animals, vehicles, and buildings. Heavy rains, deforestation, construction on unstable slopes, and earthquakes increase the chances of a landslide.

A rapid movement of a large mass of mud is a **mudflow**. Mudflows happen when a large amount of water mixes with soil and rock. The water causes the slippery mud to flow rapidly downslope. Mudflows happen in mountainous regions after deforestation has occurred or when a long dry season is followed by heavy rains. Volcanic eruptions or heavy rains on volcanic ash can produce some of the most dangerous mudflows. Mudflows of volcanic origin are called lahars. Lahars can travel at speeds greater than 80 km/h and can be as thick as wet cement.

This landslide in California was caused by heavy rains.

17 Identify List five events that can trigger a mass movement.

_____

_____

_____

_____

_____

A

B

👁 Visualize It!

18 Infer On which slope, A or B, would a landslide be more likely to occur? Explain your reasoning.

_____

_____

Visual Summary

To complete this summary, fill in the blanks with the correct word or phrase. You can use this page to review the main concepts of the lesson.

Erosion and Deposition by Wind, Ice, and Gravity

Wind forms dunes and desert pavement.

19 Wind forms dunes through:

_____

20 Wind forms desert pavement through:

_____

Ice erodes and deposits rock.

21 Alpine glaciers make landforms such as:

_____

_____

_____

22 Continental glaciers make landforms such as:

_____

_____

Gravity pulls materials downward.

23 Type of slow mass movement: _____

24 Three major types of rapid mass movement:

_____

_____

_____

25 Claims • Evidence • Reasoning Make a claim about the role that gravity plays in almost all examples of erosion and deposition. Summarize evidence to support the claim and explain your reasoning.

Lesson Review

Vocabulary

Use a term from the section to complete each sentence below.

1 When an obstacle causes wind to slow down and deposit materials, the materials pile up and eventually form a _____

2 Large masses of flowing ice called _____ are typically found near Earth's poles and in other cold regions.

3 Very fine sediments called _____ can be carried by wind over long distances.

4 As glaciers retreat, they leave behind deposits of _____

Key Concepts

5 Claims • Evidence • Reasoning Make a claim about how glaciers can cause deposition. Summarize evidence to support the claim and explain your reasoning.

_____
_____
_____
_____

6 Compare Compare and contrast how wind and glaciers abrade rock.

_____
_____
_____
_____

7 Distinguish What is the difference between creep and a landslide?

_____
_____
_____
_____

Critical Thinking

Use the diagram to answer the question below.

8 Synthesize Which of the four locations would be the best and worst places to build a house? Rank the four locations and explain your reasoning.

_____
_____
_____
_____
_____

9 Integrate Wind erosion occurs at a faster rate in deserts than in places with a thick layer of vegetation covering the ground. Why do you think this is the case?

_____
_____
_____
_____
_____
_____

FOCUS ON **FLORIDA**

SC.6.E.6.2 Recognize that there are a variety of different landforms on Earth's surface such as coastlines, dunes, rivers, mountains, glaciers, deltas, and lakes and relate these landforms as they apply to Florida.

Tampa Bay Estuary

Tampa Bay

Protecting a Rich Ecosystem

Tampa Bay is home to an enormous number of animals—from microscopic plankton to the great blue heron. The largest open-water estuary in Florida covers more than 1,000 square kilometers. Despite its large area, the Bay is very shallow. The average depth is four meters. This wide expanse of warm, shallow water supports important habitats like mangrove forests, marshes, and underwater seagrass beds. It provides a home to more than 200 species of fish. However, the Bay's ecosystem is threatened by pollution. Nitrogen runoff from residential areas is the chief pollutant. It changes the chemistry of the water and kills the phytoplankton. In 1991, the government created the Tampa Bay Estuary Program (TBEP) as part of a program to restore bays in the United States. The TBEP conducts ongoing research on how to protect the bay and its diversity. In order to work with people who know the area well, the TBEP often asks for advice from the community.

Manatee

Protecting Manatees

Florida has become a year-long home to manatees. These gentle marine mammals grow to an average length of three meters and can weigh up to 1,500 kilograms. Manatees are an important part of their ecosystem. They maintain seagrass beds with their grazing. However, while they are feeding on seagrass, near the surface of the water, manatees can be injured or even killed in collisions with boats. Almost all manatees in Florida have scars from collisions.

You can help protect the manatee population by:

- watching out for them in shallow, coastal waters, near seagrass beds;
- following the speed limit signs for boats; and
- keeping trash out of the water.

Take It Home!

Create a poster that informs people of 10 ways they can protect the wildlife and different habitats in Tampa Bay. Include photos or illustrations in your poster.

Brown pelican

Birds of the Bay

The different habitats in Tampa Bay attract about twenty-five species of birds. Key habitats for these birds include islands, mudflats, seagrass meadows, and open waters. Islands provide protection for nests from predators and other disturbances. Mudflats and seagrass meadows offer fishing grounds for shorebirds like the brown pelican. Open waters are ideal habitats for birds like loons and ducks.

The birds in Tampa Bay make their homes on some of the area's most desirable waterfront real estate. As a result, many bird habitats are under threat from development and increased human presence. We can help protect bird populations by being respectful of nesting sites by keeping their habitats free of litter.

Spoonbills feed on a mangrove island in the Tampa Bay estuary

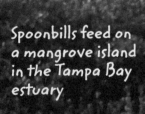

Math Connection

Aerial surveys show that there were 6,620 manatees in Florida in January through February of 2017. Complete the table. Round your answers to the nearest whole number. Check that your numbers add to the total number of manatees.

Region	Percentage of population	Number of Manatees
Upper St. Johns	4	
Atlantic Coast	46	
Southwest Florida	38	
Northwest Florida	12	

Landforms and Florida

ESSENTIAL QUESTION

How do landforms relate to Florida's geology?

By the end of this lesson, you should be able to describe some of the landforms found on Earth's surface and give examples of landforms found in Florida.

Forests, swamps, lakes, islands, and rivers provide shelter for many endangered plants and animals in and near the Florida Everglades.

SC.6.E.6.2 Recognize that there are a variety of different landforms on Earth's surface such as coastlines, dunes, rivers, mountains, glaciers, deltas, and lakes and relate these landforms as they apply to Florida.

Quick Labs
- Exploring Landforms
- How Can Materials on Earth's Surface Change?

Engage Your Brain

1 Predict Check T or F to show whether you think each statement is true or false.

T	F	
☐	☐	Florida has been covered by glaciers in the past.
☐	☐	Florida has several mountains.
☐	☐	Florida is one of the flattest of the 50 states.
☐	☐	Rivers can erode land and deposit sediment.

2 Explain Imagine you are assigned to make a brochure welcoming visitors to the state of Florida. What kinds of landforms and sites would you recommend and why?

_____

_____

_____

_____

_____

_____

_____

_____

ACTIVE READING

3 Synthesize The term *delta* was first used to describe a landform by an ancient Greek historian named Herodotus. He coined the term after the Greek letter △. Use the Greek letter and the example sentence to write your own definition of a *delta*.

Term	Greek letter
delta	△

Example sentence
The Mississippi River forms a large <u>delta</u> as the river flows into the Gulf of Mexico.

delta:

_____

_____

Vocabulary Terms
- **mountain**
- **lake**
- **river**
- **coastline**

4 Apply As you learn the definition of each vocabulary term in this lesson, create your own definition or sketch to help you remember the meaning of the term.

Build, Break, and Move

ACTIVE READING

5 Identify As you read, underline the characteristics of mountains.

👁 Visualize It!

6 Claims • Evidence • Reasoning Make a claim about which other states might have sediments from the Appalachian Mountains. Summarize evidence to support the claim and explain your reasoning.

_____

_____

_____

_____

_____

What is a mountain?

A **mountain** is a region of increased elevation on Earth's surface that rises to a peak. One way a mountain can form is when the collision of tectonic plates causes the Earth's crust to uplift, or rise. Another way mountains form is through the eruption of volcanoes.

The highest point in Florida is Britton Hill near the Alabama border, which is 105 m in elevation. Mountains typically have an elevation of at least 300 m, meaning Florida does not have mountains! In fact, Florida and Louisiana tie for second place on a list of states with the lowest average elevation.

Mountains are important sources of *sediment*. Sediment refers to any pieces of rock that have been broken down from existing rock over time. Sediments can be transported to new locations by the actions of wind, ice, and water. For example, a portion of the Appalachian Mountains have become rounded and worn down, as shown below. Sediment from the Appalachian Mountains is continually being transported to areas including Florida. In fact, millions of years ago these sediments formed layers of sedimentary rock, which helped build up the land that is Florida today.

Sediments from the Appalachian Mountains were transported to Florida.

The rounded hills of the Appalachian Mountains in Shenandoah National Park, Virginia.

What is a glacier?

How can mountains get broken down into sediments? One method is through the action of glaciers. A **glacier** (GLAY•sher) is a mass of gradually moving or flowing ice. As snow and ice build on a mountain, the glacier can begin to move down the mountain. Glaciers scrape and relocate rocks as they move, forming sediments. In the photo below, a glacier is moving down through mountains in Alaska, creating sediments. Glaciers can be found at high elevations and near Earth's poles.

An *ice sheet* is a very large glacier that covers a large area. Approximately 18,000 years ago, much of Canada and the northern portion of the United States were covered by an ice sheet. During this glacial period, the sea level on Earth was reduced as the water was stored in the ice. As a result, the land area of Florida was much larger than it is today. Once the ice sheet began to melt, sediments were deposited throughout the United States. In addition, the sea level rose again, altering Florida's shape and size.

i Think Outside the Book

8 Apply The sand on most beaches was originally produced by the erosion of rock. Imagine you are a piece of sand on a beach in Florida. Describe your life, beginning as a rock at the top of a mountain and ending as a grain of sand on the beach.

👁 Visualize It!

7 Claims • Evidence • Reasoning Make a claim about what might happen to the sea level if all the water in Earth's glaciers were suddenly released. Summarize evidence to support the claim and explain your reasoning.

_____

_____

_____

The glacier is slowly flowing down the mountain.

This glacier in Alaska is depositing sediment directly into the ocean.

Let's Hit the Water!

What is a lake?

Florida has approximately 30,000 lakes of varying size. A **lake** is a body of fresh or salt water that is surrounded by land. Lakes are fed by streams and rivers that carry water and sediment. The largest lake in Florida is Lake Okeechobee (oh•kih•CHOH•bee). This lake is part of a larger water system, called a watershed, that includes the Everglades wetlands area in South Florida.

Many of the lakes in Florida are sinkhole lakes. A sinkhole is a hole in the ground caused by the collapse of an underground cavern. Often, sinkholes become plugged by sediments and later get filled by water, forming sinkhole lakes. Lake Eola in the photo below is a sinkhole lake. If the plugs in a sinkhole are opened, it is like draining the water from a bathtub. In 1999, Lake Jackson near Tallahassee, Florida, drained as the sediment plug opened and the water flowed out, almost draining the entire lake.

ACTIVE **READING**

9 Identify How does a sinkhole lake form?

_____

_____

_____

Lake Eola in downtown Orlando, Florida, is a sinkhole lake.

What is a river?

Rivers are one method of transporting sediment. A **river** is a large, natural stream of water that flows into an ocean or other large body of water, such as a lake. Rivers start as smaller flowing bodies of water, called streams, at higher elevations. The streams can combine to eventually form rivers that flow along a channel. In Florida, most of the rivers are relatively short and do not flow quickly because of the flat elevation of the state.

Rivers change course over time as they break down the river banks, or sides of the river, and deposit sediment. During times of excessive flow, rivers can flood, leading to significant damage to human structures and farm areas. Examples of Florida rivers include the St. Johns, the Apalachicola (ap•uh•lach•ih•KOH•luh), the Suwannee (suh•WAH•nee), and the Peace.

👁 Visualize It!

10 Identify The shaded area at the tip of Florida represents the approximate location of Everglades National Park. How can lakes and rivers in Florida supply water to the Everglades?

_____

_____

_____

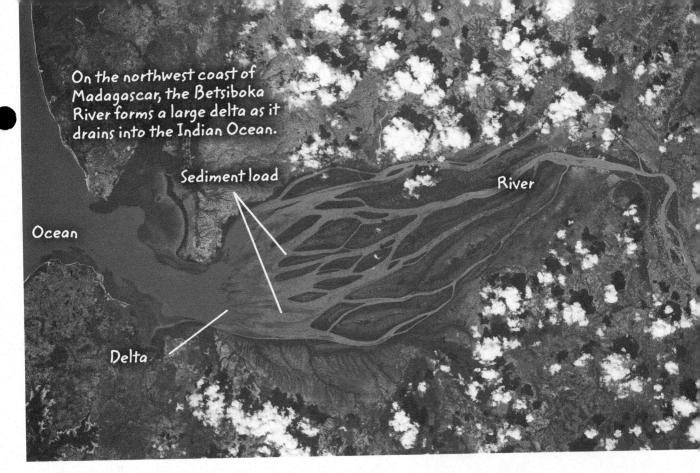

On the northwest coast of Madagascar, the Betsiboka River forms a large delta as it drains into the Indian Ocean.

Sediment load

River

Ocean

Delta

What is a delta?

When a river reaches a lake, ocean, or other body of water, the sediments carried in a river can form a delta. A **delta** (DEL•tuh) is a deposit, formed by sediment, that accumulates at the mouth of a river. These landforms are often, but not always, triangular in shape.

Deltas form as rivers slow down when they reach other bodies of water. When a river is no longer confined within a river channel, the velocity, or speed, of the water is reduced. Once velocity is reduced, the river deposits the sediments previously suspended in the water. The sediment then builds up and extends out from the shore to form a delta.

Most of Florida's rivers carry a limited amount of sediment and do not flow very fast. Therefore, Florida rivers do not form large or significant deltas. An exception to this is the Apalachicola River in the Florida Panhandle. The river is part of a larger river system that begins in the Appalachian Mountains and ends in the Florida Panhandle. Sediments are carried in the river and deposited into the Gulf of Mexico, forming deltas.

ACTIVE **READING**

11 Identify As you read, fill in the form below to summarize what you learn about deltas.

Delta

Definition
_____
_____
_____

Formation
_____
_____
_____
_____
_____

Example
_____
_____
_____

Surf's Up

What is a coastline?

Florida has a long coastline. A **coastline** is a dynamic boundary between land and the ocean. Coastlines can vary from rocky coasts with high, sharp cliffs, to gently sloping sandy beaches. A number of factors control the characteristics of coastlines including waves, wind, sediment supply, tides, and the geology of the region.

Coastlines are *dynamic*, or constantly changing. One way a coastline can change is by the action of ocean waves. Ocean waves can slowly break down rock-forming sediments along a coastline. Tides can then carry these sediments towards the coast, or away from it. In addition, sea level can change over time, changing the shape and size of coastlines.

The coastline of Florida offers many recreational areas and important shipping ports. On the western coast of Florida, the coastline forms where the land meets the Gulf of Mexico. Beaches there include Pensacola Beach and Clearwater Beach. On the eastern coast, Florida meets the Atlantic Ocean. Beaches include Flagler Beach, Daytona Beach, and Cocoa Beach.

ACTIVE READING

12 Identify As you read, underline the factors that can change the characteristics of a coastline.

Florida has more than 1,900 km of coastline.

13 Claims • Evidence • Reasoning Make a claim about why coastlines are important. Provide evidence as to why coastlines might be important to the environment or to humans. Explain your reasoning.

_____

_____

_____

_____

_____

Dunes on Florida's Gulf Island National Seashore

What is a dune?

Sand does not easily stay in one location because of the small size of sand grains. Mounds of sand, as seen in the photo below, often form as wind carries and then deposits sand particles. A dune is a mound of wind-deposited sand. Dunes are found in both desert and coastal regions. In the desert, winds can be very strong. Sand gets carried and deposited into varying sizes of dunes, from small hills to mountain-sized.

Coastal dunes form along coastlines. The shape of a beach, the sand supply, the wind direction, and the type of sand can determine the types of dunes formed. Dunes can have a variety of shapes including star-shaped, crescent, and straight dunes. In Florida, coastal dunes are fairly small and are found behind sandy beaches. The dunes offer important protection for many species of plants and animals. Unfortunately, dunes can be destroyed as a result of human activities and natural processes.

Many conservation efforts are used to protect dunes. For example, various types of vegetation, such as sea oats, can be planted on a dune surface. The root systems of these plants help to hold the sand in place, as shown in the photo below. Fences are also installed to help maintain dunes by slowing the wind. Many locations have sand ladders, or wooden walkways, that prevent human trampling of the dunes.

Human activities can affect the location and amount of sand on a beach.

Sea oats

Dune fence

◉ Visualize It!

14 Explain How can a fence protect dunes in Florida?

_____

_____

_____

_____

Visual Summary

To complete this summary, check the box that indicates true or false. You can use this page to review the main concepts of the lesson.

Mountains and glaciers produce sediment.

T   F

☐   ☐   **15** Sediment from the Appalachian Mountains helped form Florida.

Lakes and rivers are part of Florida watersheds.

T   F

☐   ☐   **16** A river carrying sediment can flow into a lake.

Landforms

Coastlines have dunes formed by the wind.

T   F

☐   ☐   **17** Dunes can occur on coastlines or in the desert.

Deltas form as rivers slow down.

T   F

☐   ☐   **18** Deltas commonly form where rivers meet land surfaces.

19 Claims • Evidence • Reasoning Make a claim about how processes in other states, and even other countries, affect landforms in Florida. Provide evidence and explain your reasoning.

Lesson Review

Vocabulary

Fill in the blank with the term that best completes the following sentences.

1 A _____ may form where a river enters a large body of water, such as a lake or an ocean.

2 A _____ is a large body of water surrounded by land.

3 Changes in sea level can result from water being locked inside a _____.

4 An elevated surface formed by volcanoes or when tectonic plates move together is a _____.

Key Concepts

5 Identify List four specific examples of different landforms in Florida by completing the table below.

Type of landform	Example

6 Explain How are sediments created and how do those sediments make new landforms?

_____

_____

_____

7 Claims • Evidence • Reasoning Although there are no glaciers in Florida, make a claim about how glaciers have affected Florida. Provide evidence and explain your reasoning.

_____

_____

_____

Critical Thinking

Use this map to answer the following questions.

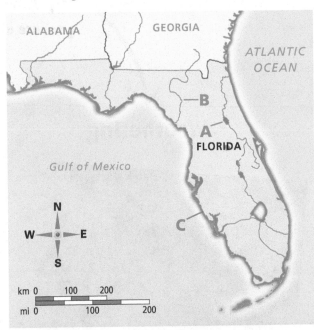

8 Identify Which location is most likely to have a dune? Explain.

_____

_____

9 Apply In location B, what can you conclude about the sediments carried in the river?

_____

_____

10 Claims • Evidence • Reasoning Many of the lakes in Florida are sinkhole lakes. Make a claim about the geology beneath Florida's surface. Provide evidence and explain your reasoning.

_____

_____

_____

_____

Landforms
and **Florida**
are affected by

Weathering

Erosion and
Deposition by
Water, Wind, Ice,
and **Gravity**

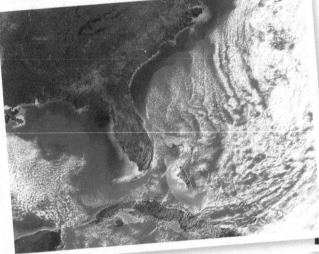

1 Interpret The graphic organizer above shows that the landforms of Florida are affected by different types of erosion. Which agent of erosion do you think affects Florida landforms the most?

_____

_____

_____

2 Contrast Distinguish between physical weathering and chemical weathering.

_____

_____

_____

_____

3 Categorize What agent is responsible for the formation of the Florida landforms called dunes?

_____

_____

4 Claims • Evidence • Reasoning Make a claim about how living things contribute to the physical and chemical weathering of rocks. Summarize evidence to support the claim and explain your reasoning.

_____

_____

_____

_____

_____

Vocabulary

Name _____

Fill in the blank with the term that best completes the following sentences.

1   Thick deposits of windblown, fine-grained sediment are known as

_____.

2   The process by which rocks break down as a result of chemical reactions is called

_____.

3   The fan-shaped mass of sediment deposited by a stream into an ocean or a lake
is called a(n) _____.

4   The rock material deposited by glaciers as they melt and retreat is called

_____.

5   _____ is the breaking down and wearing away of rock
material by the mechanical action of other rock.

Key Concept

Identify the choice that best completes the statement or answers the question.

6   While on a trip, Veronica saw the landforms shown in the following pictures.

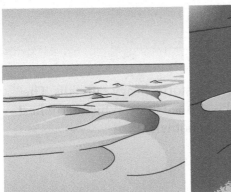 

Which of the following processes formed the landforms shown?

A the transport and deposition of sediment by ice

B the transport and deposition of sediment by water

C the transport and deposition of sediment by wind

D the transport and deposition of sediment by gravity

7 All types of glaciers erode the land as they move slowly across it. How would you describe the landscape made by alpine glaciers compared to the landscape made by continental glaciers?

F Alpine glaciers create U-shaped valleys, and continental glaciers create V-shaped valleys.

G Alpine glaciers produce rugged landscapes, and continental glaciers produce flat landscapes.

H Alpine glaciers form smooth landscapes, and continental glaciers form hilly landscapes.

I Alpine glaciers make flattened landscapes, and continental glaciers make uneven landscapes.

8 Florida has more natural lakes than any other state in the southeastern United States. With the exception of some sinkhole lakes, Florida's lakes tend to be very shallow. The table below gives some information about four Florida lakes.

Lake	Surface area (acres)	Average depth (ft)
Annie	90	68
George	46,000	10
Okeechobee	467,000	11
Washington	4,364	13

Based on the evidence, which lake is **most likely** to be a sinkhole lake?

A Lake Annie

B Lake Okeechobee

C Lake George

D Lake Washington

9 Marley has a vegetable garden in her yard. During a storm, heavy rain falls. The rain runs over the garden, and some of the soil is washed away. Which term **best** describes this movement of soil from one place to another?

F deposition

H erosion

G discharge

I weathering

10 Wind can affect a landscape in many ways. In the desert, wind can remove sediment near the surface, leaving gravel behind. The gravel becomes packed and smooth. What is the term for what is formed by this process?

A desert gravel

C desert concrete

B desert asphalt

D desert pavement

11 Sediments from mountains many kilometers away are now in the area known as Florida. Which is the **best** reasoning for how most of these sediments moved so far away from where the mountains are now?

F The wind blew the sediments there.

G The sediments were transported and deposited by streams and rivers.

H This range of mountains used to be much farther south than it is now.

I Rocks form more small, easily transported sediment on the southern side of mountains.

12 Riley rubs two rocks together. She notices that some of the surface of one of the rocks was worn away to form small particles. What has happened to that rock?

A It was eroded.   **C** It was exfoliated.

B It was dissolved.   **D** It was weathered.

13 Rainwater fills a crack in a rock. The water freezes in a cold climate. After the water thaws, it evaporates. The crack left behind is larger than it was originally.

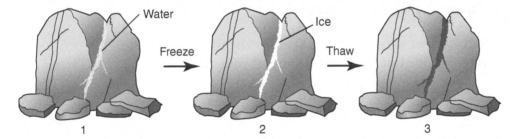

What is the physical weathering factor?

F air   **H** rock

G ice   **I** flowing water

14 For millions of years, large amounts of glacial ice formed on Earth, covering huge areas of land. It then melted, or receded. When large amounts of glacial ice formed, large amounts of water froze. When the glacial ice melted, it released water into the oceans. Based on this evidence, which claim describes the effect glaciers had on the formation of Florida?

A Florida's coastlines were eroded only during cold periods.

B Florida's coastlines were eroded only during warm periods.

C Different parts of Florida's coastlines were eroded during warm and cold periods.

D Florida's mountains were eroded only during warm periods.

15 Sandy beaches make up most of the Florida coastline. Beach sand is the product of abrasion. Which is an example of abrasion of a rock?

F a color change due to exposure to air

G a shape change due to exposure to wind

H a hole forming due to a reaction with water

I a layer falling off due to a lessening of pressure

16 What are two processes that result in rocks being broken down into smaller pieces?

A sunlight and glacial melting

B chemical weathering and physical weathering

C chemical weathering and deposition

D physical weathering and humus

Critical Thinking

Answer the following question in the space provided.

17 Make a claim about whether water is a cause of either chemical weathering, physical weathering, or both. Cite evidence to support your claim.

_____

_____

_____

_____

_____

18 Make a claim about how water and gravity work together to erode soil, sediment, and rock. Use two examples to explain your reasoning. _____

_____

_____

_____

19 Make a claim about how water deposits soil, sediment, and rock. Use two examples to explain your reasoning. _____

_____

_____

_____

Human Impact on Earth

FLORIDA BIG IDEA 6

Earth Structures

The Cape Sable dam cuts through Cape Sable in Everglades National Park.

What Do You Think?

The construction of buildings, roads, parking lots, and other structures like dams and bridges can affect our water resources in a variety of ways. In what ways does human activity affect the environment? As you explore this unit, gather evidence to help you state and support a claim.

Human Impact on Earth

CITIZEN **SCIENCE**

Investigating Water Resources

All of the water that we use comes from natural resources. Most of the water that is used in Florida is freshwater that comes from underground aquifers.

1 **Think About It**

What makes fresh surface water and groundwater such valuable resources?

_____

_____

How does human activity affect the availability of fresh water?

_____

_____

_____

Rain barrels collect rainwater for use at home.

② Ask A Question

Where does your water come from?

With a partner, research the source of the water used by your community. Consider contacting your local utility company as a source of information.

Things to Consider

- ☐ How do our water supplies get replenished?
- ☐ What are the most common uses for water?

③ Make A Plan

A Describe the environment that surrounds your local water source.

_____

_____

B Describe threats to your local water supply and how your water supply can be protected.

Threats	Ways to Protect Water Supply

C Determine what happens to wastewater and how it cycles through your environment.

_____

_____

_____

_____

🏠 Take It Home!

Trace the water used in your home to its source. Use a map to determine the route by which the water you use must be transported from its source.

Natural Resources

ESSENTIAL **QUESTION**

What are Earth's natural resources?

By the end of this lesson, you should be able to understand the types and uses of Earth's natural resources.

Light produced from electrical energy helps people see at night. Some regions of Earth are still mostly dark once the sun sets. The people living in some of these regions rely more on sunlight.

SC.7.E.6.6 Identify the impact that humans have had on Earth, such as deforestation, urbanization, desertification, erosion, air and water quality, changing the flow of water.

Lesson Labs

Quick Labs
- How Is That Made?
- Renewable or Not?
- Production Impacts

Exploration Lab
- Natural Resources Used at Lunch

 ## Engage Your Brain

1 Predict Check T or F to show whether you think each statement is true or false.

T	F	
☐	☐	Energy from the sun can be used to make electricity.
☐	☐	All of Earth's resources will last forever.
☐	☐	Food, cloth, rope, lumber, paper, and rubber come from plants.
☐	☐	Human activity can negatively affect Earth's resources.

2 Describe Name one item that you use everyday. Describe how you think that item is made.

_____
_____
_____
_____
_____
_____
_____

ACTIVE **READING**

3 Apply Many scientific words, such as *natural* and *resource*, also have everyday meanings. Use context clues to write your own definition for each underlined word.

Oranges are a <u>natural</u> source of vitamin C.

natural:

_____
_____

His curly hair is <u>natural</u>.

natural:

_____
_____

A dictionary is a useful <u>resource</u> for learning words.

resource:

_____
_____

In the desert, water is a limited <u>resource</u>.

resource:

_____
_____

Vocabulary Terms
- **natural resource**
- **renewable resource**
- **nonrenewable resource**
- **fossil fuel**
- **material resource**
- **energy resource**

4 Identify This list contains the key terms you'll learn in this lesson. As you read, circle the definition of each term.

It's Only Natural

What are natural resources?

What do the water you drink, the paper you write on, the gasoline used in cars, and the air you breathe have in common? All of these come from Earth's natural resources. A **natural resource** is any natural material that is used by humans, such as air, soil, minerals, water, petroleum, plants, and animals.

The Earth's natural resources provide everything needed for life. The energy we get from many of these resources, such as petroleum and wind, originally comes from the sun's energy. The atmosphere contains the air we breathe, controls air temperatures, and produces rain. Rainfall from the atmosphere renews the water in oceans, rivers, lakes, and streams in the water cycle. In turn, these water sources provide food and water for drinking, cleaning, and other uses. The Earth's soil provides nutrients and a place for plants to grow. Plants provide food for some animals and humans. Petroleum is used to make fuels for cars and other machines, and also to make plastics. All of these natural resources are used to make products that make people's lives more convenient.

ACTIVE **READING**

5 Identify As you read, underline examples of natural resources.

👁 Visualize It!

6 Illustrate Draw or label the missing natural resources.

A

Bauxite is a rock that is used to make aluminum.

How can we categorize natural resources?

There are many different types of natural resources. Some can be replaced more quickly than others. Thus, a natural resource may be categorized as a renewable resource or a nonrenewable resource.

i Think Outside the Book

7 Claims • Evidence • Reasoning
Make a claim about why water can be a renewable or nonrenewable resource. Summarize evidence to support each claim and explain your reasoning to a classmate.

◯ Renewable

Some natural resources can be replaced in a relatively short time. A **renewable resource** is a natural resource that can be replaced at the same rate at which the resource is consumed. Solar energy, water, and air are considered renewable resources. However, renewable resources can be used up too quickly. For example, trees are renewable. But some forests are being cut down faster than new forests can grow to replace them. Some renewable resources are considered to be *inexhaustible resources* (in'•ig•ZAW•stuh•buhl REE•sawrs•iz) because the resources can never be used up. Solar energy and wind energy from the sun are examples of these resources.

◯ Nonrenewable

A **nonrenewable resource** is a resource that forms at a rate that is much slower than the rate at which it is consumed. Some natural resources, like minerals, form very slowly. Iron ore, aluminum, and copper are important minerals. A **fossil fuel** is a nonrenewable resource formed from buried remains of plants and animals that lived long ago. For example, coal is a fossil fuel that takes millions of years to form. Oil and natural gas are other types of fossil fuels. Once these resources are used up, humans will have to find other resources to use instead. Some renewable resources, such as water, may also be considered nonrenewable if they are not used wisely.

8 Compare List some examples of renewable and nonrenewable resources.

Renewable Resources	Nonrenewable Resources

B

Natural fibers from cotton plants are processed to make fabric.

Material World

How do we use natural resources?

When you turn on a computer, take a shower, or eat food, you are using natural resources. A variety of natural resources are used to make common objects. The energy required for many of the activities that we do also comes from natural resources. Earth's natural resources can be divided into material resources and energy resources depending on how the resource is used.

As Material Resources

A **material resource** is a natural resource that humans use to make objects or to consume as food or drink. These resources can come from Earth's atmosphere, crust, fresh waters and oceans, and from organisms, such as plants and animals.

Earth's atmosphere provides the oxygen needed by plants and animals, including humans. Minerals and rock in Earth's crust are used for construction and other industries. Salt, a mineral, comes from ocean water. Fresh water sources and the oceans provide drinking water and food. Some plants, such as cotton, produce fibers that are woven into cloth or braided into ropes. Trees supply fruit crops, lumber, and paper. The sap of some trees is used to make rubber and maple syrup. Animals provide meat, leather, and dairy and egg products.

10 State Your Claim Make a claim about what other items you can think of are made of wood.

_____

_____

_____

_____

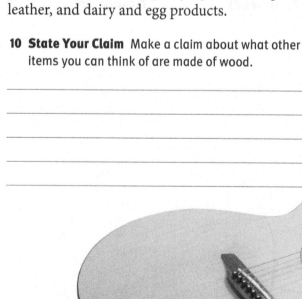

Trees are a material resource when they are used to make products, such as this guitar.

◯ As Energy Resources

Energy resources drive the world. An **energy resource** is a natural resource that humans use to generate energy. Most of the energy used by humans comes from fossil fuels. When fossil fuels are burned, they release energy, usually in the form of heat. Power plants and machines use that heat to produce mechanical and electrical energy. In turn, electrical energy is used to power lights and most of the appliances we use every day.

Other energy resources include moving water, solar power, and wind power. Trees supply fuel in the form of heat. Horses, camels, and other animals are used as transportation in some places. All of these resources are renewable energy resources.

Trees are energy resources when they are burned in a campfire.

◉ Visualize It!

11 Claims • Evidence • Reasoning
Make a claim about what two types of energy are generated from fire. Summarize evidence to support each claim and explain your reasoning to a classmate.

_____

_____

12 List Think about all the products you use every day. Fill in the chart with three of these products and the resources needed to make them or use them.

Product	Material and Energy Resources Needed
computer	plastic, metal, glass, electricity

Visual Summary

To complete this summary, circle the correct word. You can use this page to review the main concepts of the lesson.

Natural resources can be categorized as nonrenewable resources or renewable resources depending on how quickly they can be replaced.

13 Bauxite is a nonrenewable / renewable resource.

14 Cotton plants are a nonrenewable / renewable resource.

Natural Resources

A material resource can be used to make objects or to consume as food or drink. An energy resource is used to generate energy.

15 Trees that are used to make paper products are material resources / energy resources.

16 **Claims • Evidence • Reasoning** Make a claim about how a natural resource could be used as both a material resource and an energy resource. Summarize evidence to support your claim providing examples of each. Explain your reasoning.

Lesson Review

Vocabulary

Fill in the blank with the term that best completes the following sentences.

1 Nonrenewable and renewable are the two categories of _____.

2 A(n) _____ can be used to make objects.

Key Concepts

3 Evaluate Why are natural resources important to humans? Explain your reasoning.

_____

_____

_____

_____

4 Identify Give one example of a material resource and one example of an energy resource.

_____

_____

5 Claims • Evidence • Reasoning Make a claim about how nonrenewable resources and renewable resources differ. Provide evidence to support your claim and explain your reasoning.

_____

_____

_____

_____

6 List Name two material resources, one renewable and one nonrenewable. Explain your answer.

_____

_____

_____

Critical Thinking

Use the graph to answer the following three questions.

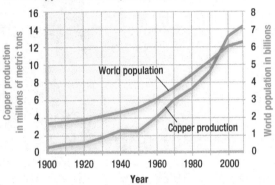

World Copper Production, 1900–2004

Sources: U.S. Bureau of Mines, U.S. Geological Survey, and U.S. Census Bureau

7 Interpret In what year was the most copper produced?

_____

8 Claims • Evidence • Reasoning Make a claim about the trend in copper production over the past 100 years. Use evidence to support your claim and explain your reasoning.

_____

_____

_____

9 State Your Claim Copper is used in making electronic devices. Make a claim about how the use of copper might change as copper becomes more scarce.

_____

_____

_____

10 Claims • Evidence • Reasoning Make a claim about how human activity affects Earth's natural resources. Provide evidence to support your claim.

_____

_____

_____

Human Impact on Land

ESSENTIAL QUESTION

What impact can human activities have on land resources?

By the end of this lesson, you should be able to identify the impact that human activity has on Earth's land.

Human activities can carve up land features. A tunnel was cut into this mountain in Zion National Park, Utah, so that people may move around easily.

SC.7.E.6.6 Identify the impact that humans have had on Earth, such as deforestation, urbanization, desertification, erosion, air and water quality, changing the flow of water.

©Nature Animals/Alamy

© Houghton Mifflin Harcourt Publishing Company

Lesson Labs

Quick Labs
- Debating Human Impact
- Roots and Erosion

 ## Engage Your Brain

1 Predict Check T or F to show whether you think each statement is true or false.

T   F

☐   ☐   Urban areas have more open land than rural areas do.

☐   ☐   Many building materials are made from land resources.

☐   ☐   Soil provides habitat for plants but not animals.

☐   ☐   Soil can erode when trees are removed from an area.

2 Illustrate Draw a picture of an object or material that is taken from the land and that is commercially important.

ACTIVE READING

3 Synthesize You can often define an unknown word if you know the meaning of its word parts. Use the word parts to make an educated guess about the meaning of the words *land degradation* and *deforestation*.

Word part	Meaning
degrade	to damage something
deforest	to remove trees from an area
-ation	action or process

land degradation:

_____

_____

deforestation:

_____

_____

Vocabulary Terms
- urbanization
- land degradation
- desertification
- deforestation

4 Apply As you learn the definition of each vocabulary term in this lesson, create your own definition or sketch to help you remember the meaning of the term.

Land of Plenty

Why is land important?

It is hard to imagine human life without land. Land supplies a solid surface for buildings and roads. The soil in land provides nutrients for plants and hiding places for animals. Minerals below the land's surface can be used for construction materials. Fossil fuels underground can be burned to provide energy. Land and its resources affect every aspect of human life.

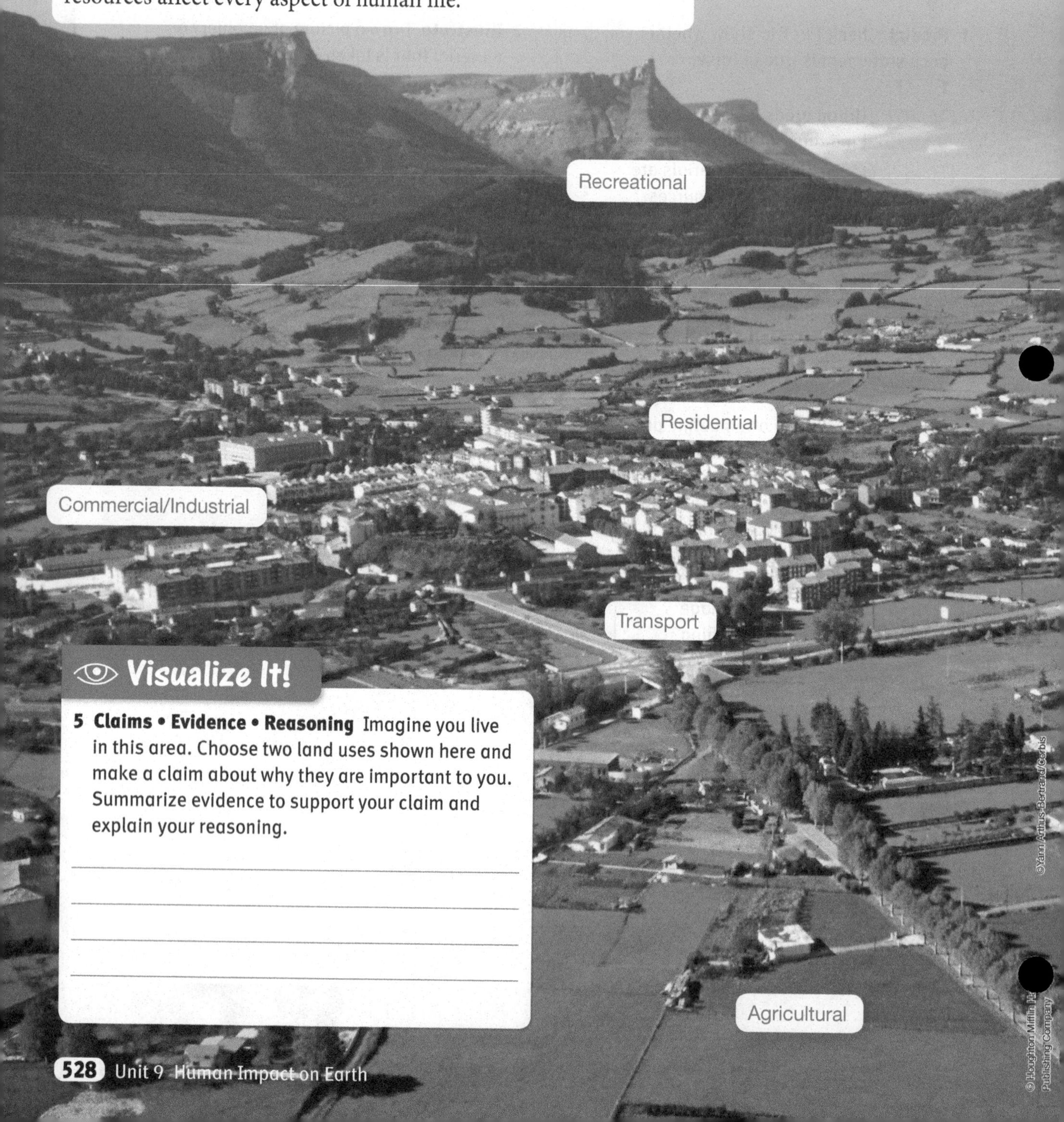
Recreational
Residential
Commercial/Industrial
Transport
Agricultural

©Yann Arthus-Bertrand/Corbis

Visualize It!

5 Claims • Evidence • Reasoning Imagine you live in this area. Choose two land uses shown here and make a claim about why they are important to you. Summarize evidence to support your claim and explain your reasoning.

____

____

____

____

What are the different types of land use?

We live on land in urban or rural areas. Cities and towns are urban areas. Rural areas are open lands that may be used for farming. Humans use land in many ways. We use natural areas for *recreation*. We use roads that are built on land for *transport*. We grow crops and raise livestock on *agricultural* land. We live in *residential* areas. We build *commercial* businesses on land and extract resources such as metals and water from the land.

Recreational

Natural areas are places that humans have left alone or restored to a natural state. These wild places include forests, grasslands, and desert areas. People use natural areas for hiking, bird-watching, mountain-biking, hunting, and other fun or recreational activities.

Transport

A large network of roads and train tracks connect urban and rural areas all across the country. Roads in the U.S. highway system cover 4 million miles of land. Trucks carry goods on these highways and smaller vehicles carry passengers. Railroads carrying freight or passengers use over 120,000 miles of land for tracks. Roads and train tracks are often highly concentrated in urban areas.

Agricultural

Much of the open land in rural areas is used for agriculture. Crops such as corn, soybeans, and wheat are grown on large, open areas of land. Land is also needed to raise and feed cattle and other livestock. Agricultural land is open, but very different from the natural areas that it has replaced. Farmland generally contains only one or two types of plants, such as corn or cotton. Natural grasslands, forests, and other natural areas contain many species of plants and animals.

6 Identify As you read, underline the ways rural areas differ from urban areas.

Residential

Where do you call home? People live in both rural and urban areas. Rural areas have large areas of open land and low densities of people. Urban areas have dense human populations and small areas of open land. This means that more people live in a square km of an urban area than live in a square km of a rural area. **Urbanization** is the growth of urban areas caused by people moving into cities. When cities increase in size, the population of rural areas near the city may decrease. When an area becomes urbanized, its natural land surface is replaced by buildings, parking lots, and roads. City parks, which contain natural surfaces, may also be built in urban areas.

Commercial and Industrial

As cities or towns expand, commercial businesses are built too, and replace rural or natural areas. Industrial businesses also use land resources. For example, paper companies and furniture manufacturers use wood from trees harvested on forest land. Cement companies, fertilizer manufacturers, and steel manufacturers use minerals that are mined from below the land's surface. Commercial and industrial development usually includes development of roads or railways. Transporting goods to market forms the basis of commerce.

7 Identify What effects does urbanization have on land?

_____

_____

_____

_____

_____

_____

_____

Why is soil important?

Soil is a mixture of mineral fragments, organic material, water, and air. Soil forms when rocks break down and dead organisms decay. There are many reasons why soil is important. Soil provides habitat for organisms such as plants, earthworms, fungi, and bacteria. Many plants get the water and nutrients they need from the soil. Because plants form the base of food webs, healthy soil is important for most land ecosystems. Healthy soil is also important for agricultural land, which supplies humans with food.

ACTIVE READING

8 Identify As you read, underline the ways that soil is important to plants.

It Is a Habitat for Organisms

Earthworms, moles, badgers, and other burrowing animals live in soil. These animals also find food underground. *Decomposers* are organisms that break down dead animal and plant material, releasing the nutrients into the soil. Decomposers such as fungi and bacteria live in soil. Soil holds plant roots in place, providing support for the plant. In turn, plants are food for herbivores and are habitats for organisms such as birds and insects. Many animals on Earth depend on soil for shelter or food.

It Stores Water and Nutrients

Falling rain soaks into soil and is stored between soil particles. Different types of soil can store different amounts of water. Wetland soils, for example, store large amounts of water and reduce flooding. Soils are also part of the nutrient cycle. Plants take up nutrients and water stored in soil. Plants and animals that eat them die and are broken down by decomposers such as bacteria and earthworms. Nutrients are released back into the soil and the cycle starts again.

👁 Visualize It!

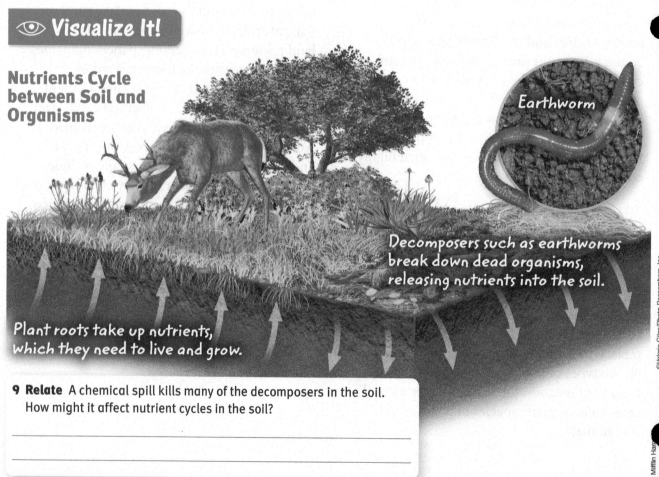

Nutrients Cycle between Soil and Organisms

Earthworm

Decomposers such as earthworms break down dead organisms, releasing nutrients into the soil.

Plant roots take up nutrients, which they need to live and grow.

9 Relate A chemical spill kills many of the decomposers in the soil. How might it affect nutrient cycles in the soil?

_____

_____

Dust Bowl

In the 1930s, huge clouds of dusty soil rolled across the southern Great Plains of the United States. Areas that were once farmlands and homesteads were wiped out. What caused the soil to blow away?

Drought and Overuse

Farmers who settled in the southern Great Plains overplowed and overgrazed their land. When severe drought hit in 1931, topsoil dried out. Winds lifted the soil and carried it across the plains in huge storms that farmers called "black blizzards." The drought and dust storms continued for years.

Modern Day Dust Bowl

Today in northwest China another dust bowl is forming. Large areas of farmland were made there by clearing the natural vegetation and plowing the soil. Herds of sheep and cattle are overgrazing the land, and large dust storms are common.

ℹ️ Extend

10 Identify What type of land use by people contributed to the Dust Bowl? Does it remain a common use of land today?

11 Claims • Evidence • Reasoning Research another area under threat from overuse. Make a claim about what is causing the problem. Summarize evidence to explain your reasoning.

12 Illustrate Do one of the following to show how the Dust Bowl or the area you researched affected society: make a poster, write a play, write a song, or draw a cartoon strip. Present your findings to the class.

Footprints

How can human activities affect land and soil?

Human activities can have positive and negative effects on land and soil. Some activities restore land to its natural state, or increase the amount of fertile soil on land. Other activities can degrade land. **Land degradation** is the process by which human activity and natural processes damage land to the point that it can no longer support the local ecosystem. Urbanization, deforestation, and poor farming practices can all lead to land degradation.

i Think Outside the Book

13 Claims • Evidence • Reasoning
Make a claim about how you could help lessen the impact of urbanization on the land in the area where you live. Summarize evidence to support the claim and explain your reasoning.

ACTIVE READING

14 Identify As you read, underline the effects that urbanization can have on land.

○ Urban Sprawl

When urbanization occurs at the edge of a city or town, it is called *urban sprawl*. Urban sprawl replaces forests, fields, and grasslands with houses, roads, schools, and shopping areas. Urban sprawl decreases the amount of farmland that is available for growing crops. It decreases the amount of natural areas that surround cities. It increases the amount of asphalt and concrete that covers the land. Rainwater runs off hard surfaces and into storm drains instead of soaking into the ground and filling aquifers. Rainwater runoff from urban areas can increase the erosion of nearby soils.

○ Erosion

Erosion (ih•ROH•zhuhn) is the process by which wind, water, or gravity transports soil and sediment from one place to another. Some type of erosion occurs on most land. However, erosion can speed up when land is degraded. Roots of trees and plants act as anchors to the soil. When land is cleared for farming, the trees and plants are removed and the soil is no longer protected. This exposes soil to blowing wind and running water that can wash away the soil, as shown in this photo.

Nutrient Depletion and Land Pollution

Crops use soil nutrients to grow. If the same crops are planted year after year, the same soil nutrients get used up. Plants need the right balance of nutrients to grow. Farmers can plant a different crop each year to reduce nutrient loss. Pollution from industrial activities can damage land. Mining wastes, gas and petroleum leaks, and chemical wastes can kill organisms in the soil. U.S. government programs such as Superfund help to clean up polluted land.

Desertification

When too many livestock are kept in one area, they can overgraze the area. Overgrazing removes the plants and roots that hold topsoil together. Overgrazing and other poor farming methods can cause desertification. **Desertification** (dih•zer•tuh•fih•KAY•shuhn) is the process by which land becomes more desertlike and unable to support life. Without plants, soil becomes dusty and prone to wind erosion. Deforestation and urbanization can also lead to desertification.

Deforestation

The removal of trees and other vegetation from an area is called **deforestation**. Logging for wood can cause deforestation. Surface mining causes deforestation by removing vegetation and soil to get to the minerals below. Deforestation also occurs in rain forests, as shown in the photo, when farmers cut or burn down trees so they can grow crops. Urbanization can cause deforestation when forests are replaced with buildings. Deforestation leads to increased soil erosion.

👁 Visualize It!

15 Claims • Evidence • Reasoning Make a claim about how human activity affected the forest in this photo. Use evidence to support your claim and explain your reasoning.

_____
_____
_____
_____
_____

Visual Summary

To complete this summary, circle the correct word or phrase.
You can use this page to review the main concepts of the lesson.

Humans use land in different ways.

16 Crops are grown on recreational/agricultural land.

Human Impact on Land

Soil is important to all organisms, including humans.

17 Decomposers/plants that live in soil break down dead matter in the soil.

Human activities can affect land and soil.

18 Poor farming practices and drought can lead to desertification/urbanization.

19 Claims • Evidence • Reasoning Make a claim about how concentrating human populations in cities help to conserve agricultural and recreational land. Summarize evidence to support your claim and explain your reasoning.

Lesson Review

Vocabulary

Draw a line to connect the following terms to their definitions.

1 urbanization

2 deforestation

3 land degradation

4 desertification

A the removal of trees and other vegetation from an area

B the process by which land becomes more desertlike

C the process by which human activity can damage land

D the formation and growth of cities

Key Concepts

5 **Contrast** How are natural areas different from rural areas?

_____

_____

_____

_____

6 **Relate** How might deforestation lead to desertification?

_____

_____

_____

_____

7 **Claims • Evidence • Reasoning** Think of an animal that eats other animals. Make a claim about why soil would be important to this animal. Provide evidence to support your claim and explain your reasoning.

_____

_____

_____

_____

Critical Thinking

Use this photo to answer the following questions.

8 **Analyze** What type of land degradation is occurring in this photo?

_____

9 **Claims • Evidence • Reasoning** The type of soil damage shown in the photo can also occur in urban areas. Make a claim about how urbanization could lead to this type of degradation. Summarize evidence to support your claim and explain your reasoning.

_____

_____

_____

_____

_____

_____

10 **Apply** What kinds of land uses are around your school? Write down each type of land use. Then describe how one of these land uses might affect natural systems.

_____

_____

_____

_____

_____

PEOPLE IN SCIENCE

SC.7.E.6.6 Identify the impact that humans have had on Earth, such as deforestation, urbanization, desertification, erosion, air and water quality, changing the flow of water.

Angel Montoya

CONSERVATION BIOLOGIST

In 1990, Angel Montoya was a student intern working at Laguna Atascosa National Wildlife Refuge in Texas. He became interested in the Aplomado falcon, a bird of prey that disappeared from the southwestern United States during the first half of the 20th century. Montoya decided to go looking for the raptors. He found a previously unknown population of Aplomados in Chihuahua, Mexico. His work helped to make it possible for the falcons to be reintroduced to an area near El Paso, Texas.

Restoration of the Aplomado falcon became Angel's lifework. He has monitored and researched the falcon since 1992. He helps release falcons that have been raised in captivity back into the wild and monitors falcons that have already been released. It isn't easy to keep tabs on a falcon, however. "Their first year they are pretty vulnerable, because they haven't had parents," Montoya says. "Just like juveniles, they're always getting into trouble. But I think they will do just fine."

Angel Montoya releases an Aplomado falcon back into the wild.

JOB BOARD

Environmental Engineering Technician

What You'll Do: Work closely with environmental engineers and scientists to prevent or fix environmental damage. Take care of water and wastewater treatment systems, as well as equipment used for recycling. Test water and air quality and keep good records.

Where You Might Work: In a water treatment facility, or an environmental laboratory.

Education: an associate's degree in engineering technology.

Other Job Requirements: Good communication skills and the ability to work well with others.

Agronomist

What You'll Do: Study the best ways to grow crops and work with farmers to help them use their land better, and get better yields. Agronomists are scientists who study crops and soil.

Where You Might Work: On a farm, in an agricultural business, for the U.S. Department of Agriculture or state or local government agencies, or for seed companies. Agronomists may work both in fields and in laboratories.

Education: a four-year college degree in agronomy, agriculture, or soil conservation.

PEOPLE IN SCIENCE NEWS

YUMI Someya

Fueling the Family Business

Yumi Someya's family had worked in recycling for three generations, cleaning and recycling used cooking oil. In Japan, many people enjoy fried foods. They often throw out the used cooking oil. Yumi's family business collected used oil, cleaned it, and sold it for reuse.

When Yumi traveled to Nepal, she was caught in a landslide. She learned that deforestation was one cause of the landslide and began to think about environmental issues. When she returned home, she worked with her father to find new uses for the used cooking oil. They experimented with fertilizer and soap. Then, in 1992, they learned about biodiesel—fuel made from recycled soybean oil. They thought that used cooking oil might work to fuel cars, too. With a team of researchers, they created Vegetable Diesel Fuel (VDF).

Now, VDF fuels the company's oil-collecting trucks and some Tokyo buses. Yumi hopes to eventually recycle all of the cooking oil used in Japan.

Human Impact on Water

ESSENTIAL **QUESTION**

What impact can human activities have on water resources?

By the end of this lesson, you should be able to explain the impacts that humans can have on the quality and supply of fresh water.

Humans and other organisms depend on clean water to survive. More than half of the material inside humans is water.

SC.7.E.6.6 Identify the impact that humans have had on Earth, such as deforestation, urbanization, desertification, erosion, air and water quality, changing the flow of water.

© Aurora Open/Justin Bailie/Getty Images

© Houghton Mifflin Harcourt Publishing Company

Lesson Labs

Quick Labs
- Ocean Pollution from Land
- Turbidity and Water Temperature
- Modeling Groundwater

Exploration Lab
- Filtering Water

Engage Your Brain

1 Analyze Write a list of the reasons humans need water. Next to this list, write a list of reasons fish need water. Are there similarities between your two lists?

2 Identify Circle the word that correctly completes the following sentences. The man in this photo is testing *water/air* quality. The flowing body of water next to the man is a *river/lake*.

ACTIVE READING

3 Synthesize You can often define an unknown word if you know the meaning of its word parts. Use the word parts and the sentence below to make an educated guess about the meaning of the word *nonrenewable*.

Word part	Meaning
renew	restore, make like new
-able	able to be
non-	not

Example sentence
Some of Earth's <u>nonrenewable</u> resources include coal and oil.

nonrenewable:

_____

_____

_____

_____

_____

Vocabulary Terms
- water pollution
- point-source pollution
- nonpoint-source pollution
- thermal pollution
- eutrophication
- potable
- reservoir

4 Identify This list contains the key terms you'll learn in this lesson. As you read, circle the definition of each term.

Close up of a mayfly larva

Water, Water

Organisms need clean water for life and good health. For example, young mayflies live in water, humans drink water, and brown pelicans eat fish they catch in water.

Why is water important?

Earth is the only planet with large amounts of water. Water shapes Earth's surface and affects Earth's weather and climates. Most importantly, water is vital for life. Every living thing is made mostly of water. Most life processes use water. Water is an important natural resource. For humans and other organisms, access to clean water is important for good health.

There is lots of water, so what's the problem?

About 97% of Earth's water is salty, which leaves only 3% as fresh water. However, as you can see from the graph, over two-thirds of Earth's fresh water is frozen as ice and snow. But a lot of the liquid water seeps into the ground as groundwater. That leaves much less than 1% of Earth's fresh liquid water on the surface. Water is vital for people, so this small volume of fresh surface water and groundwater is a limited resource.

Areas with high densities of people, such as cities, need lots of fresh water. Cities are getting bigger, and so the need for fresh water is increasing. *Urbanization* (ER•buh•ny•zhay•shuhn) is the growth of towns and cities that results from the movement of people from rural areas into the urban areas. The greater demand for fresh water in cities is threatening the availability of water for many people. Fresh water is becoming a natural resource that cannot be replaced at the same rate at which it is used.

Distribution of Earth's Fresh Water

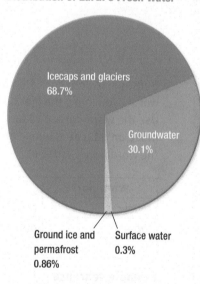

Icecaps and glaciers 68.7%

Groundwater 30.1%

Ground ice and permafrost 0.86%

Surface water 0.3%

👁 Visualize It!

5 Gather Evidence What percentage of fresh water on Earth is frozen? What percentage of fresh water is liquid?

_____

_____

Everywhere...

Where do we get fresh water?

Fresh water may fall directly as precipitation, or may melt from ice and snow. Earth's fresh liquid water is found as surface water and groundwater. *Surface water* is any body of water above the ground. It includes liquid salt or fresh water, or solid water, like snow and ice. Water may seep below the surface to become *groundwater*. Groundwater is found under Earth's surface, in spaces in rocks or in soil, where it can be liquid or frozen.

⬭ Aquifers and Groundwater

Aquifers and ground ice are forms of groundwater. An *aquifer* is a body of rock or sediment that can store a lot of water, and that allows water to flow easily through it. Aquifers store water in spaces, called *pores*, between particles of rock or sediment. Wells are dug into aquifers to reach the water. In polar regions, water is often frozen in a layer of soil called *permafrost*.

⬭ Rivers, Streams, and Lakes

Rivers, streams, and most lakes are fresh surface waters. A stream or river may flow into a bowl-shaped area, which may fill up to form a lake. Many millions of people around the world depend on fresh water that is taken from rivers and fresh water lakes.

What are water quality and supply?

Water quality is a measure of how clean or polluted water is. Water quality is important because humans and other organisms depend on clean water to survive. It is vital for living things to not only have water, but also to have clean water. Dirty, contaminated water can make us sick or even kill us.

Water supply is the availability of water. Water supply influences where and when farmers grow crops, and where people can build cities. *Water supply systems* carry water from groundwater or surface waters so people can use the water. The systems can be a network of underground pipes, or a bucket for scooping water from a well. A shortage of clean, fresh water reduces quality of life for people. Many people in developing countries do not have access to clean, fresh water.

© Houghton Mifflin Harcourt Publishing Company © Caroline Penn/Corbis; (i) ©Caroline Penn/Corbis

ACTIVE READING

6 List What are the different sources of fresh water?

_____

_____

ⓘ Think Outside the Book

7 Claims • Evidence • Reasoning Keep a water diary for a day. Record every time you use water. At the end of the day, make a claim about how you could reduce your water usage. Summarize evidence to support the claim and explain your reasoning.

Many people do not have a water supply to their homes. Instead, they have to go to a local stream, well, or pump to gather water for cooking, cleaning, and drinking.

Under Threat

What threatens fresh water quality?

When waste or other material is added to water so that it is harmful to organisms that use it or live in it, **water pollution** (WAW•ter puh•LOO•shuhn) occurs. It is useful to divide pollution sources into two types. **Point-source pollution** comes from one specific site. For example, a major chemical spill is point-source pollution. Usually this type of pollution can be controlled once its source is found. **Nonpoint-source pollution** comes from many small sources and is more difficult to control. Most nonpoint-source pollution reaches water supplies by runoff or by seeping into groundwater. The main sources of nonpoint-source pollution are city streets, roads and drains, farms, and mines.

ACTIVE **READING**

8 Identify As you read, underline the sources of water pollution.

Thermal Pollution

Any heating of natural water that results from human activity is called **thermal pollution**. For example, water that is used for cooling some power plants gets warmed up. When that water is returned to the river or lake it is at a higher temperature than the lake or river water. The warm water has less oxygen available for organisms that live in the water.

Chemical Pollution

Chemical pollution occurs when harmful chemicals are added to water supplies. Two major sources of chemical pollution are industry and agriculture. For example, refineries that process oil or metals and factories that make metal or plastic products or electronic items all produce toxic chemical waste. Chemicals used in agriculture include pesticides, herbicides, and fertilizers. These pollutants can reach water supplies by seeping into groundwater. Once in groundwater, the pollution can enter the water cycle and can be carried far from the pollution source. *Acid rain* is another form of chemical pollution. It forms when gases formed by burning fossil fuels mix with water in the air. Acid rain can harm both plants and animals. It can lower the pH of soil and water, and make them too acidic for life.

Biological Pollution

Many organisms naturally live in and around water, but they are not normally polluters. *Biological pollution* occurs when live or dead organisms are added to water supplies. Wastewater may contain disease-causing microbes from human or animal wastes. *Wastewater* is any water that has been used by people for such things as flushing toilets, showering, or washing dishes. Wastewater from feed lots and farms may also contain harmful microbes. These microbes can cause diseases such as dysentery, typhoid, or cholera.

Eutrophication

Fresh water often contains nutrients from decomposing organisms. An increase in the amount of nutrients in water is called **eutrophication** (yoo•TRAWF•ih•kay•shuhn). Eutrophication occurs naturally in water. However, *artificial eutrophication* occurs when human activity increases nutrient levels in water. Wastewater and fertilizer runoff that gets into waterways can add extra nutrients which upset the natural biology of the water. These extra nutrients cause the fast growth of algae over the water surface. An overgrowth of algae and aquatic plants can reduce oxygen levels and kill fish and other organisms in the water.

Water can become polluted by human activities in many different ways.

Chemical Pollution
Sulfur in smoke and vehicle exhausts contributes to the acidification of rain, leading to acid rain. Acid rain can affect areas far from the point of pollution.

Biological pollution

Biological Pollution
Animal and human wastes can get washed into a water supply in runoff, or through leaking pipes.

Thermal pollution

Eutrophication

Chemical pollution

9 Claims • Evidence • Reasoning Make a claim about how human activity is impacting water quality in this image. Summarize evidence to support the claim and explain your reasoning.

_____

_____

_____

10 Apply Identify one point-source and one nonpoint-source of pollution in this image.

_____

_____

_____

How is water quality measured?

Before there were scientific methods of testing water, people could only look at water, taste it, and smell it to check its quality. Scientists can now test water with modern equipment, so the results are more reliable. Modern ways of testing water are especially important for finding small quantities of toxic chemicals or harmful organisms in water.

Water is a good solvent. So, water in nature usually contains dissolved solids, such as salt and other substances. Because most dissolved solids cannot be seen, it is important to measure them. Measurements of water quality include testing the levels of dissolved oxygen, pH, temperature, dissolved solids, and the number and types of microbes in the water. Quality standards depend on the intended use for the water. For example, drinking water needs to meet much stricter quality standards than environmental waters such as river or lake waters do.

Water Quality Measurement

Quality measurement	What is it?	How it relates to water quality
Dissolved solids	a measure of the amount of ions or microscopic suspended solids in water	Some dissolved solids could be harmful chemicals. Others such as calcium could cause scaling or build-up in water pipes.
pH	a measure of how acidic or alkaline water is	Aquatic organisms need a near neutral pH (approx. pH 7). Acid rain can drop the pH too low (acidic) for aquatic life to live.
Dissolved oxygen (DO)	the amount of oxygen gas that is dissolved in water	Aquatic organisms need oxygen. Animal waste and thermal pollution can decrease the amount of oxygen dissolved in water.
Turbidity	a measure of the cloudiness of water that is caused by suspended solids	High turbidity increases the chance that harmful microbes or chemicals are in the water.
Microbial load	the identification of harmful bacteria, viruses or protists in water	Microbes such as bacteria, viruses, and protists from human and animal wastes can cause diseases.

11 State Your Claim Make a claim about the relationship between increased turbidity and the likelihood of something harmful being in the water.

_____

How is water treated for human use?

ACTIVE READING

12 Identify As you read, number the basic steps in the water treatment process.

Natural water may be unsafe for humans to drink. So, water that is to be used as drinking water is treated to remove harmful chemicals and organisms. Screens take out large debris. Then chemicals are added that make suspended particles stick together. These particles drop out of the water in a process called *flocculation*. Flocculation also removes harmful bacteria and other microbes. Chlorine is often added to kill microbes left in the water. In some cities, fluoride is added to water supplies to help prevent tooth decay. Finally, air is bubbled through the water. Water that is suitable to drink is called **potable** water. Once water is used, it becomes wastewater. It enters the sewage system where pipes carry it to a wastewater treatment plant. There the wastewater is cleaned and filtered before being released back into the environment.

Drinking water is often mixed in large basins to help remove chemicals and harmful organisms. Paddles stir the water in the basins.

Who monitors and protects our water quality?

ACTIVE READING

13 Identify As you read, underline the government agency that is responsible for enforcing water quality rules.

If a public water supply became contaminated, many people could get very sick. As a result, public water supplies are closely monitored so that any problems can be fixed quickly. The Safe Drinking Water Act is the main federal law that ensures safe drinking water for people in the United States. The act sets strict limits on the amount of heavy metals or certain types of bacteria that can be in drinking water, among other things. The Environmental Protection Agency (EPA) has the job of enforcing this law. It is responsible for setting the standards drinking water must meet before the water can be pumped into public water systems. Water quality tests can be done by trained workers or trained volunteers.

Samples of water are routinely taken to make sure the water quality meets the standards required by law.

Supply and Demand

How does water get to the faucet?

In earlier times, humans had to live near natural sources of fresh water. Over time, engineers developed ways to transport and store large amounts of water. So, humans can now live in places where fresh water is supplied by water pipes and other infrastructure. The ability to bring fresh water safely from its source to a large population has led to the urbanization of cities.

○ Creating Water Supply Systems

Freshwater supply is often limited, so we have found ways to store and transport water far from its source to where it is used. Surface water is collected and pumped to places where people need it. Groundwater can be found by digging wells into aquifers. Water can be lifted from a well by hand in buckets. It can be pumped into pipes that supply homes, farms, factories and cities. Piped water supply systems can deliver water over great distances to where humans need it. Water supply and storage systems are expensive to build and maintain.

👁 Visualize It!

A public water supply includes the water source, the treatment facilities, and the pipes and pumps that send it to homes, industries, businesses, and public facilities.

Water treatment and distribution

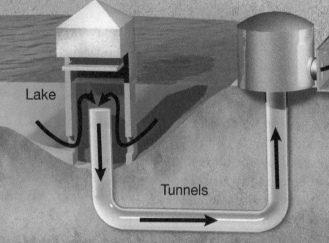

A Water can be moved far away from its source by pumping it through pipes to large urban areas.

Intake

Chemicals added

Lake

Mixing basins

Settling basins

Tunnels

Water treatment plant

B Water is treated to make it potable.

○ Changing the Flow of Water

Pumping and collecting groundwater and surface waters changes how water flows in natural systems. For example, a **reservoir** (REZ•uhr•vwohr) is a body of water that usually forms behind a dam. Dams stop river waters from flowing along their natural course. The water in a reservoir would naturally have flowed to the sea. Instead, the water can be diverted into a pipeline or into artificial channels called *canals* or *aqueducts*.

What threatens our water supply?

ACTIVE READING

14 Identify As you read, underline the things that are a threat to water supply.

As the human use of water has increased, the demand for fresh water has also increased. Demand is greater than supply in many areas of the world, including parts of the United States. The larger a population or a city gets, the greater the demand for fresh water. Increased demand for and use of water can cause water shortages. Droughts or leaking water pipes can also cause water shortages. Water is used to keep our bodies clean and healthy. It is also used to grow crops for food. Water shortages threaten these benefits.

15 Infer Why would a larger city have a larger demand for water? Explain your reasoning.

_____

_____

_____

_____

_____

_____

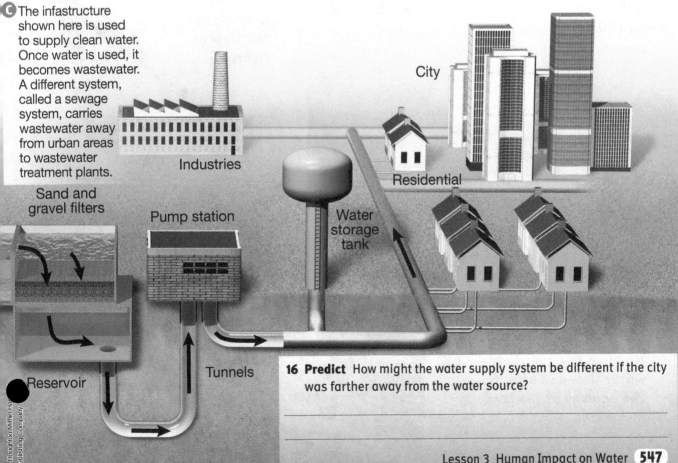

Ⓒ The infastructure shown here is used to supply clean water. Once water is used, it becomes wastewater. A different system, called a sewage system, carries wastewater away from urban areas to wastewater treatment plants.

Sand and gravel filters

Pump station

Water storage tank

Industries

City

Residential

Reservoir

Tunnels

16 Predict How might the water supply system be different if the city was farther away from the water source?

_____

_____

How do efforts to supply water to humans affect the environment?

Growing urban populations place a greater demand on water supplies. Efforts to increase water supply can affect the environment. For example, building dams and irrigation canals changes the natural flow of water. The environment is physically changed by construction work. The local ecology changes too. Organisms that live in or depend on the water may lose their habitat and move away or die.

Aquifers are often used as freshwater sources for urban areas. When more water is taken from an aquifer than can be replaced by rain or snow, the water table can drop below the reach of existing wells. Rivers and streams may dry up and the soil that once held aquifer waters may collapse, or *subside*. In coastal areas, the overuse of groundwater can cause seawater to seep into the aquifer in a process called *saltwater intrusion*. In this way, water supplies can become contaminated with salt water.

Increasing population in an area can also affect water quality. The more people that use a water supply in one area, the greater the volume of wastewater that is produced in that area. Pollutants such as oil, pesticides, fertilizers, and heavy metals from city runoff, from industry, and from agriculture may seep into surface waters and groundwater. In this way, pollution could enter the water supply. This pollution could also enter the water cycle and be carried far from the initial source of the pollution.

ACTIVE READING

17 Claims • Evidence • Reasoning Make a claim about how an increased demand on water can affect the water quality. Provide evidence to support your claim and explain your reasoning.

_____

_____

_____

_____

_____

_____

Digging irrigation canals changes the flow of rivers.

Building dams disrupts water flow and affects the ecology of the land and water.

Irrigating arid areas changes the ecology of those areas.

Death of a Sea

The Aral Sea in Central Asia was once the world's fourth-largest inland salty lake. But it has been shrinking since the 1960s. In the 1940s, the courses of the rivers that fed the lake were changed to irrigate the desert, so that crops such as cotton and rice could be grown. By 1997, the lake was down to 20% of its original volume, and down to 10% by 2017. The freshwater flow into the lake was reduced and evaporation caused the lake to become so salty that most of the plants and animals in it died or left the lake.

By 2017, only about 10% of the water originally in the Aral Sea remained and had split into several smaller lakes.

Polluted Land

The Aral Sea is also heavily polluted by industrial wastes, pesticides, and fertilizer runoff. Salty dust that is blown from the dried seabed damages crops and pollutes drinking water. The salt- and dust-laden air cause serious public health problems in the Aral Sea region. One of the more bizarre reminders of how large the lake once was are the boats that lie abandoned on the exposed sea floor.

ℹ️ Extend

18 Identify What human activity has created the situation in the Aral Sea?

19 Apply Research the impact that of one of these two large water projects has had on people and on the environment: The Three Gorges Dam or the Columbia Basin Project.

20 Claims • Evidence • Reasoning Research a current or past water project in the area where you live. Make a claim about the benefits of the project for people in the area. Make another claim about what risks there might be to the environment. Summarize evidence to support the claim and explain your reasoning.

Visual Summary

To complete this summary, fill in the blanks with the correct word or phrase. You can use this page to review the main concepts of the lesson.

Human Impact on Water

Organisms need clean water for life and good health.

Distribution of Earth's Fresh Water

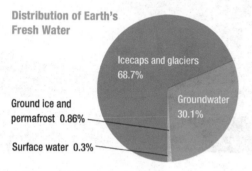

Icecaps and glaciers 68.7%

Groundwater 30.1%

Ground ice and permafrost 0.86%

Surface water 0.3%

21 Earth's fresh liquid water is found as surface water and _____

Water pollution can come from many different sources.

22 Runoff from farmland into a river is an example of _____ source pollution.

Federal laws set the standards for potable water quality. Water quality is constantly monitored.

23 Dissolved solids, pH, temperature, and dissolved oxygen are measures of _____.

Ensuring a constant supply of water for people can change the environment.

24 A _____ is a body of water that forms when a dam blocks a river.

25 Claims • Evidence • Reasoning Make a claim about the difference between water quality and water supply. Summarize evidence to support the claim and explain your reasoning.

Lesson Review

Vocabulary

Fill in the blank with the term that best completes the following sentences.

1 _____ water is a term used to describe water that is safe to drink.

2 The addition of nutrients to water by human activity is called artificial _____.

3 _____ pollution comes from many small sources.

Key Concepts

Complete the table below with the type of pollution described in each example.

Example	Type of pollution (chemical, thermal, or biological)
4 Identify A person empties an oil can into a storm drain.	
5 Identify A factory releases warm water into a local river.	
6 Identify Untreated sewage is washed into a lake during a rain storm.	

7 Describe Name two ways in which humans can affect the flow of fresh water.

_____

_____

_____

8 Claims • Evidence • Reasoning Make a claim about why water quality needs to be monitored. Support your claim with evidence and explain your reasoning.

_____

Critical Thinking

Use this graph to answer questions 9 and 10.

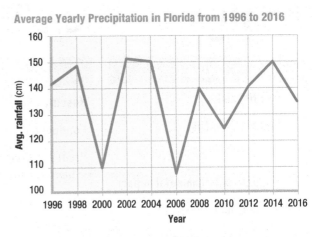

Average Yearly Precipitation in Florida from 1996 to 2016

Source: National Climatic Data Center

9 Analyze Which year had the least precipitation?

_____

10 Infer What effect might many years of low precipitation have on water supply?

_____

_____

11 Claims • Evidence • Reasoning Make a claim about whether a single person or animal could be a cause of point-source pollution. Use evidence to support your claim and explain your reasoning.

_____

_____

_____

12 Claims • Evidence • Reasoning In times of hot, dry, weather, some cities may ban the use of garden sprinklers. Make a claim about why this rule would be made. Summarize evidence to support the claim and explain your reasoning.

_____

_____

SC.7.N.1.5 Describe the methods used in the pursuit of a scientific explanation as seen in different fields of science such as biology, geology, and physics.

S.T.E.M. ENGINEERING & TECHNOLOGY
Analysis—Risk/Benefit

Skills
✔ Identify risks
✔ Identify benefits
Evaluate cost of technology
✔ Evaluate environmental impact
✔ Propose improvements
✔ Propose risk reduction
✔ Compare technologies
✔ Communicate results

Objectives
Research a desalination process.
Conduct a risk/benefit analysis of a desalination process.
Predict actions that may be taken to decrease the risks or improve the benefits of desalination.

Identifying Risks and Benefits of Desalination

Although our planet has a lot of water, vast areas of Earth are dry. Most of the water is too salty to use for drinking or to grow crops. Millions of people struggle to get enough drinking water. Many countries cannot grow enough food because of water shortages. If we could find an inexpensive and safe way to turn salt water into fresh water, people in drier parts of the world could benefit. Fresh water could be used to irrigate crops, and some dry areas could be turned into productive farmland. The removal of salt from salt water is called *desalination*. However, desalination technology is not appropriate for all areas of the world. There are a number of difficulties associated with this technology.

The Sahara Desert

1 Brainstorm What is a benefit of getting fresh water from the sea?

_____

_____

_____

_____

_____

What Methods of Desalination Are Being Tried?

Thousands of desalination facilities exist worldwide. More than a dozen methods of desalination can be used effectively. However, most desalination occurs by the *multistage flash distillation* process. In this method, seawater is boiled so that the water turns to steam, leaving the salt behind. Then the steam is cooled and becomes liquid fresh water. This process must be repeated at different temperatures and pressures to remove as much salt as possible. It takes large amounts of energy to boil the water and run the pressure pumps.

Another desalination method is called *reverse osmosis*. Reverse osmosis uses high pressure to force water through a membrane. This membrane does not allow salt and other substances to pass through. So the liquid on the other side of the membrane is fresh water.

2 Apply What resources does multistage flash distillation require?

_____

_____

_____

_____

3 Claims • Evidence • Reasoning Research two desalination methods. Make a claim about the benefits of each method. Summarize evidence to support the claim and explain your reasoning.

_____

_____

Farmland made possible by irrigation

Reverse osmosis module

Water storage tanks

Desalination facility

 **You Try It!**

Now it's your turn to research a method of desalination and perform a risk/benefit analysis.

✋ You Try It!

Now it's your turn to more thoroughly research a method of desalination and perform a risk/benefit analysis. You will be comparing your analysis with the work of other class members.

Reverse osmosis desalination plant

① Identify Risks

Choose a desalination method to research. As you learn about your chosen desalination method, write down the risks or challenges this method has. They may be financial, social, or anything else that applies. Also, list the web sites you consulted.

_____
_____
_____
_____
_____

② Identify Benefits

What are the benefits to this method that would make it worth pursuing?

_____
_____
_____
_____

③ Evaluate Environmental Impact

How will this technology affect the land? How will it affect the atmosphere? If salt is returned to the sea, how could it affect marine life?

_____
_____
_____
_____
_____
_____

(4) Propose Improvements

What could be done to make this method even better? Can it be combined with another technology or process to enhance its benefits?

_____

_____

_____

(5) Propose Risk Reduction

Is there anything that can be done to reduce the risks? Would combining it with another technology or process make it safer?

_____

_____

_____

(6) Compare Technology

Discuss your analysis with classmates who chose different technologies. Record the ways in which the method you researched seems better or worse than the methods your classmates researched.

_____

_____

_____

(7) Communicate Results

Overall, do you think the desalination method you researched should be used much more than it is? What is its best feature? What recommendations would you make about its use, including where it should be located?

_____

_____

_____

_____

_____

_____

Human Impact on the Atmosphere

ESSENTIAL QUESTION

How do humans impact Earth's atmosphere?

By the end of this lesson, you should be able to identify the impact that humans have had on Earth's atmosphere.

Human activities that involve burning fuels, such as driving vehicles and keeping buildings cool, can cause air pollution.

SC.7.E.6.6 Identify the impact that humans have had on Earth, such as deforestation, urbanization, desertification, erosion, air and water quality, changing the flow of water.

Quick Labs
- Collecting Air-Pollution Particles
- Identifying Noise Pollution
- Concrete versus Vegetation

 Engage Your Brain

1 Identify Check T or F to show whether you think each statement is true or false.

T	F	
☐	☐	Human activities can cause air pollution.
☐	☐	Air pollution cannot affect you if you stay indoors.
☐	☐	Air pollution does not affect places outside of cities.
☐	☐	Air pollution can cause lung diseases.

2 Analyze The photo above shows the same city as the photo on the left, but on a different day. How are these photos different?

_____
_____
_____
_____

ACTIVE **READING**

3 Apply Use context clues to write your own definitions for the words *contamination* and *quality*.

Example sentence
You can help prevent food <u>contamination</u> by washing your hands after touching raw meat.

contamination:

_____
_____
_____

Example sentence
The good sound <u>quality</u> coming from the stereo speakers indicated they were expensive.

quality:

_____
_____
_____

Vocabulary Terms
- greenhouse effect
- air pollution
- particulate
- smog
- acid precipitation
- air quality

4 Apply As you learn the definition of each vocabulary term in this lesson, create your own definition or sketch to help you remember the meaning of the term.

AIR
What Is It Good For?

Why is the atmosphere important?

If you were lost in a desert, you could survive a few days without food and water. But you wouldn't last more than a few minutes without air. Air is an important natural resource. The air you breathe forms part of Earth's atmosphere. The *atmosphere* (AT•muh•sfeer) is a mixture of gases that surrounds Earth. Most organisms on Earth have adapted to the natural balance of gases found in the atmosphere.

It Provides Gases That Organisms Need to Survive

Oxygen is one of the gases that make up Earth's atmosphere. It is used by most living cells to get energy from food. Every breath you take brings oxygen into your body. The atmosphere also contains carbon dioxide. Plants need carbon dioxide to make their own food through photosynthesis (foh•toh•SYN•thuh•sys).

It Absorbs Harmful Radiation

High-energy radiation from space would harm life on Earth if it were not blocked by the atmosphere. Fast-moving particles, called *cosmic rays,* enter the atmosphere every second. These particles collide with oxygen, nitrogen, and other gas molecules and are slowed down. A part of the atmosphere called the *stratosphere* contains ozone gas. The ozone layer absorbs most of the high-energy radiation from the sun, called *ultraviolet radiation* (UV), that reaches Earth.

It Keeps Earth Warm

Without the atmosphere, temperatures on Earth would not be stable. It would be too cold for life to exist. The **greenhouse effect** is the way by which certain gases in the atmosphere, such as water vapor and carbon dioxide, absorb and reradiate thermal energy. This slows the loss of energy from Earth into space. The atmosphere acts like a warm blanket that insulates the surface of Earth, preventing the sun's energy from being lost. For this reason, carbon dioxide and water vapor are called *greenhouse gases.*

ACTIVE READING

5 Explain How is Earth's atmosphere similar to a warm blanket?

_____

_____

What is air pollution?

The contamination of the atmosphere by pollutants from human and natural sources is called **air pollution**. Natural sources of air pollution include volcanic eruptions, wildfires, and dust storms. In cities and suburbs, most air pollution comes from the burning of fossil fuels such as oil, gasoline, and coal. Oil refineries, chemical manufacturing plants, dry-cleaning businesses, and auto repair shops are just some potential sources of air pollution. Scientists classify air pollutants as either gases or particulates.

ACTIVE READING

6 Identify As you read, underline sources of air pollution.

👁 Visualize It!

7 Analyze Which one of these images could be both a natural or a human source of air pollution? Explain your reasoning.

_____

_____

_____

_____

Factory emissions

Vehicle exhaust

Forest fires and wildfires

⃝ Gases

Gas pollutants include carbon monoxide, sulfur dioxide, nitrogen oxide, and ground-level ozone. Some of these gases occur naturally in the atmosphere. These gases are considered pollutants only when they are likely to cause harm. For example, ozone is important in the stratosphere, but at ground level it is harmful to breathe. Carbon monoxide, sulfur dioxide, and nitrogen dioxide are released from burning fossil fuels in vehicles, factories, and homes. They are a major source of air pollution.

⃝ Particulates

Particle pollutants can be easier to see than gas pollutants. A **particulate** (per•TIK•yuh•lit) is a tiny particle of solid that is suspended in air or water. Smoke contains ash, which is a particulate. The wind can pick up particulates such as dust, ash, pollen, and tiny bits of salt from the ocean and blow them far from their source. Ash, dust, and pollen are common forms of air pollution. Vehicle exhaust also contains particulates. The particulates in vehicle exhaust are a major cause of air pollution in cities.

It Stinks!

What pollutants can form from vehicle exhaust?

In urban areas, vehicle exhaust is a common source of air pollution. Gases such as carbon monoxide and particulates such as soot and ash are in exhaust fumes. Vehicle exhaust may also react with other substances in the air. When this happens, new pollutants can form. Ground-level ozone and smog are two types of pollutants that form from vehicle exhaust.

ACTIVE READING

8 Identify As you read, underline how ground-level ozone and smog can form.

Ground-Level Ozone

Ozone in the ozone layer is necessary for life, but ground-level ozone is harmful. It is produced when sunlight reacts with vehicle exhaust and oxygen in the air. You may have heard of "Ozone Action Days" in your community. When such a warning is given, people should limit outdoor activities because ozone can damage their lungs.

Smog

Smog is another type of pollutant formed from vehicle exhaust. **Smog** forms when ground-level ozone and vehicle exhaust react in the presence of sunlight. Smog is a problem in large cities because there are more vehicles on the roads. It can cause lung damage and irritate the eyes and nose. In some cities, there can be enough smog to make a brownish haze over the city.

◉ Visualize It!

Some compounds in smoke and exhaust are harmful by themselves. And some compounds in smoke and exhaust can react in the atmosphere to form other pollutants such as smog and acid precipitation.

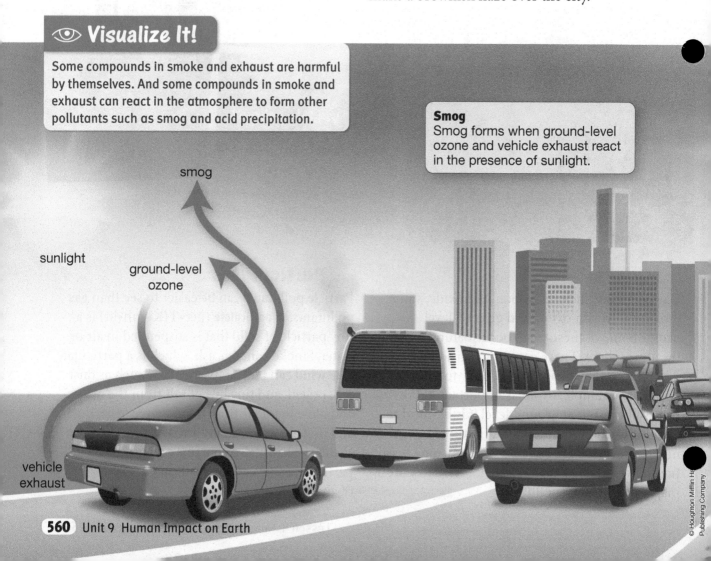

smog

sunlight

ground-level ozone

vehicle exhaust

Smog
Smog forms when ground-level ozone and vehicle exhaust react in the presence of sunlight.

How does pollution from human activities produce acid precipitation?

ACTIVE READING

9 Identify As you read, underline how acid precipitation forms.

Precipitation (prih•sip•ih•TAY•shuhn) such as rain, sleet, or snow that contains acids from air pollution is called **acid precipitation**. Burning fossil fuels releases sulfur dioxide and nitrogen oxides into the air. When these gases mix with water in the atmosphere, they form sulfuric acid and nitric acid. Precipitation is naturally slightly acidic. When carbon dioxide in the air and water mix, they form carbonic acid. Carbonic acid is a weak acid. Sulfuric acid and nitric acid are strong acids. They can make precipitation so acidic that it is harmful to the environment.

What are some effects of acid precipitation?

Acid precipitation can cause soil and water to become more acidic than normal. Plants have adapted over long periods of time to the natural acidity of the soils in which they live. When soil acidity rises, some nutrients that plants need are dissolved. These nutrients get washed away by rainwater. Bacteria and fungi that live in the soil are also harmed by acidic conditions.

Acid precipitation may increase the acidity of lakes or streams. It also releases toxic metals from soils. The increased acidity and high levels of metals in water can sicken or kill aquatic organisms. This can disrupt habitats and result in decreased biodiversity in an ecosystem. Acid precipitation can also erode the stonework on buildings and statues.

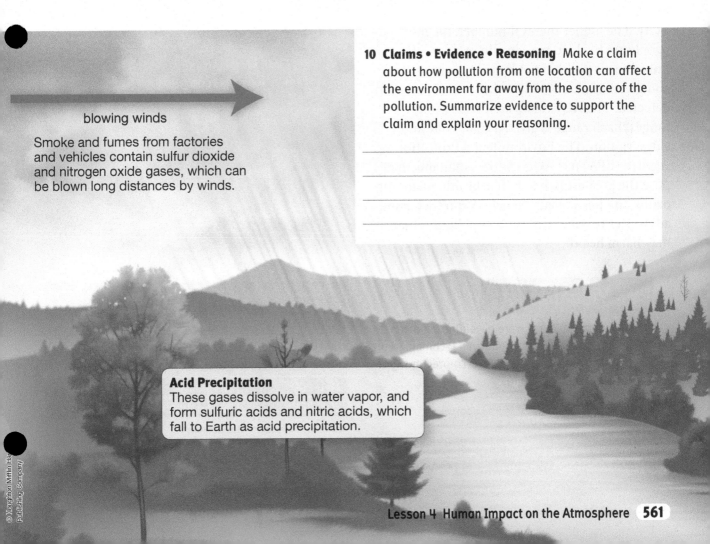

blowing winds

Smoke and fumes from factories and vehicles contain sulfur dioxide and nitrogen oxide gases, which can be blown long distances by winds.

10 Claims • Evidence • Reasoning Make a claim about how pollution from one location can affect the environment far away from the source of the pollution. Summarize evidence to support the claim and explain your reasoning.

_____

_____

_____

_____

Acid Precipitation
These gases dissolve in water vapor, and form sulfuric acids and nitric acids, which fall to Earth as acid precipitation.

How's the AIR?

What are measures of air quality?

Measuring how clean or polluted the air is tells us about **air quality**. Pollutants reduce air quality. Two major threats to air quality are vehicle exhausts and industrial pollutants. The air quality in cities can be poor. As more people move into cities, the cities get bigger. This leads to increased amounts of human-made pollution. Poor air circulation, such as a lack of wind, allows air pollution to stay in one area where it can build up. As pollution increases, air quality decreases.

Air Quality Index

The Air Quality Index (AQI) is a number used to describe the air quality of a location such as a city. The higher the AQI number, the more people are likely to have health problems that are linked to air pollution. Air quality is measured and given a value based on the level of pollution detected. The AQI values are divided into ranges. Each range is given a color code and a description. The Environmental Protection Agency (EPA) has AQIs for the pollutants that pose the greatest risk to public health, including ozone and particulates. The EPA can then issue advisories to avoid exposure to pollution that may harm health.

Indoor Air Pollution

The air inside a building can become more polluted than the air outside. This is because buildings are insulated to prevent outside air from entering the building. Some sources of indoor air pollution include chlorine and ammonia from household cleaners and formaldehyde from furniture. Harmful chemicals can be released from some paints and glues. Radon is a radioactive gas released when uranium decays. Radon can seep into buildings through gaps in their foundations. It can build up inside well-insulated buildings. *Ventilation*, or the mixing of indoor and outside air, can reduce indoor air pollution. Another way to reduce indoor air pollution is to limit the use of items that create the pollution.

Daily Peak Air Quality Index
Tuesday, June 21, 2009
Source: US Environmental Protection Agency

Air Quality Index (AQI) values	Levels of health concern
0–50	Good
51–100	Moderate
101–150	Unhealthy for sensitive groups
151–200	Unhealthy
201–300	Very unhealthy

Source: **US Environmental Protection Agency**

Color codes based on the Air Quality Index show the air quality in different areas.

👁 Visualize It!

11 Recommend If you were a weather reporter using this map, what would you recommend for people living in areas that are colored orange? Explain your reasoning.

_____

_____

_____

_____

12 State Your Claim If this were your house, make a claim about three actions you could take to decrease the sources of indoor air pollution.

Nitrogen oxides from unvented gas stove, wood stove, or kerosene heater

Chlorine and ammonia from household cleaners

Chemicals from dry cleaning

Fungi and bacteria from dirty heating and air conditioning ducts

Chemicals from paint strippers and thinners

Gasoline from car and lawn mower

Formaldehyde from furniture, carpeting, particleboard, and foam insulation

Carbon monoxide from car left running

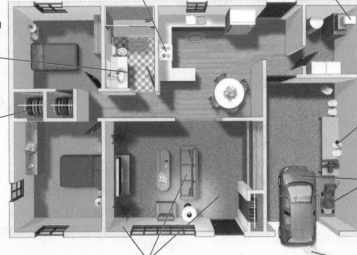

How can air quality affect health?

Daily exposure to small amounts of air pollution can cause serious health problems. Children, elderly people, and people with asthma, allergies, lung problems, and heart problems are especially vulnerable to the effects of air pollution. The short-term effects of air pollution include coughing, headaches, and wheezing. Long-term effects, such as lung cancer and emphysema, are dangerous because they can cause death.

ℹ Think Outside the Book

13 Claims • Evidence • Reasoning Think about the community in which you live. Make a claim about different things in your community and the surrounding areas that might affect the air quality where you live. Summarize evidence to support the claim and explain your reasoning.

Air Pollution and Your Health

Short-term effects	Long-term effects
coughing	asthma
headaches	emphysema
difficulty breathing	allergies
burning/itchy eyes	lung cancer
	chronic bronchitis

14 Identify Imagine you are walking next to a busy road where there are a lot of exhaust fumes. Circle the effects listed in the table that you are most likely to have while walking.

© Houghton Mifflin Harcourt Publishing Company

Things Are CHANGING

How are humans changing Earth's climate?

The burning of fossil fuels releases greenhouse gases, such as carbon dioxide, into the atmosphere. The atmosphere today contains about 43% more carbon dioxide than it did in the mid-1700s, and that level continues to increase. Average global temperatures have also risen in recent decades.

Many people are concerned about how the greenhouse gases from human activities add to the observed trend of increasing global temperatures. Earth's atmosphere and other systems work together in complex ways, so it is hard to know exactly how much the extra greenhouse gases change the temperature. Climate scientists make computer models to understand the effects of climate change. Models predict that average global temperatures are likely to rise another 4.5 °C (8.0 °F) by the year 2100.

A Sunlight (radiant energy) passes through the windows of the car.

B Energy as heat is trapped inside by the windows.

C The temperature inside the car increases.

👁 Visualize It!

15 Synthesize How is a car with closed windows a good analogy of the atmosphere's greenhouse effect?

_____

_____

_____

_____

What are some predicted effects of climate change?

ACTIVE READING

16 Identify As you read, underline some effects of an increasing average global temperature.

Scientists have already noticed many changes linked to warmer temperatures. For example, some glaciers and the Arctic sea ice are melting at the fastest rates ever recorded. A warmer Earth will lead to changes in rainfall patterns, rising sea levels, and possibly more severe storms. These changes will have many negative impacts for life on Earth. Other predicted effects include drought in some regions and increased precipitation in others. Farming practices and the availability of food is also expected to be impacted by increased global temperatures. Such changes will likely have political and economic effects on the world, especially in developing countries.

Melt water pours from an iceberg that broke away from the Jakobshavn Glacier in West Greenland.

How is the ozone layer affected by air pollution?

In the 1980s, scientists reported an alarming discovery about Earth's protective ozone layer. Over the polar regions, the ozone layer was thinning. Chemicals called *chlorofluorocarbons* (klor•oh•flur•oh•kar•buhns) (CFCs) were causing ozone to break down into oxygen, which does not block harmful ultraviolet (UV) rays. The thinning of the ozone layer allows more UV radiation to reach Earth's surface. UV radiation is dangerous to organisms, including humans, as it causes sunburn, damages DNA (which can lead to cancer), and causes eye damage.

CFCs once had many industrial uses, such as coolants in refrigerators and air-conditioning units. CFC use has now been banned, but CFC molecules can stay in the atmosphere for about 100 years. So, CFCs released from a spray can 30 years ago are still harming the ozone layer today.

The dark blue area on this map shows the size of the ozone hole over the South Pole.

17 Infer How might these penguins near the South Pole be affected by the ozone hole?

_____

_____

_____

Source: NASA

Satellite image of Arctic summer sea ice in September 1979.

Source: NASA

Satellite image of Arctic summer sea ice in September 2007.

 18 Claims • Evidence • Reasoning Make a claim about how melting sea ice effects people living in coastal areas. Summarize evidence to support the claim and explain your reasoning.

_____

_____

Visual Summary

To complete this summary, fill in the blanks with the correct word or phrase. You can use this page to review the main concepts of the lesson.

Human activities are a major cause of air pollution.

19 Two types of air pollutants are gases and _____.

Car exhaust is a major source of air pollution in cities.

smog

20 _____ is formed when exhausts and ozone react in the presence of sunlight.

Human Impact on the Atmosphere

Air quality and levels of pollution can be measured.

Air Quality Index (AQI) values	Levels of health concern
0–50	Good
51–100	Moderate
101–150	Unhealthy for sensitive groups
151–200	Unhealthy
201–300	Very unhealthy

21 As pollution increases, _____ decreases.

Climate change may lead to dramatic changes in global weather patterns.

22 The melting of polar ice is one effect of _____.

23 Claims • Evidence • Reasoning Make a claim about the following statement: Each of your breaths, every tree that is planted, and every vehicle on the road affects the composition of the atmosphere. Use evidence to support your claim and explain your reasoning.

_____

_____

Lesson Review

Vocabulary

Draw a line to connect the following terms to their definitions.

1 Air pollution

2 Greenhouse effect

3 Air quality

4 Particulate

5 Smog

A tiny particle of solid that is suspended in air or water

B the contamination of the atmosphere by the introduction of pollutants from human and natural sources

C pollutant that forms when ozone and vehicle exhaust react with sunlight

D a measure of how clean or polluted the air is

E the process by which gases in the atmosphere, such as water vapor and carbon dioxide, absorb and release energy as heat

Key Concepts

6 Identify List three effects that an increase in urbanization can have on air quality.

_____

_____

_____

7 Relate How are ground-level ozone and smog related?

_____

_____

_____

8 Claims • Evidence • Reasoning Make a claim about how human health is affected by changes in air quality. Provide evidence to support the claim, and explain your reasoning.

_____

_____

_____

Critical Thinking

Use this graph to answer the following questions.

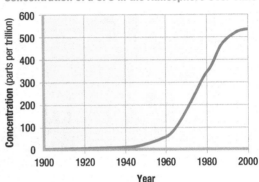

Concentration of a CFC in the Atmosphere Over Time

9 Analyze At what time in the graph did CFCs begin building up in the atmosphere?

_____

_____

10 Synthesize Since the late 1970s, the use of CFCs has been reduced, with a total ban in 2010. But CFCs can stay in the atmosphere for up to 100 years. In the space below, draw a graph showing the concentration of CFCs in the atmosphere over the next 100 years.

11 Claims • Evidence • Reasoning Make a claim about the importance of humans controlling the amount of human-made pollution. Summarize evidence to support the claim, and explain your reasoning.

_____

_____

_____

_____

_____

Protecting Earth's Water, Land, and Air

ESSENTIAL QUESTION

How can Earth's resources be used wisely?

By the end of this lesson, you should be able to summarize the value of conserving Earth's resources and the effect that wise stewardship has on land, water, and air resources.

Picking up litter to clean streams or rivers is one way we can help preserve Earth's natural resources.

SC.7.E.6.6 Identify the impact that humans have had on Earth, such as deforestation, urbanization, desertification, erosion, air and water quality, changing the flow of water.

© Houghton Mifflin Harcourt Publishing Company

© Tim Pannell/Corbis

 Lesson Labs

Quick Labs
• Cleaning Water
• How Can an Oil Spill Be Cleaned Up?
• Soil Erosion

Engage Your Brain

1 Predict Check T or F to show whether you think each statement is true or false.

T	F	
☐	☐	Conservation is the overuse of natural resources.
☐	☐	It is everybody's job to be a good steward of Earth's resources.
☐	☐	Reforestation is the planting of trees to repair degraded lands.
☐	☐	Alternative energy sources, like solar power, increase the amount of pollution released into the air.

2 Describe Have you ever done something to protect a natural resource? Draw a picture showing what you did. Include a caption.

ACTIVE READING

3 Synthesize You can often guess the meaning of a word from its context, or how it is used in a sentence. Use the sentence below to guess the meaning of the word *stewardship*.

Example sentence
Stewardship of water resources will ensure that there is plenty of clean water for future generations.

stewardship:

_____

_____

Vocabulary Terms
• conservation
• stewardship

4 Apply As you learn the definition of each vocabulary term in this lesson, create your own definition or sketch to help remember the meaning of the term.

Keeping It Clean

What are conservation and stewardship?

In the past, some people have used Earth's resources however they wanted, without thinking about the consequences. They thought it didn't matter if they cut down hundreds of thousands of trees or caught millions of fish. They also thought it didn't matter if they dumped trash into bodies of water. Now we know that it does matter how we use resources. Humans greatly affect the land, water, and air. If we wish to keep using our resources in the future, we need to conserve and care for them.

ACTIVE READING

5 Identify As you read, underline the definitions of *conservation* and *stewardship*.

○ Conservation: Wise Use of Resources

Conservation (kahn•sur•VAY•shuhn) is the wise use of natural resources. By practicing conservation, we can help make sure that resources will still be around for future generations. It is up to everybody to conserve and protect resources. When we use energy or create waste, we can harm the environment. If we conserve whenever we can, we reduce the harm we do to the environment. We can use less energy by turning off lights, computers, and appliances. We can reuse shopping bags, as in the picture below. We can recycle whenever possible, instead of just throwing things away. By doing these things, we take fewer resources from Earth and put less pollution into the water, land, and air.

👁 Visualize It!

6 Describe How are the people in the picture below practicing conservation?

_____

_____

_____

This old tire is being used as a planter instead of being thrown away.

○ Stewardship: Managing Resources

Stewardship (stoo•urd•SHIP) is the careful and responsible management of a resource. If we are not good stewards, we will use up a resource or pollute it. Stewardship of Earth's resources will ensure that the environment stays clean enough to help keep people and other living things healthy. Stewardship is everybody's job. Governments pass laws that protect water, land, and air. These laws determine how resources can be used and what materials can be released into the environment. Individuals can also act as stewards. For example, you can plant trees or help clean up a habitat in your community. Any action that helps to maintain or improve the environment is an act of stewardship.

7 Compare Fill in the Venn diagram to compare and contrast conservation and stewardship.

Stewardship

Both

Conservation

Turning empty lots into gardens improves the environment and provides people with healthy food.

Sea turtles are endangered. Scientists help sea turtles that have just hatched find their way to the sea.

👁 Visualize It!

8 Identify How is the person in the picture to the right practicing stewardship?

_____

_____

_____

Water Wise!

How can we preserve water resources?

Most of the Earth's surface is covered by water, so you might think there is lots of water for humans to use. However, there is actually very little fresh water on Earth, so people should use freshwater resources very carefully. People should also be careful to avoid polluting water, because the quality of water is important to the health of both humans and ecosystems. Because water is so important to our health, we need to keep it clean!

○ By Conserving Water

If we want to make sure there is enough water for future generations, we need to reduce the amount of water we use. In some places, if people aren't careful about using water wisely, there soon won't be enough water for everyone. There are many ways to reduce water usage. We can use low-flow toilets and showerheads. We can take shorter showers. In agriculture and landscaping, we can reduce water use by installing efficient irrigation systems. We can also use plants that don't need much water. Only watering lawns the amount they need and following watering schedules saves water. The photo below shows a simple way to use less water—just turn off the tap while brushing your teeth!

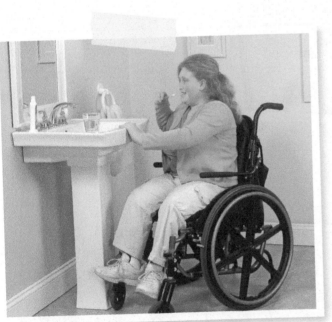

Do the Math

You Try It

9 Calculate How much fresh water is on Earth?

Solve

Each square on the grid equals 1%. Use the grid to fill in the percentage of each type of water found on Earth.

Earth's Water

☐ Salt water _____

☐ Ice (fresh water) _____

☐ Fresh liquid water _____

10 State Your Claim Make a claim about some ways you can reduce the amount of water you use.

- *Turn off the tap when brushing my teeth.*

- _____
  _____

- _____
  _____

- _____
  _____

© Houghton Mifflin Harcourt Publishing Company

◯ With Water Stewardship

Humans and ecosystems need clean water. The diagram below shows how a community keeps its drinking water clean. The main way to protect drinking water is to keep pollution from entering streams, lakes, and other water sources. Laws like the Clean Water Act and Safe Drinking Water Act were passed to protect water sources. These laws indicate how clean drinking water must be and limit the types of chemicals that businesses and private citizens can release into water. These laws also help finance water treatment facilities. We can help protect water by not throwing chemicals in the trash or dumping them down the drain. We can also use nontoxic chemicals whenever possible. Reducing the amount of fertilizer we use on our gardens also reduces water pollution.

For healthy ecosystems and safe drinking water, communities need to protect water sources. The first step to protecting water sources is keeping them from becoming polluted.

Protecting Water Resources

Water testing makes sure water is safe for people to drink. It also helps us find out if there is a pollution problem that needs to be fixed.

Water treatment plants remove pollution from wastewater before it is reused or put back into the environment.

Without clean water to drink, people can get sick. Clean water is also important for agriculture and natural ecosystems.

👁 Visualize It!

11 Claims • Evidence • Reasoning
Make a claim about what steps a community should take to manage its water resources. Use evidence to support your claim and explain your reasoning.

_____

_____

This Land Is Your Land

ACTIVE READING

12 Identify As you read this page and the next, underline ways that we can protect land resources.

How can we preserve land resources?

People rely on land resources for recreation, agriculture, transportation, commerce, industry, and housing. If we manage land resources carefully, we can make sure that these resources will be around for generations and continue to provide resources for humans to use. We also need to make sure that there are habitats for wild animals. To do all these things, we must protect land resources from overuse and pollution. Sometimes we need to repair damage that is already done.

○ Through Preservation

Preservation of land resources is very important. *Preservation* means protecting land from being damaged or changed. Local, state, and national parks protect many natural areas. These parks help ensure that many species survive. Small parks can protect some species. Other species, such as predators, need larger areas. For example, wolves roam over hundreds of miles and would not be protected by small parks. By protecting areas big enough for large predators, we also protect habitats for many other species.

Yosemite National Park is one of the oldest national parks in the country. Like other national, state, and local parks, Yosemite was formed to preserve natural habitats.

Think Outside the Book

13 Claims • Evidence • Reasoning
Plant and animal species depend on land resources. Make a claim about how you can help an endangered plant or animal species living in your area. Summarize evidence to support the claim and explain your reasoning

Through Reforestation

People use the wood from trees for many things. We use it to make paper and to build houses. We also use wood to heat homes and cook food. In many places, huge areas of forest were cut down to use the wood and nothing was done to replant the forests. Now when we cut trees down, they are often replanted, as in the picture at right. We also plant trees in areas where forests disappeared many years ago in order to help bring the forests back. The process of planting trees to reestablish forestland is called *reforestation*. Reforestation is important, but we can't cut down all forests and replant them. It is important to keep some old forests intact for the animals that need them to survive.

Through Reclamation

In order to use some resources, such as coal, metal, and minerals, the resources first have to be dug out of the ground. In the process, the land is damaged. Sometimes, large areas of land are cleared and pits are dug to reach the resource. Land can also be damaged in other ways, including by development and agriculture. *Reclamation* is the process by which a damaged land area is returned to nearly the condition it was in before people used it. Land reclamation, shown in the lower right photo, is required for mines in many states once the mines are no longer in use. Many national and state laws, such as the Surface Mining and Reclamation Act and the Resource Conservation and Recovery Act, guide land reclamation.

Reforestation

A mine being reclaimed

👁 Visualize It!

14 Claims • Evidence • Reasoning Make claims about the similarities between reforestation and reclamation. Summarize evidence to support your claims and explain your reasoning

_____

_____

_____

_____

One way to reduce urban sprawl is to locate homes and businesses close together.

○ Through Reducing Urban Sprawl

Urban sprawl is the outward spread of suburban areas around cities. As we build more houses and businesses across a wider area, there is less land for native plants and animals. Reducing urban sprawl helps to protect land resources. One way to reduce sprawl is to locate more people and businesses in a smaller area. A good way to do this is with vertical development—that means constructing taller buildings. Homes, businesses, and even recreational facilities can be placed within high-rise buildings. We also can reduce sprawl using mixed-use development. This development creates communities with businesses and houses very close to one another. Mixed-use communities are also better for the environment, because people can walk to work instead of driving.

○ Through Recycling

Recycling is one of the most important things we can do to preserve land resources. *Recycling* is the process of recovering valuable materials from waste or scrap. We can recycle many of the materials that we use. By recycling materials like metal, plastic, paper, and glass, we use fewer raw materials. Recycling aluminum cans reduces the amount of bauxite that is mined. We use bauxite in aluminum smelting. Everyone can help protect land resources by recycling. Lots of people throw away materials that can be recycled. Find out what items you can recycle!

Bauxite mine

15 Apply Aluminum is mined from the ground. Recycling aluminum cans decreases the need for mining bauxite. Paper can also be recycled. How does recycling paper preserve trees?

_____

_____

⃝ Through Using Soil Conservation Methods

Soil conservation protects soil from erosion or degradation by overuse or pollution. For example, farmers change the way they plow in order to conserve soil. Contour plowing creates ridges of soil across slopes. The small ridges keep water from eroding soils. In strip cropping, two types of crops are planted in rows next to each other to reduce erosion. Terracing is used on steep hills to prevent erosion. Areas of the hill are flattened to grow crops. This creates steps down the side of the hill. *Crop rotation* means that crops with different needs are planted in alternating seasons. This reduces the prevalence of plant diseases and makes sure there are nutrients for each crop. It also ensures that plants are growing in the soil almost year-round. In no-till farming, soils are not plowed between crop plantings. Stalks and cover crops keep water in the soils and reduce erosion by stopping soil from being blown away.

ACTIVE READING

16 Identify As you read this page, underline five methods of soil conservation.

👁 Visualize It!

Terracing involves building leveled areas, or steps, to grow crops on.

In contour plowing, crop rows are planted in curved lines along land's natural contours.

Strip cropping prevents erosion by creating natural dams that stop water from rushing over a field.

17 Analyze Which two soil conservation techniques would be best to use on gentle slopes?

☐ contour plowing

☐ crop terracing

☐ strip cropping

18 Analyze Which soil conservation technique would be best to use on very steep slopes?

☐ contour plowing

☐ crop terracing

☐ strip cropping

Into Thin Air

19 Identify Underline the sentences that explain the relationship between burning fossil fuels and air pollution.

How can we reduce air pollution?

Polluted air can make people sick and harm organisms. Air pollution can cause the atmosphere to change in ways that are harmful to the environment and to people. There are many ways that we can reduce air pollution. We can use less energy. Also, we can develop new ways to get energy that produces less pollution. Everybody can help reduce air pollution in many different ways.

◯ Through Energy Conservation

Energy conservation is one of the most important ways to reduce air pollution. Fossil fuels are currently the most commonly used energy resource. When they are burned, they release pollution into the air. If we use less energy, we burn fewer fossil fuels.

There are lots of ways to conserve energy. We can turn off lights when we don't need them. We can use energy-efficient lightbulbs and appliances. We can use air conditioners less in the summer and heaters less in the winter. We can unplug electronics when they are not in use. Instead of driving ourselves to places, we can use public transportation. We can also develop alternative energy sources that create less air pollution. Using wind, solar, and geothermal energy will help us burn less fossil fuel.

Using public transportation, riding a bike, sharing rides, and walking reduce the amount of air pollution produced by cars.

Many cities, such as Los Angeles, California, have air pollution problems.

Energy can be produced with very little pollution. These solar panels help us use energy from the sun and replace the use of fossil fuels.

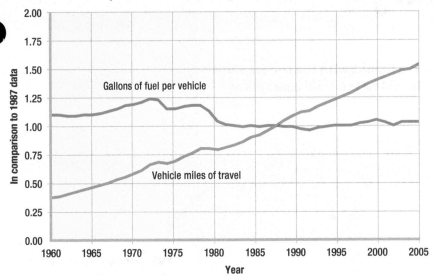

Vehicle Fuel Consumption and Miles Traveled, 1960–2005

Gallons of fuel per vehicle

Vehicle miles of travel

In comparison to 1987 data

Year

Source: U.S. Department of Transportation

👁 Visualize It!

20 Claims • Evidence • Reasoning
Make a claim about how vehicle fuel consumption in comparison to miles traveled has changed since 1960. Use evidence to support your claim and explain your reasoning.

_____

_____

_____

_____

_____

_____

⚪ Through Technology

There are lots of ways to generate energy without creating much air pollution. By developing these alternative energy sources, we can reduce the amount of pollution created by burning fossil fuels. Wind turbines generate clean power. So do solar panels that use energy from the sun. We also can use power created by water flowing through rivers or moving with the tides. Geothermal energy from heat in Earth's crust can be used to generate electricity. Hybrid cars get energy from their brakes and store it in batteries. They burn less gas and release less pollution. Driving smaller cars that can go farther on a gallon of gas also reduces air pollution.

⚪ Through Laws

Governments in many countries work independently and together to reduce air pollution. They monitor air quality and set limits on what can be released into the air. In the United States, the Clean Air Act limits the amount of toxic chemicals and other pollutants that can be released into the atmosphere by factories and vehicles. It is up to the Environmental Protection Agency to make sure that these limits are enforced. Because air isn't contained by borders, some solutions must be international. The Kyoto Protocol is a worldwide effort to limit the release of greenhouse gases— pollution that can warm the atmosphere.

21 Summarize List three ways air pollution can be reduced.

• _____

_____

• _____

_____

• _____

_____

New technologies, such as this compact fluorescent lightbulb (CFL), help limit air pollution. CFL bulbs use less energy to make the same amount of light.

Visual Summary

To complete this summary, fill in the blanks with the correct word or phrase. You can use this page to review the main concepts of the lesson.

Protecting Water, Land, and Air

Water resources are important to our health.

22 A community's water supply can be protected by:
- conserving water
- preventing pollution
- _____
- treating wastewater

Land resources are used to grow food and make products.

23 Land resources can be protected by:
- preservation
- reclamation and reforestation
- reducing urban sprawl
- _____
- soil conservation

Everybody needs clean air to breathe.

24 The main way to reduce air pollution is to:

_____

_____

_____

_____

_____

_____

25 **Claims • Evidence • Reasoning** Make claims about how you personally act as a steward of water, land, and air resources. Summarize evidence to support your claims and explain your reasoning

Lesson Review

Vocabulary

Fill in the blank with the term that best completes the following sentences.

1 _____ is the wise use of natural resources.

2 _____ is the careful and responsible management of a resource.

Key Concepts

3 Claims • Evidence • Reasoning How can water pollution be prevented? Use evidence to support your claims and explain your reasoning.

_____

_____

_____

Fill in the table below.

Example	Type of land resource conservation
4 Identify A county creates a park to protect a forest.	
5 Identify A mining company puts soil back in the hole and plants grass seeds on top of it.	
6 Identify A logging company plants new trees after it has cut some down.	
7 Identify A plastic milk bottle is turned into planks for a boardwalk to the beach.	
8 Identify Instead of building lots of single houses, a city builds an apartment building with a grocery store.	

9 Gather Evidence Technology has helped decrease air pollution in recent years. Summarize evidence to support this claim.

_____

_____

10 State Your Claim Make a claim about why it is important to protect Earth's water, land, and air resources.

_____

_____

Critical Thinking

11 Claims • Evidence • Reasoning Land reclamation can be expensive. Make a claim about how recycling materials can lead to spending less money on reclamation. Summarize evidence to explain your reasoning.

_____

_____

_____

Use the graph to answer the following question.

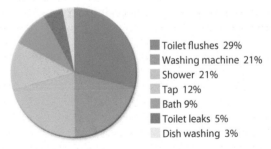

Average Water Usage of U.S. Household

- Toilet flushes 29%
- Washing machine 21%
- Shower 21%
- Tap 12%
- Bath 9%
- Toilet leaks 5%
- Dish washing 3%

12 Analyze The graph above shows water use in the average U.S. household. Using the graph, identify three effective ways a household could conserve water.

_____

_____

_____

Protecting Earth's Water, Land, and Air —is important to preserve→ **Natural Resources**

Natural Resources are affected by **Human Impact on Land**

Human Impact on the Atmosphere

Human Impact on Water

1 Interpret The Graphic Organizer above shows that humans can have an impact on Earth's natural resources. List two examples of ways in which humans can have an impact on natural resources.

_____

_____

_____

_____

_____

2 Integrate How can erosion on land impact water quality?

_____

_____

_____

_____

3 Claims • Evidence • Reasoning Make a claim about how increasing human population affects land resources, water resources, and the atmosphere. Summarize evidence to support your claim and explain your reasoning.

_____

_____

_____

_____

_____

_____

_____

_____

_____

_____

_____

_____

Vocabulary

Name _____

Check the box to show whether each statement is true or false.

T	F		
☐	☐	**1**	Air quality is a measure of how clean or polluted the air is.
☐	☐	**2**	Potable water is suitable for drinking.
☐	☐	**3**	Conservation is the wise use of natural resources.
☐	☐	**4**	Land degradation is the process by which humans restore damaged land so that it can support the local ecosystem.
☐	☐	**5**	Stewardship of Earth's resources helps make sure that the environment remains healthy.

Key Concepts

Identify the choice that best completes the statement or answers the question.

6 Ms. Chan drew the picture below, which shows a common landscaping practice.

How can this practice cause pollution?

A It pollutes nearby soil when animals track mud from one place to another.

B It pollutes drinking water in the home when chemicals seep into underground pipes.

C It pollutes water when runoff carries chemicals from the soil to local streams and lakes.

D It pollutes the air above the location when chemicals break down and produce gases.

7 Andrea would like to start an environmental conservation club at her school. She is making a poster to describe what the club will do. Which activity could she list that would be part of conservation?

F Learn how to save water.

G Learn how to nurse a sick pet.

H Learn how to build a campfire.

I Learn how to balance a budget.

8 The atmosphere helps regulate Earth's temperature so that life can exist. It also provides the oxygen and carbon dioxide that organisms need to live. Air is an important natural resource that forms part of the atmosphere. Which of these statements provides a **main** reason that air is an important natural resource?

A Air affects surface currents in the oceans.

B Air gives animals and humans a means of transportation.

C Air protects organisms from harmful radiation from the sun.

D Air provides a way for harmful pollutants to move away from Earth.

9 Erosion is the process by which soil and sediment are moved from one place to another. Erosion takes place naturally, but it can be accelerated by human activity. Which of these human activities **least** contributes to land erosion?

F urban sprawl

G planting trees

H surface mining

I improper plowing of furrows

10 The town of Winchester recently built a reservoir that will store drinking water for the town. Which of the following could cause contamination of the water and lead to health-related problems?

A water stewardship

B a water treatment facility

C increase in fertilizer use

D use of nontoxic chemicals

Name _____

11 Air pollution makes it difficult for some people to breathe. It can also cause serious health problems like asthma and allergies. Which of these choices gives the **best** description of air pollution?

F the circulating of pollutants in enclosed spaces

G the long-term health issues related to the quality of the air in cities

H the contamination of the atmosphere by pollutants from human and natural sources

I the pollution that results from changes in the atmosphere, such as the rate of global warming

12 The ozone hole is an area of depleted ozone in Earth's atmosphere. It forms over the Antarctic at the beginning of spring in the Southern Hemisphere, which is August. Which of the following human activities has the **greatest** effect on the ozone in Earth's atmosphere?

A the use of oil in automobile engines

B the use of airplanes in the atmosphere

C the use of satellites in orbit around Earth

D the use of chlorofluorocarbons in refrigeration

13 Ignacio plans to start a recycling program in his neighborhood. He wants to begin by collecting waste materials, such as glass bottles and metal cans. To convince people to help out, he makes a poster explaining how recycling benefits his community. How could recycling waste materials benefit a community?

F It reduces the amount of work that people must do to get rid of wastes.

G It reduces the amount of land area that would be mined for new materials.

H It reduces the amount of land used for storing and recycling waste materials.

I It reduces the amount of energy used because no energy is needed to recycle materials.

Critical Thinking

Answer the following questions in the space provide.

14   The atmosphere is important to life on Earth. Could it be considered a natural
resource? Use at least two examples as evidence to support your claim and
explain your reasoning.

_____

_____

_____

_____

15   The picture below is of a dam built on a river.

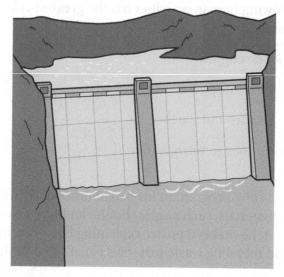

How does a dam affect the surrounding landscape behind and in front of the dam?
Explain your reasoning.

_____

_____

How does a dam affect the fish that live breed in that river? Explain your reasoning.

_____

_____

Energy in the Earth System

Waves transfer energy to the beach, which removes sand.

FLORIDA **BIG IDEA?**

Earth Systems and Patterns

What Do You Think?

In many places, the beach is being washed away by ocean waves and currents. Town officials in those areas often opt for expensive, beach re-nourishment plans where offshore sand is dredged and placed on the beach. They argue that it is necessary for tourism because people love to visit the beach. In contrast, environmentalists argue that this is a useless plan. As you explore this unit, gather evidence to help you state and support or refute the environmentalist claim.

Energy in the Earth System

CITIZEN SCIENCE

Clearing the Air

In some areas, there are many vehicles on the roads every day. Some of the gases from vehicle exhaust react with sunlight to form ozone. There are days when the concentration of ozone is so high that it becomes a health hazard. Those days are especially difficult for people who have problems breathing. What can you do to reduce gas emissions?

1 Think About It

A How do you get to school every day?

_____

_____

B How many of the students in your class come to school by car?

_____

Gas emissions are high during rush-hour traffic.

② Ask a Question

How can you reduce the number of vehicles students use to get to school one day each month?

With your teacher and classmates, brainstorm different ways in which you can reduce the number of vehicles students use to get to school.

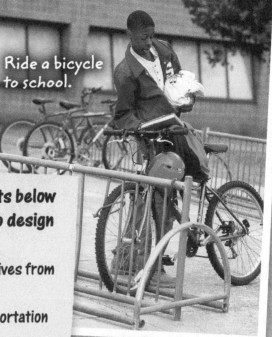

Ride a bicycle to school.

Check off the points below as you use them to design your plan.

☐ how far a student lives from school

☐ the kinds of transportation students may have available to them

③ Make a Plan

A Write down different ways that you can reduce the number of vehicles that bring students to school.

_____
_____
_____
_____
_____
_____
_____

B Create a short presentation for your principal that outlines how the whole school could become involved in your vehicle-reduction plan. Write down the points of your presentation in the space below.

_____
_____
_____
_____
_____
_____
_____

C In the space below, design a sign-up sheet that your classmates will use to choose how they will come to school on the designated day.

 Take It Home!

Give your presentation to an adult. Then have them brainstorm ways in which they can reduce gas emissions every day.

Earth's Spheres

ESSENTIAL **QUESTION**

How do matter and energy move through Earth's spheres?

By the end of this lesson, you should be able to describe Earth's spheres, give examples of their interactions, and explain the flow of energy that makes up Earth's energy budget.

Emperor penguins spend time on land and need to breathe in oxygen from the air.

These penguins also swim and hold their breath for about 18 minutes as they hunt for fish. What do you have in common with these penguins?

SC.6.E.7.4 Differentiate and show interactions among the geosphere, hydrosphere, cryosphere, atmosphere, and biosphere.

Lesson Labs

Quick Labs
- Explaining Earth's Systems
- Analyzing Weather Patterns

S.T.E.M. Lab
- Change and Balance Between Spheres

 Engage Your Brain

1 Predict Check T or F to show whether you think each statement is true or false.

T F
- ☐ ☐ Earth is made up completely of solid rocks.
- ☐ ☐ Animals live only on land.
- ☐ ☐ Water in rivers often flows into the ocean.
- ☐ ☐ Air in the atmosphere can move all over the world.

2 Analyze Think about your daily activities, and list some of the ways in which you interact with Earth.

_____

_____

_____

_____

_____

_____

_____

ACTIVE **READING**

3 Synthesize You can often define an unknown word if you know the meaning of its word parts. Use the word parts and sentence below to make an educated guess about the meaning of the word *geosphere*.

Word part	Meaning
geo-	earth
-sphere	ball

Example sentence:
Water flows across the surface of the geosphere.

geosphere:

_____

_____

Vocabulary Terms

- Earth system
- geosphere
- hydrosphere
- cryosphere
- atmosphere
- biosphere
- energy budget

4 Apply As you learn the definition of each vocabulary term in this lesson, create your own notecards to help you remember the meaning of the term.

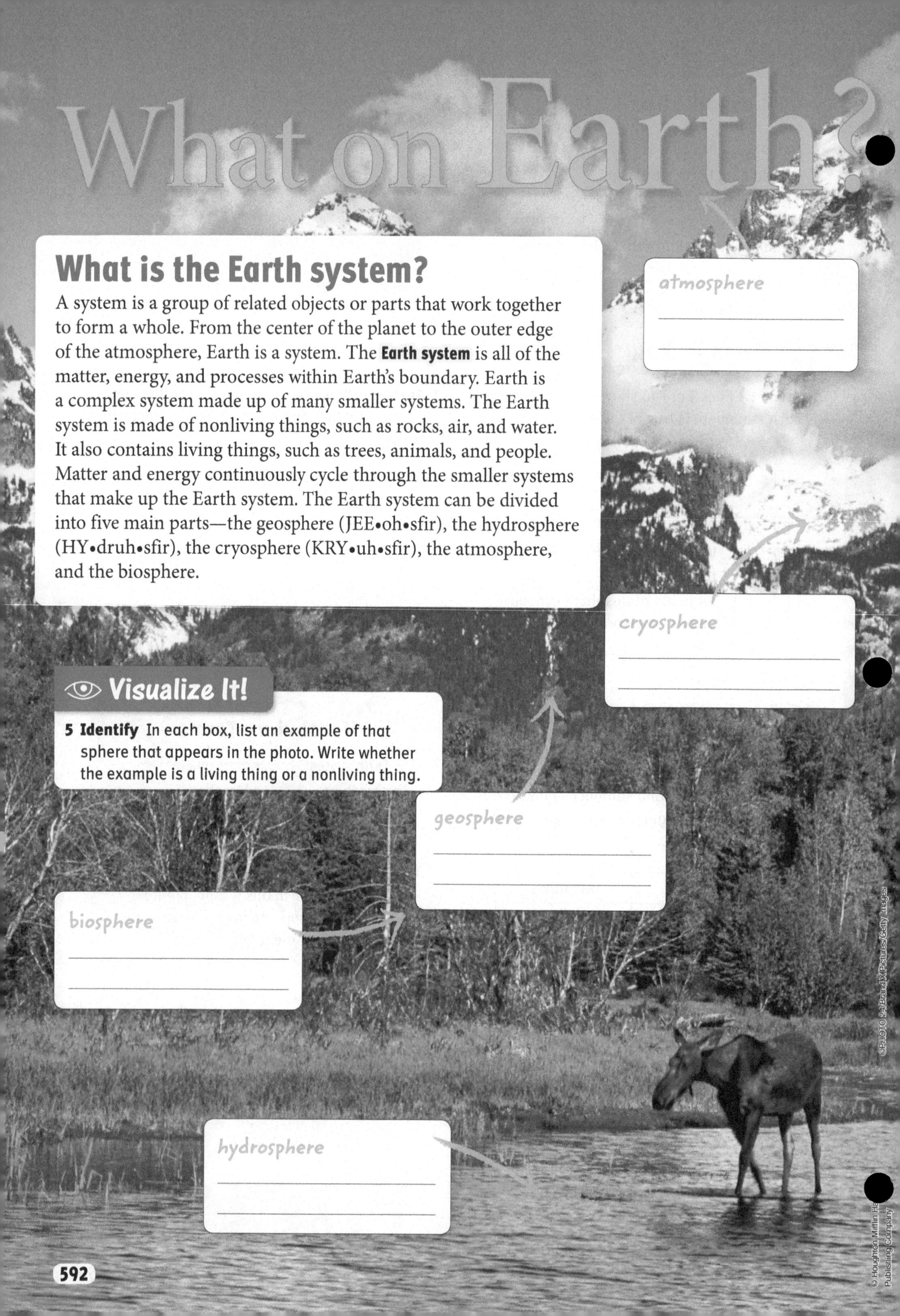

What is the Earth system?

A system is a group of related objects or parts that work together to form a whole. From the center of the planet to the outer edge of the atmosphere, Earth is a system. The **Earth system** is all of the matter, energy, and processes within Earth's boundary. Earth is a complex system made up of many smaller systems. The Earth system is made of nonliving things, such as rocks, air, and water. It also contains living things, such as trees, animals, and people. Matter and energy continuously cycle through the smaller systems that make up the Earth system. The Earth system can be divided into five main parts—the geosphere (JEE•oh•sfir), the hydrosphere (HY•druh•sfir), the cryosphere (KRY•uh•sfir), the atmosphere, and the biosphere.

atmosphere
_____
_____

cryosphere
_____
_____

👁 Visualize It!

5 Identify In each box, list an example of that sphere that appears in the photo. Write whether the example is a living thing or a nonliving thing.

geosphere
_____
_____

biosphere
_____
_____

hydrosphere
_____
_____

What is the geosphere?

ACTIVE READING

6 Identify As you read, underline what each of the three different compositional layers of the geosphere is made up of.

The **geosphere** is the mostly solid, rocky part of Earth. It extends from the center of Earth to the surface of Earth. The geosphere is divided into three layers based on chemical composition: the crust, the mantle, and the core.

The thin, outermost layer of the geosphere is called the crust. It is made mostly of silicate minerals. The crust beneath the oceans is called oceanic crust and is only 5 to 10 km thick. The continents are made of continental crust and range in thickness from about 35 to 70 km. Continental crust is thickest beneath mountain ranges.

The mantle lies below the crust. The mantle is made of hot, very slow-flowing, solid rock. The mantle is about 2,900 km thick. It is made of silicate minerals that are denser than the silicates in the crust.

The central part of Earth is the core, which has a radius of about 3,500 km. It is made of iron and nickel and is the densest layer. The core is actually composed of a solid inner core and a liquid outer core.

Crust
The crust is the thin, rigid outermost layer of Earth.

Mantle
The mantle is the hot layer of rock between Earth's crust and core. The mantle is denser than Earth's crust.

Core
The core is Earth's center. The core is about twice as dense as the mantle.

7 Summarize Fill in the table below with the characteristics of each of the geosphere's compositional layers.

Compositional layer	Thickness	Relative density
crust	5–10 km (oceanic) 35–70 km (continental)	least dense

Got Water?

What is the hydrosphere?

The **hydrosphere** is the part of Earth that is liquid water. Ninety-seven percent of all of the water on Earth is the salt water found in the oceans. Oceans cover 71% of Earth's surface. The hydrosphere also includes the fresh water in lakes, rivers, and marshes. Rain and the water droplets in clouds are also parts of the hydrosphere. Even water that is underground is part of the hydrosphere.

The water on Earth is constantly moving. It moves through the ocean in currents because of wind and differences in the density of ocean waters. Water also moves from Earth's surface to the air by evaporation. It falls back to Earth as rain. It flows in rivers and through rocks under the ground. It even moves into and out of living things.

ACTIVE READING

8 Identify What are two things through which water moves?

_____

_____

👁 Visualize It!

9 Claims • Evidence • Reasoning After your read, make a claim about which sphere the water in each photo is part of. Support your claim with evidence and explain your reasoning.

A

Water droplets form clouds.

Water flows over Earth's surface.

B

What is the cryosphere?

Earth's **cryosphere** is made up of all of the frozen water on Earth. Therefore, all of the ice, sea ice, glaciers, ice shelves, and icebergs are a part of the cryosphere. So is permafrost, the frozen ground found at high latitudes. Most of the frozen water on Earth is found in the ice caps in Antarctica and in the Arctic. However, glaciers are found in mountains and at high latitudes all over the world. The amount of frozen water in most of these areas often changes with the seasons. These changes, in turn, play an important role in Earth's climate and in the survival of many species.

10 Compare Fill in the Venn diagram to compare and contrast the hydrosphere and the cryosphere.

Hydrosphere   Both   Cryosphere

Ships can get stuck in sea ice.

C

D

Water moves in ocean currents across huge distances.

What a Gas!

What is the atmosphere?

The **atmosphere** is mostly made of invisible gases that surround Earth. The atmosphere extends outward about 500 to 600 km from the surface of Earth. But most of the gases lie within 8 to 50 km of Earth's surface. The main gases that make up the atmosphere are nitrogen and oxygen. About 78% of the atmosphere is nitrogen. Oxygen makes up 21% of the atmosphere. The remaining 1% is made of many other gases, including argon, carbon dioxide, and water vapor.

The atmosphere contains the air we breathe. The atmosphere also absorbs some of the energy from the sun's rays. This energy helps keep Earth warm enough for living things to survive and multiply. Uneven warming by the sun gives rise to winds and air currents that move air and energy around the world.

Some gases in the atmosphere absorb and reflect harmful ultraviolet (UV) rays from the sun, protecting Earth and its living things. The atmosphere also causes space debris to burn up before reaching Earth's surface and causing harm. Have you ever seen the tail of a meteor across the sky? Then you have seen a meteoroid burning up as it moves through the atmosphere!

Do the Math

You Try It

11 Identify Fill in the blank in the key with the percentage of oxygen in the atmosphere.

The Composition of the Atmosphere

- ■ Nitrogen 78%
- □ Oxygen _____%
- ■ Other gases 1%

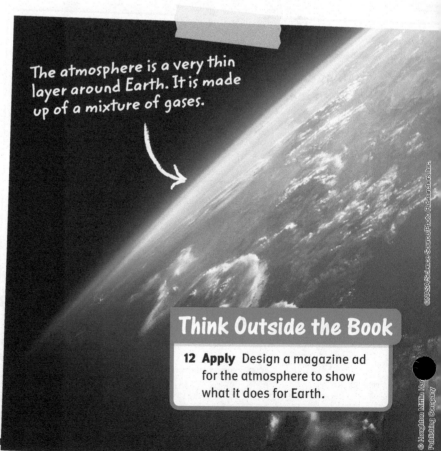

The atmosphere is a very thin layer around Earth. It is made up of a mixture of gases.

Think Outside the Book

12 Apply Design a magazine ad for the atmosphere to show what it does for Earth.

© Houghton Mifflin Harcourt Publishing Company

What is the biosphere?

The **biosphere** is made up of living things and the areas of Earth where they are found. The rocks, soil, oceans, lakes, rivers, and lower atmosphere all support life. Organisms have even been found deep in Earth's crust and high in clouds. But no matter where they live, all organisms need certain factors to survive.

Many organisms need oxygen or carbon dioxide to carry out life processes. Liquid water is also important for most living things. Many organisms also need moderate temperatures. You will not find a polar bear living in the Sahara, because it is too hot for the bear. However, some organisms do live in extreme environments, such as in ice at the poles and at volcanic vents on the sea floor.

A stable source of energy is also important for life. For example, plants and algae use the energy from sunlight to make their food. Other organisms get their energy by eating these plants or algae.

ACTIVE **READING**

13 Identify What factors are needed for life?

_____

_____

These giant tubeworms live on the deep ocean floor where it is pitch dark. The tubeworms depend on nutrients produced by bacteria that grow inside their bodies. The bacteria take in compounds from the water and turn them into forms the worms can use.

The hair on the sloth looks green because it has algae in it. The green color helps the sloth hide from predators. This is very useful because the sloth moves very, very slowly.

(tr, b) ©Houghton Mifflin Harcourt Publishing Company. (cr) ©Blaine Harrington III/Corbis, (sloth) ©Gardner/Alamy, (crabs) ©OAR/National Undersea Research Program (NURP); Texas A&M Univ.

i ◉ **Visualize It!**

14 Claims • Evidence • Reasoning After your read, make a claim about what would happen if the biosphere in this picture stopped interacting with the atmosphere. Use evidence to support your claim and explain your reasoning.

_____

_____

_____

_____

_____

_____

_____

What's the Matter?

How do Earth's spheres interact?

Earth's spheres interact as matter and energy change and cycle between the five different spheres. A result of these interactions is that they make life on Earth possible. Remember that the Earth system includes all of the matter, energy, and processes within Earth's boundary.

If matter or energy never changed from one form to another, life on Earth would not be possible. Imagine what would happen if there were no more rain and all of the freshwater drained into the oceans. Most of the life on land would quickly die. But how do these different spheres interact? An example of an interaction is when water cycles between land, ocean, air, and living things. To move between these different spheres, water absorbs, releases, and transports energy all over the world in its different forms.

Rain provides water for living things.

Ⓐ

Decomposing organisms release nutrients into the soil.

Ⓑ

By Exchanging Matter

Earth's spheres interact as matter moves between spheres. For example, the atmosphere interacts with the hydrosphere or cryosphere when water vapor condenses to form clouds. An interaction also happens as water from the hydrosphere or cryosphere evaporates to enter the atmosphere.

In some processes, matter moves through several spheres. For example, some bacteria in the biosphere remove nitrogen gas from the atmosphere. These bacteria then release a different form of nitrogen into the soil, or geosphere. Plants in the biosphere use this nitrogen to grow. When the plant dies and decays, the nitrogen is released in several forms. One of these forms returns to the atmosphere.

ACTIVE READING

16 Identify What is the relationship between Earth's spheres and matter?

_____

By Exchanging Energy

Earth's spheres also interact as energy moves between them. For example, plants use solar energy to make their food. Some of this energy is passed on to animals that eat plants. Some of the energy is released into the atmosphere as heat as the animals move. Some energy is released into the geosphere when organisms die and decay. In this case, energy has entered the biosphere and moved into the atmosphere and geosphere.

Energy also moves back and forth between spheres. For example, solar energy re-emitted by Earth's surface warms up the atmosphere, creating winds. Winds create waves and surface ocean currents that travel across Earth's oceans. When warm winds and ocean currents reach colder areas, thermal energy is transferred to the colder air and water, and warms them up. In this case, the energy has cycled between the atmosphere and the hydrosphere.

Icebergs melt in the sun.

D

Waves break where the sea floor is shallow.

C

Balancing the Budget

What is the source of Earth's energy?

ACTIVE READING

17 Identify As you read, underline the sources of Earth's energy.

Almost all of Earth's energy comes from the sun. Part of this solar energy is reflected into space. The rest is absorbed by Earth's surface. A tiny fraction of Earth's energy comes from ocean tides and geothermal sources such as lava and magma.

Energy on Earth moves through and between the five Earth spheres. These spheres are open systems that constantly exchange energy with each other. Energy is transferred between spheres, but it is not created anew or destroyed. It simply moves between spheres or changes into other forms of energy.

In any system, input must equal output in order to keep the system balanced. The same is true for the flow of energy through Earth's spheres. In Earth's energy system, any addition in energy must be balanced by an equal subtraction of energy. For example, energy taken away from the atmosphere may be added to the oceans or to the geosphere. Earth's **energy budget** is a way to keep track of energy transfers into and out of the Earth system.

The chart on the next page shows the net flow of energy that forms Earth's energy budget. Energy from the sun may be reflected back to space or absorbed by Earth's surface. Earth radiates energy into space in the form of heat.

When Earth's energy flow is balanced, global temperatures stay relatively stable over long periods of time. But sometimes changes in the system cause Earth's energy budget to become unbalanced.

The sun is Earth's main source of energy.

Think Outside the Book

18 Claims • Evidence • Reasoning
Make a claim about how energy can never be created or destroyed. Summarize evidence to support the claim by an example in your daily life and explain your reasoning.

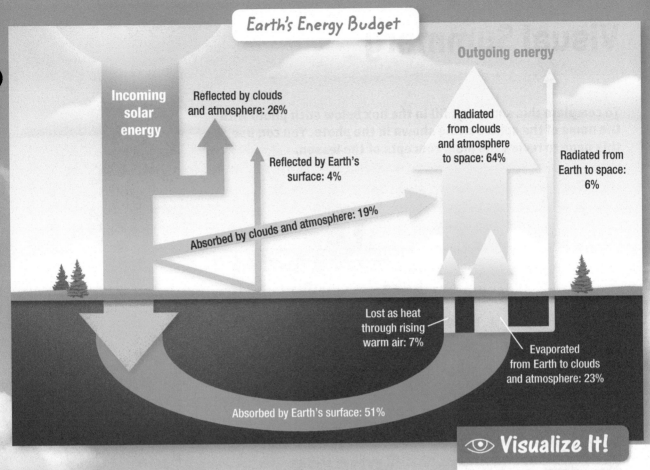

Earth's Energy Budget

Incoming solar energy

Reflected by clouds and atmosphere: 26%

Reflected by Earth's surface: 4%

Absorbed by clouds and atmosphere: 19%

Outgoing energy

Radiated from clouds and atmosphere to space: 64%

Radiated from Earth to space: 6%

Lost as heat through rising warm air: 7%

Evaporated from Earth to clouds and atmosphere: 23%

Absorbed by Earth's surface: 51%

👁 **Visualize It!**

19 Describe Describe what happens to solar energy as it enters Earth's atmosphere.

_____

_____

_____

What can disturb Earth's energy budget?

An unbalanced energy budget can increase or decrease global temperatures and disrupt the balance of energy in Earth's system. Two things that can disturb Earth's energy budget are an increase in greenhouse gases and a decrease in polar ice caps.

Greenhouse Gases

Greenhouse gases, such as carbon dioxide and water vapor, absorb energy from Earth's surface and keep that energy in the atmosphere. An increase in greenhouse gases decreases the amount of energy radiated out to space. Earth's temperatures then rise over time, which may lead to climate changes.

Melting Polar Ice

Bright white areas such as the snow-covered polar regions and glaciers reflect sunlight. In contrast, bodies of water and bare rock appear dark. They tend to absorb solar radiation. When snow and ice melt, the exposed water and land absorb and then radiate more energy back into the atmosphere than the snow or ice did. Earth's atmosphere becomes warmer, leading to increased global temperatures and climate changes.

Visual Summary

To complete this summary, fill in the box below each photo with the name of the sphere being shown in the photo. You can use this page to review the main concepts of the lesson.

20 _____

Earth's Spheres

21 _____

24 _____

23 _____

22 _____

25 Claims • Evidence • Reasoning Make a claim that any two of Earth's spheres interact. Provide evidence to support your claim. Explain your reasoning.

Lesson Review

Vocabulary

Underline the term that best completes each of the following sentences.

1 The ice caps in the Antarctic and the Arctic are a part of the *geosphere/cryosphere/biosphere*.

2 Most of the water on Earth can be found in the *biosphere/hydrosphere/geosphere*.

3 The *hydrosphere/geosphere/atmosphere* protects organisms that live on Earth by blocking out harmful UV rays from the sun.

Key Concepts

Location	Sphere
4 Identify Forms a thin layer of gases around Earth	
5 Identify Extends from Earth's core to Earth's surface	
6 Identify Extends from inside Earth's crust to the lower atmosphere	

7 Describe What does the Earth system include?

8 Analyze Which spheres are interacting when a volcano erupts and releases gases into the air?

9 Identify What are the two most abundant gases in the atmosphere?

10 Describe How do Earth's spheres interact?

Critical Thinking

Use this graph to answer the following question.

Earth's Solar Energy Balance

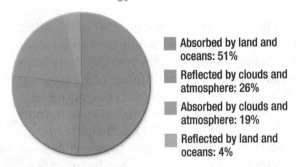

- Absorbed by land and oceans: 51%
- Reflected by clouds and atmosphere: 26%
- Absorbed by clouds and atmosphere: 19%
- Reflected by land and oceans: 4%

11 Infer Which parts of the graph would increase if all of Earth's polar ice melts? Which parts would decrease?

12 Identify Name two ways in which the Earth system relies on energy from the sun.

13 Analyze How does the biosphere rely on the other spheres for survival?

14 Claims • Evidence • Reasoning Most of Earth's liquid water is in the oceans and is not drinkable. What evidence supports this claim? What must be done so humans can drink it? Explain your reasoning.

PEOPLE IN SCIENCE

SC.6.N.2.3 Recognize that scientists who make contributions to scientific knowledge come from all kinds of backgrounds and possess varied talents, interests, and goals.

Evan B. Forde

OCEANOGRAPHER

Pillow lava on the ocean floor, seen from Alvin

Evan B. Forde is an oceanographer at the Atlantic Oceanographic and Meteorological Laboratory in Miami, Florida. His main areas of study have included looking at the different processes occurring in the U.S. east coast submarine canyons. To study these canyons, Evan became the first African American to participate in research dives in underwater submersibles—machines that can take a human being under water safely—such as *Alvin*. He is currently studying how conditions in the atmosphere relate to the formation of hurricanes.

Evan graduated with degrees in Geology and Marine Geology and Geophysics from Columbia University in New York City. Along with his scientific research, he is committed to science education. He has developed and taught courses on Tropical Meteorology at the University of Miami. Keeping younger students in mind, he created an oceanography course for middle-school students through the Miami-Dade Public Libraries. Evan speaks often to students about oceanography and the sciences, and is involved with many community youth projects.

🌐 Social Studies Connection

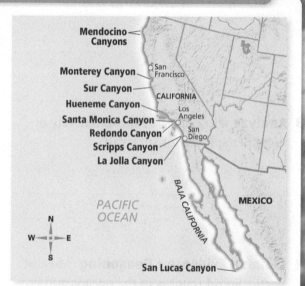

Research the Monterey Submarine Canyon shown on the map. Find out its size and if it is still considered one of the largest canyons off the Pacific Coast. Research the kind of organisms that can live there.

JOB BOARD

Wind Turbine Technician

What You'll Do: Operate and maintain wind turbine units, including doing repairs and preventative maintenance.

Where You Might Work: You will need to travel often to the different wind farms that have wind turbines. Some technicians may have the chance to travel to wind farms in different countries to complete repairs on wind turbines.

Education: Typically, technicians will graduate from a wind energy program. Technicians should have a solid understanding of math, meteorology, computer, and problem solving skills.

Other Job Requirements: To do these tasks, you will need to climb wind towers as high as 125 meters, so it is helpful if you do not have a fear of heights.

Environmental Engineering Technician

What You'll Do: Help environmental engineers and scientists prevent, control, and get rid of environmental hazards. Inspect, test, decontaminate, and operate equipment used to control and help fix environmental pollution.

Where You Might Work: Offices, laboratories, or industrial plants. Most technicians have to complete field work, so they do spend time working outdoors in all types of weather.

Education: You will need an associate's degree in environmental engineering technology, environmental technology, or hazardous materials information systems technology.

Wind turbine

The Atmosphere

ESSENTIAL QUESTION

What is the atmosphere?

By the end of this lesson, you should be able to describe the composition and structure of the atmosphere and explain how the atmosphere protects life and insulates Earth.

The atmosphere is a very thin layer compared to the whole Earth. However, it is essential for life on our planet.

©NASA

SC.6.E.7.9 Describe how the composition and structure of the atmosphere protects life and insulates the planet.

Quick Labs
- Modeling Air Pressure
- Rising Heat
- The Sun's Angle and Temperature

 Engage Your Brain

1 Predict Check T or F to show whether you think each statement is true or false.

T F

☐ ☐ Oxygen is in the air we breathe.

☐ ☐ Pressure is not a property of air.

☐ ☐ The air around you is part of the atmosphere.

☐ ☐ As you climb up a mountain, the temperature usually gets warmer.

2 Explain Does the air in this balloon have mass? Explain your reasoning.

_____

_____

_____

_____

ACTIVE **READING**

3 Synthesize Many English words have their roots in other languages. Use the ancient Greek words below to make an educated guess about the meanings of the words *atmosphere* and *mesosphere*.

Greek word	Meaning
atmos	vapor
mesos	middle
sphaira	ball

atmosphere:

_____

_____

mesosphere:

_____

_____

Vocabulary Terms

- atmosphere
- air pressure
- thermosphere
- mesosphere
- stratosphere
- troposphere
- ozone layer
- greenhouse effect

4 Apply As you learn the definition of each vocabulary term in this lesson, create your own definition or sketch to help you remember the meaning of the term.

Up and Away!

What is Earth's atmosphere?

The mixture of gases that surrounds Earth is the **atmosphere**. This mixture is most often referred to as air. The atmosphere has many important functions. It protects you from the sun's damaging rays and also helps to maintain the right temperature range for life on Earth. For example, the temperature range on Earth allows us to have an abundant amount of liquid water. Many of the components of the atmosphere are essential for life, such as the oxygen you breathe.

A Mixture of Gases and Small Particles

As shown below, the atmosphere is made mostly of nitrogen gas (78%) and oxygen gas (21%). The other 1% is other gases. The atmosphere also contains small particles such as dust, volcanic ash, sea salt, and smoke. There are even small pieces of skin, bacteria, and pollen floating in the atmosphere!

Water is also found in the atmosphere. Liquid water, as water droplets, and solid water, as snow and ice crystals, are found in clouds. But most water in the atmosphere exists as an invisible gas called water vapor. Under certain conditions, water vapor can change into solid or liquid water. Then, snow or rain might fall from the sky.

👁 Visualize It!

5 Identify Fill in the missing percentage for oxygen.

Nitrogen is the most abundant gas in the atmosphere.

Oxygen is the second most abundant gas in the atmosphere.

The remaining 1% of the atmosphere is made up of argon, carbon dioxide, water vapor, and other gases.

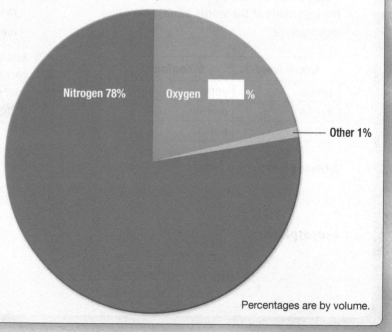

Composition of the Atmosphere

Nitrogen 78% Oxygen ___%

Other 1%

Percentages are by volume.

© Houghton Mifflin Harcourt Publishing Company

(bkgd) ©Image Source/Getty Images

How do pressure and temperature change in the atmosphere?

The atmosphere is held around Earth by gravity. Gravity pulls gas molecules in the atmosphere toward Earth's surface, causing air pressure. **Air pressure** is the measure of the force with which air molecules push on an area of a surface. At sea level, air pressure is over 1 lb for every square centimeter of your body. That is like carrying a 1-liter bottle of water on the tip of your finger!

However, air pressure is not the same throughout the atmosphere. Although there are many gas molecules that surround you on Earth, there are fewer and fewer gas molecules in the air as you move away from Earth's surface. So, as altitude increases, air pressure decreases.

As altitude increases, air temperature also changes. These changes are mainly due to the way solar energy is absorbed in the atmosphere. Some parts of the atmosphere are warmer because they contain a high percentage of gases that absorb solar energy. Other parts of the atmosphere contain less of these gases and are cooler.

ACTIVE READING

6 Identify As you read, underline what happens to temperature and to pressure as altitude increases.

7 Explain Your Reasoning Why does a mountain climber need an oxygen supply at very high altitudes, even though the air still contains 21% oxygen?

_____

_____

_____

At high altitudes such as the top of Mount Everest, air pressure and temperature are lower than they are at sea level.

Look Way Up

What are the layers of the atmosphere?

Earth's atmosphere is divided into four layers, based on temperature and other properties. As shown at the right, these layers are the troposphere (TROH•puh•sfir), stratosphere (STRAT•uh•sfir), mesosphere (MEZ•uh•sfir), and thermosphere (THER•muh•sfir). Although these names sound complicated, they give you clues about the layers' features. *Tropo-* means "turning" or "change," and the troposphere is the layer where gases turn and mix. *Strato-* means "layer," and the stratosphere is where gases are layered and do not mix very much. *Meso-* means "middle," and the mesosphere is the middle layer. Finally, *thermo-* means "heat," and the thermosphere is the layer where temperatures are highest.

Think Outside the Book

8 Describe Research the part of the thermosphere called the ionosphere. Describe what the aurora borealis is.

The aurora borealis occurs in the thermosphere.

Thermosphere

The **thermosphere** is the uppermost layer of the atmosphere. The temperature increases as altitude increases because gases in the thermosphere absorb high-energy solar radiation. Temperatures in the thermosphere can be 1,500 °C or higher. However, the thermosphere feels cold. The density of particles in the thermosphere is very low. Too few gas particles collide with your body to transfer heat energy to your skin.

Mesosphere

The **mesosphere** is between the thermosphere and stratosphere. In this layer, the temperature decreases as altitude increases. Temperatures can be as low as −120 °C at the top of the mesosphere. Meteoroids begin to burn up in the mesosphere.

Stratosphere

The **stratosphere** is between the mesosphere and troposphere. In this layer, temperatures generally increase as altitude increases. Ozone in the stratosphere absorbs ultraviolet radiation from the sun, which warms the air. An ozone molecule is made of three atoms of oxygen. Gases in the stratosphere are layered and do not mix very much.

Troposphere

The **troposphere** is the lowest layer of the atmosphere. Although temperatures near Earth's surface vary greatly, generally, temperature decreases as altitude increases. This layer contains almost 80% of the atmosphere's total mass, making it the densest layer. Almost all of Earth's carbon dioxide, water vapor, clouds, air pollution, weather, and life forms are in the troposphere.

Visualize It!

In the graph, the green line shows pressure change with altitude. The red line shows temperature change with altitude.

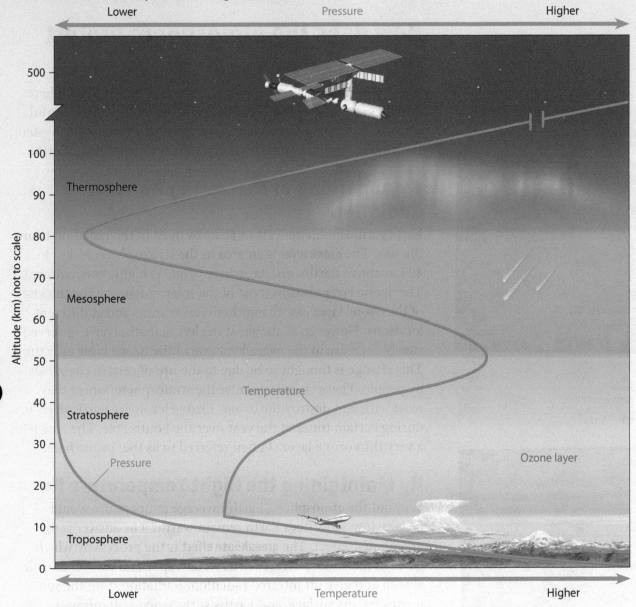

The layers of the atmosphere are defined by changes in temperature.

9 Claims • Evidence • Reasoning
Make a claim about the change in air pressure and temperature in each layer of the atmosphere. Provide evidence and explain your reasoning to a classmate.

Layer	Air pressure	Temperature
Thermosphere	decreases	
Mesosphere		
Stratosphere		
Troposphere		

Here Comes.

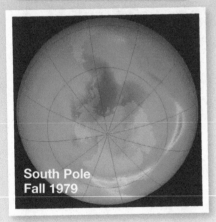

South Pole
Fall 1979

Less ozone   More ozone

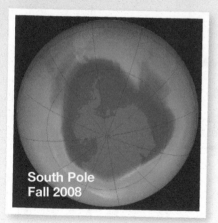

South Pole
Fall 2008

10 Gather Evidence How did the ozone layer over the South Pole change between 1979 and 2008?

_____

_____

_____

How does the atmosphere protect life on Earth?

The atmosphere surrounds and protects Earth. The atmosphere provides the air we breathe. It also protects Earth from harmful solar radiation and from space debris that enters the Earth system. In addition, the atmosphere controls the temperature on Earth.

By Absorbing or Reflecting Harmful Radiation

Earth's atmosphere reflects or absorbs most of the radiation from the sun. The **ozone layer** is an area in the stratosphere, 15 km to 40 km above Earth's surface, where ozone is highly concentrated. The ozone layer absorbs most of the solar radiation. The thickness of the ozone layer can change between seasons and at different locations. However, as shown at the left, scientists have observed a steady decrease in the overall volume of the ozone layer over time. This change is thought to be due to the use of certain chemicals by people. These chemicals enter the stratosphere, where they react with and destroy the ozone. Ozone levels are particularly low during certain times of the year over the South Pole. The area with a very thin ozone layer is often referred to as the "ozone hole."

By Maintaining the Right Temperature Range

Without the atmosphere, Earth's average temperature would be very low. How does Earth remain warm? The answer is the greenhouse effect. The **greenhouse effect** is the process by which gases in the atmosphere, such as water vapor and carbon dioxide, absorb and give off infrared radiation. Radiation from the sun warms Earth's surface, and Earth's surface gives off infrared radiation. Greenhouse gases in the atmosphere absorb some of this infrared radiation and then reradiate it. Some of this energy is absorbed again by Earth's surface, while some energy goes out into space. Because greenhouse gases keep energy in the Earth system longer, Earth's average surface temperature is kept at around 15°C (59°F). In time, all the energy ends up back in outer space.

ACTIVE READING

11 List Name two examples of greenhouse gases.

_____

_____

the Sun ...

The Greenhouse Effect

Greenhouse gas molecules absorb and emit infrared radiation.

Atmosphere without Greenhouse Gases

Without greenhouse gases in Earth's atmosphere, radiation from Earth's surface is lost directly to space.
Average Temperature: -18°C

Atmosphere with Greenhouse Gases

With greenhouse gases in Earth's atmosphere, radiation from Earth's surface is lost to space more slowly, which makes Earth's surface warmer.
Average Temperature: 15°C

____ sunlight   ____ infrared radiation

The atmosphere is much thinner than shown here.

👁 Visualize It!

12 Claims • Evidence • Reasoning
Make a claim about how greenhouse gases affect Earth. Gather evidence to support this claim. Explain your reasoning.

Visual Summary

To complete this summary, fill in the blanks with the correct word or phrase. You can use this page to review the main concepts of the lesson.

Both air pressure and temperature change within the atmosphere.

13 As altitude increases, air pressure
_____

The atmosphere protects Earth from harmful radiation and helps to maintain a temperature range that supports life.

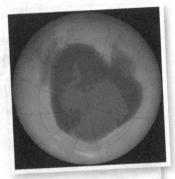

14 Earth is protected from harmful solar radiation by the
_____

The
Atmosphere

The atmosphere is divided into four layers, according to temperature and other properties.

15 The four layers of the atmosphere are the
_____
_____
_____
_____

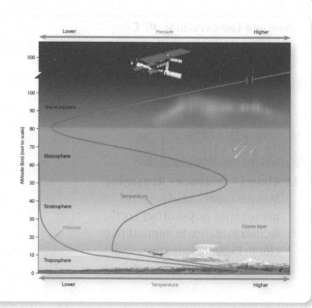

16 Explain Your Reasoning What do you think Earth's surface would be like if the Earth did not have an atmosphere? Explain your reasoning.

Lesson Review

Vocabulary

Fill in the blanks with the terms that best complete the following sentences.

1 The _____ is a mixture of gases that surrounds Earth.

2 The measure of the force with which air molecules push on a surface is called _____ .

3 The _____ is the process by which gases in the atmosphere absorb and reradiate heat.

Key Concepts

4 List Name three gases in the atmosphere.

_____

_____

5 Identify What layer of the atmosphere contains the ozone layer?

_____

6 Identify What layer of the atmosphere contains almost 80% of the atmosphere's total mass?

_____

7 Describe How and why does air pressure change with altitude in the atmosphere?

_____

_____

_____

_____

8 Explain Your Reasoning What is the name of the uppermost layer of the atmosphere? Why does it feel cold there, even though the temperature can be very high?

_____

_____

_____

Critical Thinking

9 Hypothesize What would happen to life on Earth if the ozone layer was not present?

_____

_____

10 Claims • Evidence • Reasoning A friend says that temperature increases as altitude increases because you're moving closer to the sun. Is this true? Gather evidence to support or refute your friend's claim. Explain your reasoning.

_____

_____

11 Predict Why would increased levels of greenhouse gases contribute to higher temperatures on Earth?

_____

_____

Use this graph to answer the following questions.

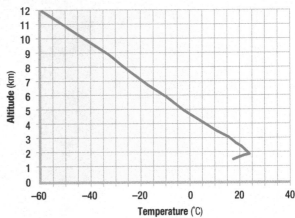

Changes in Temperature with Altitude

Source: National Weather Service. Data taken at Riverton, Wyoming, 2001

12 Analyze The top of Mount Everest is at about 8,850 m. What would the approximate air temperature be at that altitude? _____

13 Analyze What is the total temperature change between 3 km and 7 km above Earth's surface? _____

Energy Transfer

ESSENTIAL QUESTION

How does energy move through Earth's system?

By the end of this lesson, you should be able to summarize the three mechanisms by which energy is transferred through Earth's system.

Ice absorbs energy from the sun. This can cause ice to melt—even these icicles in Antarctica.

SC.6.E.7.1 Differentiate among radiation, conduction, and convection, the three mechanisms by which heat is transferred through Earth's system. **SC.6.E.7.4** Differentiate and show interactions among the geosphere, hydrosphere, cryosphere, atmosphere, and biosphere. **SC.6.E.7.5** Explain how energy provided by the sun influences global patterns of atmospheric movement and the temperature differences between air, water, and land.

✋ Lesson Labs

Quick Labs
- How Does Color Affect Temperature?
- Modeling Convection

Exploration/S.T.E.M. Lab
- The Heat from the Sun

Exploration Lab
- Stop the Energy Transfer

🧠 Engage Your Brain

1 Describe Fill in the blank with the word or phrase that you think correctly completes the following sentences.

An example of something hot is

_____

An example of something cold is

_____

The sun provides us with

_____

A thermometer is used to measure

_____

2 Explain your reasoning If you placed your hands around this mug of hot chocolate, what would happen to the temperature of your hands? Why do you think this would happen?

_____

_____

_____

_____

_____

_____

ACTIVE **READING**

3 Apply Many scientific words, such as *heat*, are used to convey different meanings. Use context clues to write your own definition for each meaning of the word *heat*.

The student won the first <u>heat</u> of the race.

heat:

_____

_____

The man wondered if his rent included <u>heat</u>.

heat:

_____

_____

Energy in the form of <u>heat</u> was transferred from the hot pan to the cold counter.

heat:

_____

_____

Vocabulary Terms

- temperature
- thermal energy
- thermal expansion
- heat
- radiation
- convection
- conduction

4 Identify This list contains the vocabulary terms you'll learn in this lesson. As you read, circle the definition of each term.

Hot and Cold

How are energy and temperature related?

All matter is made up of moving particles, such as atoms or molecules. When particles are in motion, they have kinetic energy. Because particles move at different speeds, each has a different amount of kinetic energy.

Temperature (TEMM•per•uh•choor) is a measure of the average kinetic energy of particles. The faster a particle moves, the more kinetic energy it has. As shown below, the more kinetic energy the particles of an object have, the higher the temperature of the object. Temperature does not depend on the number of particles. A teapot holds more tea than a cup. If the particles of tea in both containers have the same average kinetic energy, the tea in both containers is at the same temperature.

Thermal energy is the total kinetic energy of particles. A teapot full of tea at a high temperature has more thermal energy than a teapot full of tea at a lower temperature. Thermal energy also depends on the number of particles. The more particles there are in an object, the greater the object's thermal energy. The tea in a teapot and a cup may be at the same temperature, but the tea in the pot has more thermal energy because there is more of it.

◉ Visualize It!

5 Explain Your Reasoning Which container holds particles with the higher average kinetic energy? Explain your reasoning.

_____

_____

particle motion

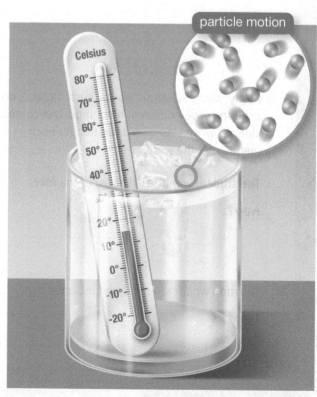

particle motion

© Houghton Mifflin Harcourt Publishing Company

What is thermal expansion?

When the temperature of a substance increases, the substance's particles have more kinetic energy. Therefore, the particles move faster and move apart. As the space between the particles increases, the substance expands. The increase in volume that results from an increase in temperature is called **thermal expansion**. Most substances on Earth expand when they become warmer and contract when they become cooler. Water is an exception. Cold water expands as it gets colder and then freezes to form ice.

Thermal expansion causes a change in the density of a substance. *Density* is the mass per unit volume of a substance. When a substance expands, its mass stays the same but its volume increases. As a result, density decreases. Differences in density that are caused by thermal expansion can cause movement of matter. For example, air inside a hot-air balloon is warmed, as shown below. The air expands as its particles move faster and farther apart. As the air expands, it becomes less dense than the air outside the balloon. The less-dense air inside the balloon is forced upward by the colder, denser air outside the balloon. This same principle affects air movement in the atmosphere, water movement in the oceans, and rock movement in the geosphere.

7 Explain your reasoning Why would an increase in the temperature of the oceans contribute to a rise in sea level?

_____
_____
_____
_____

6 Claims • Evidence • Reasoning
What might happen to the hot-air balloon if the air inside it cooled down? Gather evidence and explain your reasoning.

_____
_____

When the air in this balloon becomes hotter, it becomes less dense than the surrounding air. So, the balloon goes up, up, and away!

Getting Warm

ACTIVE READING

ACTIVE READING

8 Identify As you read, underline the direction of energy transfer between objects that are at different temperatures.

What is heat?

You might think of the word *heat* when you imagine something that feels hot. But heat also has to do with things that feel cold. In fact, heat is what causes objects to feel hot or cold. You may often use the word *heat* to mean different things. However, in this lesson, the word *heat* has only one meaning. **Heat** is the energy that is transferred between objects that are at different temperatures.

Energy Transferred Between Objects

When objects that have different temperatures come into contact, energy will be transferred between them until both objects reach the same temperature. The direction of this energy transfer is always from the object with the higher temperature to the object with the lower temperature. When you touch something cold, energy is transferred from your body to that object. When you touch something hot, like the pan shown below, energy is transferred from that object to your body.

👁 Visualize It!

9 Explain your reasoning Draw an arrow to show the direction in which energy is transferred between the pan and the oven mitts. Explain your reasoning

This pan is being removed from the oven and is very hot.

© Houghton Mifflin Harcourt Publishing Company

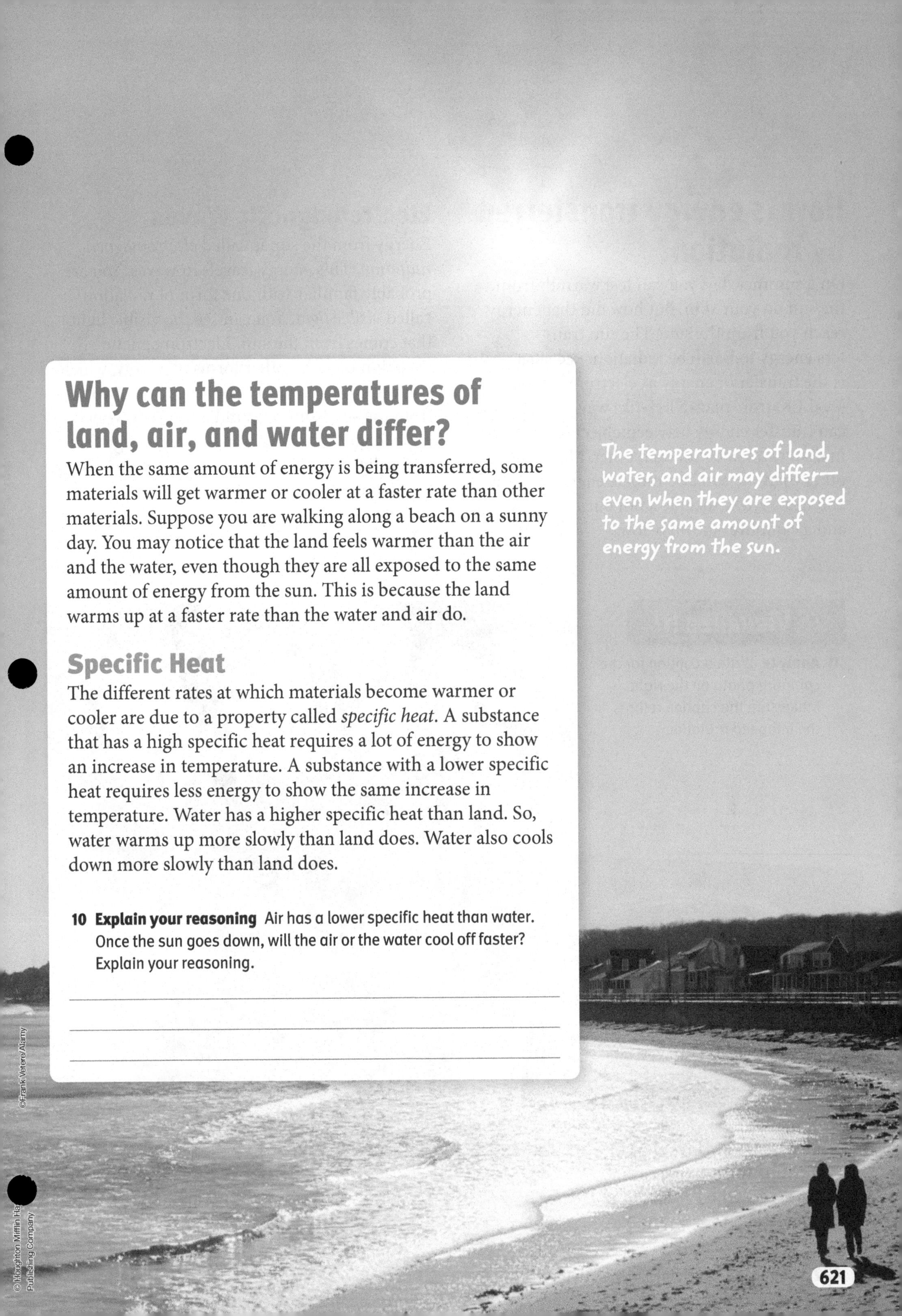

Why can the temperatures of land, air, and water differ?

When the same amount of energy is being transferred, some materials will get warmer or cooler at a faster rate than other materials. Suppose you are walking along a beach on a sunny day. You may notice that the land feels warmer than the air and the water, even though they are all exposed to the same amount of energy from the sun. This is because the land warms up at a faster rate than the water and air do.

Specific Heat

The different rates at which materials become warmer or cooler are due to a property called *specific heat*. A substance that has a high specific heat requires a lot of energy to show an increase in temperature. A substance with a lower specific heat requires less energy to show the same increase in temperature. Water has a higher specific heat than land. So, water warms up more slowly than land does. Water also cools down more slowly than land does.

10 **Explain your reasoning** Air has a lower specific heat than water. Once the sun goes down, will the air or the water cool off faster? Explain your reasoning.

_____

_____

_____

The temperatures of land, water, and air may differ— even when they are exposed to the same amount of energy from the sun.

Heat

How is energy transferred by radiation?

On a summer day, you can feel warmth from the sun on your skin. But how did that energy reach you from the sun? The sun transfers energy to Earth by radiation. **Radiation** is the transfer of energy as electromagnetic (ee•LEK•troh•mag•NEH•tik) waves. Radiation can transfer energy between objects that are not in direct contact with each other. Many objects other than the sun also radiate energy as light and heat. These include a hot burner on a stove and a campfire, shown below.

Electromagnetic Waves

Energy from the sun is called *electromagnetic radiation*. This energy travels in waves. You are probably familiar with one form of radiation called *visible light*. You can see the visible light that comes from the sun. Electromagnetic radiation includes other forms of energy, which you cannot see. Most of the warmth that you feel from the sun is infrared radiation. This energy has a longer wavelength and lower energy than visible light. Higher-energy radiation includes x-rays and ultraviolet light.

👁 Visualize It!

11 Analyze Write a caption for the campfire photo on the right. Make sure the caption relates the image to radiation.

_____

_____

_____

Energy from this hot burner is being transferred by radiation.

Energy from the sun is transferred through space.

Where does radiation occur on Earth?

We live almost 150 million km from the sun. Yet almost all of the energy on Earth is transmitted from the sun by radiation. The sun is the major source of energy for processes at Earth's surface. Receiving that energy is absolutely vital for life on Earth. The electromagnetic waves from the sun also provide energy that drives the water cycle.

When solar radiation reaches Earth, some of the energy is reflected and scattered by Earth's atmosphere. But much of the energy passes through Earth's atmosphere and reaches Earth's surface. Some of the energy that Earth receives from the sun is absorbed by the atmosphere, geosphere, and hydrosphere. Then, the energy is changed into thermal energy. This thermal energy may be reradiated into the Earth system or into space. Much of the energy is transferred through Earth's systems by the two other ways—convection and conduction.

> ## Think Outside the Book
>
> **13 Gather Evidence** Research ultraviolet radiation from the sun and its role in causing sunburns.

12 Summarize Give two examples of what happens when energy from the sun reaches Earth.

_____

_____

_____

_____

Heating Up

How is energy transferred by convection?

Have you ever watched a pot of boiling water, such as the one below? If so, you have seen convection. **Convection** (kun•VECK•shuhn) is the transfer of energy due to the movement of matter. As water warms up at the bottom of the pot, some of the hot water rises. At the same time, cooler water from other parts of the pot sink and replace the rising water. This water is then warmed and the cycle continues.

Convection Currents

Convection involves the movement of matter due to differences in density. Convection occurs because most matter becomes less dense when it gets warmer. When most matter becomes warmer, it undergoes thermal expansion and a decrease in density. This less-dense matter is forced upward by the surrounding colder, denser matter that is sinking. As the hot matter rises, it cools and becomes more dense. This causes it to sink back down. This cycling of matter is called a *convection current*. Convection most often occurs in fluids, such as water and air. But convection can also happen in solids.

wax

convection current

energy sources

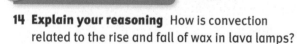

i 👁 **Visualize It!**

14 Explain your reasoning How is convection related to the rise and fall of wax in lava lamps?

Where does convection occur on Earth?

If Earth's surface is warmer than the air, energy will be transferred from the ground to the air. As the air becomes warmer, it becomes less dense. This air is pushed upward and out of the way by cooler, denser air that is sinking. As the warm air rises, it cools and becomes denser and begins to sink back toward Earth's surface. This cycle moves energy through the atmosphere.

Convection currents also occur in the ocean because of differences in the density of ocean water. More dense water sinks to the ocean floor, and less dense water moves toward the surface. The density of ocean water is influenced by temperature and the amount of salt in the water. Cold water is denser than warmer water. Water that contains a lot of salt is more dense than less-salty water.

Energy produced deep inside Earth heats rock in the mantle. The heated rock becomes less dense and is pushed up toward Earth's surface by the cooler, denser surrounding rock. Once cooled near the surface, the rock sinks. These convection currents transfer energy from Earth's core toward Earth's surface. These currents also cause the movement of tectonic plates.

ACTIVE READING

15 Name What are three of Earth's spheres in which energy is transferred by convection?

_____

_____

◉ Visualize It!

16 Apply Draw the convection current that could occur in the body of water in this image. Explain your reasoning.

Convection currents occur throughout the Earth system.

Ouch!

How is energy transferred by conduction?

Have you ever touched an ice cube and wondered why it feels cold? An ice cube has only a small amount of energy, compared to your hand. Energy is transferred to the ice cube from your hand through the process of conduction. **Conduction** (kun•DUHK•shuhn) is the transfer of energy from one object to another object through direct contact.

Direct Contact

Remember that the atoms or molecules in a substance are constantly moving. Even a solid block of ice has particles in constant motion. When objects at different temperatures touch, their particles interact. Conduction involves the faster-moving particles of the warmer object transferring energy to the slower-moving particles in the cooler object. The greater the difference in energy of the particles, the faster the transfer of energy by conduction occurs.

ACTIVE READING

17 Apply Name two examples of conduction that you experience every day.

_____

_____

_____

_____

These desert sands would feel hot because of conduction.

Where does conduction occur on Earth?

Energy can be transferred between the geosphere and the atmosphere by conduction. When cooler air molecules come into direct contact with the warm ground, energy is passed to the air by conduction. Conduction between the ground and the air happens only within a few centimeters of Earth's surface.

Conduction also happens between particles of air and particles of water. For example, if air transfers enough energy to liquid water, the water may evaporate. If water vapor transfers energy to the air, the kinetic energy of the water decreases. As a result, the water vapor may condense to form liquid water droplets.

Inside Earth, energy transfers between rock particles by conduction. However, rock is a poor conductor of heat, so this process happens very slowly.

© Houghton Mifflin Harcourt Publishing Company
(bkgd) ©Jean-Claude Winkler/Getty Images; (inset) ©alfred/©Travel/Stockbyte/Getty Images

Visualize It!

18 Claims • Evidence • Reasoning Make a claim about whether conduction also occurs in a city like the one shown below. Use evidence to support your claim. Explain your reasoning.

_____
_____
_____
_____
_____

19 Summarize Complete the following spider map by describing the three types of energy transfer. One answer has been started for you.

Radiation
Transfer of energy as
_____

_____

Types of Energy Transfer

_____

Visual Summary

To complete this summary, fill in the blanks with the correct word or phrase. You can use this page to review the main concepts of the lesson.

Energy Transfer

Heat is the energy that is transferred between objects that are at different temperatures.

20 The particles in a hot pan have _____ kinetic energy than the particles in a cool oven mitt.

Energy can be transferred in different ways.

21 The three ways that energy can be transferred are labeled in the image as

A: _____

B: _____

C: _____

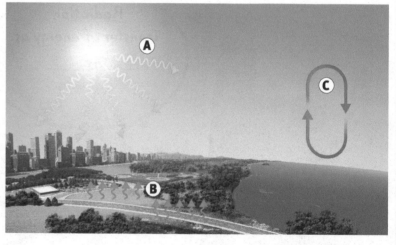

22 **Claims • Evidence • Reasoning** Make a claim about what type of energy transfer is responsible for making your feel cold when you are swimming in cool water. Use evidence to explain your reasoning.

Lesson Review

Vocabulary

In your own words, define the following terms.

1 radiation

_____

_____

2 convection

_____

_____

3 conduction

_____

_____

Key Concepts

4 Compare What is the difference between temperature, thermal energy, and heat?

_____

_____

5 Describe What is happening to a substance undergoing thermal expansion?

_____

_____

_____

6 Identify What is the main source of energy for most processes at Earth's surface?

_____

7 Claims • Evidence • Reasoning Make a claim about what happens when two objects at different temperatures touch. Identify one place where it occurs in Earth system. Provide evidence, and explain your reasoning.

_____

_____

8 Identify What is an example of convection in Earth system?

_____

Critical Thinking

9 Apply Why can metal utensils get too hot to touch when you are cooking with them?

_____

_____

_____

10 Explain Your Reasoning You are doing an experiment outside on a sunny day. The temperature of some sand is 28°C. The temperature of some water is 25°C. Explain the difference in temperatures.

_____

_____

_____

Use this image to answer the following questions.

11 Analyze Name one example of where energy transfer by radiation is occurring.

_____

12 Analyze Name one example of where energy transfer by conduction is occurring.

_____

13 Analyze Name one example of where energy transfer by convection is occurring.

_____

SC.6.N.1.1 Define a problem from the sixth grade curriculum, use appropriate reference materials to support scientific understanding, plan and carry out scientific investigation of various types, such as systematic observations or experiments, identify variables, collect and organize data, interpret data in charts, tables, and graphics, analyze information, make predictions, and defend conclusions.

S.T.E.M. ENGINEERING & TECHNOLOGY

Engineering Design Process

Skills		Objectives
Identify a need		Explain how a need for clean energy has driven a technological solution.
Conduct research		Describe two examples of wind-powered generators.
✓ Brainstorm solutions		Design a technological solution to a problem.
✓ Select a solution		Test and modify a prototype to achieve the desired result.
Design a prototype		
✓ Build a prototype		
✓ Test and evaluate		
✓ Redesign to improve		
✓ Communicate results		

Building a Wind Turbine

During the Industrial Revolution, machines began to replace human and animal power for doing work. From agriculture and manufacturing to transportation, machines made work faster and easier. However, these machines needed fuel. Fossil fuels, such as coal, oil, and gasoline, powered the Industrial Revolution and are still used today. But burning fossil fuels produces waste products that harm the environment. In addition, fossil fuels will eventually run out. As a result, we need to better understand alternative, renewable sources of energy.

Brainstorming Solutions

There are many sources of energy besides fossil fuels. One of the most abundant renewable sources is wind. A wind turbine is a device that uses energy from the wind to turn an axle. The turning axle can be attached to other equipment to do jobs such as pumping water, cutting lumber, or generating electricity. To generate electricity, the axle spins magnets around a coiled wire. This causes electrons to flow in the wire. Flowing electrons produce an electric current. Electric current is used to power homes and businesses or electrical energy can be stored in a battery.

1 Brainstorm What are other possible sources of renewable energy that could be used to power a generator?

_____

_____

_____

_____

_____

_____

_____

HAWTs must be pointed into the wind to work. A motor turns the turbine to keep it facing the wind. HAWT blades are angled so that wind strikes the front of the blades, and then pushes the blades as it flows over them. Because wind flows over the blades fairly evenly, there is little vibration. So HAWTs are relatively quiet, and the turbines last a long time.

Wind direction

Blade moves counterclockwise

The Modern Design

There are two general types of modern wind turbines. A horizontal-axis wind turbine (HAWT) has a main axle that is horizontal, and a generator at the top of a tall tower. A vertical-axis wind turbine (VAWT) has a main axle that is vertical, and a generator at ground level. The blades are often white or light gray, to blend with the clouds. Blades can be more than 40 meters (130 ft) long, supported by towers more than 90 meters (300 ft) tall. The blade tips can travel more than 320 kilometers (200 mi) per hour!

2 Claims • Evidence • Reasoning Make a claim about what problems may have been encountered as prototypes for modern wind turbines were tested. Use evidence to support your claim, and explain your reasoning.

VAWTs do not need to be pointed into the wind to work. The blades are made so that one blade is pushed by the wind while the other returns against the wind. But because each blade moves against the wind for part of its rotation, VAWTs are less efficient than HAWTs. They also tend to vibrate more and, as a result, make more noise.

Wind direction

Blade moves against the wind

Blade moves with the wind

✋ You Try It!

Now it's your turn to design a wind turbine that will generate electricity and light a small bulb.

You Try It!

Now it's your turn to design an efficient wind turbine that will generate enough electricity to light a small bulb.

Materials

✓ assorted wind turbine parts
✓ fan
✓ gears
✓ small bulb
✓ small motor
✓ socket

① Brainstorm solutions

Brainstorm ideas for a wind turbine that will turn an axle on a small motor. The blades must turn fast enough so that the motor generates enough electricity to light a small bulb. Fill in the table below with as many ideas as you can for each part of your wind turbine. Circle each idea you decide to try.

Type of axis	Shape of turbine	Attaching axis to motor	Control speed

② Select a solution

From the table above, choose the features for the turbine you will build. In the space below, draw a model of your wind turbine idea. Include all the parts and show how they will be connected.

S.T.E.M. ENGINEERING & TECHNOLOGY

(3) Build a prototype

Now build your wind turbine. As you built your turbine, were there some parts of your design that could not be assembled as you had predicted? What parts did you have to revise as you were building the prototype?

_____

_____

_____

_____

(4) Test and evaluate

Point a fan at your wind turbine and see what happens. Did the bulb light? If not, what parts of your turbine could you revise?

_____

_____

_____

_____

(5) Redesign to improve

Choose one part to revise. Modify your design and then test again. Repeat this process until your turbine lights up the light bulb.

_____

_____

_____

_____

(6) Communicate results

Which part of the turbine seemed to have the greatest effect on the brightness of the light bulb?

_____

_____

_____

_____

Wind in the Atmosphere

ESSENTIAL QUESTION

What is wind?

By the end of this lesson, you should be able to explain how energy provided by the sun causes atmospheric movement, called wind.

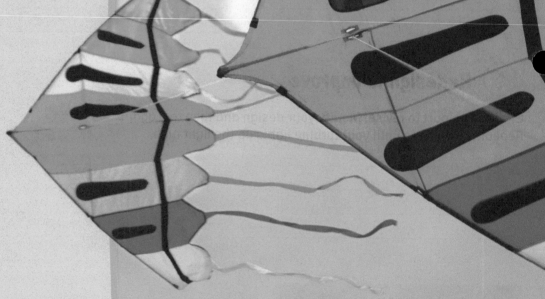

Although you cannot see wind, you can see how it affects things like these kites.

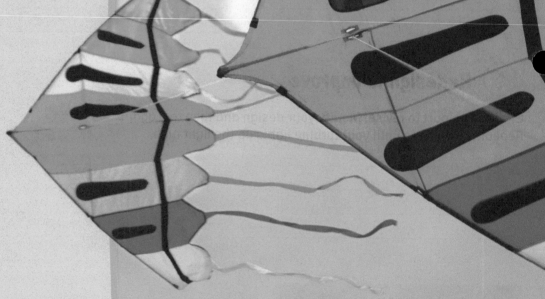

SC.6.E.7.3 Describe how global patterns such as the jet stream and ocean currents influence local weather in measurable terms such as temperature, air pressure, wind direction and speed, and humidity and precipitation. **SC.6.E.7.5** Explain how energy provided by the sun influences global patterns of atmospheric movement and the temperature differences between air, water, and land.

Lesson Labs

Quick Labs
• Modeling the Coriolis Effect
• Flying with the Jet Stream

Engage Your Brain

1 Predict Check T or F to show whether you think each statement is true or false.

T	F	
☐	☐	The atmosphere is often referred to as air.
☐	☐	Wind does not have direction.
☐	☐	During the day, there is often a wind blowing toward shore from the ocean or a large lake.
☐	☐	Cold air rises and warm air sinks.

2 Explain your reasoning If you ran over a nail and punctured this bicycle tire, what would happen to the air inside of the tire? Why do you think that would happen? Explain your reasoning.

_____

_____

ACTIVE READING

3 Synthesize You can often define an unknown phrase if you know the meaning of its word parts. Use the word parts below to make an educated guess about the meanings of the phrases *local wind* and *global wind*.

Word part	Meaning
wind	movement of air due to differences in air pressure
local	involving a particular area
global	involving the entire Earth

local wind:

_____

_____

global wind:

_____

_____

Vocabulary Terms

• wind
• Coriolis effect
• global wind
• jet stream
• local wind

4 Identify This list contains the vocabulary terms you'll learn in this lesson. As you read, circle the definition of each term.

Blow It Out!

What causes wind?

The next time you feel the wind blowing, you can thank the sun! The sun does not warm the whole surface of the Earth in a uniform manner. This uneven heating causes the air above Earth's surface to be at different temperatures. Cold air is more dense than warmer air is. Colder, denser air sinks. When denser air sinks, it places greater pressure on the surface of Earth than warmer, less-dense air does. This results in areas of higher air pressure. Air moves from areas of higher pressure toward areas of lower pressure. The movement of air caused by differences in air pressure is called **wind**. The greater the differences in air pressure, the faster the air moves.

Areas of High and Low Pressure

Cold, dense air at the poles creates areas of high pressure at the poles. Warm, less-dense air at the equator forms an area of lower pressure. This pressure gradient results in global movement of air. However, instead of moving in one circle between the equator and the poles, air moves in smaller circular patterns called *convection cells,* shown below. As air moves from the equator, it cools and becomes more dense. At about 30°N and 30°S latitudes, a high-pressure belt results from the sinking of air. Near the poles, cold air warms as it moves away from the poles. At around 60°N and 60°S latitudes, a low-pressure belt forms as the warmed air is pushed upward.

👁 Visualize It!

5 Identify In the white oval area on the map, draw the convection cell that was left out. Use a pencil to indicate warm air and a pen to indicate cool air.

The warming and cooling of air produces pressure belts every 30° of latitude.

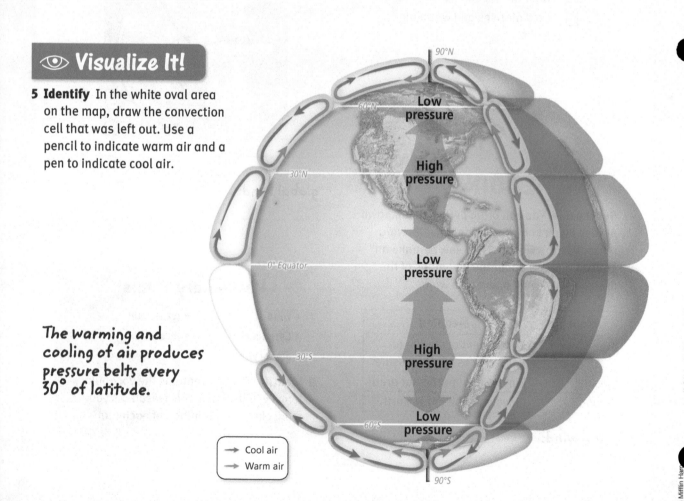

How does Earth's rotation affect wind?

Pressure differences cause air to move between the equator and the poles. If Earth was not rotating, winds would blow in a straight line. However, winds are deflected, or curved, due to Earth's rotation, as shown below. The apparent curving of the path of a moving object from an otherwise straight path due to Earth's rotation is called the **Coriolis effect** (kawr•ee•OH•lis ih•FEKT). This effect is most noticeable over long distances.

Because each point on Earth makes one complete rotation every day, points closer to the equator must travel farther and, therefore, faster than points closer to the poles do. When air moves from the equator toward the North Pole, it maintains its initial speed and direction. If the air travels far enough north, it will have traveled farther east than a point on the ground beneath it. As a result, the air appears to follow a curved path toward the east. Air moving from the North Pole to the equator appears to curve to the west because the air moves east more slowly than a point on the ground beneath it does. Therefore, in the Northern Hemisphere, air moving to the north curves to the east and air moving to the south curves to the west.

👁 Visualize It!

7 Label In the white ovals on the map, draw the direction and path of the winds that would occur at those locations on Earth.

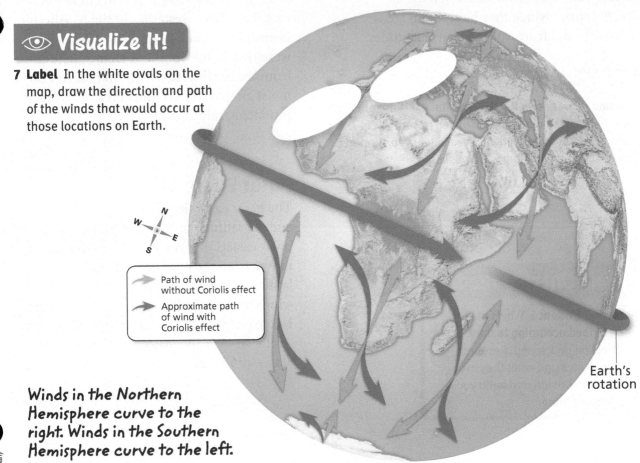

Path of wind without Coriolis effect

Approximate path of wind with Coriolis effect

Earth's rotation

Winds in the Northern Hemisphere curve to the right. Winds in the Southern Hemisphere curve to the left.

Blowin Around

What are examples of global winds?

Recall that air travels in circular patterns called convection cells that cover approximately 30° of latitude. Pressure belts at every 30° of latitude and the Coriolis effect produce patterns of calm areas and wind systems. These wind systems occur at or near Earth's surface and are called **global winds**. As shown at the right, the major global wind systems are the *polar easterlies* (EE•ster•leez), the *westerlies* (WES•ter•leez), and the *trade winds*. Winds such as polar easterlies and westerlies are named for the direction from which they blow. Calm areas include the doldrums and the horse latitudes.

ACTIVE READING

8 Claims • Evidence • Reasoning Make a claim about what direction something is moving toward if it is being carried by westerlies. Use evidence to support your claim, and explain your reasoning.

_____

_____

i Think Outside the Book

9 Gather Evidence Winds are described according to their direction and speed. Research wind vanes and what they are used for. Design and build your own wind vane.

Trade Winds

The trade winds blow between 30° latitude and the equator in both hemispheres. The rotation of Earth causes the trade winds to curve to the west. Therefore, trade winds in the Northern Hemisphere come from the northeast, and trade winds in the Southern Hemisphere come from the southeast. These winds became known as the trade winds because sailors relied on them to sail from Europe to the Americas.

Westerlies

The westerlies blow between 30° and 60° latitudes in both hemispheres. The rotation of Earth causes these winds to curve to the east. Therefore, westerlies in the Northern Hemisphere come from the southwest, and westerlies in the Southern Hemisphere come from the northwest. The westerlies can carry moist air over the continental United States, producing rain and snow.

Polar Easterlies

The polar easterlies blow between the poles and 60° latitude in both hemispheres. The polar easterlies form as cold, sinking air moves from the poles toward 60°N and 60°S latitudes. The rotation of Earth causes these winds to curve to the west. In the Northern Hemisphere, polar easterlies can carry cold Arctic air over the majority of the United States, producing snow and freezing weather.

© Houghton Mifflin Harcourt Publishing Company

Visualize It!

10 Identify Label the polar easterlies, the westerlies, and the trade winds in the white boxes on the map.

90°N

Ⓐ

60°N

Ⓑ

Horse latitudes

30°N

Ⓒ

Doldrums

0° Equator

Horse latitudes

30°S

60°S

90°S

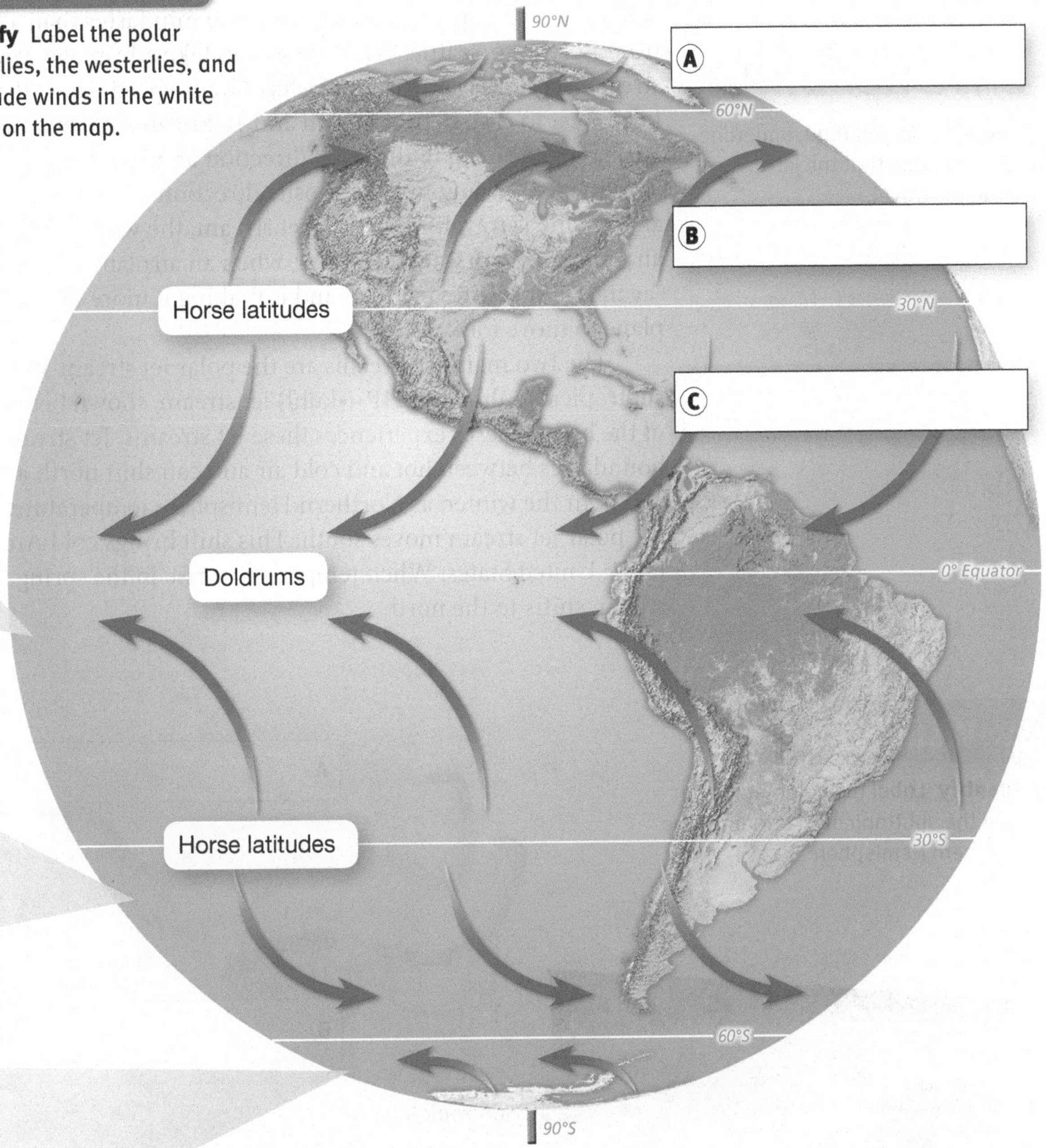

The Doldrums and Horse Latitudes

The trade winds of both hemispheres meet in a calm area around the equator called the *doldrums* (DOHL•druhmz). Very little wind blows in the doldrums because the warm, less-dense air results in an area of low pressure. The name doldrums means "dull" or "sluggish." At about 30° latitude in both hemispheres, air stops moving and sinks. This forms calm areas called the *horse latitudes*. This name was given to these areas when sailing ships carried horses from Europe to the Americas. When ships were stalled in these areas, horses were sometimes thrown overboard to save water.

The Jet Streams

A flight from Seattle to Boston can be 30 min faster than a flight from Boston to Seattle. Why? Pilots can take advantage of a jet stream. **Jet streams** are narrow belts of high-speed winds that blow from west to east, between 7 km and 16 km above Earth's surface. Airplanes traveling in the same direction as a jet stream go faster than those traveling in the opposite direction of a jet stream. When an airplane is traveling "with" a jet stream, the wind is helping the airplane move forward. However, when an airplane is traveling "against" the jet stream, the wind is making it more difficult for the plane to move forward.

The two main jet streams are the polar jet stream and the subtropical (suhb•TRAHP•i•kuhl) jet stream, shown below. Each of the hemispheres experiences these jet streams. Jet streams follow boundaries between hot and cold air and can shift north and south. In the winter, as Northern Hemisphere temperatures cool, the polar jet stream moves south. This shift brings cold Arctic air to the United States. When temperatures rise in the spring, this jet stream shifts to the north.

11 Identify As you read, underline the direction that the jet streams travel.

👁 Visualize It!

12 Identify Label the polar jet stream and the subtropical jet stream in the Northern Hemisphere.

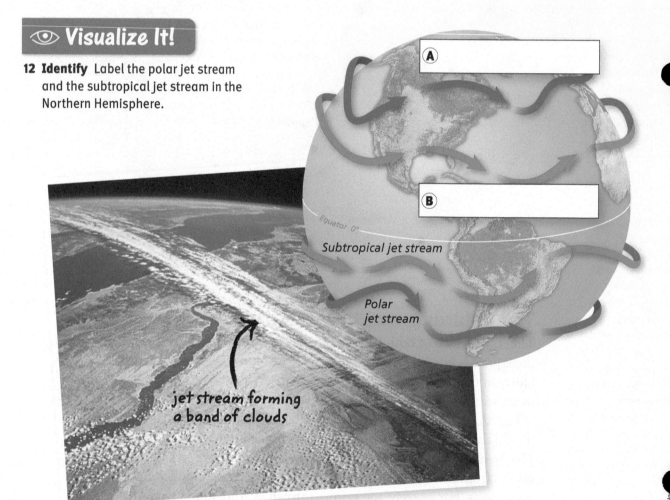

Subtropical jet stream

Polar jet stream

Equator 0°

jet stream forming a band of clouds

(bl) ©NASA/Science Source/Photo Researchers, Inc.

© Houghton Mifflin Ha Publishing Company

Desert Trades

How does some of the Sahara end up in the Americas?
Global winds carry it.

Trade Wind Carriers
Trade winds can carry
Saharan dust across the
Atlantic Ocean to Florida
and the Caribbean.

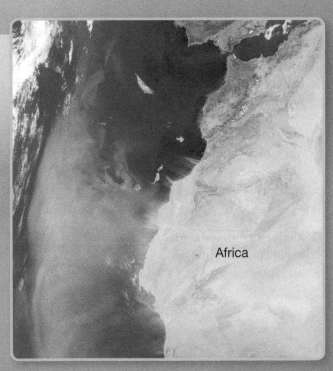

Africa

Florida Meets the Sahara
This hazy skyline in Miami is the result
of a dust storm. Where did the dust
come from? It all started in the Sahara.

The Sahara
The Sahara is the world's largest
hot desert. Sand and dust storms
that produce skies like this are
very common in this desert.

ℹ **Extend**

13 Explain your reasoning Look at a map and
explain how trade winds carry dust from the
Sahara to the Caribbean.

14 Gather Evidence Investigate the winds
that blow in your community. Where do they
usually come from? Identify the wind system
that could be involved.

15 Claims • Evidence • Reasoning How did the
winds play a role in distributing radioactive
waste that was released after an explosion
at the Chernobyl Nuclear Power Plant in
Ukraine? Gather evidence. Explain your
reasoning. Present your findings as a map
illustration or in a poster.

Feelin' Breezy

ACTIVE READING

16 Identify As you read, underline two examples of geographic features that contribute to the formation of local winds.

What are examples of local winds?

Local geographic features, such as a body of water or a mountain, can produce temperature and pressure differences that cause local winds. Unlike global winds, **local winds** are the movement of air over short distances. They can blow from any direction, depending on the features of the area.

Sea and Land Breezes

Have you ever felt a cool breeze coming off the ocean or a lake? If so, you were experiencing a sea breeze. Large bodies of water take longer to warm up than land does. During the day, air above land becomes warmer than air above water. The colder, denser air over water flows toward the land and pushes the warm air on the land upward. While water takes longer to warm than land does, land cools faster than water does. At night, cooler air on land causes a higher-pressure zone over the land. So, a wind blows from the land toward the water. This type of local wind is called a land breeze.

👁 Visualize It!

17 Analyze Label the areas of high pressure and low pressure.

sea breeze

Ⓑ _____ pressure

Ⓐ _____ pressure

land breeze

Ⓓ _____ pressure

Ⓒ _____ pressure

Valley and Mountain Breezes

Areas that have mountains and valleys experience local winds called mountain and valley breezes. During the day, the sun warms the air along the mountain slopes faster than the air in the valleys. This uneven heating results in areas of lower pressure near the mountain tops. This pressure difference causes a valley breeze, which flows from the valley up the slopes of the mountains. Many birds float on valley breezes to conserve energy. At nightfall, the air along the mountain slopes cools and moves down into the valley. This local wind is called a mountain breeze.

👁 **Visualize It!**

18 Analyze Label the areas of high pressure and low pressure.

valley breeze

Ⓑ _____ pressure

Ⓐ _____ pressure

mountain breeze

Ⓓ _____ pressure

Ⓒ _____ pressure

Visual Summary

To complete this summary, circle the correct word or phrases. You can use this page to review the main concepts of the lesson.

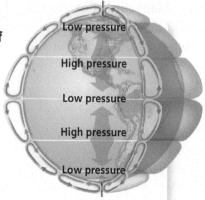

Wind is the movement of air from areas of higher pressure to areas of lower pressure.

19 Cool air sinks, causing an area of high / low air pressure.

Global wind systems occur on Earth.

20 High-speed wind between 7 km and 16 km above Earth's surface is a jet stream / mountain breeze.

Wind in the Atmosphere

Geographic features can produce local winds.

21 During the day, an area of high / low air pressure forms over water and a sea / land breeze occurs.

22 **Claims • Evidence • Reasoning** Would there be winds if the air above Earth's surface were the same temperature everywhere? Use evidence to support your claim. Explain your reasoning.

Lesson Review

Vocabulary

Fill in the blanks with the term that best completes the following sentences.

1 Another term for air movement caused by differences in air pressure is

_____.

2 Pilots often take advantage of the
_____ , which are
high-speed winds between 7 km and
16 km above Earth's surface.

3 The apparent curving of winds due to
Earth's rotation is the _____.

Key Concepts

4 Explain How does the sun cause wind?

_____

_____

_____

5 Claims • Evidence • Reasoning If Earth
did not rotate, what would happen to the
global winds? Provide evidence, and explain
your reasoning.

_____

_____

_____

6 Explain Your Reasoning How do
convection cells in Earth's atmosphere cause
high- and low-pressure belts?

_____

_____

_____

7 Describe What factors contribute to global
winds? Identify areas where winds are weak.

_____

_____

8 Identify Name a latitude where each of the
following occurs: polar easterlies, westerlies,
and trade winds.

_____

_____

Critical Thinking

9 Predict How would local winds be affected
if water and land absorbed and released heat
at the same rate? Explain your reasoning.

_____

_____

10 Compare How is a land breeze similar to a
sea breeze? How do they differ?

_____

_____

_____

Use this image to answer the following questions.

11 Analyze What type of local wind would
you experience if you were standing in the
valley? Explain your reasoning.

_____

_____

12 Infer Would the local wind change if it
were nighttime? Explain.

_____

_____

SC.6.N.3.1 Recognize and explain that a scientific theory is a well-supported and widely accepted explanation of nature and is not simply a claim posed by an individual. Thus, the use of the term theory in science is very different than how it is used in everyday life.

Evaluating Claims

Scentific methods teach us how to evaluate ideas or claims to find out if they are credible, and if our explanations are reliable and logical. We can apply critical thinking to all matters in life—even to things like deciding what detergent to buy or what to eat.

Ever since the 1930s, the legend of the Loch Ness monster living in their deep lake had become part of everyday life for the people of Inverness, Scotland. But there has been much controversy over whether or not the Loch Ness monster really exists. Who do we believe? In this case, using scientific thinking to evaluate the credibility of the claim can help.

Tutorial

Consider the evidence surrounding the Loch Ness monster claim—does the creature exist or not? How will you evaluate the evidence to come to a conclusion? Follow the steps below to shape your argument.

1 What were the methods used to collect the data? Think critically and find out why an explanation or claim has been accepted by looking at the experiments, data, and methods used to support the idea.

2 Has the data presented been tested with further observations? Think about whether the evidence supports the explanation or claim. Sometimes, facts are used to support a claim even though they cannot be retested or reproduced.

3 Is there any evidence that contradicts the explanation or claim? Is there a reasonable alternative explanation? It is important to know whether any evidence casts doubt on the explanation or claim.

Huge monster found in Scotland! Could it be a surviving dinosaur?

This is a famous photograph from 1934, showing the Loch Ness monster. In 1994, the person who took the photograph reported the "monster" as being only 14 inches tall and created by fastening an artificial head to a toy submarine.

AP PHOTO

You Try It!

Evaluating whether or not scientific evidence supports a claim can be useful in science and in everyday life. Read the brochure below, and assess the validity of the claims as you answer the questions that follow.

Geo-Vento Energy

Let Us Install Wind Turbines at Your School

The use of wind turbines to generate electrical energy at your school will:

Save nonrenewable resources!

Save money!

Say "goodbye" to electric bills!

Geo-Vento offers the following proof:

- A school in Cape Cod, MA, generates all of its electrical energy from wind turbines. This school no longer pays any electric bills.

- It is a well-established theory that wind is an excellent energy source throughout the United States. No more electric bills for anyone!

1 Evaluating Methods Evaluate the claims made in the brochure. What evidence in the brochure supports these claims?

_____

_____

_____

_____

2 Determining Factual Accuracy Is the evidence in the brochure related to the claims that are made? Explain your reasoning.

_____

_____

_____

3 Communicating Results Can you think of evidence that might disprove the claims that are made? Share your answer with your classmates and record their ideas.

_____

_____

_____

_____

_____

4 Claims • Evidence • Reasoning Do you think the theory offered as proof is scientific? Why might this statement not be widely accepted? Use evidence to support your claim and explain your reasoning.

_____

_____

_____

_____

5 Forming Alternative Hypotheses Write a claim that is a reasonable alternative to one of the claims made in the brochure. Consider and list the evidence you need to back it up.

_____

_____

_____

_____

 Take It Home!

With an adult, find a newspaper or magazine that appears to make scientific claims about a product. Carefully evaluate the claims and determine whether you think they are valid. Bring the ad to class and be prepared to share your evaluation.

Ocean Currents

ESSENTIAL QUESTION

How does water move in the ocean?

By the end of this lesson, you should be able to describe the movement of ocean water, explain what factors influence this movement, and explain why ocean circulation is important in the Earth system.

This iceberg off the coast of Newfoundland broke off an Arctic ice sheet and drifted south on ocean surface currents.

SC.6.E.7.3 Describe how global patterns such as the jet stream and ocean currents influence local weather in measurable terms such as temperature, air pressure, wind direction and speed, and humidity and precipitation.

 Lesson Labs

Quick Labs
• Can Messages Travel on Ocean Water?
• The Formation of Deep Currents

 Engage Your Brain

1 Predict Check T or F to show whether you think each statement is true or false.

T	F	
☐	☐	Ocean currents are always cold.
☐	☐	Continents affect the directions of currents.
☐	☐	Currents only flow near the surface of the ocean.
☐	☐	Wind affects currents.
☐	☐	The sun affects currents near the surface of the ocean.

This image shows sea ice caught in ocean currents.

2 Analyze What can you learn about ocean currents from this image?

_____

_____

ACTIVE **READING**

3 Synthesize You can often define an unknown word if you know the meaning of its word parts. Use the word parts and sentence below to make an educated guess about the meaning of the word *upwelling*.

Word part	Meaning
up-	from beneath the ground or water
well	to rise

Example Sentence
In areas where <u>upwelling</u> occurs, plankton feed on nutrients from deep in the ocean.

 upwelling:

_____

_____

Vocabulary Terms
• ocean current   • deep current
• surface current   • convection current
• Coriolis effect   • upwelling

4 Apply As you learn the definition of each vocabulary term in this lesson, create your own definition or sketch to help you remember the meaning of the term.

Going with the Flow

What are ocean currents?

The oceans contain streamlike movements of water called **ocean currents**. Ocean currents that occur at or near the surface of the ocean, caused by wind, are called **surface currents**. Most surface currents reach depths of about 100 m, but some go deeper. Surface currents also reach lengths of several thousand kilometers and can stretch across oceans. An example of a surface current is the Gulf Stream. The Gulf Stream is one of the strongest surface currents on Earth. The Gulf Stream transports, or moves, more water each year than is transported by all the rivers in the world combined.

Infrared cameras on satellites provide images that show differences in temperature. Scientists add color to the images afterward to highlight the different temperatures, as shown below.

ACTIVE **READING**

5 Identify As you read, underline three factors that affect surface currents.

What affects surface currents?

Surface currents are affected by three factors: continental deflections, the Coriolis effect, and global winds. These factors keep surface currents flowing in distinct patterns around Earth.

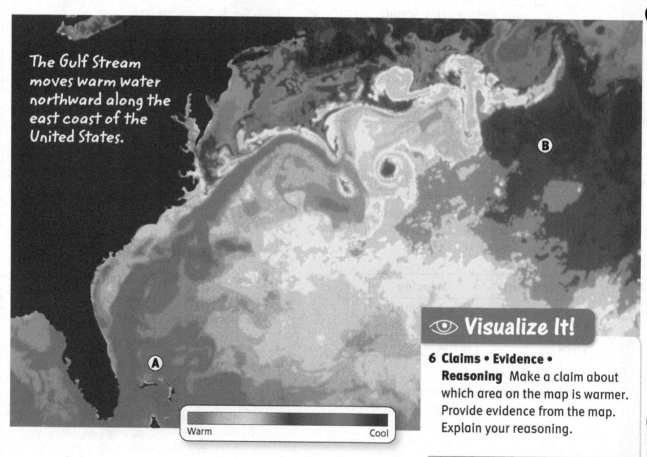

The Gulf Stream moves warm water northward along the east coast of the United States.

A

B

Warm   Cool

Visualize It!

6 Claims • Evidence • Reasoning Make a claim about which area on the map is warmer. Provide evidence from the map. Explain your reasoning.

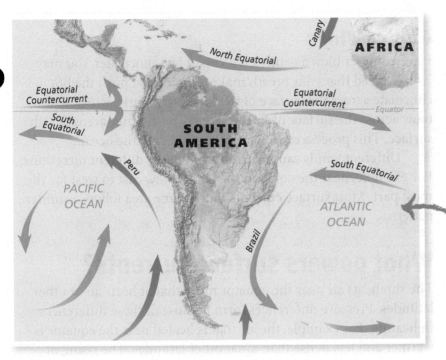

7 Identify Circle areas on the map where ocean currents have been deflected by a land mass.

Currents change direction when they meet continents.

Continental Deflections

If Earth's surface were covered only with water, surface currents would simply travel continually in one direction. However, water does not cover the entire surface of Earth. Continents rise above sea level over about one-third of Earth's surface. When surface currents meet continents, the currents are deflected and change direction. For example, the South Equatorial Current turns southward as it meets the coast of South America.

The Coriolis Effect

Earth's rotation causes all wind and ocean currents, except on the equator, to be deflected from the paths they would take if Earth did not rotate. The deflection of moving objects from a straight path due to Earth's rotation is called the **Coriolis effect** (kawr•ee•OH•lis ih•FEKT). Earth is spherical, so Earth's circumference at latitudes above and below the equator is shorter than the circumference at the equator. But the period of rotation is always 24 hours. Therefore, points on Earth near the equator travel faster than points closer to the poles.

The difference in speed of rotation causes the Coriolis effect. For example, wind and water traveling south from the North Pole actually go toward the southwest instead of straight south. Wind and water deflect to the right because the wind and water move east more slowly than Earth rotates beneath them. In the Northern Hemisphere, currents are deflected to the right. In the Southern Hemisphere, currents are deflected to the left.

The Coriolis effect is most noticeable for objects that travel over long distances, without any interruptions. Over short distances, the difference in Earth's rotational speed from one point to another point is not great enough to cause noticeable deflection.

In the Northern Hemisphere, currents are deflected to the right.

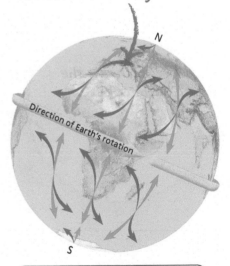

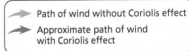

→ Path of wind without Coriolis effect
→ Approximate path of wind with Coriolis effect

Global Winds

Have you ever blown gently on a cup of hot chocolate? You may have noticed that your breath makes ripples that push the hot chocolate across the surface of the liquid. Similarly, winds that blow across the surface of Earth's oceans push water across Earth's surface. This process causes surface currents in the ocean.

Different winds cause currents to flow in different directions. For example, near the equator, the winds blow east to west for the most part. Most surface currents in the same area follow a similar pattern.

What powers surface currents?

The sun heats air near the equator more than it heats air at other latitudes. Pressure differences form because of these differences in heating. For example, the air that is heated near the equator is warmer and less dense than air at other latitudes. The rising of warm air creates an area of low pressure near the equator. Pressure differences in the atmosphere cause the wind to form. So, the sun causes winds to form, and winds cause surface currents to form. Therefore, the major source of the energy that powers surface currents is the sun.

8 Analyze Fill in the cause-and-effect chart to show how the sun's energy powers surface ocean currents.

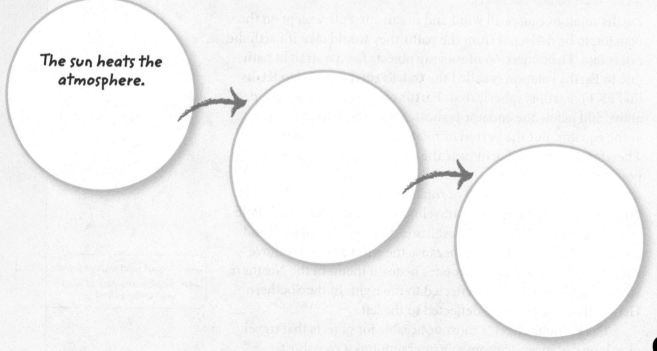

The sun heats the atmosphere.

Global Surface Winds

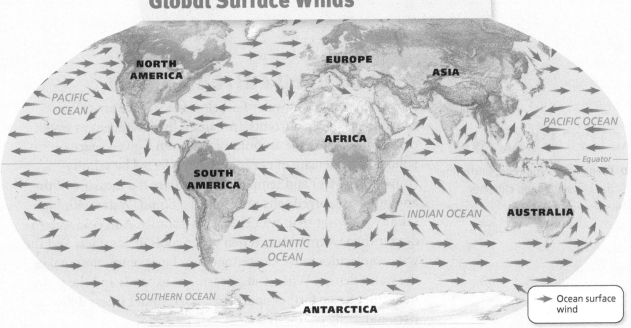

NORTH AMERICA

EUROPE

ASIA

PACIFIC OCEAN

PACIFIC OCEAN

AFRICA

Equator

SOUTH AMERICA

INDIAN OCEAN

AUSTRALIA

ATLANTIC OCEAN

SOUTHERN OCEAN

ANTARCTICA

→ Ocean surface wind

Global Surface Currents

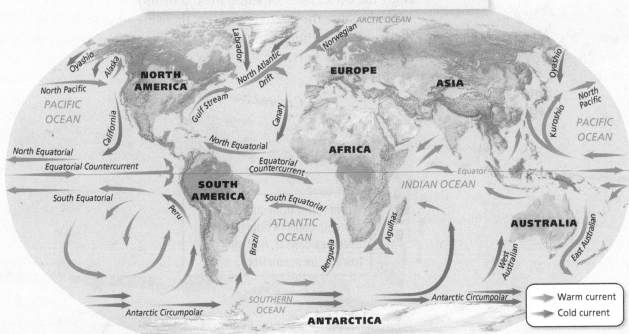

ARCTIC OCEAN

Labrador

Norwegian

Oyashio

Alaska

North Pacific

NORTH AMERICA

North Atlantic Drift

EUROPE

ASIA

Oyashio

North Pacific

PACIFIC OCEAN

Gulf Stream

Canary

Kuroshio

PACIFIC OCEAN

California

North Equatorial

AFRICA

North Equatorial

Equatorial Counturcurrent

Equatorial Countercurrent

Equator

INDIAN OCEAN

South Equatorial

SOUTH AMERICA

South Equatorial

AUSTRALIA

East Australian

Peru

Brazil

ATLANTIC OCEAN

Agulhas

Benguela

West Australian

Antarctic Circumpolar

SOUTHERN OCEAN

Antarctic Circumpolar

→ Warm current
→ Cold current

ANTARCTICA

◉ Visualize It!

9 Gather Evidence Circle the same area on each map. Describe what you observe about these two areas.

_____

_____

_____

Current Events

How do deep currents form?

Movements of ocean water far below the surface are called **deep currents**. Deep currents are caused by differences in water density. *Density* is the amount of matter in a given space or volume. The density of ocean water is affected by salinity (suh•LIN•ih•tee) and temperature. *Salinity* is a measure of the amount of dissolved salts or solids in a liquid. Water with high salinity is denser than water with low salinity. And cold water is denser than warm water. When water cools, it contracts and the water molecules move closer together. This contraction makes the water denser. When water warms, it expands and the water molecules move farther apart. The warm water is less dense, so it rises above the cold water.

When ocean water at the surface becomes denser than water below it, the denser water sinks. The water moves from the surface to the deep ocean, forming deep currents. Deep currents flow along the ocean floor or along the top of another layer of denser water. Because the ocean is so deep, there are several layers of water at any location in the ocean. The deepest and densest water in the ocean is Antarctic Bottom Water, near Antarctica.

ACTIVE READING

10 Identify As you read, underline the cause of deep currents.

Polar region

Convection current

B — Warm water from surface currents cools in polar regions, becomes denser, and sinks toward the ocean floor.

C — Deep currents carry colder, denser water in the deep ocean from polar regions to other parts of Earth.

◉ Visualize It!

11 Illustrate Complete the drawing at part B on the diagram.

What are convection currents?

As you read about convection currents, refer to the illustration below. Surface currents and deep currents are linked in the ocean. Together they form convection currents. In the ocean, a **convection current** is a movement of water that results from density differences. Convection currents can be vertical, circular, or cyclical. Think of convection currents in the ocean as a conveyor belt. Surface currents make up the top part of the belt. Deep currents make up the bottom part of the belt. Water from a surface current may become a deep current in areas where water density increases. Deep current water then rises up to the surface in areas where the surface current is carrying low-density water away.

How do convection currents transfer energy?

Convection currents transfer energy. Water at the ocean's surface absorbs energy from the sun. Surface currents carry this energy to colder regions. The warm water loses energy to its surroundings and cools. As the water cools, it becomes denser and it sinks. The cold water travels along the ocean bottom. Then, the cold water rises to the surface as warm surface water moves away. The cold water absorbs energy from the sun, and the cycle continues.

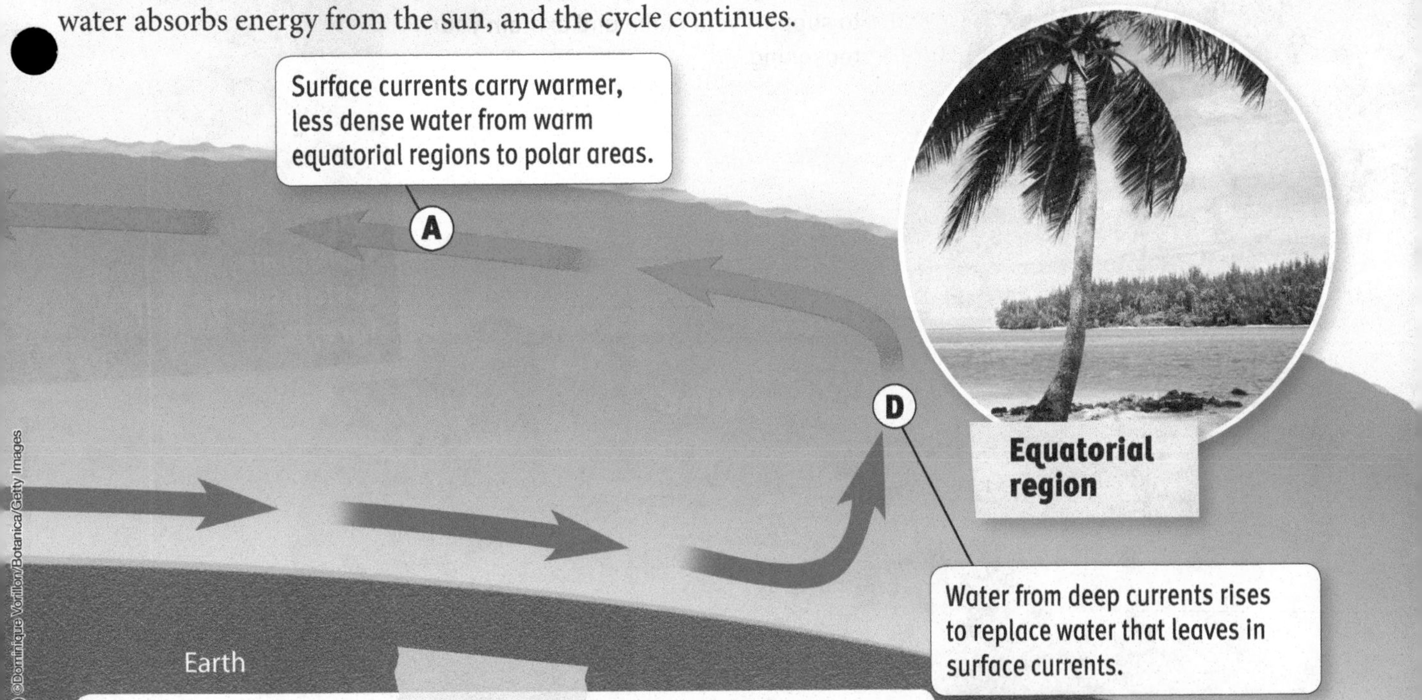

i Think Outside the Book

12 **Apply** Write an interview with a water molecule following a convection current. Be sure to include questions and answers. Can you imagine the temperature changes the molecule would experience?

Surface currents carry warmer, less dense water from warm equatorial regions to polar areas.

A

D

Equatorial region

Water from deep currents rises to replace water that leaves in surface currents.

Earth

i 13 **Claims • Evidence • Reasoning** Make a claim about how convection currents are important in the Earth systems. Provide evidence to support your claim. Explain your reasoning.

_____

_____

Note: Drawing is not to scale.

That's Swell!

What is upwelling?

At times, winds blow toward the equator along the northwest coast of South America and the west coast of North America. These winds cause surface currents to move away from the shore. The warm surface water is then replaced by cold, nutrient-rich water from the deep ocean in a process called **upwelling**. The deep water contains nutrients, such as iron and nitrate.

Upwelling is extremely important to ocean life. The nutrients that are brought to the surface of the ocean support the growth of phytoplankton (fy•toh•PLANGK•tuhn) and zooplankton. These tiny plants and animals are food for other organisms, such as fish and seabirds. Many fisheries are located in areas of upwelling because ocean animals thrive there. Some weather conditions can interrupt the process of upwelling. When upwelling is reduced, the richness of the ocean life at the surface is also reduced.

ACTIVE **READING**

14 Identify As you read, underline the steps that occur in upwelling.

The livelihood of these Peruvian fishermen depends on upwelling.

15 Claims • Evidence • Reasoning
What might happen to the fisheries if upwelling stopped? Provide evidence to support your claim and explain your reasoning.

_____
_____
_____
_____
_____

On the coast of California, upwelling sustains large kelp forests.

Wind

Warm surface water

During upwelling, cold, nutrient-rich water from the deep ocean rises to the surface.

WHY IT MATTERS

Hitching a Ride!

What do coconuts, plankton, and sea turtles have in common? They get free rides on ocean currents.

World Travel

When baby sea turtles are hatched on a beach, they head for the ocean. They can then pick up ocean currents to travel. Some travel from Australia to South America on currents.

Sprouting Coconuts!

This sprouting coconut may be transported by ocean currents to a beach. This transport explains why coconut trees can grow in several areas.

Fast Food

Diatoms are a kind of phytoplankton. They are tiny, one-celled plants that form the basis of the food chain. Diatoms ride surface currents throughout the world.

i Extend

16 Identify List three organisms transported by ocean currents.

17 Gather Evidence Investigate the Sargasso Sea. State why a lot of plastic collects in this sea. Find out whether any plastic collects on the shoreline nearest you.

18 Claims • Evidence • Reasoning Plastic and other debris can collect in the ocean. Gather evidence to support this claim and explain your reasoning.

Traveling the World

What do ocean currents transport?

Ocean water circulates through all of Earth's ocean basins. The paths are like the main highway on which ocean water flows. If you could follow a water molecule on this path, you would find that the molecule takes more than 1,000 years to return to its starting point! Along with water, ocean currents also transport dissolved solids, dissolved gases, and energy around Earth.

ACTIVE READING

19 Identify As you read, underline the description of how energy reaches the poles.

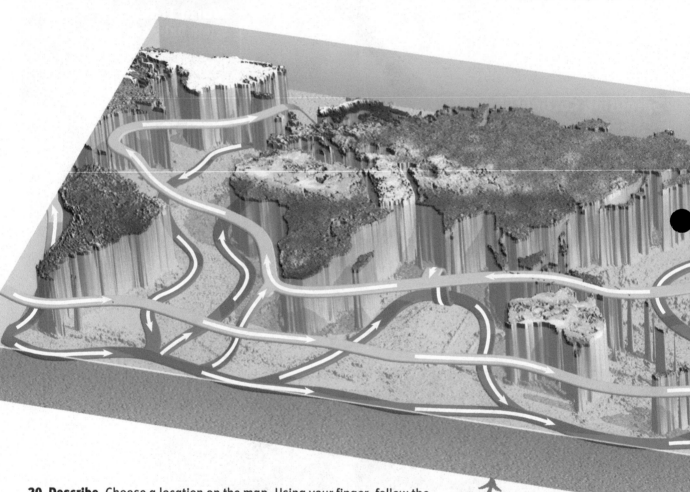

20 Describe Choose a location on the map. Using your finger, follow the route you would take if you could ride a current. Describe your route. Include the direction you go and the landmasses you pass.

_____

_____

_____

_____

_____

Antarctica is not shown on this map, but the currents at the bottom of the map circulate around Antarctica.

Ocean Currents Transport Energy

Global ocean circulation is very important in the transport of energy in the form of heat. Remember that ocean currents flow in huge convection currents that can be thousands of kilometers long. These convection currents carry about 40% of the energy that is transported around Earth's surface.

Near the equator, the ocean absorbs a large amount of solar energy. The ocean also absorbs energy from the atmosphere. Ocean currents carry this energy from the equator toward the poles. When the warm water travels to cooler areas, the energy is released back into the atmosphere. Therefore, ocean circulation has an important influence on Earth's climate.

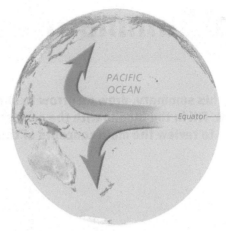

In the Pacific Ocean, surface currents transport energy from the tropics to latitudes above and below the equator.

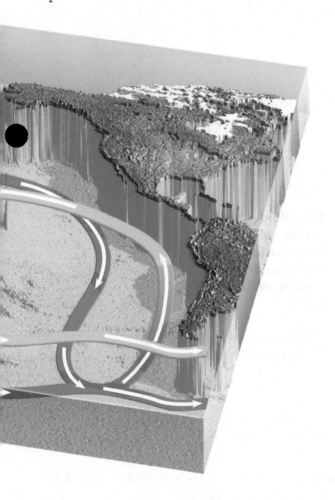

Ocean Currents Transport Matter

Besides water, ocean currents transport whatever is in the water. The most familiar dissolved solid in ocean water is sodium chloride, or table salt. Other dissolved solids are important to marine life. Ocean water contains many nutrients—such as nitrogen and phosphorus—that are important for plant and animal growth.

Ocean water also transports gases. Gases in the atmosphere are absorbed by ocean water at the ocean surface. As a result, the most abundant gases in the atmosphere—nitrogen, oxygen, argon, and carbon dioxide—are also abundant in the ocean. Dissolved oxygen and carbon dioxide are necessary for the survival of many marine organisms.

21 Claims • Evidence • Reasoning Other matter besides water are transported by ocean currents. Gather evidence to support this claim and explain your reasoning.

_____
_____
_____
_____
_____

Visual Summary

To complete this summary, draw an arrow to show each type of ocean current. Fill in the blanks with the correct word. You can use this page to review the main concepts of the lesson.

Surface currents are streamlike movements of water at or near the surface of the ocean.

22 The direction of a surface current is affected by

_____ ,

_____ ,

and _____

Deep currents are streamlike movements of ocean water located far below the surface.

23 Deep currents form where the

_____

of ocean water increases.

Ocean Currents

A convection current in the ocean is any movement of matter that results from differences in density.

24 A convection current in the ocean transports matter and

_____

Upwelling is the process in which warm surface water is replaced by cold water from the deep ocean.

25 The cold water from deep in the ocean contains

_____

26 Claims • Evidence • Reasoning Investigate patterns of global circulation. Make a claim about how global circulation works. Summarize evidence to support the claim and explain your reasoning.

Lesson Review

Vocabulary

Fill in the blanks with the terms that best complete the following sentences.

1 _____ are streamlike movements of water in the ocean.

2 The _____ causes currents in open water to move in a curved path rather than a straight path.

3 _____ causes cold, nutrient-rich waters to move up to the ocean's surface.

Key Concepts

4 Explain Your Reasoning How does the sun provide energy for surface ocean currents?

_____

_____

_____

_____

5 Explain Your Reasoning State how a deep current forms.

_____

_____

_____

6 Explain Your Reasoning How does a convection current transports energy around the globe? Explain your reasoning.

_____

_____

_____

7 List Write the three factors that affect surface ocean currents.

_____

_____

Critical Thinking

Use this diagram to answer the following questions.

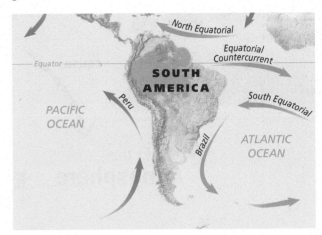

8 Apply Explain why the direction of the South Equatorial current changes.

_____

_____

_____

_____

9 Claims • Evidence • Reasoning Make a claim about how the direction of the South Equatorial current would be different if South America were not there. Provide evidence and explain your reasoning.

_____

_____

_____

_____

10 Explain Your Reasoning. Describe how surface currents would be affected if Earth did not rotate.

_____

_____

_____

_____

_____

Energy Transfer

happens throughout

causes → **Wind** in the **Atmosphere**

causes → **Ocean Currents**

Earth's Spheres

including → The **Atmosphere**

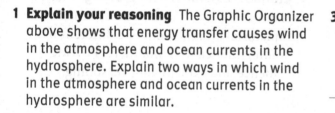

1 Explain your reasoning The Graphic Organizer above shows that energy transfer causes wind in the atmosphere and ocean currents in the hydrosphere. Explain two ways in which wind in the atmosphere and ocean currents in the hydrosphere are similar.

_____

_____

_____

_____

2 Contrast Describe the ways in which radiation, conduction, and convection transfer energy in the atmosphere.

_____

_____

_____

_____

3 Apply How could a lake be considered a part of one of Earth's spheres during one season and part of another sphere during another season?

_____

_____

_____

4 Claims • Evidence • Reasoning A student makes a statement, "The term *heat* applies to only those things that are considered hot." Make a claim about whether this claim is true or false. Gather evidence and explain your reasoning.

_____

_____

_____

Vocabulary

Name _____

Check the box to show whether each statement is true or false.

T	F		
☐	☐	**1**	Radiation is a measure of the average kinetic energy of the particles in an object.
☐	☐	**2**	Thermal expansion is the increase in volume that results from an increase in temperature.
☐	☐	**3**	The stratosphere is the top layer of Earth's atmosphere.
☐	☐	**4**	A jet stream is a wide band of low-speed winds that flow in the middle atmosphere.

Key Concepts

Identify the choice that best completes the statement or answers the question.

5 Meggie measures the wind speed every day for 7 weeks. She constructs the following line graph of the average weekly wind speed.

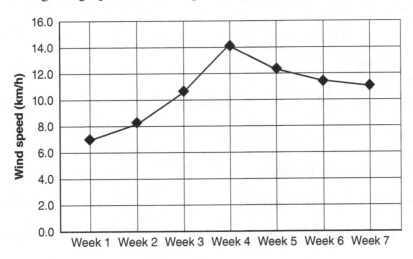

How many of the 7 weeks experience average wind speeds **greater than** 7.9 km/h?

A 4 weeks

B 5 weeks

C 6 weeks

D 7 weeks

6 Bob knows that water in a geyser is warmed by energy from deep within Earth. To investigate this process, he warms 2 L of water from 25 °C to 100 °C. Which property of the water will decrease?

F density

G volume

H kinetic energy

I thermal energy

7 Carly draws a map of surface currents in the Atlantic Ocean. On her map, she includes the major wind belts for the same area. Her map is similar to the one shown below.

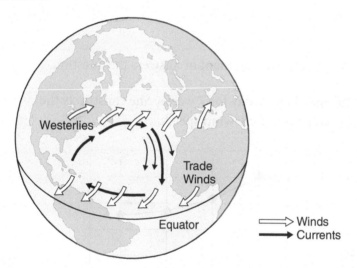

If Carly wants to add wind belts for the part of the Atlantic just south of the equator, how should she draw the arrows?

A The arrows should curve upward to the left.

B The arrows should curve upward to the right.

C The arrows should curve downward to the left.

D The arrows should curve downward to the right.

8 Sometimes fires burn large areas of forests that are part of the biosphere. Other than the biosphere, which of Earth's other spheres is a forest fire **most likely** to affect?

F geosphere

G cryosphere

H atmosphere

I hydrosphere

9 In the 18th century, the trade winds played an important role in England's merchant fleet crossing the Atlantic Ocean. This is how the trade winds got their name. In the tropics, in which direction do the trade winds drive equatorial ocean currents?

A eastward

B northward

C southward

D westward

10 Ginny enjoys mountain climbing. Today, she is climbing Mt. Sheridan, which is the tallest mountain she's ever climbed. When Ginny makes it to the top, she notices that it is more difficult to catch her breath. At higher elevations, why is it harder for Ginny to breathe?

F At higher altitudes, the air is too cold.

G At higher altitudes, the air pressure is lower.

H At higher altitudes, the air contains too much nitrogen.

I At higher altitudes, the air contains too much carbon dioxide.

11 The gases that make up Earth's atmosphere are commonly referred to as air. Air consists of major gases and trace gases. What is air?

A a mixture

B a molecule

C an element

D a compound

12 Matthew and Mei measure the temperature of the water in a lake at different times of the day. The following table shows their data at four different times.

Time	Temperature (°C)
9:00 a.m.	12
11:00 a.m.	14
3:00 p.m.	16
5:00 p.m.	13

At what time was the thermal energy of the lake water the **greatest**?

F 9:00 a.m.

G 11:00 a.m.

H 3:00 p.m.

I 5:00 p.m.

13 The continent of Antarctica is covered with an ice sheet. Which part of the Earth system includes the ice sheet?

A biosphere

C hydrosphere

B cryosphere

D atmosphere

Critical Thinking

Answer the following questions in the space provided.

14 The picture below shows a situation that causes local winds.

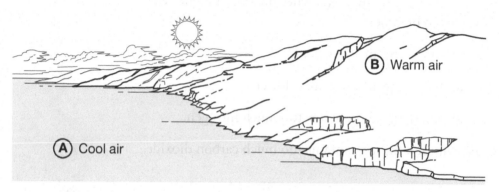

Draw an arrow on the picture to show which way the wind will blow. Make a claim about why the wind blows in that direction and name this type of local wind.

_____

_____

15 Suppose you were a superhero that could fly up through the atmosphere while feeling the temperature and air pressure change around you. Describe your trip in a paragraph, naming the four main atmospheric layers and telling how the temperature and air pressure change as you pass through each.

_____

_____

_____

_____

_____

Weather and Climate

FLORIDA BIG IDEA?

Earth Systems and Patterns

A tropical storm sends waves crashing into property.

What Do You Think?

At times the weather can change very quickly. In severe weather, people and pets can get hurt, and property can be damaged. Can you think of ways to keep people, pets, and property safe? As you explore this unit, gather evidence to help you state and support a claim.

UNIT 11

Weather and Climate

CITIZEN SCIENCE

Exit Strategy

When there is an emergency, knowing what to do helps keep people as safe as possible. So what's the plan?

① Think About It

A Do you know what to do if there were a weather emergency while you were in school?

_____

B What kinds of information might you need to stay safe? List them below.

_____
_____
_____
_____
_____

Floods can happen very quickly during a bad storm.

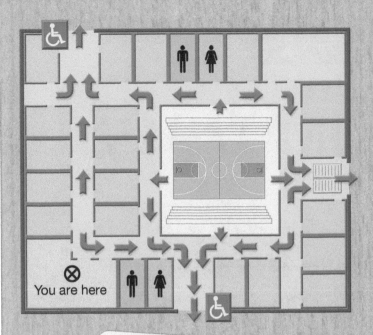

② Ask a Question

How well do you know your school's emergency evacuation plan? Obtain a copy of the school's emergency evacuation plan. Read through the plan and answer the following questions as a class.

A Is the emergency evacuation plan/map easy for students to understand?

_____

_____

B How would you know which way to go?

_____

_____

_____

C How often do you have practice drills?

_____

_____

You are here

EMERGENCY EVACUATION ROUTE

③ Propose and Apply Improvements

A Using what you have learned about your school's emergency evacuation plan, list your ideas for improvements below.

_____

_____

_____

_____

_____

_____

B Develop and give a short oral presentation to your principal about your proposal on ways to improve the school's emergency evacuation plan. Write the main points of your presentation below.

_____

_____

_____

_____

_____

C As a class, practice the newly improved emergency evacuation plan. Describe how well the improved emergency evacuation plan worked.

_____

_____

_____

_____

_____

_____

_____

_____

⌂ Take It Home!

With an adult, create an emergency evacuation plan for your family or evaluate your family's emergency evacuation plan and propose improvements.

The Water Cycle

ESSENTIAL QUESTION

How does water change state and move around on Earth?

By the end of this lesson, you should be able to describe the water cycle and the different processes that are part of the water cycle on Earth.

Water from the ocean evaporates, forms clouds, then falls back into the ocean when it rains. Can you think of other ways water travels between Earth and Earth's atmosphere?

SC.6.E.7.2 Investigate and apply how the cycling of water between the atmosphere and hydrosphere has an effect on weather patterns and climate.
SC.6.E.7.4 Differentiate and show interactions among the geosphere, hydrosphere, cryosphere, atmosphere, and biosphere.

Lesson Labs

Quick Labs
- Modeling the Water Cycle
- Can You Make It Rain in a Jar?
- Reaching the Dew Point

Exploration Lab
- Changes in Water

Engage Your Brain

1 Predict Circle the word or phrase that best completes the following sentences.

The air inside a glass of ice would feel *warm/cold/room temperature*.

Ice would *melt/evaporate/remain frozen* if it were left outside on a hot day.

Water vapor will *condense on/evaporate from/ melt into* the glass of ice from the air.

The ice *absorbs energy from/maintains its energy/releases energy into* the surroundings when it melts.

2 Analyze Using the photo above, solve the word scramble to answer the question: What happens to ice as it warms up?

T I   G A C N S E H   E A S T T

_____

ACTIVE **READING**

3 Synthesize You can often define an unknown word if you know the meaning of the word's origin. Use the meaning of the words' origins and the sentence below to make an educated guess about the meaning of *precipitation* and *evaporation*.

Latin word	Meaning
praecipitare	fall
evaporare	spread out in vapor or steam

Example sentence
Precipitation, in the form of rain, helps replace the water lost by evaporation from the lake.

precipitation:

_____

evaporation:

_____

Vocabulary Terms
- water cycle
- evaporation
- transpiration
- sublimation
- condensation
- precipitation

4 Apply As you learn the definition of each vocabulary term in this lesson, write out a sentence using that term to help you remember the meaning of the term.

What goes up...

What is the water cycle?

Movement of water between the atmosphere, land, oceans, and even living things makes up the **water cycle**. Rain, snow, and hail fall on the oceans and land because of gravity. On land, ice and water flow downhill. Water flows in streams, rivers, and waterfalls such as the one in the photo, because of gravity. If the land is flat, water will collect in certain areas forming ponds, lakes, and marshland. Some water will soak through the ground and collect underground as groundwater. Even groundwater flows downhill.

Water and snow can move upward if they turn into water vapor and rise into the air. Plants and animals also release water vapor into the air. In the air, water vapor can travel great distances with the wind. Winds can also move the water in the surface layer of the ocean by creating ocean currents. When ocean currents reach the shore or colder climates, the water will sink if it is cold enough or salty enough. The sinking water creates currents at different depths in the ocean. These are some of the ways in which water travels all over Earth.

👁 Visualize It!

5 Claims • Evidence • Reasoning Make a claim about the importance of the movement of water between the atmosphere, land, oceans, and living things. Summarize evidence to support the claim and explain your reasoning.

_____

_____

_____

_____

_____

How does water change state?

Water is found in three states on Earth: as liquid water, as solid water ice, and as gaseous water vapor. Water is visible as a liquid or a solid, but it is invisible as a gas in the air. Water can change from one state to another as energy is absorbed or released.

Water absorbs energy from its surroundings as it *melts* from solid to liquid. Water also absorbs energy when it *evaporates* from liquid to gas, or when it *sublimates* from solid to gas. Water releases energy into its surroundings when it *condenses* from gas to liquid. Water also releases energy when it *freezes* from liquid to solid, or *deposits* from gas to solid. No water is lost during these changes.

ACTIVE **READING**

6 Identify As you read, underline each process in which energy is absorbed or released.

👁 **Visualize It!**

7 Analyze Under each photo, write an example of where you might find water in that state of matter.

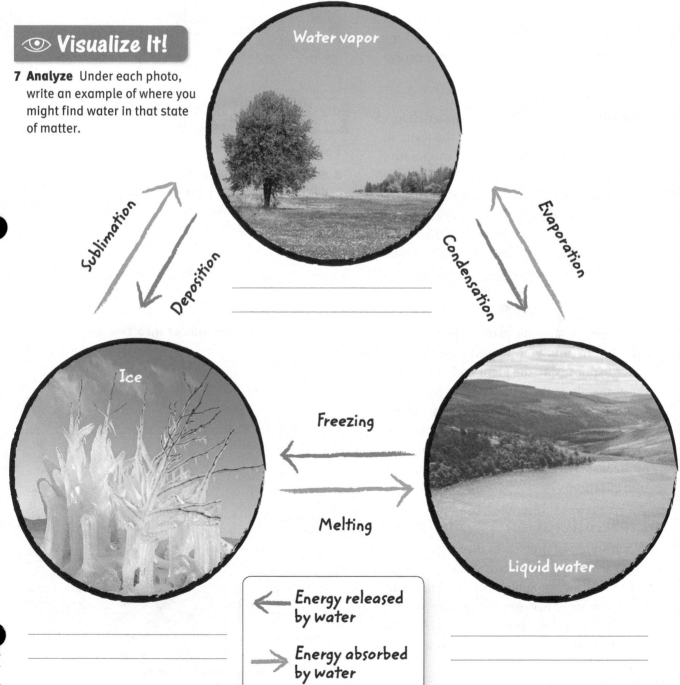

Water vapor

Sublimation

Deposition

Condensation

Evaporation

Ice

Freezing

Melting

Liquid water

← Energy released by water

→ Energy absorbed by water

The evaporating water leaves behind a dry, cracked lake bed.

How does water reach the atmosphere?

Water reaches the atmosphere as water vapor in three ways: evaporation (i•VAP•uh•ray•shuhn), transpiration (tran•spuh•RAY•shuhn), and sublimation (suhb•luh•MAY•shuhn). It takes a lot of energy for liquid or solid water to turn into water vapor. The energy for these changes comes mostly from the sun, as solar energy.

○ Evaporation

Evaporation occurs when liquid water changes into water vapor. About 90% of the water in the atmosphere comes from the evaporation of Earth's water. Some water evaporates from the water on land. However, most of the water vapor evaporates from Earth's oceans. This is because oceans cover most of Earth's surface. Therefore, oceans receive most of the solar energy that reaches Earth.

○ Transpiration

Like many organisms, plants release water into the environment. Liquid water turns into water vapor inside the plant and moves into the atmosphere through stomata. Stomata are tiny holes that are found on some plant surfaces. This release of water vapor into the air by plants is called **transpiration**. About 10% of the water in the atmosphere comes from transpiration.

○ Sublimation

When solid water changes directly to water vapor without first becoming a liquid, it is called **sublimation**. Sublimation can happen when dry air blows over ice or snow, where it is very cold and the pressure is low. A small amount of the water in the atmosphere comes from sublimation.

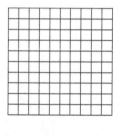 **Do the Math**

You Try It

8 Gather Evidence Show the percentage of water vapor in the atmosphere that comes from evaporation by coloring the equivalent number of squares in the grid.

Water moves into the air.

⊙ Visualize It!

9 Identify Fill in the circles beside each red heading at left with the label of the arrow showing the matching process in this diagram.

What happens to water in the atmosphere?

Water reaches the atmosphere as water vapor. In the atmosphere, water vapor mixes with other gases. To leave the atmosphere, water vapor must change into liquid or solid water. Then the liquid or solid water can fall to Earth's surface.

◯ Condensation

Remember, **condensation** (kahn•den•SAY•shuhn) is the change of state from a gas to a liquid. If air that contains water vapor is cooled enough, condensation occurs. Some of the water vapor condenses on small particles, such as dust, forming little balls or tiny droplets of water. These water droplets float in the air as clouds, fog, or mist. At the ground level, water vapor may condense on cool surfaces as dew.

◯ Precipitation

In clouds, water droplets may collide and "stick" together to become larger. If a droplet becomes large enough, it falls to Earth's surface as precipitation (pri•sip•i•TAY•shuhn). **Precipitation** is any form of water that falls to Earth from clouds. Three common kinds of precipitation shown in the photos are rain, snow, and hail. Snow and hail form if the water droplets freeze. Most rain falls into the oceans because most water evaporates from ocean surfaces and oceans cover most of Earth's surface. But winds carry clouds from the ocean over land, increasing the amount of precipitation that falls on land.

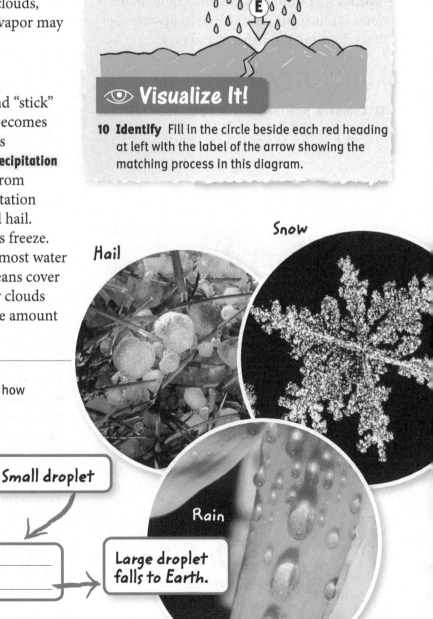

Water returns to Earth's surface.

D

E

◉ Visualize It!

10 Identify Fill in the circle beside each red heading at left with the label of the arrow showing the matching process in this diagram.

Hail

Snow

Rain

11 Summarize Fill in the boxes to describe how precipitation forms.

[_____] → Small droplet → [_____] → Large droplet falls to Earth.

How does water move on land and in the oceans?

After water falls to Earth, it flows and circulates all over Earth. On land, water flows downhill, both on the surface and underground. However, most of Earth's precipitation falls into the oceans. Ocean currents move water around the oceans.

Runoff and Infiltration

All of the water on land flows downhill because of gravity. Streams, rivers, and the water that flows over land are types of *runoff*. Runoff flows downhill toward oceans, lakes, and marshlands.

Some of the water on land seeps into the ground. This process is called *infiltration* (in•fil•TRAY•shuhn). Once undergound, the water is called *groundwater*. Groundwater also flows downhill through soil and rock.

ACTIVE READING

12 Compare How do runoff and groundwater differ?

_____

_____

_____

👁 Visualize It!

13 Support Your Claim Write a caption describing how water is moving in the diagram above.

_____

_____

Icebergs can be carried over long distances by ocean currents.

Ice Flow

Much of Earth's ice is stored in large ice caps in Antarctica and Greenland. Some ice is stored in glaciers at high altitudes all over Earth. Glaciers cover about 10% of Earth's surface. Glaciers can be called "rivers of ice" because gravity also causes glaciers to flow slowly downhill. Many glaciers never leave land. However, some glaciers flow to the ocean, where pieces may break off, as seen in the photo, and float far out to sea as icebergs.

Ocean Circulation

Winds move ocean water on the surface in great currents, sometimes for thousands of miles. At some shores, or if the water is very cold or salty, it will sink deep into the ocean. This movement helps create deep ocean currents. Both surface currents and deep ocean currents transport large amounts of water from ocean to ocean.

©Marco Simoni/Robert Harding World Imagery/Getty Images

© Houghton Mifflin Harcourt Publishing Company

Water Works

What does the water cycle transport?

In the water cycle, each state of water has some energy in it. This energy is released into or absorbed from its surroundings as water changes state. The energy in each state of water is then transported as the water moves from place to place. Matter is also transported as water and the materials in the water move all over Earth. Therefore, the water cycle moves energy and matter through Earth's atmosphere, land, oceans, and living things.

Think Outside the Book

14 Claims • Evidence • Reasoning Make a claim about how the water cycle transfers energy. Summarize evidence to support the claim and explain your reasoning.

Energy

Energy is transported in the water cycle through changes of state and by the movement of water from place to place. For example, water that evaporates from the ocean carries energy into the atmosphere. This movement of energy can generate hurricanes. Also, cold ocean currents can cool the air along a coastline by absorbing the energy from the air and leaving the air cooler. This energy is carried away quickly as the current continues on its path. Such processes affect the weather and climate of an area.

Matter

Earth's ocean currents move vast amounts of water all over the world. These currents also transport the solids in the water and the dissolved salts and gases. Rivers transfer water from land into the ocean. Rivers also carry large amounts of sand, mud, and gravel as shown below. Rivers form deltas and floodplains, where some of the materials from upstream collect in areas downstream. Rivers also carve valleys and canyons, and carry the excess materials downstream. Glaciers also grind away rock and carry the ground rock with them as they flow.

Visualize It!

15 Identify What do rivers, such as the ones in the photo, transport?

____

____

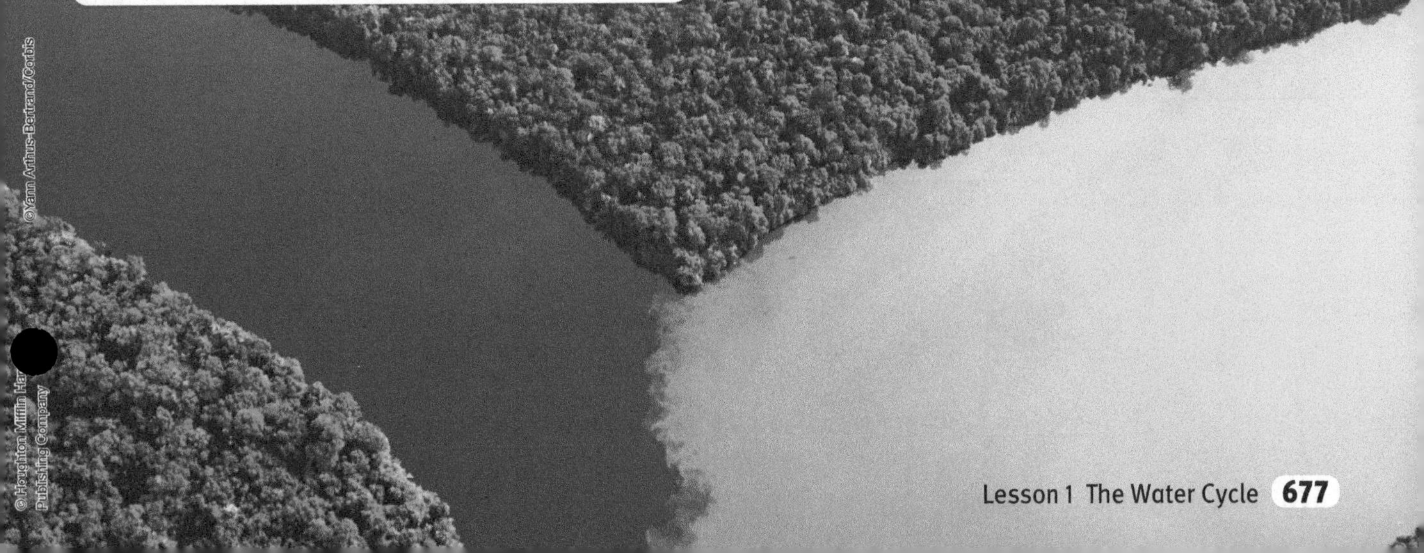

👁 Visualize It!

The Water Cycle

Water is continuously changing state and moving from place to place in the water cycle. This diagram shows these processes and movements.

16 Identify Label each arrow to show which process the arrow represents.

17 Identify Shade in the arrows that indicate where water is changing state.

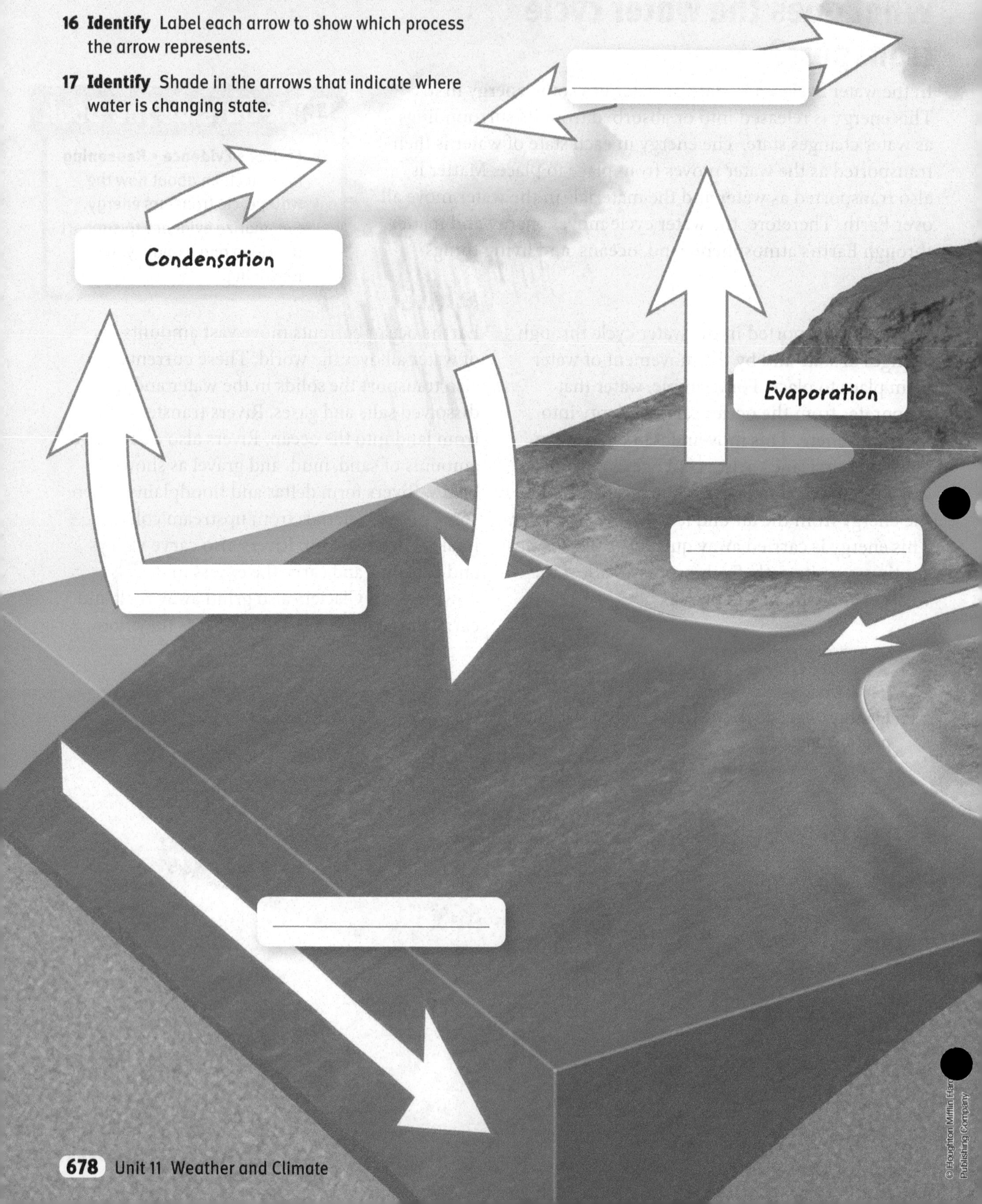

Condensation
Evaporation

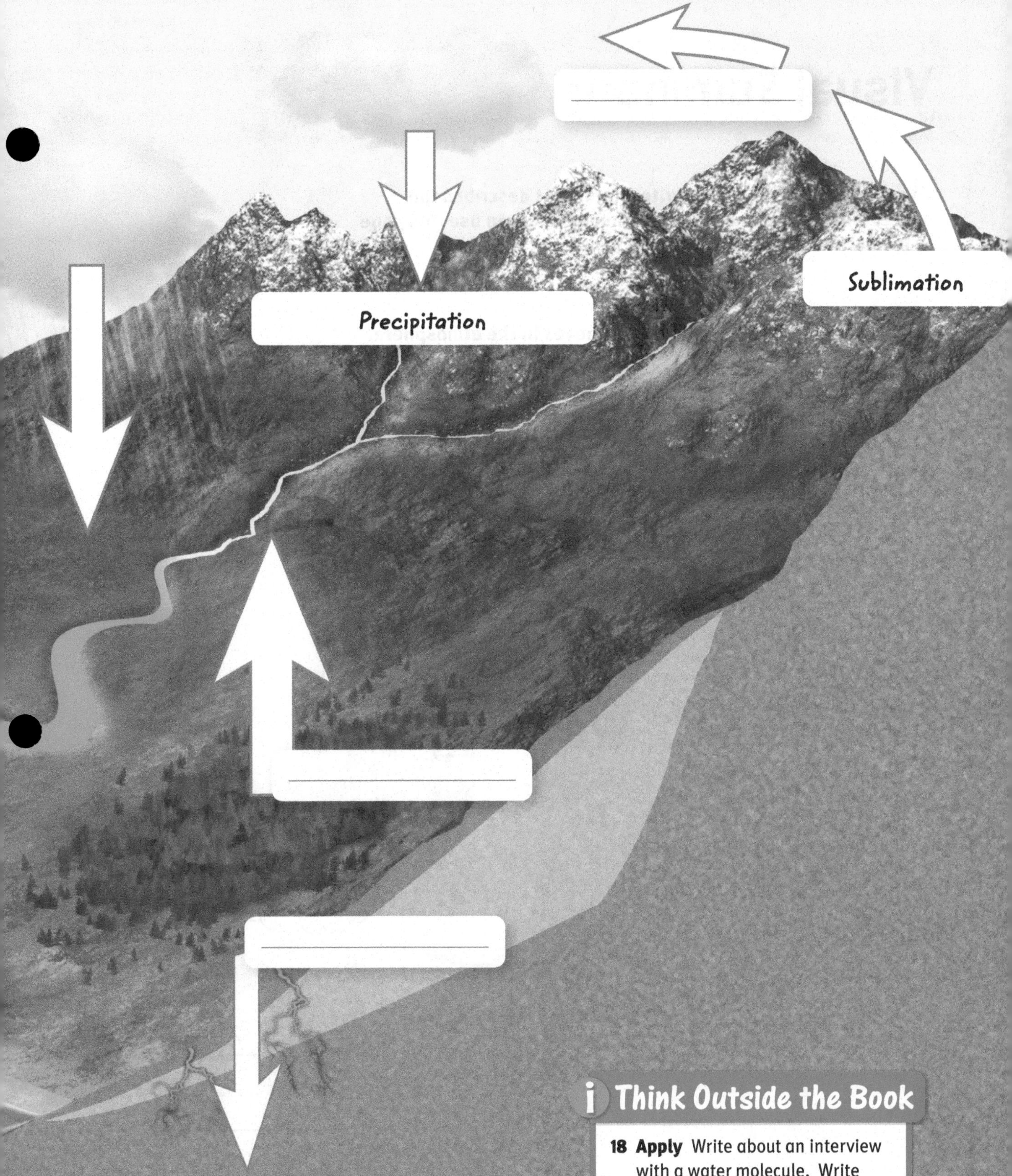

Precipitation

Sublimation

_____

_____

_____

i) Think Outside the Book

18 **Apply** Write about an interview with a water molecule. Write a story, or design a pamphlet describing one possible trip that a water molecule could take through the water cycle. Share your project with classmates.

Visual Summary

To complete this summary, write a term that describes the process happening in each of the images. You can use this page to review the main concepts of the lesson.

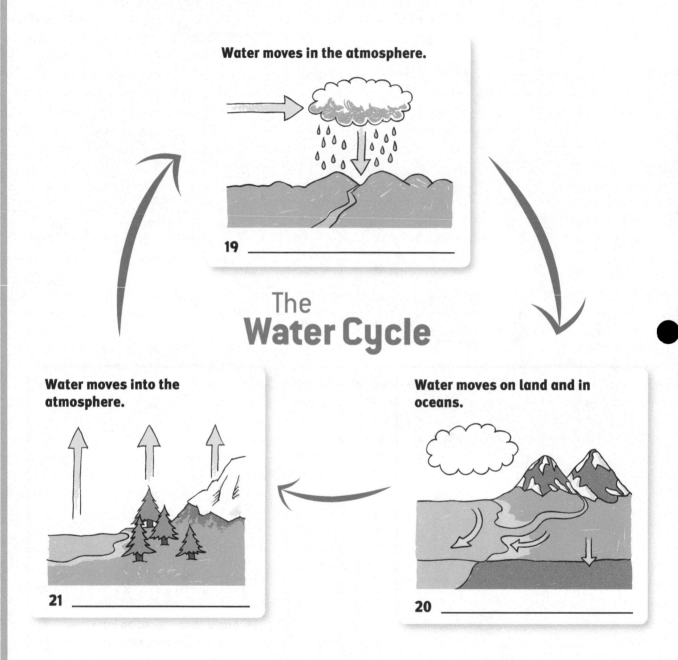

Water moves in the atmosphere.

19 _____

The **Water Cycle**

Water moves into the atmosphere.

21 _____

Water moves on land and in oceans.

20 _____

22 Claims • Evidence • Reasoning Make a claim about how the Earth's climate and the water cycle would be affected if less solar energy reached Earth. Summarize evidence to support the claim and explain your reasoning.

Lesson Review

Vocabulary

Write the correct label A, B, C, or D under each term to indicate the definition of that term.

1 water cycle

_____

2 evaporation

_____

3 precipitation

_____

4 condensation

_____

A The change of state from a liquid to a gas

B The change of state from a gas to a liquid

C The movement of water between the atmosphere, land, oceans, and living things

D Any form of water that falls to Earth's surface from the clouds

Key Concepts

5 Identify List the three ways in which water reaches the atmosphere and tell which way accounts for most of the water in the atmosphere.

_____

_____

_____

6 Classify Which of the processes of the water cycle occur by releasing energy?

_____

_____

7 Identify What happens to water once it reaches Earth's surface?

_____

_____

_____

8 Summarize Describe how three common types of precipitation form.

_____

_____

Critical Thinking

Use the image below to answer the following question.

9 Apply Describe the energy changes occurring in the process shown above.

_____

_____

10 Infer Why does the amount of water that flows in a river change during the year?

_____

_____

11 Explain Your Reasoning During a storm, a tree fell over into a river. Use evidence to support your explanation of what happened to the tree.

_____

_____

_____

_____

12 Evaluate Warm ocean currents cool as they flow along a coastline, away from the equator. Explain what is transported and how.

_____

_____

Elements of Weather

ESSENTIAL QUESTION

What is weather and how can we describe different types of weather conditions?

By the end of this lesson, you should be able to describe elements of weather and explain how they are measured.

Weather stations placed all around the world allow scientists to measure the elements, or separate parts, of weather.

A researcher checks an automatic weather station on Alexander Island, Antarctica.

SC.6.E.7.2 Investigate and apply how the cycling of water between the atmosphere and hydrosphere has an effect on weather patterns and climate.
SC.6.E.7.3 Describe how global patterns such as the jet stream and ocean currents influence local weather in measurable terms such as temperature, air pressure, wind direction and speed, and humidity and precipitation.

Lesson Labs

Quick Labs
- Cloud Cover
- Coastal Climate Model

 Engage Your Brain

1 Predict Check T or F to show whether you think each statement is true or false.

T	F	
☐	☐	Weather can change every day.
☐	☐	Temperature is measured by using a barometer.
☐	☐	Air pressure increases as you move higher in the atmosphere.
☐	☐	Visibility is a measurement of how far we can see.

2 Describe Use at least three words that might describe the weather on a day when the sky looks like the picture above.

_____

_____

_____

_____

ACTIVE **READING**

3 Distinguish The words *weather*, *whether*, and *wether* all sound alike but are spelled differently and mean entirely different things. You may have never heard of a *wether*—it is a neutered male sheep or ram.

Circle the correct use of the three words in the sentence below.

The farmer wondered *weather / whether / wether* the cold *weather / whether / wether* had affected his *weather / whether / wether*.

Vocabulary Terms

- weather
- humidity
- relative humidity
- dew point
- precipitation
- air pressure
- wind
- visibility

4 Apply As you learn the definition of each vocabulary term in this lesson, create your own definition or sketch to help you remember the meaning of the term.

Wonder about Weather?

What is weather?

Weather is the condition of Earth's atmosphere at a certain time and place. Different observations give you clues to the weather. If you see plants moving from side to side, you might infer that it is windy. If you see a gray sky and wet, shiny streets, you might decide to wear a raincoat. People talk about weather by describing factors such as temperature, humidity, precipitation, air pressure, wind, and *visibility* (viz•uh•BIL•i•tee).

What is temperature and how is it measured?

Temperature is a measure of how hot or cold something is. An instrument that measures and displays temperature is called a *thermometer*. A common type of thermometer uses a liquid such as alcohol or mercury to display the temperature. The liquid is sealed in a glass tube. When the air gets warmer, the liquid expands and rises in the tube. Cooler air causes the liquid to contract and fill less of the tube. A scale, often in Celsius (°C) or Fahrenheit (°F), is marked on the glass tube.

Another type of thermometer is an electrical thermometer. As the temperature becomes higher, electric current flow increases through the thermometer. The strength of the current is then translated into temperature readings.

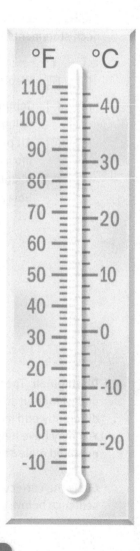

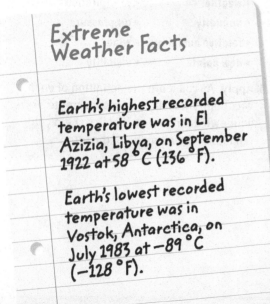

Extreme Weather Facts

Earth's highest recorded temperature was in El Azizia, Libya, on September 1922 at 58 °C (136 °F).

Earth's lowest recorded temperature was in Vostok, Antarctica, on July 1983 at −89 °C (−128 °F).

👁 Visualize It!

5 Identify Color in the liquid in the thermometer above to show Earth's average temperature in 2009 (58 °F). Write the Celsius temperature that equals 58 °F on the line below.

_____

What is humidity and how is it measured?

As water evaporates from oceans, lakes, and ponds, it becomes water vapor, or a gas that is in the air. The amount of water vapor in the air is called **humidity**. As more water evaporates and becomes water vapor, the humidity of the air increases.

Humidity is often described through relative humidity. **Relative humidity** is the amount of water vapor in the air compared to the amount of water vapor needed to reach saturation. As shown below, when air is saturated, the rates of evaporation and condensation are equal. Saturated air has a relative humidity of 100%. A psychrometer (sy•KRAHM•i•ter) is an instrument that is used to measure relative humidity.

Air can become saturated when evaporation adds water vapor to the air. Air can also become saturated when it cools to its dew point. The **dew point** is the temperature at which more condensation than evaporation occurs. When air temperature drops below the dew point, condensation forms. This can cause dew on surfaces cooler than the dew point. It also can form fog and clouds.

ACTIVE READING

6 Identify Underline the name of the instrument used to measure relative humidity.

> 👁 **Visualize It!**

7 Sketch In the space provided, draw what happens in air that is below the dew point.

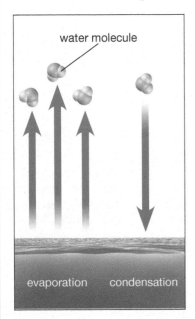

water molecule

evaporation   condensation

In unsaturated air, more water evaporates into the air than condenses back into the water.

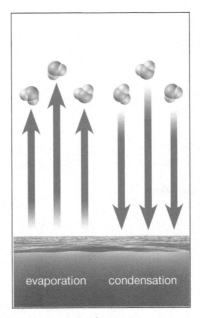

evaporation   condensation

In saturated air, the amount of water that evaporates equals the amount that condenses.

When air cools below its dew point, more water vapor condenses into water than evaporates.

8 Explain Your Reasoning Explain the process that causes dew to form on grass overnight.

_____

_____

What is precipitation and how is it measured?

Water vapor in the air condenses not only on Earth's surfaces, but also on tiny particles in the air to form clouds. When this water from the air returns to Earth's surface, it falls as precipitation. **Precipitation** is any form of water that falls to Earth's surface from the clouds. The four main forms of precipitation are rain, snow, hail, and sleet.

Rain is the most common form of precipitation. Inside a cloud, the droplets formed by condensation collide and form larger droplets. They finally become heavy enough to fall as raindrops. Rain is measured with a rain gauge, as shown in the picture below. A funnel or wide opening at the top of the gauge allows rain to flow into a cylinder that is marked in centimeters.

Snow forms when air temperatures are so low that water vapor turns into a solid. When a lot of snow has fallen, it is measured with a ruler or meterstick. When balls or lumps of ice fall from clouds during thunderstorms it is called *hail*. Sleet forms when rain falls through a layer of freezing air, producing falling ice.

Visualize It!

9 Claims • Evidence • Reasoning Make a claim about the ways in which all types of precipitation are alike. Summarize evidence to support the claim and explain your reasoning.

_____

_____

_____

Snow
Snow can fall as single ice crystals or ice crystals can join to form snowflakes.

Rain
Rain occurs when the water droplets in a cloud get so big they fall to Earth.

Sleet
Small ice pellets fall as sleet when rain falls through cold air.

Hail
Hailstones are layered lumps of ice that fall from clouds.

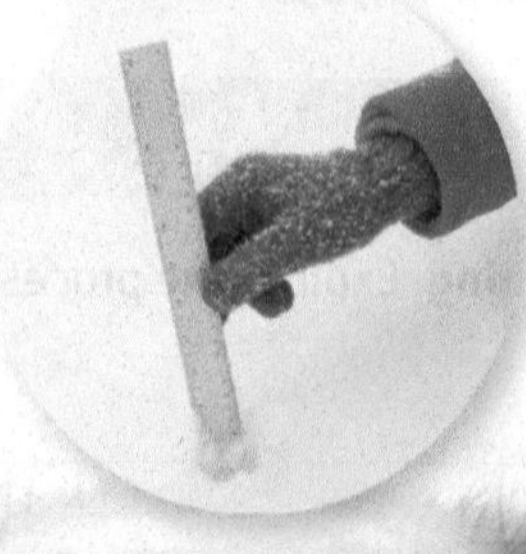

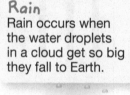

10 Measure How much rain has this rain gauge collected?

_____

Watching Clouds

EYE ON THE ENVIRONMENT

Cirrus Clouds

Cumulus Clouds

Stratus Clouds

As you can see above, cirrus (SIR•uhs) clouds appear feathery or wispy. Their name means "curl of hair." They are made of ice crystals. They form when the wind is strong.

Cumulus (KYOOM•yuh•luhs) means "heap" or "pile." Usually these clouds form in fair weather but if they keep growing taller, they can produce thunderstorms.

Stratus (STRAY•tuhs) means "spread out." Stratus clouds form in flat layers. Low, dark stratus clouds can block out the sun and produce steady drizzle or rain.

If you watch the sky over a period of time, you will probably observe different kinds of clouds. Clouds have different characteristics because they form under different conditions. The shapes and sizes of clouds are mainly determined by air movement. For example, puffy clouds form in air that rises sharply or moves straight up and down. Flat, smooth clouds covering large areas form in air that rises gradually.

 Extend

11 Gather Evidence Recall the last time you observed clouds. At what period of the day are you most likely to notice what type of cloud is in the sky?

12 Research Word parts are used to tell more about clouds. Look up the word parts *-nimbus* and *alto-*. What are cumulonimbus and altostratus clouds?

The Air Out There

What is air pressure and how is it measured?

Scientists use an instrument called a *barometer* (buh•RAHM•i•ter) to measure air pressure. **Air pressure** is the force of air molecules pushing on an area. The air pressure at any area on Earth depends on the weight of the air above that area. Although air is pressing down on us, we don't feel the weight because air pushes in all directions. So, the pressure of air pushing down is balanced by the pressure of air pushing up.

Air pressure and density are related; they both decrease with altitude. Notice in the picture that the molecules at sea level are closer together than the molecules at the mountain peak. Because the molecules are closer together, the pressure is greater. The air at sea level is denser than air at high altitude.

Air pressure and density are lower at a high altitude.

Air pressure and density are higher at sea level.

◉ Visualize It!

13 Identify Look at the photos below and write whether wind direction or wind speed is being measured.

Anemometer

An anemometer measures:

_____

Wind vane

A wind vane measures:

_____

What is wind and how is it measured?

Wind is air that moves horizontally, or parallel to the ground. Uneven heating of Earth's surface causes pressure differences from place to place. These pressure differences set air in motion. Over a short distance, wind moves directly from higher pressure toward lower pressure.

An anemometer (an•uh•MAHM•i•ter) is used to measure wind speed. It has three or four cups attached to a pole. The wind causes the cups to rotate, sending an electric current to a meter that displays the wind speed.

Wind direction is measured by using a wind vane or a windsock. A wind vane has an arrow with a large tail that is attached to a pole. The wind pushes harder on the arrow tail due to its larger surface area. This causes the wind vane to spin so that the arrow points into the wind. A windsock is a cone-shaped cloth bag open at both ends. The wind enters the wide end and the narrow end points in the opposite direction, showing the direction the wind is blowing.

What is visibility and how is it measured?

Visibility is a measure of the transparency of the atmosphere. Visibility is the way we describe how far we can see, and it is measured by using three or four known landmarks at different distances. Sometimes not all of the landmarks will be visible. Poor visibility can be the result of air pollution or fog.

Poor visibility can be dangerous for all types of travel, whether by air, water, or land. When visibility is very low, roads may be closed to traffic. In areas where low visibility is common, signs are often posted to warn travelers.

ACTIVE READING

14 Explain What are two factors that can affect visibility?

_____

_____

Fog forms as land cools overnight, causing water vapor in the air above the land to condense.

What are some ways to collect weather data?

Many forms of technology are used to gather weather data. The illustration below shows some ways weather information can be collected. Instruments within the atmosphere can make measurements of local weather conditions. Satellites can collect data from above the atmosphere.

i 👁 Visualize It!

15 Claims • Evidence • Reasoning Make a claim about the benefits of stationary and moving weather collection. Summarize evidence to support the claim and explain your reasoning.

_____

_____

_____

Satellite

Airplane

Ground station

Moving
Some forms of technology report changing measurements along their paths.

Stationary
Some forms of technology provide measurements from set locations.

Weather buoy

Ship

Visual Summary

To complete this summary, fill in the blanks with the correct word or phrase. You can use this page to review the main concepts of the lesson.

Elements of Weather

Weather is a condition of the atmosphere at a certain time and place.

16 Weather is often expressed by describing _____, humidity, precipitation, air pressure, wind, and visibility.

Visibility describes how far into the distance objects can be seen.

19 Visibility can be affected by air pollution and ____ _____

Humidity describes the amount of water vapor in the air.

17 The amount of moisture in the air is commonly expressed as _____ humidity.

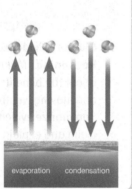

evaporation   condensation

Precipitation occurs when the water that condenses as clouds falls back to Earth in solid or liquid form.

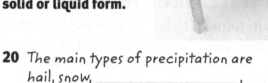

20 The main types of precipitation are hail, snow, _____, and rain.

Uneven heating of Earth's surface causes air pressure differences and wind.

18 Wind moves from areas of _____ pressure to areas of _____ pressure.

21 Claims • Evidence • Reasoning Make a claim about which weather instruments are best to take on a 3-month field study to measure how the weather on a mountaintop changes over the course of a season. Summarize evidence to support the claim and explain your reasoning.

Lesson Review

Vocabulary

In your own words, define the following terms.

1 weather _____

_____

2 humidity _____

_____

3 air pressure _____

_____

4 visibility _____

_____

Key Concepts

Weather element	Instrument
5 Identify Measures temperature	
	6 Identify Is measured by using a barometer
7 Identify Measures relative humidity	
	8 Identify Is measured by using a rain gauge or meterstick
9 Identify Measures wind speed	

10 List What are four types of precipitation?

_____

_____

Critical Thinking

11 Apply Explain how wind is related to the uneven heating of Earth's surfaces by the sun.

_____

_____

_____

_____

12 Support Your Claim Why does air pressure decrease as altitude increases? Explain your reasoning.

_____

_____

13 Synthesize What is the relative humidity when the air temperature is at its dew point?

The weather data below was recorded from 1989–2009 by an Antarctic weather station similar to the station in the photo at the beginning of this lesson. Use these data to answer the questions that follow.

	Jan.	Apr.	July	Oct.
Mean max. temp. (°C)	2.1	−7.4	−9.9	−8.1
Mean min. temp. (°C)	−2.6	−14.6	−18.1	−15.1
Mean precip. (mm)	9.0	18.04	28.5	16.5

14 Identify Which month had the lowest mean minimum and maximum temperatures?

_____

15 Claims • Evidence • Reasoning Make a claim about the most likely form of precipitation that will fall at this location. Summarize evidence to support the claim and explain your reasoning.

_____

SC.6.N.1.1 Define a problem from the sixth grade curriculum, use appropriate reference materials to support scientific understanding, plan and carry out scientific investigation of various types, such as systematic observations or experiments, identify variables, collect and organize data, interpret data in charts, tables, and graphics, analyze information, make predictions, and defend conclusions.

S.T.E.M. ENGINEERING & TECHNOLOGY

Evaluating Technological Systems

Skills	Objectives
✓ Identify inputs	Analyze weather forecasting as a system.
✓ Identify outputs	Identify the inputs and outputs of a forecasting system.
✓ Identify system processes	Interpret weather data to generate a weather map.
Evaluate system feedback	
Apply system controls	
✓ Communicate results	

Using Data in Systems

A system is a group of interacting parts that work together to do a job. Technological systems process inputs and generate outputs. An input is any matter, energy, or information that goes into a system. Outputs are matter, energy, or information that come out of the system. When you use a computer, the data set that is entered is the input. The computer delivers your output on the monitor or the printer.

Weather Data Go Into a System

What do you do if you have an outdoor activity planned tomorrow? You probably check the weather forecast to help you decide what to wear. Meteorologists are scientists who use data from different sources to find out what is happening in the atmosphere. Weather data are the input. The data set is processed by computers that perform complex calculations to generate weather models. Weather forecast systems combine 72 hours of data from weather stations, weather balloons, radar, aircraft, and weather satellites to show what is happening in Earth's atmosphere now and to predict what will happen in the future.

1 **Support Your Claim** How is a television weather forecast part of a technological system? Explain your reasoning.

_____

_____

The atmosphere is a system that can have dramatic outputs. Those outputs are inputs into a weather forecasting system.

©Craig Aurness/Corbis

Forecast Data Come Out of the System

Weather maps are one type of output from a weather forecasting system. On a weather map you can find information about moving air. The numbered lines on a weather map are called *isobars*. Isobars connect areas that have the same atmospheric pressure. Isobars center around areas of high and low pressure. An area of high pressure (H) indicates a place where cool, dense air is falling. An area of low pressure (L) indicates a place where warm, less dense air is rising. Pressure differences cause air to move. The leading edge of a cool air mass is called a *cold front*. The leading edge of a warm air mass is called a *warm front*. On a weather map, blue lines with triangles show cold fronts and red lines with half circles show warm fronts.

The direction of the triangles or half circles on a map shows which way a front is moving. Wind direction is described in terms of the direction from which the wind is blowing. A west wind is blowing from west to east.

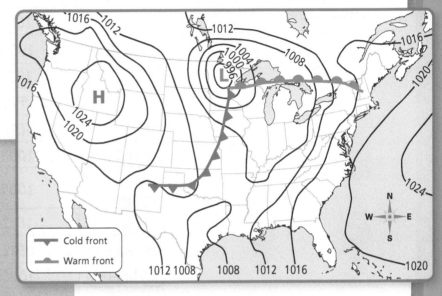

Cold front

Warm front

Anemometer (wind speed)

Wind vane (wind direction)

2 Analysis How would you describe the wind direction behind the warm and cold fronts shown on the map? Explain your reasoning.

_____

_____

_____

Weather instruments constantly measure conditions in the atmosphere and deliver data.

Barometer (air pressure) & **Rain gauge** (precipitation)

Thermometer (temperature) & **Hygrometer** (humidity)

 You Try It!

Now it's your turn to use weather data to make a forecast.

✋ You Try It!

Now it's your turn to become part of the weather forecasting system. The table and map on these pages show some weather data for several cities in the United States. You will use those data to analyze weather and make predictions.

① Identify Inputs

Which information in the table will you use to determine where the high and low pressure areas may be located?

_____

_____

_____

City	Barometric pressure (mbar)	Wind direction	Temperature (°F)
Atlanta	1009	S	63
Chicago	1012	W	36
Cleveland	1006	S	35
Denver	1021	S	34
New York	990	S	58
Billings	1012	SW	28
Spokane	1009	SW	27
Los Angeles	1009	W	68
Dallas	1012	NW	50
Memphis	1012	NW	45
Orlando	1006	S	78
Raleigh	998	S	60

② Identify Outputs

What outputs from weather stations are included on a weather map?

_____

_____

③ Identify System Processes

How will you process the information in the table and on the map to make predictions? Describe how you will use the inputs to develop an output.

_____

_____

_____

④ Communicate Results

Use data from the table and the map to answer the questions below.

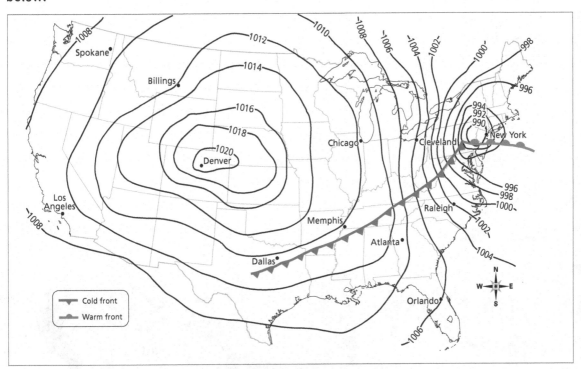

A According to the data in the table, where are the centers of the high and low pressure systems at this time? Mark them on the map using an H or an L.

B Add the temperature listed in the table for each city to the map.

C **State Your Claim** Imagine that you are a meteorologist in Atlanta and this is the current map. What temperature change would you predict over the next few hours? Explain your reasoning.

_____

_____

_____

_____

D **Support Your Claim** What pressure change would you predict for Denver over the next few days? Explain your reasoning.

_____

_____

_____

_____

What Influences Weather?

ESSENTIAL **QUESTION**

How do the water cycle and other global patterns affect local weather?

By the end of this lesson, you should be able to explain how global patterns in Earth's system influence weather.

SC.6.E.7.2 Investigate and apply how the cycling of water between the atmosphere and hydrosphere has an effect. **SC.6.E.7.3** Describe how global patterns such as the jet stream and ocean currents influence local weather in measurable terms such as temperature, air pressure, wind direction and speed, and humidity and precipitation.

The weather doesn't always turn out the way you want. But learning about the factors that affect weather can help you plan your next outing.

 **Lesson Labs**

Quick Lab
- The Angle of the Sun's Rays
- Modeling Air Movement by Convection
- Wind and Temperature

 Engage Your Brain

1 Predict Check T or F to show whether you think each statement is true or false.

T	F	
☐	☐	The water cycle affects weather.
☐	☐	Air can be warmed or cooled by the surface below it.
☐	☐	Warm air sinks, cool air rises.
☐	☐	Winds can bring different weather to a region.

2 Explain How can air temperatures along this coastline be affected by the large body of water that is nearby?

_____

_____

_____

ACTIVE **READING**

3 Infer A military front is a contested armed frontier between opposing forces. A *weather front* occurs between two air masses, or bodies of air. What kind of weather do you think usually happens at a weather front?

_____

_____

_____

_____

_____

Vocabulary Terms
- air mass
- front
- jet stream

4 Apply As you learn the definition of each vocabulary term in this lesson, create your own definition or sketch to help you remember the meaning of the term.

Water, Water

How does the water cycle affect weather?

Weather is the short-term state of the atmosphere, including temperature, humidity, precipitation, air pressure, wind, and visibility. These elements are affected by the energy received from the sun and the amount of water in the air. To understand what influences weather, then, you need to understand the water cycle.

The *water cycle* is the continuous movement of water between the atmosphere, the land, the oceans, and living things. In the water cycle, shown to the right, water is constantly being recycled between liquid, solid, and gaseous states. The water cycle involves the processes of evaporation, condensation, and precipitation.

Evaporation occurs when liquid water changes into water vapor, which is a gas. Condensation occurs when water vapor cools and changes from a gas to a liquid. A change in the amount of water vapor in the air affects humidity. Clouds and fog form through condensation of water vapor, so condensation also affects visibility. Precipitation occurs when rain, snow, sleet, or hail falls from the clouds onto Earth's surface.

ACTIVE READING

5 List Name at least 5 elements of weather.

_____

_____

_____

👁 Visualize It!

6 Summarize Describe how the water cycle influences weather by completing the sentences on the picture.

(A) *Evaporation affects weather by* _____

_____

_____

© Houghton Mifflin Harcourt Publishing Company

Everywhere . . .

B Condensation **affects weather by** _____
_____
_____

C Precipitation **affects weather by** _____
_____
_____

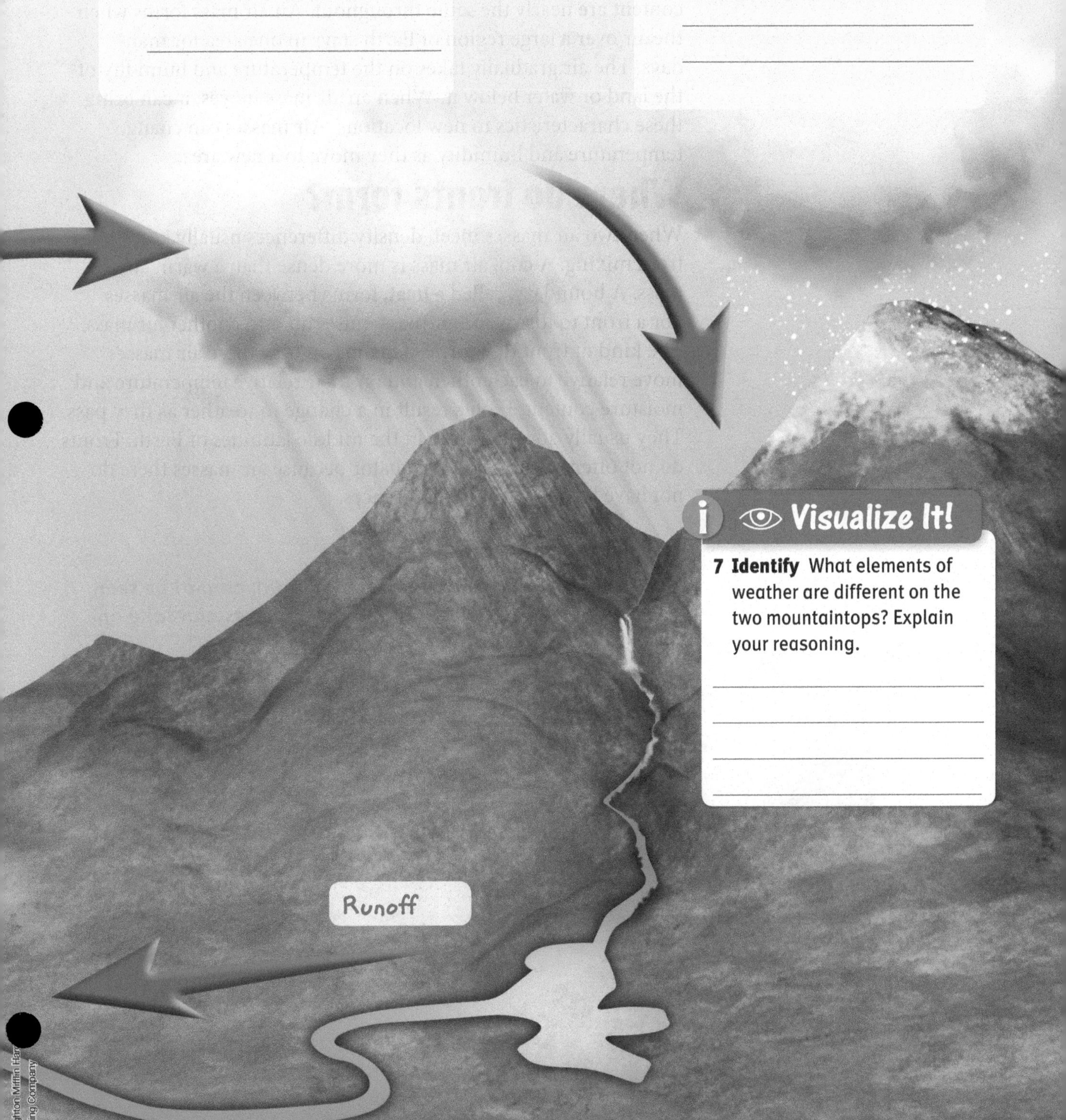

Runoff

7 Identify What elements of weather are different on the two mountaintops? Explain your reasoning.

_____
_____
_____
_____

Putting Up a **Front**

How do air masses affect weather?

You have probably experienced the effects of air masses—one day is hot and humid, and the next day is cool and pleasant. The weather changes when a new air mass moves into your area. An **air mass** is a large volume of air in which temperature and moisture content are nearly the same throughout. An air mass forms when the air over a large region of Earth stays in one area for many days. The air gradually takes on the temperature and humidity of the land or water below it. When an air mass moves, it can bring these characteristics to new locations. Air masses can change temperature and humidity as they move to a new area.

Where do fronts form?

When two air masses meet, density differences usually keep them from mixing. A cool air mass is more dense than a warm air mass. A boundary, called a **front**, forms between the air masses. For a front to form, one air mass must run into another air mass. The kind of front that forms depends on how these air masses move relative to each other, and on their relative temperature and moisture content. Fronts result in a change in weather as they pass. They usually affect weather in the middle latitudes of Earth. Fronts do not often occur near the equator because air masses there do not have big temperature differences.

The boundary between air masses, or front, cannot be seen, but is shown here to illustrate how air masses can take on the characteristics of the surface below them.

Air masses that form above water are moist.

Air masses that form above land are dry.

Cold Fronts Form Where Cold Air Moves under Warm Air

Warm air is less dense than cold air is. So, a cold air mass that is moving can quickly push up a warm air mass. If the warm air is moist, clouds will form. Storms that form along a cold front are usually short-lived but can move quickly and bring heavy rain or snow. Cooler weather follows a cold front.

9 Claims • Evidence • Reasoning Make a claim about the type of weather to expect when a cold front is headed for your area. Summarize evidence to support the claim and explain your reasoning.

_____

_____

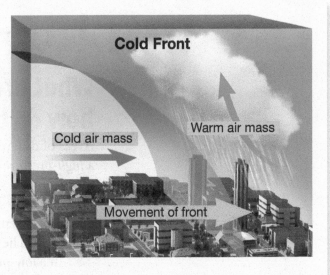

Cold Front

Cold air mass

Warm air mass

Movement of front

Warm Fronts Form Where Warm Air Moves over Cold Air

A warm front forms when a warm air mass follows a retreating cold air mass. The warm air rises over the cold air, and its moisture condenses into clouds. Warm fronts often bring drizzly rain and are followed by warm, clear weather.

10 Identify The rainy weather at the edge of a warm front is a result of

☐   the cold air mass that is leaving.

☐   the warm air rising over the cold air.

☐   the warm air mass following the front.

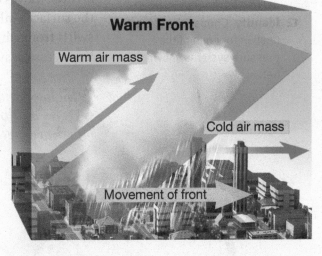

Warm Front

Warm air mass

Cold air mass

Movement of front

Stationary Fronts Form Where Cold and Warm Air Stop Moving

In a stationary front, there is not enough wind for either the cold air mass or the warm air mass to keep moving. So, the two air masses remain in one place. A stationary front can cause many days of unchanging weather, usually clear.

11 Explain Your Reasoning When could a stationary front become a warm or cold front?

_____

_____

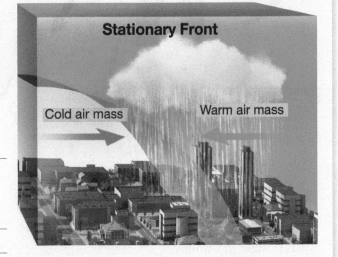

Stationary Front

Cold air mass

Warm air mass

Feeling the Pressure!

What are pressure systems, and how do they interact?

Areas of different air pressure cause changes in the weather. In a *high-pressure system*, air sinks slowly down. As the air nears the ground, it spreads out toward areas of lower pressure. Most high-pressure systems are large and change slowly. When a high-pressure system stays in one location for a long time, an air mass may form. The air mass can be warm or cold, humid or dry.

In a *low-pressure system*, air rises and so has a lower air pressure than the areas around it. As the air in the center of a low-pressure system rises, the air cools.

The diagram below shows how a high-pressure system can form a low-pressure system. Surface air, shown by the black arrows, moves out and away from high-pressure centers. Air above the surface sinks and warms. The green arrows show how air swirls from a high-pressure system into a low-pressure system. In a low-pressure system, the air rises and cools.

A high-pressure system can spiral into a low-pressure system, as illustrated by the green arrows below. In the Northern Hemisphere, air circles in the directions shown.

© Houghton Mifflin Harcourt Publishing Company

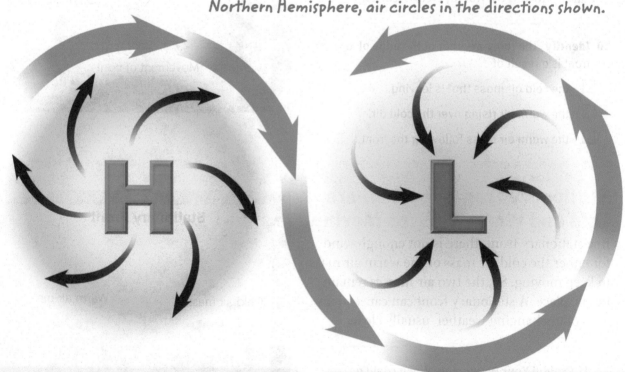

Visualize It!

12 Identify Choose the correct answer for each of the pressure systems shown below.

Ⓐ In a high-pressure system, air
- [ ] rises and cools.
- [ ] sinks and warms.

Ⓑ in a low-pressure system, air
- [ ] rises and cools.
- [ ] sinks and warms.

How do different pressure systems affect us?

When air pressure differences are small, air doesn't move very much. If the air remains in one place or moves slowly, the air takes on the temperature and humidity of the land or water beneath it. Each type of pressure system has it own unique weather pattern. By keeping track of high- and low-pressure systems, scientists can predict the weather.

High-Pressure Systems Produce Clear Weather

High-pressure systems are areas where air sinks and moves outward. The sinking air is denser than the surrounding air, and the pressure is higher. Cooler, denser air moves out of the center of these high-pressure areas toward areas of lower pressure. As the air sinks, it gets warmer and absorbs moisture. Water droplets evaporate, relative humidity decreases, and clouds often disappear. A high-pressure system generally brings clear skies and calm air or gentle breezes.

Low-Pressure Systems Produce Rainy Weather

Low-pressure systems have lower pressure than the surrounding areas. Air in a low-pressure system comes together, or converges, and rises. As the air in the center of a low-pressure system rises, it cools and forms clouds and rain. The rising air in a low-pressure system causes stormy weather.

A low-pressure system can develop wherever there is a center of low pressure. One place this often happens is along a boundary between a warm air mass and a cold air mass. Rain often occurs at these boundaries, or fronts.

👁 Visualize It!

13 Match Label each picture as a result of a high- or low-pressure system. Then, draw a line from each photo to its matching air-pressure diagram.

Ⓐ

Ⓑ

Warm air rises

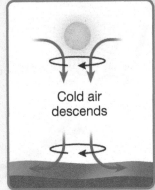

Cold air descends

Windy Weather

How do global wind patterns affect local weather?

Winds are caused by unequal heating of Earth's surface—which causes air pressure differences—and can occur on a global or on a local scale. On a local scale, air-pressure differences affect both wind speed and wind direction at a location. On a global level, there is an overall movement of surface air from the poles toward the equator. The heated air at the equator rises and forms a low-pressure belt. Cold air near the poles sinks and creates high-pressure centers. Because air moves from areas of high pressure to areas of low pressure, it moves from the poles to the equator. At high altitudes, the warmed air circles back toward the poles.

Temperature and pressure differences on Earth's surface also create regional wind belts. Winds in these belts curve to the east or the west as they blow, due to Earth's rotation. This curving of winds is called the *Coriolis effect* (kawr•ee•OH•lis eff•EKT). Winds would flow in straight lines if Earth did not rotate. Winds bring air masses of different temperatures and moisture content to a region.

Belts of global winds circle Earth. The winds in these belts curve to the east or west. Between the global wind belts are calm areas.

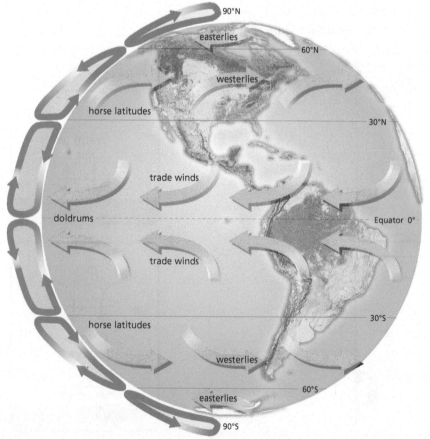

© Houghton Mifflin Ha
Publishing Company

How do jet streams affect weather?

Long-distance winds that travel above global winds for thousands of kilometers are called **jet streams**. Air moves in jet streams with speeds that are at least 92 kilometers per hour and are often greater than 180 kilometers per hour. Like global and local winds, jet streams form because Earth's surface is heated unevenly. They flow in a wavy pattern from west to east.

Each hemisphere usually has two main jet streams, a polar jet stream and a subtropical jet stream. The polar jet streams flow closer to the poles in summer than in winter. Jet streams can affect temperatures. For example, a polar jet stream can pull cold air down from Canada into the United States and pull warm air up toward Canada. Jet streams also affect precipitation patterns. Strong storms tend to form along jet streams. Scientists must know where a jet stream is flowing to make accurate weather predictions.

ACTIVE READING

15 State Your Claim Identify two ways a jet stream affects weather. Support your claim with evidence.

_____

_____

_____

In winter months, the polar jet stream flows across much of the United States.

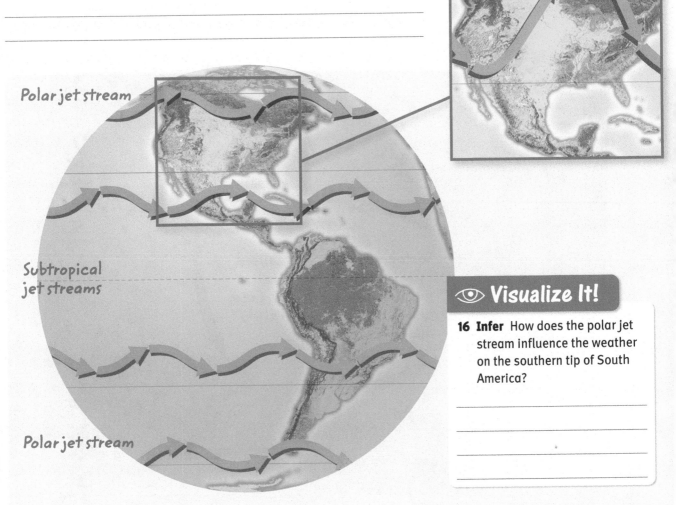

Polar jet stream

Subtropical jet streams

Polar jet stream

👁 Visualize It!

16 Infer How does the polar jet stream influence the weather on the southern tip of South America?

_____

_____

_____

_____

Ocean Effects

How do ocean currents influence weather?

The same global winds that blow across the surface of Earth also push water across Earth's oceans, causing surface currents. Different winds cause currents to flow in different directions. The flow of surface currents moves energy as heat from one part of Earth to another. As the map below shows, both warm-water and cold-water currents flow from one ocean to another. Water near the equator carries energy from the sun to other parts of the ocean. The energy from the warm currents is transferred to colder water or to the atmosphere, changing local temperatures and humidity.

Oceans also have an effect on weather in the form of hurricanes and monsoons. Warm ocean water fuels hurricanes. Monsoons are winds that change direction with the seasons. During summer, the land becomes much warmer than the sea in some areas of the world. Moist wind flows inland, often bringing heavy rains.

Warm current
Cold current

Surface currents are caused by winds. They distribute energy across Earth's surface, changing local temperature and humidity.

Cool Ocean Currents Lower Coastal Air Temperatures

As currents flow, they warm or cool the atmosphere above, affecting local temperatures. The California current is a cold-water current that keeps the average summer high temperatures of coastal cities such as San Diego around 26 °C (78 °F). Cities that lie inland at the same latitude have warmer averages. The graph below shows average monthly temperatures for San Diego and El Centro, California.

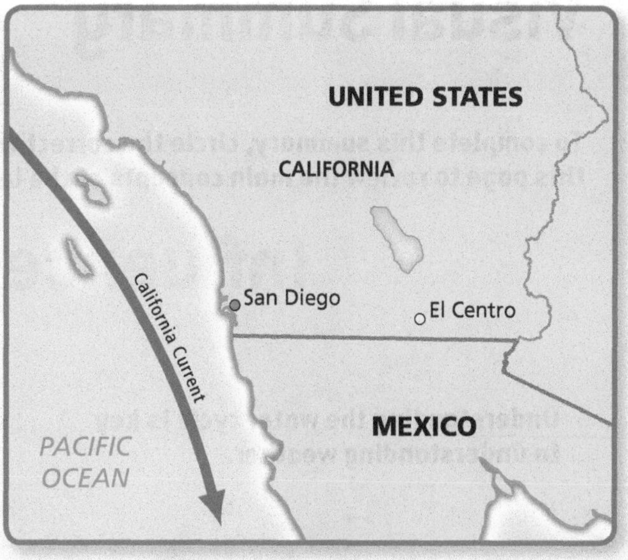

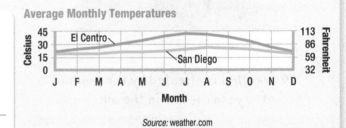

👁 Visualize It!

18 Support Your Claim Why are temperatures in San Diego, California, usually cooler than they are in El Centro, California? Explain your reasoning.

_____

_____

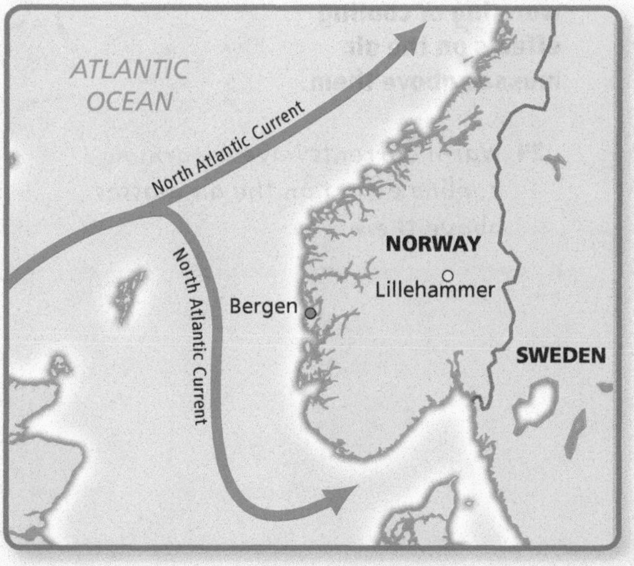

Average Monthly Temperatures

Source: weather.com

Warm Ocean Currents Raise Coastal Air Temperatures

In areas where warm ocean currents flow, coastal cities have warmer winter temperatures than inland cities at similar latitudes. For example, temperatures vary considerably from the coastal regions to the inland areas of Norway due to the warmth of the North Atlantic Current. Coastal cities such as Bergen have relatively mild winters. Inland cities such as Lillehammer have colder winters but temperatures similar to the coastal cities in summer.

👁 Visualize It!

19 Identify Circle the city that is represented by each color in the graph.

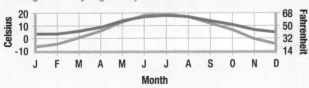

■ Lillehammer/Bergen

■ Lillehammer/Bergen

Average Monthly High Temperatures

Source: worldweather.org

Visual Summary

To complete this summary, circle the correct word. You can use
this page to review the main concepts of the lesson.

Influences of Weather

Understanding the water cycle is key to understanding weather.

20 Weather is affected by the amount of oxygen / water in the air.

Pressure differences from the uneven heating of Earth's surface cause predictable patterns of wind.

23 Global wind patterns occur as, due to temperature differences, air rises / sinks at the poles and rises / sinks at the equator.

A front forms where two air masses meet.

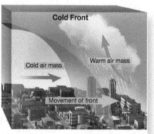

Cold Front

Cold air mass   Warm air mass

Movement of front

21 When a warm air mass and a cool air mass meet, the warm / cool air mass usually moves upward.

Global ocean surface currents can have warming or cooling effects on the air masses above them.

24 Warm currents have a warming / cooling effect on the air masses above them.

Low-pressure systems bring stormy weather, and high-pressure systems bring dry, clear weather.

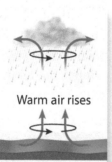

Warm air rises

22 In a low-pressure system, air moves upward / downward.

25 **Claims • Evidence • Reasoning** Make a claim about how air masses cause weather to change. Summarize evidence to support the claim and explain your reasoning.

Lesson Review

Vocabulary

For each pair of terms, explain how the meanings of the terms differ.

1 *front* and *air mass*

_____

_____

_____

2 *high-pressure system* and *low-pressure system*

_____

_____

_____

3 *jet streams* and *global wind belts*

_____

_____

_____

Key Concepts

4 **Apply** If the weather becomes stormy for a short time and then becomes colder, which type of front has most likely passed?

_____

5 **Describe** Explain how an ocean current can affect the temperature and the amount of moisture of the air mass above the current and above nearby coastlines.

_____

_____

_____

6 **Claims • Evidence • Reasoning** Make a claim about how the water cycle affects weather. Summarize evidence to support the claim and explain your reasoning.

_____

_____

_____

_____

Critical Thinking

Use the diagram below to answer the following question.

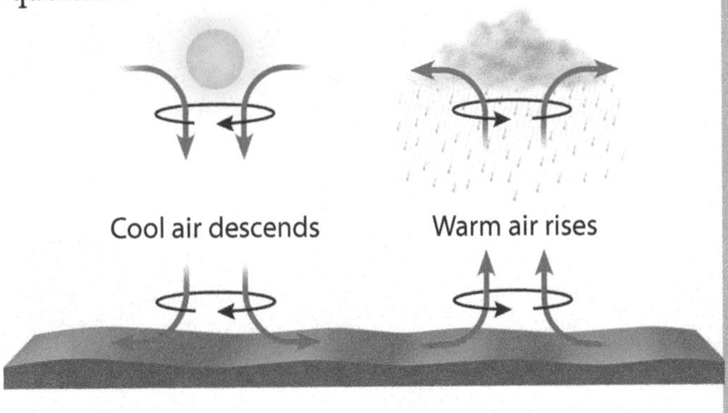

Cool air descends   Warm air rises

7 **Interpret** How does the movement of air affect the type of weather that forms from high-pressure and low-pressure systems?

_____

_____

_____

_____

_____

8 **Support Your Claim** How does the polar jet stream affect temperature and precipitation in North America? Explain your reasoning.

_____

_____

_____

_____

9 **Describe** Explain how changes in weather are caused by the interaction of air masses.

_____

_____

_____

_____

_____

_____

![Florida] FOCUS ON **FLORIDA**

SC.6.E.7.7 Investigate how natural disasters have affected human life in Florida.

Florida's Weather
Community

Storm chasing in the armored Tornado Intercept Vehicle 2

Storm Chasers

During a storm, most people try to escape it, take shelter, and hide. But there are a few people that run *after* storms! These people are known as storm chasers. They chase storms to gather information for scientific research. Storm chasers often have a training in meteorology and work for government agencies like the National Oceanic and Atmospheric Administration.

In southern states like Florida, storm chasing occurs during the summer months. Using special equipment, storm chasers track weather data to find a storm. Sometimes they drive for hours without finding a single storm. But on other days, they'll get lucky.

Keeping Pets Safe

In 2017, Florida was hit by the devastating Hurricane Irma. Along with many of the displaced human citizens, countless numbers of pets were also victims. The Humane Society of the United States along with the American Society for the Prevention of Cruelty to Animals (ASPCA) coordinated efforts with animal organizations throughout Florida to make sure that pets were included in safety and evacuation procedures.

Thousands of animals were transported to an emergency animal shelter in South Carolina, as well as to others based around the country. In addition, these organizations formed water rescue teams to help save animals in danger from flooding. To assist residents evacuating with pets, pet-friendly shelters were set up across the state, and the governor requested hotels that normally ban pets accept them during the storm.

To prepare for Hurricane Floyd, flamingos at the Miami Zoo were rounded up and kept indoors.

Pick three cities or towns in Florida. Research annual rainfall for those places. Compare the results in a bar graph. Which place has the greatest amount of precipitation? Which place has the least? Find out where in the state each place is located. How does the location affect the annual precipitation?

A rain gauge can measure the amount of rainfall an area receives.

The Community Collaborative Rain, Hail & Snow Network (or CoCoRaHS)

You may not be able to control the weather, but you could help track it! The Community Collaborative Rain, Hail & Snow Network (CoCoRaHS) is a unique volunteer network whose main goal is to track and measure precipitation. People of all ages can participate—you just need an interest in reporting weather conditions. As a volunteer, every time rain, hail, or snow arrives in your area, you will measure the precipitation from as many places as possible. Measurements have to take place around the same time every day, usually around 6:00 a.m. to 8:00 a.m. The equipment volunteers use includes a high capacity plastic rain gauge, a foil-covered foam hail pad, a set of metal hail pad mounting clips, and a package of information and forms for recording data. The information sent in by CoCoRaHS volunteers is used by government agencies, scientists, and many other people in your community.

During Florida's storm season, hurricanes can damage or destroy property.

 Take It Home!

Look up the weather forecast for your area. Record the predicted amounts of precipitation for the next five days. On each day, measure the amount of precipitation or look up the actual data. How do the predicted data compare with the actual data?

Severe Weather and Weather Safety

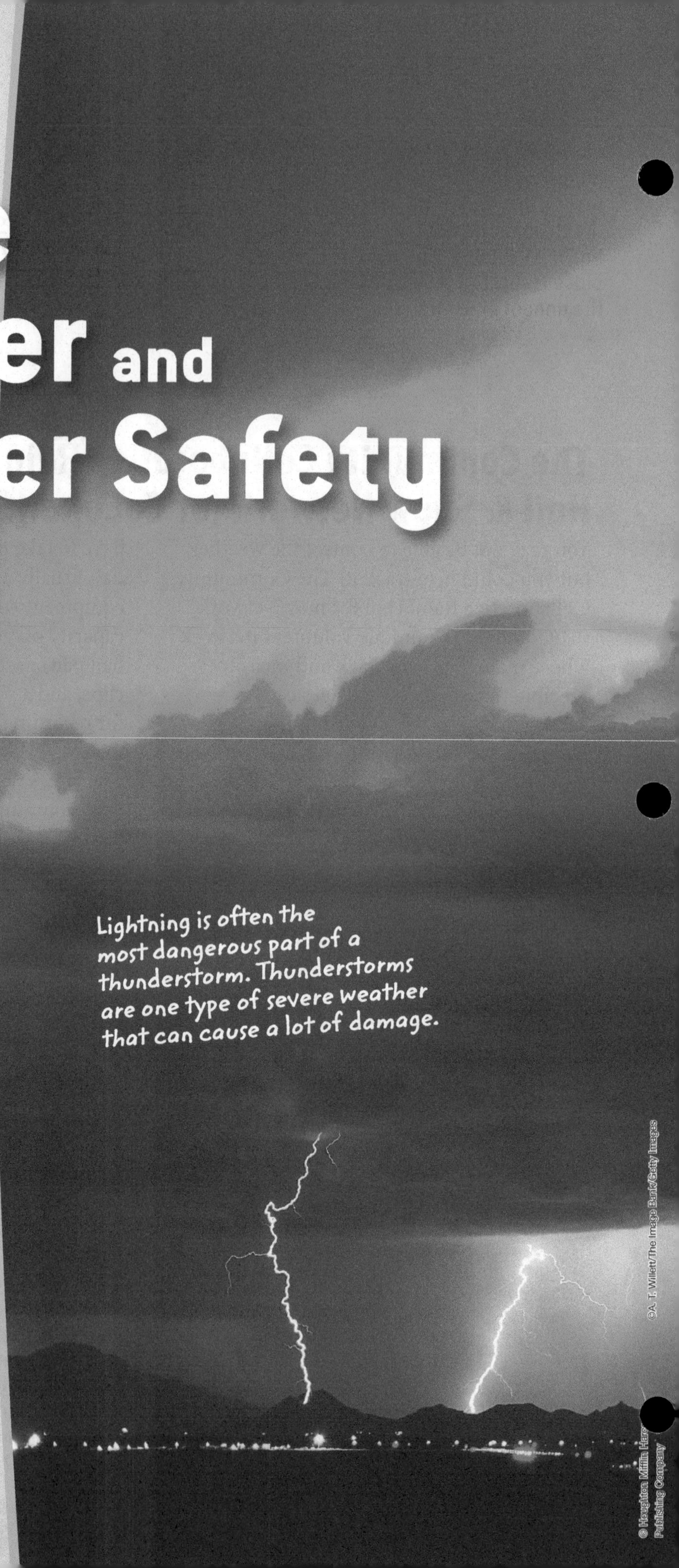

ESSENTIAL QUESTION

How can humans protect themselves from hazardous weather?

By the end of this lesson, you should be able to describe the major types of hazardous weather and the ways human beings can protect themselves from hazardous weather and from sun exposure.

Lightning is often the most dangerous part of a thunderstorm. Thunderstorms are one type of severe weather that can cause a lot of damage.

SC.6.N.1.1 Define a problem from the curriculum, use appropriate reference materials to support scientific understanding, plan and carry out scientific investigation of various types, such as systematic observations or experiments, identify variables, collect and organize data, interpret data in charts, tables, and graphics, analyze information, make predictions, and defend conclusions.
SC.6.E.7.8 Describe ways human beings protect themselves from hazardous weather and sun exposure. **HE.6.C.1.3** Identify environmental factors that affect personal health.

✋ Lesson Labs

Quick Labs
- Create Your Own Lightning
- The Speed of Sound
- Sun Protection

Exploration Lab
- Preparing for Severe Weather

⚙ Engage Your Brain

1 Describe Fill in the blanks with the word or phrase that you think correctly completes the following sentences.

A _____ forms a funnel cloud and has high winds.

A flash or bolt of light across the sky during a storm is called _____

_____ is the sound that follows lightning during a storm.

One way to protect yourself from the sun's rays is to wear _____

2 Identify Name the weather event that is occurring in the photo. What conditions can occur when this event happens in an area?

_____
_____
_____
_____
_____

ACTIVE **READING**

3 Synthesize Use the sentence below to help you make an educated guess about what the term *storm surge* means. Write the meaning below.

Example sentence
Flooding causes tremendous damage to property and lives when a <u>storm surge</u> moves onto shore.

storm surge:

_____
_____
_____
_____

Vocabulary Terms

- thunderstorm
- lightning
- thunder
- hurricane
- storm surge
- tornado

4 Apply As you learn the definition of each vocabulary term in this lesson, create your own definition or sketch to help you remember the meaning of the term.

☑ Take Cover!

What do we know about thunderstorms?

SPLAAAAAT! BOOOOM! The loud, sharp noise of thunder might surprise you, and maybe even make you jump. The thunder may have been joined by lightning, wind, and rain. A **thunderstorm** is an intense local storm that forms strong winds, heavy rain, lightning, thunder, and sometimes hail. A thunderstorm is an example of severe weather. Severe weather is weather that can cause property damage and sometimes death.

Thunderstorms Form from Rising Air

Thunderstorms get their energy from humid air. When warm, humid air near the ground mixes with cooler air above, the warm air creates an updraft that can build a thunderstorm quickly. Cold downdrafts bring precipitation and eventually end the storm by preventing more warm air from rising.

Step 1
In the first stage, warm air rises and forms a cumulus cloud. The water vapor releases energy when it condenses into cloud droplets. This energy increases the air motion. The cloud continues building up.

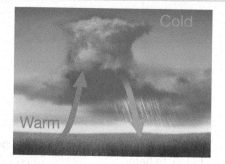

Step 2
Ice particles may form in the low temperatures near the top of the cloud. As the ice particles grow large, they begin to fall and pull cold air down with them. This strong downdraft brings heavy rain or hail.

Step 3
During the final stage, the downdraft can spread out and block more warm air from moving upward into the cloud. The storm slows down and ends.

👁 Visualize It!

5 Claims • Evidence • Reasoning Make a claim about the role of warm air in the formation of thunderstorms. Summarize evidence to support the claim and explain your reasoning.

_____

_____

_____

Lightning is a Discharge of Electrical Energy

If you have ever shuffled your feet on a carpet, you may have felt a small shock when you touched a doorknob. If so, you have experienced how lightning forms. **Lightning** is an electric discharge that happens between a positively charged area and a negatively charged area. While you walk around, electrical charges can collect on your body. When you touch someone or something else, the charges jump to that person or object in a spark of electricity. In a similar way, electrical charges build up near the tops and bottoms of clouds as pellets of ice move up and down through the clouds. Suddenly, a flash of lightning will spark from one place to another.

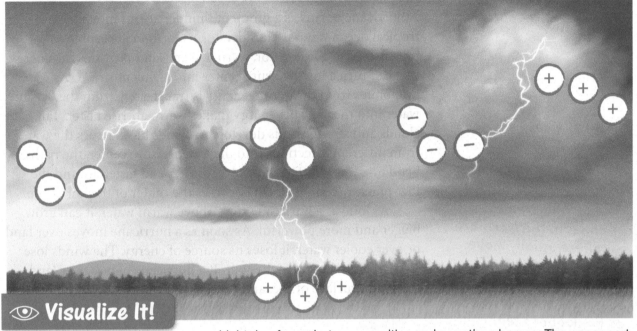

Visualize It!

6 Label Fill in the positive and negative charges in the appropriate spaces provided.

Lightning forms between positive and negative charges. The upper part of a cloud usually carries a positive electric charge. The lower part of the cloud carries mainly negative charges. Lightning is a big spark that jumps between parts of clouds, or between a cloud and Earth's surface.

Thunder Is a Result of Rapidly Expanding Air

ACTIVE READING

7 Identify As you read, underline the explanation of what causes thunder during a storm.

When lightning strikes, the air along its path is heated to a high temperature. The superheated air quickly expands. The rapidly moving air causes the air to vibrate and release sound waves. The result is **thunder**, the sound created by the rapid expansion of air along a lightning strike.

You usually hear thunder a few seconds after you see a lightning strike, because light travels faster than sound. You can count the seconds between a lightning flash and the sound of thunder to figure out about how far away the lightning is. For every 3 seconds between lightning and its thunder, add about 1 km to the lightning strike's distance from you.

✓ Plan Ahead!

ACTIVE READING

8 Identify As you read, underline the definition of *hurricane*.

What do we know about hurricanes?

A **hurricane** is a tropical low-pressure system with winds blowing at speeds of 119 km/h (74 mi/h) or more—strong enough to uproot trees. Hurricanes are called typhoons when they form over the western Pacific Ocean and cyclones when they form over the Indian Ocean.

Hurricanes Need Water to Form and Grow

A hurricane begins as a group of thunderstorms moving over tropical ocean waters. Thunderstorms form in areas of low pressure. Near the equator, warm ocean water provides the energy that can turn a low-pressure center into a violent storm. As water evaporates from the ocean, energy is transferred from the ocean water into the air. This energy makes warm air rise faster. Tall clouds and strong winds develop. As winds blow across the water from different directions into the low-pressure center, the paths bend into a spiral. The winds blow faster and faster around the low-pressure center, which becomes the center of the hurricane.

As long as a hurricane stays above warm water, it can grow bigger and more powerful. As soon as a hurricane moves over land or over cooler water, it loses its source of energy. The winds lose strength and the storm dies out. If a hurricane moves over land, the rough surface of the land reduces the winds even more.

Hurricanes in the Northern Hemisphere usually move westward with the trade winds. Near land, however, they will often move north or even back out to sea.

Hurricane Ike moves into the Gulf of Mexico on September 10, 2008.

Atlantic Ocean

Path of Hurricane Ike

Gulf of Mexico

Caribbean Sea

©NOAA via Getty Images

Hurricanes Can Cause Extensive Damage

A hurricane can pound a coast with huge waves and sweep the land with strong winds and heavy rains. The storms cause damage and dangerous conditions in several ways. Hurricane winds can lift cars, uproot trees, and tear the roofs off buildings. Hurricanes may also produce tornadoes that can cause even more damage. Heavy rains from hurricanes may make rivers overflow their banks and flood nearby areas. When a hurricane moves into a coastal area, it also pushes a huge mass of ocean water known as a **storm surge**. In a storm surge, the sea level rises several meters, backing up rivers and flooding the shore. A storm surge can be the most destructive and deadliest part of a hurricane. Large waves add to the damage. A hurricane may affect an area for a few hours or a few days, but the damage may take weeks or even months to clean up.

ACTIVE READING

9 Claims • Evidence • Reasoning Describe three dangers associated with hurricanes. Summarize evidence to support the claim and explain your reasoning.

_____

_____

Hurricane Matthew moved very close to the coasts of Florida, Georgia, South Carolina and North Carolina, in early October 2016. Matthew made one official U.S. landfall on Oct. 8 southeast of McClellanville, South Carolina, as a Category 1 hurricane with 75 mph winds.

Think Outside the Book

10 Claims • Evidence • Reasoning Use a map of ocean currents to make a claim about why hurricanes are more likely to make landfall in Florida than in California. Summarize evidence to support the claim and explain your reasoning to a classmate.

☑ Secure Loose Objects!

What do we know about tornadoes?

A **tornado** is a destructive, rotating column of air that has very high wind speeds and that is sometimes visible as a funnel-shaped cloud. A tornado forms when a thunderstorm meets horizontal winds at a high altitude. These winds cause the warm air rising in the thunderstorm to spin. A storm cloud may form a thin funnel shape that has a very low pressure center. As the funnel reaches the ground, the higher-pressure air rushes into the low-pressure area. The result is high-speed winds, which cause the damage associated with tornadoes.

Clouds begin to rotate, signaling that a tornado may form.

The funnel cloud becomes visible as the tornado picks up dust from the ground or particles from the air.

The tornado moves along the ground before it dies out.

Think Outside the Book

11 Illustrate Read the description of the weather conditions that cause tornadoes and draw a sketch of what those conditions might look like.

Most Tornadoes Happen in the Midwest

Tornadoes happen in many places, but they are most common in the United States in *Tornado Alley*. Tornado Alley reaches from Texas up through the midwestern United States, including Iowa, Kansas, Nebraska, and Ohio. Many tornadoes form in the spring and early summer, typically along a front between cool, dry air and warm, humid air.

Tornadoes Can Cause Extensive Damage

The danger of a tornado is mainly due to the high speed of its winds. Winds in a tornado's funnel may have speeds of more than 400 km/h. Most injuries and deaths caused by tornadoes happen when people are struck by objects blown by the winds or when they are trapped in buildings that collapse.

ACTIVE READING

12 Identify As you read, underline what makes a tornado so destructive.

13 Summarize In the overlapping sections of the Venn diagram, list the characteristics that are shared by the different types of storms. In the outer sections, list the characteristics that are specific to each type of storm.

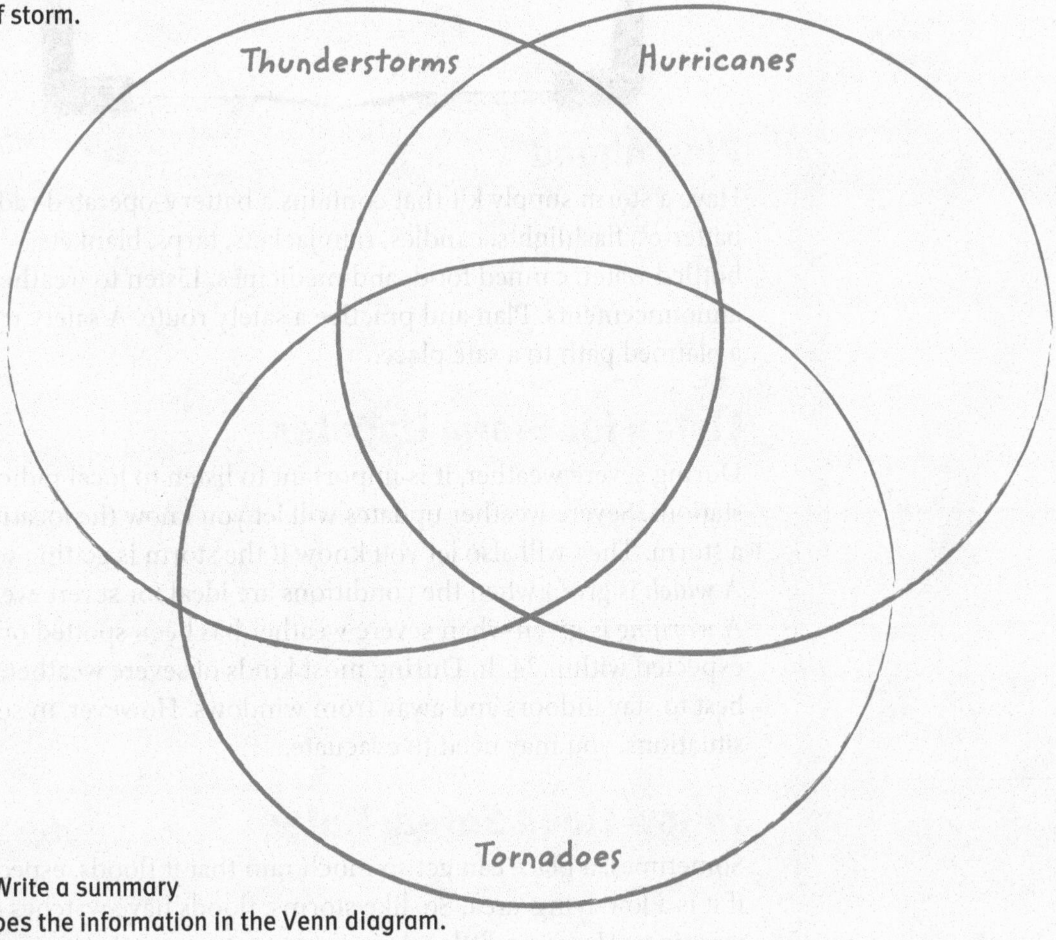

Thunderstorms

Hurricanes

Tornadoes

14 Conclude Write a summary that describes the information in the Venn diagram.

_____

_____

_____

_____

☑ Be Prepared!

What can people do to prepare for severe weather?

Severe weather is weather that can cause property damage, injury, and sometimes death. Hail, lightning, high winds, tornadoes, hurricanes, and floods are all part of severe weather. Hailstorms can damage crops and cars and can break windows. Lightning starts many forest fires and kills or injures hundreds of people and animals each year. Winds and tornadoes can uproot trees and destroy homes. Flooding is also a leading cause of weather-related deaths. Most destruction from hurricanes results from flooding due to storm surges.

> ### ⓘ Think Outside the Book
>
> **15 Claims • Evidence • Reasoning**
> Create a safety plan based on research of severe weather in your area. Summarize evidence to support your safety plan and explain your reasoning.

Plan Ahead

Have a storm supply kit that contains a battery-operated radio, batteries, flashlights, candles, rain jackets, tarps, blankets, bottled water, canned food, and medicines. Listen to weather announcements. Plan and practice a safety route. A safety route is a planned path to a safe place.

Listen for Storm Updates

During severe weather, it is important to listen to local radio or TV stations. Severe weather updates will let you know the location of a storm. They will also let you know if the storm is getting worse. A *watch* is given when the conditions are ideal for severe weather. A *warning* is given when severe weather has been spotted or is expected within 24 h. During most kinds of severe weather, it is best to stay indoors and away from windows. However, in some situations, you may need to evacuate.

Follow Flood Safety Rules

Sometimes, a place can get so much rain that it floods, especially if it is a low-lying area. So, like storms, floods have watches and warnings. However, little advance notice can usually be given that a flood is coming. A flash flood is a flood that rises and falls very quickly. The best thing to do during a flood is to find a high place to stay until it is over. You should always stay out of floodwaters. Even shallow water can be dangerous because it can move fast.

What can people do to stay safe during thunderstorms?

Stay alert when thunderstorms are predicted or when dark, tall clouds are visible. If you are outside and hear thunder, seek shelter immediately and stay there for 30 min after the thunder ends. Heavy rains can cause sudden, or flash, flooding, and hailstones can damage property and harm living things.

Lightning is one of the most dangerous parts of a thunderstorm. Because lightning is attracted to tall objects, it is important to stay away from trees if you are outside. If you are in an open area, stay close to the ground so that you are not the tallest object in the area. If you can, get into a car. Stay away from ponds, lakes, or other bodies of water. If lightning hits water while you are swimming or wading in it, you could be hurt or killed. If you are indoors during a thunderstorm, avoid using electrical appliances, running water, and phone lines.

How can people stay safe during a tornado?

Tornadoes are too fast and unpredictable for you to attempt to outrun, even if you are in a car. If you see or hear a tornado, go to a place without windows, such as basement, a storm cellar, or a closet or hallway. Stay away from areas that are likely to have flying objects or other dangers. If you are outside, lie in a ditch or low-lying area. Protect your head and neck by covering them with your arms and hands.

How can people stay safe during a hurricane?

If your family lives where hurricanes may strike, have a plan to leave the area, and gather emergency supplies. If a hurricane is approaching your area, listen to weather reports for storm updates. Secure loose objects outside, and cover windows with storm shutters or boards. During a storm, stay indoors and away from windows. If ordered to evacuate the area, do so immediately. After a storm, be aware of downed power lines, hanging branches, and flooded areas.

16 Apply What would you do in each of these scenarios?

Scenario	What would you do?
You are swimming at an outdoor pool when you hear thunder in the distance.	
You and your family are watching TV when you hear a tornado warning that says a tornado has been spotted in the area.	
You are listening to the radio when the announcer says that a hurricane is headed your way and may make landfall in 3 days.	

☑ Use Sun Sense!

How can people protect their skin from the sun?

ACTIVE READING

17 Identify As you read, underline when the sun's ray's are strongest during the day.

Human skin contains melanin, which is the body's natural protection against ultraviolet (UV) radiation from the sun. The skin produces more melanin when it is exposed to the sun, but UV rays will still cause sunburn when you spend too much time outside. It is particularly important to protect your skin when the sun's rays are strongest, usually between 10 A.M and 4 P.M.

Know the Sun's Hazards

It's easy to notice the effects of a sunburn. Sunburn usually appears within a few hours after sun exposure. It causes red, painful skin that feels hot to the touch. Prolonged exposure to the sun will lead to sunburn in even the darkest-skinned people. Sunburn can lead to skin cancer and premature aging of the skin. The best way to prevent sunburn is to protect your skin from the sun, even on cloudy days. UV rays pass right through clouds and can give you a false feeling of protection from the sun.

Wear Sunscreen and Protective Clothing

Even if you tan easily, you should still use sunscreen. For most people, a sun protection factor (SPF) of 30 or more will prevent burning for about 1.5 h. Babies and people who have pale skin should use an SPF of 45 or more. In addition, you can protect your skin and eyes in different ways. Seek the shade, and wear hats, sunglasses, and perhaps even UV light-protective clothing.

Have fun in the sun! Just be sure to protect your skin from harmful rays.

How can people protect themselves from summer heat?

Heat exhaustion is a condition in which the body has been exposed to high temperatures for an extended period of time. Symptoms include cold, moist skin, normal or near-normal body temperature, headache, nausea, and extreme fatigue. *Heat stroke* is a condition in which the body loses its ability to cool itself by sweating because the victim has become dehydrated.

Limit Outdoor Activities

When outdoor temperatures are high, be cautious about exercising outdoors for long periods of time. Pay attention to how your body is feeling, and go inside or to a shady spot if you are starting to feel light-headed or too warm.

Drink Water

Heat exhaustion and heat stroke can best be prevented by drinking 6 to 8 oz of water at least 10 times a day when you are active in warm weather. If you are feeling overheated, dizzy, nauseous, or are sweating heavily, drink something cool (not cold). Drink about half a glass of cool water every 15 min until you feel like your normal self.

Drinking water is one of the best things you can do to keep yourself healthy in hot weather.

18 Describe List all the ways the people in the photo of the beach may have protected themselves from overexposure to the sun.

_____
_____
_____
_____
_____
_____
_____
_____

Know the Signs of Heat Stroke

ACTIVE READING

19 Identify Underline signs of heat stroke in the paragraph below.

Heat stroke is life threatening, so it is important to know the signs and treatment for it. Symptoms of heat stroke include hot, dry skin; higher than normal body temperature; rapid pulse; rapid, shallow breathing; disorientation; and possible loss of consciousness.

What to Do In Case of Heat Stroke

☐ Seek emergency help immediately.

☐ If there are no emergency facilities nearby, move the person to a cool place.

☐ Cool the person's body by immersing it in a cool (not cold) bath or using wet towels.

☐ Do not give the person food or water if he or she is vomiting.

☐ Place ice packs under the person's armpits.

Visual Summary

To complete this summary, circle the correct word or phrase.
You can use this page to review the main concepts of the lesson.

Severe Weather

Thunderstorms are intense weather systems that produce strong winds, heavy rain, lightning, and thunder.

20 One of the most dangerous parts of a thunderstorm is lightning / thunder.

A hurricane is a large, rotating tropical weather system with strong winds that can cause severe property damage.

21 An important step to plan for a hurricane is to buy raingear / stock a supply kit.

Tornadoes are rotating columns of air that touch the ground and can cause severe damage.

22 The damage from a tornado is mostly caused by associated thunderstorms / high-speed winds.

It is important to plan ahead and listen for weather updates in the event of severe weather.

23 One of the biggest dangers of storms that produce heavy rains or storm surges is flooding / low temperatures.

Prolonged exposure to the sun can cause sunburn, skin cancer, and heat-related health effects.

24 One of the best ways to avoid heat-related illnesses while in the sun is to stay active / drink water.

25 **Claims • Evidence • Reasoning** Make a claim that identifies three ways severe weather can be dangerous. Summarize evidence to support the claim and explain your reasoning.

Lesson Review

Vocabulary

Draw a line that matches the term with the correct definition.

1 hurricane

2 tornado

3 severe weather

4 thunderstorm

5 storm surge

A a huge mass of ocean water that floods the shore

B a storm with lightning and thunder

C a violently rotating column of air stretching to the ground

D weather that can potentially destroy property or cause loss of life

E a tropical low-pressure system with winds of 119 km/h or more

Key Concepts

6 Thunder is caused by _____

7 An electrical discharge between parts of clouds or a cloud and the ground is called _____

8 The sun's ultraviolet rays can cause skin damage including sunburn and even skin _____

9 **Explain** How can a person prepare for hazardous weather well in advance?

10 **Claims • Evidence • Reasoning** Make a claim about ways people can stay safe during storms with high wind and heavy rains. Summarize evidence to support the claim and explain your reasoning.

Critical Thinking

Use the map below to answer the following question.

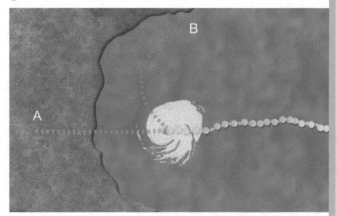

11 **Interpret** Would a hurricane be more likely to remain a hurricane if it reached point A or point B? Explain your answer.

12 **State Your Claim** Why do hurricanes form in tropical latitudes? Explain your reasoning.

13 **Describe** What two weather conditions are needed for tornadoes to form?

14 **Explain** Why is hail sometimes dangerous? Explain your reasoning.

15 **Summarize** What can you do to avoid overexposure to the sun's rays?

Natural Disasters
in Florida

ESSENTIAL QUESTION

How do natural disasters affect Florida?

By the end of this lesson, you should be able to describe the natural disasters that affect Florida, including their economic impact and their effects on people.

Tornadoes can touch down anywhere in Florida—including downtown Miami. This 1997 tornado injured five people and caused a massive power outage.

SC.6.E.7.7 Investigate how natural disasters have affected human life in Florida. **HE.6.C.1.3** Identify environmental factors that affect personal health.

Quick Labs
- Create an Emergency Preparedness Kit
- Modeling a Hurricane

Engage Your Brain

1 Predict Check T or F to show whether you think each statement is true or false.

T F
☐ ☐ It is safe to explore sinkholes.

☐ ☐ Thunderstorms can cause flash floods.

☐ ☐ Florida experiences more hurricanes than any other state.

☐ ☐ Tornadoes are rare in Florida.

2 Assess What natural disasters do you think could affect the house shown below?

_____

_____

_____

ACTIVE READING

3 Synthesize You can often determine the meaning of a word when you look at context clues, or how the word is used in a sentence. Use the sentence below to guess the definition of *muck fire*.

Example sentence:
Muck fires start when lightning strikes the ground and the dead matter making up the soil starts to burn.

muck fire:

_____

_____

Vocabulary Terms
- sinkhole
- wildfire
- muck fire

4 Apply As you learn the definition of each vocabulary term in this lesson, create your own definition or sketch to help you remember the meaning of the term.

When It Rains, It Pours

Which parts of a thunderstorm can be dangerous?

Florida has lots of thunderstorms. Thunderstorms often happen in the summer when the air over the land is warm and moist. Cooler air over the Gulf of Mexico or the Atlantic Ocean blows toward the land. The cool air pushes the warm, moist air upward. As the moist air rises, it begins to cool. The moisture in the cooling air condenses into large, dark clouds. Thunderstorms result from these large clouds. Thunderstorms can be very dangerous and may cause lots of damage in Florida. Heavy rains, hail, lightning, and high winds are all dangers associated with thunderstorms.

Heavy Rain and Flash Floods

Thunderstorms can produce very heavy rains in a short period of time. When this occurs, the soil may not be able to absorb all of the rain. Instead, the water may rush into streambeds, drainage ditches, and valleys. The water can quickly accummulate and cause a flash flood. A *flash flood* is a sudden, local flood of great volume and short duration. Flash floods can be extremely powerful and dangerous. These floods can occur in a few minutes and can wash away people, cars, and even houses! Because of the speed and power of a flash flood, stay away from streams if thunderstorms are in the area. If a stream rises high enough to cover a road, do not cross the road even if you are in a large vehicle.

Hail

Severe thunderstorms sometimes produce hail. Hailstones are chunks of ice that fall as precipitation. Hail first starts as small ice crystals near the top of a thunderstorm cloud where the air is very cold. As the ice falls downward into a warmer part of the cloud, it is covered in a thin layer of water. Strong winds may then drive the forming hail upward again. The thin layer of water freezes and the hail grows larger. Hailstones may be lifted and dropped many times in this way until they become as large as grapefruit! These hailstones can smash car windows and damage roofs and other property. They can even kill livestock. Smaller hail can also cause damage. For example, small hail can bruise plants, damaging crops.

hailstones

ACTIVE READING

5 Claims • Evidence • Reasoning Describe the effects hail can have on property. Summarize evidence to support the claim and explain your reasoning.

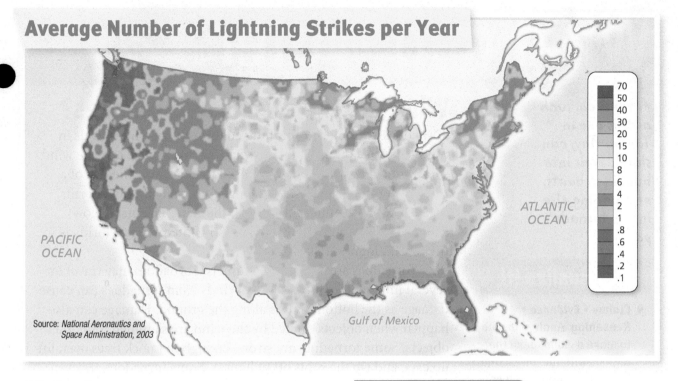

Average Number of Lightning Strikes per Year

PACIFIC
OCEAN

ATLANTIC
OCEAN

Gulf of Mexico

| 70 |
| 50 |
| 40 |
| 30 |
| 20 |
| 15 |
| 10 |
| 8 |
| 6 |
| 4 |
| 2 |
| 1 |
| .8 |
| .6 |
| .4 |
| .2 |
| .1 |

Source: *National Aeronautics and Space Administration, 2003*

Lightning

Look at the map above. The map shows that Florida is often struck by lightning. In fact, Florida has more injuries and deaths caused by lightning than any other state. So, what is lightning, exactly? Lightning is an electric discharge that takes place in clouds or between a cloud and the ground. There are several types of lightning, but cloud-to-ground lightning is the most dangerous to people. If it strikes a person, it can seriously injure or kill them. Lightning may also damage power lines and property. In addition, lightning can start fires. Some of these fires help maintain Florida's ecosystems, while other fires are dangerous to people and property.

High Wind

Thunderstorms can produce intense winds that blow 50–160 km/h. These winds can be strong enough to blow trees down. They can also knock down power lines. Thunderstorms can produce sudden, dangerous bursts of air that move toward the ground and then spread out. These downburst winds are so strong that they are sometimes mistaken for tornadoes. They can destroy crops, knock down buildings or airplanes, and even move cars!

👁 Visualize It!

6 Identify Which part of the country experiences the most lightning strikes?

_____

_____

lightning

Think Outside the Book

7 Apply In your journal, write about some experiences you've had with thunderstorms.

Wind and Water

A tornado, such as this one in Tampa Bay, can slam debris into buildings, boats, or anything else in the tornado's path.

👁 Visualize It!

9 Claims • Evidence • Reasoning Analyze the map to make a claim about the regions with the lowest and highest risk for tornadoes. Summarize evidence to support the claim and explain your reasoning.

_____

_____

What are the effects of tornadoes?

Tornadoes are violently spinning columns of air. High winds in thunderstorms often produce tornadoes. In fact, the average wind speeds in thunderstorms can be used to determine the risk of a tornado forming. Because Florida gets so many thunderstorms, tornadoes are common throughout the state. The map below shows risk areas across the continental United States. Florida is in the second highest risk area for tornadoes.

Tornadoes are shaped like funnels. Tornadoes may travel for several miles before breaking up. Winds from tornadoes can cause damage as the bottom moves along the ground. Damage can also happen when objects carried by the wind are slammed into other objects. Some tornadoes are strong enough to knock trees over, lift up cars, and rip the roofs off of houses. Some tornadoes are even strong enough to completely flatten a well-built building.

ACTIVE READING

8 Claims • Evidence • Reasoning Make a claim about the effects of a tornado. Summarize evidence to support the claim and explain your reasoning.

_____

_____

Risk of Tornadoes

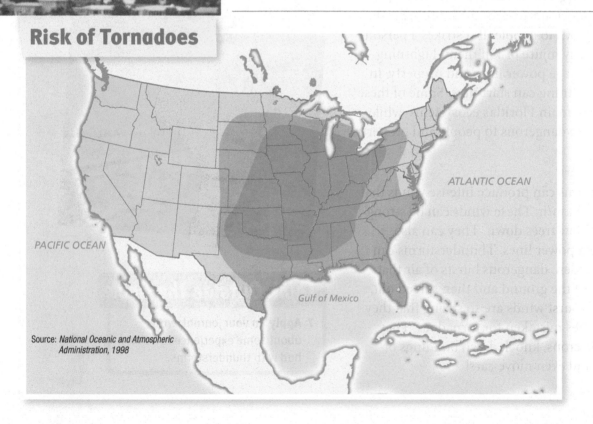

PACIFIC OCEAN

ATLANTIC OCEAN

Gulf of Mexico

Source: *National Oceanic and Atmospheric Administration, 1998*

What are the effects of floods?

Floods are very common in Florida because the state is relatively flat, a great deal of rainfall is received, and, in some areas, the rock layer under the soil doesn't let water through easily. When heavy rain occurs, low-lying areas can become flooded. Any homes and buildings in these areas may be threatened by rising water, which can cause millions of dollars in property damage. In addition, flooded roads are very dangerous to drive on, and fast-moving water can sweep people away. Finally, floodwater can enter the drinking-water supply and contaminate the water with pollutants. Contaminated water is unsafe to drink.

In addition to inland flooding, much of Florida is at risk from flooding from the ocean. During hurricanes, water from the ocean can be pushed up onto land when a storm surge hits. A *storm surge* is a swell of water that builds up in the ocean due to a hurricane's heavy winds. A storm surge can be especially devastating when the tide is high. It can also cause rivers to back up and flood. Coastal areas and islands can be totally covered by ocean water. Because of this, the Florida Keys are especially at risk from storm surges. You will learn more about storm surges later in this lesson.

Only emergency and rescue vehicles should attempt to drive through floodwaters.

10 Gather Evidence List four of the effects of flooding.

- _____
- _____
- _____
- _____

Weathering the Storm

What are the effects of hurricanes?

Hurricanes are low-pressure systems with thunderstorms and winds that circle around a central "eye." The winds circling the eye must sustain speeds of at least 119 km/h for the storm to be classified as a hurricane.

Hurricanes form over warm ocean water. If a hurricane travels over cold water, it will die out. Hurricanes usually occur in summer in the northern hemisphere. Hurricane season runs from June 1 to November 30. Because Florida is near the warm waters of the Gulf of Mexico, the Atlantic Ocean, and the Caribbean Sea, Florida is hit by more hurricanes than any other state.

Hazards to People

Hurricanes are the most violent storms on Earth. They can be deadly. Because of this danger, government officials often order citizens to evacuate when a hurricane is about to strike. However, the area still may not be safe even after the hurricane has ended. Floodwaters from the hurricane can lead to drownings. Roads may be covered by debris, causing car accidents. Broken tree limbs and damaged structures can fall on people. Broken electric lines may lead to electrocution. Because of widespread power outages, many people use generators for electricity. If not used properly, generators can cause carbon monoxide poisoning. Due to all these hazards, you should not return to an area affected by a hurricane until officials say it is safe to do so.

◉ Visualize It!

11 Claims • Evidence • Reasoning Make a claim about which areas of Florida are most likely to be hit by a category 4 hurricane. Summarize evidence to support the claim and explain your reasoning.

_____

_____

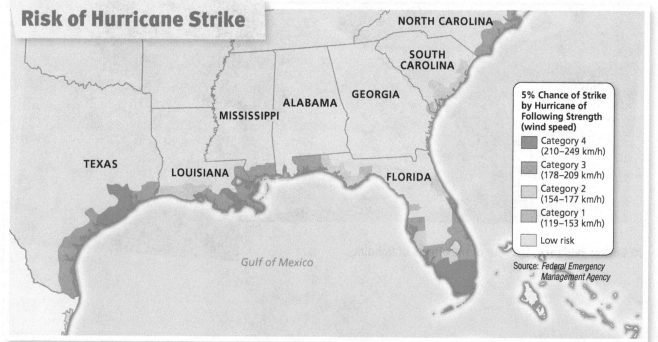

Risk of Hurricane Strike

NORTH CAROLINA

SOUTH CAROLINA

GEORGIA

ALABAMA

MISSISSIPPI

TEXAS

LOUISIANA

FLORIDA

Gulf of Mexico

5% Chance of Strike by Hurricane of Following Strength (wind speed)

- Category 4 (210–249 km/h)
- Category 3 (178–209 km/h)
- Category 2 (154–177 km/h)
- Category 1 (119–153 km/h)
- Low risk

Source: *Federal Emergency Management Agency*

Damage to Property

Florida's flat land makes it vulnerable to the full force of hurricane winds. Because of this, hurricanes striking Florida can cause an enormous amount of property damage. For major hurricanes, it typically costs several billion dollars to repair the damage.

Larger hurricanes can affect more areas than smaller hurricanes, but the destructive power of a hurricane is also related to its strength. Category 1 hurricanes are the weakest because they have the slowest winds (119–153 km/h). Category 5 hurricanes have the fastest winds (greater than 250 km/h). Winds can rip roofs off buildings or slam objects against structures. In addition, a great deal of damage can be caused by a storm surge because of the power of rising ocean water. The impact of a storm surge depends on the direction of the wind and whether the tide is high when a hurricane hits.

ACTIVE READING

12 Gather Evidence How do hurricane winds affect property?

_____

_____

👁 Visualize It!

During a regular high tide, the waters don't cause floods or damage.

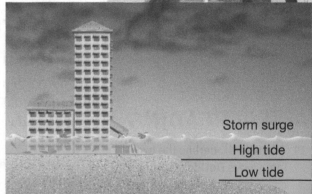

Storm surges push waters far above the high tide level and cause severe flooding.

13 Apply When a hurricane approaches land, people living directly on the coast should always evacuate when told to do so by authorities. Use the information in the diagrams to explain why.

_____

_____

_____

More Recipes for Disaster

These strawberry plants have been covered in ice to protect them from cold weather.

ACTIVE READING

14 **Identify** Underline the two main ways Florida's economy can be hurt by cold weather spells.

What are the effects of cold weather?

We don't often think about cold weather in many parts of Florida. But when cold weather does strike, it can damage crops, harm the tourism industry, and be dangerous to people. Cold weather can also make the roads icy and hazardous to drive on.

In Florida, farmers may protect crops from freezing weather by covering them or spraying them with water. The water freezes and forms a layer of ice, which traps some heat in the plant. This process keeps the developing fruit from freezing. However, if temperatures stay too low for too long, the crop will be damaged.

Because Florida usually has mild weather, many homes do not have adequate heating and insulation. As a result, people in Florida may have trouble staying warm during cold weather. Electricity can be disrupted by an ice storm, which may result in near-freezing temperatures inside houses. People who are exposed to cold weather for a long time may fall dangerously ill. If the weather gets too cold, wear several layers of dry clothing and use safe heating devices.

What are the effects of sinkholes?

Sinkholes are a danger in some parts of Florida. **Sinkholes** are holes in the ground that form when a cave collapses. In Florida, sinkholes often form where limestone is eroded by ground water, making a cave. The cave's roof falls in when ground water supporting the roof drains away. The map below shows that sinkholes are one of the major landforms in the state.

Sinkholes can swallow cars, damage homes, and even destroy whole city blocks! People can be killed when sinkholes form. Look at the photo of the sinkhole below. Nobody was killed when this sinkhole formed, but a road caved in. Sinkholes can cause millions of dollars of damage. In addition, sinkholes can disrupt services by breaking underground telephone lines, sewer lines, and more.

Sinkholes can lead to the contamination of a town's water supply. Anything that goes into a sinkhole can enter the ground water, which is used for drinking water by many Floridians. So, trash should not be dumped in a sinkhole. And because sinkholes can collapse further, you should stay away from them.

ACTIVE READING

15 Identify Underline at least five effects of sinkholes.

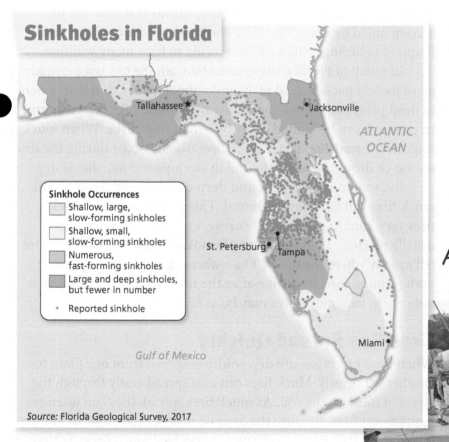

Sinkholes in Florida

Tallahassee ★

Jacksonville

ATLANTIC OCEAN

Sinkhole Occurrences
- Shallow, large, slow-forming sinkholes
- Shallow, small, slow-forming sinkholes
- Numerous, fast-forming sinkholes
- Large and deep sinkholes, but fewer in number
- • Reported sinkhole

St. Petersburg • Tampa

Miami

Gulf of Mexico

Source: Florida Geological Survey, 2017

A sinkhole in Plant City, Florida

W SAMMANDS D

👁 Visualize It!

16 Analyze What type of sinkholes would you expect to find around Jacksonville?

_____

_____

Up in Flames

What do we know about wildfires?

Wildfires are uncontrolled fires burning in natural areas. Every 3 to 5 years, there is an increase in the number of wildfires that burn in Florida. This cycle of wildfires coincides with the state's natural climatic cycles. Wildfires increase during periods of dry weather and drought.

ACTIVE READING

17 Identify Underline the sentences below that describe how a muck fire typically starts.

Fires Are Often Caused by Lightning

Wildfires usually start when lightning ignites dry trees or grasses. After the dry season, dry grass and trees may catch fire easily. Florida has frequent, intense lightning storms that may not be accompanied by much rain. The combination of dry plants and frequent lightning strikes causes Florida to have many wildfires.

In much of Florida, the ground beneath the top layer is made up of loosely packed dead plant and animal matter. Soil that is rich in dead plant and animal matter is called *muck*. Like dry grass and trees, muck can be ignited easily by a lightning strike. When muck is ignited, a **muck fire** starts. Muck fires usually occur during the dry season or droughts, when the soil in swamps and marshes is dry.

Because muck can be found deep under the top layer of soil, muck fires can burn underground. This property makes muck fires very hard to extinguish because, even though muck fires usually produce a large amount of smoke, firefighters often cannot tell exactly where the fire is. The embers of muck fires may burn underground for a long time after the fire on the surface has been put out. In fact, muck fires may burn for weeks.

Fires Can Spread Quickly

When trees or grasses are dry, wildfires spread from one plant to another very easily. Muck fires can also spread easily through the layers of muck in the soil. As muck fires spread, they can often re-ignite forest fires. Because the organic matter in the soils of Florida is loosely packed, there is plenty of air to feed muck fires. As the fire spreads underground, it can burn tree roots. When the trees fall, the underground fire may restart a surface fire.

Wildfires in the Continental United States, 1994–2013

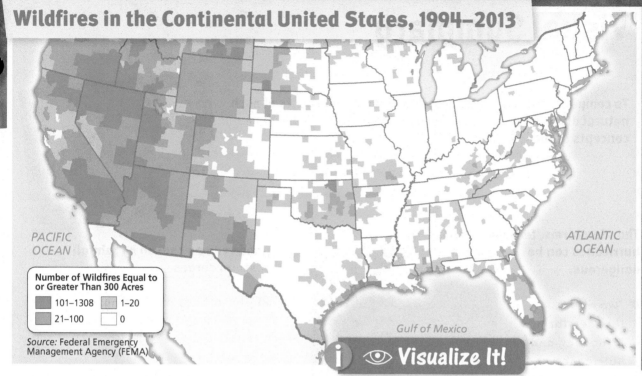

PACIFIC
OCEAN

ATLANTIC
OCEAN

Gulf of Mexico

Number of Wildfires Equal to or Greater Than 300 Acres

101–1308	1–20
21–100	0

Source: Federal Emergency
Management Agency (FEMA)

Fires Destroy Property

More and more homes in Florida are built in wilderness areas that are prone to fires. Most of the Florida developments in rural areas or near wilderness have burned in the last 100 years. In 2016, just over 3,000 wildfires occurred in Florida. They burned over 74,000 acres of land, causing damage to homes and other structures in their paths. However, 500,000 acres were burned. These fires temporarily destroyed the habitats of many animals, but the fires added nutrients to the soil and helped renew the plant life in the ecosystems.

There are several things you can do to stay safe from fires. First, know whether your home is in a fire-prone area. Second, many plants are resistant to fire. Plant these near your home. Third, have a disaster plan and supplies in your home and car. Last, if a wildfire is occuring in your area, listen to local radio or TV stations for the latest information and evacuation instructions.

ⓘ 👁 Visualize It!

18 Claims • Evidence • Reasoning Explain why certain parts of the country are more susceptible to wildfires. Provide evidence to support the claim. Explain your reasoning.

_____

_____

This truck was caught in a wildfire.

19 Summarize Make a checklist of safety measures you can take to protect yourself and your family from wildfires.

_____

_____

_____

_____

_____

_____

Visual Summary

To complete this summary, describe at least two effects of each natural disaster shown. You can use this page to review the main concepts of the lesson.

Natural Disasters

Thunderstorms, tornadoes, and hurricanes can be dangerous.

20 Two effects of thunderstorms, tornadoes, and/or hurricanes:

_____
_____
_____
_____

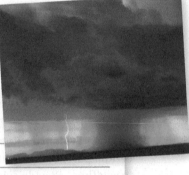

Floods can be caused by rainfall or storm surges.

21 Two effects of flooding:

_____
_____
_____
_____
_____
_____

Cold weather can impact Florida's economy.

22 Two effects of cold weather:

_____
_____
_____
_____
_____

Sinkholes are common in Florida.

23 Two effects of sinkholes:

_____
_____
_____
_____
_____

Fires can spread quickly with little warning.

24 Two effects of fires:

_____
_____
_____
_____

25 **Claims • Evidence • Reasoning** Make a claim about how thunderstorms can cause flooding and fires, Provide evidence with factors supporting your claim. Explain your reasoning.

Lesson Review

Vocabulary

Fill in the blank with the term that best completes the following sentences.

1 A(n) _____ can form when water supporting the roof of a cavern drains and the roof falls.

2 A fire burning uncontrolled in a natural area is called a(n) _____

Key Concepts

3 Identify What are the dangers associated with thunderstorms?

_____

_____

_____

4 Describe Describe how a tornado can endanger property and people.

_____

_____

_____

5 State Your Claim How can floodwater affect the public drinking water supply?

_____

_____

_____

6 Explain Why is Florida susceptible to sinkholes?

_____

_____

_____

7 Explain Your Reasoning How can you protect yourself from the cold?

_____

_____

Critical Thinking

Use the table to answer the following questions.

Top Six Deadliest U.S. Hurricanes				
Rank	Name (Landfall location)	Year	Category	Deaths
1	Galveston Hurricane (Galveston, TX)	1900	4	8,000–12,000
2	Okeechobee Hurricane (West Palm Beach, FL)	1928	4	2,500–3,000
3	Hurricane Katrina (Louisiana and Mississippi)	2005	3	1,500
4	The Cheniere Caminada Hurricane (Louisiana)	1893	4	1,100–1,400
5	Sea Islands Hurricane (South Carolina and Georgia)	1893	3	1,000–2,000
6	Georgia-South Carolina Hurricane (South Carolina and Georgia)	1881	2	700

8 Gather Evidence Where have the majority of the hurricanes listed made landfall? Use evidence from the graph to support this claim and explain your reasoning.

_____

_____

9 Gather Evidence Did the deadliest hurricane happen recently or in the past? Use evidence from the table to support this claim and explain your reasoning.

_____

_____

10 Relate Which area would be most likely to experience wildfires: a wet area with many lightning strikes, a dry area with few lightning strikes, or a dry area with many lightning strikes? Explain your reasoning.

_____

_____

PEOPLE IN SCIENCE

SC.6.N.2.3 Recognize that scientists who make contributions to scientific knowledge come from all kinds of backgrounds and possess varied talents, interests, and goals.

J. Marshall Shepherd

METEOROLOGIST AND CLIMATOLOGIST

J. Marshall Shepherd

Dr. Marshall Shepherd, who works at the University of Georgia, has been interested in weather since he made his own weather-collecting instruments for a school science project. Although the instruments he uses today, like computers and satellites, are much larger and much more powerful than the ones he made in school, they give him some of the same information.

In his work, Dr. Shepherd tries to understand weather events, such as hurricanes and thunderstorms, and relate them to current weather and climate change. He once led a team that used space-based radar to measure rainfall over urban areas. The measurements confirmed that the areas downwind of major cities experience more rainfall in summer than other areas in the same region. He explained that the excess heat retained by buildings and roads changes the way the air circulates, and this causes rain clouds to form.

While the most familiar field of meteorology is weather forecasting, research meteorology is also used in air pollution control, weather control, agricultural planning, climate change studies, and even criminal and civil investigations.

Social Studies Connection

An almanac is a type of calendar that contains various types of information, including weather forecasts and astronomical data, for every day of the year. Many people used almanacs before meteorologists started to forecast the weather. Use an almanac from the library or the Internet to find out what the weather was on the day that you were born.

JOB BOARD

Atmospheric Scientist

What You'll Do: Collect and analyze data on Earth's air pressure, humidity, and winds to make short-range and long-range weather forecasts. Work around the clock during weather emergencies like hurricanes and tornadoes.

Where You Might Work: Weather data collecting stations, radio and television stations, or private consulting firms.

Education: A bachelor's degree in meteorology, or in a closely related field with courses in meteorology, is required. A master's degree is necessary for some jobs.

Airplane Pilot

What You'll Do: Fly airplanes containing passengers or cargo, or for crop dusting, search and rescue, or fire-fighting. Before flights, check the plane's control equipment and weather conditions. Plan a safe route. Pilots communicate with air traffic control during flight to ensure a safe flight and fill out paperwork after the flight.

Where You Might Work: Flying planes for airlines, the military, radio and tv stations, freight companies, flight schools, farms, national parks, or other businesses that use airplanes.

Education: Most pilots will complete a four-year college degree before entering a pilot program. Before pilots become certified and take to the skies, they need a pilot license and many hours of flight time and training.

Snow Plow Operator

What You'll Do: In areas that receive snowfall, prepare the roads by spreading a mixture of sand and salt on the roads when snow is forecast. After a snowfall, drive snow plows to clear snow from roads and walkways.

Where You Might Work: For public organizations or private companies in cities and towns that receive snowfall.

Education: In most states, there is no special license needed, other than a driver's license.

Climate

ESSENTIAL QUESTION

How is climate affected by energy from the sun and variations on Earth's surface?

By the end of this lesson, you should be able to describe the main factors that affect climate and explain how scientists classify climates.

Earth has a wide variety of climates, including polar climates like the one shown here. What kind of climate do you live in?

SC.6.E.7.2 Investigate and apply how the cycling of water between the atmosphere and hydrosphere has an effect on weather patterns and climate. **SC.6.E.7.5** Explain how energy provided by the sun influences global patterns of atmospheric movement and the temperature differences between air, water, and land. **SC.6.E.7.6** Differentiate between weather and climate

Lesson Labs

Quick Labs
- Modeling a Front
- Factors That Affect Climate
- Modeling El Niño

 ## Engage Your Brain

1 Predict Check T or F to show whether you think each statement is true or false.

T	F	
☐	☐	Locations in Florida and Oregon receive the same amount of sunlight on any given day.
☐	☐	Temperature is an important part of determining the climate of an area.
☐	☐	The climate on even the tallest mountains near the equator is too warm for glaciers to form.
☐	☐	Winds can move rain clouds from one location to another.

2 Infer Volcanic eruptions can send huge clouds of gas and dust into the air. These dust particles can block sunlight. How might the eruption of a large volcano affect weather for years to come?

_____
_____
_____
_____

ACTIVE READING

3 Synthesize You can often define an unknown word if you know the meaning of its word parts. Use the word parts and sentence below to make an educated guess about the meaning of the word *topography*.

Word part	Meaning
topos-	place
-graphy	writing

Example sentence
The topography of the area is varied, because there are hills, valleys, and flat plains all within a few square miles.

topography:

_____
_____

Vocabulary Terms
- weather
- climate
- latitude
- topography
- elevation
- surface currents

4 Apply As you learn the definition of each vocabulary term in this lesson, create your own definition or sketch to help you remember the meaning of the term.

How's the Climate?

5 Identify As you read, underline two elements of weather that are important in determining climate.

What determines climate?

Weather conditions change from day to day. **Weather** is the condition of Earth's atmosphere at a particular time and place. **Climate**, on the other hand, describes the weather conditions in an area over a long period of time. For the most part, climate is determined by temperature and precipitation (pree•SIP•uh•tay•shuhn). But what factors affect the temperature and precipitation rates of an area? Those factors include latitude, wind patterns, elevation, locations of mountains and large bodies of water, and nearness to ocean currents.

Temperature

Temperature patterns are an important feature of climate. Although the average temperature of an area over a period of time is useful information, using only average temperatures to describe climate can be misleading. Areas that have similar average temperatures may have very different temperature ranges.

A temperature range includes all of the temperatures in an area, from the coldest temperature extreme to the warmest temperature extreme. Organisms that thrive in a region are those that can survive the temperature extremes in that region. Temperature ranges provide more information about an area and are unique to the area. Therefore, temperature ranges are a better indicator of climate than are temperature averages.

👁 Visualize It!

6 State Your Claim How might the two different climates shown below affect the daily lives of the people who live there?

_____

_____

_____

_____

_____

Desert region

Polar region

Precipitation

Precipitation, such as rain, snow, or hail, is also an important part of climate. As with temperature, the average yearly precipitation alone is not the best way to describe a climate. Two places that have the same average yearly precipitation may receive that precipitation in different patterns during the year. For example, one location may receive small amounts of precipitation throughout the year. This pattern would support plant life all year long. Another location may receive all of its precipitation in a few months of the year. These months may be the only time in which plants can grow. So, the pattern of precipitation in a region can determine the types of plants that grow there and the length of the growing season. Therefore, the pattern of precipitation is a better indicator of the local climate than the average precipitation alone.

i Think Outside the Book

8 Apply With a classmate, discuss what condition, other than precipitation, is likely related to better plant growth in the temperate area shown directly below than in the desert on the bottom right.

👁 Visualize It!

7 Gather Evidence Match the climates represented in the bar graph below to the photos by writing *A, B,* or *C* in the blank circles.

Annual Precipitation in Three Climates

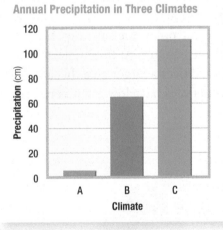

○ There are enough resources in the area for plants to thickly cover the ground.

○ Some plants that grow in deserts have long roots to reach the water deep underground.

○ Conditions in a tropical forest allow lots of plants to grow quickly and closely together.

Here Comes the Sun!

How is the sun's energy related to Earth's climate?

The climate of an area is directly related to the amount of energy from the sun, or *solar energy*, that the area receives. This amount depends on the latitude (LAHT•ih•tood) of the area. **Latitude** is the angular distance in degrees north and south from the equator. Different latitudes receive different amounts of solar energy. The available solar energy powers the water cycle and winds, which affect the temperature, precipitation, and other factors that determine the local climate.

Latitude Affects the Amount of Solar Energy an Area Receives and that Area's Climate

Latitude helps determine the temperature of an area, because latitude affects the amount of solar energy an area receives. The figure below shows how the amount of solar energy reaching Earth's surface varies with latitude. Notice that the sun's rays travel in lines parallel to one another. Near the equator, the sun's rays hit Earth directly, at almost a 90° angle. At this angle, the solar energy is concentrated in a small area of Earth's surface. As a result, that area has high temperatures. At the poles, the sun's rays hit Earth at a lesser angle than they do at the equator. At this angle, the same amount of solar energy is spread over a larger area. Because the energy is less concentrated, the poles have lower temperatures than areas near the equator do.

ACTIVE READING

9 Identify As you read, underline how solar energy affects the climate of an area.

👁 Visualize It!

10 Claims • Evidence • Reasoning Make a claim about the difference between the sun's rays that strike at the equator and the sun's rays that strike at the poles. Provide evidence with factors supporting your claim. Explain your reasoning.

_____

_____

_____

_____

The amount of solar energy an area receives depends on latitude.

Drawing is not to scale.

The Sun Powers the Water Cycle

It is easy to see how the water cycle affects weather and climate. For example, when it rains or snows, you see precipitation. In the water cycle, energy from the sun warms the surface of the ocean or other body of water. Some of the liquid water evaporates, becoming invisible water vapor, a gas. When cooled, some of the vapor condenses, turning into droplets of liquid water and forming clouds. Some water droplets collide, becoming larger. Once large enough, they fall to Earth's surface as precipitation.

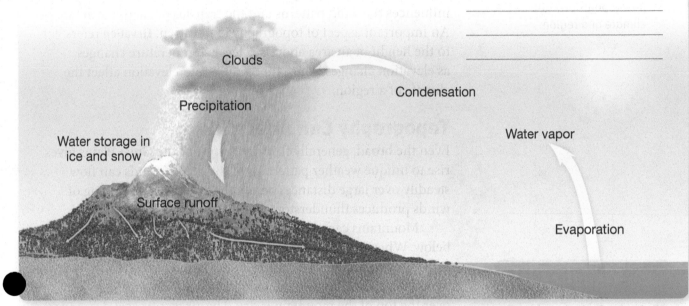

Clouds

Precipitation

Condensation

Water vapor

Water storage in ice and snow

Surface runoff

Evaporation

The Sun Powers Wind

The sun warms Earth's surface unevenly, creating areas of different air pressure. As air moves from areas of higher pressure to areas of lower pressure, it is felt as wind, as shown below. Global and local wind patterns transfer energy around Earth's surface, affecting global and local temperatures. Winds also carry water vapor from place to place. If the air cools enough, the water vapor will condense and fall as precipitation. The speed, direction, temperature, and moisture content of winds affect the climate and weather of the areas they move through.

Warm, less dense air rises, creating areas of low pressure.

Cold, more dense air sinks, creating areas of high pressure.

Wind forms when air moves from a high-pressure area to a low-pressure area.

Warm surface

Cool surface

Latitude Isn't Everything

How do Earth's features affect climate?

ACTIVE READING

12 Identify As you read, underline how topography affects the climate of a region.

On land, winds have to flow around or over features on Earth's surface, such as mountains. The surface features of an area combine to form its **topography** (tuh•POG•ruh•fee). Topography influences the wind patterns and the transfer of energy in an area. An important aspect of topography is elevation. **Elevation** refers to the height of an area above sea level. Temperature changes as elevation changes. Thus, topography and elevation affect the climate of a region.

Topography Can Affect Winds

Even the broad, generally flat topography of the Great Plains gives rise to unique weather patterns. On the plains, winds can flow steadily over large distances before they merge. This mixing of winds produces thunderstorms and even tornadoes.

Mountains can also affect the climate of an area, as shown below. When moist air hits a mountain, it is forced to rise up the side of the mountain. The rising air cools and often releases rain, which supports plants on the mountainside. The air that moves over the top of the mountain is dry. The air warms as it descends, creating a dry climate, which supports desert formation. Such areas are said to be in a *rain shadow*, because the air has already released all of its water by the time that it reaches this side of the mountain.

> 👁 **Visualize It!**

13 Apply Circle the rain gauge in each set that corresponds to how much rain each side of the mountain is likely to receive.

The Rain Shadow Effect

The Wet Side Air rises up the mountainside. The rising air cools and releases precipitation. The precipitation supports a lush plant community in this area.

The Dry Side Dry air flows over the mountain and warms as it sinks. The warm air absorbs moisture and creates conditions under which deserts may develop.

Elevation Influences Temperature

Elevation has a very strong effect on the temperature of an area. If you rode a cable car up a mountain, the temperature would decrease by about 6.5 °C (11.7 °F) for every kilometer you rose in elevation. Why does it get colder as you move higher up? Because the lower atmosphere is mainly warmed by Earth's surface that is directly below it. The warmed air lifts to higher elevations, where it expands and cools. Even close to the equator, temperatures at high elevations can be very cold. For example, Mount Kilimanjaro in Tanzania is close to the equator, but it is still cold enough at the peak to support a permanent glacier. The example below shows how one mountain can have several types of climates.

👁 Visualize It!

14 Apply Circle the thermometer that shows the most likely temperature for each photo at different elevations.

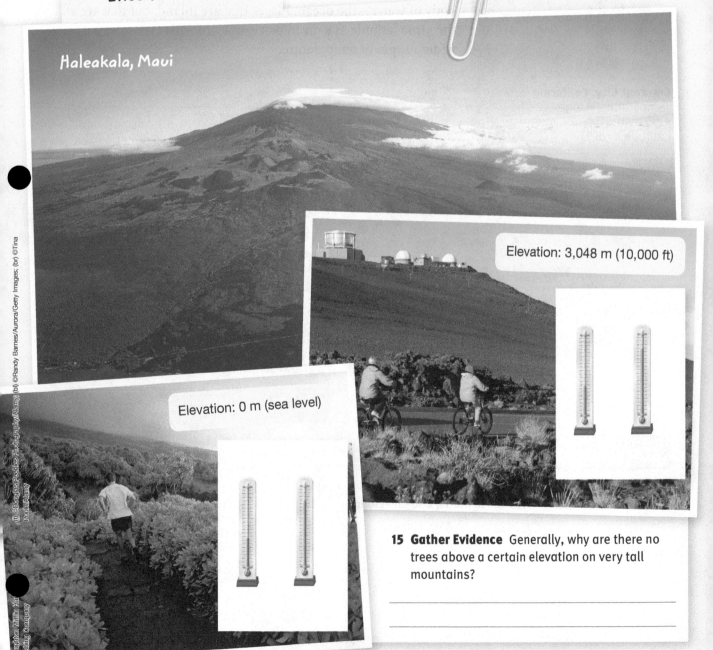

Effects of Elevation

Haleakala, Maui

Elevation: 3,048 m (10,000 ft)

Elevation: 0 m (sea level)

15 Gather Evidence Generally, why are there no trees above a certain elevation on very tall mountains?

_____

_____

Waterfront Property

How do large bodies of water affect climate?

Large bodies of water, such as the ocean, can influence an area's climate. Water absorbs and releases energy as heat more slowly than land does. So, water helps moderate the temperature of nearby land. Sudden or extreme temperature changes rarely take place on land near large bodies of water. The state of Michigan, which is nearly surrounded by the Great Lakes, has more moderate temperatures than places far from large bodies of water at the same latitude. California's coastal climate is also influenced by a large body of water—the ocean. Places that are inland, but that are at the same latitude as a given place on California's coast, experience wider ranges of temperature.

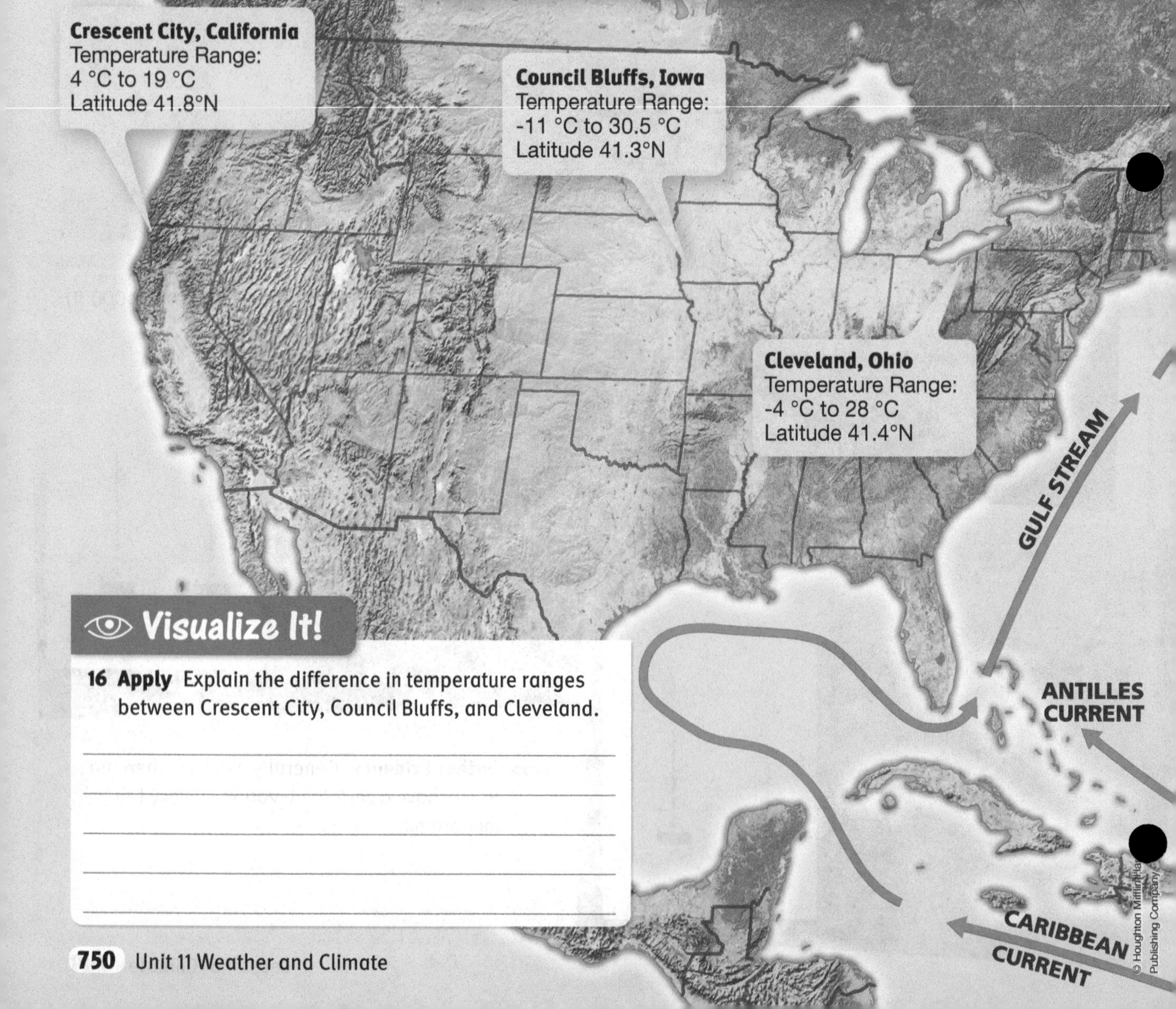

Crescent City, California
Temperature Range:
4 °C to 19 °C
Latitude 41.8°N

Council Bluffs, Iowa
Temperature Range:
-11 °C to 30.5 °C
Latitude 41.3°N

Cleveland, Ohio
Temperature Range:
-4 °C to 28 °C
Latitude 41.4°N

GULF STREAM

ANTILLES CURRENT

CARIBBEAN CURRENT

👁 Visualize It!

16 Apply Explain the difference in temperature ranges between Crescent City, Council Bluffs, and Cleveland.

_____

_____

_____

_____

_____

How do ocean currents affect climate?

An *ocean current* is the movement of water in a certain direction. There are many different currents in the oceans. Ocean currents move water and distribute energy and nutrients around the globe. The currents on the surface of the ocean are called **surface currents.** Surface currents are driven by winds and carry warm water away from the equator and carry cool water away from the poles.

Cold currents cool the air in coastal areas, while warm currents warm the air in coastal areas. Thus, currents moderate global temperatures. For example, the Gulf Stream is a surface current that moves warm water from the Gulf of Mexico northeastward, toward Great Britain and Europe. The British climate is mild because of the warm Gulf Stream waters. Polar bears do not wander the streets of Great Britain, as they might in Natashquan, Canada, which is at a similar latitude.

NORWAY CURRENT

Natashquan, Canada
Temperature Range:
-18 °C to 14 °C
Latitude: 50.2°N

London, England
Temperature Range:
2 °C to 22 °C
Latitude 51.5°N

LABRADOR CURRENT

NORTH ATLANTIC CURRENT

GULF STREAM

ATLANTIC OCEAN

17 Support Your Claim How do currents distribute heat around the globe?

_____
_____
_____

👁 Visualize It!

18 Infer How do you think that the Canary current affects the temperature in the Canary Islands? Explain your reasoning.

_____
_____
_____

CANARY CURRENT

Canary Islands, Spain
Temperature Range:
12 °C to 26 °C
Latitude 28°N

NORTH EQUATORIAL CURRENT

Zoning Out

What are the three major climate zones?

Earth has three major types of climate zones: tropical, temperate, and polar. These zones are shown below. Each zone has a distinct temperature range that relates to its latitude. Each of these zones has several types of climates. These different climates result from differences in topography, winds, ocean currents, and geography.

ACTIVE READING

19 Identify Underline the factor that determines the temperature ranges in each zone.

Temperate

Temperate climates have an average temperature below 18 °C (64 °F) in the coldest month and an average temperature above 10 °C (50 °F) in the warmest month. There are five temperate zone subclimates: marine west coast climates, steppe climates, humid continental climate, humid subtropical climate, and Mediterranean climate. The temperate zone is characterized by lower temperatures than the tropical zone. It is located between the tropical zone and the polar zone.

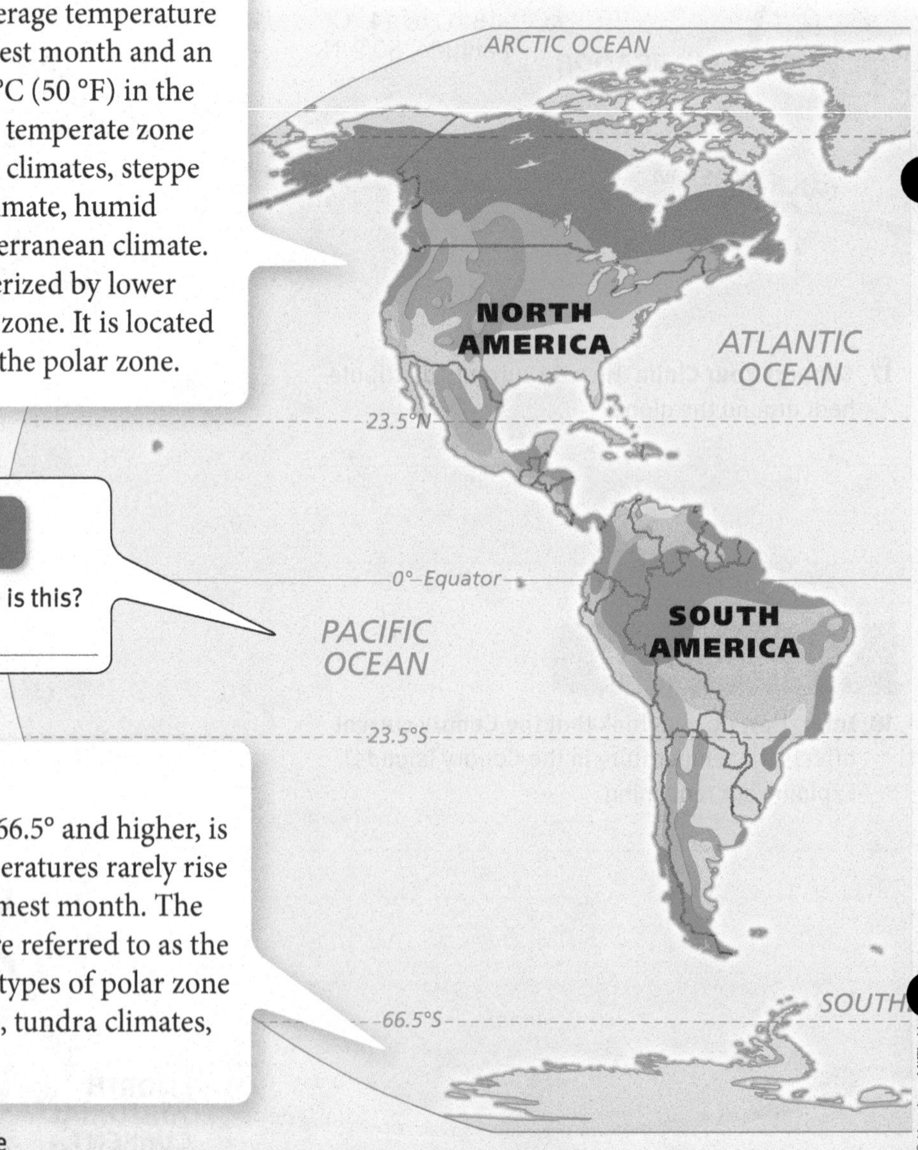

ARCTIC OCEAN
NORTH AMERICA
ATLANTIC OCEAN
23.5°N
0°-Equator
PACIFIC OCEAN
SOUTH AMERICA
23.5°S
66.5°S
SOUTH

Visualize It!

20 Label What climate zone is this?

___

Polar

The polar zone, at latitudes of 66.5° and higher, is the coldest climate zone. Temperatures rarely rise above 10 °C (50 °F) in the warmest month. The climates of the polar regions are referred to as the *polar climates.* There are three types of polar zone subclimates: subarctic climates, tundra climates, and polar ice cap climates.

21 Summarize Fill in the table for either the factor that affects
climate or the effect on climate the given factor has.

Factor	Effect on climate
Latitude	
	Cooler temperatures as you travel up a tall mountain
Winds	
	Moderates weather so that highs and lows are less extreme
Surface ocean currents	
	Impacts wind patterns and the transfer of energy in an area

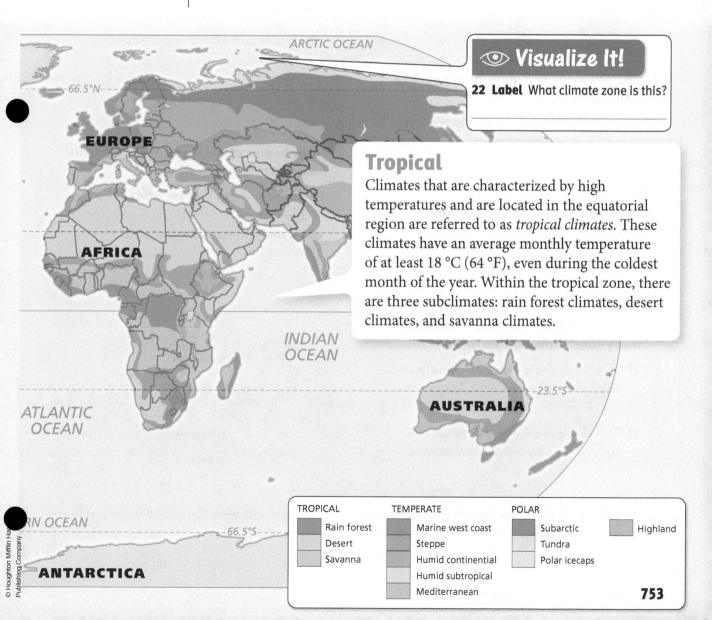

Visualize It!

22 Label What climate zone is this?

Tropical

Climates that are characterized by high
temperatures and are located in the equatorial
region are referred to as *tropical climates*. These
climates have an average monthly temperature
of at least 18 °C (64 °F), even during the coldest
month of the year. Within the tropical zone, there
are three subclimates: rain forest climates, desert
climates, and savanna climates.

TROPICAL	TEMPERATE	POLAR	
Rain forest	Marine west coast	Subarctic	Highland
Desert	Steppe	Tundra	
Savanna	Humid continential	Polar icecaps	
	Humid subtropical		
	Mediterranean		

ARCTIC OCEAN

66.5°N

EUROPE

AFRICA

INDIAN OCEAN

23.5°S

AUSTRALIA

ATLANTIC OCEAN

RN OCEAN

66.5°S

ANTARCTICA

Visual Summary

To complete this summary, circle the correct word or phrase.
You can use this page to review the main concepts of the lesson.

Climate

Rain   Water vapor   Wind

Winds transfer energy and moisture to new places.

24 Winds can affect the amount of precipitation in/elevation of an area.

Temperature and precipitation are used to describe climate.

23 Climate is the characteristic weather conditions in a place over a short/long period.

Large bodies of water and ocean currents both affect climate.

26 Large bodies of water affect the climate of nearby land when cool waters absorb energy as heat from the warm air/cold land.

Both topography and elevation affect climate.

25 Temperatures decrease as elevation increases/decreases.

There are three main climate zones and many subclimates within those zones.

27 The three main types of climate zones are polar, temperate, and equatorial/tropical.

28 The three main climate zones are determined by elevation/latitude.

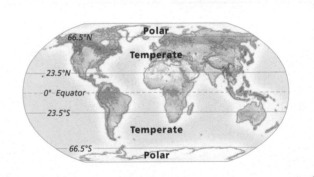

66.5°N   Polar

Temperate

23.5°N

0° Equator

23.5°S

Temperate

66.5°S   Polar

29 **Claims • Evidence • Reasoning** Explain how temperature changes with elevation and latitude Provide evidence with factors supporting your claim. Explain your reasoning.

Lesson Review

Vocabulary

In your own words, define the following terms.

1 topography

_____

_____

2 climate

_____

_____

Key Concepts

Fill in the table below.

Factor	Effect on Climate
3 Identify Latitude	
4 Identify Elevation	
5 Identify Large bodies of water	
6 Identify Wind	

7 Explain What provides Great Britain with a moderate climate? How?

_____

_____

8 State Your Claim What are two characteristics used to describe the climate of an area?

_____

Critical Thinking

Use the image below to answer the following question.

9 Support Your Claim Location A receives nearly 200 cm of rain each year, while Location B receives only 30 cm. Explain why Location A gets so much more rain. Use the words *rain shadow* and *precipitation* in your answer.

_____

_____

_____

_____

10 Gather Evidence What climate zone are you in if the temperatures are always very warm? Where is this zone located on Earth?

_____

11 Claims • Evidence • Reasoning Make a claim about how the sun's energy affects the climate of an area. Provide evidence with factors supporting your claim. Explain your reasoning.

_____

_____

_____

_____

UNIT **11**
Summary

What **Influences Weather?**

Elements of Weather

averaged over time determine

Climate

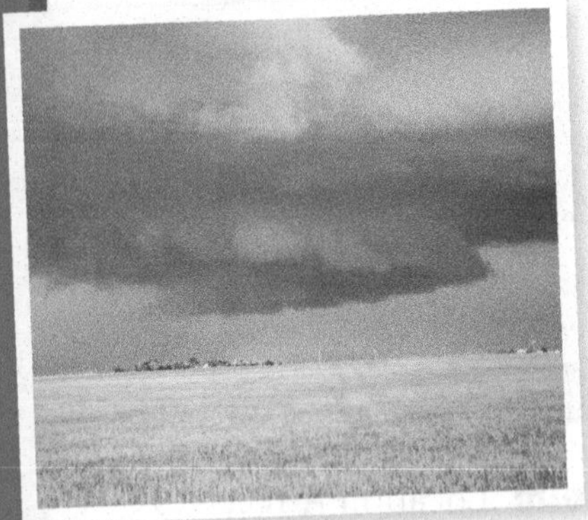

The Water Cycle

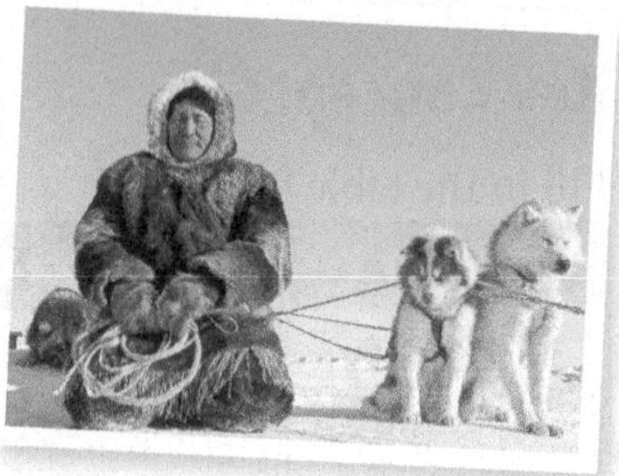

Severe Weather and Weather Safety

are connected to

Natural Disasters in Florida

1 Gather Evidence The graphic organizer above shows that the water cycle influences weather and climate. Explain why this is true.

2 Explain Your Reasoning Why is knowing about hurricane safety particularly important to Florida residents?

3 Distinguish Describe the difference between weather and climate.

4 Support Your Claim *Weather safety* means that people should be prepared for certain types of bad weather. Explain your reasoning.

Vocabulary

Name _____

Fill in each blank with the term that best completes the following sentences.

1 _____ is the ratio of the amount of water vapor in the air to the amount of water vapor needed to reach saturation at a given temperature.

2 A(n) _____ is a violently rotating column of air stretching from a cloud to the ground.

3 _____ is the characteristic weather conditions in an area over a long period of time.

4 A long period of climate cooling during which ice sheets spread beyond the polar regions is called a(n) _____.

Key Concepts

Identify the choice that best completes the statement or answers the question.

5 The temperatures in Gainesville, Florida, vary more than the temperatures in Miami, Florida, do. The map shows the locations of both of these cities.

How can the locations of the two cities explain the differences in their temperature ranges?

A Gainesville is farther north than Miami is, so latitude will make its temperatures vary more widely.

B Miami is closer to the ocean, and winds from the ocean cause its temperatures to vary greatly.

C Miami is closer to the ocean, which affects its climate by keeping its temperatures more consistent.

D Gainesville is farther inland, which affects its climate by keeping it warmer at night and colder during the day.

6 Human skin contains melanin. Melanin helps protect the skin from which environmental factor?

F extreme humidity

H ultraviolet rays from the sun

G subzero temperatures

I acid rain

7 The jet stream usually stays too far north to affect Florida's weather. What is the jet stream?

A the spinning of the air in the same direction as Earth's rotation

B the spinning of the air in the opposite direction of Earth's rotation

C the movement of air from an area of high pressure to an area of low pressure

D a narrow band of strong winds that blows in the upper region of the atmosphere

8 The following is a map of the continental United States. Four areas are labeled *A*, *B*, *C*, and *D*.

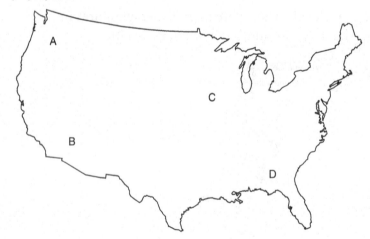

Where is a hurricane **most likely** to happen?

F point A

G point B

H point C

I point D

Name _____

9 Florida beaches are known for their white sand, clear ocean water, and palm trees. A picture of a Florida beach is shown below.

Which elements shown add water vapor to the atmosphere?

A palm trees only

B ocean water only

C ocean water and sand

D palm trees and ocean water

10 If a warm wind passes over snow, the snow can be heated rapidly. When this happens, the snow can change directly into water vapor without first becoming liquid water. What is the correct term for this process?

F deposition

G melting

H evaporation

I sublimation

11 Eliana measures the outdoor temperature each day for a week at exactly 3:00 p.m. The temperatures she records are all between 25 °C and 30 °C. Eliana concludes that the climate of her area is tropical. What is the **most** important reason why her study and conclusion may **not** be correct?

   A She recorded the temperature at only one time of day instead of more often.

   B She made her conclusion based only on temperature and not also on precipitation.

   C She made her conclusion based on only 1 week of data instead of over a long period of time.

   D She did not calculate the humidity, air pressure, and wind conditions when she made her conclusion.

12 For several days, the weather where Cheyenne lives was cool. When the temperature did warm, Cheyenne noticed that it was also very windy. How could winds influence the temperature?

   F Winds transfer energy around Earth.

   G Winds are caused by the energy of the sun.

   H Winds move because of differential warming of the air.

   I Winds transfer energy from the air to the ground.

13 Florida is susceptible to muck fires. Which of the following conditions explains Florida's risk of muck fires?

   A Florida has relatively flat topography and is located at or near sea level.

   B Limestone exists at or near the ground surface in most areas of Florida.

   C Florida has frequent, intense thunderstorms that are accompanied by intense lightning.

   D The lower layers of soil are made of organic material that can become very dry during droughts.

Name _____

14 Visitors to Florida sometimes complain about the high humidity. What does high humidity indicate?

F a cool temperature

G a high-pressure system

H an approaching cold front

I a high amount of water vapor in the air

15 During a winter storm, Annabelle observes hail falling in her yard. After the hailstorm, rain falls. Which statement correctly describes hail and rain?

A Hail and rain are both solids.

B Hail and rain are both liquids.

C Hail is a liquid, and rain is a solid.

D Hail is a solid, and rain is a liquid.

16 The sun's energy influences climate in different ways. For example, the latitudes at the equator receive more energy from the sun and therefore have warmer temperatures. How does the sun's energy **most directly** influence precipitation in a climate?

F The sun's energy drives the water cycle, which determines precipitation.

G The sun's energy creates wind patterns that bring precipitation to different areas.

H The sun's energy controls the amount of condensation and therefore precipitation.

I The sun's energy starts the water cycle by causing percolation, which leads to precipitation.

17 Elevation is the measure of how high something is above a reference point. What is the **most** common reference point used to refer to the elevation of natural landforms?

A sea level

B lake level

C land level

D river level

Critical Thinking

Answer the following questions in the space provided.

18 The map below shows the three different climate zones on Earth.

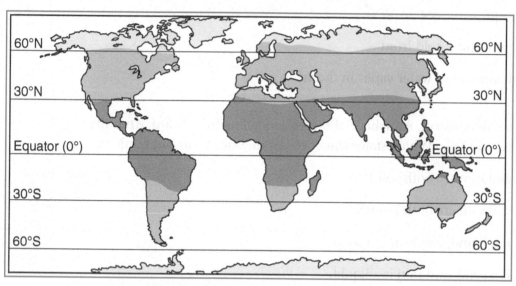

Label each climate zone on the map. Then describe the temperature and precipitation typical of each zone.

_____

_____

_____

Make a claim about how latitude affects the climate of each zone. Cite evidence to support your claim.

_____

_____

_____

19 Even if you do not live on a coast, the movement of water in the oceans and water vapor in the atmosphere over the oceans does affect your weather. Make a claim about how the water cycle and the global movement of water through ocean currents and winds affect the climate of your local region. Cite evidence to support your claim and explain your reasoning.

_____

_____

_____

_____

_____

⟨Technology⟩
and ⟨Coding⟩

This breathtaking image of Earth was taken from the International Space Station, an international laboratory orbiting Earth. The operation of the International Space Station is controlled by 52 computers and millions of lines of computer code. Its many high-tech features include solar panels that power the laboratory and a human-like robotic astronaut.

This is Robonaut 2, a robot designed to do routine maintenance at the International Space Station.

(bg) © NASA (in) © NASA

Data Driven

What is computer science?

If you like computer technology and learning about how computers work, computer science might be for you. *Computer science* is the study of computer technology and how data is processed, stored, and accessed by computers. Computer science is an important part of many other areas, including science, math, engineering, robotics, medicine, game design, and 3D animation.

Computer technology is often described in terms of *hardware,* which are the physical components, and *software,* which are the programs or instructions that a computer runs. Computer scientists must understand how hardware and software work together. Computer scientists may develop new kinds of useful computer software. Or they may work with engineers to improve existing computer hardware.

The first electronic computer, the computer ENIAC (Electronic Numerical Integrator And Computer), was developed at the University of Pennsylvania in 1946.

The integrated circuit (IC), first developed in the 1950s, was instrumental in the development of small computer components.

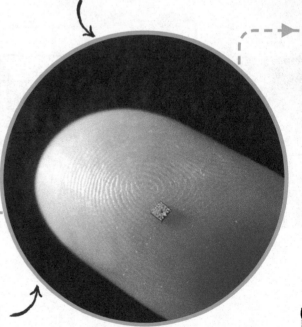

The development of the IC made it possible to reduce the overall size of computers and their components and to increase their processing speed.

How has computer technology changed over time?

Modern digital computer technology is less than 100 years old. Yet in that short amount of time, it has advanced rapidly. The earliest digital computers could perform only a limited number of tasks and were the size of an entire room. Over the decades, engineers continued to develop smaller, faster, and more powerful computers. Today's computers can process hundreds of millions of instructions per second!

Computer scientists and engineers think about what people want or need from computer technology. The most advanced hardware is not useful if people do not know how to use it. So computer scientists and engineers work to create software that is reliable, useful, and easy to use. Today's tablet computers, cell phones, and video game consoles can be used without any special training.

Advances in digital computer technology have helped make computers cheaper and easier to operate, which has allowed many more people to work and play with them.

1 **Claims • Evidence • Reasoning** Make a claim about whether modern computers are simpler or more complex than early computers. Summarize evidence to support the claim and explain your reasoning.

_____

_____

Computer Logic

What do computer scientists do?

Many people enjoy developing computer technology for fun. Learning how to create mobile phone games or Internet-enabled gadgets can be rewarding hobbies. For some people, that hobby may one day become a career in computer science. Working in computer science is a bit like solving a puzzle. Applying knowledge of how computers work to solve real-world problems requires collaboration, creativity, and logical, step-by-step thinking.

This is a kayak folded up.

They collaborate across many disciplines

Computers are valuable tools in math and science because they can perform complex calculations very quickly. Computers are useful to many other fields, too. For example, animators use computer technology to create realistic lighting effects in 3D animated films. Mechanics use computers to diagnose problems in car systems. For every field that relies on special software or computer technology, there is an opportunity for computer scientists and engineers to collaborate and develop solutions for those computing needs. Computer scientists must be able to define and understand the problems presented to them and to communicate and work with experts in other fields to develop the solutions.

Computational origami is a computer program used to model the ways in which different materials, including paper, can be folded. It combines computer science and the art of paper folding to create new technologies, such as this kayak.

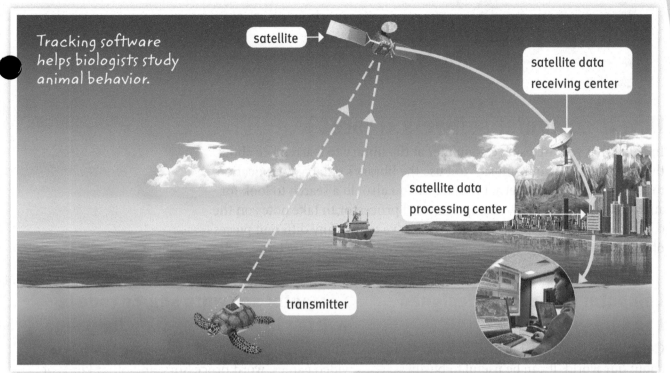

Tracking software helps biologists study animal behavior.

satellite

satellite data receiving center

satellite data processing center

transmitter

They help solve real-world problems

Some computer scientists carry out theoretical research. Others apply computer science concepts to develop software. Theoretical computer science and practical software development help solve real-world problems. For example, biologists need ways to safely and accurately track endangered animals. Computer science theories on artificial intelligence and pattern recognition have been applied to advanced animal-tracking technologies, such as satellite transmitters and aerial cameras. New kinds of image processing software now allow biologists to analyze the collected data in different ways.

They use logical, step-by-step thinking

Computers perform tasks given to them, and they do this very well. But in order to get the results they expect, computer scientists and programmers must write very accurate instructions. Computer science and programming requires logical thinking, deductive reasoning, and a good understanding of cause-and-effect relationships. When designing software, computer scientists must consider every possible user action and how the computer should respond to each action.

2 Support Your Claim Make a claim about how computer science is helping this scientist do her research. Support your claim with evidence from the image.

_____

_____

_____

Transmitters can be attached to animals to help track their movements.

Up to <Code>

How is computer software created?

Imagine that you are using a computer at the library to learn more about the history of electronic music. You use the library's database application to start searching for Internet resources. You also do a search to look for audio recordings. Finally, you open a word processor to take notes on the computer. Perhaps without realizing it, you've used many different pieces of software. Have you ever wondered how computer software is created?

Computer software is designed to address a need

Computer software can help us to learn more about our world. It can be useful to business. Or it can simply entertain us. Whatever its purpose, computer software should fulfill some human want or need. The first steps in creating software are precisely defining the need or want being addressed and planning how the software will work.

Computer software source code is written in a programming language

The instructions that tell a computer how to run video games, word processors, and other kinds of software are not written in a human language. They are written in a special programming language, or *code*. JavaScript, C++, and Python are examples of programming languages. Programming languages—like human languages—must follow certain rules in order to be understood by the computer. A series of instructions written in a programming language is called *source code*.

Identifying what need a computer program addresses is one of the first development steps.

Source code is revised

Sometimes, programmers make mistakes in their code. Many programming environments have a feature that alerts the programmer to certain errors, such as spelling mistakes in commands, missing portions of code, or logical errors in the sequence of instructions. However, many mistakes go undetected, too. Some errors may cause the program to function incorrectly or not at all. When this happens, the programmer must identify the error, correct it, and test the software again.

3 **Identify** This source code contains an error. Infer where the error is located. What does this code "tell" the computer to do? Write your answers below.

_____

_____

_____

Computer software is user tested and revised

Once the software is created, it must be tested thoroughly to make sure it does not fail or behave in unexpected ways. It must also be tested to ensure that it meets users' needs. The creators of a piece of software might observe how people use it. Or they might ask users to provide feedback on certain features and test the software again.

```
13
14   # Scores are not tied, so check
15   # which player wins the round
16 ▾ if player1_score > player2_score:
17       print ("Player 1 wins!")
18 ▾ else:
19       prnt ("Player 2 wins!")
20
```

```
! Syntax error, line 19
```

Test running a program is important for finding and fixing errors in the code.

Play it Safe

How should I work with computers?

It is easy to lose track of time when you're sitting in front of a computer or game console. It's also easy to forget that things you say or do online can be seen and shared by many different people. Here are some tips for using computers safely and responsibly.

✓ Maintain good posture

Time can pass by quickly when you are working on a computer or another device. Balance computer time with other activities, including plenty of physical activity. When you are sitting at a computer, sit upright with your shoulders relaxed. Your eyes should be level with the top of the monitor and your feet should be flat on the ground.

✓ Observe electrical safety

Building your own electronics projects can be fun, but it's important to have an understanding of circuits and electrical safety first. Otherwise, you could damage your components or hurt yourself. The potential for an electrical shock is real when you open up a computer, work with frayed cords, or use ungrounded plugs or attempt to replace parts without understanding how to do so safely. Ask an adult for help before starting any projects. Also, avoid using a connected computer during thunderstorms.

head and neck in a straight, neutral position

shoulders are relaxed

wrists are straight

feet are flat on the ground

Good posture will help you avoid the aches and injuries related to sitting in front of a computer for a long time.

✓ Handle and maintain computers properly

Be cautious when handling and transporting electronic devices. Dropping them or spilling liquids on them could cause serious damage. Keep computers away from dirt, dust, liquids, and moisture. Never use wet cleaning products unless they are specifically designed for use on electronics. Microfiber cloths can be used to clear smudges from device screens. Spilled liquids can cause circuits to short out and hardware to corrode. If a liquid spills on a device, unplug it and switch it off immediately, remove the battery and wipe up as much of the liquid inside the device as possible. Don't switch the device back on until it is completely dry.

✓ Do not post private information online

Talk to your family about rules for Internet use. Do not use the Internet to share private information such as photographs, your phone number, or your address. Do not respond to requests for personal details from people you do not know.

✓ Treat yourself and others with respect

It is important to treat others with respect when on the Internet. Don't send or post messages online that you wouldn't say to someone in person. Unfortunately, not everyone acts respectfully while online. Some people may say hurtful things to you or send you unwanted messages. Do not reply to unwanted messages. Alert a trusted adult to any forms of contact, such as messages or photos, that make you feel uncomfortable.

4 Apply Fill in the chart below with a suitable response to each scenario.

SCENARIO	YOUR RESPONSE
You receive a text message from an online store asking for your home address.	
You've been lying down in front of a laptop, and you notice that your neck is feeling a little sore.	
You need to take a laptop computer with you on your walk to school.	
You want to try assembling a robotics kit with a friend.	
Someone posts unfriendly comments directed at you.	

Career in Computing: Game Programmer

What do video game programmers do?

Creating your own universe with its own set of rules is fun. Just ask a programmer who works on video games!

What skills are needed in game programming?

A programmer should know how to write code, but there are other important skills a programmer needs as well. An understanding of physics and math is important for calculating how objects move and interact in a game. Game programmers usually work on a team with other people, such as artists, designers, writers, and musicians. They must be able to communicate effectively, and ideally, the programmer should understand the other team members' roles.

How can I get started with game development?

You don't need a big budget or years of experience to try it out. There are books, videos, and websites that can help you get started. When you're first experimenting with game development, start small. Try making a very simple game like Tic-Tac-Toe. Once you've mastered that, you can try something more complex.

5 Claims • Evidence • Reasoning Make a claim about why working on a team would be important to the game development process. Summarize evidence to support the claim and explain your reasoning.

_____

_____

_____

Glossary

Pronunciation Key

Sound	Symbol	Example	Respelling	Sound	Symbol	Example	Respelling
ă	a	pat	PAT	ngk	ngk	bank	BANGK
ā	ay	pay	PAY	ŏ	ah	bottle	BAHT'l
âr	air	care	KAIR	ō	oh	toe	TOH
ä	ah	father	FAH•ther	ô	aw	caught	KAWT
är	ar	argue	AR•gyoo	ôr	ohr	roar	ROHR
ch	ch	chase	CHAYS	oi	oy	noisy	NOYZ•ee
ĕ	e	pet	PET	ŏŏ	u	book	BUK
ĕ (at end of a syllable)	eh	settee lessee	seh•TEE leh•SEE	ōō	oo	boot	BOOT
				ou	ow	pound	POWND
ĕr	ehr	merry	MEHR•ee	s	s	center	SEN•ter
ē	ee	beach	BEECH	sh	sh	cache	CASH
g	g	gas	GAS	ŭ	uh	flood	FLUHD
ĭ	i	pit	PIT	ûr	er	bird	BERD
ĭ (at end of a syllable)	ih	guitar	gih•TAR	z	z	xylophone	ZY•luh•fohn
				z	z	bags	BAGZ
ī	y eye (only for a complete syllable)	pie island	PY EYE•luhnd	zh	zh	decision	dih•SIZH•uhn
				ə	uh	around broken focus	uh•ROWND BROH•kuhn FOH•kuhs
îr	ir	hear	HIR	ər	er	winner	WIN•er
j	j	germ	JERM	th	th	thin they	THIN THAY
k	k	kick	KIK				
ng	ng	thing	THING	w	w	one	WUHN
				wh	hw	whether	HWETH•er

A

abrasion (uh•BRAY•zhuhn) the process by which rock is reduced in size by the scraping action of other rocks driven by water, wind, and gravity (465)
abrasión proceso por el cual se reduce el tamaño de las rocas debido al efecto de desgaste de otras rocas arrastradas por el agua, el viento o la gravedad

absolute dating any method of measuring the age of an event or object in years (442)
datación absoluta cualquier método que sirve para determinar la edad de un suceso u objeto en años

absolute magnitude a measure of how bright a star would be if it were seen from a standard distance (107)
magnitud absoluta una medida del brillo que tendría una estrella vista desde una distancia estándar

acid precipitation (AS•id prih•sip•ih•TAY•shun) precipitation, such as rain, sleet, or snow, that contains a high concentration of acids, often because of the pollution of the atmosphere (466, 561)
precipitación ácida precipitación tal como lluvia, aguanieve o nieve, que contiene una alta concentración de ácidos debido a la contaminación de la atmósfera

air mass a large body of air throughout which temperature and moisture content are similar (700)
masa de aire un gran volumen de aire, cuya temperatura y cuyo contenido de humedad son similares en toda su extensión

air pollution the contamination of the atmosphere by the introduction of pollutants from human and natural sources (559)
contaminación del aire la contaminación de la atmósfera debido a la introducción de contaminantes provenientes de fuentes humanas y naturales

air pressure the measure of the force with which air molecules push on a surface (609, 688)
presión del aire la medida de la fuerza con la que las moléculas del aire empujan contra una superficie

air quality (AIR KWAHL•ih•tee) a measure of the pollutants in the air that is used to express how clean or polluted the air is (562)
calidad de aire una medida de los contaminantes presentes en el aire que se usa para expresar el nivel de pureza o contaminación del aire

alluvial fan a fan-shaped mass of rock material deposited by a stream when the slope of the land decreases sharply (475)
abanico aluvial masa en forma de abanico de materiales depositados por un arroyo cuando la pendiente del terreno disminuye bruscamente

aphelion (uh•FEE•lee•uhn) in the orbit of a planet or other body in the solar system, the point that is farthest from the sun (135)
afelio en la órbita de un planeta u otros cuerpos en el sistema solar, el punto que está más lejos del Sol

apparent magnitude the brightness of a star as seen from Earth (106)
magnitud aparente el brillo de una estrella como se percibe desde la Tierra

artificial satellite any human-made object placed in orbit around a body in space (278)
satélite artificial cualquier objeto hecho por los seres humanos y colocado en órbita alrededor de un cuerpo en el espacio

asteroid a small, rocky object that orbits the sun; most asteroids are located in a band between the orbits of Mars and Jupiter (196)
asteroide un objeto pequeño y rocoso que se encuentra en órbita alrededor del Sol; la mayoría de los asteroides se ubican en una banda entre las órbitas de Marte y Júpiter

asthenosphere the solid, plastic layer of the mantle beneath the lithosphere; made of mantle rock that flows very slowly, which allows tectonic plates to move on top of it (346)
astenosfera la capa sólida y plástica del manto, que se encuentra debajo de la litosfera; está formada por roca del manto que fluye muy lentamente, lo cual permite que las placas tectónicas se muevan en su superficie

astronomical unit the average distance between Earth and the sun; approximately 150 million kilometers; symbol: AU (160)
unidad astronómica la distancia promedio entre la Tierra y el Sol; aproximadamente 150 millones de kilómetros; símbolo: UA

atmosphere a mixture of gases that surrounds a planet, moon, or other celestial body (596)
atmósfera una mezcla de gases que rodea un planeta, una luna, u otros cuerpos celestes

atom the smallest unit of an element that maintains the properties of that element (312)
átomo la unidad más pequeña de un elemento que conserva las propiedades de ese elemento

B

barrier island a long ridge of sand or narrow island that lies parallel to the shore (480)
isla barrera un largo arrecife de arena o una isla angosta ubicada paralela a la costa

beach an area of the shoreline that is made up of deposited sediment (480)
playa un área de la costa que está formada por sedimento depositado

biosphere the part of Earth where life exists; includes all of the living organisms on Earth (597)
 biosfera la parte de la Tierra donde existe la vida; comprende todos los seres vivos de la Tierra

C

centripetal force (sehn•TRIP•ih•tuhl) the inward force required to keep a particle or an object moving in a circular path (138)
 fuerza centrípeta la fuerza hacia adentro que se requiere para mantener en movimiento una partícula o un objeto en un camino circular

chemical weathering (KEM•ih•kuhl WETH•er•ing) the chemical breakdown and decomposition of rocks by natural processes in the environment (466)
 desgaste químico la descomposición química que sufren las rocas por procesos naturales del entorno

cleavage in geology, the tendency of a mineral to split along specific planes of weakness to form smooth, flat surfaces (319)
 exfoliación en geología, la tendencia de un mineral a agrietarse a lo largo de planos débiles específicos y formar superficies lisas y planas

climate the weather conditions in an area over a long period of time (422)
 clima las condiciones del tiempo en un área durante un largo período de tiempo

coastline (KOHST•lyn) a location where land and ocean surface meet (506)
 costa el lugar donde se encuentran la superficie del terreno y la del océano

comet (KAHM•it) a small body that gives off gas and dust as it passes close to the sun; a typical comet moves in an elliptical orbit around the sun and is made of dust and frozen gases (194)
 cometa un cuerpo pequeño que libera gas y polvo al pasar cerca del Sol; un cometa típico está formado por polvo y gases congelados y sigue una órbita elíptica alrededor del Sol

compound a substance made up of atoms or ions of two or more different elements joined by chemical bonds (312)
 compuesto una sustancia formada por átomos de dos o más elementos diferentes unidos por enlaces químicos

compression (kuhm•PRESH•uhn) stress that occurs when forces act to squeeze an object (371)
 compresión estrés que se produce cuando distintas fuerzas actúan para estrechar un objeto

condensation (kahn•den•SAY•shuhn) the change of state from a gas to a liquid (675)
 condensación el cambio de estado de gas a líquido

conduction (kuhn•DUHK•shuhn) the transfer of energy as heat through a material (626)
 conducción la transferencia de energía en forma de calor a través del contacto directo

conservation (kahn•sur•VAY•shuhn) the wise use of and preservation of natural resources (570)
 conservación el uso inteligente y la preservación de los recursos naturales

convection (kuhn•VECK•shuhn) the movement of matter due to differences in density that are caused by temperature variations; can result in the transfer of energy as heat (345, 624)
 convección el movimiento de la materia debido a diferencias en la densidad que se producen por variaciones en la temperatura; puede resultar en la transferencia de energía en forma de calor

convection current any movement of matter that results from differences in density; may be vertical, circular, or cyclical (655)
 corriente de convección cualquier movimiento de la materia que se produce como resultado de diferencias en la densidad; puede ser vertical, circular o cíclico

convergent boundary the boundary between tectonic plates that are colliding (358)
 límite convergente el límite entre placas tectónicas que chocan

core the central part of Earth below the mantle (345)
 núcleo la parte central de la Tierra, debajo del manto

Coriolis effect (kawr•ee•OH•lis ih•FEKT) the curving of the path of a moving object from an otherwise straight path due to Earth's rotation (637)
 efecto de Coriolis la desviación de la trayectoria recta que experimentan los objetos en movimiento debido a la rotación de la Tierra

creep the slow downhill movement of weathered rock material (494)
 arrastre el movimiento lento y descendente de materiales rocosos desgastados

crust the thin and solid outermost layer of Earth above the mantle (345)
 corteza la capa externa, delgada y sólida de la Tierra, que se encuentra sobre el manto

cryosphere (KRY•oh•sfir) one of Earth's spheres where water is in solid form, including snow cover, floating ice, glaciers, ice caps, ice sheets, and frozen ground permafrost (595)
 criosfera una de las esferas de la Tierra donde el agua se encuentra en estado sólido en forma de capas de nieve, hielos flotantes, glaciares, campos de hielo, capas de hielo continentales y porciones de suelo permanentemente congeladas permafrost

crystal natural solid substance that has a definite geometric shape (313)
 cristal sustancia sólida natural que tiene una forma geométrica definida

D

data (DAY•tuh) information gathered by observation or experimentation that can be used in calculating or reasoning (23)
datos la información recopilada por medio de la observación o experimentación que puede usarse para hacer cálculos o razonar

day the time required for Earth to rotate once on its axis (214)
día el tiempo que se requiere para que la Tierra rote una vez sobre su eje

deep current a streamlike movement of ocean water far below the surface (654)
corriente profunda un movimiento del agua del océano que es similar a una corriente y ocurre debajo de la superficie

deforestation (dee•fohr•ih•STAY•shuhn) the removal of trees and other vegetation from an area (533)
deforestación la remoción de árboles y demás vegetación de un área

deformation (dee•fohr•MAY•shuhn) the bending, tilting, and breaking of Earth's crust; the change in the shape of rock in response to stress (368, 379)
deformación el proceso de doblar, inclinar y romper la corteza de la Tierra; el cambio en la forma de una roca en respuesta a la tensión

delta (DEL•tuh) a mass of material deposited in a triangular or fan shape at the mouth of a river or stream (475)
delta un depósito de materiales en forma de triángulo o abanico ubicado en la desembocadura de un río

dependent variable (dih•PEN•duhnt VAIR•ee•uh•buhl) in a scientific investigation, the factor that changes as a result of manipulation of one or more independent variables (23)
variable dependiente en una investigación científica, el factor que cambia como resultado de la manipulación de una o más variables independientes

deposition the process in which material is laid down (329, 472)
deposición el proceso por medio del cual un material se deposita

desertification (dih•zer•tuh•fih•KAY•shuhn) the process by which human activities or climatic changes make areas more desertlike (533)
desertificación el proceso por el cual las actividades humanas o los cambios climáticos hacen que un área se vuelva más parecida a un desierto

dew point at constant pressure and water vapor content, the temperature at which the rate of condensation equals the rate of evaporation (685)
punto de rocío a presión y contenido de vapor de agua constantes, la temperatura a la que la tasa de condensación es igual a la tasa de evaporación

divergent boundary the boundary between two tectonic plates that are moving away from each other (359)
límite divergente el límite entre dos placas tectónicas que se están separando una de la otra

dune a mound of wind-deposited sand that moves as a result of the action of wind (489)
duna un montículo de arena depositada por el viento que se mueve como resultado de la acción de éste

dwarf planet a celestial body that orbits the sun, is round because of its own gravity, but has not cleared its orbital path (191)
planeta enano un cuerpo celeste que orbita alrededor del Sol, es redondo debido a su propia fuerza de gravedad, pero no ha despejado los alrededores de su trayectoria orbital

E

Earth system all of the nonliving things, living things, and processes that make up the planet Earth, including the solid Earth, the hydrosphere, the atmosphere, and the biosphere (592)
sistema terrestre todos los seres vivos y no vivos y los procesos que componen el planeta Tierra, incluidas la Tierra sólida, la hidrosfera, la atmósfera y la biosfera

earthquake a movement or trembling of the ground that is caused by a sudden release of energy when rocks along a fault move (378)
terremoto un movimiento o temblor del suelo causado por una liberación súbita de energía que se produce cuando las rocas ubicadas a lo largo de una falla se mueven

eclipse (ih•KLIPS) an event in which the shadow of one celestial body falls on another (228)
eclipse un suceso en el que la sombra de un cuerpo celeste cubre otro cuerpo celeste

elastic rebound the sudden return of elastically deformed rock to its undeformed shape (379)
rebote elástico ocurre cuando una roca deformada elásticamente vuelve súbitamente a su forma no deformada

electromagnetic spectrum all of the frequencies or wavelengths of electromagnetic radiation (258)
espectro electromagnético todas las frecuencias o longitudes de onda de la radiación electromagnética

element a substance that cannot be separated or broken down into simpler substances by chemical means; all atoms of an element have the same atomic number (312)
elemento una sustancia que no se puede separar o descomponer en sustancias más simples por medio de métodos químicos; todos los átomos de un elemento tienen el mismo número atómico

elevation the height of an object above sea level (748)
  elevación la altura de un objeto sobre el nivel del mar

empirical evidence (em•PIR•ih•kuhl EV•ih•duhns) the observations, measurements, and other types of data that people gather and test to support and evaluate scientific explanations (10)
  evidencia empírica las observaciones, mediciones y demás tipos de datos que se recopilan y examinan para apoyar y evaluar explicaciones científicas

energy budget (EN•er•jee BUJ•it) a way to keep track of energy transfers into and out of the Earth system (600)
  presupuesto energético forma de llevar la cuenta de las transferencias de energía dentro y fuera de un sistema

energy resource a natural resource that humans use to generate energy (523)
  recurso energético un recurso natural que utilizan los humanos para generar energía

engineering (en•juh•NIR•ing) the application of science and mathematics to solve real-life problems (44)
  ingeniería la aplicación de las ciencias y las matemáticas para resolver problemas de la vida diaria

epicenter (EP•i•sen•ter) the point on Earth's surface directly above an earthquake's starting point, or focus (378)
  epicentro el punto de la superficie de la Tierra que queda justo arriba del punto de inicio, o foco, de un terremoto

equinox (EE•kwuh•nahks) the moment when the sun appears to cross the celestial equator (218)
  equinoccio el momento en que el Sol parece cruzar el ecuador celeste

erosion the process by which wind, water, ice, or gravity transports soil and sediment from one location to another (329, 472)
  erosión el proceso por medio del cual el viento, el agua, el hielo o la gravedad transporta tierra y sedimentos de un lugar a otro

eutrophication (yoo•TRAWF•ih•kay•shuhn) an increase in the amount of nutrients, such as nitrates, in a marine or aquatic ecosystem (542)
  eutrofización un aumento en la cantidad de nutrientes, tales como nitratos, en un ecosistema marino o acuático

evaporation the change of state from a liquid to a gas (674)
  evaporación el cambio de estado de líquido a gas

experiment (ik•SPEHR•uh•muhnt) an organized procedure to study something under controlled conditions (20)
  experimento un procedimiento organizado que se lleva a cabo bajo condiciones controladas para estudiar algo

fault (FAWLT) a break in a body of rock along which one block moves relative to another (370)
  falla una grieta en un cuerpo rocoso a lo largo de la cual un bloque se mueve respecto de otro

floodplain an area along a river that forms from sediments deposited when the river overflows its banks (475)
  llanura de inundación un área a lo largo de un río formada por sedimentos que se depositan cuando el río se desborda

focus the location within Earth along a fault at which the first motion of an earthquake occurs (378)
  foco el lugar dentro de la Tierra a lo largo de una falla donde ocurre el primer movimiento de un terremoto

folding the bending of rock layers due to stress (369)
  plegamiento fenómeno que ocurre cuando las capas de roca se doblan debido a la compresión

fossil the trace or remains of an organism that lived long ago, most commonly preserved in sedimentary rock (415)
  fósil los indicios o los restos de un organismo que vivió hace mucho tiempo, comúnmente preservados en las rocas sedimentarias

fossil fuel a nonrenewable energy resource formed from the remains of organisms that lived long ago; examples include oil, coal, and natural gas (521)
  combustible fósil un recurso energético no renovable formado a partir de los restos de organismos que vivieron hace mucho tiempo; algunos ejemplos incluyen el petróleo, el carbón y el gas natural

front the boundary between air masses of different densities and usually different temperatures (700)
  frente el límite entre masas de aire de diferentes densidades y, normalmente, diferentes temperaturas

galaxy (GAL•eck•see) a collection of stars, dust, and gas bound together by gravity (94)
  galaxia un conjunto de estrellas, polvo y gas unidos por la gravedad

gas giant a planet that has a deep, massive atmosphere, such as Jupiter, Saturn, Uranus, or Neptune (176)
  gigante gaseoso un planeta con una atmósfera masiva y profunda, como por ejemplo, Júpiter, Saturno, Urano o Neptuno

geocentric (jee•oh•SEN•trik) describes something that uses Earth as the reference point (122)
  geocéntrico término que describe algo que usa a la Tierra como punto de referencia

geologic column an ordered arrangement of rock layers that is based on the relative ages of the rocks and in which the oldest rocks are at the bottom (435)
  columna geológica un arreglo ordenado de capas de rocas que se basa en la edad relativa de las rocas y en el cual las rocas más antiguas están al fondo

geosphere the mostly solid, rocky part of Earth; extends from the center of the core to the surface of the crust (593)
  geosfera la capa de la Tierra que es principalmente sólida y rocosa; se extiende desde el centro del núcleo hasta la superficie de la corteza terrestre

glacial drift the rock material carried and deposited by glaciers (490)
  deriva glacial el material rocoso que es transportado y depositado por los glaciares

glacier (GLAY•sher) a large mass of ice that exists year-round and moves over land (490)
  glaciar una masa grande de hielo que existe durante todo el año y se mueve sobre la tierra

global wind (GLOH•buhl WIND) the movement of air over Earth's surface in patterns that are worldwide (638)
  viento global el movimiento del aire sobre la superficie terrestre según patrones globales

gravity a force of attraction between objects that is due to their masses (134, 224)
  gravedad una fuerza de atracción entre dos objetos debido a sus masas

greenhouse effect the warming of the surface and lower atmosphere of Earth that occurs when water vapor, carbon dioxide, and other gases absorb and reradiate thermal energy (558, 612)
  efecto invernadero el calentamiento de la superficie y de la parte más baja de la atmósfera, el cual se produce cuando el vapor de agua, el dióxido de carbono y otros gases absorben y vuelven a irradiar la energía térmica

groundwater the water that is beneath Earth's surface (476)
  agua subterránea el agua que está debajo de la superficie de la Tierra

half-life the time required for half of a sample of a radioactive isotope to break down by radioactive decay to form a daughter isotope (442)
  vida media el tiempo que se requiere para que la mitad de una muestra de un isótopo radiactivo se descomponga por desintegración radiactiva y forme un isótopo hijo

heat the energy transferred between objects that are at different temperatures (620)
  calor la transferencia de energía entre objetos que están a temperaturas diferentes

heliocentric (hee•lee•oh•SEN•trik) sun-centered (122)
  heliocéntrico centrado en el Sol

hot spot a volcanically active area of Earth's surface, commonly far from a tectonic plate boundary (398)
  mancha caliente un área volcánicamente activa de la superficie de la Tierra que comúnmente se encuentra lejos de un límite entre placas tectónicas

humidity the amount of water vapor in the air (685)
  humedad la cantidad de vapor de agua que hay en el aire

hurricane (HER•ih•kayn) a severe storm that develops over tropical oceans and whose strong winds of more than 119 km/h spiral in toward the intensely low-pressure storm center (716)
  huracán una tormenta severa que se desarrolla sobre océanos tropicales, con vientos fuertes que soplan a más de 119 km/h y que se mueven en espiral hacia el centro de presión extremadamente baja de la tormenta

hydrosphere the portion of Earth that is water (594)
  hidrosfera la porción de la Tierra que es agua

hypothesis (hy•PAHTH•eh•sys) a testable idea or explanation that leads to scientific investigation (22)
  hipótesis una idea o explicación que conlleva a la investigación científica y que se puede probar

ice core (YS KOHR) a long cylinder of ice obtained from drilling through ice caps or ice sheets; used to study past climates (423)
  testigo de hielo un cilindro largo de hielo que se obtiene al perforar campos de hielo o capas de hielo continentales; se usa para estudiar los climas del pasado

igneous rock rock that forms when magma cools and solidifies (330)
  roca ígnea una roca que se forma cuando el magma se enfría y se solidifica

independent variable (in•dih•PEN•duhnt VAIR•ee•uh•buhl) in a scientific investigation, the factor that is deliberately manipulated (23)
  variable independiente en una investigación científica, el factor que se manipula deliberadamente

jet stream a narrow band of strong winds that blow in the upper troposphere (640, 705)
  corriente en chorro un cinturón delgado de vientos fuertes que soplan en la parte superior de la troposfera

K

Kuiper Belt a region of the solar system that is just beyond the orbit of Neptune and that contains small bodies made mostly of ice (192)
cinturón de Kuiper una región del Sistema Solar que comienza justo después de la órbita de Neptuno y que contiene planetas enanos y otros cuerpos pequeños formados principalmente de hielo

Kuiper Belt object one of the hundreds or thousands of minor planet-sized objects that orbit the sun in a flat belt beyond Neptune's orbit (192)
objeto del cinturón de Kuiper uno de los cientos o miles de objetos del tamaño de un planeta menor que orbitan alrededor del Sol en un cinturón plano, más allá de la órbita de Neptuno

L

lake (LAYK) a filled or partially filled basin of fresh or salt water surrounded by land (504)
lago una cuenca de agua dulce o salada total o parcialmente llena y rodeada de tierra

land degradation (LAND deg•ruh•DAY•shuhn) the process by which human activity and natural processes damage land to the point that it can no longer support the local ecosystem (532)
degradación del suelo el proceso por el cual la actividad humana y los procesos naturales dañan el suelo de modo que el ecosistema local no puede subsistir

landslide the sudden movement of rock and soil down a slope (495)
derrumbamiento el movimiento súbito hacia abajo de rocas y suelo por una pendiente

latitude (LAHT•ih•tood) the angular distance north or south from the equator; expressed in degrees (746)
latitud la distancia angular hacia el norte o hacia el sur del ecuador; se expresa en grados

launch (LAWNCH) the process of setting a rocket or spacecraft in motion (290)
lanzamiento el proceso por el cual se pone en movimiento un cohete o nave espacial

lava magma that flows onto Earth's surface; the rock that forms when lava cools and solidifies (392)
lava magma que fluye a la superficie terrestre; la roca que se forma cuando la lava se enfría y se solidifica

law a descriptive statement or equation that reliably predicts events under certain conditions (8)
ley una ecuación o afirmación descriptiva que predice sucesos de manera confiable en determinadas condiciones

life cycle analysis (LYF SY•kuhl uh•NAL•sis) the evaluation of the materials and energy used for the manufacture, transportation, sale, use, and disposal of a technology (59)
análisis del ciclo de vida la evaluación de los materiales y la energía usados para la fabricación, transporte, veta, uso y eliminación de una tecnología

lightning an electric discharge that takes place between two oppositely charged surfaces, such as between a cloud and the ground, between two clouds, or between two parts of the same cloud (715)
relámpago una descarga eléctrica que ocurre entre dos superficies que tienen carga opuesta, como por ejemplo, entre una nube y el suelo, entre dos nubes o entres dos partes de la misma nube

light-year the distance that light travels in one year; about 9.46 trillion kilometers (96)
año luz la distancia que viaja la luz en un año; aproximadamente 9.46 trillones de kilómetros

lithosphere the solid, outer layer of Earth that consists of the crust and the rigid upper part of the mantle (346)
litosfera la capa externa y sólida de la Tierra que está formada por la corteza y la parte superior y rígida del manto

local wind (LOH•kuhl WIND) the movement of air over short distances; occurs in specific areas as a result of certain geographical features (642)
viento local el movimiento del aire a través de distancias cortas; se produce en áreas específicas como resultado de ciertas características geográficas

loess (LOH•uhs) fine-grained sediments of quartz, feldspar, hornblende, mica, and clay deposited by the wind (489)
loess sedimentos de grano fino de cuarzo, feldespato, hornblenda, mica y arcilla depositados por el viento

luminosity (loo•muh•NAHS•ih•tee) the actual brightness of an object such as a star (107)
luminosidad el brillo real de un objeto, como por ejemplo, una estrella

lunar phases the different appearances of the moon from Earth throughout the month (226)
fases lunares la diferente apariencia que tiene la Luna cuando se ve desde la Tierra a lo largo del mes

luster the way in which a mineral reflects light (319)
brillo la forma en que un mineral refleja la luz

magma (MAG•muh) the molten or partially molten rock material containing trapped gases produced under the Earth's surface (392)
magma el material rocoso total o parcialmente fundido que contiene gases atrapados que se producen debajo de la superficie terrestre

mantle the layer of rock between the Earth's crust and core (345)
manto la capa de roca que se encuentra entre la corteza terrestre y el núcleo

material resource a natural resource that humans use to make objects or to consume as food and drink (522)
recurso material un recurso natural que utilizan los seres humanos para fabricar objetos o para consumir como alimento o bebida

matter anything that has mass and takes up space (312)
materia cualquier cosa que tiene masa y ocupa un lugar en el espacio

mesosphere (MEZ•uh•sfir) 1. the strong, lower part of the mantle between the asthenosphere and the outer core, 2. the layer of the atmosphere between the stratosphere and the thermosphere and in which temperature decreases as altitude increases (346, 610)
mesosfera 1. la parte fuerte e inferior del manto que se encuentra entre la astenosfera y el núcleo externo, 2. la capa de la atmósfera que se encuentra entre la estratosfera y la termosfera, en la cual la temperatura disminuye al aumentar la altitud

metamorphic rock a rock that forms from other rocks as a result of intense heat, pressure, or chemical processes (330)
roca metamórfica una roca que se forma a partir de otras rocas como resultado de calor intenso, presión o procesos químicos

meteor a bright streak of light that results when a meteoroid burns up in Earth's atmosphere (198)
meteoro un rayo de luz brillante que se produce cuando un meteoroide se quema en la atmósfera de la Tierra

meteorite a meteoroid that reaches Earth's surface without burning up completely (198)
meteorito un meteoroide que llega a la superficie de la Tierra sin quemarse por completo

meteoroid a relatively small, rocky body that travels through space (198)
meteoroide un cuerpo rocoso relativamente pequeño que viaja en el espacio

mineral a naturally formed, inorganic solid with a crystalline structure (312)
mineral un sólido inorgánico formado naturalmente que tiene una estructura cristalina

model a pattern, plan, representation, or description designed to show the structure or workings of an object, system, or concept (38)
modelo un diseño, plan, representación o descripción cuyo objetivo es mostrar la estructura o funcionamiento de un objeto, sistema o concepto

mountain an area of significantly increased elevation on Earth's surface, usually rising to a summit (502)
montaña elevación considerable sobre la superficie terrestre que alcanza su punto más alto en la cima

muck fire a fire that burns organic material in the soil (736)
incendio de subsuelo incendio que quema el material orgánico del suelo

mudflow the flow of a mass of mud or rock and soil mixed with a large amount of water (495)
flujo de lodo el flujo de una masa de lodo o roca y suelo mezclados con una gran cantidad de agua

NASA the National Aeronautics and Space Administration (290)
NASA la Administración Nacional de Aeronáutica y del Espacio

natural resource any natural material that is used by humans, such as water, petroleum, minerals, forests, and animals (520)
recurso natural cualquier material natural que es utilizado por los seres humanos, como agua, petróleo, minerales, bosques y animales

neap tide a tide of minimum range that occurs during the first and third quarters of the moon (239)
marea muerta una marea que tiene un rango mínimo, la cual ocurre durante el primer y el tercer cuartos de la Luna

nonpoint-source pollution pollution that comes from many sources rather than from a single specific site; an example is pollution that reaches a body of water from streets and storm sewers (542)
contaminación no puntual contaminación que proviene de muchas fuentes, en lugar de provenir de un solo sitio específico; un ejemplo es la contaminación que llega a una masa de agua a partir de las calles y los drenajes

nonrenewable resource a resource that forms at a rate that is much slower than the rate at which the resource is consumed (521)

recurso no renovable un recurso que se forma a una tasa que es mucho más lenta que la tasa a la que se consume

nuclear fusion the process by which nuclei of small atoms combine to form a new, more massive nucleus; the process releases energy (150)

fusión nuclear el proceso por medio del cual los núcleos de átomos pequeños se combinan y forman un núcleo nuevo con mayor masa; el proceso libera energía

O

observation the process of obtaining information by using the senses; the information obtained by using the senses (21)

observación el proceso de obtener información por medio de los sentidos; la información que se obtiene al usar los sentidos

ocean current a movement of ocean water that follows a regular pattern (650)

corriente oceánica un movimiento del agua del océano que sigue un patrón regular

Oort cloud a spherical region that surrounds the solar system, that extends from the Kuiper Belt to almost halfway to the nearest star, and that contains billions of comets (195)

nube de Oort una región esférica que rodea al Sistema Solar, que se extiende desde el cinturón de Kuiper hasta la mitad del camino hacia la estrella más cercana y contiene miles de millones de cometas

orbit the path that a body follows as it travels around another body in space (134)

órbita la trayectoria que sigue un cuerpo al desplazarse alrededor de otro cuerpo en el espacio

oxidation (ahk•sih•DAY•shuhn) a chemical reaction in which a material combines with oxygen to form new material; in geology, oxidation is a form of chemical weathering (466)

oxidación una reacción química en la que un material se combina con oxígeno para formar un material nuevo; en geología, la oxidación es una forma de desgaste químico

ozone layer the layer of the atmosphere at an altitude of 15 to 40 km in which ozone absorbs ultraviolet solar radiation (612)

capa de ozono la capa de la atmósfera ubicada a una altitud de 15 a 40 km, en la cual el ozono absorbe la radiación solar

P - Q

Pangaea (pan•JEE•uh) the supercontinent that formed 300 million years ago and that began to break up 200 million years ago (353)

Pangea el supercontinente que se formó hace 300 millones de años y que comenzó a separarse hace 200 millones de años

parallax (PAIR•uh•laks) an apparent shift in the position of an object when viewed from different locations (122)

paralaje un cambio aparente en la posición de un objeto cuando se ve desde lugares distintos

particulate (per•TIK•yuh•lit) a tiny particle of solid that is suspended in air or water (559)

material particulado una pequeña partícula de material sólido que se encuentra suspendida en el aire o el agua

penumbra (pih•NUHM•bruh) the outer part of a shadow such as the shadow cast by Earth or the moon in which sunlight is only partially blocked (228)

penumbra la parte exterior de la sombra como la sombra producida por la Tierra o la Luna en la que la luz solar solamente se encuentra bloqueada

parcialmente perihelion (perh•uh•HEE•lee•uhn) the point in the orbit of a planet at which the planet is closest to the sun (135)

perihelio el punto en la órbita de un planeta en el que el planeta está más cerca del Sol

physical weathering (FIZ•ih•kuhl WETH•er•ing) the mechanical breakdown of rocks into smaller pieces that is caused by natural processes and that does not change the chemical composition of the rock material (462)

desgaste físico el rompimiento mecánico de una roca en pedazos más pequeños que ocurre por procesos naturales y que no modifica la composición química del material rocoso

planet (PLAN•it) a relatively large spherical body that orbits a star (93)

planeta un cuerpo esférico relativamente grande que orbita alrededor de una estrella

planetary ring a disk of matter that encircles a planet and consists of numerous particles in orbit, ranging in size from dust grains up to objects tens of meters across (178)

anillo planetario un disco de materia que rodea un planeta y está compuesto por numerosas partículas en órbita que pueden ser desde motas de polvo hasta objetos de diez metros

planetesimal (plan•ih•TES•ih•muhl) a small body from which a planet originated in the early stages of development of the solar system (141)

planetesimal un cuerpo pequeño a partir del cual se originó un planeta en las primeras etapas de desarrollo del Sistema Solar

plate tectonics the theory that explains how large pieces of the lithosphere, called plates, move and change shape (356)

    tectónica de placas la teoría que explica cómo las grandes partes de litosfera, denominadas placas, se mueven y cambian de forma

point-source pollution pollution that comes from a specific site (542)

    contaminación puntual contaminación que proviene de un lugar específico

potable suitable for drinking (545)

    potable que puede beberse

precipitation (pri•sip•i•TAY•shuhn) any form of water that falls to Earth's surface from the clouds; includes rain, snow, sleet, and hail (675, 686)

    precipitación cualquier forma de agua que cae de las nubes a la superficie de la Tierra; incluye a la lluvia, nieve, aguanieve y granizo

probe (PROHB) an uncrewed vehicle that carries scientific instruments into space to collect scientific data (277)

    sonda espacial un vehículo sin tripulación que transporta instrumentos científicos al espacio para recopilar información científica

prominence a loop of relatively cool, incandescent gas that extends above the photosphere and above the sun's edge as seen from Earth (155)

    protuberancia una espiral de gas incandescente y relativamente frío que, vista desde la Tierra, se extiende por encima de la fotosfera y la superficie del Sol

prototype (PROH•tuh•typ) a test model of a product (47)

    prototipo prueba modelo de un producto

Pugh chart (PYOO CHART) a table used to compare the features of multiple items, such as technological products or solutions (60)

    tabla de Pugh una tabla que se usa para comparar las características de muchos elementos, como productos o soluciones tecnológicas

R

radiation (ray•dee•AY•shuhn) the transfer of energy as electromagnetic waves (622)

    radiación la transferencia de energía en forma de ondas electromagnéticas

radioactive decay the process in which a radioactive isotope tends to break down into a stable isotope of the same element or another element (442)

    desintegración radiactiva "el proceso por medio del cual un isótopo radiactivo tiende a desintegrarse y formar un isótopo estable del mismo elemento o de otro elemento

radiometric dating (ray•dee•oh•MET•rik DAYT•ing) a method of determining the absolute age of an object by comparing the relative percentages of a radioactive parent isotope and a stable daughter isotope (443)

    datación radiométrica un método para determinar la edad absoluta de un objeto comparando los porcentajes relativos de un isótopo radiactivo precursor y un isótopo estable hijo

relative dating any method of determining whether an event or object is older or younger than other events or objects (428)

    datación relativa cualquier método que se utiliza para determinar si un acontecimiento u objeto es más viejo o más joven que otros acontecimientos u objetos

relative humidity (REL•uh•tiv hyoo•MID•ih•tee) the ratio of the amount of water vapor in the air to the amount of water vapor needed to reach saturation at a given temperature (685)

    humedad relativa la proporción de la cantidad de vapor de agua que hay en el aire respecto a la cantidad de vapor de agua que se necesita para alcanzar la saturación a una temperatura dada

renewable resource a natural resource that can be replaced at the same rate at which the resource is consumed (521)

    recurso renovable un recurso natural que puede reemplazarse a la misma tasa a la que se consume

reservoir (REZ•uhr•vwohr) an artificial body of water that usually forms behind a dam (547)

    represa una masa artificial de agua que normalmente se forma detrás de una presa

revolution (reh•vuh•LOO•shun) the motion of a body that travels around another body in space; one complete trip along an orbit (215)

    revolución el movimiento de un cuerpo que viaja alrededor de otro cuerpo en el espacio; un viaje completo a lo largo de una órbita

rift zone an area of deep cracks that forms between two tectonic plates that are pulling away from each other (334)

    zona de rift un área de grietas profundas que se forma entre dos placas tectónicas que se están alejando una de la otra

risk-benefit analysis (risk•BEN•uh•fit uh•NAL•ih•sis) the comparison of the risks and benefits of a decision or product (58)

    análisis de riesgo-beneficio la comparación de los riesgos y los beneficios de una decisión o de un producto

river (RIV•er) a large natural stream of water that flows across land surfaces within a channel (504)

    río un gran curso de agua natural que fluye a través de superficies de terreno y dentro de un canal

rock cycle the series of processes in which rock forms, changes from one type to another, is destroyed, and forms again by geologic processes (332)

    ciclo de las rocas la serie de procesos por medio de los cuales una roca se forma, cambia de un tipo a otro, se destruye y se forma nuevamente por procesos geológicos

rockfall the rapid mass movement of rock down a steep slope or cliff (495)

 desprendimiento de rocas el movimiento rápido y masivo de rocas por una pendiente empinada o un precipicio

rotation the spin of a body on its axis (214)

 rotación el giro de un cuerpo alrededor de su eje

S

sandbar a low ridge of sand deposited along the shore of a lake or sea (480)

 barra de arena un arrecife bajo de arena depositado a lo largo de la orilla de un lago o del mar

satellite (SAT'l•yt) a natural or artificial body that revolves around a planet (224)

 satélite un cuerpo natural o artificial que gira alrededor de un cuerpo celeste que tiene mayor masa

sea-floor spreading the process by which new oceanic lithosphere sea floor forms when magma rises to Earth's surface at mid-ocean ridges and solidifies, as older, existing sea floor moves away from the ridge (354)

 expansión del suelo marino el proceso por medio del cual se forma nueva litósfera oceánica suelo marino cuando el magma sube a la superficie de la Tierra en las dorsales oceánicas y se solidifica, a medida que el antiguo suelo marino existente se aleja de la dorsal oceánica

season (SEE•zuhn) a division of the year that is characterized by recurring weather conditions, and determined by both Earth's tilt relative to the sun and Earth's position in its orbit around the sun (218)

 estación una de las partes en que se divide el año que se caracteriza por condiciones climáticas recurrentes y que está determinada tanto por la inclinación de la Tierra con relación al Sol como por la posición que ocupa en su órbita alrededor del Sol

sedimentary rock a rock that forms from compressed or cemented layers of sediment (330)

 roca sedimentaria una roca que se forma a partir de capas comprimidas o cementadas de sedimento

shear stress (SHIR STRES) stress that occurs when forces act in parallel but opposite directions, pushing parts of a solid in opposite directions (370)

 tensión de corte el estrés que se produce cuando dos fuerzas actúan en direcciones paralelas pero opuestas, lo que empuja las partes de un sólido en direcciones opuestas

shoreline the boundary between land and a body of water (477)

 orilla el límite entre la tierra y una masa de agua

sinkhole a circular depression that forms when rock dissolves, when overlying sediment fills an existing cavity, or when the roof of an underground cavern or mine collapses (735)

 depresión una depresión circular que se forma cuando la roca se funde, cuando el sedimento suprayacente llena una cavidad existente, o al colapsarse el techo de una caverna o mina subterránea

smog (SMAHG) air pollution that forms when ozone and vehicle exhaust react with sunlight (560)

 esmog contaminación del aire que se produce cuando el ozono y sustancias químicas como los gases de los escapes de los vehículos reaccionan con la luz solar

solar flare an explosive release of energy that comes from the sun and that is associated with magnetic disturbances on the sun's surface (155)

 erupción solar una liberación explosiva de energía que proviene del Sol y que se asocia con disturbios magnéticos en la superficie solar

solar nebula (SOH•ler NEB•yuh•luh) a rotating cloud of gas and dust from which the sun and planets formed (139)

 nebulosa solar una nube de gas y polvo en rotación a partir de la cual se formaron el Sol y los planetas

solar system the sun and all of the planets and other bodies that travel around it (93)

 Sistema Solar el Sol y todos los planetas y otros cuerpos que se desplazan alrededor de él

solstice (SAHL•stis) the point at which the sun is as far north or as far south of the equator as possible (218)

 solsticio el punto en el que el Sol está tan lejos del ecuador como es posible, ya sea hacia el norte o hacia el sur

spectrum (SPEK•truhm) a range of electromagnetic radiation that is ordered by wavelength or frequency, such as the band of colors that is produced when white light passes through a prism (258)

 espectro una gama de radiación electromagnética ordenada por longitud de onda o frecuencia, como la banda de colores que se produce cuando la luz blanca pasa a través de un prisma

spinoff a commercialized product incorporating NASA technology or "know how" that benefits the public (296)

 derivado de la tecnología espacial un producto comercializado que incorpora la tecnología o la pericia de la NASA para beneficio del público

spring tide a tide of increased range that occurs two times a month, at the new and full moons (238)

 marea viva una marea de mayor rango que ocurre dos veces al mes, durante la luna nueva y la luna llena

star a large celestial body that is composed of gas and that emits light; the sun is a typical star (94)

 estrella un cuerpo celeste grande que está compuesto de gas y emite luz; el Sol es una estrella típica

stewardship (stoo•urd•SHIP) behavior that leads to the protection, conservation, and reclamation of natural resources (571)
gestión ambiental responsable comportamiento que hace posible la protección, la conservación y el rescate de los recursos naturales

storm surge a local rise in sea level near the shore that is caused by strong winds from a storm, such as those from a hurricane (717)
marea de tempestad un levantamiento local del nivel del mar cerca de la costa, el cual es resultado de los fuertes vientos de una tormenta, como por ejemplo, los vientos de un huracán

stratosphere the layer of the atmosphere that lies between the troposphere and the mesosphere and in which temperature increases as altitude increases; contains the ozone layer (610)
estratosfera la capa de la atmósfera que se encuentra entre la troposfera y la mesosfera y en la cual la temperatura aumenta al aumentar la altitud; contiene la capa de ozono

streak the color of a mineral in powdered form (318)
veta el color de un mineral en forma de polvo

sublimation the process in which a solid changes directly into a gas (674)
sublimación el proceso por medio del cual un sólido se transforma directamente en un gas

subsidence the sinking of regions of the Earth's crust to lower elevations (334)
hundimiento del terreno el hundimiento de regiones de la corteza terrestre a elevaciones más bajas

sunspot a dark area of the photosphere of the sun that is cooler than the surrounding areas and that has a strong magnetic field (154)
mancha solar un área oscura en la fotosfera del Sol que es más fría que las áreas que la rodean y que tiene un campo magnético fuerte

superposition (soo•per•puh•ZISH•uhn) a principle that states that younger rocks lie above older rocks if the layers have not been disturbed (429)
superposición un principio que establece que las rocas más jóvenes se encontrarán sobre las rocas más viejas si las capas no han sido alteradas

surface current a horizontal movement of ocean water that is caused by wind and that occurs at or near the ocean's surface (650, 751)
corriente superficial un movimiento horizontal del agua del océano que es producido por el viento y que ocurre en la superficie del océano o cerca de ella

technology (tek•NAHL•uh•jee) the application of science for practical purposes; the use of tools, machines, materials, and processes to meet human needs (45)
tecnología la aplicación de la ciencia con fines prácticos; el uso de herramientas, máquinas, materiales y procesos para satisfacer las necesidades de los seres humanos

tectonic plate a block of lithosphere that consists of the crust and the rigid, outermost part of the mantle (356)
placa tectónica un bloque de litosfera formado por la corteza y la parte rígida y más externa del manto

tectonic plate boundary (tek•THAN•ik PLAYT BOWN•duh•ree) the edge between two or more plates classified as divergent, convergent, or transform by the movement taking place between the plates (379)
límite de placa tectónica el borde entre dos o más placas clasificado como divergente, convergente o transformante por el movimiento que se produce entre las placas

temperature (TEM•per•uh•chur) a measure of how hot or cold something is; specifically, a measure of the average kinetic energy of the particles in an object (618)
temperatura una medida de qué tan caliente o frío está algo; específicamente, una medida de la energía cinética promedio de las partículas de un objeto

tension (TEN•shun) stress that occurs when forces act to stretch an object (371)
tensión estrés que se produce cuando distintas fuerzas actúan para estirar un objeto

terrestrial planet one of the highly dense planets nearest to the sun; Mercury, Venus, Mars, and Earth (160)
planeta terrestre uno de los planetas muy densos que se encuentran más cerca del Sol; Mercurio, Venus, Marte y la Tierra

theory the explanation for some phenomenon that is based on observation, experimentation, and reasoning; that is supported by a large quantity of evidence; and that does not conflict with any existing experimental results or observations (9)
teoría una explicación sobre algún fenómeno que está basada en la observación, experimentación y razonamiento; que está respaldada por una gran cantidad de pruebas; y que no contradice ningún resultado experimental ni observación existente

thermal energy the total kinetic energy of a substance's atoms (618)
energía térmica la energía cinética de los átomos de una sustancia

thermal expansion an increase in the size of a substance in response to an increase in the temperature of the substance (619)
expansión térmica un aumento en el tamaño de una sustancia en respuesta a un aumento en la temperatura de la sustancia

thermal pollution a temperature increase in a body of water that is caused by human activity and that has a harmful effect on water quality and on the ability of that body of water to support life (542)

contaminación térmica un aumento en la temperatura de una masa de agua, producido por las actividades humanas y que tiene un efecto dañino en la calidad del agua y en la capacidad de esa masa de agua para permitir que se desarrolle la vida

thermosphere the uppermost layer of the atmosphere, in which temperature increases as altitude increases (610)

termosfera la capa más alta de la atmósfera, en la cual la temperatura aumenta a medida que la altitud aumenta

thunder the sound caused by the rapid expansion of air along an electrical strike (715)

trueno el sonido producido por la expansión rápida del aire a lo largo de una descarga eléctrica

thunderstorm a usually brief, heavy storm that consists of rain, strong winds, lightning, and thunder (714)

tormenta eléctrica una tormenta fuerte y normalmente breve que consiste en lluvia, vientos fuertes, relámpagos y truenos

tidal range the difference in levels of ocean water at high tide and low tide (238)

rango de marea la diferencia en los niveles del agua del océano entre la marea alta y la marea baja

tide the periodic rise and fall of the water level in the oceans and other large bodies of water (236)

marea el ascenso y descenso periódico del nivel del agua en los océanos y otras masas grandes de agua

topography (tuh•POG•ruh•fee) the size and shape of the land surface features of a region, including its relief (748)

topografía el tamaño y la forma de las características de una superficie de terreno, incluyendo su relieve

tornado a destructive, rotating column of air that has very high wind speeds and that may be visible as a funnel-shaped cloud (718)

tornado una columna destructiva de aire en rotación cuyos vientos se mueven a velocidades muy altas y que puede verse como una nube con forma de embudo

trace fossil a fossilized structure, such as a footprint or a coprolite, that formed in sedimentary rock by animal activity on or within soft sediment (417)

fósil traza una estructura fosilizada, como una huella o un coprolito, que se formó en una roca sedimentaria por la actividad de un animal sobre sedimento blando o dentro de éste

trade-off (TRAYD•awf) the giving up of one thing in return for another, often applied to the engineering design process (56)

compensación pérdida de una cosa a cambio de otra, con frecuencia aplicado al proceso de diseño en ingeniería

transform boundary the boundary between tectonic plates that are sliding past each other horizontally (359)

límite de transformación el límite entre placas tectónicas que se están deslizando horizontalmente una sobre otra

transpiration the process by which plants release water vapor into the air through stomata; also the release of water vapor into the air by other organisms (674)

transpiración el proceso por medio del cual las plantas liberan vapor de agua al aire por medio de los estomas; también, la liberación de vapor de agua al aire por otros organismos

troposphere the lowest layer of the atmosphere, in which temperature drops at a constant rate as altitude increases; the part of the atmosphere where weather conditions exist (610)

troposfera la capa inferior de la atmósfera, en la que la temperatura disminuye a una tasa constante a medida que la altitud aumenta; la parte de la atmósfera donde se dan las condiciones del tiempo

umbra a shadow that blocks sunlight, such as the conical section in the shadow of the Earth or the moon (228)

umbra una sombra que bloquea la luz solar, como por ejemplo, la sección cónica en la sombra de la Tierra o la Luna

unconformity (uhn•kuhn•FAWR•mih•tee) a break in the geologic record created when rock layers are eroded or when sediment is not deposited for a long period of time (431)

disconformidad una ruptura en el registro geológico, creada cuando las capas de roca se erosionan o cuando el sedimento no se deposita durante un largo período de tiempo

uniformitarianism (yoo•nuh•fohr•mi•TAIR•ee•uh•n iz•uhm) a principle that geologic processes that occurred in the past can be explained by current geologic processes (414)

uniformitarianismo un principio que establece que es posible explicar los procesos geológicos que ocurrieron en el pasado en función de los procesos geológicos actuales

universe space and all the matter and energy in it (97)

universo el espacio y toda la materia y energía que hay dentro de él

uplift the rising of regions of the Earth's crust to higher elevations (334)
    levantamiento la elevación de regiones de la corteza terrestre a elevaciones más altas

upwelling the movement of deep, cold, and nutrient-rich water to the surface (656)
    surgencia el movimiento de las aguas profundas, frías y ricas en nutrientes hacia la superficie

urbanization (ER•buh•ny•zhay•shuhn]) the growth of urban areas caused by people moving into cities (529)
    urbanización el crecimiento de las áreas urbanas producido por el desplazamiento de personas hacia las ciudades

vent an opening at the surface of the Earth through which volcanic material passes (392)
    chimenea una abertura en la superficie de la Tierra a través de la cual pasa material volcánico

visibility the distance at which a given standard object can be seen and identified with the unaided eye (689)
    visibilidad la distancia a la que un objeto dado es perceptible e identificable para el ojo humano

volcano a vent or fissure in Earth's surface through which magma and gases are expelled (392)
    volcán una chimenea o fisura en la superficie de la Tierra a través de la cual se expulsan magma y gases

water cycle the continuous movement of water between the atmosphere, the land, the oceans, and living things (672)
    ciclo del agua el movimiento continuo del agua entre la atmósfera, la tierra, los océanos y los seres vivos

water pollution (WAW•ter puh•LOO•shuhn) waste matter or other material that is introduced into water and that is harmful to organisms that live in, drink, or are exposed to the water (542)
    contaminación del agua material de desecho u otro material que se introduce en el agua y que daña a los organismos que viven en el agua, la beben o están expuestos a ella

wavelength the distance between two adjacent crests or troughs of a wave (258)
    longitud de onda la distancia entre dos crestas o senos adyacentes de una onda

weather the short-term state of the atmosphere, including temperature, humidity, precipitation, wind, and visibility (684, 744)
    tiempo el estado de la atmósfera a corto plazo que incluye la temperatura, la humedad, la precipitación, el viento y la visibilidad

weathering the natural process by which atmospheric and environmental agents, such as wind, rain, and temperature changes, disintegrate and decompose rocks (329, 369, 462)
    meteorización el proceso natural por medio del cual los agentes atmosféricos o ambientales, como el viento, la lluvia y los cambios de temperatura, desintegran y descomponen las rocas

wildfire (WYLD•fyr) an unplanned fire in land that is undeveloped except for roads and power lines and other such structures (736)
    incendio forestal un incendio imprevisto en terrenos que no están urbanizados excepto por la presencia de carreteras, cables eléctricos y otras estructuras de ese tipo

wind the movement of air caused by differences in air pressure (636, 688)
    viento el movimiento de aire producido por diferencias en la presión barométrica

year the time required for the Earth to orbit once around the sun (215)
    año el tiempo que se requiere para que la Tierra le dé la vuelta al Sol una vez

Index

Page numbers for definitions are printed in **boldface** type.
Page numbers for illustrations, maps, and charts are printed in *italics*.

pure substances. *See also* compounds; elements; matter; Ptolemy, 124
Pyrenees Mountains, 372
pyroclastic materials, **393**

R

radiation (of energy), **622**. *See also* solar radiation
radiation, electromagnetic (EM), 152
radiation, sun and, 152
radio waves, 258, 263
radioactive decay, **442**
radiocarbon dating, 445
radiometric dating, **443**, 445
  methods, 445
  determining age of Earth, 447
rain, 686, 728
recreational use of land, 529
recycling, **576**
reef crest, 587
reflecting telescope, **276**
reforestation, **575**
relative dating, **426–437**
relative humidity, **685**
  psychrometer, **685**
remote-sensing satellites, 264, 278
renewable resource, 521
repetition of experiments, 28–**29**
replication
  of experiments, 29
reservoir, **547**
residential use of land, 529
retrograde rotation, **162**
revenue, space exploration and Florida, 294
reverse faults, 171
revolution of planets, **215**
ridge push, 360, 361
rift zone, **334**
river, 504, 541
rock, **330–337**
  classes of, 330–331
  cycle, 332–334
  igneous, **330**, 331
  metamorphic, **330–331**
  ordered, 432
  organisms buried in, 316
  process affecting, 329
  relative age of, 429, 433–435
  sedimentary, 430
rocket, liquid-propellant, 2
rock fall, 495
runoff, **676**
rotation, 153
  Earth-moon-sun relationship, 134, 135
  of Earth, 214
  of the sun, 153

S

saltwater intrusion, 548
sandbar, 480

sand dune, 506, 507
SARSAT instruments, 280
satellite, **224**, 264. *See also* space exploration; space images
  combined satellite images, 280
  for collecting weather information, 279
  for communication, 282
  for monitoring changes over time, 265, 279
  for relaying information to distant locations on Earth, 282
  for search-and-rescue operations, 280
  for studying Earth's surface features, 264, 278
  Global Positioning System (GPS), 283
Saturn, 178
  atmosphere of Titan, 179
  Cassini's visit to, 179, 277
  planetary ring system of, **178**
  statistics, 178
  water geysers of Enceladus, 179
Schirra, Wally, 290
science, 6–7
scientific explanation, 6
  collecting and organizing data, 46
  data, 46
  experiment, 46
  observation, 46
scientific investigation, 20–30
  collecting and organizing data, 25
  data, 34
  defining a problem, 24
  dependent variable, 23
  drawing and defending conclusions, 25
  experiment, 20
  hypothesis, 22–27
  identifying variables, 25
  independent variable, 23
  interpreting data and analyzing information, 25
  observation, 20, 21–23
  planning for, 24
  predictions, 24
  quality and, 28–29
  repetition of, 28–29
  replication of, 28–29
  types of, 20
scientific knowledge, 4–15
scientific theory, 7–9
  difference from law, 8
  evidence for, 10
  examples, 9
sea breeze, 642
sea cave, 479
sea-floor
  age, 354
  magnetic properties, 354
  ocean trenches, 355
  sediments, 422
  spreading, 354
sea-floor sediments, 422
sea-floor spreading, **354**

sea oats, 507
sea turtles, 297
search-and-rescue operations satellites, 280
seasons, 217
  on your Uranus, 181
sediment, **502**. *See also* erosion and deposition by water
sedimentary rock, 319, **330**
  composition and texture of, 419
  determination and age of, 429, 447
  disturbance of and layers of, 430–431
  Earth's history shown in, 419
sediments, sea-floor, 422
shear stress, **370**
shield volcanoes, 393
Shenandoah Mountains, 502
Shepherd, J. Marshall, 740
shoreline, **477**
short-period comets (Kuiper Belt), 195
Sierra Nevada's, 373
silicate mineral 316
sinkhole, 735
sinkhole lake, 504
Sirius, 106
slab pull, 360, 361
sleet, 686
Sloan Digital Sky Survey Camera, 88
Skylab space station, 290, 291, 296
small bodies in the solar system, 188–200
  asteroids, 190, **196**
  comets, 190, **194**
  dwarf planets, 190
  Kuiper Belt objects (KBOs), 190
  meteoroids, meteors, and 198
  meteorites, 190
smog, 559
snow, 686
soil
  conservation of, 577
  human impact on, 538, 548
  importance of, 530
Sojourner, 172, 290, 291
solar activity, 154
  prominences, **154**
  solar flares, **154**
  sunspots, **154**
solar eclipse, 225
solar flares, 154, **155**
solar nebula, **139**
solar radius, 109
soar system, **93**, 118–119, 120, 122. *See also* gas giant planets; heading under specific bodies; moon (Earth's); moons; small bodies in the solar system; sun; terrestrial planets
solar system information, 139–143
  protoplanetary disk, **141**, 142
  protostellar disk, 139
  solar nebula, **139**
solar system historical models, 120–128